THE RISE OF AMERICAN AIR POWER
THE CREATION OF ARMAGEDDON

THE RISE OF
American Air Power
The Creation of Armageddon

MICHAEL S. SHERRY

Yale University Press
New Haven and London

Designed by James J. Johnson
and set in Fairfield Medium types.
Printed in the United States of America by
Vail-Ballou Press, Inc., Binghamton, New York.

Library of Congress Cataloging-in-Publication Data

Sherry, Michael S., 1945–
   The rise of American air power

   Bibliography: p.
   Includes index.
   1. Aeronautics, Military—United States—History. 2. Air
power—History. 3. Bombing, Aerial—United States—
History. I. Title.
UG633.S457   1987   358.4′00973   86–19003
ISBN 0–300–03600–0 (cloth)
        0–300–04414–3 (pbk.)

*The paper in this book meets the guidelines for
permanence and durability of the Committee on
Production Guidelines for Book Longevity of the Council
on Library Resources.*

10   9   8   7   6   5   4   3

Contents

Illustrations

following page 146

1, 2. "The Angel of Death" and "His New Toy" accompanied article by M. W. Royse, "The Next War in the Air," *Nation*, 9 May 1923, 537.

3. "'The FUTURE'" appeared in Francis Trevelyan Miller, *The World in the Air: The Story of Flying in Pictures* (New York and London, 1930), vol. 2, 328.

4. Map showing air routes to Japanese cities, from *United States News*, 31 October 1941, 18–19. Copyright © 1941, by The United States News Publishing Corporation.

5. Model airplanes in Union Station, *Life*, 29 September 1942, 33. Photograph by Nelson Morris. Courtesy LIFE Picture Service.

6. Illustration of "clouds of planes" in *Life*, 19 January 1942, 18. Illustration by A. Leydenfrost.

7, 8. Boeing advertisements appeared in *Life*, 22 March 1943, 63, and *Life*, 10 July 1944, 85, and in other mass circulation magazines. By permission of the Boeing Company.

9. Nash-Kelvinator ad appeared in *Life*, 12 October 1942, 1. Courtesy White Consolidated Industries.

10. Philco ad appeared in *Life*, 15 May 1944, 1. Courtesy White Consolidated Industries.

11. Propaganda poster, "Plane Warning." Courtesy National Archives, Still Picture Branch, 44-PA-978.

12. Propaganda poster, "Sucker Bet." Courtesy National Archives, Still Picture Branch, 179-WP-1027.

Preface

Four decades after the end of World War II, visible reminders of the bomber's destructiveness are few: an occasional memorial to the victims of bombing or a ruined building (the Kaiser Wilhelm Church in West Berlin and the Peace Memorial in Hiroshima) preserved as testimony to wartime devastation. Often dwarfed by new construction, these ruins sometimes appear out of place, too inconsequential as reminders of past fury. In Eastern Europe, the inadequacies of socialist reconstruction perversely enhanced remembrance, for the rubble took decades to clear, but even there the physical testimony has mostly disappeared. What testimony remains is largely implicit: all those shining, rebuilt city centers do remind, in passing, that something else once stood there. Other testimony may be exhumed some day in archeological digs uncovering the unexploded bomb or the foundation of some forgotten building. An astonishing sign of human capacity to recover, the disappearance of the traces of aerial warfare parallels the passing of vivid recollection. As John Hersey noted in 1985 about Kiyoshi Tanimoto, one of Hiroshima's survivors: "His memory, like the world's, was getting spotty."[1]

This book is primarily an explanation, not a remembrance, of the rise of strategic air war. But fragile remembrance today follows naturally from two of my major themes: the profound difficulties people faced in comprehending air war even as it unfolded, and the manner in which thinking about bombing before August 6, 1945, has shaped attitudes and approaches to the nuclear question. Almost as soon as Hiroshima was destroyed, the reflex reaction of most observers was to regard the atomic age as revolutionary and the previous history of air war as irrelevant, just as earlier commentators on the bomber tended to dismiss the previous history of warfare. In both cases, declarations of the past's irrelevance masked the persistence of old habits. This book examines that persistence, showing how ideas about air war, and indeed the habit of regarding bombing as an abstract idea, developed in the prenuclear era and persisted beyond it. In that regard, an inability to imagine in the 1980s what it was like in Berlin, Tokyo, or Hiroshima in 1945 reflects a recurrent and disturbing quality in all modern thinking about aerial warfare.

The title of this book refers to three related developments in aerial warfare: the creation of an apocalyptic mentality, consisting of expectations of ultimate danger and destruction that were both frightening and reassuring; the creation of the apparatus for realizing that danger; and the creation of the modern nuclear dilemma. For the most part, the last is suggested obliquely in this account; aware of the wealth of material on nuclear warfare, and suspicious that most of it provided little historical perspective, I decided to examine the rise of strategic bombing from the turn of the century through the end of World War II. In the perspective I establish, the danger of nuclear armageddon, as well as perceptions of that danger, was created less by the invention of nuclear weapons than by the attitudes and practices established before 1945.

I also concentrate on the rise of American air power, seeking to explain the origins, preeminence, and uses of that power. Of course, a book limited to that story and to the prenuclear era cannot fully explain the dilemma of our times. The warplane was the product of international technology, ideas, and relations, and while I have not systematically attempted a global history of air power, I have selectively drawn on ideas and developments abroad, especially in Great Britain, whose prophets, inventors, and warriors usually found a receptive audience in the United States. But the rise of American air power is the key to the modern dilemma.

I also concentrate on what Americans have expected of and learned from strategic bombing. Their perspectives on the bomber are crucial, for the warplane was created in imagination before it was invented as a practical weapon. The bomber was the product of extravagant dreams and dark forebodings about the role it might play in war and peace. Moreover, because the airplane had numerous peacetime uses, many of them stimulating grand hopes in their own right, it often developed without much attention to its possible role in war. Peaceful uses so meshed with military applications that each often evolved under the cover of the other, in ways familiar from the later evolution of nuclear and space technology. Thus, an understanding of American air power and of the problem of aerial warfare can be achieved only in the context of cultural and intellectual history. The ways people have thought about air power proved so remarkably consistent, despite rapidly changing technology over a half-century, that a mere recital of a particular invention or an individual bombing raid sheds little light on the appeals and uses of air power. The bomber in imagination is the most compelling and revealing story.

A history of American air power might be written from other perspectives—tactics, technologies, organizations, and campaigns—some of which are already well developed by other writers. After all, ideas about air power did not evolve wholly apart from tangible developments. Practical limitations imposed sharp restraints on the translation of ideas into action, often more so than statesmen or warriors initially realized. Because that was so, my account necessarily becomes lengthier and more complex once it reaches World War II; the simplicity of war possible in imagination diminished in execution. The interplay of ideas and actions, theory and technology, dreams and deeds constitutes a significant focus of this account. But I emphasize that practical developments were usually secondary to imagination in shaping strategic air war.

At the same time, to treat bombing simply as an abstraction—as a strategy or horrible fantasy or set of statistics—would be to repeat a persistent error in a half-century's preoccupation with the bomber: the tendency to regard it (and finally the atomic bomb) as more potent in imagination than in its capacity to kill and destroy. In part for that reason, I examine not only what people thought about bombers but what bombing actually did, especially in the massive campaigns of World War II that preceded use of the atomic weapon. Only a full appreciation of those campaigns can establish how the problem of air war became acute long before the nuclear age.

This account may strike some readers as unduly harsh toward American leaders, especially those generals, Henry Harley Arnold and Curtis E. LeMay, who championed the most destructive forms of bombing. But it should also emerge that the limitations of these men were generally the product of the political, cultural, and intellectual environment in which they worked. At times military men did better than civilians in overcoming that environment, and rarely did they do much worse. Limited or ambitious men, both in and out of the military, often sanctioned a kind of casual brutality. Yet their roles do more to illustrate than to explain why the story unfolded as it did. Similarly, while they often quarreled with each other, generating those feuds and conflicts that are the stuff of much military history, in the end it is more instructive to trace what diverse groups had in common as they thought about and practiced aerial warfare.

Some readers may also find my explanation of American war-making unduly or unfairly critical, especially in its suggestion of how racist attitudes and assumptions helped shape the bombing campaign against Japan. As the inevitably skeptical question puts it: if Americans were racist in incinerating Japanese cities, then how can one explain Britain's firebombing of Hamburg and Dresden? The answer, it seems to me, is relatively simple: similar consequences can arise out of different motives and impulses. Of course, British and American bombing had much in common as well, but Japanese–American racial antagonisms added special fuel to the combustible mix of wartime motives for bombing. By the same token, racism was hardly the only impulse behind American bombing: I suggest that among policymakers, if not in the public at large, a technological fanaticism often governed actions, an approach to making war in which satisfaction of organizational and professional drives loomed larger than the overt passions of war.

The methods I have employed in researching and writing this story are familiar ones. A large literature of published sources is available. At many points I have also drawn heavily from archival sources, although they are often exasperatingly uneven in quality and quantity. My use of oral history, a popular technique in recent decades, has been limited. I have followed chronology in a broad way, but I sometimes set it aside to characterize certain moods, ideas, and practices that defy precise chronological placement.

Above all, I have emphasized the diversity of the appeals that air power has had for Americans. The result is a somewhat eclectic explanation of how Americans came to embrace strategic bombing, but this is deliberate, for it is important not to see the bomber as satisfying merely the needs of particular interest groups or the strategic demands of particular campaigns. The diversity of its appeals made the bomber a unique weapon and helped its rise to first place in national strategy and policy. Particular arguments for or against the bomber might come and go, but a host of others was always available. Like most important changes in how nations behave, the rise of American air power rested on arguments whose collective force was greater than the sum of their parts. In the end, the United States often accepted air power regardless of the merits of specific arguments, leaving us a legacy with which we still grapple.

A note on terminology. I have tried to avoid the special language of military organizations. While at times I refer to the Army Air Corps, an official designation applying to the period 1926–41, or to the Army Air Forces (AAF), the wartime designation, I often refer to the "air force" or the "American air force," a generic term for the aviation of the United States Army, which went through numerous bureaucratic mutations to which the reader need not be subjected and did not attain independence from the army until after World War II. When I refer to "airmen," I usually mean military aviators, primarily those within the United States Army except where the context indicates otherwise.

Many readers will be aware of several recent books relevant to my topic, including some which, to this writer's consternation, appeared just as this book was going into production. At the last moment, I briefly and selectively drew on three of special importance: Ronald Schaffer's *Wings of Judgment;* Paul Boyer's *By the Bomb's Early Light;* and John Dower's *War Without Mercy.* Future scholars will wish to make further use of these and other recent sources and to pursue the dialogue on important issues that they, hopefully along with my own work, establish.

Many people contributed to this book. At Northwestern University, Karen Halttunen and Sarah Maza provided support and guidance; in differing ways, Robert Wiebe and David Joravsky helped me to broaden and sharpen the book's perspective; Betty Jo Dobbs made suggestive comments about how to understand science and scientists; Robert Finlay worked with astonishing tenacity to help me edit the book into more manageable form. Richard Chapman gave assistance and countless corrections at all stages; Leo Ribuffo provoked me to sharpen my criticism; Abby Solomon listened to my complaints and gave valuable advice; George Roeder offered wide-ranging suggestions and boundless enthusiasm. My debt to archivists is as great as any author's; all cannot be mentioned, but William Cunliffe of the National Archives was once again tireless in searching for records and wise in commenting upon how I used them. In tracking down records and gaining perspective on a key figure, Forrest C. Pogue, the biographer of George C. Marshall, provided critical assistance at the beginning and end of this project. My editor at Yale University Press, Charles Grench, mixed support and skepticism in just the right combination. Two typists, June Schuster and Joan Stahl, worked with a cumbersome technology and a capricious author to prepare the manuscript. Several organizations extended financial assistance: the National Endowment for the Humanities provided the bulk of support for research, supplemented by grants from Northwestern University and the Eleanor Roosevelt Foundation; the Rockefeller Foundation funded a year's leave, enabling me to draft the manuscript; Northwestern University covered most of the costs of preparing the manuscript. Richard Davis provided friendship and a quiet refuge where I could review my own work critically. James Beal was patient and understanding in the face of my many absences to work on this book; I owe him a special debt.

Lake Winnipesaukee, New Hampshire
September 1985

Evanston, Illinois
June 1986

THE RISE OF AMERICAN AIR POWER
THE CREATION OF ARMAGEDDON

The Age of Fantasy

Before the final battle in *A Connecticut Yankee in King Arthur's Court,* the hero's companion boasts, "We shan't have to leave our fortress, now, when we want to blow up civilization." After his electric battlefield has done its work, Hank Morgan, the Yankee genius, surveys the results. "Of course we could not count the dead, because they did not exist as individuals, but merely as homogeneous protoplasm, with alloys of iron and buttons."[1] Mark Twain's fantasy, full of doubt about the future of mankind and men's wars, satirized the attractions and dangers of a dehumanized technology of war: destructive passion disguised as cold science, peril clothed in progress, imperialism masked as ingenuity. In the decades after Twain wrote, the attractions were more persuasive, especially when men and women anticipated the role that aircraft might play.

THE LIMITS OF FANTASY

Twain had not foreseen the airplane, but in imagining more generally the consequences of modern weaponry, he had established a perspective within which the airplane might have been viewed. By the time his prophecy appeared in 1889, a substantial predictive literature about flight already existed; it proliferated over the next twenty-five years of technological development capped by the Wright brothers' first powered flight in 1903. Moreover, this literature flourished in the context of an explosive growth in other military technologies and in the acquisition of armaments, armies, and navies by the world's major powers.

Throughout the period, military uses for aircraft were hardly unforeseen. More than any other modern weapon, the bomber was imagined before it was invented. In a century of primitive experiments with balloons and then with dirigibles, nearly every claim later advanced by strategists of air war was already mentioned. After 1900, the

1

first demonstrations of heavier-than-air craft usually had unmistakable military implications, or took place in public view of governments' interest in those implications. They were obvious to Europeans after the first flights across the English Channel. In the United States, the initial wave of publicity regarding the airplane as a practical machine came in 1908, when the Wright brothers demonstrated their invention over the capital for the U.S. Army Signal Corps. For days, thousands watched in awe at the miracle of flight, and the event stirred lavish predictions about how the airplane would change the affairs of the nation and humankind. That event, like others, precipitated little foreboding. Even when prophets detected dangers, they usually converted them into virtues.

Fantasy followed optimistic paths in part because of certain unique properties of the airplane. It may be true that "guns, like everything else, have their social history," one rooted in identifiable social, economic, and national interests. But inasmuch as the airplane was never merely a weapon of war, its development confronts the social historian with a greater challenge than other devices of modern warfare. As Winston Churchill once said, "The submarine, to do it justice, has never made any claim to be a blessing, or even a convenience." The submarine, the machine gun, and the tank sometimes fired the imagination (of Jules Verne, for example) but did not touch the range of interests, aspirations, and activities that the airplane would.[2]

Never viewed solely as a weapon, the airplane was the instrument of flight, of a whole new dimension in human activity. Therefore it was uniquely capable of stimulating fantasies of peacetime possibilities for lifting worldly burdens, transforming man's sense of time and space, transcending geography, knitting together nations and peoples, releasing humankind from its biological limits. Flight also resonated with the deepest impulses and symbols of religious and particularly Christian mythology—nothing less than Christ's ascension. Its realization, then, served as a powerful metaphor for heavenly aspirations and even, among the literal-minded, as the palpable vehicle for achieving them. Not surprisingly, prediction preceded innovation and ran far ahead of technology even after invention occurred.

As metaphor for so many human aspirations, flight stimulated fantasies that were by no means consistently positive. In prehistory, in ancient cultures yielding legends like that of Icarus, in Da Vinci's work on flying machines, in the hysterical reactions of Parisian crowds to the first balloon ascents, and in the outpouring of predictive literature at the close of the nineteenth century, flight had seemed both dangerous and attractive, symbol of vision and arrogance. Likewise with speculation about the impact of flight upon warfare. Eighteenth-century Parisians imagined "our cities in fire, our harvests ravaged, our fortresses destroyed," even their wives and daughters ravished by "lovers and thieves descending our chimneys."[3] Manned flight suggested a wide range of wartime possibilities on which dreamers could speculate and over which, once flying became a reality, men and women would argue.

The variety of these conflicting images of danger and promise made the airplane harder to ignore than other prospective weapons, made thinking about it more complex, and made its development more difficult to trace. In breadth of impact on humankind, especially in capacity to stir the imagination, only the railroad and the steamship approached the airplane, although few commentators explored the precedent they offered about changes in warfare, and only nuclear energy was comparable for a later age. The warplane had its social history, but a complicated one that went beyond national interests or parochial influence, peculiar conceptions of war, and war itself. Air war had its origins in the complicated relationships among fantasy, patterns of technological improvisation, and the immediate context of war and peace.

Of these, fantasy was sometimes the most important, certainly the most revealing. Of course, people imagined the impact of flight on warfare in imperfect ways. But the themes that arose proved remarkably persistent. The reasons people feared or welcomed the warplane were often the same in 1900 as they would be in 1940, or even in 1980. The tension between large hopes and dark fears about the warplane, between apocalyptic apprehensions and dreams of deliverance, was also lasting. The nature of the airplane alone did not make for such constancy. Vivid, often mistaken predictions about air war said less about technology or the imperfections of imagination than about the cultures which would build and use bombers. If they do not always explain why nations would bomb one another, they at least suggest how they would justify bombing or why they sometimes needed little justification at all.

Fantasy about how flight might affect warfare fed on the technological progress and accelerating militarism of the European world at the century's turn. By 1900, the major European powers had some four million men in uniform and a capacity to mobilize perhaps ten times that number. More than that, they were increasingly conscious of their technological rivalry, especially in naval armaments, the race for which even distant upstarts like the United States and Japan now joined. Free from the burden of a major war for thirty years, Europeans were nonetheless troubled as well by how they might reconcile a developing faith in peace with evidence of escalating armaments and international tensions. It was not a simple fear of war, but rather a desire to deny that fear and reconcile it to the faith in peace that stimulated an extensive literature about new weapons. The gravity of hopes and fears regarding war and technology, and the style adopted in appealing to a new mass readership, gave that literature its distinctive character.

Prophecy about new weapons did not come so freely to Americans at the turn of the century as it did to Europeans. Some Americans did see military purpose in the airplane, but more with an eye to commercial possibilities than to war itself. Samuel P. Langley, the venerable scientist whose crowning effort at powered flight dropped "like a handful of mortar" into the Potomac River, coaxed a grant from the United States Army in 1898 with vague promises as to how his machines might change warfare. But Langley cared most about his experiments and their financing, little about war.[4]

In the American Army's Signal Corps, overseer of a feeble effort at military aviation, some of the pioneer fliers naturally took war more seriously. They had read daring predictions for air power, like that made in Chicago in 1893 by a British officer who foresaw the day when "the arrival of the aerial fleet over the enemy capital will probably conclude the campaign." They could speculate, as one American officer did in 1908, that powerful airships would some day be so frightening that they would "make war less likely in the future than in the past." But military men were generally reticent or uncertain about the future of the warplane, despite the later claims of some to early foresightedness. It could hardly have been otherwise. Blériot's flight across the English Channel in 1909 made some Englishmen, already primed by years of scare literature about invasion from across or under the Channel, moan that England was "no longer an island." It could prompt no similar terrors in the United States, an ocean away from potential enemies; hence prophecy about new weapons was sparse, or it came, like Twain's complex fantasy, in a context far different from war as people thought of it. In Ignatius Donnelly's apocalyptic account of class warfare, the airship was the workingman's instrument of brutal revenge against his oppressors as well as the vehicle of flight to a new Eden—in short, a tool for Donnelly in his attempt (common in the 1890s) to trace the future of an America falling victim to class divisions.[5]

Still, not all Americans were mute. Though the context was civil rather than international war, Donnelly's fantasy foreshadowed a half-century's preoccupation with the bomber as instrument of vengeance rather than victory and as catalyst to bloody class conflict. In other prophecies, Americans struck the same themes of confidence and foreboding more extensively developed in the predictive literature of Europeans. Seers on both sides of the Atlantic took comfort in the very awfulness of imagined warplanes. Precisely because the "birds of hell" would bring "shrieks of agony" and leave men "crazed with fear," they would also leave "the capital of a great nation, a great army, costly defenses and armament, all at the mercy of few hundred bird men." Airplanes, it was hoped, might end "war as we had known it." The sight, the sound, even the prospect of aeronautical terrors might make nations end war speedily or capitulate before war began or even banish war altogether. Such predictions shaded off into another category of prophecy, one that saw a less direct but no less benign implication for war in the airplane's advent. Stefan Zweig saw in Blériot's flight the seeds of "a European community spirit, a European national consciousness" making national frontiers "useless" because "the spirit of these times . . . visibly seeks unity and world brotherhood!" In the United States, the romanticism of other possibilities was even more fervid. Poets extolled aviators as "winged Argonauts of trackless air" whose "Golden Fleece" would be "Man's Brotherhood." One American transformed the airplane into "a mechanical messiah whose coming would wondrously transform life and society," as her vision has been described: it seemed that "the airplane had irrevocably cleaved history into two epochs." It was even leading to "the emergence of an 'aerial' person" according to the prominent feminist Charlotte Perkins Gilman.[6]

These were predictions not so much about the impact of the airplane on war or peace as about the expected salutary course of technological progress. People did not look at the airplane and then deduce its impact on human affairs. Rather, they took

general propositions about the benefits of technology and applied them as confidently to
the imagined airplane as they did to other weapons and inventions—or more confidently, since the airplane was endowed with more virtues. It was as easy for some to
prophesy, as Victor Hugo did in 1864, that flying machines would make armies "vanish, and with them the whole business of war, exploitation and subjugation" as it was
for others to proclaim how the machine gun "would compel all nations to keep peace
towards each other." This habit was not entirely new, for centuries earlier John Donne
had concluded that "the numbers of men slain now, since the invention of Artillery,
are much lesse than before, when the sword was the executioner."[7]

Now it was an article of faith. The airplane was like a host of other weapons
invented or imagined in the nineteenth century and celebrated for their capacity to
"diminish the evils of war." To John Hay, the American secretary of state, these
weapons demonstrated "the plain lesson of history that the periods of peace have been
longer protracted as the cost and destructiveness of war have increased." Hay's assumption was similar to Jack London's confidence that "the marvelous and awful
machinery of warfare . . . today defeats its own end. Made pre-eminently to kill, its
chief effect is to make killing quite the unusual thing." An American newspaper
caught the same mood succinctly: "Behind the images of carnage shines the light of
universal peace." The predictive literature of the times, I. F. Clarke has argued, was
almost unanimous "in claiming that war had become too terrible to continue, or that it
had become so rapid in its results that the modern battle was now far more humane
than the dreadful engagements of the bad old days." Just as with the other new
inventions, there were opposing predictions about the airplane as well, some that
dismissed it as a harmless, if amusing toy or a practical but pedestrian aid to armies and
navies. But these predictions provided counterpoint, not corrective, to the faith that, in
the modern world, "the greatest destroyer is the greatest philanthropist."[8]

That faith was perhaps not so naive as later generations often thought. The
prophets of peace recognized the destructiveness of modern weaponry, so much so that
faith in peace became a necessity, not just the product of complacent idealism. The
alternative was to face terrors too awesome to contemplate. Altering international rules
first laid down in 1899, the Hague Conference of 1907 banned "bombardment, by
whatever means" of "undefended" cities and structures, but prohibition alone provided
scant comfort.[9] Elaborate international agreements and diverse peace movements rested in part upon regarding the machine gun and the bomber as yet another sign of man's
progress.

Their proponents tried gamely to place such weapons in service to higher goals.
They saw preparedness as compatible with peace, not primarily because new weapons
would deter aggressors, but because they would deter or shorten war itself by making it
too horrible for intelligent citizens to entertain or endure. It therefore seemed plausible
for an American politician to urge that the way "to lessen human warfare" was to
"cultivate the highest chemistry and make the most deadly armament." War might not
disappear altogether—historical experience as well as gleanings from Darwin made

that seem unlikely, just as confidence in the efficacy of some types of war made it seem undesirable. Still, it might be shortened, humanized, or confined to inferior peoples for whom it served as an agent of progress. If so, Europeans could still, in Clarke's words, "have their wars and enjoy them."[10]

War itself was not unthinkable, only endless and meaningless war. Far from ignoring new weapons, the prewar generation often exaggerated their destructiveness in order to assert their power to compel peace. Sentiments seemingly opposed to each other—hope for peace and fear of modern weapons—coexisted comfortably because this generation found hope in their very terror. It displayed a morbid fascination with them only to wish them away. But it did serve notice of their imminence.

The times seemed to bear witness to that trust. A century of technological progress had also seen relative peace in Europe. The brevity and decisiveness of most wars that did occur seemed only to validate the claim that scientific advancement and economic interdependence were making protracted war impractical or unthinkable. Not even Americans realized that their Civil War prefigured the enormous increases in defensive firepower and economic resources which would make battle more costly and less conclusive. When so many other social problems seemed conquerable by science, it made sense to think that science might also diminish the evil of war.

Behind such reasoning lay a deeper faith in the capacity of men and women to make rational decisions about their fate. On the eve of World War I, Norman Angell's *The Great Illusion*, the most famous expression of that faith, argued that economic interdependence among progressive nations made war senseless. War might happen, he said, but it would do nobody any good if it did, for it would sever the connections of credit and commerce on which all depended. Read as a prediction of what harm war might bring, *The Great Illusion* was reasonable prophecy; but as a prediction of man's new rationality, it missed the mark in a way that expressed its times well. It also influenced later proponents of peace through aviation, who saw aviation as spinning a web of international connectedness.

Reactions to new weapons were also shaped by concern about the destruction of men's souls rather than men's bodies. In an age nursing both great hopes and substantial fears about the fate of the individual, war was still seen as the foremost arena for the demonstration of heroic potential; the chief danger of the dreadnought or the machine gun or the airplane was that they might make men superfluous or anonymous in war. Even Alfred Thayer Mahan, champion of the modern American navy, feared that new battleships carrying only long-range guns would create in commanders an "indisposition to close" with the enemy. It was possible as well to worry that passionless strife might make men more savage, given the assumption that "terror and punishment were useful checks on the human impulse to prolong war."[11]

People dealt with these fears in several ways. Past wars could be rewritten to glorify the individual's heroic achievements and give meaning to bitter sacrifices, as Americans often did with their Civil War—missing how Cold Harbor and Sherman's march set a precedent for an age of impersonal destruction. Legions of professional military officers met the danger of new weapons simply by denying that the weapons would do much to change warfare, by resisting their use, or by redoubling their enthusiasm for the cavalry charge and the offensive à outrance. Others celebrated the men who mastered the new machines as a new kind of technological hero. They hoped that the power and precision of new weapons would free soldiers from the regimented confines of close-order formations, so necessary when guns were inaccurate. Such weapons, Harvard President Charles W. Eliot argued, would force "every modern army to imitate what used to be called Indian warfare." Aerial dogfights in World War I later seemed to confirm how machines would expand rather than constrict opportunities for individual derring-do. [12]

Prophets of air war hinted at another, more disturbing opportunity for heroism. They did not escape the preoccupation of the age with will and courage. But they socialized those qualities, making them the virtues of the masses at home as well as of the individual soldiers at the front. Victory would be decided in a nightmarish contest of national wills, the loser the nation that quailed before the prospect of aerial attack on its capital or succumbed to mass panic at the first "knock-out" blow.

Visions of aerial war thus united two different concerns about warfare—the modernist's emphasis on scientific destruction and the nation in arms and the traditionalist's faith in demonstrations of courage and élan as decisive in battle. Such demonstrations were now the responsibility of the nation itself, as it resolved to mobilize huge resources and dared to risk destruction. In that bleak vision, the agencies of destruction were new and impersonal, but at least traditional values remained useful.

It was also possible to disassociate war technology from war itself, seeing it as a sign of cultural progress and racial superiority. Scientists and engineers sometimes approached the invention of the airplane in the same spirit they employed in developing light bulbs or phonographs. Whatever their ultimate uses, these devices brought the joy of problem solving and served as signs of man's triumph over nature. The press, too, celebrated new instruments of destruction as examples of beauty and scientific creativity or as evidence of a new industrial bounty which would make nations less greedy and warlike toward each other. For a generation fearful of race decline, the new technology also seemed to buttress the dominant position of the white race. Occasional fantasies granted licence for using the new weapons against supposed racial inferiors in a way intolerable in thinking about war among one's brethren. Bombers might unleash on China and Japan "a rain of death to every breathing thing, a rain that exterminates the hopeless race." [13]

The visions of air war that emerged before World War I were shaped by these broad currents of racism and faith in progress as well as by certain habits of style and form already established in the sensational predictive literature about war. That literature exploited the passions and patriotism of a new mass readership by dealing with international rivalries and technological change in absolutist categories of victory and defeat, disaster and deliverance. It rarely allowed for subtler possibilities or, in an age of more pressing concerns about dreadnoughts and mass armies, for extended attention to the airplane itself. Predictions about air war were too few, too inchoate, and too remote from immediate dangers to allow an argument about its future to be fully joined.

The extremes of hope for the warplane's capacity to revolutionize warfare and offhand dismissal of its importance defined not so much a spectrum of opinion as a chasm of less emotionally satisfying possibilities that few people could explore. Those who thought about the future of air war—rarely the statesmen or generals who would later make the decisions—had few alternatives from which to choose. They were told that terror from the sky would eliminate the burden of carnage on the ground and costly armadas at sea by shocking armies and nations into quick surrender and perhaps even into a permanent peace. Or they could take comfort in the assurance that the airplane would scarcely change warfare at all, serving only to improve observation and communication (as balloons were already doing) or to add a bit of firepower to the battlefield.

Only one man located the grimmer terrain between these polarized possibilities. To be sure, H. G. Wells could not always resist the pull of extravagant hopes for the airplane. In *The World Set Free* (1914) Wells showed mankind awakening to the necessity of a world government to rescue it from total war, although only after so many years of global destruction by air that the fantasy was at best bleakly utopian. And *The World Set Free* was Wells's weaker prophecy, more striking for its forecast of atomic bombs and radioactive poisoning than for its insight into the evolution of air war.

The War in the Air (1908) was at once more apocalyptic and more realistic. A war begun by German air raids on American cities expands into a global struggle in which the Asiatic nations prove as adept as Europeans in the arts of destruction from the skies. The Asiatics are no more successful in gaining a decision, however, and the world plunges into "a universal guerrilla war" from which there is no escape.

While other commentators based predictions about the airplane on their comfortable assumptions about Western civilization, Wells drew on his fundamental pessimism about it. For him, the airplane was the logical product of the thoughtless militarism of the time, the lazy faith in the certainty of progress, and the "destructive scramble" of the great powers to extend their "economic exploitation." Likewise, the bomber could topple that civilization not just because it could kill and destroy, but because it would rip apart its economic and political fabric. Political convulsion, economic chaos, famine, and pestilence would be the real sources of civilization's collapse. Death and destruction by bombing would only be their catalysts. Wells's nightmare vision succeeded in part because he alone saw air war in its broadest context, as both the product and the downfall of Western civilization.[14]

Wells also had a subtler appreciation of nationalism and crowd psychology. He took the emerging notion of a knockout aerial blow to the national will and gave it a new and dismaying twist. In *The War in the Air* the brief, relatively light attack on New York City forces quick capitulation by panicky municipal officials. But far from producing national surrender, it only fires the indignation and patriotism of the masses, who demand that the fight continue, thereby plunging the nation into an all-out war. The knockout blow fells only the orderly process of government, not the blind urge to fight on; it yields no mercifully brief decision, only long descent into global destruction. If Wells misjudged the capacity of governments to retain their authority amid national calamity, he understood, with an eye to the Paris Commune, the popular passions and national tenacity which would make a myth of the notion of a decisive, paralyzing attack from the air.

A sensible appreciation of the military limitations of the airplane led him to much the same conclusion. Warplanes "could inflict immense damage; they could reduce any organised Government to a capitulation in the briefest space, but they could not disarm, much less could they occupy, the surrendered areas below. They had to trust the pressure upon the authorities below of a threat to renew the bombardment. It was their sole resource." "The Germans," he added, "had struck at the head, and the head was conquered and stunned—only to release the body from its rule." Even turning part of New York City into "a furnace of crimson flames" brought no victory. Wells's key insight was that aerial warfare was "at once enormously destructive and entirely indecisive." It might inflict incalculable bloodshed rather than freeing man from it. [15]

In imagining vast aerial armadas rising almost overnight into the skies, Wells grossly underestimated the economical and technical demands of air war—a misjudgment made by many others for decades. The awesomeness of the destruction he foresaw also taxed Wells's capacity for dramatization: terrible events were viewed through the eyes of a hapless and negligible victim. In between the abstract and the individual lay possibilities of vast destruction that even Wells could not fully capture. His own penchant for apocalyptic visions did not allow him to consider whether nations might learn to live, however badly, with this new weapon, harnessing it to older forms of warfare, but neither abolishing it as he urged nor succumbing to all its dangers as he feared.

Still, Wells rose above his contemporaries by recognizing the complexities of the new weapon, by rejecting a simple choice between the trivial and the millennial predictions that others made, and by exploring that chasm between them. He tried to see the warplane as a horrid but limited weapon, neither unthinkable nor blessed. Coming from a writer of international fame and influence, his warning did not go unnoticed. It also changed the prevailing outlook very little.

FANTASY AND IMPROVISATION

Although visions like Wells's revealed contemporary expectations, they did little to guide the practical development of military aviation in its first years. That development derived from technical and tactical improvisations connected only loosely to the larger visions. Speculation about the warplane usually came from those who had little to do with invention, from poets and futurists and politicians. When generals, aviators, and technicians began toying with the warplane before World War I, they improvised both technology and doctrine, often indifferent toward grander prophecies, though sometimes goaded into action by the politicians and pundits who mouthed them.

Scientists and inventors provided little guidance. The Wright brothers had no great scheme for employing warplanes when they began securing military contracts in Europe and, after a rebuff, in America. Concerned with the patent and financial issues raised by those contracts, they pondered its military utility only passingly. They knew that the airplane's initial use would be military. But they were naive about their power to control that use, slow to see any role for the plane beyond observation and quick to calm their unease about bombing and strafing with platitudes. At the end of World War I, Orville Wright could still reassure himself that "the aeroplane has made war so terrible that I do not believe any country will again care to start a war."[16]

Few inventors and developers—Count von Zeppelin with his dirigibles was one exception—had more imagination than the Wrights. Bacon and Da Vinci had secreted their designs for a host of dreadful weapons "on account of the evil nature of man," as Da Vinci put it. In their time, scientists "tended to be more obedient, or at least more vocal about obedience, to moral and Christian principles." The airplane's inventors did not so much reject those principles as ignore them. Alexander Graham Bell, for decades deeply involved in aeronautical research, explained during the Spanish-American War, "I am not ambitious to be known as the inventor of a weapon of destruction" but added that "I must say the problem—simply as a problem—fascinates me." The plane's wartime use was often just a secondary concern to its creators. Thus the pace of technological progress governed the warplane's development, not because men were somehow driven by its sheer force, but in part because they abdicated responsibility to it.[17]

The reticence of the airplane's inventors about its moral and strategic implications did not stem from lack of sophistication. Far from being the "folklore technologists" that myth sometimes made them out to be, they succeeded because they appreciated the scientific method, participated in an embryonic community of aeronautical experts, knew the virtues of institutionalized research, and recognized that only government could offer them capital and a market.[18] But as theorists and moralists of war, they had little to suggest. They offered only the raw materials which, as Elting Morison has commented regarding the navy, "were brought into successful combination by minds not interested in the instruments for themselves but in what they could do for them."[19] Only a later generation of scientists sometimes felt sufficiently compelled or confident to tell military men how to use their inventions.

Among American army and navy fliers, the second group responsible for early developments in military aviation, practical concerns and patterns of improvisation were also dominant. Money was one preoccupation—the army hesitated to fund aviation at all. Staying alive was another—one-fourth of the first contingent of flying officers died in training. They crashed too often or left aviation too soon or were too low in rank to worry about doctrine and strategy. Between 1910 and 1912, they were among the world's first aviators to experiment with firing guns and dropping bombs from planes, but they leapt to few conclusions as a result. As for the Signal Corps, its interest was limited to the airplane's role in reconnaissance and communications.

Military aviation was even then a public issue, but political debate did little to clarify conceptions of the airplane's purpose. A struggle over where to place aviation in the military system—one destined to plague military politics for decades—was already beginning. But that struggle did as much to sidetrack thinking about the airplane's purpose as to inform it, partly because it encouraged exaggerated claims from partisans, partly because it focused attention on the organizational forms rather than on the strategic substance of air power.

True, it was possible to imagine that the airplane would some day be more than "merely an added means of communication, observation and reconnaissance," as the assistant secretary of war characterized it in 1913.[20] By 1916 even the army's general staff, never given to a generous view of the airplane's potential, recommended aviation's eventual separation from the Signal Corps, while Congress was already considering a proposal for a cabinet-level department of aviation. During the war, aviation was finally removed from the Signal Corps' authority and might have become an independent service had the war gone on longer.

But young airmen like William Mitchell and Henry Harley Arnold, who would later lead the fight for aviation's autonomy, were content before 1917 to remain wards of the Signal Corps, unsure as yet that they had either the doctrine or the political resources to fly on their own. In the navy, more accustomed to technological change and to projecting American power abroad, a few officers were more venturesome. They foresaw a place for naval aviation in defending the Philippines, the first of generations of officers who looked to air power as an economical way to defend American interests in the Far East. They also weighed development of aircraft carriers and bombing missions for their planes. Neither before nor during World War I did the navy do much with these possibilities, limiting its aviation largely to reconnaissance and coastal defense.[21]

Before World War I, then, military aviation was hardly more than a casual improvisation, even in Europe, where popular fears of doomsday occasionally prompted hurried efforts to build warplanes. On the eve of World War I, the major powers could each claim only about fifty to one hundred planes, none ready to fight. "In fact," as Robin Higham succinctly put it, "exactly what they were there for was not very clear."[22] Success in military aviation had less to do with national talents or needs than with the accidents of war. The Germans were developing dirigibles whose potential for bombing intrigued them and alarmed the British. But the Italians led in aviation because their war with the Turks in 1911–12 accelerated their aviation program. They carried out the first bombing operations since Austrian balloonists tossed a few explosives on Venice in 1849. The Italians' effort also prompted the first moral controversy over a bombing incident. But the Italians did not become a major air power, although their effort was impressive until the start of World War II. The American armed forces, eventually to be supreme in the air, numbered their planes and pilots in the dozens, spent a pittance on aviation compared to other major powers, and by 1914 had lost whatever lead they earlier held. Whatever the deeper national needs or traits that eventually fostered American supremacy—such as a knack for technology or a fondness for inexpensive and decisive victories—they were not much in evidence before World War I. Americans showed no special rush to develop warplanes, no peculiar interest or talent that matched or exceeded that of other major powers.

Historians sometimes list the factors that retarded the development of military aviation in the United States and abroad—the primitiveness of technology and the unpredictability of its development, the resistance of military bureaucracies to change and the paucity of institutional mechanisms to promote it, the lack of urgency about national security and the preoccupation with naval armaments. Undoubtedly such forces were at work. Yet merely to recite them is to suggest that somehow progress should have come more quickly. There was no reason that it should have. Only war and a new set of attitudes toward national security could make that happen. Until 1914, the airplane inspired hopes and fears to which the casual efforts of the time bore little relation.

THE TEST OF WAR

In war the improvisational pattern continued. Airplanes, undifferentiated as to design or purpose at the start of the war, soon proliferated into different types, with conflicting organizations and doctrines to employ them. The issue became less whether to use aircraft in war than how. Even late in the war, battlefield (tactical) uses had priority: for reconnaissance, observation, and artillery spotting; for command of the air space while performing those functions; and for strafing troops and enemy positions. Most field commanders wanted nothing more from their aircraft. The stalemate of slaughter on the ground, far from encouraging them to seek out new ways of gaining a decision, only made them hungrier for aerial resources that might somehow tip the balance in battle, thereby justifying the monstrous expenditure of men and machines and rescuing their reputations.

Aside from technological advances, what encouraged some military men to assign a more ambitious role to airplanes remains unclear. The few strategists who articulated such a role rarely indicated the source of their ideas. Probably the prewar fantasies of air war had at most an indirect influence. Instead, strategic air war* grew haphazardly. A complex mix of popular passions, political ambitions, strategic desperation, military rivalry, and wartime momentum brought the bombers to London and Cologne.

As in most wars, responsibility for introducing new terrors was unclear in this one. Precedent of course existed in artillery shelling of cities. As for aerial bombs, German planes dropped a few on Liège and Paris during the war's first weeks. The British struck German Zeppelin sheds in September 1914. The French first dropped bombs on a German city in December, just weeks before the Germans struck at Dover.

---

*Defined here as aerial attack on an enemy's capacity and will to sustain military operations, rather than on those operations themselves.

Zeppelin attacks on England followed in 1915, and soon the bombing spread to all theaters of war. Austrians and Italians traded notably punishing blows against cities. The French, wary of setting the wrong precedent for German bombers, generally confined their large effort to attacks on military and industrial targets. But by war's end, bombs had hit every capital of the warring European powers except Rome, and rumors of impending attack even darkened cities in eastern Canada and the United States.

The Zeppelin raids of 1915 marked the decisive turn. Motivated partly by rivalries and ambitions within the military, they were pressed by officers on a civilian leadership with sentimental, moral, and political qualms about bombing. The kaiser, worried about the fate of his royal cousins in London and squeamish about the nastiness of modern war, reluctantly approved the bombing program only after getting assurances that "historic buildings and private property will be spared as much as possible," stipulations that neither the state of the art nor the desires of officers could long respect. Chancellor Bethmann-Hollweg feared that unrestricted war, in the air as on the seas, might make "a very unfavourable impression on foreign neutrals, particularly in America." He of course lost the argument. [23]

The case for bombing cities developed piecemeal. German commanders promised tangible rewards: raids on British cities would supposedly force the Allies to divert precious resources from France in order to defend England, giving the Germans an edge in the great battles on the western front. This promise was indeed partly realized. When cries of anguish and indignation in England forced the hand of authorities, they gradually assembled an impressive apparatus of air defense: hundreds of fighter aircraft, antiaircraft guns, barrage balloons, searchlights, sound detectors, and communications systems. An invaluable rehearsal for 1940, this effort offered few immediate benefits for the British. Weather, navigational difficulties, and mechanical breakdowns did as much to slow the German attacks, and British antiaircraft shells proved a sometimes deadly menace to the population they tried to protect, as did the many false alarms of a hair-trigger warning system. German attacks did drain English resources; but that consideration made some authorities hesitate to invest too heavily in air defense, lest doing so invite the very German bombing they hoped to deter.

The Germans exaggerated the rewards, however. They assumed that the resources diverted would have played a critical role on the front, when aviation was in fact not that decisive as yet. Had the English government kept those resources in France, they would only have "encouraged their generals to squander even more of their manpower on futile attempts to storm impregnable positions." [24] In addition, Germany's bombing enthusiasts ignored the drain of air war on their own resources. Though numbering only in the dozens, the Zeppelins and later the lumbering Giant bombers, with a wingspread scarcely shorter than that of the B-29s of World War II, imposed a considerable cost on the Germans as well. Not for the last time, airmen employed a facile but faulty calculus.

The German command also sought to damage the English economy, directly by destruction of physical plant—a farfetched possibility given the weight and accuracy of the bombers' effort—and indirectly by causing demoralization and panic in the work force. "The German people," one communiqué warned, "has become a hard race with an iron fist. . . . The hammer is in our hands, and it will fall mercilessly and shatter the places where England is forging weapons against us." In fact, it fell randomly, noisily, but hardly mercilessly. Results were occasionally spectacular, especially when German bombers struck in darkness, as the English air defense often forced them to do. On some nights, hundreds of thousands of Londoners streamed into the tubes and tunnels under their city, production in some key industries was disrupted, and even David Lloyd George himself, who "lacked physical courage," fled the city.[25]

English terror mirrored German hopes. It was undoubtedly not just a response to the scale of the raids, each of which, as one observer commented, hardly compared to "a before-breakfast skirmish almost any morning on the Somme," and which together inflicted some fourteen hundred English fatalities during the war. Terror sprang from the unpredictability of the raids as well as from shock over the violation of accepted standards of war, a response possible only for a generation that ignored the long record of horrors in centuries of wars.[26]

Contemporaries as well as later observers exaggerated the extent and importance of the panic in England. Panic existed, perhaps more in the government than in the people themselves, as Wells predicted; but so too did a "stiffening of morale." The *Daily Mail* captured the popular response when it boasted that the Germans "imagine that by a wicked, purposeless act of murder . . . they can frighten the British people. . . . The only result in England is to remind us that the German is a Hun."[27]

Despite mixed results, some Germans hoped that the attack on English morale would yield an even greater return. Bombing English cities might provide "a basis for peace" by diminishing the enemy's "will" to wage war. Convinced of the "well-known nervousness of the [English] public" and skeptical that England was truly committed to the war effort, they believed that bombing might knock her altogether out of the war.[28]

It did not, of course, and in the end Germany abandoned strategic bombardment, never to resume it consistently even in World War II. At the same time, England took it up, more impressed by the raids than were the Germans themselves. By 1918 attacks by British and other Allied forces on German cities, not to mention the large but forgotten Italian effort, had come to dwarf Germany's record in tonnage dropped and in sophistication of tactics and strategy. The reluctant commander was General Hugh Trenchard, aptly characterized as the "father who tried to strangle the infant [strategic bombing] at birth though he later got credit for the grown man." Under Trenchard the Allies and Americans were assembling a new force of thousands of bombers to launch massive attacks in 1919 on German "industry, commerce, and population," including Berlin itself, with incendiaries and a new poison gas developed in the United States. "I would very much like if you could start up a really big fire in one of the German towns," Trenchard's superior instructed, and "I would not be too exacting as regards accuracy in bombing railway stations. . . . The German is susceptible to bloodiness, and I would not mind a few accidents due to inaccuracy."[29]

Borrowing German practice, the British reversed Germany's pattern of decision

making: whereas officers overcame civilian reluctance in Germany, in England out-
raged civilians wore down the generals' doubts about strategic bombing. But London
echoed Berlin's strategic reasoning. "Conceptually," one historian has said, "British
insight was acquired at the receiving end of German bombs." Now Allied bombing, it
seemed, might sap the enemy's strength on the front, deplete production, and unnerve
the population. In Britain's case, an additional impetus to bomb came from the apparent failure of the vaunted British navy to achieve a strategic breakthrough through
blockade—hence the "first essays in strategic bombing on the British side were framed
by the Royal Navy." As in Germany, some doubts about strategic bombing arose in
England. Like Bethmann-Hollweg, Churchill, though no opponent of bombing, questioned whether any "terrorization of the civil population . . . would compel the Government of a great nation to surrender."[30]

Doubts like Churchill's never halted air raids, in part because rational calculations about damaging the enemy were never the sole motivation for the strategic
bombing conducted by either side. Bombing escalated through a series of challenges
and responses, raids and reprisals, all initiated as much to satisfy popular demands for
revenge and punishment against supposed war crimes as to achieve any tangible gain.
Lloyd George's reply to a restive crowd in London—"We shall bomb Germany with
compound interest!"—nicely caught that spirit. A Leipzig newspaper, gloating about
how an attack on London struck "the heart which pumps the life-blood into the arteries
of the brutal huckster nation," exploited the same mood in Germany: "At last, the long
yearned for punishment has fallen on England, this people of liars and hypocrites."[31]

So-called reprisal raids went so far beyond the misdeed that provoked them that no
calculated desire to even the score or deter further wrongs could have alone inspired
them. The target of attack was not so much the enemy as the flagging spirits of one's
compatriots. Air war, like no other weapon in the modern arsenal, satisfied yearnings
for blood and punishment among peoples deeply wounded by war and deprived of
decisive victories. Only sea blockade was comparable, and it worked too slowly to
satisfy passions in the same way. In terms of practical effect, air war could not, this
soon, meet prewar fantasies. In the passions that motivated air war, however, it offered
a Wellsian reality.

It also raised a moral issue, although in a war that blunted sensibilities not even
the bombing of cities could stir an extended moral debate. Outrage at what the enemy
did predictably overwhelmed self-doubt. To some observers, the very nature of modern
war made moral questions irrelevant. "The Germans had a perfect right to bomb
London," one peer instructed the House of Lords, reminding them that as countries
became arsenals of war, notions of undefended places and distinctions between civilian
and military activities broke down. English clergymen protested that reprisal bombing
"would permanently lower the standard of honourable conduct between nation and
nation" and damage England's special role as "a trustee of international morality in
war-time." But by 1917, when these strictures were issued, "honourable conduct"
seemed a hollow standard indeed.[32]

Hopes for a sterner code to guide judgment on bombing were faint. They rested on the prudence and apology with which bombing and reprisal were sometimes defended, on the embarrassed avoidance and heated denials of the clergy's concerns, or on rationalizations which betrayed troubled consciences. Passing bows to legal and moral standards at least meant that they were still implicit elements in the moral calculations men made. "The lineaments of justice," Michael Walzer has said, are suggested by "the unchanging character of the lies soldiers and statesmen tell."[33]

Soldiers and statesmen often applied a practical test to moral issues. Bethmann-Hollweg begged that Germany avoid "irritating the chauvinistic and fanatical instincts of the English nation without cause." Yet as Admiral Alfred von Tirpitz had already argued, what was indefensible if done "without cause" seemed justified if inflicted with sufficiently majestic force: "Single bombs from flying machines are wrong; they are odious when they hit and kill an old woman. . . . [But] if one could set fire to London in thirty places, then what in a small way is odious would retire before something fine and powerful. All that flies and creeps should be concentrated on that city."[34] Tirpitz's twisted logic was not entirely irrelevant to the moral issue at hand. He, like other people in the war, did feel forced to make moral calculations about the relationship between ends and means. What limited their debate was partly the carelessness of those calculations.

The principal element in the moral case for strategic bombing was that it would rescue humanity from the horrors of stalemated, industrialized war, making conflict either so mercifully decisive or so mercilessly horrible that it could not continue. Bombing could not do this, however. Instead of breaking from the attitudes and conditions which led to slaughter on the battlefield, air war expressed and in some ways aggravated them. Never the cheap weapon some thought it to be, air power consumed the same enormous technological and economic resources that sustained the ground war: by November 1918, the British and French had produced one hundred thousand aircraft and were employing over a half-million people in their production. On the front, it intensified the destructiveness of firepower, as aerial observation guided artillery fire with unprecedented accuracy. At the same time, given a war in which the British could use 321 trainloads of shells in one seventeen-day barrage at Passchendaele—a year's production of fifty-five thousand war workers—tactical aircraft could make no decisive addition to firepower, especially as soldiers burrowed further underground. Only when German forces began faltering anyway could air power give the Allied armies a significant advantage in battle.

Warplanes, used in part in response to the futility of the offensive à outrance on the ground, were hurled into battle with the same offensive abandon. Good tactical reasons were advanced for so doing. It was pointed out that planes could not guard territory like isolated sentries on duty without being picked off one by one; they had to seek out the enemy and attack in force. And attack in force they did, as commanders like Trenchard sent hundreds of planes to battle: against the German spring offensive in 1918 the British expended over 1,000 of the 1,232 craft they had on hand at the start. About fifty-five thousand airmen met their death in the war—a negligible figure by the standards of ground combat, but an appalling loss rate given the size of the air forces involved. Leadership was partly the problem, for some air commanders were old infantry or cavalry officers baffled by these new machines. Others were young, too inexperienced to handle the large forces suddenly in their charge. They were forced to improvise tactics, ill-equipped to analyze results, and prone to make excessive claims for their weapon. Like other new weapons of the day, the airplane did little "except to increase the efficiency of the slaughter."[35] The battlefield may have been the most practical arena in which to employ the airplane. At the same time, it was also the least decisive because the stalemate on land was so massive, deeply determined, and resistant to change that whatever advantage superior aviation offered was insufficient to break it.

That alone perhaps argued for its strategic employment. Yet in that capacity too, air power could not sustain hopes that it would transcend the conditions and attitudes that prevailed in ground warfare. Commanders spent their aircraft in the same futile charges against the enemy. Even air defense against strategic bombing took an offensive form, guided by the assumption that real defense was impossible except by destroying the enemy's bases and factories. Destructive without being decisive, strategic bombing threatened only to nationalize the battle of attrition on the ground, testing how long entire peoples rather than armies could exhaust each other, provoking civilian populations into a grim offensive against each other that mimicked what the soldiers did on the battlefield. Far from transcending the horrors of modern war, military aviation—like submarines and poison gas, two other weapons deemed capable of the decisive breakthrough—had the moral utility only of democratizing those horrors still further.

Observers until 1917, Americans brought little new insight to these matters. Determined to keep at arm's length from their allies, they still followed strategic doctrines established by the Fochs and Trenchards more often than they realized. Upon entering the war, most Americans had few firm views on the morality and strategy of employing the air weapon other than a general revulsion at its more ruthless uses, deep faith in America's productive capacity, and a vague hope that "clouds of planes" traveling the "million roads to Berlin" might yield a quick and inexpensive victory. Headlines like "GREATEST OF ALL AERIAL FLEETS TO CRUSH THE TEUTONS" expressed a confidence in air power uncluttered by concern about moral, strategic, and logistical obstacles.[36] Moreover, Americans were too remote from the danger of air war, too late to develop a capacity for bombing, and too muddled in their lines of authority to permit argument about bombing to be fully joined.

Some American proponents of air power did promise quick release from the stalemate of war: "The land may be trenched and mined; guns and bayonets form an impossible barrier. The sea may be mined and netted and the submarine lurks in its depths. But the highways of the air are free lanes, unconquered as yet by any nation. America's great opportunity lies before her. The road to Berlin lies through the air. The eagle must end this war." Every day's delay in building planes "means three or four thousand more Americans that will not come back at all, or will come back crippled and of no use at all." "By no other means" except air power, the *New York Times* argued, "can we so quickly or so surely render valuable aid to our allies. . . . Airplanes can be rapidly built. . . . Money is all that is lacking." This apparently naive American faith in air power was shared by the French government, which quickly turned to the United States for planes, and by English newspapers which promised tens of thousands of American machines in breathtakingly short time.[37]

The views of officials responsible for aviation were as formless in April 1917 as those in the press and public. Their journeys to the battlefields of Europe soon sharpened their outlook. First to go was Major William Mitchell, a zealous advocate of military aviation even though a latecomer to it. His somewhat unreliable *Memoirs of World War I* portrayed him as horrified by the senseless slaughter he observed during the Nivelle Offensive in the spring of 1917 and determined to find a more effective way to wage war. Pugnacious and ambitious, he instructed John J. Pershing that strategic bombing could have "a greater influence on the ultimate decision of the war than any other arm."[38] But Mitchell's advocacy of such bombing did not evolve in the straightforward way later imagined by both defenders and detractors. Trenchard, apparently the major influence on him during his first months in France, preached the virtues of massed air power concentrated in the hands of one commander and used offensively. Mitchell still applied such maxims largely to battlefield situations.

Less famous visitors to France were as important as Mitchell. The Bolling Mission, sent to evaluate requirements for aviation, was favorably taken by the potential for long-range bombardment, and by fall of 1917 some air officers were promising that night missions could "put an end to the war far more quickly than sending one or two million men to line the trenches." Over the following months an organization took shape in France designed to plan a strategic bombing effort. In one officer's bleak view, bombing was necessary "in order that we may not only wreck Germany's manufacturing centers but wreck them more completely than she will wreck ours next year." With round-the-clock bombing, the enemy's "manufacturing works . . . and the morale of the workmen would be shattered." Even the army's Chief of Staff, Peyton March, seemed attracted by ambitious talk of new bombers able to strike fifteen hundred miles from their bases with a bomb load of forty-five hundred pounds.[39]

It was largely just talk. The enchanting prospect of an armada of American bombers bringing swift and painless victory, part of the vision of an efficient and disciplined America, fell victim to the production failures, tangled communications, and faulty planning that embarrassed Woodrow Wilson and the progressives. The voluntaristic system of organizing war production assumed that "the wheels of private enterprise spun freely even while neatly meshed with those of public authority."[40] With no way in practice to mesh the two, gears clogged, output stopped, strategy and logistics became disconnected. Responsible officials, desperate to meet production quotas regardless of strategic specifics, stamped out the planes that were easiest to make—trainers and observation craft and obsolete types that would never darken the skies over Essen or Berlin. Despite mammoth appropriations, not one night bomber made it from factory to front. Even production of lesser aircraft was disappointing.. That sorry performance appeared even worse, as Secretary of War Newton Baker recognized, because of naive claims made for the airplane and for American uniqueness:

> We were dealing with a miracle. The airplane itself was too wonderful and new, too positive a denial of previous experience, to brook the application of any prudential restraints which wise people would have known how to apply to ordinary industrial and military developments. As a consequence, the magicians of American industry were expected to do the impossible for this new and magical agency, and this expectation was increased by the feverish earnestness with which all Americans desired that our country should appear speedily, worthily, and decisively in the war.[41]

The production failure left the American Air Service with no real strategic force of its own, only borrowed planes and deferred hopes for an aerial offensive in 1919 that would never happen. The war likewise left aviators an uncertain legacy. Held in check by ground commanders, struggling to learn the art of command, prone to bitter feuds with comrades and superiors, and deprived of a full test of the bomber's potential, they could not expound a coherent theory of strategic bombardment or develop an unqualified commitment to it. Mitchell's finest hour came when he directed a superior force of some fifteen hundred planes against German forces in the Saint-Mihiel salient. They made a significant contribution to the Allied advance. But according to Mitchell's most astute student, he later "grossly exaggerated" what happened there, not so much the achievement itself as its implications for strategic air power.[42] The attack was, after all, only an unusually ambitious use of tactical aviation.

Mitchell already envisaged leaping beyond the battlefield to attack the enemy's "vital centers." Yet his freedom to articulate and act on a theory of strategic air war was highly circumscribed. Indeed, one scholar has suggested, when Mitchell had to move from imagining an air force to commanding one, his "dominant conception of air power had shifted from the realm of the strategic to that of the tactical." Not even aviators, always fond of seeing themselves as free from the shackles of tradition, could entirely cease extrapolating visions of future wars from earlier experience. In the 1920s, past experience primarily meant tactical aviation. Mitchell, not to mention his less reckless or arrogant colleagues, left the war uncertain of the direction they wanted aviation to take. Doctrine would emerge gradually, the product of wartime improvisation, not a source of it. At war's end, the warning of Secretary Baker against "promiscuous bombing upon industry, commerce or population" suggested the outlines of an American debate never fully joined among military men or in the public at large.[43]

In thinking about air war, Americans were in a unique position. Isolated from the war, late to enter it, slow to bomb, and invulnerable themselves to attack, they took positions on the destruction of cities and industries without fear of consequence.

Because attention focused on the production of bombers rather than on their purpose in war, hopes for bombing were left intact yet untested. Compared to European opinion on air war, American views were casual.

What informed those views was not so much the immediate fears and challenges of the war, but cultural traditions and anxieties which encouraged Americans to look "above the battle" and permitted them both to celebrate and to ignore new weapons like the bomber.[44] The Civil War had inspired an ennobling view of war that remained powerful even on the eve of World War I. War still seemed an opportunity more for individual heroism than for mass destruction. Anxieties about the debilitating effects of machine civilization—regimentation, materialism, class cleavages—strengthened the urge to embrace war with relief. "France," David Kennedy has commented, "figures as kind of equivalent of Huck Finn's 'Territory,' a place to light out to in flight from the artificial constraints of civilized life." Among Americans at war, even among the troops in the trenches, perception was "shot through with images of knight-errantry and of grails thrillingly pursued," images reflected on a higher level by Wilsonian definitions of the war as the last of its kind. Neither American needs nor the brevity of American participation compelled the grim sense of impersonal and futile destruction so deeply felt by Europeans.[45]

In one sense, Americans realized this was a war of scientific destruction, and they organized to wage such a conflict, paying due attention to the contributions of scientists and other experts. Yet there were ways to reconcile the heroic impulse with impersonal realities. The very magnitude of the carnage was reassuring evidence "that miracles of heroism were possible in that decadent, commercial age." Armies were engines of impersonal destruction, men "mere cogs," yet men identified with the engines in a way that "turned the whole genre of attacks on technology on its head. Death through one's own machines, which, since Marx's early writings, had seemed the absurd extreme of alienation, now restored to the warriors a comfortable sense of themselves."[46]

Similarly, the warplane embodied not so much a conflict between heroic traditions and machine-age anonymity, but a happy fusion of the two. Americans in the Lafayette Escadrille could identify crudely and completely with their machines:

Two valve springs you'll find in my stomach,
Three spark plugs are safe in my lung,
The prop is in splinters inside me,
To my fingers the joy stick has clung.[47]

At the same time, to others and often to themselves, aviators were knights of the air locked in individual combat, proof that the mechanical age possessed gallantry, the only men "freed from much of the ruck and reek of war by their easy poise above it." These "gentlemen-warriors" were celebrated as exemplars of the heroic tradition, not as pioneers of a new kind of warfare. At times, war itself commanded aesthetic awe rather than dismay. An American correspondent reported from London how "wonderstruck eyes watched the drama of the skies." "In the gracious loveliness of a perfect summer's day when the sky was blue and gold and clear,'" the Gotha bombers seemed less like instruments of "death and destruction and unendurable suffering" than like "little silver birds." People "stood watching vastly interested, a little excited, but not in the least frightened."[48] Finding such reassurance and satisfaction, Americans looked away from the role of the warplane as an agent of destruction.

By November 1918, the bomber had found acceptance in both Britain and America. In Britain it inspired a lasting terror which left that nation determined to build a powerful strategic force and, even twenty years later, gave pause to Chamberlain at Munich. In America, it inspired casual fascination and easy hopes. For neither country was the test of war sufficient to challenge these reactions. As exploration of that middle ground between apocalyptic fantasy and careless dismissal, the war experience was too incomplete to confirm the Wellsian prophecy. Too much had happened in World War I for that generation to ignore the bomber, but too little had happened to appreciate fully its potential and limitations. Both extravagant hopes and unreasoning fears were still possible.

Indeed, the war seemed to make them more necessary than ever. Far from appearing an extension of the slaughter of modern war, air power seemed to many people one way to escape from it. To sustain the battered faith that technology might make war more humane, belief in the bomber's capacity to abolish war or make it decisive was required. In the midst of air war, it was possible in England to assert that although the airplane is "the most punitive weapon ever placed in the hands of mankind" it "may eventually render war so horrible as to result in its abolition altogether." Scarcely less sanguine was another English prophecy that, Wells to the contrary, "after one or two staggering blows, in which its chief cities are destroyed, and its means of communications paralysed, a country may find itself so helpless that there will be nothing for it to do but sue for peace."[49] Such sentiments displayed surprising resilience in the years to come in both Britain and America. The war experience—or more precisely, how it was remembered—made future air war seem inevitable, terrifying, and attractive.

2

The Age of Prophecy

During the 1920s, the most sensational episodes in American aviation were Billy Mitchell's demonstration in 1921 of how bombers could sink battleships and Charles Lindbergh's flight across the Atlantic in May 1927. Bracketing several years of speculation about the future of aviation, the two events signaled danger to a few observers but offered reassurance to most, particularly about how individualism could persist in the wake of mass war and in the midst of mass culture. The significance attached to the heroics of Mitchell and Lindbergh helps explain how the bomber became acceptable to Americans as an instrument of warfare. Though less forcefully than Europeans, they had learned from World War I how terrifying future aerial war might be. Yet in general their attraction to the aerial weapon deepened in the 1920s.

It did so in part because it rarely had to be tested against visible or disturbing military realities. In both Europe and the United States, military aviation stagnated. A glut of aircraft left over from the war, tight purse strings in most national treasuries, and the absence of immediate enemies curbed investment in bomber design and purchase. In much of the British Empire and for American forces in Nicaragua the bomber proved a cheap way to inflict an imperial sting on obstreperous subjects. But for these operations, aircraft left over from World War I did nicely, and if raids in far-off lands provoked occasional cries of moral anguish, they hardly seemed like a rehearsal for modern air war. Development of military aviation did not altogether cease. In particular, the French maintained a huge air force in the twenties, the Italians made strides, British air officers honed their theory of strategic bombing, and American airmen pioneered in patrolling the seas. More generally, the aircraft carrier came of age. And indirectly or surreptitiously, all the great powers prepared the way for advances in military air power by promoting civil aviation. Simply because the greatest strides and the most glamorous feats came in the civilian field, however, there was reason to believe that aviation was following a pacific course and to ignore its more disturbing potential.

Fear of and attraction to the bomber remained but drew mostly on what people remembered from World War I and imagined for a rather distant future, not on what they observed at firsthand. In the American case, attraction drew on especially subtle forces. Prophecy, political debate, and cultural imagination shaped a benign image of aviation, thereby making the bomber seem attractive as an instrument of American ideals but remote as a weapon of war. In this perspective, bombers could be divorced from bombing: their instrumental and symbolic virtues were separable from the destruction they threatened. Their danger was the dark side of a moon of shiny progress—something imaginable but out of view. As a consequence, the ideas and institutions that made it possible to bomb developed faster than inquiry into the wisdom of doing so.

PROPHECY AS REASSURANCE

The 1920s was the golden age of speculation about the airplane. Because prophecy necessarily leaped ahead of technology, it often read like fanciful or bloodless abstractions, as if designed, like science fiction, less to depict future dangers than to express current anxieties. That tendency was offset in the European case by the visible urgency of the aerial problem there, which led Europeans to speculate sooner and more boldly about the bomber than did Americans. The rehearsal for all-out air war that Europeans had just witnessed and their anxiety about the prospects for lasting peace dictated attention to air power. The French so vigorously promoted their air force that they even touched off English fears of aerial attack across the Channel. All the imperial powers experienced growing difficulties in controlling their restive empires as well as dread of the Bolshevik threat to international and internal stability. They searched for ways besides military preparedness to achieve security—the League of Nations and arms control, for example—because ravaged economies and war-weary constituents gave governments no other choice. At the same time, national fatigue also strengthened the appeal of air power as a supposedly cheap and humane weapon.

In that context, two very different men, Giulio Douhet and Basil H. Liddell Hart, articulated the emerging doctrine of strategic air power. Prophets and polemicists as much as theorists, they fleshed out ideas first sketched before and during the war and now widely aired in the press and among military men. Douhet (1869–1930), the Italian officer once imprisoned during the war for his outspoken defense of air power, gained a sympathetic hearing from Mussolini's regime, although *The Command of the Air* (1921, with later addenda), written in Italian, only slowly gained an audience as reports and translations of it spread. Liddell Hart (1895–1970), the British military critic and historian, enjoyed an esteemed career after injuries incurred on the battlefields of France forced his retirement from the British army in 1924. His flirtation with strategic air power was provocative but brief. *Paris, or the Future of War* (1925), published simultaneously in England and the United States, was a notorious tract of the times but it gained less enduring attention than Douhet's work, in part because Liddell Hart slowly soured on his own ideas.

To both men, strategic air power was the only solution to the grisly indecisiveness of ground warfare. Savage and sane critics of that warfare and the leaders who practiced it, they saw its indecisiveness not as a transient condition but a permanent affliction. World War I marked a turning point in history. Armies and navies, the traditional means of deciding conflicts, could no longer end wars; the power of the defense made their efforts futile. Even a rare offensive success so exhausted the victor that "the side which won the most military victories was the side which was defeated," Douhet noted with reference to Germany's fate in the war. Generals who still sought defeat of their opponent's armies would lead their nations to ruin, victims of the "shortsighted, if natural delusion . . . that the armed forces themselves were the real objective." Attack on those forces was only one means to the end of subduing "the enemy's will to resist."[1]

The only hope for restoring decisiveness to war was to cease battering at the enemy's strongest point, the surface forces now developed to defensive perfection, and attack the enemy's will behind the lines, just as Paris had found Achilles' weak point (the pun Liddell Hart played on in his title). For the first time in history, man could do this swiftly. "Aircraft enables us to *jump over* the army which shields the enemy government, industry and people, and *so strike direct and immediately at the seat of the opposing will and policy.*" Or, as Douhet put it, "Now it is actually populations and nations," rather than their agents, "which come to blows and seize each other's throats."[2]

Prophets of aerial apocalypse in the 1920s displayed remarkable unanimity in imagining how the bombers would do their job. Flying in numbers and with bomb loads unimaginable in World War I, fleets of aerial dreadnoughts would strike in the first hours of war, perhaps even before any declaration of war, and rain tons of explosive, incendiary, and gas or bacteriological bombs on an enemy's metropolitan centers. J. F. C. Fuller, the other major British proponent of new forms of warfare, asked his readers to

> picture, if you can, what the result will be: London for several days will be one vast raving Bedlam, the hospitals will be stormed, traffic will cease, the homeless will shriek for help, the city will be in pandemonium. What of the government at Westminster? It will be swept away by an avalanche of terror. Then will the enemy dictate his terms, which will be grasped at like a straw by a drowning man. Thus may a war be won in forty-eight hours and the losses of the winning side may be actually nil![3]

Scenarios rarely ran to much more detail than this austere sequence of attack, panic, and collapse.

After all, the prophets could foresee no real battle to describe. Armies and navies would do little more than guard borders and coastlines. In the air, most military experts agreed, defense against bombers was virtually impossible. Their speed, mobility, fire-power, and numbers would overwhelm defending fighters and antiaircraft artillery, which would do little more than shoot blindly, especially when bombers struck at night or when they attacked far from their targets by launching aerial "torpedoes" about which the 1920s featured extravagant prediction. Douhet eventually wrote off fighter planes as wasteful diversions from the strength of the "battleplane" force whose sole mission would be to launch "intensive and violent offensives" against enemy air bases, factories, and cities. Command of the air was necessary, yet rarely would it be achieved by direct confrontation between hostile air forces. An intelligent enemy would follow the same principles, but the devastation he unleashed would have to be suffered on the assumption that his will would collapse first under the crushing weight of bomber attacks.[4]

Even with his vivid imagination, Douhet could not describe what those attacks would be like. He paid little attention to determining which target systems might best be struck or how bombers would do so accurately, although his admonition to do the job fast and thoroughly was sound tactical advice. If postwar examination revealed that bombing during the Great War had been atrociously inaccurate, that only strenghtened the case for attacking whole cities and brushing aside problems of accuracy. "How could a country go on living and working under this constant threat, oppressed by the nightmare of imminent destruction and death? How indeed!" No further description was needed. *The War of 19—* (1930) bogged down in tedious orders of battle and lengthy accounts of the aerial combat which he saw as peripheral to the mission of his bombers. He could not describe what was really novel about the war he envisioned—the death and destruction on the ground—other than to note that cities would become "unapproachable flaming braziers." Beyond that, it seemed "useless . . . to elabo-rate." War against cities was terrifying but barely imaginable. The certainty of quick victory made description seem unnecessary, and the horror of bombing was perhaps enhanced by letting the reader conjure up his own nightmare. Any suggestion that events on the ground might be more complicated, might go beyond panic and sur-render, would have robbed predictions of their promise that air power could be decisive.[5]

Peace through chemistry was a variation on the promise of deliverance through technology. Armed with dubious statistics indicating that death rates from gas attacks in World War I were far lower than those from shot and shell, prophets like Liddell Hart argued that "gas may well prove the salvation of civilization from otherwise inevitable collapse in case of another world war." Nonlethal gases in particular might secure "the fruits of victory, but without the lasting evils of mass killing or destruction of property." Such optimism about the benefits of aerochemical warfare was a minority view. Yet even an apocalyptic view of airborne gas warfare also strengthened claims for its decisiveness. Besides, the proponents of aerial bombing had other ways to address the moral issues it raised, shown by Hugh Trenchard's tortured distinction between bombing "for the sole purpose of terrorising the civilian population" and bombing "to terrorise munition workers (men and women) into absenting themselves from work."

By and large, however, the moral case of the prophets rested only on their assertion that bombing would bring wars to mercifully speedy, if costly, conclusions. Since bombing was sure to be so frightful, its destructiveness aroused little worry—a terrorized populace would surrender before destruction proceeded far at all.[6]

Certainty about the bomber's efficacy rested on an appreciation of new technology, but also on unquestioned belief in the fragility of modern societies. All the achievements in which Europe once gloried—material wealth, economic interdependence, sophisticated communications—now seemed cause for the gravest worry that the home front had become hopelessly vulnerable: "A nation's nerve-system, no longer covered by the flesh of its troops, is now laid bare to attack, and, like the human nerves, the progress of civilization has rendered it far more sensitive than in earlier and more primitive times." Repeated images of "nerve centers," "vital centers," and "nerve ganglia" reflected a pervasive sense of a fragile social organism. It derived from memories of panic in the streets and mutiny in the trenches during the war and from the myth (soon skillfully exploited by the Nazis) that Germany had collapsed from within without being defeated in the field. It also stemmed from the wartime discovery of man's susceptibility to propaganda and manipulation, to the dark passions that Freud had uncovered. The new technology of mass communications, far from inducing confidence about a government's ability to control its population, spawned visions of internal collapse, with both propaganda and bombardment eroding the will to resist. Modern economic systems appeared equally brittle. Akin to the "engine and transmission of an automobile" in their "intricacy and delicacy," a nation's "industrial resources and communications form its Achilles' heel."[7]

The Achilles' heel, however, was not so much the home front in general as the war-weary and exploited urban masses. If soldiers fled combat more often than "imaginative soldiers" usually acknowledged, then surely "the workers in shop, factory, or harbor will melt away after the first losses." In focusing on working-class reaction to bombing, air power arguments fused apprehensions about a delicate social organism with commonplace fears about the economic failings of capitalism. Particularly in England, it was feared that bombing might trigger "Bolshevik upheaval." "The Red Scare could so easily be tied to the Air Scare," as one historian has put it.[8]

The next war, then, would be a test of shattered nerves. In hours, Liddell Hart speculated, London would find "the business localities and Fleet Street wrecked, Whitehall a heap of ruins, the slum districts maddened into the impulse to break loose and maraud, the railways cut, factories destroyed. Would not the general will to resist vanish, and what use would be the still determined fractions of the nation, without organization and central direction?"[9] Where Wells envisioned war sustained by stubborn, if unreasoning, patriotism, postwar prophets saw it decided quickly, above all by the disloyalty of an alienated working class.

Geography also made England's plight seem grave. The sea approaches to Britain made incoming bombers hard to detect and English cities easy to locate; German bases were close to London but Berlin was far from England's bombers. Yet geography and technology were not the sole considerations in fearing a knockout blow, for anxieties deriving from World War I gave that fear depth and intensity. At the same time, memories of war's horror magnified the bomber's promise as well as its peril. "The more rapid and terrifying the arms are," Douhet argued, "the faster they will reach vital centers and the more deeply they will affect moral resistance. Hence the more civilized war will become." True, in the wake of World War I, the humanity of modern weapons was a tattered hope, not the confident proposition it had been. Reassurance often seemed lame, as in Douhet's prediction that "cemeteries would undoubtedly grow larger, but not as large as they became before the peace signed at Versailles." Air power would deliver such a "swift and sudden blow," according to Liddell Hart, "that the ethical objection to this form of war is at least not greater than to the cannon-fodder wars of the past." So strong was the revulsion to trench warfare, however, that the old promise of escape from familiar horrors through technology persisted. To discard it altogether would have condemned Europeans to an unrelievedly grim view of the future. Faith in the future required belief in the finality of this new weapon.[10]

That belief also allowed contradictions in the air power prophecies to go unnoticed. The prophets proclaimed the revolutionary nature of their weapon, its capacity to transform warfare and to make history irrelevant. The past, in particular the bomber's ambiguous record in the world war, taught "less than nothing," Douhet announced.[11] But the past still bound the prophets. They could not really imagine a future, except one crudely extrapolated from contemporary experience. Dismissing most of the war's record, they simplistically assumed that bomb damage in a future conflict would be a simple multiple of previous experience: a tenfold increase in bomb tonnage yielding ten times the panic and dislocation. Abolishing navies, they developed a doctrine that echoed the great naval strategist Alfred Thayer Mahan in his emphasis on a single battle fleet and strangulation of an enemy's civilian economy.[12] Their uncomplicated faith in the bomber's offensive capacity mimicked the commitment of an earlier generation to the offensive à outrance on the ground and at sea. A single-minded offensive spirit, derided by the prophets as madness in conventional warfare, returned with a vengeance in their scenarios of air war. They did not see how their own weapon might evolve unpredictably, strengthening the defense as well as the offense, creating its own futile charges and bloody stalemates. They were also disconcertingly content to let the past predict the future of ground and naval warfare. Liddell Hart, with his emerging theories of fast, mechanized armies, was more flexible in this regard. But Douhet ignored the possibility that surface warfare might regain its offensive capacity—in good part because of the tactical aviation which Douhet so contemptuously dismissed.

Douhet could write movingly of the "mysterious aspect" of war. He was awed by how "whole peoples become wolves and throw themselves into torment and a bloody work of destruction, as though possessed by blind folly." Yet in the end he believed that "war is simple, like good sense," and that any conclusions other than his would "deny reason itself." As historian he appreciated the psychological complexity of war, but as prophet he discarded it. He and his fellow prophets assumed that rational calculation would rule the next great war, in the decisions made in launching it and in the resignation to defeat that civilian populations would swiftly translate into a national decision for surrender. "The normal man, immediately he recognizes a stronger, directly he realizes the hopelessness of overcoming his enemy, always yields," said Liddell Hart. There was no allowance in these predictions for the way war makes people act abnormally, no room for stoic defiance of the odds, no place for passions that sustain war beyond rational limits. Not even four years of "blind folly" suggested the wisdom of Wells's scenario.[13]

Seeking to bypass such folly, Douhet actually made it central to his definition of war: "The purpose of war is to harm the enemy as much as possible; and all means which contribute to this end will be employed, no matter what they are." Douhet confused the character of war with its purpose. Ideally at least, harming the enemy was only a means to another end, and in losing sight of that end, Douhet betrayed how his weapon could serve as the vehicle of irrationality rather than as the instrument of its defeat. If the bomber did not prove immediately decisive, if nations misused it and populations defied it, if they employed it to seek vengeance rather than victory, the next war would recreate the old stalemate of attrition warfare in horrifyingly new form, throwing humankind back to earlier centuries when siege and pillage put entire populations at hazard. Momentarily able to predict such "an inhuman, atrocious performance," Douhet refused to believe it would happen and shrank from describing the course it might follow.[14]

Liddell Hart reached the same point by a different route. He rejected destruction as an end in itself: "Of what use is decisive victory in battle if we bleed to death as a result of it?" The goal of war was nothing more than "a resumption and progressive continuance of . . . the peace-time policy." But nations often have far more ambitious or vicious goals. Passionately desiring to restore limits to the purpose and conduct of war, Liddell Hart did not acknowledge that aerial war might mark the final breakdown of such restraint. "New weapons," Liddell Hart wrote in condemning a generation of commanders, "would seem to be regarded merely as an additional tap through which the bath of blood can be filled all the sooner." More than he recognized, however, his alternative posed the same danger.[15]

Some observers argued that air war promised deliverance from the horrors of the trenches only by opening up "hideous vistas" of greater destruction. Churchill pronounced that the bomber gave mankind the means to "accomplish its own extinction." Another Englishman rightly wondered if bombing would "smash the will to war. You may only harden it, intensify it." Others feared that two combatants roughly equal in air strength might hesitate altogether to attack enemy cities, settling into an uneasy "balance of terrors" (to use a term introduced in the 1930s) or else descending into "the edifying spectacle of two nations hammering away at each other's capital, with no immediate object but mutual destruction." Of course, either outcome would upset the prophets' calculations.[16]

As the criticisms of aerial prophecy suggested, the twenties and thirties marked a shift away from the confident attitudes of earlier times about technological advances. The enemy was no longer a foreign power but "the immense destructiveness of modern weapons."[17] Similarly, in thinking about air war, possibilities were imaginable beyond the contrasting predictions of the airplane as either a trivial addition to the old ways of war or a triumph over them. Still, some who doubted that air war on cities would be quickly conclusive sometimes appeared to dismiss the danger; they, too, could hardly describe in detail the course that air war might take. Other critics resembled the prophets in argumentative style, employing an apocalyptic rhetoric which, though intended to inform and alarm, numbed the senses and carried unintended reassurances. For them as well as the prophets, air war remained a doomsday prospect more than a believable danger. They all hoped that nations would shrink from unleashing air war—its horror constituted its virtue by deterring the unthinkable from occurring.

These tendencies in the predictive literature about air war existed in the United States as well but in a rather different context. Whereas the bomber was mainly an offensive weapon to Europeans, in the United States it seemed to strengthen defense. The war games that seized popular attention in the 1920s and the predictions of men like Billy Mitchell established a comforting notion of the bomber's role. American planes, roaming maritime approaches to the continent and smashing any sea or air armada that came close, promised to make attack upon America almost impossible. To be sure, the new aerial technology also made American attack on Europe almost impossible, in that no American army could again cross the Atlantic in the face of some European enemy's air power, but that was of little consequence to most Americans, opposed as they were to any repeat of the grand crusade of 1918. In the reasoning of prophets like Mitchell, the bomber undermined the security of European nations, their capitals within such easy reach of enemy airplanes; but it might enhance America's safety, if deployed to guard the nation's oceanic moats.

That difference between European and American perspectives was more apparent than real, however. The bomber Mitchell wanted for striking into the Atlantic would have to approach, in range and size and accuracy, the aircraft capable of offensive missions against an enemy's heartland. That certainly entered Mitchell's calculations, for his oft-repeated sketches of American cities under aerial attack expressed, in thinly disguised form, opportunities he foresaw for American attack on foreign cities. In addition, European ideas of air power were familiar to American airmen, through personal contacts developed during the war and sometimes through reading what was written abroad. Liddell Hart's *Paris,* for example, quickly found an audience in the United States Army Air Service. Mitchell sketched similar ideas in official memoranda and unpublished writings, in the polemics he published in the early twenties, and at greater length in 1925 in a *Saturday Evening Post* series and in *Winged Defense.*[18]

Like his counterparts in Europe, Mitchell confidently consigned ground forces to a secondary role and naval power (except submarines) to the deep sea of obsolescence. More baldly than his European contemporaries, he also proclaimed the humanity of aerial attack on enemy "vital centers." Because bombing would democratize the horrors of war and inflict them so quickly, "either a state will hesitate to go to war, or, having engaged in war, [air power] will make the context sharper, more decisive, and more quickly finished." The passage from peril to reassurance was always jarringly sudden in Mitchell's writings. Air power, he wrote in 1930,

> is a distinct move for the betterment of civilization, because wars will be decided quickly and not drag on for years. What will the future hold for us? Undoubtedly an attack on the great centers of population. If a European country attacks the United States, New York, Chicago, Detroit, Pittsburgh and Washington will be the first targets. It is unnecessary that these cities be destroyed in the sense that every house be levelled with the gound. It will be sufficient to have the civilian population driven out of them so that they cannot carry on their usual vocations. A few gas bombs will do that.

This "quick way of deciding a war," he added, would be "really much more humane than the present methods of blowing up people to bits by cannon projectiles or butchering them with bayonets."[19]

Such reassurance was commonplace. "Jingoes," wrote the head of the army's Chemical Warfare Service in 1921, "will hesitate long before they start war in the future, knowing that they themselves" will face its "terrors." ("If this be a chemist's idea of humane warfare," a New York paper retorted, "God deliver the world from its chemists!") Air war against cities would be a "calamity," one of Mitchell's fellow airmen wrote, but one "of this magnitude would create a demand for peace that could not be denied."[20]

As in European writings on this subject, tortured arguments were frequent. Mitchell claimed that the "more terrible" weapons of recent wars had actually reduced total casualties because with their long range "the defeated side can get away with its men as they are far off from their opponents." He suggested that strategic bombing would somehow both democratize future warfare and diminish its casualties because it would confine fighting to smaller numbers of skilled specialists—he compared them with the knights of the Middle Ages—rather than mass armies. In promising the "distinct benefit to civilization" that air war would bring he offered a curious distinction: "air forces will attack centers of production . . . not so much the people themselves." Somehow, victory would ensue, his followers argued in 1926, "by terrorizing the whole population of a belligerent country while conserving life and property to the greatest extent." Air prophets were not invariably systematic thinkers.[21]

Yet inconsistencies in their argument for strategic bombardment mattered little simply because Mitchell and his contemporaries presented it as an attractive theory disconnected from American realities. The challenge for Americans was less to learn to wage strategic bombing than to guard against it. In theory, the most effective defense was to reply in kind. But inasmuch as planes of foreign powers lacked the range to attack the United States except from bases or aircraft carriers in the western Atlantic, interception, not retaliation, was sufficient. Mitchell therefore advocated a mixed air force of fighter, pursuit, and bombing aircraft, not the all-bomber force suitable only for offensive war that Douhet embraced. More cautious airmen, convinced that aerial support for the army and navy would remain a primary function, put still less emphasis on strategic bombardment.

Mitchell's limited definition of American needs in the air may also have stemmed from his modest definition of American interests. Global economic interests existed for the United States, he acknowledged; but having proclaimed the end of American "isolation," he also asserted that "America could entirely dispense of her sea-going trade if she had to, and continue to exist and defend herself," a view that not all airmen shared.[22]

Only in the Far East did war seem likely to Mitchell, and in that regard he mirrored the nation's inconsistencies regarding isolationism. Many Americans nursed a belligerent attitude toward Japan that they avoided with regard to European powers. Following suit, Mitchell imagined an offensive use of the bomber in the Far East though otherwise he stressed the defensive. Making little attempt to define American interests, Mitchell was moved perhaps by visions of race war, which triggered reckless talk on both sides of the Pacific in the 1920s. To be sure, he justified his proposed bomber force as a deterrent against Japanese attack on America's colony, the Philippine Islands. But there was almost a note of relish in his description of the course to be followed if deterrence failed. An American aerial offensive routed through Alaska and the North Pacific would be "decisive" because Japan's cities were "congested" and built from "paper and wood or other inflammable structures." The attractions of this "ideal target," already worrisome to the Japanese, would be fully realized in twenty years. In the 1920s, however, the possibilities for air war against Japan rarely generated sustained public debate, even in the military, where Mitchell's ideas circulated and apprehension of a Far Eastern war was widespread.[23]

Confusion in what military aviators claimed to expect of the bomber was in part attributable to their ambitions and intellects and to their fear of stating in public what they believed in private. But confusion also stemmed from broader circumstances. Airmen only reflected the difficulty the nation's political leadership had in defining national interests and strategic needs. Moreover, aerial technology was developing too quickly to enable anyone to reach hard judgments on strategic possibilities. In this context, there was ample room for airmen to disagree, change their minds, or hold to contradictory ideas, especially when they were agitators first and theorists second. By mid-decade, Mitchell, among others, was moving beyond continental defense and tactical employment of air power, but the process was incomplete. These pioneers believed that, given involvement in another world war, the United States might leap over the enemy's conventional defenses and use the bomber to "smash up his means of production, supply and transportation," as Mitchell put it in 1924. On occasion, politicians openly discussed the same prospects. Yet most professional airmen saw their primary task as guarding the United States from attack, not striking across the oceans at its enemies. The theory of strategic air bombardment remained largely that, an attractive doctrine contemplated at considerable psychological and geographical distance.[24]

Public debate early in the decade followed the same lines. The scarier prophecies coming out of Europe as well as similar American ideas received wide attention but usually in the context of what the war-mad European nations might do, rarely as something Americans might employ. Occasionally someone went further. Will Irwin, in his popular book *"The Next War": An Appeal to Common Sense* (1921), hinted at what the United States was capable of by stressing the American role in plans for bombing Germany in 1919 and in development of new and deadly forms of gas, about which Irwin shared the "near hysteria" of the decade.[25] Irwin suggested that the next great war would sweep the United States into it and by implication into the practice of bombing cities. A layman who rivaled professional airmen in predictive capacities, he saw entire populations pitted against each other, their bombers launching gas attacks rendering a great capital city "in one night . . . changed from a metropolis to a necropolis." In a passage borne out by the firestorms of World War II, he imagined how Paris could "suddenly become a superheated furnace . . . the population struggling, piling up, shriveling with the heat . . . the survivors ranging the open fields in the condition of starving animals." Most telling, he surpassed the professionals by capturing the psychic ease with which men could wage war by air. It "takes advantage of the limits of human imagination. If you bayonet a child, you see the spurt of blood, the curling up of the little body, the look in the eyes. . . . But if you loose a bomb on a town, you see only that you have made a fair hit." The "gallant" airmen he talked to during World War I "were thinking and talking not of the effects of their bombs but only of 'the hit.'" Beyond that, "they closed their imagination—as one must do in war."[26]

But Irwin's provocative tract triggered no extended debate about the efficacy or morality of American air power. In fact, it was not intended to, for Irwin's concern was the abolition of war by international law and organization, not contemplation of how to wage it. At most, his book was an exception that proved the rule: in an era of self-proclaimed American isolation from Europe's quarrels, the apocalyptic visions of Europeans like Douhet and Liddell Hart found expression only on the fringes of American debate.

The arguments of skeptics about air power did not penetrate far either. One presidential board appointed to investigate the aviation controversy, challenging the air prophets, contended that World War I "taught us again that man can not make a machine stronger than the spirit of man." The board condemned "the belief that new and deadlier weapons will shorten future wars" as likely to "lead to a readier acceptance of war as the solution of international difficulties." As so often with skeptics, however, in dismissing the promise of air power they also came near to dismissing its danger: "The next war may well start in the air but in all probability will wind up, as the last war did, in the mud." The skeptics' dismissal of air war on cities, like

Mitchell's vision of sturdy self-sufficiency, gave Americans the luxury of developing the bomber in the reassuring context of continental defense.[17]

PROPHECY AND POLITICS

The controversy over Mitchell's ideas merged seamlessly into a more immediate political debate, in the United States and among all the major powers, over disarmament and military budgets. Naval armaments bore the burden of that debate. But despite its slow progress, military aviation also played an inescapable role. Given the war's legacy and the ideas expounded by prophets of air power, few leaders could escape the bomber's darkening shadow, much less broader pressures from exhausted populaces to limit the burden of armaments. In England, the nation most vulnerable to air attack, expansion of the RAF was held back lest it undermine international efforts at arms control. But even in the United States, lingering hope for international cooperation, widespread desire to limit government spending, and fear of the political gains opponents might score on the disarmament issue forced a return to the conference table.

From Versailles to the eve of World War II, various leaders strove for limitations on air war with a vigor matched only by their pessimism about the odds of reaching and enforcing agreements. Quantitative restrictions on the size of air forces, qualitative ones on the most threatening kinds of aircraft, proscriptive ones against various kinds of bombing, plus visionary schemes to create an international air force—all taxed the patience and ingenuity of diplomats. The bomber, one nation's means of defense, was another's way to attack. Eager to ban the bomber from Europe, England still wanted it to police the empire. The technical obstacles to inspection and enforcement were vexatious, above all because it was too easy to convert airliners to bombers—agreement to limit naval arms faced no similar barrier. Of course, banning civilian aviation was impossible, while proposals to internationalize or cartelize it foundered on commercial jealousies and on the league's weakness.

Successes were few and limited in scope. The most drastic restriction was the ban on German military aviation written into the Versailles Treaty. The most famous disarmament gathering, the Washington Conference on the Limitation of Arms in 1921–22, established such high ceilings on aircraft carriers that it did more to promote than to retard their development. The Washington delegations threw up their hands at devising a formula for restricting the numbers, types, or bombing methods of aircraft, passing that thankless task on to jurists at the Hague court—they drafted some sensible rules, which had not gained the force of international law when war broke out in 1939. A lengthy effort at Geneva in 1932 to agree upon restrictions or rules ended in failure, notwithstanding President Herbert Hoover's dramatic proposal to abolish all offensive weapons. As for chemical and bacteriological warfare, a danger so intertwined with the aerial menace, the major powers followed much the same course. Vague restrictions were formulated at Versailles and Washington and more severe ones were written into the Geneva protocols hammered out in 1925, but these were not to take effect until ratified by the home governments of the contracting powers, which often qualified their acceptance or (in the case of the United States and Japan until the 1970s) withheld it altogether. Large-scale research into chemical warfare continued; Geneva only encouraged governments to hide it further from public view.

More far-reaching efforts to control these weapons were victims of the usual tangle of economic, bureaucratic, and strategic considerations. In the end, another consideration also held back the diplomats: if an end to air war meant only a return to slaughter in the trenches, the alternative was hardly attractive. A Harvard professor made this case for gas weapons in no uncertain terms: "however vast the destruction, however 'inhuman' the methods used, however appalling the sacrifice of life," the resolution of conflict by "some quick and overpowering blow" seemed "preferable to its alternative,—a long war . . . of mud, vermin, disease and nameless agony,—a war of starvation, exhaustion, lying, brutalization, and madness." The bomber thus retained its appeal; its restriction made sense only as part of a comprehensive disarmament. Few people liked the failure to control the bomber, and even the *New York Times,* no voice of radicalism in the matter of arms control, chastised the Washington conference for admitting "its helplessness to curtail the sinister energies of the most dangerous and destructive instrumentality of modern war, the bombing airplane." But a shared perception of danger among the great powers only overlay diverse perceptions of interest.[28]

Although futile, postwar efforts at arms control nonetheless shaped Americans' views of the bomber by establishing one context in which they pondered its significance. Less concerned than Europeans with national survival, Americans keenly debated aviation's impact on national efficiency and economy. The crux of the issue, tiresomely and sensationally debated, was whether the bomber could replace the battleship and the surface fleet as the primary instrument of coast defense. Mitchell's argument was that it could, at great savings to the taxpayer. Battleships were defenseless against bombers, useless in attacking other nations with air power, and wasteful as a way of guarding against an enemy threat from across the seas. The airplane could do the job cheaply, if freed from the clutches of the army and navy and organized into a separate service. The efficiency of air power was the *idée fixe* of all his writing, scarcely refined through fifteen years of polemics, supported by crude comparisons of the destructive power of battleships and bombers and buttressed by claims that an entire air force could be operated for the cost of "one or two battleships a year."[29]

These claims were central to the appeal of air power at the time of the Washington conference. Indeed, Senator William Borah, the man most responsible for goading the Harding administration into calling the diplomats together, seized on such claims to make the case for naval disarmament. Mitchell's sensational bombing trials against naval targets—carried out in 1921 after months of controversy, given enormous press attention, and followed up by mock raids on east coast cities by Mitchell's planes— strengthened the claims of the air power enthusiasts. When the ex-German battleship *Ostfriesland* slid into the Atlantic twenty-one minutes after Mitchell's bombers struck, the bomber seemed to many the best hope for peace and disarmament. In the extravagant predictions of the time, the burden of costly navies would soon be lightened. A Washington headline proclaiming "Airplane [the] Only Hope to Reduce Naval Armaments" captured a popular line of argument.[30] When the Washington conference assembled soon after (with Mitchell himself in the American delegation), controversy over Mitchell's experiment continued to reverberate, and renewed bombing trials would keep it up for years to follow. Hardly enough to make statesmen scrap their navies, the bomber's merits did help make possible limitations on naval arms: tonnage limits for capital ships in the famous ratio of 5 : 5 : 3 : 1.75 : 1.75 for Britain, the United States, Japan, Italy, and France, respectively.

More important for the story of air power, the controversy over the relative merits of the battleship and the bomber meant that in their first sustained look at military aviation, Americans saw it as a way to uphold New Era virtues of economy, efficiency, and technological innovation. The argument for air power appealed to widespread sentiment for the reduction of federal expenditures in the wake of the orgy of wartime spending. It also responded to postwar disillusionment with involvement in European wars by portraying a self-reliant America that would defend its shores without venturing abroad.

Above all, arguments for air power fed on a widespread image of naval armaments as the foremost expression of modern militarism.* After a long naval arms race, one widely seen as a major cause of World War I and renewed after the war's end, battleships served as the primary symbol of the burden and danger of militarism. The power of the naval lobby—dozens of senior admirals and naval bureaucrats linked with friendly congressmen and powerful industrialists—suggested that vested interests lay behind the pressure to build bigger fleets. Of course there was also an aviation industry, peopled by its share of scoundrels and fast-buck artists and dogged in the 1920s by its wartime reputation for delivering dangerous goods behind schedule for outlandish prices. But in a market saturated with surplus warplanes, the industry was in shambles for much of the 1920s, hardly a match in the public mind for the naval lobby. In addition, because airmen often crossed swords with industrialists or died because of industrial misdeeds, the prophets of air power often appeared as opponents rather than as agents of greedy capitalists; in the years after Mitchell's court-martial, his more hysterical defenders viewed him as the victim of nothing less than a vast "Air Trust" conspiracy. In sum, the call for constructing an air force seemed to come from a handful of low-level officers fighting to protect a better idea from corrupt interests.

The fighting within the military services sharpened the image of airmen as challengers of militarism and waste. Their principal opposition often came from the navy, in part because the demands of airmen for a separate department of aviation or a unified

---

*In Alfred Vagts's classic definition, militarism referred to any activity that did not contribute to the purpose of military forces—to prevent or win wars. Its contemporary meaning often emphasized something slightly different—a tendency of military institutions and their allies not only toward self-aggrandizement, but toward the promotion of war itself. See Vagts, A History of Militarism, Civilian and Military (1937, 1959), especially 13–17.

department of defense would have undercut the navy's control over its own air arm, a prospect even naval fliers did not relish. More than that, neither the range of existing airplanes nor the postwar disillusionment with fighting in Europe encouraged the air power enthusiasts to justify the bomber as a replacement for ground armies in waging war overseas, although they offered this justification out of the public eye.[31] The best case for an independent air force was to present it as a necessary, economical alternative to the fleet in defense of American coastlines.

A few heretics aside, the admirals played into the hands of the army aviators. Relegating aviation to an auxiliary role in their service, they boasted of the battleship's invulnerability to air attack—Josephus Daniels, the navy's civilian secretary, was ready to stand bareheaded on the deck of any battleship Mitchell dared to attack, certain that Mitchell would be "blown to atoms long before he gets close enough to drop salt upon the tail of the navy."[32] The navy resisted Mitchell's demands for a public test of bombers against warships, then manipulated (as did Mitchell) the ground rules for the 1921 tests to its advantage, and finally (it was alleged) harassed and spied on critics of accepted naval wisdom. Weak attempts to explain away Mitchell's success in the tests compounded the flaws in the navy's handling of the defiant aviators.

On technical and tactical matters, the navy's arguments were not without merit—aircraft faced enormous difficulty in locating ships at sea; naval construction was not a static science. But often the admirals appeared moved by selfish interests and blind faith in naval tradition. The army's response to Mitchell suggested the same pattern to some critics. Exiling him to San Antonio in 1925 and convicting him on court-martial charges later that year, the army seemed in league with the White House—Calvin Coolidge himself preferred the court-martial charges—in resisting new ideas.

In truth, the stridency rather than the substance of Mitchell's campaign accounted for much of the wrath of the brass. He did after all accuse them of "incompetency, criminal negligence, and almost treasonable administration."[33] Equally persistent but more patient airmen in both services survived, albeit with difficulties, and they sometimes resented Mitchell's self-appointed role as hero and martyr. No less important than Mitchell in the development of air power, they have faded from history because Mitchell so supremely drew all the lightning down on himself. By personalizing the issue of air power, his court-martial, along with the turmoil and intrigue which accompanied it, decisively shaped America's image of the new weapon.

Mitchell and his supporters, skillful publicists with ready access to the press, easily caricatured their opponents as foolish old men—"lineal prototypes of the champions of the long-bow"—or as petty, vindictive bureaucrats bilking the taxpayers into supporting outdated modes of warfare. "The older officers in both our services understand rifles, siege guns, and battleships," the New York Globe explained. "They do not understand aeroplanes, poison gases, aerial torpedoes." In Mitchell's view, aviation was a victim of "conservatism," a habit of basing "everything on precedent." Admiral William Fullam, one of the navy heretics, condemned officers with heads "buried in the sands of conservatism," and Admiral William Sims agreed that most naval officers were "hide-bound, unfitted and uneducated." "Fossilized admirals" were the culprit in the view of the *Toledo Times*. Mitchell, conjuring up images so useful in modern American politics, promised to "jar the bureaucrats out of their swivel chairs" and take his case "to Congress and the people." Senator Borah's enemies were those "interested in armament contracts . . . and the bureaus and bureaucracy" which would not stop until "paralyzed by the power of public opinion." The very setting of Mitchell's court-martial in a dingy building reeking of "government squalor" suggested his martyrdom by a tawdry and faceless bureaucracy, a replay of old progressive battles pitting the people against the special interests.[34]

Mitchell and the aviators seemed like courageous warriors for truth and progress. Newspapers noted his "devil-may-care recklessness" and his "romantic sort of person-age." "We may wait," the *Cleveland Press* gushed, "a hundred years for another such display of courage." To his legal counsel, Congressman Frank Reid, Mitchell was "a 1925 John Brown," who, though "crucified," will find that "his ideas will go marching on." Mitchell's detractors sometimes advanced the image of Mitchell as a rebel, only giving it a malevolent twist by accusing him of employing the "revolutionary methods of the communists" or, in John J. Pershing's charge, of being infected by the "Bolshevik bug."[35]

Marvelous public relations, Mitchell's war with the armed services paid few immediate political dividends. "Changes in military systems come about only through the pressure of public opinion or disaster in war," Mitchell believed. But appealing for air power as a money-saving measure became tricky when the opponent was Coolidge, that formidable penny pincher to whom adding another department to the government was heedless extravagance. By squeezing military budgets ("Who's gonna fight us?" he asked) Coolidge also sharpened the resistance of army leaders to air power claims.[36] By goading the navy to develop its own aviation, Mitchell also made the embarrassed admirals over into more formidable opponents. Moreover, his vision of a fortress America had political appeal but little strategic immediacy, inasmuch as no enemy was at hand to cross the oceans and land on American shores, and it kept him from forging the natural alliance with naval fliers, who saw aviation as a way to extend the nation's offensive capacity for protecting global interests. In the end, too, Mitchell's attempt, as Trenchard put it, to "convert his opponents by killing them first" cost him not only his job but considerable credibility. It gained him headlines but little support among those powerful enough to aid his cause. The attention of press and public opinion was usually fleeting and superficial, directed at the spectacle of sinking battleships and squabbling bureaucrats. After Mitchell's court-martial, much of the entertainment ended, and commentary on national defense at times barely mentioned aviation.[37]

In all likelihood, these setbacks made little difference to military aviation. Henry Harley Arnold, the air force's commanding general in World War II, later assessed the fate of Mitchell's early plans by concluding that "military aviation really couldn't have amounted to very much then, even if everybody had agreed with him."[38] Furthermore, the bitter feud of the twenties contributed to Mitchell's goals in ways that he could hardly have foreseen by strengthening the cohesiveness and commitment of his fellow army aviators. Beyond that, the image of the contending forces that developed in the 1920s made air power look curiously benign. Airmen were portrayed as the cutting edge of reform and technology and their superiors as the guardians of reaction. Yet the airmen also promised escape from the evils of scientific war as well as retreat to an America that needed no alliance, no League of Nations, no expeditionary army or navy "second to none" to protect itself. In this context, the admirals and generals stood for something modern and reprehensible—the evils of bureaucracy and militarism—in their alliance with private interests, their resort to bureaucratic machinations, their power and facelessness. For the most part, the aviators seemed to exemplify rugged individualism in an era of bureaucratic authority.

Air power derived its appeal by promising to place the glitter of modern technology in service of traditional values, above all the nation's long-standing distrust of standing armies. American security had never been effortless, and especially since the 1890s prominent Americans such as Theodore Roosevelt, moved by visions of empire abroad and unity at home, had forged a stronger army and navy. Mitchell, however, promised something more comforting. Air power, as he usually described it, would provide inexpensive security for a new generation of Americans, leaving them free from militarism and its accompanying evils—taxation, conscription, and tyranny. Americans, as C. Vann Woodward has written, traditionally "disavowed the engines and instruments of the power they did not need and proclaimed their innocence for not using them, while at the same time they passed judgment upon other nations for incurring the guilt inevitably associated with power." Leaving the nation's traditional institutions intact, air power also promised to retain inviolate America's claim to innocence and uniqueness "in a wicked world."[39]

The contests of the 1920s established air power as an alternative to a military system that had brought the world to war in 1914. In Arnold's inflated recollection, "to the American people . . . , Billy and his antiquated bombers were not so much a new weapon as the death knell of weapons. To hell with all armament; to hell with everything to do with war!"[40] Focusing attention on bureaucratic conflict, confined largely to the issue of continental defense, the debate about military aviation diminished awareness of the bomber's possible use against cities in the next great war—as, of course, did the prevailing assumption that for America there should be no such war. The organizational battle over air power overwhelmed the strategic issues, and with the bomber's proponents almost powerless, the bomber itself seemed almost benign. Americans were accepting the bomber, less because of Mitchell's persuasiveness, than because of the images of aviation that his well-publicized battles helped to establish.

THE CULTURAL CONTEXT OF PROPHECY

Bureaucratic battles over military aviation were insufficient in themselves to make the airplane a benign instrument. Complementary images flowing from other currents in the political culture added resonance to the images arising from Mitchell's struggles and also shifted attention further away from the airplane as an instrument of modern warfare.

One source was the continued evocation of combat pilots as knights of the air, the last warriors endowed with individuality in a war of anonymous millions. Holding bittersweet recollections of their experiences, some pilots themselves were reluctant to court heroic status. When Eddie Rickenbacker, the most famous American ace, rushed to print with *Fighting the Flying Circus* (1919), he also reminded Americans that "fighting in the air is not a sport. It is scientific murder."[41] Still, unlike the ground soldier, the individual flier stood out in postwar recollections of combat. Lengthy narratives of derring-do focused on what the pilots did to one another, not on their contribution to the carnage on the ground, while most other war literature treated aviation as the peripheral weapon it was; there was no *All Quiet on the Western Front* for war in the air. On screen, *Hell's Angels* (1930) "managed a mild anti-war spirit while extolling flight." When Hollywood recreated air war in *Wings* (1927), audiences apparently loved its sentimental plot of an aviator who, his best friend lost behind German lines, flies to rescue him, only to die in his comrade's arms. Similar themes were evident in Theodore Roosevelt, Jr.'s, depiction of the American ace Frank Luke: "Like some old-time frontiersman, he wanted every notch on his gun authenticated." In the 1930s, an American poet could still celebrate the chivalry in the skies of the "Knights of the world's last knighthood" and invoke mythical Greek warriors to describe airmen. Heroes of the air seemed lifted out of war altogether, serving as much-wanted reminders of the individual's continued significance in the machine age. Simultaneously, they appeared as throwbacks to an age of more gallant warfare, their courage magnified by the frailty of their machines and the odds against their survival. Given these images, it was easy to ignore the potential of airpower for "scientific murder."[42]

Evoking similar images, heroes of peacetime flying received more attention than combat aviators in the 1920s. Their exploits established the principal context in which Americans learned about aviation. Victims or practitioners of media exploitation, they enjoyed a hero-worship in which war existed only as an afterthought, and at that more often as metaphor for their deeds than as arena for the technology they promoted.

The primary example, of course, was the response to Charles Lindbergh's solo flight across the Atlantic in 1927. Despite Lindbergh's laconic protest that his feat was the product of cooperation and calculation, statesmen and journalists often saw in it a foolhardy daring akin to that of the great warrior—a Joan of Arc, the biblical David, the pilots of the Lafayette Escadrille or the Unknown Soldier of World War I. President Coolidge sent a navy cruiser to bring the Lone Eagle home; the army commissioned him a colonel; generals from the Great War toasted his bravery. Surrounding Lindbergh with the trappings of military heroism did not represent a conscious embrace of military virtues and certainly not a recognition of the military potential of aviation. Rather, in the wake of the enormous sacrifices of World War I, only war itself provided a point of reference sufficient for measuring Lindbergh's achievement.

At the same time, Lindbergh's flight also appeared to confirm the wisdom of sacrifice in the recent war. It fastened again the frayed bonds between France and the United States in a way that diplomats had failed to do. "Has any such Ambassador ever been known!" the American ambassador to France exclaimed of Lindbergh, who was hailed as "the glad reuniter of long-riven parts" back in the United States. Through Lindbergh, wartime allies celebrated commonality in the easiest of circumstances, without worry about the differences that divided them. A feat of such beneficent diplomacy was far removed from the world of guns and bombers, even if, as Lindbergh acknowledged, the military had played a role in his success by training him as a pilot and providing navigational and logistical support for his flights. Yet Lindbergh's own account in 1927 of his military training removed it as far from war as possible; he and his fellow student pilots had flown only "for the love of flying."[43]

At the core of the Lindbergh celebration was a culture's attempt to reconcile divergent ideals. Lindbergh embodied at once the promise of the machine age and the virtues of frontier individualism. Like the airmen of World War I, he suggested that the promise might be realized without the regimentation and crassness of industrialism. The *New Republic* gathered together conflicting images when it protested the decision to bring Lindbergh home "on a gray battleship with a collection of people all of the same stripe, in a kind of ship that has as much relation to the life of a sea as a Ford factory has! We might as well have put him in a pneumatic tube and shot him across the Atlantic." Again, as in the bomber–battleship controversy, the suggestion was that flight represented escape from the dehumanization of the machine, a notion echoed by a prominent English politician hailing Lindbergh's achievement as "a triumph of man over machinery." At the same time, Americans could admire the industrial discipline and cooperation that lay behind Lindbergh's deed because the final triumph was clearly an individual act. Lindbergh's "role was finally a double one," John William Ward has concluded, serving both to celebrate "the complex institutions which made modern society possible" and to reaffirm an America that was a place of "escape from institutions, from the forms of society, and from limitations put upon the free individual." As with most potent cultural images, Lindbergh's flight derived its power in the American imagination from its capacity to hold divergent ideals in suspension.[44]

His flight crystalized an image that countless other aviators helped to sustain. The press gave tireless attention to their perils and achievements. "You got an airplane, some financial backing, and a press agent, and made the first non-stop flight from one place to another place (there were still plenty of places that nobody had ever flown between)," Frederick Lewis Allen wrote while the hoopla was still fresh.[45] Records were made not only to be broken, but to be redefined in a myriad of ways—after a man had made a record, a woman could match it or someone else could fly in the opposite direction or soar over an uncharted and presumably perilous route. America's military aviators figured prominently in the race to set new records, flying across the Atlantic in 1919, nonstop coast-to-coast in 1923, around the world in 1924, and setting new speed, height, and endurance records—usually with an eye to publicity.

Preoccupation with breaking records and with the crashes that so often accompanied new ventures dominated the attention paid to aviation. In their speeches and writings, aviators were often on the defensive, pleading that the spectacular crashes described in newspapers and depicted in newsreels not blind Americans to realizing the practicality of commercial aviation. In truth, the disasters were as essential a part of aviation's image as the records set and inventions tested. They contributed to a sense of individual daring, of the machine's frailty, and of man's resourcefulness that made aviation a benign attraction, a fusion of frontier spirit and machine-age discipline. Few wanted to hear Lindbergh say that his famous flight involved slight risk.

Achievements like Lindbergh's were greeted as signposts on the road to an imminent aerial millennium. Sketched out before the war, the virtues of flight were now elaborated in a frenzy of celebration. "Aviation enthusiasts tended to view flight as a 'holy cause,'" and with religious fervor they outlined its potential to democratize, uplift, and pacify the nations that touched it. The conspicuous roles in aviation assumed by women in the late twenties and thirties popularized that perceived potential. As pilots, stunt fliers, saleswomen, and stewardesses, women served narrow interests: given the dominant image of women as less mechanically adept and physically courageous than men, their highly visible presence in the skies was deliberately contrived by the aviation and airline industry to make flying seem safe, easy, and accessible. The pioneering women fliers "domesticated the sky, purging it of associations with death and terror." For their part, these women found in aviation a socially acceptable outlet from traditional feminine roles. Privately, some felt the same sense of power and mastery usually ascribed to men, foreseeing the day when they "got the chance to fly bombers against the enemy after casualties decimated the regular male crews." Publicly, their skill at promoting aviation as an extension of the traditional domestic sphere of women made their image a culturally acceptable one. In addition, opportunities envisioned for women—and to a lesser extent for blacks—sustained the image of aviation as a kind of vertical frontier in American history, a new arena of opportunity for social mobility. At the same time, feminizing aviation further reinforced its pacific image, for women would presumably bend aviation toward benign and uplifting purposes.[46]

Extolled in terms of national progress and superiority, aviation also provided welcome counterpoint to fears about what progress might bring. "Here is Charles Lindbergh, minding a machine over 3,000 miles of ocean," observed Stuart Chase, a sophisticated cultural critic. "So close was he bound to it, that he spoke of himself and it as 'we.' In a sense he loved it, and all the world loved him for that affection. I have not heard him called a robot."[47]

For Chase, the airplane was a sign of the harmony of man and machine, one countering contemporary fears that mass production made modern culture vulgar and monotonous. As of 1929, he explained, airplane-building still employed skilled craftsmen fashioning "not disembodied standard parts . . . , but a living unity, with a character of its own." He admitted that soon aircraft assembly lines would "spew out their millions of interchangeable parts," a possibility suggested by Henry Ford's widely publicized interest in aircraft manufacturing. "We may weep for the spirit of craftsmanship here crucified," Chase conceded, but the "standardized airplane" would allow the masses to fly, and it "need send no hostages to loveliness. Her design and her medium call for the micrometer and the superlative finish of the grinding tool. These can if they choose deliver a more just and lovely thing than craftsmanship could ever achieve." Henry Ford's visionary advertisements depicting sleek aircraft landing at trim airports promised the same. As Chase's rhapsody indicated, aviation offered to fuse the best qualities of an older tradition of individual ingenuity with the benefits of the more impersonal age of the machine.[48]

Cultural commentators like Chase and the historian Charles Beard anxiously tried to balance the virtues and dangers of the machine. As they did, they noted the threat of technological war, but they also compartmentalized it, viewing it as an abscess to be cauterized from machine culture. When looking at the possibilities for air war, they raised a specter only to exorcise it.

This approach was evident in a volume that Beard edited. Beard urged readers of *Whither Mankind* (1928) to "face the assertion that wars among the various nations of machine civilization may destroy the whole order." Yet, arguing that "the whole mechanical outfit of a capitalistic country can be reproduced in about ten years," he doubted that any war could be so devastating "that human vitality and science could not restore economic prosperity and even improve upon the previous order. . . . We may admit the reality of the perils ahead without adopting the counsel of despair." Admission, not exploration, was as far as Beard could go. When he closed the volume, a passing warning about "the devastations of war" was overshadowed by the uplifting assertion that "the spirit of intelligent control . . . has a fighting chance to prevail."[49]

One source of Beard's optimism can be found in the essay "War and Peace" by Emil Ludwig, a prolific German-born writer. Science made war more horrible, he acknowledged, but it also destroyed its utility, as was evident from the problems visited upon the victors of World War I. Science "has transcended all boundaries and has intertwined the widely differentiated raw materials and industrial domains," so that no nation could hope to monopolize materials or markets by military conquest. The impersonality of scientific war also made "the idea of heroic death . . . a lie and every exhortation to win martial laurels a crime." Through history, war had been only the product of "the minds of a few" who manipulated the masses to support it. Now the machine culture would banish the "hateful words" of the warmongers. "Even the air, in which the traveller could once perceive real differences, is becoming homogenous. Wherever men are, there also is the smell of machine oil." Machines would "bring people together more quickly than could the conferences of their statesmen." They were "compelling us toward peace." The young would be educated to the horrors of war and learn that "great foreign cities are friendly neighbors which can now be reached by aeroplane in a few hours." Noting cursorily how new devices like the airplane made conflict more terrible, Ludwig concentrated on his main theme, how new inventions could help abolish war.[50] In writings like Ludwig's, the danger of modern war seemed at once more intense and more circumscribed—a far greater peril if it occurred, but one now far less likely to occur.

Despite all that World War I suggested about the problem of science and war, when concerned Americans examined the machine, they confined that problem to a small corner of their thoughts or ignored it altogether. When the Academy of Political and Social Science devoted an entire issue of its *Annals* to aviation in May 1927, only one brief article by Billy Mitchell examined its military uses. A few years later, President Hoover's prestigious Committee on Recent Social Trends examined the impact of science but omitted its implications for war entirely. In general, too, few engineers, industrialists, or scientists wrote expansively about war and military aviation. Even the brash army aviators became more cautious after Mitchell's court-martial.[51]

Those who pondered the fate of the airplane certainly differed widely in politics and temperament, journeying to a point of congruence from widely separate directions. Europeans seemed to grasp almost desperately at the airplane, knowing its terrible role in war but hoping it might prevent war. Americans either seized on it eagerly or ignored it complacently, inspired by a confidence about man's ability to control his creations. Both groped toward versions of deterrence, based upon the perilous trust that scientific war had a horror that would be its own deterrent or upon a more buoyant faith that science would simply make war impractical and unattractive.

Lindbergh asserted that his flight signified how aviation would "bring our peoples nearer together in understanding and in friendship than they have ever been." (Only late in life did he come to regard even civilian aviation as dangerous, an agent of cultural destruction rather than connectedness.) As Mitchell claimed, to oppose the progress of aviation would be to oppose civilization itself, inasmuch as "transportation is the essence of civilization." W. Jefferson Davis, a much-published expert on aeronautical law and advisor to the government, found aviation a means for realizing "President Wilson's dream of a League of Nations": traditional barriers among peoples became "invisible from the skies, and the big booming air liners go shuttling over them, weaving a pattern of new understanding, banishing insularity and prejudice, building up economic interdependence—surest safeguard against war—and fusing old antipathies in the unfailing solving of daily business intercourse." What political institutions could achieve only painfully in the way of broadened consciousness and international harmony, commerce and science would realize effortlessly. Entranced by such prospects, men were prone to look away from the dangers of aerial technology, in much the same way that people did in the 1960s when space flight was portrayed as an agent of planetary and ecological awareness.[52]

A tendency to divorce civil and military aviation strengthened optimism in the 1920s and 1930s. To be sure, army aviators skillfully exploited the connection between the two in arguing that they could perform a host of useful peacetime duties, such as aerial mapping, fire fighting, mail-flying, and route development. Henry Ford recognized that "once we know enough about commercial aeronautics, it will not be difficult to turn out military airplanes as needed and to find the proper pilots for them." The convertibility of commercial aircraft to military duties was a recognized obstacle to disarmament, especially when governments promoted military aviation "under the guise of commerce."[53] Yet recognition of a practical connection faded when people attempted to take a longer view of progress, for they assumed that civilian and military aviation were independent elements instead of common constituents of the machine culture. The patterns of aeronautical progress usually observed confirmed that comforting distinction. It was a cliché of the period that aviation had really gotten started, in World War I, as the handmaiden of war but afterward began realizing its peacetime potential. With each passing year, as commercial airlines flourished, aviation seemed less and less a military activity. Progress and peril, science and destruction, peace and war increasingly appeared separable.

For a moment, Stuart Chase seemed to confront the danger of air war unblinkingly. In a chilling look at "The Two-Hour War," which appeared in the *New Republic* and in his own *Men and Machines* in 1929, Chase distilled the decade's scare literature and its conflicting impulses about the machine and the airplane. He asked his reader to imagine that in Europe "a thousand men climb into the cockpits of a thousand aircraft" and after a few hours' flight drop their bombs

> per schedule—and so, to all intents and purposes, the civilization founded by William the Conqueror, which gave Bacon, Newton and Watt to the world, comes, in something like half an hour, to a close. Finished and done. London, Liverpool, Manchester, Lancashire, Bristol, Birmingham, Leeds—each has had its appointed place on the code of instructions, and each now duly makes its exit from the list of habitable places on the planet. Not even a rat, not even an ant, not even a roach, can survive the entire and thorough lack of habitability. Every power nerve has been cut with explosives; every living thing has ceased to breathe by virtue of diphenyl chlorarsine.

For Chase, this was no passing danger dutifully noted but almost a certainty, from which "I see no possible way out." The certainty was increased by the impossibility of comprehending it: "The persons capable of imagining the holocaust in advance are so few, and of such slight influence . . . that the world cannot realize what it now faces until it has faced it in a *fait accompli*." Nor would he exempt America from the danger: "Particularly complete would be the termination of New York. With her bridges and tunnels bombed, with her many tall buildings crashing like glorified tenpins, with her super-congestion, citizens would hardly have time to seize their check books before being summoned to the waiting rooms of the recording angel."

Yet Chase circumscribed the danger even as he magnified it. Like European prophets of air war, he found urban culture too fragile to sustain air war because "technological tenuousness" made it vulnerable to the destruction of a few key elements. He could not locate "the central intelligence to nurse a great city through a nervous breakdown." For that reason, "there is one good thing certainly to be said about the next war: it will not keep us long on edge. . . . The whole business will be over in a couple of hours. With lungs full of diphenyl chlorarsine, we shall not need to worry about anything ever again." If Chase intended this to be grim humor, it also suggested morbid release from the horrors of conventional war.

The arena of war had become both deadlier and narrower: "It hardly pays to discuss any mechanism of warfare except the airplane," Chase said, inasmuch as aviation had "reduced all other weapons . . . to so much scrap iron." Chase neatly banished the scourge of war as it had been known. There were no dangers other than air war to worry about, no intermediate possibilities between peace and holocaust; war was reduced to the problem of one weapon. Perhaps for this reason, when he posed solutions to the problem, Chase did so with astonishing dispatch, simply advising rulers to take the lead "in relentlessly suppressing war machines." Chase admired the airplane as symbol and agent of progress in the machine culture; he feared it as an instrument of war. He juxtaposed the two possibilities nicely, but they remained alongside each other, not integrally related. Hesitantly, Chase also offered hope. After the two-hour war, "the surviving West, together with the East, will then ban the machine from war—which means, of course," he added with telling simplicity, "the banishment of war. . . . Or so the conclusion hangs, neatly balanced between the hope and the belief, within my mind." He also neatly balanced terror and redemption.[54]

At midpoint between two world wars, that was where American perceptions of the airplane rested, at the intersection of peril and promise, with most people cautiously choosing the path of reassurance. They did so because the urge to see science as beneficent remained strong. Attention thus drifted away from war. The glories and the dazzle of aviation, even the struggle over military aviation, took it elsewhere. Then too, in peacetime men were inclined to worry more about what the machine culture would do to their souls and pocketbooks than to their survival. Given these concerns, they read history selectively, emphasizing how earlier developments in transportation had knit together nations and continents, downplaying how they also had intensified the scale and destructiveness of war. War itself continued to seem remote to most Americans anyway, but all the more so because the airplane would keep it distant.

A subtle process led Americans to this point. Of course, one should not exaggerate the depth or the firmness of the outlook described here; the peril and promise of air war were hardly the liveliest concerns of most Americans. Yet the haphazard nature of concern for air war in one way made attraction to it more elusive and compelling. Aviation drew on sources so diverse and inspired images so complex that responsibility for it rested everywhere—and nowhere. From that very ambiguity arose a general complicity for evading the intractable problems that arose from the advent of war in the air. In 1934, an English writer indicted his civilization for the doom that hung over it: "Mankind is Frankenstein," he lamented, and "science, especially the science of aviation, is his monster." The "nice boy" aviator, the mild-mannered scientist, the phony politician, and the unthinking masses had collaborated in the imminent death of Western civilization by the "senseless wickedness" of air war. "At none of these can we point and say 'that is the criminal!' "[55]

3

The Decline of Danger

During the 1930s, the attractions of air power that prevailed during happier days persisted, though in somewhat altered forms. Despite increasing world tensions and spreading use of the bomber in several conflicts, expectation that the United States might go to war, particularly that it would do so with the bomber as its foremost weapon, diminished for a time. The airmen's new doctrine of precision bombing, public debate about air power theories, and American responses to the bomber's use abroad all made danger appear remote. In turn, remoteness allowed technology and planning to proceed with important questions left unanswered, or even unasked.

PUBLIC IMAGE AND PROFESSIONAL DOCTRINE

As aviation was presented to Americans during the first half of the decade, its potential for peacetime uses seemed more than ever separable from its military application. To be sure, the onset of the Great Depression raised disturbing questions about the economic and social impact of technological change. But aviation was largely exempt from the doubts raised about technology. On the contrary, economic disaster encouraged Americans to see in the rapid growth of commercial aviation a rare glimmer of vitality. Not only did airlines expand rapidly, but the airplane itself appeared on the verge of democratization, near to becoming an article of mass production and consumption akin to the automobile. It seemed reasonable for a federal official to predict in 1930 that the day was near when "everybody would fly, everybody would have a plane, and aerial traffic cops would soon be busy handing out tickets." With the appropriate fanfare and modest government subsidies, prototypes of a "poor man's airplane" began rolling into public view, greeted as evidence that an automobile for the skies was around the corner.[1]

At the same time, in well-publicized events and spectacles, Americans glimpsed the growing range and power of military aviation. Army and navy aviators broke more records for speed, endurance, and range. Sleeker bombers, embodying the first real improvements in design since World War I, entered military service. The United States Army Air Corps, seeking publicity as well as strategic insight, staged bold flights, maneuvers, and war games, such as one that theoretically reduced a part of New York City to a "smoldering heap of ashes."[2]

What most Americans learned about these episodes, however, gave them little reason to see anything ominous. The extensive press coverage of air force maneuvers rarely suggested that the United States would ever bomb other countries. And some of the maneuvers were little more than stunts that backfired badly for the Air Corps. In August 1931, the National Broadcasting Company gave a blow-by-blow radio account of an attempt by army bombers to intercept and sink an old freighter, the *Mount Shasta*, in the Atlantic. But the air crews first failed to find the ship, then proved unable to sink it, and finally left it to the Coast Guard to finish off. Such a miserable performance badly embarrassed the Air Corps in its attempt to supplant the navy as the first line of coast defense.

The stormiest incident involving aviation in the early thirties, the air mail fiasco of 1934, also left the impression that military aviation, at least in American hands, was a frail instrument of war. The episode began when President Franklin Roosevelt canceled contracts issued to private business to carry the mail and ordered the Army Air Corps to do the job. Benjamin Foulois, the Chief of the Air Corps, was all too eager to prove that his organization could do so. As the *New York Times* commented, "The proponents of a separate Air Force for defense purposes see for the first time an opportunity to obtain their objective." But Foulois overplayed his hand. Equipped with obsolete planes and hampered by the inadequate facilities funded by a parsimonious Congress, the aviators found their worst enemy in some unusually severe winter weather. Disaster and embarrassment resulted, as planes crashed, pilots died, and congressmen and journalists mourned the poor boys sacrificed by a headline-hunting president. "That's legalized murder!" fumed Eddie Rickenbacker, who now, along with Lindbergh, was a backer of the aviation industry. The denouement came when Roosevelt ordered a cutback in service, while improving weather and organizational efficiency sharply reduced accidents.[3]

The whole mess had conflicting implications for military aviation. It undermined the aviator's claims that they were ready to function as an independent service. Yet it also appeared to validate their charge that conservative ground officers had short-changed the Air Corps and throttled its growth. It thereby not only compelled modest increases in appropriations for the Air Corps but climaxed still another round of controversy about the merits of an independent air force. As in previous battles over this issue, the army aviators did not achieve their goal of independence. Indeed, most had become too cautious since the Mitchell affair to pursue it openly. But they inched further along the road to organizational autonomy. Army aviation, already promoted from Air Service to Air Corps in 1926, secured establishment in 1935 of a General

Headquarters Air Force, which theoretically gathered all operational units under one command responsible only to the army chief of staff. In all, army aviation had accumulated some capital out of its own embarrassment.

These marginal gains existed largely on paper, however. The relentless squeeze on military budgets brought on by the depression overshadowed all military politics. Army leaders felt caught in a bind. They regarded aviation as the most expensive item in their budget, one whose growth would dissipate the strength of the ground army and the integrity of the officer corps. On the other hand, they feared that economizing on aviation would offend a public enamored with air power and hand over to the navy the initiative in developing aviation. The army general staff never escaped this bind. Douglas MacArthur, the chief of staff early in the 1930s, followed a shifting course. One moment he allied with pacifists and proponents of disarmament by proposing the abolition of military aviation to the World Disarmament Conference, doing so in hopes of freeing up funds for the ground army. At other times he curried support from aviators by backing creation of the General Headquarters Air Force and proclaiming the utility of air power in attacking the "vital arteries of a nation."[4] A confrontation with President Franklin Roosevelt on the budget issue reportedly left him so upset that he threatened (not for the last time) to resign and so ill that he vomited on the White House lawn. Roosevelt handled the aviation issue in a scarcely more consistent manner, flattering Mitchell while running for the presidency in 1932 but disappointing the aviators once he got into office. From this tangled web of political and budgetary considerations the Air Corps emerged with its share of total army budgets increased, but the contraction of those budgets made this at best a rearguard victory.

Beyond budgetary and organizational issues, the air mail affair reinforced the benign image of military aviation. Once again, army aviators often appeared to be the victims of established interests. More than that, the episode suggested how remote the possibility was of American engagement in actual air war. Mitchell asked the appropriate question: "If an army aviator can't fly a mail route in any sort of weather, what would we do in a war?"[5] An air force that could not carry out that humble task seemed an unlikely instrument of impersonal destruction across the seas. Furthermore, the bad news from the air mail affair seemed to coincide with evidence of waning public interest in the grander theories of air power. The press featured several articles that were highly skeptical about those theories, and Mitchell, by 1934 once again a pariah at the White House, found himself shunned by publishers, who thought he now bored his readers. In short, 1934 perhaps marked the nadir of the public image of American military aviation.

Just at that low point, however, Air Corps officers were distilling a new doctrine, one of precision bombing, that soon would enhance their status and mobilize their ranks, and later calm moral distress as the nation contemplated the next world war and the bomber's use in it. Peculiarly the brainchild of American theorists, though sometimes foreshadowed and later appropriated by airmen elsewhere, the doctrine of precision bombing had origins as complex as its implications.

Among those origins, however, ideology played a negligible role, at least in the formal deliberations of American airmen. Strong-minded, occasionally bitter about their clashes with senior army and navy officers, these men were nonetheless reticent or indifferent about the larger controversies over fascism abroad and unrest at home that aroused many Americans during the depression years. Most had entered military aviation for the excitement and glamor it offered or for the chance it seemed to offer as a new field for rapid promotion. Understandably, given how new that field was, their perspective on doctrine was parochial.

It was sharpened by professional frustrations. Rapidly promoted during World War I, Air Corps officers had endured wholesale reduction in rank after the war's end and a glacial pace of promotion thereafter. So had most other army officers, but airmen were different because of the mystique of aviation and the pack mentality induced by their training and their battles with superiors. Infantry or artillery officers also worried about dead-end careers, but at least their branches of service were not suspect in the eyes of the high command. For airmen alone, personal ambition meshed precisely with professional progress.

Walter Millis once assessed the priorities of Air Corps officers between the wars as follows: "Independent power and authority came first; to attain the goal it was next necessary to develop a 'doctrine' which would make it militarily valid; finally, with the doctrine established, it was necessary to invent a weapon which would justify the strategy." Such criticism has been commonplace, and as Millis acknowledged, hardly leveled only at air officers. Nor was it entirely fair, inasmuch as relationships among status, doctrine, and technology were more complex than Millis allowed. If airmen had been hesitant to develop doctrine, laymen would have voiced it in some fashion anyway, as indeed they often did. Yet Millis had the pattern substantially correct. Logic alone never dictated employment of air power against enemy cities and factories. Many other uses, for which a few airmen made pleas, existed for the airplanes. Air forces exposed to combat in the 1930s learned, as World War II showed more fully, that tactical aviation in support of surface forces "could often destroy the forces in the field before strategic bombers could have a paralyzing effect." But no doctrine except strategic air power satisfied the drive to achieve an independent air force that would bring personal status, power, and probably most important, professional respectability.[6]

Other differences and irritations, often petty in themselves, widened the gap between the fliers and their superiors trained in ground warfare, intensifying the drive for a doctrine that would justify independence. Aviators were set apart because they were relatively young, few in number (everyone knew everyone), low in rank, less often products of the West Point fraternity, and engaged in the most dangerous assignment (in one typical year, 2.5 percent of all army aviators died in crashes). Their one toehold in the bureaucracy, the position of assistant secretary of war for air (a civilian post), was eliminated in the budget crunch of 1933. Their weak position in the army bureaucracy encouraged them to circumvent it by courting support in Congress, the press, and the public. It also contributed to "something of a persecution complex," as one sympathetic historian has put it, a contemptuous attitude that often saw stupidity or malice in the bureaucracy's understandable stress on gradual change and discipline. Anachronisms imposed on aviators—"the somewhat ridiculous spectacle of aviators on horseback" at Maxwell Field, for example—did not help. "Anyone," Foulois later recalled, "who went against staff thinking on any subject in those days invited a reprimand for himself rather than a reward for daring to think imaginatively." Yet defiance was attractive as well as dangerous, as if "the more trouble you were in with your superiors, the higher your status among your own group." In other words, airmen made a virtue out of inferior status.[7]

Frustrated in their efforts to influence higher policy, airmen were nonetheless largely masters of their own house. Except for the two top positions, promotions (although not necessarily assignments) in the Air Corps were made by the corps itself, not by the army. On matters of doctrine, the general staff's lukewarm interest in aviation cut two ways. It required the Air Corps to perform the ritual of harmonizing its official doctrine with conservative War Department policy, downplaying aviation as an independent agent of victory and stressing its role in supporting conventional forces. But superiors rarely looked over the shoulders of the airmen once this ritual was complete. In their own institutions, most of all at the Air Corps Tactical School in Alabama, Air Corps officers were free to construct their own curriculum and dogma. The leisurely pace of life in the peacetime army gave them plenty of time to do so.

By the 1930s, both the airmen and their institutions were also mature enough to carry on their struggle in more sophisticated ways. A cohort of officers had a decade or two of experience in aviation and had passed beyond the youthful stage of infatuation with the joys of flying. The Air Corps Tactical School had established a body of literature and a tradition of theorizing about aviation. Mitchell's fate had taught airmen that glamorous stunts and daring pronouncements were insufficient to achieve recognition of air power.

The new doctrine of precision bombing was the product of their efforts and the vehicle of their ambitions. Briefly, airmen, especially at the tactical school, argued that strategic air power could contribute to victory or secure it by attacks on the enemy state, especially its economic institutions. These attacks need not be indiscriminate, indeed should be targeted at only a few key components whose destruction would disrupt the functioning of the entire state. The enemy's will or capacity to fight would then collapse.

Americans took the lead in developing daylight precision bombing for reasons historians have been hard pressed to identify. Perhaps, it has been argued, they drew on an American tradition of technical elegance—a dubious explanation, inasmuch as American technology had usually been geared more to volume than precision, and other nations with a tradition of technical elegance, such as the Germans, did not develop the same doctrine of bombing. Perhaps strategic geography played a role, inasmuch as years of defending military aviation as a weapon for intercepting ships on trackless oceans placed a high premium on navigational and bombing accuracy. Technological advances in the 1930s at least made the new doctrine more plausible. New bombsights and bombers—first the B-10, then the four-engined B-17, with its bristling armament and its long range of twenty-four hundred miles*—made accurate penetration deep into enemy territory seem possible. But airmen began formulating precision bombing doctrine before 1935, when the first B-17 flew. More demonstrably than usual, this technology was the offspring, not the parent, of doctrine.

Since doctrine preceded capability, it derived as much from strategic ideas, bureaucratic interests, and national politics as from technology. Douhet, Liddell Hart, Mitchell, and others had prepared the way by their talk of vital centers and the Achilles' heel of the modern nation, implying an enemy's vulnerability to attack on selected targets. Yet their language was more metaphorical than exact, referring to targets as small as a railroad junction and as big as an entire enemy capital. Their prevailing assumption in the 1920s that gas would be a primary agent of attack—one the Air Corps would largely discard in the 1930s—hardly suggested precision. Their influence on the Air Corps, while large on the general matter of strategic bombardment, often consisted of the convenience of invoking better-known authorities to support arguments American airmen were already developing on their own. By the time he wrote *Skyways* (1930), Mitchell had made an unqualified commitment to the primacy of strategic bombardment, but he never systematically developed the notion of daylight precision bombing, which owed more to less-remembered officers who since the twenties had argued for destruction of key plants in "a complex system of interlocking factories."[8]

Beyond the influence of particular men and ideas, four forces converged in the 1930s to make daylight precision bombing an attractive notion. First, the Air Corps needed to justify organizational independence in a more effective fashion. Mitchell's coast-defense rationale had only pitted the corps against a navy too powerful for the airmen to defeat. As late as 1938, the navy secured army agreement to its demand that the Air Corps patrol no further than one hundred miles from the coast. This was a dead-end struggle for the Air Corps. It never ceased to invoke coast defense to support its claims; even when, in the midthirties, it drafted plans for bombers with a range of up to ten thousand miles, it rested its case on their utility in guarding the sea approaches to the nation. A transparent justification that fanned the general staff's suspicions, it gave strategic debate over aviation a distinct air of unreality. In the long run, however, the struggle over patrolling the oceans was a secondary issue, because the Air Corps wanted to show how it could win a major war, not merely ward off attack. Only an offensively oriented air force could command first place in the military establishment.

The airmen's argument for independent air power was made more compelling by a second consideration, the nation's strategic position. Strategists of air power knew that

---

*Range is a misleading measure of a warplane's capability. More informative is its radius of action, the distance which it can travel and then return to base—a figure that is usually well under half the range depending on the vagaries of weather, navigation, the size of bomb loads, and the enemy's countermeasures.

the United States enjoyed the unique advantage of relative immunity to air attack. True, they often invoked the danger of such an attack to buttress the case for air power, and in the late 1930s, the prospect of German seizure of air bases in the Western Hemisphere gave the danger some plausibility. But for the foreseeable future, the United States, with probable allies abroad (especially in Europe) or bases close to likely enemies (such as the Philippines near Japan), could inflict air attack with little fear of retaliation. It was in an enviable position to exploit the fragile complexity of the modern state.

What self-interest and strategy made compelling, the nation's mood made politic. America's response to the bloodletting and disillusionment of World War I ruled out dispatch of another great army to fight abroad. In the 1920s it had been neither prudent nor especially compelling for airmen to offer their bombers as a substitute for the expeditionary armies of the past. In the 1930s, as crises abroad imperiled American interests, airmen guardedly advanced the case for a bomber force that could strike across the seas. Air power appealed as well to a deeper strain of antistatism and antimilitarism in American culture because its reliance on a small, technically sophisticated elite apparently avoided the burdens of conscription, taxation, and death. It was the perfect weapon for a nation that wanted the fruits of centralized state power without challenge to traditions of decentralized authority and individual autonomy. It had particular appeal in the Far East, where the gulf between American ambitions and American power was especially great. It would be a kind of "barely visible hand" of national power, providing influence in world affairs while preserving traditions of limited federal authority associated with the nation's long era of "free security."[9] Airmen never formulated this appeal in such explicit or sweeping terms, of course. But it had informed Mitchell's arguments for air power, and the young officers at the tactical school quite explicitly recognized the nation's large stake in world power as well as the widespread popular hostility toward using another mass expeditionary army to effect that power.

Finally, the airmen faced the continuing need to justify the bomber as not only a practical but a humane instrument of war. Memories of World War I made many Americans demand nothing less of military doctrine. In this regard, earlier prophecies had never been fully satisfying—promising quick victory, they still had portrayed the bomber as an instrument of brute terror, employing chemical weapons that were the foremost symbol of war's inhumanity to man.

Precision bombing satisfied all these forces. It promised victory independent of the other branches of the armed forces, with minimal demands on and risks for Americans, by employing the bomber as an instrument of surgical precision rather than indiscriminate horror, laying its high explosives (not gas or incendiaries) on its targets with pinpoint accuracy, incapacitating the enemy without slaughter.

The key to success was target selection, the determination of a few key components or junctions in an enemy economy whose destruction would disable the whole system. It was a task airmen knew required the skills of the engineer and the economist, although the Air Corps had no money to hire them in the 1930s. Instructors at the tactical school largely relied on impressions and data from the United States. Taking note of a power failure in New York City in 1935, for example, they reasoned that "in one stroke" eighteen bombers striking at its power system could insure that "the entire machine that we know as New York could not function . . . [and] the city would have to be evacuated." Haywood Hansell, a young officer later to be a key strategic planner, recalled how a similar lesson in "specialization, and hence, vulnerability, literally fell into our laps." Discovering a drop in delivery of controllable pitch propellers, the Air Corps learned that a simple but critical spring for the propellers all

> came from one plant and that that plant in Pittsburgh had suffered from a flood. There was a perfect and classical example. To all intents and purposes a very large portion of the entire aircraft industry . . . had been nullified just as effectively as if a great many airplanes had been individually shot up, or a considerable number of factories had been hit. That practical example set the pattern for the ideal selection of precision targets. . . . That was the kind of thing that was sought in every economy.

Transportation, steel plants, ball-bearing manufacture, food delivery systems, energy supplies, and above all electrical power contained a few vital gears whose destruction would jam vast economic systems. Selective attack would bring systemic disorganization.[10]

It would also do so quickly and cheaply. Airmen did not stipulate the numbers of aircraft or the length of time required to achieve victory, in part because they were speculating broadly instead of drawing up war plans against specific nations. But Mitchell made extravagant claims with regard to numbers—four hundred planes would do the job. "The only reason to build 2,300 airplanes is to feed hungry contractors," he promised, adding that three modern ships would "demoralize and destroy Japan." And the analogies and examples cited by the theorists at the tactical school suggested quick paralysis induced by small numbers of aircraft, though later estimates were more realistic.[11]

Enticingly precise about the key components of the modern state and how to attack them, air planners were exasperatingly vague about how defeat would follow upon their destruction. At times, following a more traditional definition of strategy, they suggested that destruction would lead to victory by undermining the war-making capacity of an enemy; deprived of the sinews of war or the means to transport them, its military forces would gradually become unable to fight on. But that line of argument presumed that the enemy's forces were the objective and promised no quick victory. More often airmen talked of destroying the "enemy's will to resist . . . centered in the mass of the people."[12] Defining the objective in that way did not mandate direct attacks on a civilian population, inasmuch as its will might be shattered when the population witnessed the paralysis of its economy or military forces. Neither did it exclude such attacks, a matter on which there was considerable hedging.

The planners' vacillation about whether the final objective would be the morale of the population or its war-making capacity was a critical weakness in their doctrine. A 1926 text asserted that "complete destruction of vital parts of the enemy's sources of supply" would lead "eventually . . . to the collapse of the whole system."[13] In the masterful evasion of Muir Fairchild, an important tactical school instructor who wrote in the wake of Poland's defeat in 1939:

> The industrial mechanisms which provide the means of war to the armed forces, and those that provide the means of sustaining a normal life to the civil population, are not separate, disconnected entities. They are joined at many vital points. If not electrical power, then the destruction of some other *common* element, will render them *both* inoperative at a single blow. The nationwide reaction to the stunning discovery that the sources of the country's power to resist and sustain itself, are being relentlessly destroyed, can hardly fail to be decisive.[14]

This was a disturbing mixture of confidence about success and evasion about how to achieve it. Admittedly, Fairchild finally considered the enemy's will as the ultimate objective, and distinctions between the will and the capacity to wage war can be arbitrary. Yet it made a great difference, in strategy and in the lives of attackers and defenders, which objective was singled out. For Fairchild, apparently, one objective was as good as another. As was often the case in strategic thinking, belief in success encouraged imprecision about how to achieve it.

This conceptual problem was equally evident in imagining what would happen once an objective was attacked. Few airmen speculated about when an enemy's will would collapse or how a discouraged populace would bring a nation to surrender. Perhaps, it was argued, "the citizens of a democracy will demand that their representatives accept peace even with defeat when their will-to-fight has completely changed to fear."[15] Combining the red scare with the air scare, this said nothing about how dictatorships would respond to war's horrors. In any event, no one worked out the ensuing chain of events in any detail. Even the references to panic in World War I that peppered writings in the 1920s largely disappeared.

Indeed, numerous flaws in American air doctrine went largely unexamined. The invincibility of the unescorted bomber formation was an article of faith; Flying Fortress was no idle choice of name for the B-17. In theory, bombing by daylight permitted the necessary precision, while the bomber's speed, thick skin, bristling armament, and high altitude provided the requisite defense. But unexpectedly strong enemy air defenses, in conjunction with foul weather and human error and all the other things that can go wrong in war, would disrupt navigational precision. Only a slight disruption in the air would translate into gross inaccuracies on the ground, especially inasmuch as Air Corps calculations on bombing accuracy already rested on shaky probability theory. And if planes nonetheless found and bombed targets accurately, their destruction still might not achieve the expected effect if the targets chosen were in fact not critical to the functioning of the enemy state, or if they had been dispersed by an enemy in anticipation of attack, or if they possessed unused capacity (slack, it was later called) so that only a surviving remnant met critical needs. By the same token, a damaged target might be repaired quickly, or some alternative to the critical bottleneck might be jerry-rigged—an alternative rail line expanded, a vital material imported, a new industrial process substituted. The Air Corps recognized that target selection involved an extraordinary economic sophistication that it lacked. The resourcefulness of combatants in World War I—albeit under conditions that seemed leisurely to visionaries of air war—might have argued for more caution on this matter. And these uncertainties, the stuff of countless later critiques of air power theory, paled before the one most obvious to Wells but least appreciated by airmen in the 1930s: if every other assumption proved valid—attack proceeded, disruption spread, paralysis set in, defeat was inflicted—it remained unclear how air power could translate defeat into surrender.

Strategic bombing theory was like the complex modern society airmen imagined, so interdependent in its assumptions that the failure of one component would unravel the whole thing. As one critic has neatly put it, the airmen "assumed that virtually every significant aspect of modern society was distinct enough to be identified for destruction, yet interdependent enough to bring about total collapse of a nation once certain links were destroyed."[16] The airmen rarely recognized such flaws in their assumptions. Of course, other military doctrines of the day had their weaknesses as well. More than that, the fliers were not challenged to explore weaknesses in strategic theory. Inasmuch as they usually justified air power to their superiors as a weapon of continental defense, the issue was rarely joined within military circles. The airmen's own world was highly insular, and their struggle with the army put a premium on consensus as well as on a dogmatism in their own affairs like that which they mocked in the general staff. The swift pace of technological progress in the 1930s also minimized doubts; if the full potential of precision bombing was not immediately realizable, some imminent development would surely close the gap between dream and reality. And of course opportunities for reality-testing were few, and when they arose, air officers thought the uses of air power in Ethiopia, Spain, and China were too primitive in technology and tactics to tell them much. The Air Corps' dismissive attitude toward past experience was neatly captured in the tactical school's motto, *Proficimus More Irrentiti* (We make our progress unhindered by custom).[17]

Another reason for overlooking the obstacles to precision bombing concerned a role for the bomber soon to be important in American policy. Air prophets had for a long time postulated the bomber's potential for deterrence and diplomatic coercion: it would ward off attack, secure victory without unleashing its fury, and even help "establish world dominion," in Mitchell's words. If air power's importance were above all political and psychological, then the practicality of its actual operations was a secondary concern. Air Corps officers, however, hestiated to explore this higher level of strategy. Insofar as they gave international politics much thought, they held to a rather commonplace notion of "ceaseless warfare among the major powers" fueled by struggle for world markets. Their task was to prepare to wage and win wars, not to formulate schemes to prevent them. Deterrence and coercion were the responsibility of the highest reaches of the War Department and the White House, charmed circles closed to airmen. Airmen did not overlook the obstacles to precision bombing because they imagined a subtle deterrent role for their bombers.[18]

The limitations of American thinking about precision bombing indicate what a short distance its proponents had traveled from Douhet, Liddell Hart, and Mitchell writing in the 1920s. In particular, the path Wells had taken twenty years earlier in exploring the psychology of air war remained largely unexplored. From one perspective, the new doctrine appeared more refined and humane in its focus on select economic targets rather than on the lives and homes of civilians and their leaders. Yet it did not clearly substitute economy for morale as an objective but rather saw economic targets as a more effective point of attack on the enemy's nerves. Dislocation of the economy superseded dismemberment of the society but with the same end in view, the destruction of the will to fight.

The similarity in objectives was important. Later, in World War II, much was made about a distinction between British night bombing to terrorize German cities and American daylight precision bombing designed to immobilize the enemy's war-making capacity. In 1945, when Americans joined the British in area bombing, much was made of the collapse of this distinction. However, although the distinction was real, it had never been clearly drawn in American doctrine. In the 1930s, Americans never decisively opted for the enemy's war-making capacity as their objective. They proposed to attack the enemy's will, only by more humane and economical methods. In Mitchell's curious distinction, which found its way into Air Corps doctrine in 1926, air attack was "a method of imposing will by terrorizing the whole population . . . while conserving life and property to the greatest extent." Later the Air Corps discreetly dropped references to "terrorizing" the enemy but still listed "attacks to intimidate civil populations" among its objectives in official doctrine and hinted at such attacks in public statements.[19]

Neither their own consciences nor the revulsion against the past war's carnage shared by many Americans permitted the airmen to be amoral technicians. As in the writings of Douhet, Liddell Hart, and Mitchell, arguments for air power carried a strong if superficial moral justification. If American airmen advanced that justification less explicitly in the 1930s, it was in part because they were largely speaking to each other, not yet urged in public to defend themselves. In 1934, a retired air officer stressed how the actual damage that gas war "can do to civilians is slight in comparison with the terror that it is capable of spreading," and he compared this mode of war with the ones practiced in World War I: "Which method then actually is the most humane? The millions of widows, orphans, and maimed from the World War could give the most convincing answers." A leading proponent of precision bombing argued that "a determined air armada . . . may actually prove to be a more convincing argument against war than all the Hague and Geneva Conventions put together." If ethical arguments were neither profound nor sustained, they were unavoidable. Scenarios of quick victory simply implied a moral justification that needed little explicit statement.[20]

As in World War I, morality and utility remained discrete but closely related categories in debate about air war. Moral means were not necessarily useful, and useful means were not necessarily moral, but for the airmen, a measure of moral validity adhered to methods of war that achieved quick victory and minimized prolonged suffering. In this regard, the historical significance of the doctrine of precision bombing was not its repudiation of moral concerns but its role in quieting consciences anxious about the future of air war. Proponents of precision bombing believed that it would reap the long-standing promise of air power without inflicting unreasonable harm to humanity. Of course, the promise of air power had always inhered in its capacity to bring terror. Precision bombing did not entirely divorce the two, but it pushed terror so far into the background, placed so much distance between the act and the result, that it had much the same effect. Like the strategy of economic blockade practiced by both English and Germans in World War I, it proposed to attack the enemy population indirectly, by disrupting and starving it rather than by blasting and burning. But if no quick victory came and the enemy's will remained the objective, then airmen might have to strike at it through systematic rather than selective destruction, that is, by direct attacks on the civilian population. If that possibility remained alive, then both the moral and practical case for precision bombing became vastly more problematic.

Mostly out of view, these tensions and potentialities in the theory of air power emerged more starkly in contemplation of war with Japan. His court-martial having cut the last bonds of discretion, Mitchell gave such contemplation a more fanciful and menacing twist than he had in the 1920s. Now he regarded American action in the Far East as an instrument of American expansion. "It is westward that our course of empire will take its way," he grandly pronounced. He also portrayed Japan as scheming to attack not only American possessions but the United States itself, constructing secret "air fortresses" from which huge fleets of aircraft would bomb American cities. The Japanese, he warned in one of the last speeches he wrote, considered the United States "a decadent military power" and believed that "we will be as easy to attack as a large jellyfish."[21]

More menacing than ever, Japan also appeared more vulnerable. Submarines could destroy Japan's commerce, and its cities were attractive targets: "These towns are built largely of wood and paper to resist the devastations of earthquakes and form the greatest aerial targets the world has ever seen. . . . Incendiary projectiles would burn the cities to the ground in short order. An attack by gas, surging down through the valleys, would completely block them out." American planes could strike easily through the Aleutians, the Kurile Islands, or Eastern Siberia. "An understanding with Russia that would allow the United States to operate through Siberia and Kamchatka would be decisive against Japan." For Mitchell, war against the "yellow military peril" seemed easy and inviting. Significantly, the humanitarian defense he usually offered for air power—as a weapon whose frightfulness would require few casualties—had no place in these musings. Destruction would be total, not selective.[22]

Undoubtedly known to the Air Corps, Mitchell's ideas were only an object of casual interest for most of the 1930s. Official plans noted the critical role aircraft might play in defense of the Philippines but assigned them no larger mission. In 1935, an important air planner pointed out the deterrent value of such bombers, which might go far "toward squelching any expansion ideas on the part of an Asiatic Power." More boldly, a student at the tactical school presented Japan as "an ideal objective for air attack," suggesting that Japanese resort to indiscriminate bombing would remove the "humanitarian" obstacles to such bombing on America's part.[23] From the Command and General Staff School came a study, "The Psychology of the Japanese Soldier," which drew on Douhet and embraced air power. When the United States faced the fanatical Japanese, it should visit slaughter on them from the air, for "meeting Japan's bayonets with bayonets is playing into her hand." The United States had to rely on its "mechanical superiority" and realize "the tremendous striking power of an air force directed at the paper cities of congested Japan." Against American bombers, "Samurai swords will be found rusty and their rice mustardized."[24]

But these early ideas about air war against Japan were infrequent and had a casual quality reflected in a lack of preparation for realizing them. No bases or plans were readied. Incendiary bombs, the mainstay of any probable air war against Japan, were not developed. Elsewhere too, inconsistency and superficiality defined the dominant attitude. To be sure, war with Japan was a concern among army and navy planners. They focused especially on the defense of the Philippines, which seemed to pose insoluble dilemmas: no one was sure how long the islands would remain in American hands, much less how the navy could defend them over the distances involved and with the limits on strength imposed by arms treaties and tight budgets. But the mere assumption that a Pacific war would be primarily a naval show discouraged participation by the Air Corps and the army in planning. Then, too, planning itself was a sideshow in the army, described by one student as "comparatively barren of strategic theory and interest" before 1938.[25]

Similar casualness and inconsistency prevailed in higher political circles and in the nation at large, which exhibited toward the Far East a "mixture of moral globalism and fear of military involvement" that could be reconciled only by "tortured argument," as Akira Iriye has written.[26] James Farley once recalled that at one of FDR's first cabinet meetings, the new president took note of Japan's vulnerability to bombing from the Aleutians, but the claim lacks verification. Roosevelt had previously been in touch with Mitchell, but he was a committed navalist, on record as condemning Mitchell's views and later as declaring chemical warfare "inhuman and contrary to what modern civilization should stand for." In 1937 and 1938, he had the State Department condemn Japanese bombing of civilians in China as "barbarous" violations of the "elementary principles" of modern morality. Secretary of State Cordell Hull also arranged an informal embargo on the sale of aviation equipment to nations using "airplanes for attack on civilian populations," with the Senate cooperating in its own "unqualified condemnation of the inhuman bombing of civilian populations."[27]

Consistency rarely bound Roosevelt. In 1934 Hull offered the Japanese ambassador a scarcely veiled threat by pointing out that Britain, another island nation once seemingly secure, could have its capital wiped out by a fleet of two thousand bombing planes and noting how an American airplane had recently flown from the United States to Japan. Such talk was perhaps one reason for another bombing scare in Japan, the second in three years. In general, however, Roosevelt did not give air power much thought before 1938. When he did consider the possibility of war with Japan he turned first to naval power, toying in 1937 and 1938 with vague schemes for an Anglo-American "peaceful blockade" of Japanese commerce or for undeclared maritime war against the Japanese. Most commentary in the media reflected Roosevelt's orientation: occasional loose talk about the tempting vulnerability of Japan's combustible cities to aerial attack, alongside a prevailing assumption that any war with Japan would be primarily naval.[28]

The casualness in contemporary speculation about air war against Japan, stemming from preoccupation with naval arms and the remoteness of actual hostilities, also reflected prevailing racial attitudes among Americans toward the Japanese. The ease and openness with which bombing Japan was mentioned and ethical considerations were disregarded had no equivalent in speculation about war against Germany or other Western nations. The attribution by some writers of vicious and grandiose designs to the Japanese justified aggressive American fantasies in the classic pattern of racist psychology: fear, contempt, and aggression mingled, each justifying but masking the other. Doubts about Japanese military capabilities in the air often rested on explicitly racial distinctions—the inferior eyes and ears of Asians supposedly made them poor fliers. Yet in part because Americans deprecated the prowess of the Japanese, mention of bombing them required little consideration of how aerial victory would be accomplished. Hence contemplation remained occasional, almost offhand.

Racism was hardly peculiar to Americans, mirrored as it was among those Japanese caught up in their own visions of racial destiny. It weaved its way through the whole course of Japanese–American relations. But in contributing to early notions about bombing Japan, it helped expose important dynamics behind the rise of American air power. Those notions revealed the aggressive fantasies about air power that aviators and other Americans usually held in check, suggesting that the humane rationale imbedded in the doctrine of precision bombing was frail and disposable. Similarly, they showed how the idea of air power was informed by fears and passions reaching far beyond the rational language of strategic calculation which airmen usually employed.

The casualness of American thinking about air war in the Far East was another indication of the state of official regard for strategic air power at mid-decade. The official view of air power was in a curious state of suspension, caught between the abstract or fanciful speculations of the Army Air Corps, the military bureaucracy's continued distrust of airmen, and the episodic and confused attention of the White

House and Congress. In an Air Corps ambitious but fearful of alienating superiors and public opinion, dreams of a great mission seeped through the cracks of more guarded propaganda for the cause. The army general staff, more alert than ever to the tactical role of aviation, bore down on the Air Corps by prohibiting production of the B-17 (beyond thirteen prototypes) and by challenging research and development for more advanced bombers. As one general staff officer put it in 1936, a proposed long-range bomber was "distinctly an airplane of aggression" that had "no place in the armament of a nation which has a National Policy of good will and a Military Policy of protection, not aggression."[29] Only after 1938 did a national policy for strategic air power begin to take shape.

PUBLIC DEBATE AND EXPERT REASSURANCE

Beyond official circles, a public debate about air power continued, one characterized by real concern and interest but giving the skeptics a small margin over those who prophesied that air power offered either total victory or supreme danger. As aerial holocaust grew closer, its danger seemed to recede. That at least was the impression conveyed by popular images of American aviation and by informed examinations of air power and the nation's strategic needs.

The American air force in particular appeared as a weapon of growing but still limited utility after the air mail affair of 1934. With Mitchell's eclipse and then his death in 1936, no well-known exponent of American air power spoke to the nation. Perhaps the most visible authorities were Henry Harley Arnold and Ira Eaker, two Air Corps officers who collaborated on three books in the late thirties and early forties, but these gave only a brief glimpse of the more terrifying possibilities of air power and emphasized the defensive aspect of American air power. Other Air Corps officials maintained a similar emphasis in public. Major General Oscar Westover, the Chief of the Air Corps, alluded to new missions for aircraft like the B-17, emphasizing their capacity to "keep us out of war" and mentioning Japan's fear of "ruthless bombardment of her tinder-box cities" by Russian bombers based at Vladivostok. In public, few aviators fleshed out these suggestions of offensive and deterrent functions for air forces.[30]

Most Americans continued to hear about the familiar scenario of aerial interception of sea or air armadas. In 1937, for example, the press reported a test ordered by Roosevelt in which an air squadron located a battleship in fog hundreds of miles off the West Coast—"the greatest happenstance in the world," Curtis LeMay admitted—and sunk it in a mock attack. Americans saw the familiar battleship–bomber controversy waged anew. A highly publicized flight of B-17s to South America that same year—LeMay was again the navigator—reworked the same theme in a hemispheric context, in line with the expanded concept of defense that the Roosevelt administration was developing. The climax of these headline-grabbing episodes came in a stunt—the Air Corps pulled out all the stops in securing newspaper and live coast-to-coast radio coverage—in which LeMay again led a flight of B-17s, this time in the interception of the Italian liner *Rex* in the Atlantic. Accompanied by dramatic photographs, a *New York Herald Tribune* article sounded the familiar defensive theme with the headline, "FLYING FORTS, 630 MILES OUT, SPOT ENEMY TROOP SHIP." All the hoopla reiterated the potential of aviation as an instrument of defense against invasion and loss of isolation.[31] So too did most of the extensive press coverage given to the B-17 and the experimental models of longer-range bombers in the late thirties. If war came, these aircraft were apparently designed to avoid the destruction of cities and seek out the enemy's troopships or war-making apparatus with fine-tuned precision, for their pilots were "trained from the beginning and at all times in 'spot' bombing instead of 'area' bombing" and were able to "drop a bomb into a pickle barrel from 18,000 feet up."[32]

Indeed, in the years before Pearl Harbor, a curious inversion of logic in debate about aircraft types moved Americans further away from recognizing the role their new bombers might play. Critics suspicious that Roosevelt was maneuvering the United States into a European war saw danger in the production of short-range tactical aircraft, inasmuch as their only foreseeable use would be to accompany American ground forces in battle against the Axis powers. Better, one writer argued, to construct three or four thousand long-range precision bombers, which could intercept an attack on the United States far from its shores. "Public uncertainty notwithstanding," he asserted, "the function of a bomber is not primarily the destruction of defenseless women and children. Neither is the bomber essentially an 'offensive' weapon." The long-range bomber, one congressman claimed in 1939, gave America "the ability to strike the enemy over the only two ways in which he can approach the United States, and that is over the Atlantic or Pacific Ocean," satisfying his wish to "have the fighting occur in somebody else's parlor rather than in my parlor." As John Chamberlain, writing in the *New Republic,* asked in criticizing the administration's interest in short-range bombers, "Isn't it at least arguable that our plane factories are being geared to turn out the types of plane needed for another overseas expeditionary force?" Thus a developing offensive capacity to bomb others remained disguised by preoccupation with protecting ourselves and preventing World War I. Big planes would protect American ideals and isolation, while little planes would undermine them.[33]

At the same time, another belief continued to grow: that air war against cities was likely to prove counterproductive, indeed, that the strategic uses of air power might be less important than the tactical. The arguments along these lines by skeptics of strategic air power, while often sound as analysis of contemporary experience or as pronouncement on the future, also diminished the dangers ahead.

The skeptics followed several lines of attack on the doctrine of strategic air war. They often began by attacking the motives of the air prophets, as when the *American Mercury* charged that "the flyers, seeking larger appropriations, have taken to playing the politician's game, i.e., conjuring up a terrible bogey, and then representing themselves as the only sorcerers capable of exorcising it." On the diplomatic level, *Commonweal,* with Hitler's threats in mind, saw in the fantasy of aerial holocaust "a new method of saber-rattling" by which "almost any pint-pot dictator could make a grand-stand play and set up a new empire overnight."[34]

Appeals to history and contemporary experience afforded skeptics a second line of attack. Hauling out statistics as avidly as the air prophets, they pointed out the little actual damage that bombing of cities had caused in World War I and its tendency to arouse rather than subdue a fighting spirit. "War will not be waged against women and children," one popular piece asserted. "Terrorism was given its trial during the World War and only wasted military resources and brought on counter-terrorism." A corollary line of argument was to deflate the threat of gas war by noting its limited utility in the last war and the impossibly large tonnages of gas that would be necessary to achieve decisive success. Puncturing the myth of bomber invincibility was another favorite theme, at times worked out by substituting for it a new myth of uncannily accurate antiaircraft systems employing new devices like the "Sperry-Wilson data computer," said to compile target data and aim guns instantly. "Perhaps sooner or later the bombing of cities will come to be officially recognized as a form of euthanasia for desperate patriots. That it will ever become a really popular pastime may be seriously doubted."[35]

Skeptics reasserted a traditional definition of war objectives and strategy. The trouble with air power, a naval officer wrote, is that it "can take nothing. It can hold nothing. *It cannot stand its ground and fight.*" A more sophisticated analysis of modern combat in *Fortune* dismissed prophecies like Douhet's as "pure romance," suggesting that no changes in technology had been decisive enough to overshadow traditional forms of warfare. A prominent army general reminded his audience "that every war must be won—finally—by sending men into enemy territory—and holding it." Mocking the prophets, he concluded: "After Samson smote the Philistines 'hip and thigh' and slew a thousand men with the jawbone of an ass, we may guess that some dreamers of that time would have equipped their military forces with asses' jawbones, exclusively. That would have been a grave mistake then, and it would be now." Similar sentiments lay at the heart of the 1934 report by a prestigious committee chaired by former Secretary of War Newton Baker, and they ran through a wide range of popular writing. Even after Poland's fall, *Harper's* ran an article entitled "Bombing Cities Won't Win the War" that maintained that "no war will be won by attacking civil populations in cities. No war will be won by the airplane alone. For it can't be and it won't be. War is won by infantry and money to buy wheat." According to *Commonweal*, it was "axiomatic that our cities are not destined for destruction from the air during the next emergency." Antiaircraft defense "has gone a long way since H. G. Wells wrote 'The War in the Air,'" too far for generals to waste planes in attacks on cities.[36]

The heart of the skeptics' argument was their belief that because air war against cities was impractical and counterproductive, it simply would not occur. Reassurance, that is, rested on the assumption that generals and politicians would rationally calculate the futility of bombing cities. The "fabric" of civilization is not going to be disrupted by such bombing, one skeptic announced: "The reader can be sure that similar calculations have been made by the staffs of all nations whom air warfare on a large scale might possibly concern, and that the ultimate futility of a policy of air terrorism has been perceived." An additional restraint would come from popular pressures to avoid air attack on enemy cities lest it trigger reprisals, civilians being likely to engage in "lynching any of their own airmen they can lay hands on" if they attempted such an attack.[37]

Repeatedly the skeptics ignored the contention of air prophets that the objective of armed force in war had changed: "no army would waste its very limited resources on the civil population. The objective of an army is the subjugation of the enemy army." Some also denied the impact of technology on the moral standards of war's conduct. "Wholesale destruction of the civil population has been a matter of humanity or inhumanity, civilization or barbarism, rather than of weapons." The same writer even denied the impact of technology on tactics: "Cavalry will still be needed and used," wars will be won "by a man with a knife in his hand."[38]

The skeptics' argument, then, fell short in several ways. By exaggerating the utility of knives and horses, some risked sounding like military Luddites. By asserting that aviation would find its most valuable role in supporting traditional forms of force, others suggested its use in situations requiring great precision, even while they had denied aviation's technological capacity against strategic targets. Most of all, by defining the objective of war as the defeat of the enemy's forces and the seizure of territory and by assuming that nations would rationally pursue that objective, they overlooked the appeal and utility of supposedly irrational uses of military force.

Writing for an American audience, Winston Churchill unwittingly demonstrated this last flaw in the skeptical argument. Churchill contended that "air bombing of the noncombatant populations for the purpose of slaughter" would be counterproductive on both moral and practical grounds: it would cost the attacking force dearly, it would "infuriate the nation" attacked (and its friends, like the United States, in case England was attacked), and it would be dissipated by measures of civil defense. Even if a population wanted to surrender, he asked in raising a much overlooked question, "how would they make their will felt?" The Germans briefly, and Churchill himself more systematically, were soon to ignore these sensible arguments. How much Churchill ever believed them may be arguable, for it was Churchill who five years earlier had described London as "the greatest target in the world, a kind of tremendous, fat, valuable cow tied up to attract the beast of prey." Perhaps his knowledge of radar later changed his mind on London's vulnerability.

In any event, Churchill did give a hint as to how the bombing of cities might yet occur. Terror bombing of urban areas might be useless, but if the RAF disrupted daylight attacks aimed at precise targets, an enemy could "only drop bombs indiscriminately upon built-up areas, protesting, of course, that there are military objectives somewhere thereabouts." Churchill had led his readers right back to the scenario he had rejected. He acknowledged that city-bombing would take place, albeit only as a reluctant or desperate attempt to use bombers of doubtful utility for other purposes or to abide by demands for vengeance or quick action. Here again was the less satisfying prospect that neither skeptics nor enthusiasts explored, bent as they were on defending or refuting bombing as a decisive weapon of rational policymakers.[39]

The assumption that war would follow a rational course might have diminished the skeptics' persuasiveness had it not been often shared by their opponents, the prophets of aerial doomsday, who still portrayed a future war of reassuring terror. A few, to be sure, left little to cling to beyond the speed of holocaust: if war struck the world's capitals and "took the lives of all their inhabitants," it would be over in a few hours. More typical was a *Readers Digest* prediction that the prospect of incendiary bombing would make it "less urgent for nations to settle their difficulties by the insanity of armed conflict."[40]

With Mitchell's voice silenced, the most lurid predictions came from England, where the fear of air war on cities remained greatest. Borrowing generously from Douhet and from England's experience in World War I (it "will be exactly reproduced on the next occasion, though on a more grandiose scale"), L. E. O. Charlton offered a mix of fact and fancy that further popularized notions of the knockout blow and push-button wars moving to swift and inexorable conclusions. His was an uncomplicated vision. Air power would operate with utter simplicity: "All it has to do is to proceed from A to B, linger a moment, and then come back." Victory would come swiftly by breaking the will of an enemy population, for after World War I no nation would again endure a "war of exhaustion"; the "will to war" would collapse before material devastation became widespread. Terrorization, he acknowledged, had satisfied a German need for blood and vengeance in World War I, but he emphasized how bombing would be a rational instrument of quick victory. Charlton also held out the possibility that an international police force would provide an "Escape from Armageddon" by monopolizing the bomber and ushering in an age of universal peace.[41]

Another English writer, John Langdon-Davies, gave to Charlton's predictions the added force of social psychology in his book *Air Raid: The Technique of Silent Approach High Explosive Panic* (1938). Civilian populations "can best be immobilized—that is irrationalized—by suspense. There is no need to smash them physically; instead they must be dislocated psychologically, and then they become more useful to the enemy alive than dead." Langdon-Davies offered prophetic insight into the psychological consequences of air raids on cities. "It is not merely that the individual feels helpless to save himself," he wrote, "it is much more a realization that the ability to take part in the communal life has vanished." Extrapolating wildly from a few firsthand experiences in Spain, he also promised that air war could so quickly force a rational decision to surrender that destruction and carnage need not worry his readers.[42]

Sometimes ideological passions twisted the prophets' view of the future. J. F. C. Fuller, the influential English military critic and historian, became hysterical about the danger of mass panic and cowardice in the face of aerial attack. Sympathetic to the English fascists, he distrusted the loyalty and steadfastness of Jewish and working-class Englishmen should war come, certain that the "terrifying moral effect of bombing" would lead to *"complete industrial paralyzation,"* a "surrender to mob violence," or "a civil war in the middle of a foreign one!" His only solution was to discipline the population, and his prescriptions dripped contempt for the masses and for democratic government.[43]

Writing after the start of the European war, the American aviator Al Williams also emphasized the political and psychological effects of air attacks on cities. Yet Williams's attraction to fascist politics and technology repeatedly diverted him from assessing the "unseen, sinister, and ominous imponderables" of air war. He sympathized with the use of air power made by Germany because it was presumably encircled by enemies. His assessment of American needs in the air became sidetracked by an outpouring of venom against England, Roosevelt, and the forces of internationalism that were supposedly dragging the United States into war. At the same time, Williams saw himself as a simple airman who hated politics and was comfortable only with his fellow flyboys. "Oh, if we could only sell this camaraderie of the air to all the rest of the world," he rhapsodized about his visits with German aviators in 1938. Enjoying Eddie Rickenbacker's blessing, Williams's book showed, in a manner similar to Charles Lindbergh's thinking, how a combination of reactionary politics and technocratic idealism provided another distraction from contemplation of future horrors.[44]

Americans could find in the writings of George Fielding Eliot an honest attempt to examine those horrors and steer a middle course between the skeptics' dismissal of air war and the prophets' embrace. A widely published commentator on issues of foreign and military policy, Eliot examined air power more thoughtfully than any other expert in America. One of a new breed of self-proclaimed realists who believed that force and calculation govern international relations, he reviewed a wide range of possibilities for the airplane in war and ruled out none. He came to believe that aviation "has restored strategical surprise" to warfare after it had become stalemated on land, making it possible, for the first time in history, to strike "at the seat and source" of enemy power "without first having to overthrow the armed forces with which he seeks to protect them." Sharing such broad assumptions with the air prophets, he stopped short of embracing their scenarios of quick victory by either terror or economic dislocation. He regarded "terrorization" as impractical and unlikely, for it would be a "gambler's throw . . . quite as likely to stiffen and harden the resistance of the stricken nation as it is to terrorize it."[45]

Still, he did not insist it would not occur. A nation might resort to it in desperation or calculate that air raids on cities, even if not quickly decisive, might induce "the opponent into an uneconomical and in the end disastrous defensive attitude." Unlike many writers, he acknowledged the possibility that the resulting air war might become deadlocked, though he thought this unlikely because two combatants rarely would be evenly matched. Avoiding the blanket generalizations of many other writers, Eliot was also careful to point out that geographical conditions greatly affected the vulnerability of nations to air attack or their capacity to employ it. In the end, he remained guardedly optimistic. Regarding the knockout aerial blow, "the weight of considered military opinion is against this possibility." Air power was more likely to realize its potential in spearheading ground and naval forces, in attacking well-defined military and economic objectives, and (he emphasized after Munich) in serving as a weapon of intimidation in diplomatic crises.[46]

Here were sensible, cautious, in many ways prophetic judgments about the future role of air power. Yet Eliot's commitment to realistic appraisal was limited when he considered how the United States might use air power. As he considered the possibility of war with Japan, he argued that the United States "could not bring direct pressure to bear upon Japan save by air raids on Japanese cities," but this was "a form of warfare against which American public opinion has set its face, and which American airmen would never be willing to carry out unless driven to do so as a measure of reprisal for like enemy conduct."[47] Not only had "reprisal" escalated air war in World War I (as Eliot knew), but Eliot's faith in the constraints of morality and public opinion overlooked the fickleness of public opinion and conflicted with his attempt to ground American policy in hardheaded calculations of interest.

In addition, Eliot's commitment to the ideals of isolation and voluntarism under-cut his appraisal of possible American strategy in the air. It is true that he belittled the notion "that all we have to do is to insure ourselves against actual invasion." Such a narrow conception of strategy, he argued, would leave American interests abroad undefended and potential enemies undeterred—only an enemy's fear of destruction, not simply a fear his offensive might fail, would make him pause. But Eliot, like so many Americans, abhorred the political and economic regimentation they assumed would accompany creation of an expeditionary army sufficient to arouse an enemy's fear of devastation. At this point, political ideals, not cold calculations of national interest, again guided Eliot's thinking. "Why should we go to war to defend freedom if we must begin by destroying it with our own hands?" Eliot reconciled the imperatives of national security and political freedom by embracing sea power, which he argued could intercept any invasion and inflict intolerable pain by blockade against an enemy.[48]

It was a curious choice on Eliot's part, defended less by strategic reasoning than by the claim that adequate naval power could be mobilized through voluntary methods. Precisely the same argument could have been made for air power, but Eliot did not foresee that the bomber could replace the battleship as the nation's foremost offensive weapon. Demonstrating the common inversion of thinking on these matters, he warn-ed against the development of short-range aircraft useful only in a land war abroad and argued for long-range bombers capable of assisting the fleet in patrolling the seas. Only in passing did he note that "if the day ever comes when hostile bombers can cross the ocean directly from foreign bases, one of the most effective insurances we can have against such a thing being attempted will be our ability to execute reprisals in kind."[49]

Most tellingly, Eliot assumed that realistic calculations of interest would govern the decisions of nations in the maw of war. At times he recognized other possibilities. Amid the excruciating strain produced by an event like the Munich crisis, he noted, people do not calculate coolly but "react like a suddenly loosened spring." In wartime, ideological and national passions can lead combatants to regard their enemy as "human scum to be wiped from the face of the earth," leading to a reenactment of "all the merciless ferocities of those Dark Ages which we have so proudly boasted were forever behind us."[50] But he did not examine how air power might be the instrument of such passions. His consistent theme was that "all contemplation of war is based on the weighing of risk against advantage." As he put it in "The Impossible War With Japan," "a war which, by reason of its perfectly-known military, geographical, and strategical factors, cannot, demonstrably, turn out to the permanent advantage of either side, a war between nations so situated that neither has anything very serious to fear from the other within its own selected sphere of influence and activity, is a war that is not going to take place. It is an impossible war." Eliot's assumption of rational calculations minimized his acknowledgment of the danger of all-out air war. Germany might be tempted to strike at London, but "the masters of modern Germany are not fools."[51] His reasoning resembled that of other experts who condemned as "arrant nonsense" the notion that "whole cities will be wiped out by flights of bombers from overseas," for "it is obvious that a foreign squadron . . . would not waste its load on residential districts, but would concentrate upon railroad yards, piers, and factories."[52] In describing their argument as "obvious," realists revealed that something more than "realism" underlay their thinking—at a minimum, an unacknowledged measure of optimism about human rationality. They offered reassurance, but it was flawed in two ways: strategic conditions might change so that bombing cities would appear profitable or rational calculations might not prevail at all.

Perhaps the most subtle and certainly the most curious speculation about air war came in a book by an Irish psychologist, Watson O'dell Pierce, who was writing and teaching in America at the time his *Air War: Its Psychological, Technical and Social Implications* was published in 1939. Pierce obliquely approached the strategic and moral issues that concerned others. His aim was to explore the social and psychological characteristics that made possible the development and use of military aviation, to examine air war as "the end product of our scientific civilization." In that Wellsian spirit, he emphasized the psychic necessity of combat aviators to achieve distance "from the messy and brutal part" of air war by turning combat into "a mechanical operation." Similarly, engineers and industrialists who made air war possible found the act of killing repugnant but the preparation of killing machines satisfying: "To be an organizer of destruction is psychologically very different from being the destroyer in person." Pierce portrayed aviation as the product of benign and malignant forces in modern society—the scientist who sought knowledge but could "prostitute his ability to the service of war for the pay of a policeman" and the imperialist who sought to achieve the fulfillment of his greed.[53]

Yet despite some probing essays into social psychology, Pierce could not define what made aviation "the end product of our scientific civilization" or what constituted its appeal to the modern spirit. Nor could he look squarely at the threat posed by air war. Like so many writers, he feared that air attack on cities would succeed because of the mass panic—illustrated for him by reactions to Orson Welles's famous "War of the Worlds" broadcast in 1938—it would trigger. Because censorship, rumor, and distortion lay at the heart of such panic, he was hopeful that the democracies' freedom of information and opinion would give them an edge in air war. But he also feared that the capitalist democracies, where the burdens of war might fall unevenly because of class, racial, and ethnic inequalities, would fall prey to internal division and subversive propaganda. Here were more echoes of long-standing fears of how the threats of class war and national war might intertwine.

In his Wellsian approach to the problem of air war, Pierce attempted to break from the rigid categories of contemporary debate. Yet if he neither minimized nor exaggerated the dangers, in the end he simply looked beyond them. Emphasizing the faultlines in modern nations which made them vulnerable to air attack, he was less interested in air war than in addressing the problems of modern civilization. "The danger" of air war "to real democracy is twofold," he wrote. "It must resist fascist aggression from the outside. It must watch that in resisting external aggression, it does not become a fascist state at home." The concern was legitimate, but it also shifted his focus away from the destruction the bomber might inflict toward the harm the victim nations might do to themselves in response. Unavoidably, too, the emphasis on the psychological effects of bombing carried with it the familiar implication that defeat in air war might come quickly, with minds shattered but bodies intact.[54]

FASCISTS' BOMBS AND DEMOCRACIES' VIRTUE

Speculation about air war had another dimension after 1935. By the late thirties, men were not only theorizing about air war but were drawing on firsthand experience with it. They anxiously examined the bomber's record in the Italian-Ethiopian war of 1935, the Spanish civil war which broke out in 1936, and the conflict between China and Japan, renewed by the latter in 1937. Writing for the *New York Times*, Herbert L. Matthews, once doubtful about the usefulness of bombing, argued that the Italian air raids on Barcelona in 1938 (they drew even more attention than the German Condor Legion's destruction of Guernica) "told what modern war means"; for him it meant that bombers "could destroy centuries of civilization in a few minutes." If Barcelona did not surrender, Langdon-Davies argued, it was only because the German and Italian masterminds of the attack cut it short lest they reveal to the world the secret of their new technique of war.[55]

In general, however, contemporary experiences altered few positions. Prophets found the evidence necessary to sustain their arguments or merely ruled the record before 1939 too inconclusive to merit much attention, while skeptics usually had their doubts reinforced. Louis Fischer, reporting admiringly on how "Madrid Keeps Its Nerve," described how bombing stiffened the morale of the Loyalists and convinced them of the rebels' desperation.[56] In the *Saturday Evening Post,* an American army officer observed that bombing had proven "disappointing to the theorists of peacetime." When Franco's rebels bombed Madrid, "Did the Madrileños sue for peace? No, they shook futile fists at the murderers in the sky and muttered, 'Swine.'" His conclusion: "Terrorism from the air has been tried and found wanting. Bombing, far from softening the civil will, hardens it." Aviation, the army man argued unsurprisingly, had scored its greatest success in close support of infantry operations.[57]

Similar conclusions were usually drawn from China. An indignant editorial in the *New York Times* judged Japanese bombing of Chinese cities "as stupid as it is brutal," doubting that "hundreds of headless coolies cluttering the debris-littered streets of Canton" did anything to "impair the strength of China's arms." One popular writer argued that air power had been effective against Chinese cities only insofar as the corrupt Nationalist government had failed to protect its people. "Wholesale bombing for sheer terrorism would be a costly, worthless gesture," he generalized; "it is a political catchword to scare you, but you won't find it in the militarist's practical handbook." From the Council on Foreign Relations came speculation in 1938 that Japan's military leaders "may have discovered that indiscriminate bombings were defeating their purpose by arousing the Chinese to more determined efforts."[58]

Few observers, whether skeptical or alarmist about the possibility of air war on cities, minimized the horror of the attacks they described or entirely ruled out their occurrence in future wars. But most played down their decisiveness and therefore, by implication or assertion, the likelihood that they would be employed in the future. Spain, *Fortune* noted, was perhaps "too Spanish" to prove a great deal, but it still indicated the failure of Douhet's theory. Only the fascist bombing of Guernica and Barcelona disturbed this prevailing line of argument. A typical conclusion was to admit that there might be another "Guernica in another major war" but to emphasize "the stupidity of the fascist military mind."[59]

At the same time, it is true, the media gave wide coverage to the air raid preparations of the major European countries, especially in the months before and after Munich. Describing massive plans for evacuation of cities, shelter-building, and gas mask distribution, they conveyed the imminence of air war and the magnitude of hysteria abroad about it. But many writers emphasized the political rather than the military dimensions of air raid precautions. "When you go to London you forget about war," one account began, suggesting the sense of unreality in British air raids preparations. Another writer went so far as to find the preparations a sham perpetrated by embattled Tories who tried to hold onto power by stirring up the fear of war and then making the masses grateful for the peace they arranged. Eliot, too, saw the preparations as "backfires against any possible flaring-up of public resistance to the policy upon which the [French and English] governments had determined."[60]

If anything, the Europeans' panic about air war confirmed a conclusion already formed from observations in Spain and China: the potency of air war on cities lay more in its threat than in its actual use; its value was more political than military. Employing the bomber for psychological terror and political intimidation appeared to be ushering in a new kind of political–military war of nerves, a kind of war to which "fascist" or "totalitarian" governments were especially inclined and for which they were especially adept. Archibald MacLeish, the American poet and playwright, gave expression to this notion in his radio play, *Air Raid*, evoking the fascist threat and challenging illusions of invulnerability to which he thought people still clung. An observer of the Spanish civil war regarded the bombing of cities as "the instrument of the dictator, rather than the general. It carries frightfulness to horizons which [the] sternest militarists are becoming afraid to reflect upon." The very fact that bombing was too inaccurate to serve military purposes made it primarily an instrument of "terrorism": after all, random and unpredictable bombing enhanced terror.[61]

Furthermore, it appeared, dictators had the power and ruthlessness to harness the psychological terror of the bomber to a broader scheme of intimidation and subversion, while holding their own populations in check during an agonizing war of nerves. The fact that the Luftwaffe was the most visibly nazified branch of the German armed forces may have lent credence to this line of reasoning. Some analysts added a further point: because fascist countries lacked the discipline, patience, or resources to win by a protracted conventional war—an accurate prediction, though in conflict with the image of ironclad control over populations—they would be all the more inclined to grab for a cheap victory by resorting to terror.[62] Opinions differed about whether the resort to terror would work and whether it reflected fascist stupidity or cunning, desperation or design. Agreement was widespread, however, that bombing cities had a special place in the hearts of fascists.

Debate on air war had taken on a political complexion that was largely missing in the 1920s, when its eventual employment was regarded as possible by all nations, regardless of their political forms or ideology. In one more way, the danger of air war had become both magnified and circumscribed—magnified in that the Axis powers now loomed as a force lacking scruples in the resort to air war, but circumscribed insofar as its use by other nations, its role as a universal weapon of war, had faded from debate. The widespread opinion in the late thirties that the Western democracies lagged far behind Germany and Italy in the development of strategic air power strengthened this perspective. So, too, did the resounding denunciations of bombing in China and Spain made by the press and by the governments of the democracies and the general emphasis on the defensive nature of British and American preparations for air war. Bombing cities was something that only fascist governments, foolishly or not, attempted.

The rise of the fascist powers and their air raids on cities were very convenient for the Western democracies. The opposing images of the two camps that were fashioned almost inverted reality. The Germans never made a concerted effort to wage strategic air war, although occasionally they shifted tactical aircraft to strategic missions when opportunity, miscalculation, or fits of desperation came into play. Later, Hitler yearned for a miracle instrument of strategic air war. But he never gave strategic air power sustained support, and it lacked solid grounding in both the technology and the doctrine of the German air force.

An impression to the contrary outside Germany may be forgiven in light of Hitler's boasts and the fascist record in Ethiopia and Spain. Exaggerating German intentions and capabilities, British and American officials thought they were following the Nazis' lead, not pioneering the course toward air war against cities. But it remained the case that, in the 1930s, only England and America seriously developed the concept and instruments of strategic air war. Of course, in both countries that development was shrouded in a fog of bureaucratic battles, governmental indecision, shifting strategies, and unarticulated purposes. In the United States, the defensive rationale for heavy bombers and the continuing struggle over air force autonomy obscured long-run trends. In England, air policy was buffeted by conflicting impulses for disarmament and air superiority and by deep divisions over whether to settle for a "shop-window" (in contemporary jargon) air force designed to impress potential enemies or to develop a bomber force capable of waging a sustained war. For reasons of deterrence, the RAF concentrated more on the bomber's role as destroyer of cities than did the Americans, who emphasized precision bombing. And by the late 1930s, a host of factors forced the RAF to stress air defense: acute anxiety about the vulnerability of English cities; growing hope, spurred by developments in radar, that air defense might yet be feasible; and the dawning realization that Bomber Command was a pitiful vehicle for the theory it espoused. These twists and turns, especially in British policy, masked Anglo-American interest in bombing cities.

Nonetheless, a fundamental orientation toward strategic bombing arose, however confused its translation into policy. In England, a profound anxiety over exposure to aerial attack fused with an equally powerful sense of England's limited moral and material resources for conventional combat. In the United States, the material resources were ample, but political tolerance for using them was not. In both countries, abhorrence and attraction combined to make air power compelling. What resulted was the apparent paradox, noted by one authority, whereby nations "whose policy was normally defensive tended towards the counter-strike deterrent theory, while those with aggressive intentions developed tactical air forces."[63] The image of air power as a fascist weapon obscured the paradox, concealing the Anglo-Americans' developing interest in strategic air war and muting their concern about the morality of that interest.

The association of air power with fascism was one reason why the ethical issues posed by air war received little attention in the 1930s. Of course, fascist bombing elicited vigorous moral condemnation, but it was largely reflexive. Few defined what was immoral about bombing cities beyond the fact that it involved killing "the wrong people" and was done by fascists, who were, ipso facto, immoral in method and intent. This simplicity of judgment was part of a larger problem, as Michael Howard has commented: "The liberal conscience in the mid-thirties was equally revolted by war and by Fascism, and so found it easy to believe that the two were one and the same." In the case of air war, labeling the fascists' bombing of civilians as murder was surely valid, but morally it was not very instructive, for much of war is murder. In retrospect, the American State Department's vigorous condemnations provide a kind of moral yardstick by which the later crumbling of American standards can be judged. At the time, reflexive condemnation offered no distinctions from other kinds of murder that even democracies practice—by siege, shelling, or economic blockade, for example— and few guidelines for the future handling of the bomber. It was unclear whether the nature of the victim or the intent of the attacker determined the moral status of bombing, and thus whether a "supreme emergency" for the democracies might sanction their own resort to the kind of bombing they had condemned.[64]

To those who gave these ethical issues extended consideration, few recourses were apparent. Bombing, John Fischer Williams recognized, came with fewer twinges of conscience because the assailant's "hands physically have no blood upon them." Rules of war might be useful, Eliot argued, not by eliminating barbaric acts but at least by providing a standard for measuring them, keeping consciences alive and thereby forcing some restraint. "It is not claimed for municipal law," he pointed out, "that it prevents illegal conduct, merely that it defines it, and lays the lawbreaker open to penalties." Yet Eliot was fair-minded and realistic enough to raise grave doubts about his own proposal for rules of air war. Reprisal was the only likely punishment for violation and it threatened "a breakdown of the whole system." No rules were easily applicable in a civilization that had already erased the distinction between civilian and soldier: "Is a troop train full of soldiers a proper military objective? Surely. Yet suppose the troop train is standing in Waterloo Station, jammed with hurrying humanity? Is an aircraft factory, busily turning out bombing planes, a proper military objective? Undoubtedly, if it is located on some remote hillside. But suppose it is in the heart of the city of Paris, with tenements all about it full of women and children?" All kinds of military objectives "cannot be attacked from the air—in the present state of bombing accuracy—without wholesale slaughter." As Williams observed, "Even when the rules of international law are strictly observed, modern war involves terrible dangers to the non-combatant and civilian population." It seemed that "the only really practical solution would be to . . . prohibit all bombing from the air," a prospect Williams confessed was quite impractical, leading him finally to declare that "the ultimate aim of law must be the disappearance of war"—an approach, Eliot pointed out, that had been tried out for a generation and found wanting.[65]

A more promising course was to define morality in terms of utility. The French Catholic philosopher Jacques Maritain argued that the bombing of cities was reprehensible not just because it was intrinsically wrong to attack innocents, but because "terror" and total war prolonged war. They defeated the very end of victory by arousing resistance, and they poisoned the peace thereafter as well. Whatever was unnecessary for victory, he maintained, was "bestiality." This was a slippery standard by which to measure acts of war, for by it the most ruthless bombing of cities was justified if it could be plausibly argued (and plausible arguments are notoriously easy to construct in war) that it would contribute to victory. Yet at least Maritain's formula provided a rough standard, and it appealed not to unenforceable rules of international law or flimsy consciences of statesmen and enraged populations, but to their practical interests: the moral might be the efficacious. At a time of growing doubt about the utility of city-bombing, it seemed to promise restraint. When war came, the reasoning employed by Maritain, while often used to justify bombing, was also the argument most successfully invoked to challenge it.[66]

The image of the bomber in American thinking changed subtly over the twenty years preceding the outbreak of the European war. In the 1920s, the danger of air war had seemed grave but abstract, remote from American concerns. By the end of the 1930s, the reality of its occurrence abroad made the danger more graphic but in some ways less urgent, for reality did not seem as bad as what had been imagined. Dread remained, but it had been diminished by application of a kind of free-market model to the issue of air war: in the marketplace of war strategies, the effective uses of air power would drive out the ineffective. The former seemed reassuringly limited: aviation would succeed most in support of conventional armaments or perhaps in attack on narrowly defined economic and military objectives; it was less useful, even counterproductive, when used in indiscriminate fashion against urban areas and civilian populations. If fascists employed it in this manner, their success was dubious, their methods involved psychological intimidation more than physical destruction, and the moral burden was now comfortably shifted to their shoulders. More reasonable men presumably recognized the futility of indiscriminate destruction.

The possibility of sustained war against cities simply eluded most people. After decades of debate, bombing cities still appeared either as the ultimate weapon or as a futile, desperate gesture. Sustained slaughter, for rational or irrational reasons, remained barely imaginable. These limits on imagination are, in retrospect, unsurprising, inasmuch as they largely remain in force a half-century later. As Harold Macmillan once chillingly observed, "We thought of air warfare in 1938 rather as people think of nuclear war today."[67] The limits on foresight and awareness of Macmillan's generation rarely resulted from willful denial of possible dangers or unwillingness to think about the issues involved.

Still, evidence was available, in the lesson provided by World War I, of the need to examine critically the impact of new weapons on warfare. The world had already once suffered grievously from the failure to anticipate the impact of the machine gun, the submarine, and the entire apparatus of industrial warfare. Moreover, the war had shown the danger of assuming that governments would make calculations about these weapons in a thoughtful or rational way. They had displayed the capacity to waste vast numbers of men in operations of marginal or negative utility, and soldiers and citizens had shown a remarkable capacity to endure this waste. Perhaps only a desperate wish that such a nightmare never recur can account for the failure to look more closely at the Great War's meaning.

In a variety of ways, the remoteness of air power formed the secret of its appeal. Air war lay on the periphery of American concerns about their security, and as some Americans imagined using it, it posed few moral or strategic dilemmas. To its detractors, its limited utility insured limited use; to its defenders, its power promised to keep war itself distant, its precision to bring quick and sanitary victory if war occurred. Where something more could be conceived, in contemplating war with Japan, the attraction was too casual to arouse much conern. For both defenders and detractors, the possibility of attack against the United States, although frequently invoked to defend American aerial armament, was farfetched. In brief, Americans could develop air power—or for that matter oppose it—without much regard for the likelihood or consequences, moral or selfish, of using it. They entered World War II with an impoverished legacy of concern about air war, with few standards by which to judge its wisdom, indeed with little feeling that standards were needed. Millis's characterization of Americans' attitudes toward their future security by 1938 applies nicely to their consideration of the bomber as well: "Thus the shadow of the future was already plain; but there was nothing with which to give it substance."[68]

Arguably, different American responses to the bomber would have made little difference. In facing Germany, the English never had the Americans' luxury of freedom from retaliation. Too, the RAF, an independent service since 1918, had less need for the self-justifying theorizing about strategic air war that characterized American airmen. It operated in an atmosphere of more urgent and sophisticated concern about the prospect of air war and the possibility that air war might be less conclusive than either the prophets or skeptics had allowed. Yet before the war the English placed great emphasis on the strategic bomber, and during the war the RAF would use the bomber with a vindictiveness unexcelled by Americans. In short, a richer legacy of debate in England did nothing to diminish the practice of strategic air war.

But the casualness of debate among Americans did this: it allowed attraction to strategic bombing to develop even when no provocation of the kind experienced by the British occurred, and it shaped how Americans defined and justified what they did when war did come. Furthermore, overlaying the differences between the United States and Great Britain in the 1930s were similarities in the sense of distance from which use of the bomber was viewed. In both, the terms of strategic debate were largely defensive; in both, the democracies' potential for bombing cities was largely hidden. For both, the Munich crisis triggered a change in thinking about the bomber and accelerated the momentum to use it. For neither did it quite appear that way at the time.

4

The Attractions of Intimidation

Writing from Paris at the height of the Munich crisis, Ambassador William Bullitt offered President Roosevelt a pithy summary of Munich's lessons: "If you have enough airplanes you don't have to go to Berchtesgaden."[1] Roosevelt understood the message. In varying ways he acted on it during the three years following the crisis of September 1938. Once again, however, contemplation of aerial holocaust and preparation to wage it easily diverged.

After the Munich crisis, it is true, the British, German, and American air forces all moved, in fumbling and differing ways, toward the use of the bomber on enemy cities. Yet from the American perspective, the specter of air war if anything continued to recede. In part this was because other considerations still intruded. Too, reports from abroad continued to suggest that the bomber, at least as a weapon of attack on civilian masses, was less terrifying in actuality than it had been in anticipation. More than that, while fear of air war remained, the bomber's deterrent value outweighed its actual military employment in American calculations. Especially in meeting the crisis in the Far East, American policymakers found the bomber an alluring instrument for minimizing, even averting, American participation in war. The mobilization of American air power rapidly accelerated without forcing attention to the terrors and limits of its use.

THE LESSONS OF "INTERNATIONAL BLACKMAIL"

In Europe, the prospect of aerial holocaust was one reason that the British and French governments appeased Hitler's demands for the Sudetenland. With Barcelona's bombing still vividly recalled, the decisiveness of a German knockout aerial blow against the capitals of the democracies was unquestioned by the summer of 1938. "*We cannot expose ourselves now to a German attack,"* a leading English general put it. *"We simply commit suicide if we do."* France's leaders feared that in the event of war "French cities would be laid in ruins" whose legacy might be "another Commune" led by radicals exploiting a frightened proletariat. The panicked efforts of governments to distribute gas masks and evacuate cities (nearly a third of Parisians fleeing their city) helped to popularize the anxieties of elites.[2]

Hysterical, ill-founded, these fears were a substitute for strategic calculations, not the product of them. British leaders never seriously analyzed whether Germany had the power and intention to launch an untried strategy of aerial attacks on French and British cities. In reality, Hitler lacked both. At a minimum, he could not have launched it without first defeating Czechoslovakia and then gaining air bases in France to put his short-legged bombers in reach of England. But British leaders, responding partly to the disarray in English and French rearmament programs, attributed to Hitler's dictatorship a demonic efficiency it lacked and to Hitler's air force the same city-busting capacity they longed to create for their own bombers—a case of "mirror imaging." The RAF had unwittingly contributed to the hysteria by propagandizing notions of the knockout blow and by exaggerating German air strength in order to buttress its own claims on the budget.[3]

More than crude projection was at work, of course. More skillful at a game all the European air powers played in the 1930s, Germany brandished a shop-window air force whose number of front-line planes hid weaknesses in training, reserves, and industrial capacity. Hitler's *Luftpolitik,* designed for home consumption as well as intimidation abroad, aggravated Anglo-French fears. Visitors to Germany like the RAF's Hugh Trenchard and America's Charles Lindbergh confirmed high-level expectations of sudden, irresistible destruction at the Luftwaffe's hands. Lindbergh, though technically astute, failed to realize that the Luftwaffe's primary orientation was tactical; correctives provided by obscure American military attachés received little attention.

Yet the decisive factor in the nail-biting summer of 1938 was not these exaggerated reports or the artful Nazi threats but the credulity of the audience that received them. Memories of panic during the Great War, years of scare literature, and distrust of the masses all came together in the Munich crisis. Perhaps there was even a measure of satisfaction in the fear of German attack, inasmuch as it had long been a promise of air power that "the very magnitude of the disaster . . . may prove to be a restraining influence," that is, that the bomber's frightfulness might deter war itself.[4] In England and France, a war-scarred generation welcomed as much as it feared the notion of a devastating air attack from Germany, lest Europe plunge again into the horrors experienced in World War I.

Roosevelt had played only a marginal role in the drama of Munich. But he observed keenly, learned quickly, and snatched the promise of American air power out of the debacle. For months he had received occasional reports on the apparent disparity between the Luftwaffe and the air forces of Germany's opponents and on the decisive role that disparity was coming to play. They came from American aircraft manufacturers, from foreign visitors to the White House, and most of all from Lindbergh and his intermediaries with the White House, Joseph Kennedy (FDR's ambassador to England) and Bullitt (ambassador to France), both also in touch with the frightened leaders of the European democracies.[5]

Of these channels, Lindbergh was at once the most troublesome and the most fruitful. He made three publicized trips to Germany, the last in October 1938, all endorsed by the American military attaché in Berlin and the Air Corps' General H. H. Arnold. There followed two secret visits in which he attempted to negotiate an extraordinary deal for French purchase of German aircraft engines. Lindbergh held a naive, if not unqualified, sympathy for the German position and the Nazi regime. His disastrous experiences with invasive American reporters had induced respect for a German "sense of decency and value which in many ways is far ahead of our own." His penchant for stereotyping national groups and for a kind of technocratic elitism led him to admire the Luftwaffe's achievements and to disparage the staunchness of England's opposition to the Nazis. But these predispositions did not lead him to atypical conclusions about European aviation nor did they prejudice those conclusions in FDR's eyes. At the height of the Munich crisis, Kennedy cabled to Washington Lindbergh's judgment that "Germany now has the means of destroying London, Paris, and Praha if she wishes to do so," and Lindbergh's counsel to accept Hitler's demands in order to avert "the loss of European civilization" and "something akin to Communism running over Europe."[6]

For almost two years Bullitt had also been cabling alarms. In November 1936, impressed by the speed of his own aerial travel through Europe, he wrote Roosevelt that "these dinky little European states can not live in an airplane civilization." It was on the twentieth of September that Bullitt made his comment that with "enough airplanes you don't have to go to Berchtesgaden."[7]

Roosevelt was drawing the same conclusion. He did so largely intuitively, for Roosevelt's view of air power swept beyond what even his military advisors (whose views he scarcely solicited anyway) counseled. As late as January 1938 his call for strengthened defenses had emphasized his traditional concern, the navy. Desperation to find some way to reverse the Nazi tide, reinforced by imitation of Hitler's methods, led Roosevelt to create an American air force that airmen had failed to achieve for years.

Roosevelt was formulating two broad ways that air power could play a decisive role in the emerging European struggle. On September 18, when immediate war still seemed likely, Roosevelt speculated that strategic bombing could help force a quick German surrender. To minimize German resistance, England, France, and the Soviet Union should resort to a sea blockade and to "pounding away at Germany from the air," confident "that the morale of the German people would crack under aerial attacks much sooner than that of the French or the English." As Harold Ickes recorded the president's predictions, Roosevelt argued that "this kind of war would cost less money, would mean comparatively few casualties, and would be more likely to succeed than a traditional war by land and sea."[8] In light of how slowly economic strangulation was known to work, his sunny view of the speed and cheapness of such a war indicated how FDR shared the prevailing belief that the terror of bombing, not its actual destruction, would work a quick victory.

As the threat of immediate war passed, Roosevelt's attention to air power as a war-fighting instrument dwindled for a while. His interest shifted to a second role for air power, that of a tool for deterrence and diplomacy. Munich, however depressing for the moment, also opened tantalizing possibilities for FDR. The challenge was not simply to forestall its repetition but to seize a leaf from Hitler's notebook.

Helping the British and French to rebuild their air forces was one way. Even before Munich the French had placed a small order for American planes and acknowledged their hopes for purchasing many more. Munich accelerated French and British interest, though the obstacles to American assistance were formidable. Roosevelt delegated responsibility to civilians, especially Treasury Secretary Henry Morgenthau, for steering a difficult course past the shoals of French pride and financial exhaustion, American neutrality legislation, suspicion of entangling alliances among congressmen and editorialists, and the military's wariness about losing technological secrets and production capacity to foreigners.

More attractive than arming others was the prospect of a commanding American aerial deterrent which would best Hitler at his own game. Pursuing that goal, on October 14 Roosevelt announced his intention to revise American defense plans and seek additional military funds (eventually the figure of $500 million was set). Privately, he began tossing about extravagant figures for an expanded American air force. By November 14, at a key meeting with eleven subordinates, he had settled on the round number of ten thousand planes for the American air force and a capacity to produce another ten thousand each year.[9]

This was "a bolt from the blue," something far beyond the airmen's own plans for expansion that autumn. Arnold recorded that Roosevelt sought "a striking force to back United States foreign policies," arguing that a ground army "would not be considered in the light of a deterrent by any foreign power, whereas a heavy striking force of aircraft would." Morgenthau set down FDR's ideas in all their boldness. Emphasizing that "sending a large army abroad was undesirable and politically out of the question," even for hemisphere defense, Roosevelt saw air power as an instrument of negotiation and intimidation:

> "I am not sure now that I am proud of what I wrote to Hitler in urging that he sit down around the table and make peace. That may have saved many, many lives now, but that may ultimately result in the loss of many times that number of lives later. When I write to foreign countries I must have something to back up my words. Had we had this summer 5,000 planes and the capacity immediately to produce 10,000 per year, even though I

might have had to ask Congress for authority to sell or lend them to the countries in Europe, Hitler would not have dared to take the stand he did."

Or as Arnold later paraphrased the president:

the President came straight out for air power. Airplanes—now— and lots of them! . . . A new regiment of field artillery, or new barracks at an Army post in Wyoming, or new machine tools in an ordnance arsenal, he said sharply, would not scare Hitler one blankety-blank-blank bit! What he wanted was airplanes!

The president's emphasis on sheer numbers of planes and his irritation at arguments for the supporting apparatus that would make them effective attested to an interest similar to Hitler's in an air force whose appearance would be more important than its use.[10]

Roosevelt was not simply letting fly another trial balloon, as he was famous for doing so often. After the military responded coolly to his ideas, he persisted, even to provoking "table-pounding" confrontations with his generals. Roosevelt threatened that if the Air Corps could not use the warplanes he wanted, the RAF certainly could. He demanded aircraft "with which to impress Germany" and on January 10 lectured top army officials that "the only check to a world war, which would be understood by Germany, would be the creation of a great [French] air force and a powerful force in this country." He was scarcely less forceful with congressional leaders, lecturing them in January that "there would not have been any Munich" if the British and French air forces had been double the size they were. Clearly, Roosevelt had his dutch up.[11]

Particularly in public, he also knew how to cast his new interest in air power in more limited and acceptable terms. Nineteen thirty-eight had brought fresh evidence of German political subversion in Latin America and of Germany's potential to attack Latin America by air should it secure bases in West Africa. Roosevelt told his conference on November 14 to prepare "to resist attack on the western hemisphere from the North Pole to the South Pole" and to have "a sufficiently large air force to deter anyone from landing in either North or South America."[12] Not news to the War Department, which was already developing plans for such a mission, the effort to strengthen hemisphere defense through air power secured the unquestioned cooperation of military officials.

In envisioning these ambitious roles for air power, Roosevelt acted on complex motives which he only sketched in private and was hardly inclined to make public. One motive was secondary, though politically risky. Roosevelt did not rearm to reemploy, but he was determined that rearmament maximize employment in an economy in renewed recession and mindful of the political advantages of economic stimulation. Roosevelt, of course, flatly denied such intentions, telling the press that "national defense is national defense and nothing else." In private he baldly confided his political motives. "These foreign orders" for airplanes, Morgenthau recorded the president as saying, "mean prosperity in this country and we can't elect a Democratic Party unless we get prosperity. . . . Let's be perfectly frank."[13]

Yet Roosevelt's initiatives, congruent as they were with schemes he had entertained before the onset of the 1938 recession, clearly had a larger purpose. A year earlier, in his famous quarantine speech, he had broached vague ideas about curbing aggression without resort to war, and in succeeding months he had toyed with the possibility of a maritime blockade of Japan. His post-Munich initiatives developed these possibilities, albeit with a shift in focus to air power. Roosevelt imagined the United States playing a decisive role in shaping world events without embarking on all-out war. He had not abandoned hope that war might be averted through some ill-defined combination of force and diplomacy. Given his conviction that Hitler had triumphed because of his superiority in the air, FDR's immediate interest lay in stiffening Anglo-French fortitude in hopes of averting any repetition of September's catastrophe. Meanwhile, he could enhance his own counterweight to the dictators' power by expanding American air power as well as by revising neutrality legislation and continuing with naval rearmament. In the event of war, as Roosevelt saw it, the United States could assist the embattled antifascist nations with its industrial, naval, and air power, harnessing American power to the energies of other nations on the front lines without overtaxing American patience, pocketbooks, and personnel.

It is futile to wonder whether, in the three years after Munich, Roosevelt was seeking to prevent war or to prepare for American participation in it, for FDR, ever one to keep his options open, had both possibilities in mind. More than that, he sought to stake out a gray area in between these two choices, to define methods of undeclared war that might secure the fruits of intervention without inflicting its full costs. Likewise, it is futile to speculate whether Roosevelt's simultaneous efforts to rearm Britain and France and expand the American air force were intentionally, even deviously, confused so that he could aid allies abroad without offending isolationists at home. American rearmament was hardly a subterfuge for aiding others. Indeed, Roosevelt openly surmounted the obstacles to French orders from American factories. In doing so, he ultimately served the unilateral objective of speeding buildup of the Army Air Corps. If anything, foreign orders bootlegged American rearmament.

Roosevelt too stubbornly pursued both aid to the French and rearmament at home to permit an argument that one held clear priority. His fondness for power, his conception of national interest, and his contempt for the Anglo-French performance at Munich left him in no mood to trust that effete allies had the tenacity to deter or fight Hitler if only America would generously supply the sinews of war. His sneer that Britain had "cringed like a coward" and caved in to "complete despair" hardly ruled out continued aid but did indicate FDR's sense of its limited utility. On January 31, 1939, Morgenthau, himself keenly interested in the French orders, told Roosevelt that "for your international speeches to be effective, you must be backed up with the best air fleet in the world." His words suggested again the administration's quest for American power that Munich had done much to accelerate. Roosevelt's references to the baleful effects of Wilson's military weakness in 1914 and 1917 indicated much the same temper.[14]

Roosevelt's concept of the indivisibility of peace also argued for a more powerful and visible American deterrent. He preached "that no nation can be safe in its will to peace so long as any other powerful nation refuses to settle its grievances at the council table." Peace was a seamless fabric, especially because of economic and technological advances that marked a break with the past. Even before the outbreak of blitzkrieg warfare, he was stressing how "the world has grown so small and weapons of attack so swift." Such language, now abstract but soon to be laced with pointed references to the impact of air power, outlined the technological rationale for a global definition of national security. The United States could respond to global insecurity by "many methods short of war, but stronger and more effective than mere words," Roosevelt promised. Roosevelt disqualified intervention "with arms" and singled out neutrality laws as an obstacle to effective policy, but his "methods short of war" clearly countenanced more than just revision in legal and economic policy. Repudiation of armed intervention did not exclude intervention by the display of arms. Methods short of war could still embrace the capacity for deterrence that rearmament implied. And in Roosevelt's developing concept of undeclared war, methods short of war shaded off imperceptibly into methods of war, although he was not ready to abandon efforts at diplomacy and disarmament hitherto tried and found wanting.[15]

For Roosevelt's purposes, air power seemed an ideal instrument, decisive yet humane, for deterring, limiting, or at the worst, waging war. Meanwhile, it also served American and hemispheric defense, objectives so uncontroversial that the expansion of American air power could proceed with minimal opposition. In short, Roosevelt had gathered together and turned to his purposes the benign images of bombardment aviation and the malignant images of warfare on the ground. And inasmuch as war-fighting uses of aviation seemed remote, rearmament in the air entailed no urgent consideration of the bomber's morality and utility. Therefore Roosevelt's new aerial policy squared with the dominant prejudices and priorities of Americans: alarm over fascist aggression, aversion to military expeditions abroad, desire to preserve American isolation, and faith in aviation as a benign technology.

Insofar as public opinion polls measured those priorities and prejudices, they were still too imperfectly formed to guide Roosevelt easily. Within a broad consensus for rearmament indicated by a November 1938 survey, 90 percent of Americans supported an increased air force, 86 percent a larger navy, 82 percent a bigger army. Only later did opinion polls suggest firmer preferences for air power: in June 1941, 73 percent of respondents preferred to strengthen the air force, only 16 percent the navy and 11 percent the army; by small but consistent margins Americans preferred to deploy naval and air power rather than ground armies in the event of their entry into the European war; weeks after Pearl Harbor, Gallup found Americans wanting to spend money on airplanes rather than on battleships by an eight-to-one margin. In November 1938, Roosevelt was intuitively anticipating and shaping the preferences Americans were coming to hold, not responding to a clear-cut mandate.[16]

Similarly, subjective readings of public opinion offered him little guidance, insofar as printed commentary on the Munich crisis represented confusing messages on how Americans judged the role of air power. The glossy press graphically conveyed the Europeans' fear of air war but said little about how that fear affected settlement of the Munich crisis. *Life* ridiculed claims of German air superiority as a ridiculous "yarn." Hitler's "victory without war," as the *New York Times* put it, was impressive but not often attributed to the threat of bombing. Unusual was the *New Republic*'s careful distinction between the reality of German air power (which it discounted) and the fear of that power: "For twenty years," Bruce Bliven wrote, "people have been told about the horrors of aerial warfare against helpless civilians," and their fear was now of "tremendous significance." By 1939 George Fielding Eliot was emphasizing that the Luftwaffe's strength, however limited, had been a supreme weapon of "international blackmail" at Munich, abetted by English authorities who carried out air raid protection with "an air of ghoulish ostentation." Likewise in 1939, Lewis Mumford warned of the "irrational forces" that governed in crisis: "It was the five thousand airplanes that Germany did *not* possess, added to the five thousand that they may doubtfully have had, that aided in the Berchtesgaden betrayal." But these sharper readings of Munich's meaning emerged slowly and offered no clear suggestion that Washington should copy Berlin's methods.[17]

In this climate of diffuse public opinion Roosevelt moved cautiously and sometimes confusingly. Through the fall of 1938 at least, grand pronouncements about the necessity of arresting aggression and rearming America were matched by stern refusal to go into details or even sketch broad strategies, except on the uncontroversial priority of hemisphere defense. At the November 14 conference, Morgenthau scotched FDR's suggestion that he go public on European air strengths as a way of mobilizing public opinion, for Morgenthau feared that the figures would only justify Neville Chamberlain's appeasement in the public's eyes—a sign that the administration accepted claims of German air superiority longer than much of the press. Press coverage of the November 14 conference first emphasized Roosevelt's interest in the economic impact of rearmament, then shifted to defense issues, but Roosevelt left the impression that the context was "continental" defense. Asked what was "the new danger which makes this continental defense necessary," he flippy responded, "Read the newspapers for the past five years." He left to his assistant secretary of war, Louis Johnson, the task of making a public call for quadrupling the American air force, but even Johnson offered a rationale that was strictly defensive.[18]

By January, Roosevelt had inched forward with his call for "methods short of war" and for specific legislation on rearmament. But meanwhile Roosevelt had done a good deal else to sow confusion. His attempt to direct some orders for airplanes to government plants deflected attention from issues of military policy. Critics eagerly attacked rearmament plans "as a cloak for further pump-priming" and "the most idiotic ever advanced in any country," sometimes suggesting that Roosevelt's foreign policy was designed to lift the nation out of depression by leading the country into war.[19] Potentially as dangerous was Roosevelt's failure to distinguish clearly between American rearmament and aid to the French. Conflating the two jeopardized the former because the latter generated such intense suspicion. The cause célèbre was the crash on January 23 of Douglas Aircraft's latest medium bomber—with a French test pilot on board. The crash blew the cover of administration secrecy about French aircraft orders, precipitated an ugly row, and sensationalized anxieties about sly Europeans taking advantage of guileless Americans and about presidential secrecy and usurpation of authority. A political battle, bound up with the complementary struggle over neutrality legislation, raged for over a year, until a final French order was negotiated after strenuous administration efforts. Critics saw American rearmament as a subterfuge for supplying planes to Europe or feared that French orders would sap the industrial capacity needed to produce American planes.[20]

Yet the jeopardy to administration plans was not fatal. It was eventually able to show that foreign orders would actually speed American rearmament—by financing plant expansion, by reducing the unit costs of airplanes purchased for the American Air Corps, and later by clearing off of American shelves large numbers of obsolescent craft which otherwise would have served as a drag on modernization of the American force. Beyond that, foreign orders diverted controversy from American rearmament. They drew the wrath of Roosevelt's opponents, generally "unilateralists"[21] opposed to entanglement with the British and French, but selling battleships would have stirred their ire just as much.

If foreign orders were a diversion, FDR's program for American air power tended to disarm his opponents, most of whom regarded battleships as instruments of a reckless foreign policy and still viewed airplanes as defenders of American isolation. To Charles Beard, the notable historian and opponent of FDR's foreign policy, the battleship was both obsolescent and inherently an instrument of "aggressive warfare." Likewise, Bruce Bliven had called for a buildup in air and coastal defenses in opposition to FDR's 1938 naval program because bombers, "far from fulfilling the prediction of the alarmists," had proven to be poor offensive weapons against cities and best suited only for tactical purposes. They were preferable as well to Lindbergh, moving toward his public role as Roosevelt's enemy, but also working with the Air Corps on the design of a new, long-range bomber, the B-29. Some critics did attack FDR's program for the Air Corps, suspecting that he wanted ten thousand American planes because "Hitler or someone for him is alleged to have claimed an air force of that size—a claim of doubtful veracity." Administration defenders gave credence to such attacks when they spoke of securing "a restraining psychological effect upon any potential foe." When Roosevelt, in defending French orders to Senate leaders, defined American security in sweeping geographical terms—not using the "frontier on the Rhine" phrase later attributed to him but conveying its substance—another uproar ensued. Yet no real debate on Roosevelt's ideas about aerial deterrence was ever joined. It could not be because he kept those ideas mostly secret and steered debate elsewhere, while critics preoccupied with naval policy offered little opposition to rearmament of the American Air Corps.[22]

By defining the issue as hemisphere defense, Roosevelt found another way to divide his opponents and establish common ground with many of them. While Herbert Hoover saw FDR's warnings of Nazi attacks on the Western Hemisphere as "sheer hysteria," other critics accepted the need for more planes to guard the Americas. They also played into Roosevelt's hands by continuing to see danger and deceit in administration plans for short-range tactical aircraft whose only foreseeable use would be to accompany American ground forces in battle on the European continent. Long-range bombers served Roosevelt's purposes and these were just what some prominent critics advocated—a fleet of several thousand precision bombers capable of intercepting an attack on the Americas by sea or air.[23]

Thus a developing capacity to intimidate or bomb others remained disguised by the preoccupation with protecting America. Far from decrying air power, many anti-interventionists sought to bend it to their purposes. In doing so, they supported the big bomber air force that Air Corps officers wanted, and they smoothed Roosevelt's path toward creating a deterrent force even as they carped at his immediate plans.

Encountering only oblique public opposition to his plans, Roosevelt faced a more formidable threat from within his administration, ironically from the military and the Air Corps itself. Air Corps' resistance to French orders was a bitter point of conflict. Arnold, promoted by FDR to chief of the Air Corps in September, accepted foreign orders in principle but sharply contested the way Roosevelt handled them, especially the end run Roosevelt made around the army by delegating Morgenthau to supervise foreign orders. When Arnold felt he had to take the heat publicly for the controversy raised by the crash of the Douglas bomber, his bitterness toward Morgenthau deepened. Arnold grudgingly acknowledged the benefits to the Air Corps of foreign purchases but remained suspicious that the French were stealing technological secrets. The conflict dragged on until March 1940, when Roosevelt, "looking directly at me . . . said there were places to which officers who did not 'play ball' might be sent, such as Guam." "Oh boy, did General Arnold get it," Morgenthau gleefully recorded. The French got what they wanted, joining the British in ordering forty-six hundred airframes and thirteen thousand engines to add to a smaller order negotiated the previous year—though little arrived in time to do the French much good.[24]

The president and his military staff also clashed over his plans for American rearmament. After decades of budgets they deemed miserly, military leaders welcomed the money Roosevelt wanted appropriated but forcefully challenged his priorities for spending it. George Marshall, newly appointed as Deputy Chief of Staff, took the lead for the army at the November 14 conference in a notable confrontation in which Roosevelt, for the first and last time, addressed the austere general as George. In the following weeks Marshall developed his own methods for balancing aerial rearmament against the other needs of the army, at a cost of some $2 billion, quadruple the figure

Roosevelt had in mind. Rarely invited to the councils of diplomacy, painfully remembering the disasters of mobilization in 1917, he and other military officers saw their job as preparing to fight, not as waging a diplomatic war of nerves, though no more than other Americans did they believe that fighting was certain to occur. Airplanes without trained fliers, good facilities, and an effective ground army could not fight.

But Marshall and the army also met Roosevelt on his own ground, challenging his belief in the deterrent value of a shop-window air force. "Airplanes will not impress foreign leaders and their general staffs," wrote Marshall's superior. "The absence or weakness in the other two elements required to make an effective air force—facilities and skilled personnel—will be known and accurately evaluated by potential enemies." Marshall increased the pressure on Roosevelt by enlisting his old mentor, John J. Pershing, to plead with the president for a balanced force. Like Arnold, he also worked on the president through an unlikely comrade, Harry Hopkins.[25]

Eventually Roosevelt altered his original proposal. He complained to his military advisors that he "had sought $500,000,000 worth of airplanes, and he was being offered everything except airplanes." He would not accept a figure of $2 billion for rearmament. But he revised the breakdown of the $500 million figure so that it included $200 million for "non-air armaments" and targeted $120 million for the logistical and training needs of the Air Corps. That left only $180 million for airplanes—a staggering sum by contemporary standards but enough for just 3,032 new planes (only half of them combat types), which would bring up the Air Corps to 5,500 by the end of 1940. Like other political leaders at this time—including Hitler, who now vainly sought to create the air force his enemies thought he had—Roosevelt could not force a decisive break with the military's traditional views on strategy.[26]

Marshall himself at times sounded almost old-fashioned on the issue of air power. He reminded one audience that it was almost always "the man with the sword, or the crossbow, or the rifle, who settled the final issue on the field. . . . I am not implying that we expect to shoot down many planes with rifle bullets," he added, but he seemed to imply that just the same. Yet Marshall received sympathetically the indoctrination in air power given him by Arnold and Frank Andrews, the commander of GHQ Air Force, and he accepted the airmen's grievances about neglect at the hands of ground army officers. His doubts were primarily political, not strategic. He distrusted the capacity of the public and its political representatives to grasp the complex but drab components of true military effectiveness: the training of soldiers and sound industrial preparedness, without which "we will be impotent, even if we have a collection of Galahads in the ranks." Air power as a strategy did not frighten him, but as a popular fixation it did. The problem "lies with the general public. They are not interested until a crisis arises," he complained, "and even then the particular matter must have some dramatic appeal, such as the photograph of a line of battleships, or of a squadron of huge bombing planes, or of the tragedy of women and children being bombed in Spain or China." A photograph of a bombed city "not only creates a profound impression upon every civilian who examines it, but it more or less fixes in his mind a specific remedy—

practical or impractical. But there is far more to this business than the bombing of cities—far, far more."[27]

As Marshall's remarks indicated, air power remained more potent and vexing as an idea than as an instrument for war. Other leaders shared his concern with the political ramifications of air power in the wake of Munich. Herbert Hoover, staunch foe of Roosevelt's foreign policy, feared that "the one condition" which could lead Americans into a European war would arise "if wholesale attacks were made upon women and children by deliberate destruction of cities from the air," although he doubted that any national leaders would undertake such "barbarism." Even as Hoover spoke, British leaders saw opportunity in the very danger the ex-president had identified. An air attack on London would cause "an explosion of American feeling" that would crush isolationism and bring America in on the British side: "Nothing would be so effective as the bombing of London, translated by air [radio broadcasting, that is] to the homes of America." Figures as diverse as Churchill, Joseph Kennedy, and Walter Lippmann shared the view (as did the Germans in their own way) that London's bombing would draw the United States into war, and in June 1939 King George VI, after a talk with Roosevelt, recorded that "if London was bombed U.S.A. would come in." As so often in the history of air war, the prospect of aerial destruction evoked ambivalent reactions of danger and temptation, and the idea of it was more compelling than the reality.[28]

Surprisingly, American air officers adopted a position on rearmament closer to Marshall's than to Roosevelt's. Arnold, too, argued the need for a balanced force, although he meant balance within the Air Corps more than between it and the army, and like Marshall he downplayed the value of sheer numbers of airplanes. This defensible professional position was still curious for the head of an organization so often bent on seizing any opportunity for expansion. Perhaps Arnold, cautious after a generation of bruising battles with his military superiors, hesitated to alienate them again by siding wholly with the president. The air mail fiasco in 1934 provided sufficient reminder of the embarrassment that could result down the line if the Air Corps undertook a mission its supporting apparatus could not sustain. Roosevelt's plans promised immediate gratification but long-term political and military dangers, loading down the Air Corps with thousands of aircraft for whose rapid obsolescence Arnold would later have to account.

Most of all, differing conceptions of high policy marked the faultline between the Air Corps and Roosevelt more than perceptions of political interest. Not a bold strategic thinker, inclined to see fighting rather than deterring war as his primary task, Arnold did not respond to Roosevelt's urgency about securing a here-and-now diplomatic counterweight to German and Japanese advances. Influenced in part by Lindbergh, Arnold shared Roosevelt's notions about the menace of the Luftwaffe, accepting the astonishing claim that "Germany has 2,000 bombers with a range of 3,300 miles" and acknowledging the key role air power had played at Munich. But he did not immediately follow the president in applying European events to American foreign policy. The professional lagged behind the layman. Even in the iconoclastic Air Corps, doctrine was, as in most military organizations, a thick accretion of years of assumptions and position papers, pressing down hard on most officers. The Air Corps had not yet systematically fashioned a view of the relationship between air power and national interests beyond defending them in actual war.[29]

More daring air officers, however, were charting Roosevelt's course. At the tactical school, Captain Laurence S. Kuter admiringly described Germany's use of air power in the Munich crisis as a kind of final stage in the evolution of warfare as Clausewitz had conceived it:

> During the past few weeks we have seen enacted what might be called an "Unwaged War"—a further streamlining of the old conventional pattern by the elimination of the actual armed conflict. Yet in this war Germany enforced her will upon England and France at Munich just as surely and almost as unceremoniously as did the latter upon Germany at Versailles, and *without* the intermediate stage of death and destruction. Germany enforced her will through the mere *threat* of armed force. Czechoslovakia was the sacrifice she demanded for a temporary and pitifully insecure peace.

All other forms of force counted for nothing before "the fear of bombs raining from the sky on Paris and London." Kuter made no exact analogy between what Hitler had accomplished with air power and what the United States might do. But his admiration for Hitler's achievement showed.[30]

Lieutenant Colonel Donald Wilson, another officer at the tactical school, carried Kuter's argument a step further. Wilson anticipated "future 'Munichs'" for which the United States should prepare by acquiring long-range bombers. Hitler had "the vision required to build an air force of heretofore unheard of proportions and at Munich it won without a struggle." The United States should not "miss the import of air striking power in the more recent bloodless wars," Wilson argued: "What could be better than a force so strong that actual conflict is thereby avoided?" Wilson envisioned using American air power to defend interests and policies beyond the hemisphere, in a manner close to Roosevelt's thinking. Wilson, however, looked not to Europe but to the Far East, citing the Panay incident as the kind of defeat that air power would have averted "by the presence in Alaska of an air force capable of exerting critical pressure against Japanese home territory. Crazy? Yes, crazy again—the same way that Hitler was crazy. . . . The sort of craziness that becomes a rational reality in light of the happenings at Munich. This sort of craziness does seem to be a powerful weapon in the new order of international relations." In short Munich warranted emulation as well as regret over Hitler's success. The key to air power's utility was not its use but the very irrationality of threatening to use it.[31]

At a higher level, Major General Frank Andrews, commander of GHQ Air Force, gave a more guarded accounting of Munich's lessons in a well publicized speech on January 16, 1939. Andrews, a forceful exponent of the independent air force and the long-range bomber, couched much of his address in the familiar terms of hemisphere defense. But he stretched this concept beyond the breaking point. "Our country should be the first to span the oceans both ways nonstop" by building bombers with "a tactical range of 10,000 miles." Most American strategists were planning to intercept any German penetration into Latin America once it began. Andrews, citing Munich, proposed something else: "to stop the aggressor nation from even planning the attack, through fear of retaliation." Air power should be seen not simply as a war-fighting instrument but "as an instrument of national policy," one capable, as Munich showed, of "toppling the diplomatic balance" and perhaps eventually creating mutual deterrence through terror between two nations both "capable of powerful air action."[32]

Officers like Kuter, Wilson, and Andrews were trying to link the aerial weapon to national policy, that is, to justify its potential not only for winning wars but for sustaining peacetime policies. They almost, but not quite, made the link. According to standard Air Corps doctrine, armed forces could serve national policy in three ways: by preserving "national existence" (an obvious function), by assisting "the active acquisition of foreign territory" (ruled out by national repudiation of territorial imperialism), and by "the coercion of enemy nations whose policies were in conflict with our own." That coercion might be necessary to protect American economic and political interests abroad, and air power held the promise of coercive power without deploying large armies of occupation which antagonized foreign subjects and drained national resources. The components of this argument for air power were scattered about in Air Corps doctrine but were never convincingly assembled. Airmen, like other officers, routinely identified economic conflict as a prime cause of war. But their dominant focus remained on how to fight wars, not on what a later generation would call politico-military strategy. Then too, some officers rightly doubted whether Americans who preferred their causes to be moral would regard economic interests as worth defending through war. Despite suggestive comments earlier by Mitchell and now by younger officers, no one articulated a vision of air power as the instrument of American economic hegemony.[33]

Thus Roosevelt's ideas on the diplomatic counterweight that air power might provide were echoed in the Air Corps, particularly among big-bomber advocates, but not strongly enough to capture Roosevelt's attention. He formed no alliance with the bomber enthusiasts, probably as yet unfamiliar with their ideas.[34] Roosevelt also did not enter the continuing fray within the War Department over production of long-range bombers. Aided by Marshall, the Air Corps' bomber advocates did reverse War Secretary Woodring's earlier decision to eliminate heavy bombers entirely from Air Corps procurement. Two hundred fifty Flying Fortresses were included in the January 1939 program for a fifty-five-hundred-plane air force. But actual orders were limited (seventy B-17s and sixteen B-24s ordered in fiscal 1940) and deliveries were slow. Even those ordered were justifiable under the coast and hemispheric doctrines of the military.[35]

Likewise, FDR's hand was not evident in the Air Corps' quest for still larger bombers. In 1938, the Joint Army–Navy Board had prohibited further development of bombers larger than the B-17, and the initiative only resumed in 1939, culminating in the B-29, first flown in 1942 and destined to fire Japanese cities. Potential use of the B-29 against Japan or Germany was recognized by 1939.[36] But when the War Department approved the B-29, neither it nor the Joint Board approved such ambitious strategic missions.

The Air Corps was left to build a new air force with hemisphere defense and aid to Britain and France as its only clearly sanctioned strategic missions. To be sure, even those missions, liberally construed, added urgency to its activities, and new strategic plans prepared by the Joint Board covered a range of contingencies, including an offensive to defeat Germany and Italy while holding a defensive line in the Pacific. But in 1939, Joint Board planning had proceeded in a vacuum, without explicit authorization from the president, who left the strategists to divine his intentions.

Not surprisingly, therefore, airmen largely kept their own counsel in 1939 when they speculated on their strategic mission, working outside the formal structure of strategic planning. Tactical school instructors, still the fountainhead of more radical air doctrine, acknowledged the immediate priority of hemispheric defense but continued to emphasize that selective attacks on an enemy's economic structure remained the ideal employment of air power. As had been the case throughout the 1930s, the Far East invited vivid speculation on air power's role, even though European events generated the most concern. On September 1, 1939, Lieutenant Colonel Carl Spaatz, Chief of the Air Corps' Plans Division, produced for Arnold a sweeping analysis of air strategy in case of conflict with Japan. Ruling out invasion of Japan as both unnecessary and unfeasible, eliminating a naval blockade (a recurrent idea of Roosevelt's) as difficult and too slow, Spaatz reached the unsurprising conclusion that strategic bombers, perhaps based on Luzon, were best fitted for the task. Spaatz offered no details regarding the methods or targets of bombing. But given Japan's industrialized economy and dense population, he thought it "probable that sustained air attack alone would be sufficient to force Japanese acquiescence in our national policies." And he added, in an echo of reactions to Munich and a prophecy of plans to come, that "the mere existence" of an American bomber force on Luzon might "restrain Japan from open and active opposition to our national policies."[37]

Spaatz's ideas added another reason to develop the B-29, which he simultaneously recommended, but apparently received no immediate follow-up. More than ever after September 1, air officers devoted attention to industrial mobilization, development of new aircraft, the continuing demands of foreign orders, and the requirements of hemispheric defense. Neither the outbreak of war in Europe nor Marshall's ascent to the post of Chief of Staff had an immediate effect on long-range strategic planning or on Roosevelt's views. Perhaps, as a contemporary account implied, Germany's limited use of the bomber against Poland that fall may have come as a relief to Roosevelt and his advisors. Air war "had assumed, in their eyes, as in everyone else's, a shape more dreadful than was to be justified by the event. All sorts of catastrophic happenings—

great air raids over Paris and London, panics in the markets, death and destruction on the wholesale plan—were momentarily expected." But the long-feared knockout blow did not materialize.[38]

Roosevelt requested the belligerents to avoid bombing open towns. Britain, France, and Germany, all too uncertain of their capabilities to take the first plunge, happily agreed. He authorized small increases in the armed forces. But he did not focus on air power as he had a year earlier, instead turning toward revisions in the neutrality laws that would permit belligerents to purchase by "cash and carry." He also reportedly came down hard on the War Department when he learned of its planning to equip an expeditionary force, insisting that "we won't send troops abroad. We need only think of defending this hemisphere." Such a statement hardly ruled out eventually "assisting the democracies with our Navy and Air Force," as reporters paraphrased the president's thinking, but it hardly emboldened planners either. Predictably, Air Corps officials continued to work the rich vein of hemisphere defense in defending appropriations for long-range bombers.[39]

"FIFTY THOUSAND PLANES A YEAR"

Germany's dramatic breakthrough in France in May 1940 spurred Roosevelt to a breakthrough of his own in air policy. For the first time in over a year, he gave air power top priority, now expressing it in terms so grandiose that they dwarfed his earlier statements. Addressing a joint session of Congress on May 16, Roosevelt called for a production capacity of "at least 50,000 planes a year," a standing force of naval and military aircraft of the same size, and renewed congressional commitment to the sale of aircraft to Britain and France. Calculated to shock Americans into rethinking their fundamental assumptions about national security, Roosevelt's address was sprinkled with references to the "swift and deadly" attacks across vast expanses that airplanes could launch. As dramatization of the primacy of air power, the message was Roosevelt's boldest.

Yet with reference to strategy the May 16 message if anything marked a retreat. Gone were the veiled references of the past to a role for American air power in altering the outcome of the struggles in Europe and Asia. The rationale was solely defensive, though defense was broadly conceived. Ticking off the flight times required for foreign aircraft to attack North America, Roosevelt portrayed the United States as vulnerable to sudden destruction. His objective was "national protection" against "the possibility of attack on vital American zones." Roosevelt had given bolder expression to the needs of American defense. But a revolutionary growth in air power was given a most traditional rationale.[40]

The address did little to guide strategists but much to reopen public debate about air power's role in preserving American isolation. Some anti-interventionists mixed enthusiasm for air power with condemnation of FDR's request for fifty thousand planes, puzzled by the anomaly of Roosevelt's bold call for such a huge force to serve such limited ends. Critics like the aviator Al Williams suspected deceit. "The airplanes are for Europe," Williams flatly declared, arguing that Roosevelt was "creating panic and terror" in order to secure planes for the British and plunge the nation into war. No other explanation seemed credible to those who preached that economy of force was the supreme virtue of air power: a few hundred or a few thousand planes could insulate the Americas from attack, an attack whose likelihood Williams disparaged in any event.[41]

Skewed by issues more political than strategic, the renewed debate on air power again informed Americans poorly about the role air power might play in the escalating world war. It was further skewed by Lindbergh, now at the center of resistance to Roosevelt, who believed that "this youngster . . . has accepted Nazi methods." Lindbergh's criticisms of Roosevelt, however strident, were not always myopic. He caught the incipient globalism of Roosevelt's policy. "If we say that our frontier lies on the Rhine, they can say that theirs lies on the Mississippi," he argued. But Lindbergh's views on air power—widely publicized and endowed with his prestige as pioneer in the air—were unenlightening about the issues Americans would face should they enter the war. Echoing the Mitchell of the midtwenties, he celebrated the invulnerability of the United States to attack by sea or air. A relatively small force—ten thousand front-line planes—could guard the approaches to America. Transatlantic attacks would some day be feasible but were of no immediate worry. "The Air defense of America is as simple as the attack is difficult."[42]

Yet once again anti-interventionists like Lindbergh prepared the ground for Roosevelt's developing emphasis on air power. It was precisely hemispheric defense that Roosevelt was now emphasizing. Lindbergh could haggle about the numbers of planes needed, but both politics and personal experience compelled him to embrace air power. Indeed, Lindbergh particularly favored the development of long-range bombers to provide an aerial version of the naval "chastity belt" around the Americas that Roosevelt had already proclaimed. Intent on keeping the United States out of war, Lindbergh did not explore what role those bombers might play in war. Nor did he pay much attention to Germany's air blitz, if only because England's successful resistance undercut his argument that aid to the Allies was futile. Between Roosevelt and Lindbergh, as between interventionists and their critics more generally, the danger and potential of the bomber were less an issue than the common coin spent to sustain political positions. This pattern persisted up to Pearl Harbor in public discourse. Air power was at once alluring, relatively noncontroversial, easily lost in the vortex of issues swirling across the United States, such as well-worn controversies over creating an independent air force and the navy's role in the air age.[43]

Some popular writers tried to be more informed. In writings like *United We Stand! Defense of the Western Hemisphere*, Hanson Baldwin gave increasing attention to air power but more to its mobilization than to its use. In passing he acknowledged that "anything seems possible, even the most Wellsian fantasia of the shape of things to come." He asked Americans to be capable of attacking an enemy's "industrial cities." He warned that "the plane has turned back the clock of history; cities are again under siege . . . the enemy now assaults with blazing oil and fire bombs the castle of our security—our homes." He accepted the role that night bombing of Germany would play and hence implicitly the destruction of large urban areas. But Baldwin placed top priority on "precision bombing of specific targets," and that as prelude to invasion of the Continent. Only when Baldwin looked beyond the war did his imagination run free. He wanted America's voice to be "heard in the far corners of the earth," and he believed that American air power might become "the future patrol force of the world," one that would "help to make the peace and keep it." The urge to find redemption in the rise of air power, now joined to visions of a *pax americana,* led an able man past contemplation of what might be done with weapons at hand.[44]

Americans could look for an authoritative view of official thinking about air strategy in *Winged Warfare* (1941), by Air Corps generals H. H. Arnold and Ira C. Eaker. But like Baldwin, they said less about the potential use of air power than about the urgency of amassing it. They offered the standard defense of precision bombing as "the most economical way of reducing a large city to the point of surrender." Yet they admitted that in Europe, "bombings are now largely reserved for the hours of darkness and for bad weather," when precision was unlikely, and that "the will of a whole nation" was an objective in war, which opened the way to wholesale destruction of cities. Nonetheless, Arnold and Eaker clung to reassurance. Reports of "attacks on civil populations" by German and British bombers resulted from "propaganda" or "mistaken identity" or "tactical errors." Their will to believe in the invulnerability and precision of bombers remained intact: "They can no more be completely stopped once they have taken the air than the big shell can be stopped once it has left the muzzle." Predictions of future bombers "spreading death and destruction 5,000 miles away" mixed with the language of precision bombing. Here, then, were confused admissions of the role bombers might play. A succeeding volume, *Army Flyer* (1942), written before Pearl Harbor but published after it, clarified little. In the free market of strategies, good uses of the bomber would drive out the bad, although the bomber's objective included "lastly the people, the workers." In any event, there was the familiar promise that air power's virtue transcended its actual use: its "threat . . . can accomplish without dropping a bomb the breakdown of opposing diplomatic morale."[45]

Popular literature, then, gave only a sidelong glance at the potential uses of American air power. So, too, did reporting on the actual air war in Europe. That war began in earnest in the summer of 1940 through a series of escalations undertaken by both sides. As early as July 8, Churchill had called for "an absolutely devastating, exterminating attack" on Germany, and he sanctioned the first raid against Berlin on August 25. By then, German planning to bomb English cities had already begun; night attacks, initiated on September 7, continued until tapering off in 1941, when the Luftwaffe turned against British shipping and prepared to move east. Neither side had a well-conceived rationale for bombing the other's cities. Hitler's intentions were particularly murky, unless he thought that terror alone was to suffice, which it was not. The British at least had a strategic doctrine and now also the sense of "a supreme emergency" justifying the bombing of Germany's cities; but the argument that such bombing was an unavoidable necessity overlooked what the bombers could have done in North African operations and in the critical Battle of the Atlantic. Like the Luftwaffe, the RAF was soon forced to bomb at night, although for a while longer the language of precision bombing provided a figleaf for attacks on the Nazis' cities and morale. Cities were the only target RAF night bombers could hit, and satisfying ones for a beleaguered power seeking revenge and straining to impress Americans and Russians with their ability to inflict it. Whatever the intentions on either side, the result for both was aimless, even counterproductive bombing campaigns. As one historian has commented, "If the object had been to stimulate the German war economy and to encourage the Germans to fight, no better technique than the clumsy [British] air offensive of 1940–1943 could have been devised." Much the same might be said of the German blitz of Britain.[46]

Covering the blitz, America's radio journalists possessed a supreme opportunity for enlightening Americans about air war on cities. Radio had seized first place in the homes of Americans as the medium for reporting events abroad and for heightening awareness of them. Having become virtual "tools of the administration" in their undisguised sympathy for the Allies and for American intervention,[47] radio's best journalists, like Edward R. Murrow, had a compelling motive for rendering dramatically the story of London in flames. And radio could cover the bombing of cities like it could no other form of war. Correspondents did not face so starkly the problems encountered on the battlefield or the seas: rapid movement, disruption of electronic communications, military censorship, impenetrable confusion. For this kind of war, at least as a friendly nation experienced it, they had a front-row seat. Immediacy was almost total.

Some, like Murrow, exploited it brilliantly for the commercial, artistic, and political purposes that guided them. As Archibald MacLeish said of Murrow, "You burned the city of London in our homes and we felt the flames that burned it. . . . You destroyed the superstition of distance and of time." Yet these purposes also turned the prism away from possible horrors. Insofar as Murrow "made Americans think of the Battle of Britain as a prelude to the bombing of New York or Washington," as his best critic puts it, he reinforced the paradigm of defense in which Americans viewed their approach to war. Sympathy for the British also called for celebration of their heroic qualities, made survival seem more possible, diminished the horrors also dramatized, especially when they were measured against the nightmare previously imagined—as, of course, did the simple failure of the Germans to win. Murrow, standing on the rooftops of London, himself personified resistance, and he communicated the less evident attractions of air war: the awe it inspired, the rallying of the spirit it induced, the national bonding it forged. "There's almost a small-town atmosphere about the place," Murrow reported from London. "I've even heard a conversation between total strangers in a railway car—something which was unthinkable in peacetime." He concluded that "class distinction" crumbled "in an air-raid shelter at three o'clock in the morning." Reporting the conviction that England would survive, Murrow unquestionably informed Americans. But to Murrow, "there are no words to describe the thing that is happening." If much of his reporting belied that claim, reticence still governed. He preferred to "talk about the people underground," about the frightened and the brave, the dislocated and the determined, almost never the dead and the wounded.

Murrow's message was hopeful. Night bombing was "serious and sensational. It makes headlines, kills people, and smashes property; but it doesn't win wars. It may be safely presumed that the Germans know . . . that several days of terror bombing will not cause this country to collapse." The implicit message was that air war against England, like that waged earlier against Spain and China, had proved its futility as well as its barbarism. It was the fascists' method of war, terrible but hardly the wave of the future. On the few occasions he mentioned Britain's efforts to reply in kind, his reporting was perfunctory, with a passing reference to the necessity of "fanaticism." Or he described the RAF bomber pilot visiting London's ruins "who had been over Germany so many times . . . and said: 'I've seen enough of this. I hope we haven't been doing the same thing in the Ruhr and Rhineland for the last three months.'" The RAF, Murrow suggested, bombed targets, not people.[48]

The print media often reinforced these hopeful messages about the blitz. They were implied in a cautious, sophisticated study titled "Air Power as World Power" that occupied the entire March 1941 issue of *Fortune*. They were sustained in popular writings, Willy Ley telling Americans that in a properly prepared city "there was no reason for anybody to die of fright" during bombing, and the journalist William L. White giving an upbeat report on his experience with bombing: "It is not nice, but if you think you would be terribly afraid, you had better go over and get bombed for a while, because you will be relieved to find that you are not." For *Commonweal* Christopher Hollis gave these messages perversely humorous expression. Reporting from England that "aerial warfare is a very mild inconvenience," he found a measure of democratic justice in the fact it was no longer just soldiers who "have the unpleasantness of being killed" in war. Like Murrow, but far more pointedly, Hollis recognized the compensations of being bombed. Germany's "gigantic psychological blunder" had served to "destroy the last vestiges of that in which lay the Germans' major hope— a defeatist mentality and a readiness to compromise with Hitler." What finally impressed Hollis "much more about the blitzkreig than its inhumanity is its complete futility." Air power, as an independent weapon, was itself "a futility."[49]

Few writers ruled out the recurrence of air war on cities, but most agreed that the blitz reinforced previous lessons about the indecisiveness of such bombing. Air power retained the appeal of employing "a greater proportion of machinery to men than any other weapon of warfare," but its importance seemed to lie more in its "tactical influence upon land and sea warfare," as *Life* commented. As a strategic weapon, its methods would be selective, not indiscriminate. *Life* reported in August 1941 its satisfaction that new British bombing of Germany "was enough to lift the hearts of all the free peoples" and welcomed the news that the British now "were dishing it out" as well as taking it. But like American air strategists, popular commentators failed to reckon with this ominous development in the bomber's use to achieve psychological satisfaction rather than military victory, or simply glossed over the critical issue of what targets an ally's bombers might seek.[50]

In several years of observing air war, Americans who paid attention to it had moved from imagination to reality in a piecemeal, gradual fashion. The slow, erratic nature of that war's escalation, plus its indecisiveness, fostered acceptance. If the war had begun with the catastrophic, knockout blow previously foreseen, the shock might have induced more intense concern about air war's morality, utility, and probability to reoccur. Piecemeal evolution of air war produced relief that reality was less terrifying than the nightmare and gave Americans time to absorb and accept this new descent into barbarism. What happened was more complex than the simple movement from horror of bombing to the "uncritical acceptance of all the claims made for the airplane by its most enthusiastic advocates." Nor was it clear that "American disapproval of Fascist bombings manifested itself in a desire for revenge, rather than a desire to abolish bombing."[51] These factors were sometimes at work, but the blitz in particular led many Americans to question more extreme claims for air power, and if some Americans welcomed revenge, few wanted it at the price of going to war. Overriding these factors were reluctance to engage the issue and lack of apparent necessity to do so: the blitz seemed to indicate that air war on cities was a passing fad.

"COMMAND OF THE AIR BY THE DEMOCRACIES"

As popular fear and anticipation of air war receded, official preparation to wage it mounted. The public had a clue to these efforts in successive reorganizations of the War Department. In November 1940 Arnold became Deputy Chief of Staff to Marshall while retaining his post as Chief of the Air Corps, a move that elevated his status and gave the Air Corps a central place in the general staff's planning. The next spring, the long vacant position of assistant secretary of war for air was filled by Robert Lovett, brought in by War Secretary Henry L. Stimson to rationalize industry's chaotic mobilization for aircraft production. In June 1941, creation of the Army Air Forces (Arnold again as Chief) marked another step toward the twin goals of air force autonomy and equality.

Mirroring these changes was a movement toward decisive acceptance by high officials of strategic air power. To be sure, the process was erratic, buffeted by demands of allies, manifold problems of mobilization, organizational confusion and service rivalries, military conservatism, and the casualness of Roosevelt's direction. Neither the money nor the productive capacity was there to turn out fifty thousand planes within a year, and the War Department quickly trimmed that figure. At that, production targets could not be met. In one week in November 1940, the Air Corps received only two combat aircraft from industry; nine months later it was still "a virtually unarmed air force." Even if production goals could be met, their value was in doubt because strategic timetables were unfathomable: a quick "triumph of mass production would, paradoxically, bring the danger of defeat by obsolescence—unless war arrived soon enough to absorb the full output of the clattering assembly lines."[52]

And yet in this confusion Roosevelt, in his own way, did lead. His fifty-thousand-plane objective, inspired by fondness for the psychological value of impressive numbers, was almost wholly his figure, dwarfing recommendations from service officers unready to think so big.[53] By stressing sheer numbers, Roosevelt intuitively grasped that the key to victory in the emerging air war was economic productivity and bureaucratic efficiency, not strategic genius.[54] He also directed energies where the military bureaucracy was most comfortable expending them: on the technical and economic problems of how to mobilize air power, not on the moral, political, and strategic issues of how to employ it. A focus on mobilization muted the vexing debate on whether or how to enter the war, responded to the anxieties of military officers who shared memories of failed mobilization during the last war, and deflected attention away from the thorny issue of the air force's role and mission. Emphasizing mobilization, Roosevelt found the lowest common denominator of thinking about air power.

At the same time, he signaled his strategic priority for long-range bombers, but, as usual, in a piecemeal and private way that minimized controversy. In June 1940 he told military planners how he imagined "the United States in the war, but with naval and air forces only," plus aid to allies. That fall he finally let Arnold out of the "dog house" and back into the White House. In February, the State Department pressed on the White House a document derived from German sources characterizing the Nazis' economic situation as "desperate" and highly vulnerable to strategic bombing. And on May 4, 1941, FDR ordered a speedup of heavy bomber production to five hundred per month in order to provide "command of the air by the democracies." This was paralleled by the heavy proportion of research and development budgets the army was now devoting to the heavy bomber.[55]

By the summer of 1941, Roosevelt was returning full circle to the thoughts he had offered in the midst of the Munich crisis. His hope in the interim years to deter or at least contain hostilities through aerial rearmament had been dashed, at least for Europe. But if the airplane had not deterred war, it might yet win it, as he had speculated in September 1938. So Churchill informed Roosevelt in July, arguing that bombing might "produce an internal convulsion or collapse" in Germany. So the president seemed to argue in talking to Hopkins, who in August 1941 characterized FDR as "a believer in bombing as the only means of gaining a victory." Hopkins, intimate with FDR and faithfully reflecting his views, himself broadcast to the British an exaggerated promise that American "airplanes [in British hands] tonight may be dropping bombs on Brest, on Hamburg, on Berlin, helping to safeguard our common heritage." Morgenthau, already convinced that the United States should use England "as a stepping stone to bomb Germany," elicited from Roosevelt another statement of faith in the bomber when he asked the president how he would "lick Hitler." Notwithstanding the failure of the blitz, FDR replied that he had been "again and again" telling the English (who did not listen, he complained) that "if they sent a hundred planes over Germany for military objectives that ten of them should bomb some of these smaller towns that have never been bombed before. . . . There must be some kind of factory in every town," and "that is the only way to break the German morale." Like many others, Roosevelt blurred the distinction between military objectives and wholesale attacks on civilians or saw the former as a convenient pretext for the latter.[56]

By now Roosevelt probably "wished to take the United States into the war" but perhaps not all the way. The arsenal policy was still vital; with the new Lend Lease law and Russia's entry into the war, a mounting proportion of American production was flowing to the Allies. But war by proxy did not alone promise victory. Air power carried that promise for Roosevelt. Events that autumn strengthened this line of thinking. The British could fight with little else but the bomber and their navy for the moment. The Russians might tie down the Nazi armies, but even optimists could not predict their eventual victory. While American naval forces were deepening their role in the undeclared Atlantic war, Congress signaled continued aversion to any intervention by American ground forces abroad when the House, on August 12, extended draftees' terms of service by a margin of just one vote and retained a ban on sending draftees beyond the hemisphere. In November Paul Douglas of the University of Chicago informed Roosevelt that Americans accepted "use of an airforce but they are opposed at present to an A.E.F. [American Expeditionary Force]." Public opinion polls were confirming these preferences. So was Walter Lippmann, who argued in September that a large ground army was "the cancer which obstructs national unity, causes discontent which subversive elements exploit, and weakens the primary measures of our defense." Should the United States go to war, its contribution to the war effort should consist "basically of Navy, Air, and manufacturing."[57]

In more guarded ways, military leaders were also embracing air power, despite the blitz and Britain's own indifferent record with the bomber. British troubles with American bombers were written off to poor handling and strategic pigheadedness. Since the British and Germans had shifted to night bombing, they simply failed to wage the war of economic strikes the Americans envisioned.[58]

In official strategic plans the bomber was gaining prominence. The broad framework of strategy in which the bomber would fit had been taking shape since the fall of 1940. The initiative came from Admiral Harold Stark, the Chief of Naval Operations, who gave cogent exposition to a Europe-first strategy. He identified defense of Britain, victory in the Atlantic, and defeat of Germany as priorities, while the United States should avert war in the Pacific and assume only a defensive posture there if it came. Roosevelt neither authorized Stark's memorandum nor formally approved the results but he tacitly accepted it as the basis of upcoming talks with British planners. Strategy now had a formal definition.[59]

American–British deliberations, conducted in secret in Washington from January 29 to March 29, 1941, reaffirmed the broad outlines of Stark's approach and sanctioned strategic air power in the waging of the war. To be sure, compromises were made and differences remained. The planners recommended "a sustained air offensive against German Military Power" only as preparatory to a land invasion of the Continent: since army and navy officers dominated the talks, a more forceful statement of the bomber's role was not to be expected. American planners also distrusted the faith of Churchill and his staff that bombardment, blockade, and peripheral campaigns could win the war without large-scale invasion, although their own president substantially shared the British view. Subsequent talks in August identified Anglo-American differences further without resolving them. The American Joint Board thought the British placed undue reliance on bombing to destroy "general civil morale." Attacks should be aimed "against specific objectives which have an immediate relation to German military power."[60]

Despite such differences within and between the British and American delegations, their prescriptions for victory accorded broadly with the strategic planning now forcefully undertaken by the Army Air Forces (AAF). The president was the catalyst to the AAF's initiative at planning. On July 9, he sent the war and navy secretaries his request for an estimate of "overall production requirements required to defeat our potential enemies."[61] Logistical needs were Roosevelt's primary concerns, but they could not be determined without making strategic assumptions, as FDR knew. For the AAF, Roosevelt's request was the opportunity to expound its vision of air war. Rather than pool its planning effort with that of the Army general staff, Arnold pressed hard for permission for his new Air War Plans Division (AWPD-1) to do its own planning. The general staff, perhaps itself overwhelmed by the magnitude of FDR's request, granted permission, acceding surprising autonomy to the AAF. Heavily staffed with bomber advocates like Haywood Hansell and Kuter from the tactical school, the AWPD wrote into basic war plans the long-standing faith in precision bombing.

AWPD/1, as the result was called, concentrated on Germany's defeat. The air planners believed that bombing alone might achieve that objective but hedged their bets because they still needed to make their plans acceptable to the general staff. Bombing would proceed with complementary objectives: to defeat Germany alone if possible, to prepare for invasion if not. Since the air force could go into action before an invasion force could be trained, a choice between those objectives seemed unnecessary for the moment anyway. A preliminary effort to subdue the German air force would be necessary, but the ultimate priority for bombing was the German economy, "presumably drawn taut," as Hansell later put it, by the massive demands of war. Scheduled to begin twenty-one months after American entry into the war, the main assault by an American force of four thousand bombers would "in six months bring much of her [Germany's] vital industry to ruin." The principal targets would be Germany's electric power system, its transportation network, and its petroleum industry.[62]

Far more sophisticated than the speculations of airmen in the 1930s, AWPD/1 was nonetheless hastily prepared and ambiguous on some critical points. Both British and German bombing had already shown how strategic air war might degenerate into futile barbarism. Supremely confident in their day bombers, the American air planners did not address this danger or the possibility that even successful precision strikes might fail to paralyze the German economy. True, they did not rule out "heavy and sustained bombing of cities" as a kind of coup de grace climaxing the success of economic attacks or decisive German setback in ground fighting. But throughout the 1930s their strategic arguments had rested on the moral assumption that precision bombing would bring swift, economical, and humane victory. The justification for strategic bombing was the alternative it offered to the carnage of ground warfare. In 1941 the air strategists saw no reason to challenge that assumption. Brushing aside the English and German experiences in 1940 and 1941, they felt no need to review the moral issue.[63]

Their pressing concerns were neither strategic nor moral but political and economic. Their attention flowed to threading AWPD/1 through the channels of the conservative general staff and to mobilizing industry for the war. To the air planners' relief, Marshall gave AWPD/1 his approval, steered it around the Joint Board, and sent it on to a sympathetic Stimson. The general staff still believed that destruction of the enemy's ground armies was the only sure path to victory. But doubts about the survival of Britain and Russia ran large in the War Department, making a land invasion of the Continent seem remote at best: hence even conservative officers acknowledged the imperative of first weakening Germany by bombing. Strategy, then, along with Roosevelt's wishes about how to fight the war, made the War Department amenable to a vision of air war that would have seemed repugnant and fanciful a few years earlier.

"THE PAPER CITIES OF JAPAN"

In 1941, American policymakers thought they had the chance to implement that vision—not immediately in Europe but in the Far East. Their efforts to do so marked the decisive transition from fantasy to attempted action.

The occasion arose when American grand strategy began conferring a new importance on the Far East. The tightening connection, real and imagined, between the Far Eastern and European crises was bringing Tokyo and Washington closer to conflict. For Tokyo, the defeat of the European colonial powers in their war with Hitler afforded Japan the chance to move south into French Indochina and toward the mineral-rich Dutch East Indies in an effort to salvage Japan's fortunes in its war with China and slip the noose of American economic sanctions. For Washington, Japanese expansion imperiled the lifeline of its European allies to their colonies and their capacity to sustain the war against Hitler. By September 1940 in particular, when the Japanese completed the Tripartite Pact with Berlin and Rome, the two crises seemed to have merged into one. Acceptance of further Japanese expansion ran the twin risks of further weakening the Allies and compromising the administration's leadership in the fight against fascism. "The people of the United States . . . reject the doctrine of appeasement," Roosevelt commented in October 1940.[64]

Yet the same global perspective that raised the Far Eastern crisis to new urgency also condemned it to second place in Washington's priorities. Operating on the Europe-first strategy, Washington tried to arrest Japanese expansion on the cheap, husbanding its resources for rearmament at home and aid to allies across the Atlantic. It was a perilous course to take. Minimal measures to deter Japanese expansion ran the risk, given the overall weakness of the American posture, of seeming only to be provocations or empty bluffs, as military leaders often feared. "The delicate line between what would deter and what would provoke," Roberta Wohlstetter has written, "was evidently the subject of much discussion, little thought, and still less agreement among policymaking officials." It was never, of course, identified. Roosevelt, charting a shifting middle course between deterrence and conciliation, never achieved the consistency that successful deterrence presupposed: "The American policymakers kept themselves as well as the Japanese guessing," notes Wohlstetter. For its more forceful advocates, a deterrent policy rested also on the conviction that Japan's power was more show than substance, its leaders ready to back down in the face of the white man's superior determination. That was the frequently stated view of Stimson, who noted that in past conflicts the Japanese had "crawled down" and retreated "like whipped puppies" when the United States stood firm. At the same time, in contrast to the view of the Japanese as emotional children (or cringing animals), the rationale for deterrence also presupposed the Japanese were shrewd calculators who would measure gains against losses and decide the latter were too weighty.[65]

After November 1940, air power increasingly emerged as the attractive, cheap deterrent, the means of escape from the strategic dilemma into which Washington had settled. Diplomacy might yet define areas of compromise or at least postpone hostilities, but alone its prospects seemed bleak. Naval power was the traditional means, but the Battle of the Atlantic sapped the strength of both British and American navies, and efforts to coordinate the British and American naval forces still available foundered on the rocks of insufficient force, Anglo–American jealousies, and the legal and political barriers against a formal American commitment to the British. Simultaneously, the American army was tied down by new hemispheric responsibilities and its expansion for a possible return to Europe. American air power, though not yet abundant, could be deployed unilaterally and economically, with no commitments to the British and few claims on American resources. Its appeal, in short, sprung from a combination of desperation about America's strategic position and enthusiasm about the chances for victory without war, as illustrated by Munich. At last, a chance to turn the fascists' methods against them seemed possible.

Initially, China seemed the place where the bomber might work its magic. The initiative came from China itself. In November 1940, T. V. Soong, Chiang Kai-shek's ambassador in Washington, approached Morgenthau about basing five hundred American planes in China for attacks on Hainan, Formosa, Japanese shipping, and even the Japanese home islands. The mastermind behind the scheme was General Claire Chennault, the retired Air Corps officer now serving as advisor to the air force of Chiang and his wife. As later described by Chennault, never one to mince words, the plan would have had American bombers eventually "burn out the industrial heart of the Empire with fire-bomb attacks on the teeming bamboo ant heaps of Honshu and Kyushu."[66] Its path smoothed by White House aide Lauchlin Currie and the journalist Joseph Alsop, Chennault's daring proposition ignited a burst of enthusiasm and activity from top civilian officials in Washington. Hard-pressed for a quick way to check Japanese advances, loathe to challenge domestic opposition to direct American entry in the war, nervous as always that the generalissimo might give up the fight, they grabbed at this new straw. Here was a way to awe the Japanese, while arrangements to funnel American planes and crews through a dummy private corporation would preserve secrecy.

Morgenthau enthusiastically told the British ambassador about the Chinese plan to "bomb Tokyo and other big cities." Such an attack, he confided to his diary, "would change the whole picture in the Far East." He found Secretary of State Cordell Hull eager to unleash the bombers, perhaps even to have them drop some tonnage on Tokyo on their way to China. Even Morgenthau confessed, "Well, Cordell, you leave me speechless." When Morgenthau presented the plan to FDR, the president was "simply delighted." Pressed by Chiang to take action, Roosevelt ordered Hull, Morgenthau, Stimson, and Navy Secretary Frank Knox to get to work on it.[67]

But the War Department had grave doubts. Morgenthau's involvement alone aroused suspicion in light of his past efforts at circumventing the military in order to aid allies. In any event, Chennault's plan seemed both extravagant and futile. The Chinese lacked the "balanced air force" without which the bombers would be useless. China's track record even with less sophisticated aircraft hardly warranted optimism about how it would handle B-17s and B-24s. Marshall admitted that if the Chinese "could get even 6 or 7 bombing trips into Japan they could cause considerable trouble there," but he believed, like Stimson and Arnold, that more likely the effort "would be a big waste." Worse, any bombers sent to China would undermine commitments to the British. As Marshall complained, "We would be asking them to delay for months the ability to bomb large cities all over Europe with facility—Berlin, Milan, even the oil fields in Roumania." All that Morgenthau could work out with the War Department was the dispatch of one hundred pursuit planes.[68]

Currie and Chennault were too zealous to let the matter rest. In May 1941 they revived the plan for "occasional incendiary bombings of Japan." Roosevelt agreed once more, but the War Department again thought it impractical. Ensnared by departmental obstructions, air aid to China continued, but never beyond handfuls of second-rate bombers. Like so many American plans for China during the war, this one proved to be an enthusiasm of the moment, fervently embraced but soon forgotten.[69]

Enthusiasm for air power continued despite abandonment of the China plan. Significantly it often infected civilians more than military officials, in part because civilian leaders tended to place more faith than officers in any form of deterrent— hence repeated proposals from Roosevelt for various forms of naval action as well. The president urged his strategists to consider "the possibility of bombing attacks [from aircraft carriers] against Japanese cities." He also apparently prompted Stark to ask

Admiral Husband Kimmel in Hawaii to "study very carefully the matter of making aircraft raids on the inflammable Japanese cities (ostensibly on military objectives), and the effect such raids might have on Japanese morale and on the diversion of their forces away from the Malay barrier." Stark had doubts about the usefulness of such raids but added, in a clear reference to Roosevelt, that *"you and I may be ordered"* to have a plan for them ready, noting too a "rising tide" of public pressure for action against Japan.[70]

Stark may also have been reflecting British pressures for action. A "really effective" air attack on Japan's cities, London's spokesmen suggested, "might well result in a public demand for the return of Japanese forces from theatres vital to us." They proposed using air power not precisely to deter war but at least to contain it cheaply so that the Anglo-Americans could keep top priority on Europe, an approach similar to Roosevelt's. But American officers, testy as always about British measures to lure American forces into the western Pacific, outlined their fish-or-cut-bait position: indecisive action seemed worse than none at all. The few American carriers in the Pacific, they complained, could only "deliver a bombing attack so ineffectual that its value would be less than as though it were undelivered but retained as a constant threat to the Japanese people." Pinprick attacks "might even raise Japanese morale and thus free their naval forces for work in the South." Implicitly, the Americans accepted the value of both aerial deterrence and actual attacks on Japanese cities. Weeks later, Stark half-seriously proposed the cruise of a powerful naval force through the North Pacific, mindful of Japan's "unholy fear of bombing." But the moment hardly seemed ripe for carrier action, when the British suggested it or at any time in 1941.[71]

Instead, Washington began moving toward employment of land-based air power to deter Japan or wage war against it. This was the most daring development in American Far Eastern strategy in the year before Pearl Harbor, though its origins remain obscured by the loss of records and the bureaucratic confusion that characterized the American government in 1941.[72] Broadly, three threads of planning, knit together by a sense of strategic desperation, converged in 1941: the older, casual speculation on the susceptibility of Japan to aerial intimidation; the strategists' rather sudden interest in the Philippines as a base for American action; and Roosevelt's episodic but forceful attraction to air power.

Of these threads, only the role of the Philippines sprung from sustained bureaucratic interest—as well it might, because it posed a classic strategic problem. Army strategists had traditionally despaired of defending the islands in the event of full-scale war with Japan. Consequently, the Philippines had been fed only scraps from the War Department's table. Before 1940, only the navy had showed a lively interest in defending the island outpost. In 1940, the army and navy began crossing paths on the Philippines issue, the navy increasingly burdened by responsibilities in the Atlantic, the army studying how a rearmed Philippines might resist attack and provide "an additional deterrent to further Japanese plans for expansion."[73]

Official doctrine continued to dismiss serious defense of the Philippines, but the ground beneath it shifted in a series of ad hoc initiatives in 1941. The impending shipment of modern aircraft to the islands elicited new hope from Douglas MacArthur and his air officers in the Philippines and from Marshall himself, who by February could comment: "If we had a single squadron of modern planes in the Philippines, it would at least give the Japanese something to think about." Doubtless Marshall was then thinking only of a tactical role for his modern planes, but Air Corps officers were bolder. By April, their Intelligence Division was canvasing other government agencies for data on economic objectives in Japan suitable as targets for American bombers. In the Philippines, Colonel Harold George initiated new plans for the defense of the islands and for air strikes against "Hainan, Formosa, and the main Japanese islands." These developments paralleled the thinking of State Department hawks, who were "confident that the Japanese structure will collapse like the Italian one once a determined and prepared resistance is made," and of the British who used the revealing Italian analogy more than the Americans, Churchill once calling the Japanese the "Wops of the Pacific." What little strength the Allies had in the Far East was at least the kind "which Japan particularly fears," air power. As Allied strategists meeting at Singapore agreed in April: "It is probable that her collapse will occur as a result of economic blockade, naval pressure and air bombardment."[74]

The interest in aerial reinforcement of the Philippines came at first in fragmentary impulses held in check by military conservatism and the Europe-first priority. But suddenly those impulses came together in July, when renewed Japanese penetration southward (this time into the unoccupied areas of Indochina), plus Germany's invasion of the Soviet Union (now agonizingly vulnerable to Japanese attack) provoked a sense of deepening crisis in the Far East. But crisis also presented opportunity. Germany's turn east placed new demands on the American arsenal to aid Russia but also lowered by a notch the urgency of supplying the British. Moreover, MacArthur was exuberant about the chances of defending the Philippines, and Congress at last seemed ready to end starvation rations for the islands. Even the worst-case scenario—a Japanese strike north against the Soviet Union, widely predicted in the American press—offered compensations: relief of pressure on the European colonial outposts to the south and the alluring prospect of access to air bases in Russia's Far Eastern territory, so close to Japanese cities. And the growing number and striking power of America's long-range bombers emboldened the architects of American policy.

Roosevelt, of course, was still intent on the use of economic sanctions to curb the Japanese. On July 26 he froze Japanese assets, a move that virtually halted Japanese trade in American goods, especially the petroleum products Japan so much needed. The relationship between that move and rearmament in the Philippines was unclear. Chronology alone suggests that the economic and military measures developed independently: the efforts of MacArthur and Marshall to deploy new air power to the Philippines and to return MacArthur to active duty as commander of American army forces in the Far East preceded news of Japan's new move south, which prompted FDR's freeze order. Eager to delay war in the Far East, most military men, particularly in the navy, were critical of the embargo as provocative and probably saw it as simply heightening the probability of war and therefore the urgency of finding some way to deter it. Roosevelt might have regarded the economic and military measures as complementary deterrents or as forming a kind of carrot-and-stick approach to Tokyo, since his original intention had been to modulate the embargo so as to leave incentives for Japan to be cautious. More likely, there was no grand design here, not even in Roosevelt's fertile mind, but simply parallel, ad hoc responses developed in competing bureaucracies and bound together only by the "careless hope"[75] that the Japanese would bow to superior force and American attention could remain where it belonged, on Europe.

If anything more guided Washington that summer, it was perhaps a model of undeclared war borrowed from the European theater and in one way or another Roosevelt's guiding star since the fall of 1938. Washington worried less about a sudden, catastrophic Japanese attack on Allied and American installations (despite Japan's reputation for surprise) than about "gradual encroachment" against Russia and/or the Europeans' colonial possessions.[76] If Japan moved in piecemeal fashion, the political problem would be acute, for Washington was hardly confident that an indirect challenge to American interests would rally the American people to enter the Asian war. At the same time, the notion of gradual encroachment may have been wishful thinking, playing into Roosevelt's preferred strategy of limited war and allowing him to believe there was time to deploy limited forces to the Far East while avoiding the full-scale hostilities that would compromise aid to Europe. As yet, after all, Roosevelt was successfully playing the game of undeclared war in the Atlantic; he did not relish the political prospects of urging full-scale use of American forces in either theater; and perhaps the Japanese themselves would be clever enough to calculate the disadvantages of provoking American entry into the war. If so, Americans would have time to build a bomber force in the Philippines and employ it in concert with other measures to force the Japanese back from an all-out confrontation with the United States. Once again, the bomber seemed less a weapon of war than a chip to play in an undeclared war of nerves.

The new mixture of urgency and opportunity brought forth action from high-level officials. By July 27, if not earlier, the Air Corps had begun work on ferrying B-17s to the Far East. In August, the War Department settled on a figure of 165 heavy bombers to be sent to the Philippines.[77] It was a bold decision. In face of the Europe-first priority, it seized most of the 220 B-17s scheduled for production over the next half-year and assigned half of all the big bombers the United States possessed to the Far East—all this when bombers were critically needed to guard the Atlantic sea-lanes, protect other outposts, train new crews, and bolster allies. The decision measured the desperation about the Far East and the optimism about the bomber's potential that arose despite the formidable practical obstacles to deployment of the big bombers. Crews worked in utmost secrecy, prepared to fire at Japanese planes, forced to follow a circuitous path down through New Guinea and Australia to minimize detection by the Japanese, flying unfamiliar routes that taxed the endurance of the bomber, landing on unknown runways that sometimes collapsed under the weight of the Fortresses, and arriving in the Philippines to ground installations poorly equipped to handle them.[78]

Roosevelt's role in this bold decision came late, if the surviving documents are a reliable guide. He apparently received his first briefing on the decision and gave it his approval during an August 7 meeting with Arnold and his military staff at the Argentia conference. The British, too, were apprised of the decision, impinging as it did on their long-frustrated hopes for American help in the Far East as well as on priorities for aid to England and the Soviet Union. No sustained discussion or controversy seemed to have ensued.[79]

But back in Washington, the planned deployment was generating a crescendo of nervous optimism. There, top officials spoke ecstatically about their forthcoming threat, none more so than Secretary Stimson. For years he had pondered how to place adequate American power in the Far East to contain the Japanese. He could hardly contain his joy about finding the solution, and it measured the enormous appeal of air power, particularly to civilians, that Stimson, this aging patriarch steeped in the ways of the ground army, now proclaimed the bomber's arrival. On September 12, the news that the first nine B-17s had arrived at Manila prompted Stimson to claim that the American bomber had "completely changed the strategy of the Pacific and lets American power back into the Islands in a way which it has not been able to do for twenty years." He informed FDR and the cabinet that nothing less than a "reversal of the strategy of the world" had been brought by the arrival of the four-engine bomber. "The President was impressed," noted Stimson, who was not past flattering himself about his own influence but in this case was probably correct.[80]

Following almost daily the progress of bomber flights to the Philippines, Stimson worked with Marshall to integrate the new air strategy with diplomacy and to fight off Roosevelt's inclination to disperse American resources too thinly. When Roosevelt considered a reduction in the army's size to facilitate increased aid abroad, Marshall prepared his case for exempting the Philippines from cuts: "Critical situation. Japan wavering. Strong air and navy forces on her flank may deter her or wean her from Axis. If Japan moves, forces in position to assist Associated [British, Dutch, Australian] Powers." Roosevelt stated his "complete agreement about the necessity for the 4-engined bombers in the Philippine Islands and Hawaii."[81]

Apparently still unsure of Roosevelt's stand, Stimson and his staff gave the president a sweeping statement on air strategy. Like military men had been doing ever since the fall of 1938, they instructed him in the complexities of an effective air force. "These planes are not individually a finished element of such air power," Stimson reminded Roosevelt, adding in an analogy the president might appreciate: "The process of commissioning a plane is not unlike the process of commissioning a battleship, and you know how long that takes." Hastening to counter any dispersal of the limited supply of planes, Stimson urged that their deployment was "not a static but a dynamic question." The new bombers should be treated as "a great pool of American power" best used now in the Philippines, not, as Arnold put it to Stimson, on missions of "doubtful efficiency" out of England against Germany. Above all, as Stimson stressed,

"A strategic opportunity of the utmost importance has suddenly arisen in the south-western Pacific. Our whole strategic possibilities of the past twenty years have been revolutionized by the events in the world in the past six months. From being impotent to influence events in that area, we suddenly find ourselves vested with the possibility of great effective power." The American bomber force was still an "imperfect threat," but "if not promptly called by the Japanese, [it] bids fair to stop Japan's march to the south and secure the safety of Singapore, with all the revolutionary consequences of such action."[82]

Soliciting Hopkins's view of Stimson's stern words, Roosevelt confessed himself "a bit bewildered" by them. But Stimson had already cleared his views with Hopkins and did so, with Marshall's help, again on October 30, and apparently no further argument with the president ensued. Even earlier, Britain's Lord Halifax told Churchill, Roosevelt was already saying "a good deal . . . about the great effect that . . . planting some heavy bombers at the Philippines was expected to have upon the Japs." On November 5, Roosevelt received from Marshall and Stark fresh assurances about the "potency" of the Philippines threat. On November 7, playing for time until the new threat was ready, Roosevelt rejected Churchill's plea for a verbal warning to Japan that might have only "an opposite effect" from deterrence and cabled the prime minister his cautious confidence that reinforcements at Singapore and the Philippines "will tend to increase Japan's hesitation." On the same day, Roosevelt polled his cabinet about "whether the people would back us up in case we struck at Japan down there." Roosevelt's phrasing, as Stimson recorded it, was vague, though significantly it included no explicit mention of Japanese attack on United States installations prior to American action. Stimson thought FDR had "the big bombers" in mind in his remarks, though among cabinet officers only he and Hull knew about them.[83]

Meanwhile, Stimson was trying to align the State Department with air strategy in order to make sure that his "imperfect threat" was not prematurely called. The problem was that even a small bomber force would not be ready until mid-December and a full force not until February or March. Stimson asked Hull to string out negotiations with Japan for at least three months. Hull, increasingly impatient about those negotiations, required further intervention from Stimson. Describing how the reinforced Philippine garrison could serve as a "diplomatic arm in forcing the Japanese to keep away from Singapore and perhaps, if we are in good luck, to shake the Japanese out of the Axis," Stimson also cautioned against premature "flamboyant announcements" about the bomber deployments. Stimson asked Hull to speak softly and give him "a very short time to get that big stick into readiness." He conveyed much the same message to the American diplomat W. Averell Harriman. Postponement of war in the Pacific was already the guiding principle, if not always the day-to-day practice, of American policy. The air strategy gave new urgency to what Marshall called "some very clever diplomacy," even "certain minor concessions" for Japanese face-saving, in order "to save the situation."[84]

By holding the Japanese in check, America's bombers might also resolve the vexatious demands of the Allies for more explicit American commitments to come to their aid in the event of war. American air power could be deployed independently and used unilaterally. It allowed the Americans and the British to move along parallel but independent tracks, as London was rushing naval reinforcements to the Far East, sharing with the Americans deterrence as their purpose and March 1942 as their deadline for building up their force. The parallel went further: in both cases the forces were too small and too hastily thrown together to be much more than a bluff, and in neither case was the weakness of the bluff fully appreciated. Meanwhile, the promise of American air power was used to satisfy not only the British but the Dutch and the Chinese. All were brought in on the new secret.[85]

By early November, Washington's plans for its Far Eastern bombers were well advanced. In the rush to get them there, in the unspoken temptation to regard their existence alone as decisive, in the careless mixture of awe and deprecation of Japanese abilities, the question of what to do with them when they reached the Philippines received hasty, sometimes conflicting answers from the military staff. The intent was grand: deter Japanese expansion, interdict it if it flowed southward, even, as both Stimson and Marshall conjectured, wean Japan from the Axis powers. As translated into operational plans, the most obvious mission for the bombers was to defend the Philippines against invasion by attacking any landing force in its ships or on the beaches. With the Philippines so neatly astride Japan's sea routes southward, the bomber could also disrupt Japanese convoys and bomb airfields on Formosa. The Philippines' proximity to Japan, long seen as their weakness, now became their advantage.

These missions, though within the range of B-17s and the B-24 Liberators now also in the pipeline, were ambitious indeed for an untried air force stationed far from home base. But War Department plans did not end there. For one thing, the bombers might be useful in situations short of war. "There is war in China and there is war in the Atlantic at the present time, but in neither case is it declared war," Marshall reminded his staff, echoing Roosevelt's views. Pending full-scale hostilities, MacArthur might carry out reconnaissance over Japanese-held territories, perhaps even over Japan itself. Believing that Japan might resort to further gradual encroachment, Marshall perhaps foresaw the bombers' use in some sort of undeclared war in the Pacific.[86]

Here lay temptation to consider even more extravagant possibilities. If Tojo and Hull gave Marshall more time and if Tokyo launched only a limited offensive, Marshall could checkmate Japan in a bolder way. Military estimates in October still listed attack on Russia as the most probable Japanese action, with attack on American installations far down the list. "They are headed north," Roosevelt advised Churchill on October 15. As late as November 26 Marshall discounted attack on the Philippines "as a probability because the hazards would be too great for the Japanese." Marshall also believed that a credible force would be in the Philippines by mid-December, though fewer than seventy heavy bombers would then be in place. Given that timetable, the

United States might have ready the ultimate deterrent to Japanese expansion: Fortresses and Liberators able to strike Japan itself. The enemy would be trapped.[87]

So Marshall told an extraordinary gathering of press bureau chiefs and senior correspondents on the morning of Saturday, November 15. Swearing the reporters to secrecy, he asked them not to upset a delicate game of deterrence he outlined. "We are preparing an offensive war against Japan, whereas the Japs believe we are preparing only to defend the Phillipines [sic]." The Japanese had not yet learned of the bomber buildup, he explained, adding (without mentioning American code-breaking efforts) that "we know what they know about us and they dont [sic] know that we know it." The moment was soon arriving to show America's hand, but adroitly. Information about the buildup must not leak through the press but "from the White House or the State Department directly to Japanese officials—presumably [Saburo] Kurusu," the Japanese special envoy flown to Washington to assist in negotiations. Privacy was critical in order to prevent a loss of face which would compel Japanese "fanatics . . . to demand war immediately." Given discretion, Japanese officials "can say to the cabinet: 'Look here. These people really mean to bomb our cities, and they have the equipment with which to do it. We'd better go slow.'" In that way, Marshall suggested, "war might be averted."

Nor, he added, was this simply a clever bluff. Even if the scheme failed and war occurred, "we'll fight mercilessly. Flying fortresses will be dispatched immediately to set the paper cities of Japan on fire," Marshall explained in language unusually graphic for him. "There won't be any hesitation about bombing civilians—it will be all-out."[88]

These were such extraordinary comments that their intent, even their authenticity, has been much debated. Marshall's scrupulous biographer, Forrest Pogue, acknowledged that the Chief of Staff overrated air power at the time but concluded that Marshall was "no Billy Mitchell" and discounted Marshall's bolder statements on bombing Japan as, if accurately recorded, betraying at most a passing excess or an attempt to hush up the press.[89] But Marshall's remarks should not be dismissed. Not one but two accounts of the conference survived, and Marshall himself graciously accepted their authenticity and correctness in 1949.[90] More important, the War Department and Marshall himself frequently considered offensive missions. As Marshall knew, the AAF was rushing to the Philippines incendiary bombs, whose utility against military targets was low and whose use the army had ignored before 1941.[91] At the same time, studies of targets in Japan, begun the previous spring, now yielded a mounting flow to the Philippines of maps, intelligence information, and target folders needed to carry out raids on Japan. The quality of this data was probably low, but the urgency of sending it was unquestioned, Marshall himself asking his key AAF aide about what information the Philippines were receiving on "what General MacArthur would attack in Japan . . . if war were declared December 1, 1941" and directing studies of "an air offensive against the Japanese empire."[92] As far back as September 12, Marshall had informed Stark that the new B-24s "can reach Osaka with a full load and Tokyo with a partial load." Stimson too knew of the developing hopes for a capacity to bomb Japan itself.[93] Staff planning documents at a variety of levels made frequent references to how Japan would "be open to aerial attack by U.S." and its cities would be "a lucrative target for bombardment aviation." Both economic and civilian targets were repeatedly identified. Granted, the full extent to which MacArthur and his staff had been briefed to undertake raids against Japan is unclear, and the whole effort had a quality of desperate improvisation.[94] But the ideas Marshall expressed on November 15, well documented also for the several weeks preceding and following it, were neither caprice nor simply bluff. As Marshall told an aide on November 1, "a strong stand meant nothing unless an actual action followed in case of necessity."[95]

Mystery about Marshall's intentions persists, however. For one thing, American bombers were not really up to the task envisioned for them. With a radius of action of about nine hundred miles when fully loaded, the B-17s near Manila could hardly reach the southernmost Ryukyus, much less the main Japanese cities, which lay some eighteen hundred miles from the bombers' bases. One solution to this large dilemma was to send the longer-legged B-24s, with slightly greater range and higher ceiling, and to stage bomber attacks out of advance bases in northern Luzon or further north on smaller Philippine islands, though bases there would be highly vulnerable to Japanese attack.[96]

Instead, as Marshall revealed on November 15, the War Department hit upon an even more fanciful scheme to solve the basing problem: bombers would shuttle between the Philippines and Soviet bases near Vladivostok or on the Kamchatka Peninsula; bases in China were also considered. After dropping bombs on Japan's cities, the Luzon-based aircraft would have only a comparatively short flight to Siberian airfields, where they would refuel, reload, and return to their main bases after dropping more bombs on Japan on the way back.

The scheme, as old as Mitchell's writings, generated enormous enthusiasm despite the impossible obstacles against realization. The practical difficulties alone were formidable. To maintain Siberian bases the AAF would have had to deliver supplies through Japanese-infested waters or maintain a difficult air ferry route through Alaska, and then work in a land alien climatically, linguistically, culturally, and politically. Some Washington officials were mindful of these problems. That they nonetheless persisted in the shuttle-bombing scheme suggests that they foresaw no prolonged campaign against Japan requiring prodigies of logistics—a few surprise missions, even as Marshall suggested simply the threat of such missions, would overawe the Asians.

The political obstacles to the Siberian arrangement were even more daunting. The Soviet Union, already in a death struggle with Germany, hardly wanted to provoke war with Japan by allowing American use of Russian bases. Still, Japan might solve that problem simply by attacking the Soviet Union. In July, air strategists were already noting how Japan "would be impressed" if the B-17s being sent to the Far East followed a route through Siberia, then "along the edge of Japan," and on to Manila, laying bare the vulnerability of "vital Japanese industrial establishments." Tenuous, even devious negotiations with the Soviets ensued. Washington, already interested in an Alaska–Siberia route for ferrying Lend-Lease aircraft to the Russians, tried to exploit conversations over that possibility to gain information needed for basing bombers in Siberia. But Stalin told Harriman in September that American crews could not ferry aircraft through Siberia lest they jeopardize Soviet neutrality with Japan.[97]

The pattern of American failure was set but not easily admitted. Bombing Japan from Vladivostok "would be a comparatively simple matter," Marshall was told in August. "The power" of an arrangement for shuttle-bombing "can hardly be over-estimated," Stimson wrote FDR on October 21; indeed it seemed enough that "it might well remove Japan from the Axis powers." Stimson took up the matter with Harriman on the same day and then sought Hull's help in making arrangements with Moscow. Staff studies continued to emphasize the decisive potential of bombing from Soviet bases. The American effort foundered, however, on the declining probability that Japan would attack Russia, on Soviet secretiveness and suspiciousness, and on American mistrust as well, for when Arnold proposed that the White House take up the matter with Stalin, the army general staff objected that Stalin might betray the scheme, even use it to provoke a Japanese–American war that would remove the Japanese threat to him. The delicate game of deterrence, so dependent on playing the Russian card, also ruled out open solicitation of Soviet help. As the formal effort to secure Soviet help was collapsing, Marshall and his staff weighed a desperate plan to fly a bomber or two from Alaska into Vladivostok, perhaps unannounced, and then onto the Philippines, over a route so untried that "both airplanes and crews might be lost"— all this to obtain the data on Soviet bases that Moscow was zealously guarding. Even after Pearl Harbor, the diplomatic effort to gain access to those bases continued. It seems, again, that Marshall's statement of November 15 was hardly whimsy.[98]

But it was certainly naive, no more so than in its trust that policymakers could manage the press and orchestrate leaks to the Japanese in a way that would frighten them into submission without forcing them into retaliation. True, perhaps Marshall's intentions were not what he said on the fifteenth; perhaps he knew the threat to attack Japan was empty but hoped it would gain credibility through carefully staged leaks. Yet if he had wanted to plant a leak, one or two reporters would have sufficed; calling in bureau chiefs was standard practice for seeking an inclusive ban on publications of secret information.[99] Most likely, Marshall wanted to preserve secrecy until the proper moment. Both he and Stimson derived from American code-breaking an overconfidence that Japanese knowledge of the bomber buildup could be detected. Stimson was "very anxious to avoid any boasting" about the deployment, preferring to let "these facts sink into the Japanese of their own impact," and he had prepared for Marshall the draft of an announcement about it "when the news breaks of the arrival of the flying fortresses at Manila." As Marshall told an aide on November 1, after December 10 "it would be advantageous for the Japanese to learn of our really effective reinforcements." Yet after his November 15 meeting with the press, any continuing efforts on Marshall's part left behind a documentary trail of only teasing bits of information. He probably met with Roosevelt immediately after his morning conference with the press, but there the trail largely ends.[100]

One possibility is that the scheme aborted because of an unplanned leak. The flight of dozens of B-17s across the Pacific was a big secret to manage. The crisis in the Far East had already invited press speculation. Back in March, Joseph Alsop had discussed the "body blow" to Japan that would come from using B-17s based in China. On August 8 and again on October 31, *U.S. News* had speculated brazenly about possible American incendiary attacks delivered from American bases or from Vladivostok on Tokyo, that "city of rice-paper and wood houses." If nothing else, such speculation illustrated the ease with which some Americans contemplated bombing Japanese cities and their confidence that Japan would be an easier mark than Germany.[101]

The critical disclosure of American plans came on November 19 from the *New York Times*'s Arthur Krock. Krock revealed the reversal in American strategy regarding the Philippines and outlined how heavy bombers based there could launch a "pincer attack" and "drop bombs on Japan, land in Siberia, refuel, and rebomb and repeat the enterprise on a return trip to Manila." What is more, Krock speculated that Japanese envoys in Washington either had learned of this plan from Roosevelt and Hull or would do so by "reading this dispatch." Either way, this new dimension to strategy would "probably have an important effect on the progress of the American-Japanese peace discussion." Here, Krock concluded, was "reassuring" news for the United States.

Krock had not attended the November 15 meeting with Marshall, but his well-informed account must have been based on it. Krock's story elicited no recorded comment from Marshall. However, it may have diminished hopes for fine-tuning the release of information just when other complications were also arising—disappointment in negotiations with the Soviets, doubts from Marshall's own air aide about the strategic wisdom of a quick attempt to bomb Japan, and delays in shipping bombers to the Philippines. But Marshall's effort apparently stumbled along, demolished only on December 7 by the ferocious surprise Japanese attack on MacArthur's airfields. A measure of how desperation and hope persisted came on December 6, when Arnold rushed to the West Coast to break a bottleneck in the flight of thirteen more B-17s to the Philippines. They only got as far as Hawaii.[102]

The Japanese, meanwhile, had only to read the American press to realize that something ominous was going on in the Philippines, and their extensive spy network there stood a good chance of observing it. Certainly Japanese leaders had long feared that American air attacks, especially incendiary raids, could leave their cities "reduced to ashes" and consume Tokyo in a conflagration more "frightful" than that caused by the great earthquake of 1923. They were particularly determined to head off any American attempt to procure or seize bases in Siberia. To that degree, American hopes for aerial deterrence rested on real enough Japanese anxieties. Moreover, coded messages intercepted by American experts showed that the Japanese had an accurate fix on the numbers of B-17s in the Philippines, although not on other elements of American aerial strength. But Japanese leaders seemed to sense no immediate danger from the Philippines, and Japanese envoys apparently received no threat of bombing from Hull, Roosevelt, or others, despite the speculation from Marshall and Krock in that regard, nor did they communicate any alarm on the basis of Krock's article.[103]

Washington's effort at deterrence failed, not only in execution, but in design. Military strategy rested on the diplomats' success in delaying the outbreak of war at least until mid-December, preferably until February or March. Yet the final diplomatic position, determined by Hull and Roosevelt without consulting the strategists and offered to the Japanese on November 26, left no room to bargain. Subtler diplomacy might not have delayed the outbreak of war, for Japan's timetable was not flexible. But the puzzle, in light of the military's tremendous hope for delay, is that it was not attempted, perhaps because grand design did not alone shape policy. The patience required to string out negotiations collided with exasperation over new signs of Japanese military action; even Stimson, the frequent proponent of delay, was, by November 27, "glad to have time" but not "at any cost of humility on the part of the United States." Stimson's bristling mood reflected intense pressures on the administration, from its own ranks as well as from allies and the press, to avoid any appearance of appeasement. Decoded Japanese messages indicated that some kind of Japanese action was now irreversible, so that statements of diplomatic position could no longer serve to delay, only to mobilize opinion and fix Japanese culpability.[104]

But confidence about the bomber may also have led the American government to overplay its hand, even at this late date. The situation in the Far East still seemed extraordinarily fluid. It was on the twenty-sixth that Marshall repeated his doubts that Japan would attack the Philippines. "Thus far we have talked in terms of the defense of the Philippines, but now the question is what we do beyond that," he said hopefully. That was also the occasion for his remarks about undeclared war. The administration still saw merit in debating the wisdom of a warning to the Japanese emperor. Only on the twenty-eighth did Stimson resign himself to the doubtfulness of securing Siberian bases. Marshall still felt it possible on the seventeenth to plead to Roosevelt "to gain time." Like other advisors, he listed possible Japanese objectives as a series of "ors"— Malaya or the Netherlands East Indies or the Burma Road or the Philippines, etc. Marshall's expectations of a limited Japanese offensive fit neatly with FDR's prevailing belief, in Hopkins's later words, that Japan "would merely use the 'one by one' technique of Germany" and avoid direct confrontation with the United States.[105]

In short, the administration expected quick Japanese action but not all-out war. In the quasi war it easily envisioned, the bombers could play a critical role by threat or by actual use—officials never made clear which because the choice depended on such unpredictable circumstances. Roosevelt may have had such a war in mind when he remarked on the twenty-seventh that the Japanese had just learned about the B-17s' deployment to the Philippines. That same day he also received Marshall's curiously elliptical recommendation that "prior to the completion of the Philippine reinforcement, military counteraction be considered only if Japan attacks or directly threatens United States, British, or Dutch territory." Presumably, military action prior to such Japanese attacks would be acceptable once sufficient bombers were in place and would be taken immediately even without direct assault on American installations if Japan attacked the Allies' holdings. That is, the United States might yet spring its own surprise. If so, Roosevelt needed, in the absence of such an assault, a pretext to enter the war and use the bombers. He may have sought it by ordering the Asiatic Fleet on naval patrols whose likely purpose, according to a careful historian, was "to provoke a *Panay*-type incident" which might "justify an American declaration of war." Given the priority Roosevelt attached to the European war, it is out of the question that he wanted war with Japan and unlikely that he sought an incident to justify declaring it. War seemed inevitable; the only hope was to delay or enter on favorable terms. For those purposes, Roosevelt may have accepted a chance to trigger the kind of undeclared war which his naval patrols in the Atlantic had helped provoke. Marshall himself was aware that under the loose authorization given MacArthur, reconnaissance missions might be flown over Japanese territory, in violation of international law, and "might cause the Japanese to fire the first shot."[106]

Any historian's case for such a provocative strategy must remain speculative in light of a documentary record that does not clarify whether Roosevelt's intentions were complex and devious, simply confused, or both. But certainly Roosevelt and his advisors were amateurs in the arts of brinksmanship and deterrence that they had been practicing since July. They presided over a jerry-rigged apparatus of policymaking that undermined their intentions to coordinate words, threats, and inducements in a way that would modify or delay action by the Japanese. They were victims of their own ambitions, not only at Pearl Harbor but in the Philippines, where despite the warning provided by the earlier attack on Hawaii, MacArthur's forces also met disaster, and airmen were soon "calling their big bombers the 'Fleeting Fortresses.'" From Manila to Washington, American leaders had foreseen—wanted to foresee—an undeclared war of nerves, not the sudden outbreak of total war, and had exaggerated the awesomeness of the mere appearance of power, the air force they sent to Luzon.[107]

In misjudging their enemy, Americans also drew on a long tradition of casual racism which made contemplation of air war against Japan easy and shallow. The strategic and moral wisdom of incinerating cities was not the issue it was in contemplating war against Germany, for which Americans had generally been wary of making bloodcurdling promises of quick victory. Americans assumed that Asians would panic or collapse in the face of bombing which Englishmen or Germans could endure. The myth of Japanese incompetence, particularly in the air, was widely shared: from the men who flew the B-17s and anticipated a "picnic" with the Japanese; to the intelligence establishment in Washington; to leaders like Marshall and Stimson, who boasted of the ease with which Americans could bomb; and to America's British allies as well. Its complement was the myth of Japanese cowardliness, for all the bellicosity attributed to them. Like all myths, these derived in part from a factual basis: Japan's profound difficulties in fighting the badly disorganized Chinese and her economic weaknesses. Those Japanese who typed Americans as shallow materialists unwilling to fight distorted the enemy as well. The point is not that Washington's air strategy in the fall of 1941 was the simple product of racism. The wish to foresee easy Japanese capitulation also derived from another legacy—arising especially out of the Munich crisis—of seeing air power as a cheap instrument of intimidation. But racist attitudes enhanced the attraction to air power, above all by minimizing the claims of conscience; assuming the Japanese would cave in quickly to American bombing, American leaders did not have to confront the possibility of killing thousands in a long aerial campaign.[108]

Most important, the story of their abortive plans suggests that the ferocity of America's final aerial assault on Japan in 1945 was not a simple response to Japanese treachery on December 7 and tenacity thereafter or to the formidable obstacles against American victory. Well before December 7, some American leaders had considered their own exercise in surprise bombing, one whose contemplation blurs the facile notions of Japanese perfidy and American vulnerability so easily enshrined for Americans in the "day of infamy." The United States was the true pioneer of strategic air war, and whereas the Japanese attack on Hawaii aimed almost wholly at traditional military objectives, American plans envisioned wholesale attack on civilians. Even before December 7, air power appealed as a vehicle for easy victory and vengeance.

The crucial element was not simply faith in American technology. Nor was it precisely faith in air power. It was faith in the idea of air power. For on the eve of Pearl Harbor, air power was still largely for Americans an idea, an alternative to war as much as a way to wage it. Its use under some circumstances was, of course, imaginable. But imagination was in a holding pattern. The approaching possibility of America's use provoked little soul-searching, especially measured against the debate over forbidding possibilities that periodically erupted in the twenties and thirties. Acceptance of air war against Japan was not yet the issue, for the bomber still promised escape from war or at least from a protracted and deadly version of it. Belief in the victory of intimidation or in the swift, surprise conquest had long allowed proponents of air power to evade troublesome moral and strategic issues. Fading from contemplation of war in Europe, it still permitted some Americans to imagine air war against Japan in a spirit of casual temptation.

5

From Intimidation to Annihilation

"Perhaps the best way to offset this initial defeat is to burn Tokyo and Osaka." That possibility, posed two days after the Pearl Harbor disaster by a key army planner, was already galvanizing the nation's officials. Frantically renewing the bid for Siberian air bases, President Roosevelt made an indirect approach to Ambassador Litvinov on the eighth, then gave Secretary of State Hull the thankless task of following up on his initiative. Although the American air force in the Philippines was mauled in the first days of hostilities, MacArthur cabled Marshall on the tenth that an attack on Japanese cities through use of Soviet airfields promised nothing less than a "golden opportunity . . . for a master stroke while the enemy is engaged in over-extended initial air efforts." Marshall concurred. The speed and magnitude of Japanese successes muted talk of a quick victory through air power. But in Manila and Washington and in London as well the hope arose that, as Churchill put it, "the burning of Japanese cities by incendiary bombs" would "bring home" to the Japanese people the foolishness of their course or at least compel Tokyo to return home some of the forces spearheading its advance.

Of course the effort to enlist Moscow failed. Litvinov rebuffed Hull's overtures, adding his sensible doubts about the utility of bombing cities. Washington and London hesitated to press Stalin too hard into action against Japan that might jeopardize Allied fortunes in the struggle against Hitler. Meanwhile, the British preferred an Allied twist on the Pearl Harbor attack by having carriers "steal up" on Japan and "ravage their cities." Washington also once again eyed China as a base for bombers attacking Japan, a prospect as hopeless as the Siberian scheme. According to General Arnold, the Army Air Forces' commanding general, "The theme song must be 'How can we bomb Japan from China.'" For the moment, it was not to be. The handful of bombers assembled for that task in the spring was diverted to the Middle East; only the token Doolittle raid would be carried out, and that not until April.[1]

These schemes to bomb Japan nonetheless revealed underlying continuities in the Anglo-American approach to air war, showing something easily forgotten, perhaps even hard to detect at the time: the enemy's sudden attack produced no quick reorientation of American ideas about the use of air power. The first impulse was to resurrect schemes concocted under different circumstances. As in many other matters, so too in the use of air power: Pearl Harbor was not the watershed it came to seem.

A decisive change in American thinking about strategic bombing did occur during World War II. Before their entry into the war, Americans who supported air power generally saw it as capable of rapidly intimidating or defeating an enemy. During the war, they came to accept it as playing a different role, that of inflicting sustained destruction on enemy homelands. Attrition and annihilation replaced speed and selectivity—virtues which initially attracted Americans to the bomber—in their vision.

But the shock of Pearl Harbor did not abruptly sweep away moral scruples against annihilation, despite a common notion that Americans go to war believing it entitles annihilative force in the pursuit of total victory. What happened instead was a gradual descent into the hell of all-out air war, a descent made so incrementally that its flames and shadows were only dimly discerned. The few existing inhibitions against destruction of enemy cities were already slipping away before Pearl Harbor. Conversely, after December 7, even professional airmen still imagined "a telling and perhaps decisive blow" by air against Japan that precluded protracted annihilation.[2] In short, acceptance of annihilation began before Pearl Harbor; realization of its likely costs, duration, and moral dilemmas only gradually emerged after December 7. Several factors in wartime political culture guided acceptance and slowed realization. Initial uncertainties about the war's course, the purposes of political leadership, the stance of air power's advocates, and the biases of prominent commentators—all these allowed concerned Americans to welcome the escalation of bombing and to ignore it, to celebrate its virtues and to overlook many of its consequences.

THE CONFUSION OF INITIAL EXPECTATIONS

Realization was slow in part because of strategic conditions abroad and political conditions at home. Despite defeats everywhere, the magnitude of the Anglo-American setback in the Far East was not immediately apparent even to high officials, much less to a public spared the full details of the disaster and exposed to misleading headlines hinting at early and easy victory. In addition, Pearl Harbor did not immediately give rise to a view of the Japanese as so fanatical or unworthy as to deserve annihilation. Two considerations crucial for justifying war on Japanese cities were not yet in view. First, while the Japanese were still on the offensive, the seemingly suicidal nature of their resistance hardly appeared; even into 1943 they sometimes retreated rather than fight to the death. Furthermore, evidence of Japanese mistreatment of prisoners of war accumulated slowly and was even more slowly released to the American public. The passions and hatreds of war mounted gradually in response to months of sustained defeat and frustration and to the manner in which dominant institutions interpreted these phenomena.

Popular expectations for the strategic course of the war remained similarly diffuse. Many Americans, moved by anglophobia or by panic over events in the Far East, challenged the administration's Europe-first priority and later its quest for unconditional surrender. Others suspected that the American stake in the Far East was imperial rather than moral or strategic. To some observers, the popular mood seemed variously listless and quixotic, given over first to "a kind of puzzled boredom about the war in general," then to spurts of excessive optimism at the first signs of success. "Daily one hears talk of the war being over in six months," commented a British observer after November's landings in North Africa. Months later, he complained about American politicians who "have poured oil on these flames . . . of national anger and humiliation," making "the Pacific front permanently a more burning issue than [the] European front is ever likely to be."[3] December 1941, then, brought practical unanimity on the necessity of victory but not on the purposes for and means of achieving it, not on the degree of it to be sought, not on the magnitude of destruction necessary to achieve it.

Beneath the widespread acceptance of the necessity of war and victory was a poor grasp of the war's costs and purposes. John Blum has reminded us that "only the United States among the great powers was 'fighting this war on imagination alone.'" Complaint about the war's unreality to Americans was a wartime commonplace, particularly when soldiers and journalists compared the stench of battle in which Americans fell with the cheerful, easy affluence so many Americans at home now enjoyed. The liberal journalist Ralph Ingersoll lamented that even on the battlefield, "fascism is still an unreal thing to the American. . . . He cannot really hate it." He "must fight simply . . . so that he can get back home—to a land that has now, in his memory, grown so lovely that there is no meanness in it." *Life* magazine repeatedly regretted that Americans had only a "Hollywood" view of the war which the administration did little to deflate (and which *Life*'s abundant consumer advertising itself did much to abet). The persistence of these complaints measured one effort at greater realism but also the difficulty of achieving it. The remoteness of air war to Americans was in part rooted in the remoteness of war itself.[4]

In strategic terms, too, there was little urgency to grapple immediately with the role of air power. Contrary to the prevailing expectation that the bombers would bear the initial brunt of the American effort, there was little for them to do over the war's first winter. Lack of bombers and bases left the army and navy largely to repel the enemy's blows. Roosevelt hardly felt free to save the new bombers coming off production lines for strategic employment, not while commanders clamored for bombers to support ground and naval operations, not while he felt it urgent to get American ground forces into action in order to blunt accusations of incompetence and to enlist popular investment in the war.

The result of all this was that the gulf between ideas and action that so long characterized the emergence of strategic air power—one at first glance so certain to disappear with war's outbreak—enjoyed remarkable persistence. Narrowing though it did after December 7, it still left plans and dreams, strategic calculations and moral concerns, free of the tests of reality for months and in some respects years to come.

Official planning for "strategic devastation"[5] remained surprisingly diffuse, in part for reasons that inhered in the very nature of air war. Ground and naval operations usually required forces highly concentrated in time and space, plunged suddenly into action on a single day or hour, with the risks and rewards telescoped into a moment's danger. Allied strategists could not easily imagine taking one-third or one-half of the forces away from invasions of Guadalcanal or North Africa without foreseeing grave consequences for their outcome. Such operations required a discrete decision for which responsibility was evident and lay clearly with a few men. Strategic air war was far more dispersed over time and space, with success riding on a prolonged campaign instead of a climactic battle, the risks and rewards more difficult to measure and slower to reveal themselves. The weight and timing of operations could be altered without fatal (or so it often seemed) jeopardy to their utility. Therefore, air war was often shaped by incremental decisions.

Furthermore, ground and naval operations often required closer coordination among branches of the armed services and the national forces of allies. Therefore, they more visibly touched on conflicting perceptions and interests, setting off livelier debate that revealed the assumptions of the parties involved. Lengthy wrangling over opening a second front in Europe or over minor operations such as those in Burma stood in marked contrast to the paucity of attention given strategic air war by the key decision makers, the American Joint Chiefs and the Anglo-American Combined Chiefs. The status of the American AAF further diminished deliberations, for Arnold was still subordinate and usually deferential to Marshall, the army chief of staff. For all these reasons, debate on aerial operations among top strategists often lacked focus and clarity.

The point should not be pressed too far. Arnold could defer to Marshall in part because the chief of staff embraced at least a moderate version of air power. From the start, controversy arose when theater commanders demanded the bombers Arnold wanted reserved for independent strategic operations. Recurrently during the war, debate erupted over whether the British or the Americans had the better method for bombing. But widespread acceptance of bombing, the apparatus of decision making, and the nature of aerial operations rarely permitted those differences to be aired explicitly.

Of course, decisions of some sort had to be made. By January 1942 the Combined Chiefs of Staff had reconfirmed the Europe-first priority and authorized the buildup of an American bomber force in Britain in 1942. But the size and mission of what became the American Eighth Air Force constantly shifted through the year. The Allies initially considered invading France as early as the autumn of 1942, an operation that would shift the function of the bombers from strategic devastation to support of ground forces.

Those prospects faded in the summer of 1942, but TORCH (the North Africa invasion) again siphoned off many of the bombers from General Ira Eaker's Eighth Bomber Command. American heavy bombers first struck occupied Europe in the summer of 1942—raiding Ploesti from Egyptian bases on June 12 and targets in France from English bases on August 17. At that, the bombers were rushed into battle prematurely in order to present Allies and Americans a show of American contribution to the European war as well as to lay claim in the headlines for the AAF's vision of its role. Not until the next year—much later and in far smaller numbers than Arnold had once hoped—could American bombers penetrate German air space. American strategic bombing, then, was at once a high priority and a distant reality in 1942.

Throughout the war, Anglo-American strategists faced two basic issues which they resolved by transforming conflict into complementarity. The weightier issue was whether strategic bombing would independently win the war in Europe or at least make any invasion essentially a coup de grace. That had been the hope of both Churchill and Roosevelt in 1941. That expectation, however, had arisen in good part from the necessity of imagining a war of limited liability, with Britain lacking the force and the United States the sanction to send ground armies into France. Pearl Harbor and the German declaration of war opened up, particularly for American officers, a return to a more traditional definition of strategy. That definition varied with its proponents, but to Marshall, the dominant American figure, it meant assigning heavy bombers a major role, first in softening up Germany by direct attacks on it, then in assisting an invasion. Bombing would be complementary to other operations. It was a formula sufficiently broad to paper over much disagreement and avert most open conflict.

But it still simmered. The formula threatened the AAF's hope to deliver the long-promised decisive blow. In 1942, Arnold still clung to that hope, trying through Harry Hopkins to reach Roosevelt, complaining of "the failure of the democracies to recognize any of those simple facts" about the dangers of dispersing bombers to ground commanders, promising "a real break in [German] morale" with heavier bombing, and finally pleading directly to the president that "air action . . . properly supported and extended by the action of surface forces will win the war." Arnold's civilian superiors, Stimson and Lovett, were offering much the same message in 1942. For his part, Hopkins was a sympathetic recipient of that message, deriving "thrill and encouragement" from the RAF's first great raids on German cities, whose "inevitable destruction" he eagerly awaited. Nor did Roosevelt disagree in principle with Arnold, but he also wanted operations on the ground started.[6]

The other conflict involved the relative merits of British night area and American daylight precision bombing. In dramatic, one-thousand-bomber raids, the RAF Bomber Command turned against German cities in the spring of 1942. Its head, Arthur Harris, sought to destroy German industrial and urban life as well as to silence his critics at home. American airmen suspected the British approach was wasteful and ineffective, but they were not inclined to press criticism of men with far more experience—to Eaker, Harris was "the senior member in our firm"[7]—as long as Americans were allowed to test their own methods. Difference was in any event transformed into virtue: the two efforts would supposedly complement rather than compete with each other.

With the major strategic differences postponed or papered over, the shape of the American bombing effort often emerged indirectly in decisions about production, logistics, and deployment instead of strategy. Roosevelt moved boldly, once again proposing figures for the output of bombers and other aircraft exceeding the AAF's request. Even bomber advocates like Lovett feared that Roosevelt would get trapped in "the old numbers racket"; manufacturers would try (as they had in World War I) to meet quotas by producing light or obsolescent aircraft; what Lovett called FDR's "fantasy" would disrupt the fragile machinery of industrial mobilization. But Arnold sided with Roosevelt, as did the War Production Board's Donald Nelson. At bottom the issue centered on whether production capabilities should shape strategy or vice versa. In the end, the president's production targets for airplanes—60,000 in 1942, 125,000 for 1943—were not met because of the high priority given to heavy bombers, but the weight of production approached the president's orders. While he attended more to mobilization than to strategy per se, Roosevelt had reaffirmed his preference for an aerial strategy wherever possible.[8]

THE LIMITS OF OFFICIAL GUIDANCE

Roosevelt shaped public expectations about the bomber as indirectly as he molded the course of official strategy. Indirection was suited both to his temperament and to the pervasive vagueness with which Americans viewed the war. As a result, Roosevelt urged Americans to mobilize for air war while also diverting attention from its conduct.

Above all, he called on Americans to produce. In doing so, he sought to make the air war abroad more real to Americans at home. At the same time, however, he aggravated the sense of distance from that war because he translated it into terms especially familiar to Americans at home—their daily tasks centered on the production effort. That effort was "even more urgent" than shooting and fighting. The "one thought for us here at home to keep uppermost," he reported on February 23, 1942, was "the fulfillment of our special task of production." Even when the tempo of American combat operations picked up, he stressed prodigies of production. "In winning this war," he told Americans on the eve of the 1944 election, "there is just one sure way to guarantee the minimum of casualties—by seeing to it that, in every action, we have overwhelming material superiority." He did sometimes describe combat, not to give Americans a feel for it, but to evoke the familiar—how many gallons of fuel they had to produce for an aerial mission, for example. Roosevelt captured one reality of this war in which production capabilities loomed so decisively. But, conforming to a culture disinclined to look at war's hardships and conscious of its economic prowess, as well as to official fears of shocking Americans, he kept the other reality of combat and destruction at a distance.[9]

Beyond emphasizing the production effort, Roosevelt said little to establish or excite expectations of the role strategic air power would play in securing victory. His few references to the air war were usually brief, anecdotal, or misleading. His April 1942 promise that "soon American Flying Fortresses will be fighting for the liberation of the darkened continent of Europe" hardly characterized the slow progress in organizing the Eighth Air Force. Reporting to Congress in September 1943 on bombing Hitler's fortress without a "roof," Roosevelt distinguished between German bombing of Britain undertaken "for the sheer sadistic pleasure of killing" and Allied aerial attacks on "carefully selected, clearly identified strategic objectives." In the few instances when reporters questioned him about bombing, he was unwilling to acknowledge or discuss the savagery of the air assault on Europe. Significantly those instances arose when places of religious or political value were threatened, such as the Vatican, the abbey at Monte Cassino, and the Swedish legation in Berlin. The fate of civilians commanded no attention comparable to that given famous buildings.[10]

Roosevelt did hint at a distinction between American bombing of Germany and Japan by suggesting that only in Germany did the bombers aim at specific economic objectives. In January 1943, he promised vaguely to "bomb them [the Japanese] constantly from the air," while the targets for Germany were more precisely described: "their war factories and utilities and seaports." Later, he held out a promise to avoid merely "inching our way forward from island to island across the vast expanse of the Pacific," and instead to take to "the skies over Japan." On June 12, 1944, he expressed the hope that "we can force the Japanese to unconditional surrender or to national suicide much more rapidly than has been thought possible." Loosely worded, these references to strategic bombing if anything declined during Roosevelt's last year of life, just when the pace of that bombing was rapidly accelerating.[11]

Roosevelt rarely spoke of the bomber as an instrument of vengeance against the enemy. In alleging Nazi responsibility for beginning air war on cities, he stated that "the Nazis and the Fascists have asked for it—and they are going to get it." But like his desire "to eliminate from the human race Nations like Germany and Japan," this was a deviation from his usual characterization of the war's purpose in positive terms of reconstituting the defeated enemies as peace-loving nations and securing a permanent peace. Unconditional surrender was demanded, but retribution he reserved for enemy leaders and war criminals alone. On the other hand, Churchill, who found "poetic justice" in aerial assault on Germany and Japan, found the rhetoric of revenge more congenial.[12]

By word, then, Roosevelt offered Americans little inducement to anticipate or desire the savagery of all-out air war. But in shaping expectations, presidents have much more than words at their disposal. Roosevelt's actions often spoke more loudly. The priority he attached to bomber production did so. Even more so did the famous raid on Japanese cities carried out on April 18, 1942, by sixteen army B-25 bombers flying from the carrier *Hornet*. That mission arose from the numerous schemes proposed before and after Pearl Harbor for bombing Japan and from Roosevelt's desire to strike a blow at Japanese morale, at the frustrations and fears of the American public, and at the wavering Chinese commitment to carry on their war. Air officers, too, hoped that air raids would force the Japanese to withdraw fighter aircraft from combat theaters, provide "a shot-in-the-arm for Generalissimo Chiang," and satisfy public opinion in the states, where "the bonus clubs have been putting up prize money for the first air attack *upon Japan*." At the State Department, the principal Far East official believed that an aerial blow on Tokyo would demoralize the Japanese and sap their confidence in the emperor.[13]

The raid's results were more mixed than American officials and a jubilant press acknowledged. General James Doolittle's bombers carried out low-level bombing runs with incendiaries and high explosives, but in flying on to Chinese bases, the planes were all lost when forced to land in Japanese-held territory (or, in one case, Siberia). As Arnold wrote to the president, "No raid is a success in which losses exceed ten per cent." Roosevelt described the raid as an attack on Japanese "war industries." In fact, the Doolittle raiders were supposed to attack by night, when the precision suggested by FDR's phrase would have been impossible; only the apprehension that the *Hornet* had been spotted sent the bombers off in daylight. Industrial and military targets had indeed been prescribed, but bombs scattered into dense residential districts. Doolittle himself was aware of the possibility of starting fires "they'll never put . . . out." Two purposes were already pulling against each other—striking terror and damaging the enemy's war-fighting capacity. Official statements and news coverage allowed Americans to enjoy the former under the latter's guise.[14]

For the Chinese, the raid caused disaster. To prevent any new raids using Chinese bases, Japanese forces pushed further inland and took punitive actions that caused the deaths of perhaps a quarter million peasants. Tokyo did withdraw some fighter forces for home defense, and the embarrassed high command, in an effort to extend its defensive lines, rushed into far-flung naval operations at Midway and elsewhere that gave American forces their first opportunity for a decisive victory—a happy consequence that few American strategists had foreseen, however. In Japan's cities, any weakening of morale induced by this first taste of destruction may well have been offset by the indignation and the opportunity for tightened government control of the populace triggered by the raid. Even in the United States, whose public opinion was the main target, the results were confused. Satisfaction was widespread but so too were new fears, along the West Coast and in Washington as well, of Japanese revenge attacks on American cities, whose defense required more diversions of American forces.

Like the simultaneous incarceration of Japanese-Americans, the Doolittle raid was designed to give satisfaction to Americans feeling powerless toward Japan. And if Roosevelt was hypocritical in denouncing Nazi barbarism while sanctioning repression at home, his use of bombing was also disturbing.[15] Of course, Pearl Harbor justified the raid in American eyes, but the strike at Pearl Harbor had been aimed at military targets, while Roosevelt's response, made after his condemnations of enemy bombing practices, promised to escalate the war into an all-out assault on enemy cities. In a moment of extreme emergency, a nation's leadership may be entitled to lift morale by actions essentially nonmilitary in immediate effect, for a nation's mood is one component of its military strength. But no such emergency existed, and bombing cities was not FDR's only choice even if the necessity of dramatic action be granted. A daring naval raid elsewhere in the Pacific or an air attack on military installations in Japan would have been feasible, similar to Japan's attacks on American forces, and no more risky than exposing one of the nation's few carriers and losing a squadron of medium bombers. By ordering the Doolittle raid, Roosevelt, through action rather than word, was not simply holding out a promise to take the offensive and secure final victory. He was setting expectations for the nature of that offensive: destruction of Japanese cities, with due revenge meted out.

That action also posed the risk of upsetting Roosevelt's own preferred strategy. That an American bomber first struck at Japan rather than at Germany aggravated popular expectations to take on Tokyo before Berlin. The Doolittle raid had been designed to curb such expectations by offering Americans a token of revenge, but there is little evidence that it succeeded in that purpose. The scare over Japanese revenge bombing suggested the contrary. So too did the expression of "exterminationist sentiment" (as one historian has called it) found in a patriotic parade in New York in June 1942, when a popular float displayed "a big American eagle leading a flight of bombers down on a herd of yellow rats which were trying to escape in all directions." And even a year after the raid, when Americans learned of the execution of some of the Doolittle fliers, indignation prompted bitter calls for revenge by bombing and other means and shook once again the American commitment to the Europe-first strategy. If Roosevelt had raised the expectations on which he would have to deliver, they were not ones with which he was uncomfortable. But he established a disturbing precedent for employing military force to meet psychological expectations. And because those expectations are usually mercurial and immeasurable, in contrast to the finite (if huge) demands of military victory, they could not be clearly satisfied and lacked criteria by which to judge when the killing should stop. In short, Roosevelt added fuel to the engine of unrestrained air war.[16]

More than most forms of military force, air power had long stimulated fears and hopes ranging far beyond its military utility. So it continued to do at the White House after the Doolittle raid. Perhaps not seriously, Roosevelt passed along to Arnold a proposal to bomb Japanese volcanoes and trigger explosions which would "convince the mass of Japanese that their gods were angry with them." FDR had already reminded military leaders of his desire for "the bombing of Japan proper from east and west," and the year would be filled with flurries of hope and futile diplomatic efforts to mount attacks from China or Russia. He also entertained another chimerical plan by Chennault—pressed by Wendell Willkie, Joseph Alsop, and Harry Hopkins—to bomb Japan into defeat within a year and welcomed a Chinese proposal to bomb power plants at Shanghai "if for no other than economic reasons," although Arnold doubted the military value of such action. Military gains doubtless attracted Roosevelt to some of these schemes, and Churchill too, who couched his hope that bombing would force Tokyo to withdraw from the battlefronts in the nursery rhyme, "Lady bird, Lady bird, fly away home, your house is aburning, your children are gone." But Roosevelt more often saw bombing as a sop to morale and to demands for assistance to the Chinese, whose leader so often threatened to drop out of the war.[17]

Of course Roosevelt was not the only public official to guide popular expectations of the bomber. Air force leaders sometimes offered louder and cruder visions of the bomber's role in war. Arnold promised that the Doolittle raid was "just the dawn of a day of wrath," portraying bombers as so fearsome that "in 60 seconds, the cumulative effort of a hundred years can be destroyed." Air power, he pronounced on another occasion, "is a war-winning weapon in its own right," the method of war "cheapest on all counts" and "by far the greatest economizer in human lives." In short, Arnold, in line with a generation's prophecy, celebrated both the destructiveness and the restraint of air power, its military utility and its capacity for vengeance. Similarly, Lovett asserted that by destroying factories, bombers can give enemy populations "their first searing lesson . . . that crime doesn't pay." Statements like these gave Americans a hint of the satisfactions beyond victory that the bomber might achieve, although air force leaders usually were more cautious in their public pronouncements.[18]

PROPAGANDA AND PROPHECY

Official words and actions constituted one influence on the expectations Americans held for the strategic air war. Another came from public advocacy of air power during the war, which often mirrored the obliqueness of Roosevelt's approach to the matter. Even more than their president, air power's proponents confused debate more than they clarified it, championed destructiveness even as they denied it, and celebrated the national genius for production with only a glimpse at its consequences in war.

That celebration was the theme in the most trivial but pervasive medium of advocacy, the corporate advertising which did much to define the war's nature and purposes simply because government was reluctant to assume that task. Advertising offered verbal and visual images of the air war that were rarely instructive about its realities. It stressed the romance of aviation and the technological prowess of American business, the fruits of which were to flow to the postwar civilian. There were exceptions, as in the Nash-Kelvinator ad linking its peacetime manufacture of refrigerators with the war against Japan: "Ice Cubes for Japan!" promised that flying boats would deliver not only bombs but "hate and vengeance" to Tojo. But even ads like Nash-Kelvinator's visually depicted air war in highly stylized or romanticized ways that rarely suggested the scope and nature of the destruction bombers might deliver and pictured airplanes more often in tactical than in strategic missions. The Boeing Company took the high road in its ads, among the finest technically and the most restrained of the war. In doing so, however, it struck another common note in wartime advertising.

Wary of inflammatory language, Boeing emphasized the company's technical achievements, both in its copy and in its high-quality photographs of soaring bombers and sophisticated production lines. Even when Boeing depicted combat, as it did with the Eighth Air Force's great Schweinfurt raids, it eschewed stylized depiction. Emphasizing accuracy and realism, it ran an official AAF photograph of the bombed target (though clouds prevented the viewer from seeing tangible destruction), while the copy stressed that its bombers destroyed factories without harming cities.

Like the president, most wartime advertising asked the viewer to see the war as a production and engineering effort and to celebrate American superiority in that regard. That approach satisfied the long-run corporate goal of winning the allegiance of customers in the postwar market. Of course, companies identified their prowess with the destruction carried out by Allied forces, but except for those firms looking to defense production as their primary postwar activity, destruction was a transitory expression of that prowess. Their long-term interest lay in playing up those technical abilities with lasting implications for the civilian market. In short, they celebrated the means of production as much as, even more than, its immediate ends. And by 1944, as the end of the war became foreseeable—and the bombing intensified—the lure of postwar markets shifted advertising further from the realities of the war.

Particularly among the airline and airplane companies eager to promote civilian air travel after the war, wartime advertising also served as a powerful vechicle for continued promotion of the Winged Gospel. Far from abating, the promise of the 1930s that the "air car" would soon be a commonplace alongside the automobile took on added attraction during the war, alongside scarcely less extravagant predictions of how giant airliners would make global travel an everyday affair. The same spirit permeated what contemporaries called "air-conditioned" educational curricula, evident in instruction about aviation and in changing styles of mapmaking and teaching geography. The fads of the forties often had distinctly militaristic and nationalistic intentions or overtones. Many were designed to prepare young Americans for air war, and the replacement of "rowboat geography" with "airplane geography," closely linked to a scholarly fixation with the new pseudoscience of geopolitics, was used to acquaint Americans with the global responsibilities they would assume in the postwar era. But the fads carried many implications. They were another promise of those rewards for winning the war that popular culture conveyed to Americans, material ease and technological marvels when the peace came. They carried forward long-held expectations of air commerce and travel as creators of the *One World* Wendell Willkie wrote about following his global air journey. The war necessarily added ambiguity to the airplane's image, yet it remained surprisingly pacific. Even the bomber's image kept shifting—the B-29 Superfortresses were renamed Peacemakers in Boeing's final wartime ads, a nice precedent for labeling the MX missile of the 1980s the Peacekeeper.[19]

Neither advertising nor official statements generated the controversy stirred by a small band of civilian publicists. Japan's success with air raids at Pearl Harbor and elsewhere gave new prominence to the role of air power in war and to a new burst of popular writing about it. Yet, often these polemics still drew attention to the politics rather than to the strategy and morality of air war. Mitchell and Douhet became subjects of hagiography, particularly by the pen of Emile Gauvreau, an astute but eccentric scandalmonger: Mitchell had been "the most unerring prophet in 500 years of military history" and the victim of a "billion dollar airplane conspiracy" embracing Wall Street and (through his marriage to Dwight Morrow's daughter) Charles Lindbergh. Mitchell's predictions on how Pearl Harbor could be attacked added another sensational dimension to his alleged martyrdom. Even to establishment commentators like the *Times*'s Arthur Krock, it was now obvious that "General Mitchell was always right," the victim of what William Bradford Huie called "the same old gold-braided bunk" still controlling the armed services. Making, like many others, an analogy to the hapless French, Huie regarded Mitchell as one of "our De Gaulles," darkly noting that "France waited too late to replace her Gamelins with De Gaulles."[20]

These propagandists wanted unification of the armed services and superiority among them for the air force. Their enemies were the Joint Chiefs, indulged by Roosevelt and backed by a vast bureaucracy committed to sending battleships and infantrymen off to pointless slaughter. Of course, in these accounts, strategy and politics were intertwined. Their authors paraded a vision of "victory through air power," as Alexander P. de Seversky titled his 1942 manifesto, the most discussed of the war. But their accusations of corruption, conspiracy, and incompetence were as arresting as their strategic arguments. Not their least appeal was their spiteful but satisfying explanation of disaster at Pearl Harbor. They spoke to familiar issues largely rooted in domestic politics, and critical as they often were of the air force, they sometimes provoked a political response. Arnold, believing that de Seversky pursued publicity instead of his responsibilities as principal owner of Republic Aviation, turned the power of federal contracting against him, while Lovett worked through Walter Lippmann to secure a more favorable public image of the Army Air Forces.[21]

De Seversky and like-minded writers nonetheless set the tone of public debate about air power for two years after Pearl Harbor. They sometimes presented an almost effortless path to victory. In William Bradford Huie's view, American bombers could strike Berlin or Tokyo "with city-block accuracy without a bombardier's ever seeing anything on the ground," seeking "not to destroy every building in the block; but to destroy the one building in the block where bearings for the Focke-Wulf planes are being made." Victory would require little fighting on the ground. In *The Coming Battle of Germany* (1942), William Ziff thought an invasion of Europe not only unnecessary but impossible. Inasmuch as Americans were avengers, not conquerors like the Germans, they should happily settle for the destruction of Germany by air, though perhaps they would not have to carry it out, for "at the first sign of real disaster the neuroticism, the inner turmoil, the wild fears and hatreds of these people, will boil to the surface." In a typical argument, Ziff urged Americans to avoid "a war of attrition" with the "rivers of blood" that would flow in a conventional war, without acknowledging the destructiveness of a war of aerial attrition in which even the Allies, he predicted, would lose twenty-five hundred planes per month.[22]

The prophets were in fact increasingly pressed to bridge the gulf between prewar myth and wartime reality. Old metaphors of easy victory persisted in promises that "a knockout blow against these [enemy] citadels must bring inevitable collapse, just as a house of cards collapses when the base cards are removed." But the same writer warned that such a blow would be "an undertaking of the greatest magnitude," requiring thousands of bombers over Germany for an unspecified number of months.[23]

Allan Michie, a reporter for *Fortune* and other magazines, struggled to bridge the gulf. He recognized early in 1942 how disappointing the performance of American daylight bombers had been. He lamented how "supercharged advertisements" and "statements from overzealous government and service officials" had satisfied "national pride" but misled Americans about the difficulties ahead. Yet Michie also thought it possible "within the next two months to triple or quadruple our bomber striking force," bring Germany "to her knees before the end of the summer of 1943," and leave Anglo-American armies free to "walk across Europe." Success would come in part if the AAF made the painful decision to switch to night bombing and help the British multiply the number of "dead" German cities. Such savagery undercut the old moral rationale for strategic bombing. Michie gloried in the RAF's destruction of cities, yet maintained that the objectives of bombing should be economic. In short, writers like Michie were tracing for their readers the shift in bombing methods from selective paralysis to sustained destruction, while struggling to minimize the moral and military questions such a shift raised.[24]

It was de Seversky, the colorful Russian-American aviator and manufacturer, who most grandly revealed and brutally resolved the tensions in thinking about air power building for a generation. In the tradition of futurist writing like that of his mentor Mitchell, de Seversky couched aggressive designs in the guise of what others might do, beginning with a sketch of the United States under awesome aerial attack by an unnamed enemy waging "systematic, scientific" destruction, "the planned wrecking of a great nation." Proposing a fleet of aerial leviathans capable of circumnavigating the globe, he was also following Mitchell's vision of aggressive isolationism, portraying an American air force patrolling the world without having to depend on allies and bases overseas. Not all disciples of Mitchell took that direction. De Seversky, however, sounded nationalist themes.[25]

De Seversky also worked both sides of the aisle in the debate between selective disruption and systematic devastation. On the one hand, since civilians had proven they could endure tremendous bombing, their morale was a dubious target, economic objectives were preferable in wars against advanced nations, and precision bombing could disable them: "by piercing vital organs and nerve centers the entire mechanism can be paralyzed." Here was the old, familiar, and enticing organic metaphor. But the language of precision faded as de Seversky pronounced that "there is just one target: the whole country" and proposed a strategy of "extermination" and "total destruction" of the enemy.[26]

With de Seversky, the old defense for American bombing methods, whose virtue had been elegance and restraint, crumbled. De Seversky salvaged the case for bombing by arguing that at least armies and navies need no longer waste treasure and lives: no small virtue for a nation plunging into world war. But more than that, he offered a political argument that turned the defects of bombing—its inaccuracy and its destructiveness—into virtues. "The conduct of war will be determined by whether the purpose is to destroy the enemy or to capture him, whether the prey must be killed or trapped alive." In America's case, it seemed clear that "because we have no imperial purposes, but in every case want only to remove a threat to the normal life of the world, American strategy must be geared for the war of elimination," a task for which the bomber was ideal. In short, with an irony de Seversky did not appreciate, a brutal strategy arose from America's benign purpose.[27]

Surprisingly, there was little challenge to de Seversky's assumptions. True, to analysts like Hanson Baldwin, prophets like de Seversky were "false gods." But Baldwin accepted a large role for strategic bombing, including the night bombing of German cities practiced by the British. Significantly, George Fielding Eliot found that the weakness of an exclusively aerial strategy lay not in its savagery but its restraint. It might win the war. "But it is not the quickest way to win the war, for it is neither using all our power, nor is it absorbing the enemy's reserve strength in all categories." To idle Allied armies and navies seemed foolish, for "the most humane way to fight a war is to prosecute it with the utmost fury until victory is won; this will always cost less in lives." These propositions were deeply grounded in sound doctrine and military tradition but offered only utilitarian arguments against an air strategy. And because Eliot and Baldwin viewed war as the application of rational calculations on the most efficient means of victory, they could not appreciate air power's attraction as a weapon of vengeance.[28]

War had attenuated the spectrum of debate on air power. Where once alternatives (however arbitrary) had been offered in the clash between prophets and skeptics, now public argument was largely confined to disagreement over the techniques and proportions of the air war. Even the prophets sometimes backed away from their more extreme claims for air power as the sole instrument of victory.[29] In short, Americans were given no alternative to substantial reliance on widespread destruction by air as one method to win the war. Strategic as well as moral debate had not ceased, but it ran in narrow channels. This, more than specific claims and counterclaims, defined how Americans thought about what bombers might do.

Reaction to de Seversky's book indicated this trend. While technicians took issue with the soundness of his predictions and some of the religious press criticized their moral implications, a more common note was generous approval. Here was a book of "tremendous charm" and "surgeon-like reasoning." De Seversky was ranked with Mitchell, Admiral Mahan, and Clausewitz as strategist and contributor to the "philosophy of conflict" (a judgment that has not stood the test of time). He was, like Mitchell, cast as a lonely hero battling the "stubborn wall of opposition" erected by the bureaucracy of the War Department and the Air Corps. Such a view not only overlooked de Seversky's own vested interest as aircraft manufacturer but made it appear that the

AAF—whose leadership a *Nation* reviewer equated to "the management of a peanut wagon"—was far too reactionary to bomb with the zeal de Seversky proposed. As it had for two decades, the alleged conservatism of government officials obscured official embrace of strategic bombing. If their manner of running the war was "fully as serious as treason," then destruction of the enemy by air seemed remote indeed. Working these old political accusations, many reviewers said little about the destruction de Seversky proposed.[30]

Approval and adroit promotion gave de Seversky's ideas broad and sustained exposure. Condensed in *Readers Digest,* the book was purchased in 1942 for movie production by Walt Disney. An odd but fruitful partnership between prophet and animator ensued. It was a commercially risky film, so Disney worked closely with the Gallup organization, whose market research was designed not only to promote the film but, by divining public interests and tastes, to help shape its content.[31]

De Seversky was Disney's chief collaborator and, with his heavy Russian accent, the rather curious star of the film. Two-thirds of the film was animation, but the live footage featured de Seversky, presented as a dishonored prophet like Mitchell. The film thereby reduced the complex forces behind the growth of military aviation to a stirring story of individual struggle. In line with market research showing a public interest in bombing Tokyo, that city's destruction "was saved for the final triumphant scene of the film—the reward which America would reap should it have the courage and wisdom to follow Seversky's advice." To underscore de Seversky's thesis that air power obviated the grim task of conquering Japan's far-flung outposts, the animation showed giant American bombers flying from Alaska and striking at Japanese factories and ports. Then the bombers dissolved into an American eagle whose talons, in a prolonged sequence of orgiastic destruction, rend and tear at the Japanese octopus whose tentacles surrender their grip on Japan's conquests. Finally, the camera offered a global view of the octopus dissolving into the burned ruins of Japan, while the soundtrack poured out "America the Beautiful" and the final words, VICTORY THROUGH AIR POWER, appeared. As with the book, the formal argument was for a sure and relatively easy method of victory, but vengeance was the very patriotic theme. Reduced to animation, air war was at once glorified, trivialized, and dehumanized, becoming "a carnival of destruction, relieved of all such imponderables as human beings, ideals and causes and effects."[32]

The film's impact need not be overestimated. Although Disney pressured Simon and Schuster to bring out a cheap paperback edition of the book in order to promote the film, box office gross was not impressive. The Disney version drew praise from the *New York Times* but also criticism as "a conglomeration of animated cartoon styles, mostly bad." Some animated scenes were visually effective, but also crudely and obviously propagandistic. Most of all, James Agee rightly noted, "there were no suffering and dying enemy civilians . . . no civilians at all, in fact," indeed hardly any people in the film. And yet the best scrutiny of the film came from movie critics whose challenge was not authoritative in strategic terms or widely disseminated. More powerful judges apparently reacted enthusiastically, if the rumor is accurate that Churchill prevailed on Roosevelt to view the film at the Quebec conference in August 1943, and in turn Roosevelt pressed it upon the Joint Chiefs.[33]

Perhaps what both book and film reflected most accurately was the ease with which Americans were making distinctions between their enemies, saving their greatest fury for the Japanese. True, the film was rarely overtly racist; instead, a technological determinism governed. Yet where Germany was symbolized by an iron ring, Japan was given the form of a loathsome octopus, and the final vicious scene, what Agee called Disney's "gay dreams of holocaust," unmistakably promised special treatment for Japan.

Hollywood rarely broached directly the subject of Japan's final fate from the air. Indeed, except in animation, strategic bombing defied dramatic visual depiction. In most films, Hollywood, collaborating closely with the AAF, glorified the air force, its men, and its bombers. True to Hollywood's conventions, "it often seemed that the Army Air Corps Chorus was hovering around every corner" and the product was "pure sentimentalized corn." The latter was most evident in *A Guy Named Joe,* in which Spencer Tracy, killed in a suicidal attack on a German aircraft carrier, returns to earth as counselor to green airmen.

A few of Hollywood's better films, however, downplayed the sentimental and, like *Victory Through Air Power,* cultivated popular expectations for a virtuous campaign of annihilation against Japan. Assisted by Hap Arnold and William Faulkner, Howard Hawks employed a style of gritty realism in *Air Force* (1943), the story of a B-17 crew who arrive at Oahu amid the Japanese attack and fly on to the Philippines to help American forces there. He also reassured Americans about their virtues in an age of technological warfare: the crewmen were not bloodthirsty patriots, but efficient technicians moved by personal loss and indignation over Japanese treachery, and the unfounded portrayal of Japanese fifth columnists in Hawaii (which prompted an eloquent protest from Norman Thomas) set up the bomber as an instrument of righteous indignation. In fact, the B-17 *Mary Ann* was the star of the film: if initially perceived as a "mechanized freight train" flown by a "mechanical brain," *Mary Ann* emerged as a battle-scarred heroine endowed with her own indomitable spirit and in whom the crew invested its loyalty. Most important, *Mary Ann* finally finds her true purpose: her first mission (intercepting Japanese ships approaching the Philippines) fit the classic defensive rationale for the bomber, but as the film ends the bomber departs to attack Tokyo, in a visual promise that Americans' wish for Japan's annihilation will be fulfilled. A later film—*The Purple Heart* (1944), about the torture and trial of the Doolittle aviators who fell into Japanese hands—gave explicit expression to that implicit promise of vengeance: a doomed American flier warns his captors that American bombers will "blacken your skies and burn your cities to the ground and make you get down on your knees and beg for mercy. This is your war . . . and it won't be finished until your dirty little empire is wiped off the face of the earth!"[34]

THE LIMITS OF JOURNALISM

Journalistic reporting and commentary offered another source of expectations about the bomber's role in the war as well as of possible challenges to the preferences of officials and propagandists. Often, however, the media left the popular imagination impoverished because its coverage was constricted by the nature of air war, the purposes of commercial journalism, and the politics of the war. The reporting of bombing raids was a good case in point.

When the Allies had been on the receiving end of strategic bombing, all the advantages of immediacy and vividness in reporting had lain with the air war. These disappeared when British and American bombers took to the skies. Photographs could not translate the enemy's destruction on the ground into compelling images: taken at high altitudes, often under unfavorable conditions of smoke and clouds, they recorded scenes of bombed-out cities that were monotonously similar and in which the viewer (and often even the professional analyst) was hard-pressed to discern the scale and nature of the destruction. Words, like photographs, could only convey abstract, anonymous, and repetitive images of the destruction below. Alternative images—from low-level aerial reconnaissance, from captured enemy photographs, from neutral newspapers—were few in quantity or suspect as enemy propaganda.

In contrast, ground and naval operations could be observed at closer hand. Making better copy, they attracted journalists and impressed editors eager to sell by capturing public attention. As American land and sea offensives intensified in 1943 and 1944, coverage of them crowded out accounts of the strategic air war—just as the latter was reaching its maximum fury. The air war had too much glamor and importance to be ignored, but photographers and writers usually turned to aspects of it they could convey vividly—combat in the sky, the bombers themselves, and the crews: the men and technology passing in and out of missions, but not the results. The impersonality and abstractness of air war, which have become almost clichés of modern times, were reinforced by the commercial and artistic considerations which governed wartime reporting. In a war waged at home only in imagination, a special effort was required to grasp what bombers did.

Coverage of the air war, like that of all the war, was also limited by political considerations. Journalists could only witness what authorities permitted and report only what censors passed on. The RAF's head of Bomber Command, Arthur Harris, pleaded for openness, but superiors overruled him. Both the RAF and AAF banned reporters from accompanying bomber missions until 1943, and even then journalists could hardly observe the action well enough to contest official claims. Edward R. Murrow's blunt description of a Berlin raid as "a massive blow of retribution" in which "men die in the sky while others are roasted alive in their cellars" was unusual.[35]

In any event, few reporters were inclined to contest official claims. They saw themselves as enlisted in the war effort, their task that of establishing confidence in

Allied virtue and victory and commanders. Journalists did sometimes probe and question. But more often, as a Canadian reporter later confessed, "we were a propaganda arm of our governments. . . . We were cheerleaders." What the reporter did best in these circumstances was to capture the heroics, the sufferings and failings of the individual soldier, as Ernie Pyle did. Such reporting was by no means always celebratory or single-mindledly patriotic, but it did shift away from broader issues of strategy, politics, and morality, and it meant that "the more the importance of the individual soldier was reduced by technology, the more correspondents concentrated on writing about him."[36] Finally, there was the need to view the war in uplifting and reassuring ways. If American participation in World War II lacked the naive idealism of that of the First World War, Americans still needed to view the war as a positive experience. Neither editors nor officials wished to present it as too shocking, although fears of public complacency gradually loosened restrictions on grimmer portrayals of combat.

The best combat reporting challenged American expectations of easy victory through application of superior technology. Released a few months after American forces suffered shocking losses on the island in November 1943, Robert Sherrod's *Tarawa* reported the sacrifices of American soldiers as well as their naive hopes on the eve of battle that the naval and air barrage might make the landing a cakewalk. To rely on technology "was the American way to fight a war," he commented. But with the enemy squirreled away underground, "there was no way to defeat the Japanese except by extermination," and "airpower could not win the war alone. . . . The road to Tokyo would be lined with the grave of many a foot soldier." Sherrod blamed expectations to the contrary on the censors and rewrite men who "gave the impression that any American could lick any twenty Japs" and on home front affluence and illusions of ease—the mood of a nation "wallowing in unprecedented prosperity," as he bitterly put it.[37]

Yet the savagery Sherrod described may have cut an unintended way. Presented as the grim necessity Americans had to accept, that savagery also made any alternative to a war of mutual "extermination" seem attractive. As the young John F. Kennedy wrote his parents shortly before Tarawa: "When I read that we will fight the Japs for years if necessary and will sacrifice hundreds and thousands if we must—I always like to check from where he is talking—it's seldom out here." Kennedy hoped that "perhaps all of that won't be necessary—and it can all be done by bombing."[38]

The best reporters, like Sherrod, usually viewed the air war from the perspective, literal and strategic, of the ground soldiers. Few journalists of equivalent talent covered the strategic bombing effort. Many accounts of action in the air continued the romantic tradition of glorifying individual efforts and sacrifices, particularly early in the war, with the Eagle Squadron of American fliers serving in the RAF, Doolittle's raiders, and Chennault's Flying Tigers. In part because early action was small-scale, the old gladiators-of-the-sky tradition persisted. True, particularly in the Pacific war, the enemy supposedly lacked the chivalric qualities attributed to him in the First World War.

Robert Scott, Jr.'s *God Is My Co-Pilot,* in which God hardly appeared, mixed racial hatred with a cheerful zest for air combat: "Personally, every time I cut Japanese columns to pieces in Burma, strafed Japs swimming from boats we were sinking, or blew a Jap pilot to hell out of the sky, I just laughed in my heart and knew that I had stepped on another black-widow spider or scorpion." Scott recorded brutalities by Americans that he condemned when carried out by the enemy, and likewise recklessness by Americans which was merely suicidal fanaticism when mirrored in Japanese actions. But however skewed, the focus on individual feats was widely sustained.[39]

New circumstances pulled against it, however. If individual heroism was still the salient quality observed, it took on a certain grimness. While some crewmen relished combat and the enemy's destruction, such passion was rare. The enemy was usually faceless, almost an incidental element of the story; crews had "no personal feeling against Germans" or an "impersonal attitude toward the enemy, so hard for Europeans . . . to understand." Emotion ran strongest in loyalty to comrades and the service. The bombers themselves were often the heroes of accounts.[40]

In fact, hatred of the enemy was generally strongest among the civilians furthest removed from him, but even Americans at home attempted to view this war more coolly than they had the First World War. In part the changing nature of air war, in which bureaucracy and the machine threatened to dwarf the individual, accounted for these different emotional attitudes. As a consequence, the struggle to reconcile a romantic view of military aviation with modern realities defined much of the writing on the air war. Already in May 1942, *Saturday Review* saw in the airman a new elite, a new "Hero for America," indeed "a new human type" whose "task is usually destructive," but "it is not civilization that he wants to destroy."[41]

In November 1942 John Steinbeck's *Bombs Away: The Story of a Bomber Team,* which he wrote for the Army Air Forces, appeared. Steinbeck struggled to find the familiar and the redemptive in the modern work of bombing. For him, the war brought welcome release from the despair and disunity of the "directionless depression." The air force provided men the "antidote for the poisons of this idleness and indirection," much as Steinbeck earlier thought the government's agricultural camps had given purpose to the dustbowl refugees of *The Grapes of Wrath.*[42]

Steinbeck acknowledged that the pilot as individualist hero was gone, but he tried to sustain the American attachment to individualism in the new cooperative setting. On the one hand, he emphasized the modernity of the airman, who has no "ecstatic anticipation of Valhalla, honor, and glory, but . . . fights to win and to survive." This "isn't a war of speeches and frothy hatred. It is a technical job, a surgeon's job. There is only time for hatred among civilians. Hatred does not operate a bombsight." In some ways Steinbeck's airman was the prototype of the "organization man" widely seen after the war as the dominant character type of American culture: the bomber crewman recognized the superiority of the group to the individual; the bomber team "is truly a democratic organization" which banished arbitrary, paternal authority; the good crewman internalized organizational values, for he "shall know the reasons for orders rather than . . . obey blindly and perhaps stupidly." The airman was cool, cooperative, controlled. On the other hand, by invoking the concept of the team, Steinbeck also grounded the character and values of his airmen in familiar virtues and institutions. *Bombs Away* fairly dripped sports analogies: the air crew was "the greatest team in the world," and the airmen's war "the Big League in the toughest game we have ever been up against, with the pennant the survival and the future of the whole nation." Far from being a wrenching change, service in the air force harnessed skills and attitudes learned on boyhood baseball teams and hunting trips and in encounters with the family car.[43]

Steinbeck's outpouring of images and analogies betrayed tensions in his effort to reconcile past and present. Crewmen supposedly sprang from the frontier tradition of the "Kentucky hunter and the Western Indian-fighter." Exchanging rifle for turret, "the American boy simply changes the nature of his game. Instead of raiding Sioux or Apache, instead of buffalo or antelope, he lays his sights on Zero or Heinkel, on Stuka or Messerschmitt." But frontier individualists often abandoned the team and fled organized society. The sports analogy was also a troublesome way to reconcile past and present, for modern sports raised up a physical elite within which individuals sought glory, sometimes at the expense of the team. According to Steinbeck, "the cadets are drawn from a cross-section background of America but they are the top part of the cross section." Seeing a democratic elite, Steinbeck saw no tension between democracy and elitism. Stressing that the bomber crew had to cooperate democratically to fly successfully, he neglected their lack of choice about where to fly and what to bomb.[44]

Steinbeck's portrayal was uneasy because he sought to compress two differing views of America into his perspective on the airman. Like Lindbergh fifteen years earlier, the airman was presented as both individualist and joiner, relic of the past and harbinger of the new era, free spirit and disciplined technician, democrat and superman, "Dan'l Boone and Henry Ford."[45] Steinbeck was not necessarily wrong, for disparate qualities coexist in the American character. But Steinbeck did not acknowledge how uneasily the characteristics with which he endowed airmen mingled. To liken crewmen to quail hunter and pony express rider was surely comforting, capturing what Americans wanted to see in themselves, and in soldiers and sailors as well as airmen. But it was also misleading because it did not suggest what these Americans would have to do, and become, in war.

Steinbeck updated a tradition of looking at new weapons. Like his predecessors (if with fewer of their doubts), he pushed away terror by finding that new technologies liberated old virtues and gave rise to new ones. Like them, he considered how new devices shaped men's characters, not how character contributed to new devices and their destructive uses. Later, after the war, Steinbeck granted that he had crossed the line between journalism and advocacy. "We were all part of the war effort," he wrote. Correspondents were not "liars." But, he added, "it is in the things not mentioned that the untruth lies." In *Bombs Away*, many things were not mentioned.[46]

Especially neglected were the destructive nature and intent of bombing. "For a long time we hated the idea of the heavy bomber. It was considered only an offensive weapon designed to carry bomb loads to enemy cities to destroy them." But the battles of the Coral Sea and Midway "have demonstrated that our heavy bomber is our greatest weapon for the defense of our coast against invasion," Steinbeck argued, unaware of how poorly the land-based bombers had performed at Midway. Steinbeck admitted that enemy countries, not just ships at sea, would be bombed. But airmen "knew the mathematics of destruction. Guns and ammunition and food that does not arrive is more important than a bomb dropped in the Wilhelmstrasse." It still appeared, as it had before Pearl Harbor, that in the free market of the bomber's uses, good ones would drive out pointlessly destructive ones.[47]

A later sketch of the airman by Brendan Gill, one of the talented writers at the *New Yorker* during the war, succeeded where Steinbeck failed, in part because the accumulation of experience in bombing by 1944 facilitated realism. Too, in the "Young Man Behind Plexiglas" Gill let the airman speak for himself. Through Ted Hallock, a twenty-two-year-old bombardier who had completed thirty B-17 missions in Europe, Gill identified some of the same virtues and characteristics Steinbeck had, but their meaning was ambiguous, the tone somber. Hallock saw himself less as a member of a team than as "a cog in one hell of a big machine," one he both admired and resented, all the while knowing that "fliers have to be expendable, . . . that's what Eaker and Doolittle had us trained for. That's what war is." Analogous to his position in the air force was his relationship to his bombsight, about which "the more I found out . . . the more ingenious and inhuman it seemed. It was something bigger . . . than any one man was intended to comprehend." Indeed, he wondered "if I've been a cog in one thing after another since the day I was born." Hallock's guiding metaphor was the machine, not the playing field, his dominant mood bewildered, sometimes angry, sometimes resigned.

Where Steinbeck saw easy transition to the demands of military life, Hallock struggled. He was courageous but not heroic, content when his bomber was shot up to ditch in Switzerland until his crewmates decided to try for England. Trying to reconcile his wartime position to the antiwar politics he had imbibed in the thirties, he discovered in England "that there were people in the world who looked the same as us but thought differently from us," and he "began to wonder if the Germans were maybe as much different from the English and us as a lot of writers and politicians claimed." He did not directly question what he did. But he noted that pilots seemed eager to fly again, perhaps "because they're really flying the ship. When you're only one of the hired hands, who's being carried along to do the dirty work, to drop the bombs and do the killing, you don't feel so good about it." In the end, feeling "cheated out of a good big chunk of our lives," Hallock divined no special meaning in what he had done, only hoping that eventually he would feel that "all that cannonfodder stuff never happened."[48]

This bittersweet portrait fleshed out the flier far more than Steinbeck had done. Where Steinbeck's men had been temporarily adrift but deeply rooted in American traditions, Hallock had an uncertain place in his own culture, whose dominant quality was its quiet regimentation of powerless men. Technology informed the lives of both Steinbeck's men and Hallock, but where Steinbeck saw an effortless fit between man and machine, Hallock felt an alien presence. In 1944, another observer, the historian Dixon Wecter, in "Children of the Machine Age," found fliers to be men with "little interest in the life of ideas or social values," men who "emotionally are often immature. . . . They are types of modern man, whose command of technology is vastly superior to the control of his own group plans and destinies."[49] Hallock did search for ideas and values, but like Wecter's veterans, he was captive of the machine and adrift.

Writers like Gill and Wecter raised at least oblique doubts about the values informing the bombing effort and the costs exacted from the men involved, although by the time such writing appeared in 1944 "the bloom was off the war books," as Sherrod later put it.[50] Readers of *Life* were led along a course similar to that traced from Steinbeck to Gill, from easy celebration to growing complexity. *Life* ran its share of flattering pieces on American fliers, on the precision and effectiveness of their bombing, on the hope that air war, "relatively cheap in men," might avert the "nightmare" of ground warfare. But *Life* usually shied away from offering panaceas for easy victory. It sometimes discounted the ferocity of British night raids on Hamburg and other German cities, writing off reports of massive civilian casualties as enemy propaganda. Still, its photographs generally told of indiscriminate destruction. And by May 1944, articles like "The Chimneys of Leipzig," based on the story of three repatriated American girls, grimly portrayed the destruction of German cities. By 1944, *Life* was also detailing the early failures and costly successes of the Eighth Air Force, emphasizing that "to crush a strong and widely dispersed industrial power by air is an extremely complicated and costly business."[51]

Since no serious bombing of Japan occurred until June 1944, *Life* had little to report on the strategic air war in the Far East. Its suggestions were usually implicit, as when it ran photographs of Japanese dead incinerated in the great Tokyo earthquake and fire of 1923. The photographs at least made the point that Japanese cities would be easy targets for firebombing. Indeed, *Life*'s photographs relating to the Pacific war were generally more graphic and suggestive than those for Europe. Yet its characterizations of the Japanese enemy gradually became more complex. Perhaps the Japanese saw human life as "essentially cheap" because of horrible experiences like the 1923 fire as much as because of "the tradition of the Samurai." In a lavish photographic essay that appeared in September 1944, *Life* noted that "war is the closest of all relationships between nations," and as if to emphasize the common humanity of the warring cultures, its photos of Japanese in everyday tasks, even the sheer vividness of these color photographs, humanized an enemy once regarded only as bucktoothed, ugly, and menacing.[52]

But these changes came only after a deluge of propaganda, often crudely racist, about the Japanese. Any doubts they raised about the utility and morality of the Allied bombing effort arose too late to affect a momentum of effort by 1944 fully accelerated. Similarly, in England a lively debate developed only after the RAF's bombing was already reaching its wartime peak. The debate over air power—itself a debate on limited terms—had already receded, and naval and ground operations were crowding the air war off the front pages. In sum, what Americans could learn from the media about the air war was not always blindly praiseworthy of bombing or simplistically degrading of the enemy, but even a limited appreciation of the war's complexity came mostly after the course of bombing was already set.

THE LIMITS OF CONTROVERSY

Public opinion polls, which might have clarified public debate, were surprisingly uninstructive. True, along with much subjective evidence they indicated consistent if not clear-cut distinctions between views of the nation's two enemies. Americans were more likely to describe pejoratively the Japanese than the Germans and especially later in the war to view the Japanese people, not just their government, as America's enemy. No one doubted that the Japanese were the more hated enemy, in good part for racial reasons. An equally telling difference between views of the two enemies, however, lay in the pervasive shallowness of American knowledge of the Far East. As Jerome Bruner commented in 1944, "Probably never has a modern nation fought an enemy about which she knew so little as we of Japan."[53]

Early in the war, Americans expected victory to come more easily over Japan than over Germany, although such expectations diminished with time. By decisive majorities, they expressed their desire to bomb Japan's cities and to move the bulk of American air power to the Pacific. But there were no precisely comparable questions asked about bombing German cities. Unless the absence of such questions alone is evidence that bombing Germany generated less interest, comparisons are difficult, although most Americans probably thought that bombing could more easily defeat Japan than Germany. Taken collectively, these polls probably indicated a desire to prosecute strategic air war to its fullest but also substantial doubt about the prophets' claims that doing so could almost alone win the war. But questions about bombing both Japan and Germany also disappeared from the polls after mid-1943. This inattention to issues raised by strategic bombing after mid-1943 paralleled the decline in public debate and media attention to them following the initial wave of air power tracts.[54]

Americans came to and expressed their acceptance of strategic air power in more complex and indirect ways than polls could reveal. Just as before World War II, the attraction of air power lay in the diversity of its appeals, none so compelling alone as to focus concerted debate about the bomber, and many distantly related to the conduct of war itself. The distance, physical and psychological, from which Americans viewed the war reinforced this diffuseness. No single argument for air power emerged triumphant, no decisive clamor to unleash it arose. Instead, war tempered the persuasiveness of claims by both extreme skeptics and prophets—a sensible reaction to the war but one that muted debate among Americans still further.

Air power offered the promise of easy victory and vengeance against their enemies.

Yet most Americans, like their leaders, deferred final judgment on that promise, preferring to set aside the wrangling about theory and just give air power its chance. Insofar as Americans sought vengeance, they usually let it emerge as a consequence of policies whose stated purpose was the destruction of economic and military objectives, or let British night bombers provide it. Japan's punishment was more avidly and openly welcomed, and words were often strident, but Japan would not come within reach of American air power until the war's last year, except for Doolittle's promissory note on things to come. Above all, Americans preferred to view the bombing effort in the categories—production and technology—that reflected their virtues and avoided explicit questions about moral and military purposes. The media demonstrated some awareness of the nature of bombing operations late in the war, but then to help Americans appreciate and sustain the costs of war, not to raise fundamental questions about its content.

Perhaps the acceptance of strategic air war meant that Americans had suspended moral debate, accepted the bomber on utilitarian grounds, and revealed again their supposed "tendency to refer to war in absolute terms."[55] But while the religious and pacifist press sometimes displayed that tendency, its stance and role in wartime debate also revealed more complex reasons for the acceptance of air war.

Implicitly or explicitly, it is true, the religious press often confessed its inability to advocate restraints on the conduct of air war. Reacting to the Doolittle raid, the *Christian Century* could only express regret about the intensification of air war and "commit to the mercy of God those upon whom the bombs may fall." One source of restraint, arising out of prewar law and theology, lay in the test of utility, the principle that "greater violence must not be used than is necessary to achieve the purpose in view.'" But there seemed no way "to draw a line between discriminate and indiscriminate bombing." Indeed, it seemed "idle to try to put a check upon the way in which weapons are used. If we fight at all, we fight all out." More than that, the *Christian Century* assumed that bombing did have military utility. That left the religious press no alternative except to do what *Commonweal* did: condemn the bombing of cities as "indefensible morally, no matter how efficacious militarily." Such condemnation set a high moral standard but was consigned to practical irrelevancy because few Americans would sacrifice a weapon whose utility even *Commonweal* felt forced to acknowledge. That acknowledgment was perhaps the most telling component of the dissenters' position. With surprising ease, they relinquished the argument that might most effectively have rooted moral concerns in practical conduct of the war—the possibility that much bombing served little military purpose.[56]

It was addressed, however, by the English pacifist Vera Brittain in *Massacre by Bombing*, a tract published in the United States early in 1944 and given front-page coverage by the *New York Times*. By arguing that bombing could be justified only if there was "absolute certainty" that it would shorten the war, Brittain admitted that bombing might have its place. But she argued that the bombing of German cities had failed to offer convincing evidence in that regard and in the meantime had caused untold suffering. In the past, laws of war at least "bore witness to the survival of some fragments of a Christian conscience among the combatants." But in World War II, "the contesting parties pay little heed to the former decencies and chivalries." Brittain was trying to establish standards by which the brutalities of bombing could at least be measured, even if not stopped. Her target was conscience as much as deeds.

In that effort she succeeded to some degree, in part by flushing out the mood of vengeance usually shrouded by utilitarian arguments for bombing. The writer Mac-Kinlay Kantor justified "socking the rapacious German nation with every pound of high explosive available" as necessary for punishing aggression and deterring its recurrence, while other responses spoke of bombing as justified repayment for Nazi crimes. Here indeed was evidence that bombing satisfied more than just hopes for victory. (Just before the controversy arose over Brittain's declaration, a statement on the bombing of Monte Cassino by General Dwight Eisenhower was released warning that the same problem could arise on the battlefield, for "the phrase 'military necessity' is sometimes used where it would be more truthful to speak of military convenience or even of personal convenience.")

Other responses to Brittain published by the *Times* refused to justify bombing in terms of retribution or revenge. For these writers, as for Brittain, moral justification inhered in military utility and in the saving of Allied casualties bound to result from the imminent invasion of France. They disagreed with Brittain about the utility of bombing but acknowledged that it was not yet proven. More than that, so Anne O'Hare McCormick worried, the Allies preferred a solely military path to German surrender, failing to exploit Germany's internal weakness through rhetoric as well as through bombs. "Words are still cheaper than lives or planes. But so far neither Mr. Churchill nor Mr. Roosevelt has said anything to counter the German propaganda that the peace will be worse than the war." If not entirely fair to Roosevelt and Churchill, McCormick had at least addressed the problem of politics and morality raised by the bombing campaign, by asking if nations at war were bound to end the bloodletting through the least destructive means as long as fundamental objectives were secured.

Between the celebration of revenge by Kantor and the suspicions of overkill by McCormick stood a more commonplace reaction to the bombing, the kind of bland denial demonstrated by the *New Republic*. The liberal weekly deplored "bombing defenseless people merely to instil terror in them" but implied there were no defenseless people in modern war, and besides, "so far as we are aware," terror bombing "is not the practice of the RAF and the AAF." The truth was that most of the liberal press was too concerned for the political outcome of the war to have much interest in its military conduct. Dissent from the course of bombing was confined to the fringes of American politics, and even there few mounted an effective case that bombing ran beyond the requirements of victory. That so few did—that even dissenters usually accepted the military utility of bombing—measured again, from still another perspective, the persuasiveness of the air power argument.[57]

Still, the brief controversy over Brittain's tract, even the hair-trigger reactions of those who condemned her outright, suggested that moral debate was not suspended. Even total war did not erase all moral sensibilities about bombing. That was the case in Great Britain, where direct knowledge of bombing's horrors induced some doubts about the wisdom and legitimacy of all-out air war.[58] In the United States, too, exposed as it had been for a generation to horrific as well as benign literature about the bomber, moral argument was not entirely discarded. To be sure, it was often crude. Yet even retribution was, to its proponents, a moral as well as political imperative. A corollary to retribution was the claim that "war is a conflict of peoples, not of armies." In the words of a contributor to the *New Republic,* "The natural enemy of every American man, woman and child is the Japanese man, woman and child." The nation might spare the civilian if the enemy could be defeated without harming him, but if not, "he reverts to his fundamental position as . . . prime target." Thus, "unnecessary destruction is not unnecessary when it becomes necessary"—necessary to win, that is. Protection of civilians was a luxury, not a fundamental right to be abridged only in extremis.[59]

Of course that argument was no novelty by World War II. Invoked to justify siege, blockade, and submarine warfare, it was also not novel to aerial warfare. It drew its moral force from an all-too-real historical development, the rapacious demands made by modern states on their entire populations in the pursuit of victory, and it was a difficult argument to refute. But as usually invoked, it was a repugnant argument, although a moral one of sorts. It ignored any distinction between civilians who were willing workers and others who were conscripts of the state. It placidly assumed that their killing would measurably advance the cause of victory. It fatally undercut the moral indignation that Americans earlier had expressed over Japanese bombing in China and German bombing in Europe.

Perhaps because that argument was repugnant, some Americans resorted to another, slipperier defense of bombing: that civilian deaths were acceptable as the accidental by-product of the destruction of legitimate targets. That is, lack of the intention to harm absolved the destroyer of moral responsibility. Persistent in both British and American circles, this argument took on the quality of ritual denial inasmuch as civilian deaths could be incurred as long as they were not openly desired. More forthright was de Seversky's bland explanation of how rationalization could operate: "the kind of large-scale demolition which would be looked upon as horrifying vandalism when undertaken by soldiers on the ground can be passed off as a technical preparation or 'softening' [for invasion or occupation] when carried out by aerial bombing." Finally, the bombing of civilians was made acceptable by the claim that it "would be a kindness—even to the enemy," for decisive ferocity would in the long run save enemy lives.[60]

Troubled Americans acknowledged the widespread killing of civilians, accepted their innocence, labeled their killing murder—then designated it as justifiable homicide, as the only recourse if victory were to be secured and Allied casualties minimized. Yet the nature of the necessity they invoked must be examined. Few Americans (and they not very plausibly) could argue that survival itself was at stake. By necessity, most

Americans did not mean the prospect of imminent and complete destruction, a contingency which might justify strategic devastation of enemy cities. Instead, they meant the requirements of victory, total victory at that, and with minimum suffering and loss for the victors. For them, that argument had a compelling moral sanction. It also was dangerously open-ended, for it could justify almost any action that accelerated triumph. Perhaps the best that might be said of their reasoning is that its sanction extended only to the limit of victory, excluding the pursuit of vengeance and other goals whose criteria were even less measurable.

In the end, what characterized debate on bombing was not the absence of moral argument, but its casualness. The circumstances and characteristics of air war, not just moral laziness, helped to make argument casual. Americans entered the war with little tradition of realistic debate about air power to draw upon. Until 1944, they waged a war of limited offensives in which their bombers came into play only slowly, in which the production effort commanded much popular attention, and in which journalists and politicians were ill-equipped or disinclined to raise moral issues. To those who sought vengeance, bombing offered it without much need to proclaim it. To those who sought a narrower justification for air power, seeing its morality as inhering in its utility, measuring that utility was critical for maintaining limits on destruction. But utility was an imponderable: the gains of air war were rarely quantifiable in terms of acreage conquered or armies surrendered, and they were inseparable from progress made in other ways, such as invasions assisted and armies immobilized. Even after the war, gains resisted precise characterization. During the war, their intangible nature confused and perhaps exhausted intelligent debate on the morality and efficacy of bombing.

These circumstances were more permissive than determinative, for where they differed somewhat, as in England, debate was at best modestly more informed. But they were strengthened by broader characteristics of the war. Argument about bombing was crude because categories of argument about the war itself were crude. What Americans learned of the war usually shielded them from addressing its consequences in human terms. Various forms of a moral argument were advanced but sometimes as sops to troubled consciences or to the needs of public relations, and never did argument rise to the level of sustained debate. It hardly seemed that it could, given the imponderables at issue, and a more general sense of futility or indifference about any possibility of arresting the ferocity of the war.

But casual attitudes toward bombing did not arise solely from the circumstances of the war. The distance from which Americans viewed air war, as either prospect or reality, had always been great. The capacity of the bomber to secure easy vengeance in the guise of military necessity had long been one of its attractions. Its promise to reduce or end bloodletting on the ground had been an even stronger attraction after World War I. The moral and imaginative effort required to bridge the gap between promise and reality had always been immense. If people in the relative luxury of peace could not reconcile their benign and horrific images of air war, they were hardly more likely to do so in the maw of war.

THE IMPORTANCE OF AWARENESS

Casual attitudes certainly helped Americans to accept bombing, but the case can be made that they did little to shape the actual course of bombing. The example of the British, so terribly knowledgeable about air war but so bent on unleashing the bomber's fury against German cities, apparently strengthens that case. If Americans had known more and confronted better what they did know, they might not have objected more. Even if they had, their government might have followed the same course.

Did American leaders fashion that course partly in response to public opinion? Direct evidence is, not surprisingly, slight, though more abundant regarding the Pacific war. Yet public pressures did not need to be overt, or overtly recorded, to be felt. They needed little restatement in part because they had been felt keenly by men like Marshall and Roosevelt even before Pearl Harbor—by then, they had already anticipated wartime pressures and come to share many of the assumptions behind them. After December 7, public opinion was evident in the wide attention given to the prophets of victory through air power, in the applause for the Doolittle raid and early Anglo-American efforts against Germany, and in fears expressed about mounting American casualties. National leaders shared those fears. According to Averell Harriman, "Roosevelt was very much affected by World War I" and "had a horror of American troops landing again on the continent and becoming involved in . . . trench warfare with all its appalling losses." Marshall, himself acutely sensitive to casualty figures, made a special effort to keep Roosevelt informed of them "because you get hardened to these things and you have to be very careful to keep them always in the forefront of your mind." Roosevelt also recognized the limits on American tolerance of sacrifices in another world war and knew that, as Harriman put it, "if the great armies of Russia could stand up to Germans," the strategic opportunity existed to limit American losses. No similar opportunity existed in the Pacific, which only made the incentive to employ air power there more intense.[61]

At the same time, pressure to employ air power was not strong enough to lead the Roosevelt administration into an exclusive reliance on it. Alarm about casualties did not always push policymakers toward expanding the strategic role of bombers. With the invasion of Europe imminent, 1944 opened with widespread "anticipation of vast American losses."[62] Insofar as Allied leaders responded to that anxiety, they diverted the heavy bombers away from Germany into a massive effort to weaken German defenses in France against invading forces. More broadly, countervailing considerations reined in a rush to air power: it was still too untested a weapon to place all bets on it, and even where an aerial strategy was more concertedly pressed, as was the case in the war against Japan, formidable undertakings on the ground and at sea were required to secure bases placing Japan within reach of American bombers.

What facilitated official reliance on air power was less irresistible public pressures than the previous acceptance and general attractiveness of strategic bombing. The congruence of official and public expectations was indicated simply by the lack of friction between them. Another consideration inviting use of air power, then, lay in the lack of political conflict that its use entailed.

A more alert and concerned citizenry might have made a difference, not by fostering an empty public ritual of handwringing about the morality of bombing, but in more substantive ways. First, a distinction between the use of bombing for military purposes and its employment to satisfy political and emotional ends might have forced the bombing effort into narrower channels. If leaders rarely stoked the fires of vengeance and hegemony openly they did little by word to bank them and a good deal by action to fan them. Had they not and had others examined the bombing effort more critically, a greater obligation might have been placed on commanders to justify the military utility of missions.

Contemporary leaders were themselves alert to this possibility. They were fearful that popular perceptions of inhumanity in the bombing effort might affect its course, the political image of the United States, and the fate of the air force and its ambitions. Privately, they worried—in General Ira Eaker's warning late in the war—that "we should never allow the history of this war to convict us of throwing the strategic bomber at the man in the street."[63] Publicly, their concern found expression in repeated assertions of the virtue of American precision bombing and in denials, sometimes valid and often not, that such bombing had been abandoned in favor of less discriminate targeting. In an international context, they made numerous efforts to explain why Allied bombers killed civilians in occupied countries whose loyalty the United States courted. Most important, in the few cases where the constraints of popular opinion seemed substantial—in the matter of bombing Rome, for example—American leaders made considerable efforts to operate within them.

To be sure, it is unfair to impose on historical subjects a latter-day notion of restraint, as if they should have freed themselves from passions which were inherent in the war. Yet contemporaries had before them not merely an abstract standard of the acceptable limits of force, but a historical record full of cautionary lessons. It was, after all, a staple of commentary that military actions during World War I outran defensible military and political purposes: unrestricted submarine warfare had not always served German purposes, nor had the dispatch of hordes of infantry against impenetrable defenses served a useful end. That war might develop an uncontrollable momentum was known to articulate Americans during World War II; indeed, their own Civil War offered much the same lesson. Given how much Americans had World War I in mind as they waged the second war, their insensitivity to that lesson is striking.

The dominant image of air power, as a revolutionary weapon that broke from the past, discouraged careful attention to these depressing precedents from past wars. The parallels between the two world wars did not seem close enough: futile infantry charges consumed a nation's own population as well as its enemy's, while massive bombing raids, unless they provoked a response in kind, killed the enemy far more than one's own. So the defenders of air power argued, although the reality was more complicated. It was not just Anglo-American air power that saved the lives of many British and American soldiers. "The truth is that in every war *somebody* has to deal with the enemy's main body; in the Second World War it was the Russians."[64] Usually overlooking that truth, both critics and proponents of air power failed to probe more subtly the lessons of World War I.

Restraining wartime practice, more skeptical attitudes might also have made a longer-term difference, leading Americans to view themselves, their victory, their war, and their weapons more modestly. Some Americans, including many in generals' uniforms, did view the bombing as at best a dirty if necessary business. Had more done so, the tendency of Americans to see their role in the war self-righteously might have diminished, and along with it that sense of virtue that Americans carried into the postwar world. It would have been harder to equate technological superiority with moral superiority and take the latter "to be a permanent quality which not only explains past victories, but also justifies the national claim to be the lawgiver and arbiter of mankind," as Hans Morgenthau complained in 1950. Likewise, the air force's shining image and dominance in strategy during the postwar years would have been more difficult to maintain. Whether such outcomes be regarded as baneful or desirable, they surely would have made a difference. Whether they might have happened is indicated by the contrasting British experience. After the war, what Walzer calls "The Dishonoring of Arthur Harris," the RAF's Bomber Commander, "at least went some small distance toward reestablishing a commitment to the rules of war and the rights they protect." Although a declining Britain cast its lot with strategic air power after the war, attitudes derived from the war in part accounted for British pressures upon the United States not to use the bomber in various cold war crises. As Walzer says, dishonoring a man seems a "cruel" way to establish standards. As it was for Churchill in Harris's case, it would have been hypocritical for a Truman or an Eisenhower to dishonor an Arnold, Eaker, or LeMay for actions so broadly sanctioned. But if they had, a different course of history might have resulted.[65]

It might have in another, even more far-reaching way. What moral debate that did occur about bombing focused on the near-term danger of harm to the enemy. Almost invisible was the danger it posed to those who triumphantly unleashed it. Briefly, it caught the eye of the *New Yorker:* "Once again, in their collective reaction to the destruction of Berlin, New Yorkers have demonstrated that they don't know what fear is." The magazine agreed with other commentary arguing that "it serves the bastards right . . . that it was a necessary action, efficiently and economically carried out . . . that each individual should shoulder his share of the moral responsibility for it." But the *New Yorker* added ominously:

One implication, however, is still, as far as we know, fluttering around untrapped. Nobody has pointed out that the destruction of Berlin established the fact that it is now possible to destroy a city and that every city, but for the hairline distinction between the potential and the actual, is afire, its landmarks gone and its population homeless. From where we sit, the flames are clearly visible.[66]

Shaped by culture, politics, geography, and the nature of air war, the distance from which Americans viewed the bombing not only enhanced its attractiveness in the immediate struggle, but blinded awareness of future perils.

Bombing in the American Imagination:
A Visual Essay

The Angel of Death

His New Toy

The
FUTURE
*"A New Heaven
and a New Earth"*

Drawing by
H. RAYMOND
BISHOP

What is to be the next Great Epoch in Human Progress? We can reach but one conclusion: "The whole World united into a great Brotherhood of Nations through the Power of the AERIAL AGE."

Contrasting images from the 1920s expressed the dichotomous views of the airplane that characterized the years between the wars. "The Angel of Death" (1) and "His New Toy" (2) captured fears of armaments and militarism that were commonplace in the first years after World War I, although more often felt toward naval weaponry. " 'The FUTURE: A New Heaven and a New Earth' " (3) captured the benign view of aviation as a force for peace that became dominant later in the decade, in the wake of Lindbergh's flight and the spread of commercial aviation.

BOMBER LANES TO JAPAN

Flying Time From
Strategic
Points

U.S.S.R.

MONGOLIA

MANCHOU[...]

LAKE BAIKAL

CHINA

Chungking

8 Hours

7¼ Hours

INDIA

Hong kong

13 Hours

SIAM

INDO-
CHINA

CHINA
SEA

7½ Hours

AFRICA

INDIAN OCEAN

Cavité
PHILIPPINES

Singapore

BORNEO

(4) A two-page illustration in the United States News *instructed readers, even before Pearl Harbor, on how vulnerable Japan's cities were to firebombing; it accorded neatly with developing plans in the War Department for possible air attack on Japan from the*

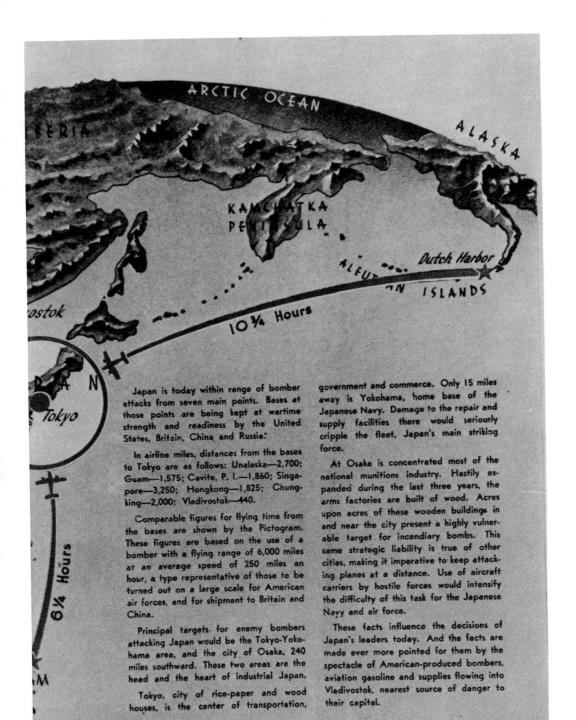

Japan is today within range of bomber attacks from seven main points. Bases at those points are being kept at wartime strength and readiness by the United States, Britain, China and Russia:

In airline miles, distances from the bases to Tokyo are as follows: Unalaska—2,700; Guam—1,575; Cavite, P. I.—1,860; Singapore—3,250; Hongkong—1,825; Chungking—2,000; Vladivostok—440.

Comparable figures for flying time from the bases are shown by the Pictogram. These figures are based on the use of a bomber with a flying range of 6,000 miles at an average speed of 250 miles an hour, a type representative of those to be turned out on a large scale for American air forces, and for shipment to Britain and China.

Principal targets for enemy bombers attacking Japan would be the Tokyo-Yokohama area, and the city of Osaka, 240 miles southward. These two areas are the head and the heart of industrial Japan.

Tokyo, city of rice-paper and wood houses, is the center of transportation,

government and commerce. Only 15 miles away is Yokohama, home base of the Japanese Navy. Damage to the repair and supply facilities there would seriously cripple the fleet, Japan's main striking force.

At Osaka is concentrated most of the national munitions industry. Hastily expanded during the last three years, the arms factories are built of wood. Acres upon acres of these wooden buildings in and near the city present a highly vulnerable target for incendiary bombs. This same strategic liability is true of other cities, making it imperative to keep attacking planes at a distance. Use of aircraft carriers by hostile forces would intensify the difficulty of this task for the Japanese Navy and air force.

These facts influence the decisions of Japan's leaders today. And the facts are made ever more pointed for them by the spectacle of American-produced bombers, aviation gasoline and supplies flowing into Vladivostok, nearest source of danger to their capital.

Pictogram
Title Reg.   U. S. Pat. Office

Philippines. Partially obscured in this reproduction is the 6-1/2-hour path from Guam—the route American bombers would eventually follow—and the shortest route of all, 1-3/4 hours from Vladivostok, where Americans repeatedly but futilely hoped to gain air bases.

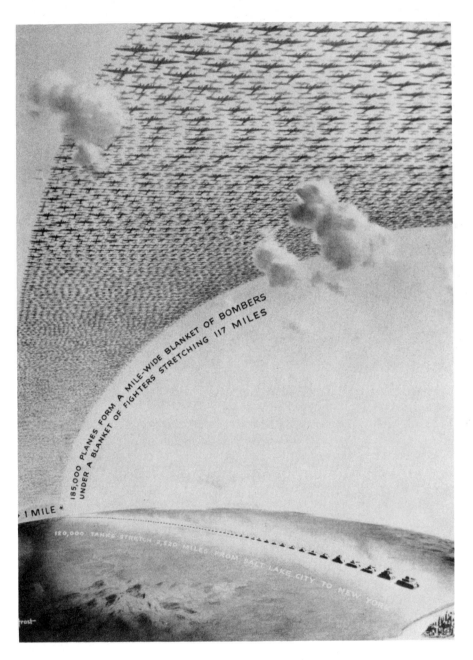

185,000 PLANES FORM A MILE-WIDE BLANKET OF BOMBERS
UNDER A BLANKET OF FIGHTERS STRETCHING 117 MILES

◂ I MILE ▸

120,000 TANKS STRETCH 7,520 MILES FROM SALT LAKE CITY TO NEW YORK

*Americans' visual environment during the war repeatedly invited them to recognize the
dominance of air power and the need to maximize aircraft production. Thousands of
travelers through Chicago's Union Station saw a display of model airplanes across the
station ceiling and millions of* Life's *readers saw this photograph (5) of the display.* Life
*also visualized the ascendancy of air power in a wartime illustration (6) of "the clouds of
planes and armadas of tanks that the U.S. must forge to win the war."*

The skin of freedom's teeth

When free America first struck back at totalitytyranny, Boeing Flying Fortresses* put teeth in our aerial offensive . . . smiting the enemy with death from the substratosphere.

In the photograph above, you see the aluminum "skin" that covers the wings of the Boeing B-17. To speed the output of the thirty-two-ton Fortresses, aluminum alloy sheets were needed of greater dimension than it is practical to manufacture.

On the machine pictured above, developed by Boeing tooling engineers, standard aluminum alloy stock is automatically spot-welded into "super-sheets"

up to 14 feet wide and any desired length. Many times faster than flush-riveting, the Boeing automatic feed spot-welding tables make 65 controlled welds a minute, enabling Boeing to meet the extremely high U. S. Army requirements while maintaining quantity production. And the elimination of rivets reduces "drag" and increases speed in flight.

This is merely one of more than 100,000 special tools and templates developed by Boeing for the faster production of the Flying Fortress. Like many other Boeing-developed tools, it has been widely adopted by American aircraft manufacturers.

And tooling is but one of more than *twenty-five* different fields of engineering activity at Boeing . . . fields which might seem, to the uninitiated, a far cry from Flying Fortresses, Stratoliners,* globe-girdling Clippers and other Boeing-designed and Boeing-built airplanes.

• • •

It is this diverse skill and experience in manufacturing, tooling, engineering research and design which will some day make the phrase "Built by Boeing" a hall-mark of better products for free men in a better world.

The B-29 shown here without its armament. The plane in the background is a Boeing Flying Fortress

Shortening the road to Tokyo

When word flashed around the world that B-29 Superfortress crews had ended the training stage and gone into action against Japan, it was cheering news. But behind that news is a deeper significance. For the Boeing Superfortress marks the greatest single advance in aviation since the war began.

Many details of the B-29's performance must still remain military secrets but it can be stated without qualification that this is the most potent weapon of air warfare ever developed. Half again as large as the Flying Fortress, the Superfortress is faster, carries far heavier bombload and has greater range than any other bomber in combat today.

The same Boeing engineering staff that designed the B-17 Flying Fortress — improved it over a period of years and had it ready for action when war came —is responsible for the Boeing B-29. Working closely with the Army Air Forces Materiel Command, these men have incorporated in the new Superfortress many of Boeing's unique principles of design proved in combat where the Forts, manned by the matchless Army Air Forces flight crews, have so consistently carried out their precision bombing missions and weathered the toughest sky battles of the war. Only the keen engineering vision and production skill which enabled Boeing to give America the 247, first

modern-type commercial transport — the Flying Fortress — the famous Stratoliners and transocean Clippers — could have done this job — in time.

So highly do military authorities regard the need for this new Boeing bomber that they have requested several of the nation's largest aircraft factories, in addition to the Boeing plants, to build it.

How many of the B-29 Superfortresses are to be built, and where and how they will be used, must remain restricted information. But you can rest assured that in the hands of courageous, keenly trained American crews these great ships are a formidable weapon for Victory.

DESIGNERS OF THE FLYING FORTRESS · THE NEW B-29 SUPERFORTRESS · THE STRATOLINER · TRANSOCEAN CLIPPERS **BOEING**

FINISH THE FIGHT WITH WAR BONDS

Boeing, one of the largest wartime producers of military aircraft and designer of the B-17 and B-29 bombers, consistently emphasized marvels of technology and production more than destruction in its advertising, linking those marvels with promises of postwar comfort and convenience for civilian travelers. 7 (March 1943); 8 (July 1944).

ICE CUBES FOR JAPAN !

Listen, *Tojo*—when you hear that *kar-rump* some night and the factory walls start sliding into the sea—look out, it's one of those new "ice cubes" from Nash-Kelvinator!

We are building *plenty* of them just for you—huge Kelvinators that fly and ice cubes that hurt.

Monster metal-bellied flying boats—growing on Nash-Kelvinator assembly lines—to whisk the Navy's men and material to any spot you raise your head! Giant Vought-Sikorsky cargo carriers built *complete*—and not in ones or twos, but in fleet upon fleet!

Want to hear some more?

Then listen—that angry hum coming out of the East—

They are the propellers built by Nash-Kelvinator, built by the many thousands!

And that mighty roar you'll soon be hearing is the voice of the most powerful engine ever placed in a pursuit ship. It will take the Navy's new *Corsair* higher, faster than any "Zero" in your stable.

They're coming, Tojo—coming from men who, in building last year's refrigerators and automobiles, thought only of a nation's health and happiness.

But now, it's hate and vengeance and the remembrance of a thousand Axis wrongs that are guiding their hands . . . beating every production record in Nash-Kelvinator history by two and three.

Look out, Tojo, *the nights are growing longer.*

• • •

NASH-KELVINATOR CORPORATION

Corporate advertising more often emphasized the destructiveness of bombing early in the war, when few American bombers were active; later in the war, as bombing intensified, advertisers looked to peacetime markets. Nash-Kelvinator's October 1942 ad "Ice Cubes for Japan!" (9) suggested the link to peacetime comforts by its title but also bluntly promised

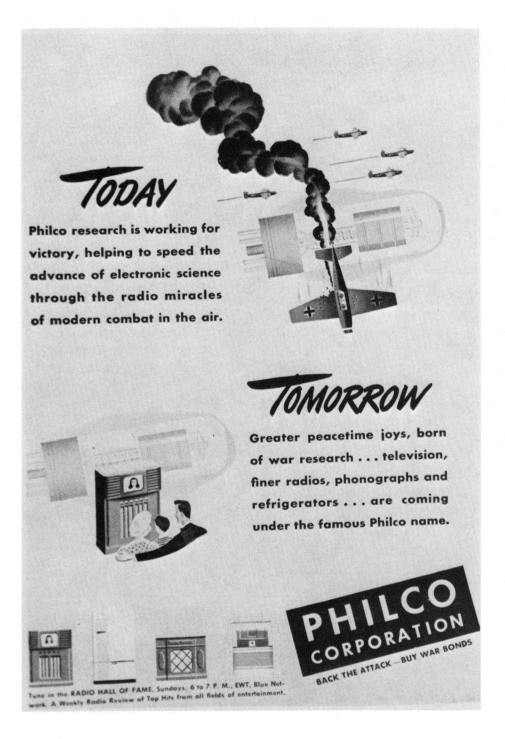

readers that aviation would bring "hate and vengeance" to Japan. By both visual and verbal messages, Philco's May 1944 ad (10), like Boeing's, asked readers to look beyond the destructiveness of aviation and consider the wartime pleasures and peacetime conveniences that flowed from the technology of aviation.

Propaganda posters (11, 12), designed to encourage volume and quality in the production of munitions, frequently suggested bombing as a fitting form of punishment for subhuman enemies. The Japanese were depicted as rats or apes more often than the Germans, but even when, as here, such caricatures were applied to both, distinctions remained: the German figures are recognizable as Hitler, while the Japanese figures might be any or every Japanese; the Japanese are rendered as cruder and visually impaired; and the knife-wielding Japanese are presented as technologically more primitive.

Another wartime propaganda poster (13) designed to promote production shifted the focus away from the usual wartime paradigm of attacking the enemy to an older one dominant in the 1930s—military aviation as a means to defend helpless civilians.

(14) The Army Air Forces adopted the techniques of Hollywood to simulate reality for crews—one of many wartime efforts to simulate conditions in Japan. Shown here, on a motion picture sound stage, is a model of Tokyo Bay (top and in background) used in the production of training films designed to brief aircrews slated to attack Japanese targets.

GIANT BROOD FROM THE EAGLE'S EYRIE

On June 17, 1944, the front page of the Chicago Tribune *celebrated the start of B-29 attacks on Japan by linking the bombers with an angry American eagle taking flight toward destruction; fittingly, the eagle was newly hatched, for it would be several months before the B-29s really began to deliver on the promise offered here (15). The* New York

"SOME NEW JAPANESE PRINTS."

Times *celebrated realization of that promise in its Sunday, May 20, 1945, edition with a typically caricatured, subhuman, and bewildered Japanese viewing the destruction of Japan's firebombed cities (16).*

The visual environment rarely gave Americans a full appreciation of what their bombers did to Japan. The typical military photograph, like this one (17) taken in the wake of a heavy attack on Tokyo on May 25–26, 1945, could only imply, not reveal, the destruction below, which was obscured by billowing clouds.

(18) A rare Japanese photograph of citizens and soldiers amid the destruction of an
unidentified Japanese city gives a hint of the realities which Americans could not observe in
the occasional photographs they saw of Japan's bombing.

Japanese photographs show victims of fire attacks on unidentified Japanese cities. The clothed bodies (19) were probably the victims of some form of asphyxiation; the baby and

parent (20), closely resembling victims of atomic attack, most likely died from the intense heat generated in firestorms.

Only at war's end could low-level photography begin revealing for Americans the full extent of the damage done in incendiary attacks. A Life photograph (21) which appeared on September 19, 1945, showed Tokyo at the end of the war. An American military

photograph (22) taken in September 1945 testified to the destruction of an unidentified Japanese city on Honshu, with a partially demolished POW camp in the foreground. Some structures appear intact in these photographs, but appearances could be misleading: the walls of concrete buildings often survived incendiary attack, but fire gutted them.

An American military photograph (23) taken in September 1945 showed that the destruction of Tokyo—although vast, as indicated by the whitened areas—was not complete, and that the railroad system at least partially survived.

LIFE

20, 1945   Vol. 19, No. 8

WING SHOWS MORE GRAPHICALLY THAN AERIAL PHOTOGRAPHS (PP. 26-27) EFFECT OF ATOMIC BOMB HIT ON HIROSHIMA. SMOKE BILLOWS 40,000 FEET

In the immediate wake of Hiroshima, a Life illustration (24) gave verbal and visual testimony to a continuity sustained through conventional and atomic bombing: the difficulty of presenting visually the realities of bomb damage. The copy accompanying the drawing, indicating that it "shows more graphically than aerial photographs [the] effect of [the] atomic bomb hit on Hiroshima," was quite accurate in that Life's accompanying photographs revealed little indeed. But even the drawing, replicating the billowing clouds that obscured destruction in photographs of firebombed cities, suggested scarcely more.

6

The Dynamics of Escalation

"You can't hit a town like Cologne without its having a definite effect upon the morale of the entire German people," said General H. H. Arnold in December 1942.[1] The Americans were not yet able to hit Cologne or any town in Germany, but many welcomed the British effort to do so without quarter and shared British illusions about its efficacy. In light of those illusions, it is clear that professional officers had difficulty viewing the air war any more realistically than did the general public. For a variety of reasons, including the role of strategic realities and perceptions, they too maintained a distance on the air war, especially when that war intensified in 1944. Certainly intelligent men tried to formulate intelligent plans. But plans and actions diverged in ways that leaders often were either helpless to resist or incapable of comprehending.

1942–43: THE PERILS OF DISPERSION

One reason they diverged was that forces were scattered in ways that strategists had not foreseen—to the North African theater, for example, where the Army Air Forces gained much of its first experience. Its participation there was at best reluctant, retarding as it did the buildup of the Eighth Air Force in England and confined as it was largely to support of surface forces moving against the Germans and Italians. Most bombing done by Allied air forces in North Africa was hardly strategic. Yet there were compensations. For Arnold, even a North African campaign was preferable to the diversion of bombers to the Pacific—the navy's desire—inasmuch as it carried the promise of further bases from which to carry out strategic attacks on Italy and Germany. The same promise allowed Arnold to swallow another distasteful decision, to follow up TORCH with operations against Sicily and Italy. And if still subordinated to a sea–land offensive, AAF commanders, supported by Eisenhower, nonetheless gained independence and unity of command in tactical matters.

147

But the AAF's success in Africa as a cooperative arm could also backfire, since it provided support for those arguing that the cooperative role should be dominant. At best, TORCH's impact on the air force's strategic fortunes was double-edged, depleting Eaker's Eighth Air Force but allowing it time to mount an independent campaign by delaying the invasion of northwestern Europe. But through the autumn of 1942, the new time-lease was used to little avail. True, bombing accuracy was encouraging, despite wild misses like the time bombers struck a French town one hundred miles away from their target. Likewise, the bombers seemed to take an encouraging toll of enemy fighters, so much so that even British newsmen and officers muted their earlier skepticism about American bombing methods. They joined American air force leaders in the mistaken belief that the Luftwaffe was on the wane and the chance for decisive air attack on Germany was near, if only they could stop those diversions.

But the toll of enemy fighters soon shriveled when intelligence officers sifted through the overlapping claims submitted by green crews. "We were living in a fool's paradise, far as that stuff was concerned," Curtis LeMay later recalled, and postwar scrutiny indicated that even the revised figures were grossly optimistic.[2] Raids against highly fortified German submarine pens on France's western coast—critical targets with the Battle of the Atlantic hanging in balance—showed disappointing results. Other raids into France and Holland were little more than combat training missions. As the new year approached, AAF leaders were jittery about the future of the daylight campaign.

The disappointments were not solely the AAF's responsibility, although they were exacerbated by its misleading claims on the Eighth's initial accomplishments. Weather, always the greatest impediment to success, played havoc with every aspect of operations. TORCH gutted the Eighth's ranks and often diverted what bombers remained to support of North African operations. With rarely even one hundred bombers operational, Eaker could counter his detractors by pointing out that they were proving themselves right by denying him sufficient force. However, before the Casablanca conference not even Arnold and Eaker knew the depth of Churchill's desire to convert the AAF into a night-bombing force like Bomber Command or of his sneering attitude toward the Americans' "most obstinate perseverance in this [daylight bombing] method."[3]

By the time Roosevelt and Churchill met at Casablanca on January 14, 1943, Arnold had heard of Churchill's intentions. Never squeamish about putting a subordinate on the line, Arnold rushed Eaker from England to defend daylight strategic operations. Eaker personally took his case to Churchill, assembling the arguments for the daylight bomber, principally the economy of force achievable through greater precision. Eaker's position was tricky, for he had little new to say to the British, and he had to defend the Eighth Air Force without appearing to derogate the RAF's contribution. As before, the best tack was to deny conflict: British and American operations would be complementary, not competitive, the British destroying urban areas, the Americans hitting bottleneck targets or marking them by fire for British attack at night. Together they would engage the German air force and cause German war-weariness by round-the-clock bombing. Twenty-four-hour operations would also head off the hopeless congestion in Britain's airfields and air space sure to result if both British and American bombers were squeezed into the same schedule. Arguing from operational necessity just as the British had in defending their switch to night bombing, Eaker also asserted that his bombers had to strike by day because they were built to do so and the crews were trained only in that method; to switch to the dark would halt the AAF's offensive altogether for months. Too, only the daylight bomber could engage the German fighter force, depleting it so as to facilitate further bombing as well as ground operations.

There was troublesome logic here. Arguments from operational necessity allowed means to dictate ends—bombing forces, British or American, did what they could do best, not necessarily what it was best to do. Shooting down German fighters became a major achievement of the American bombers, but the initial intention had been to destroy the German air force in its factories and on its airfields. If now it was to be done substantially through the attrition of combat, the task could be grim indeed, especially without long-range fighter escort.

These dangers and anomalies went largely unscrutinized. Other issues, especially a renewed quarrel about the relative priorities of the European and Pacific theaters, dominated the conference. The conferees deliberated little about how strategic bombing would bring about the enemy's defeat. It was a lapse understandable in light of the imponderables involved, the political questions that would have to be solved, and perhaps also the undertone of confidence entering Allied discussions: expanding resources and opportunities made hard questions about alternative routes to victory less pressing. The crisis over the Eighth Air Force was seen as a tactical, not a strategic, problem. The issue was how best to bomb, not how to win the war through bombing, and the tidy round-the-clock formula averted hard choices even on that matter.

Eaker and Arnold won their case with Churchill and the Combined Chiefs. The upshot of the conference for the Anglo-American air forces was essentially a codification of previous agreements and inclinations. The Combined Chiefs' formula directed Allied bombers both to destroy the "German military, industrial and economic system" and to undermine "the morale of the German people to a point where their capacity for armed resistance is fatally weakened." The ambiguous wording—"fatally weakened" was a wonderful example—left unanswered the question of what kind of invasion would be required and how its timing would fit with the schedule of bombing. Furthermore, the specific objectives listed—submarine construction yards, the aircraft industry, transportation, oil production, and other enemy industries—left broad latitude to air force commanders and bore little relation to the campaign of area destruction that the RAF mounted with increasing fury. The Allies also accorded the RAF broad authority over Eighth Air Force operations, reserving to American commanders "the technique and method to be employed." Commanding unquestionably the junior force, American leaders were for the moment content with that provision.[4]

Now Arnold and Eaker had more time but only, as it turned out, to meet unexpected challenges. With continued diversions of bombers, trained crews, and shipping to other operations, the Eighth could not attack Germany in force until May, dispatching 279 bombers on the twenty-ninth. The bulk of Eaker's effort remained directed at German submarines: construction yards in Germany and the concrete pens on the French coast. That campaign substantially failed, not for lack of accuracy but because of enemy resiliency. Entire French port towns were leveled until, as Germany's Admiral Karl Doenitz declared, "No dog nor cat is left in these towns. Nothing but the submarine shelters remain."[5] Of course, they were all the German navy needed. Likewise, sub-building yards in Germany were struck, but little reduction in production resulted. In what became a recurrent pattern, Allied intelligence also badly underestimated Nazi resourcefulness. Meanwhile, resentment grew in occupied countries over the heavy civilian casualties inflicted by American raids, including those against French and Belgian factories and transportation facilities. Prewar theory had not even anticipated that problem. At best, the Eighth's gains in the first half of 1943 took the form of hard-won lessons in the tactics, politics, and critical analysis of strategic operations. Earlier hopes of demolishing the German air force were dashed by increasingly effective enemy fighter tactics as well as by the Eighth's inability to strike with the force on which those hopes rested.

Arnold and Marshall beat their wings in impatience. Both approached Roosevelt for greater support for the bombing campaign. Marshall advised the president that, owing to lack of numbers, the airmen "have never been able even to approximate the techniques in which they have built up the proposition of daylight precision bombing." Arnold held out to Harry Hopkins the lure of an attack on German ball-bearing production which "would probably wreck all German industry." He pleaded that all he required for success was "the green light from the Commander in Chief to accumulate an adequate air striking force in England." In truth, there was little Roosevelt could do. He had already given the bombing campaign strong support. To do more would have jeopardized other operations and plunged Roosevelt into interservice and inter-Allied rivalries. Only when political considerations of Allied unity arose was he willing to take that step.[6]

Failing to make headway up the chain of command, Arnold vented his frustration against Allies and subordinates. He complained bitterly that the British had no intention of invading Europe, preferring instead an early surrender by Germany that would leave it intact as a buffer against the Soviet Union. He hectored his staff, especially Eaker, about a host of failings. For his part, Eaker was already furious about lagging shipments and the sagging morale of his overworked men. A sharp-tongued polemicist, he sent Arnold a scathing indictment of Washington for diverting elsewhere the forces it had promised him, throwing in a lengthy discussion of how the Russians might well feel betrayed by the American failure to take on Germany proper and react in a way "everyone who can remember August of 1939 knows well." Eaker's outburst did not silence Arnold for long, and finally Eaker protested that he was not "a horse which needs to be ridden with spurs." Meanwhile in June, Arnold leveled a blast at all of his combat commanders, warning that "we are not in a position to ignore costs and to win by brute force alone." With the recent controversy over French and Belgian casualties in mind, he added that "careless inaccurate bombing" could poison "international amity for years after the war is over." Each airman was reminded that "he is handling a weapon which can be either the scourge or the savior of humanity according to how well he uses it."[7]

Arnold's upbraiding of his commanders was not just empty posturing. He appreciated the tendency of a huge and widely scattered organization to slip out of its chief's control and settle into comfortable routine. But these injunctions also revealed his confusion and anxiety at the midpoint of war. Only a few months earlier he had seemed indignant about the very qualms he now raised, maintaining that "this is brutal war and . . . the way to stop the killing of civilians is to cause so much damage and destruction and death that civilians will demand that their government cease fighting. This doesn't mean that we are making civilians or civilian institutions a war objective, but we cannot 'pull our punches' because some of them may get killed."[8] Now in June he sought, by presenting the bomber as "either the scourge or the savior of humanity," to draw on the faded dualism of prewar argument and posit illusory choices. Certainly he feared that the "fondest hopes" of air power advocates, as he put it in June, were now in jeopardy. His personal health as precarious as that of the air force, he may as well have despaired of his own fortunes.

In a war of vast organizations and impersonal strategies, an individual leader's impact was not always decisive. But Arnold showed how personal and organizational anxiety provided one spur to escalation of the air war. It was not necessarily Arnold's intention to make that war more costly or brutal—efficiency, the clean kill, promised large rewards for the man and the air force. But intention and result did not always correlate.

How they could diverge was already evident in the spring of 1943, when the British and Americans once again reviewed bombing policy. The occasion arose in May when Eaker's command presented its operating plan for the Combined Bomber Offensive (Operation POINTBLANK as it was codenamed) to the Joint and Combined Chiefs. On some points, Eaker's plan represented a dubious but politically necessary compromise. By placing priority on submarine yards and bases, the plan did not reason from operational necessity—from what the bomber could do—and instead, despite mounting appreciation of how invulnerable the submarine targets were, responded to assessments of what needed to be done in winning the Atlantic battle. With more success, the AAF also employed B-24s in direct aerial operations against the subs at sea. But to admit that the submarine war was better won that way would have undercut longstanding claims for the air forces as an independent strategic weapon. In that sense, organizational goals were perhaps foremost in the Eaker plan.

The determination of bombing strategy and methods could be surprisingly casual. The strategists reviewing Eaker's plan did dovetail the bomber offensive with the planned invasion, partly because they had by then set a date for the invasion. Too, Marshall now put the greatest stress on success of the bomber offensive, seeing it as essential if dwindling reserves of manpower were not to be exhausted by invasion and casualties were not to become intolerable. Without bombing, invasion "would be a visionary matter," he told the Joint Chiefs on May 15. But otherwise Allied strategists focused on the tactics and logistics involved in carrying out the Eaker plan, offering little scrutiny of its strategic rationale. Though nominally a blueprint for RAF operations as well, Eaker's plan in fact spoke largely to the American effort. Allied strategists made little provision for coordinating the RAF and AAF campaigns, instead retreating again into the comfortable formula that the two were "entirely complementary."[9]

This was hardly the case. Without the closest cooperation, the RAF might destroy vast urban areas but leave important industries still substantially functioning; similarly, the AAF could attack those industries without achieving the cumulative effect desired. The two forces operated "along lines not so nearly parallel as some of the Americans originally had assumed."[10] By pursuing divergent objectives, the Allies honored only in the breach a fundamental maxim of strategic air war (indeed, of all war) on which the better prophets had insisted: limiting objectives, adhering to them tenaciously, attacking them repeatedly. Indeed, only by abiding by that rule could Allied air forces salvage what military and moral virtue remained in their weapon. Widely dispersed efforts threatened to cause—to use an anachronistic but appropriate term—overkill: redundant and pointless destruction.

1943: THE COLLAPSE OF RESTRAINTS

The potential for overkill was borne out in the summer of 1943, as Bomber Command struck German cities with increasing ferocity, Eaker responded to Arnold's lash with raids against Nazi industries, and in the Mediterranean theater, where most American bombers were still stationed, the AAF attacked Italian targets. In bombing Rome, the AAF successfully avoided most of the religious and historical buildings whose threatened destruction had bothered Allied consciences. Before and after the Rome raid of July 19, the RAF aimed its blunter sword at Italy's northern cities. Striking a powerful blow at Italian morale and Mussolini's government, the two air forces achieved the war's most decisive demonstration of old promises that the bomber would win wars through shock rather than sustained destruction. But Mussolini's government was by then a hollow shell, its collapse too easy to permit large claims for air power. Furthermore, so slight had been enemy opposition to the Rome attack that General Carl Spaatz thought the raid "too easy" to prove much of interest to the air force.[11]

Meanwhile, from England the Anglo-American air forces opened major offensives. In tonnage as well as havoc wreaked Bomber Command still shouldered the heavier burden. Its main technique, pioneered in 1942 with the thousand-plane raids, remained massive assaults with incendiaries on urban areas. By 1943, the technique had much advanced because new tactics and devices aided target identification, the control of bomber operations, and confusion of enemy defenses. Harris first waged the widely touted Battle of the Ruhr but achieved his greatest and most revealing success in four furious assaults on Hamburg during late July and early August.

At Hamburg, everything came together for Harris. The city's location by water gave it a vivid profile to the eyes of men and radar, one rarely possible in the air war on Germany. Bomber Command addressed the chronic problem of "creep-back"—the tendency of aerial "fringe merchants" to bomb short of the aiming point and thereby disperse the whole bombing pattern—simply by turning it into a virtue: exploiting the tendency by laying out a carpet of bomb drops. Most critically, the RAF finally introduced "Window"—bundles of aluminum-coated strips which overwhelmed enemy radar. Earlier withheld for fear that the Germans would copy it—they did, since few technical advances in the war waited long for mimicry—Window temporarily blinded fighter defenses. Even the weather cooperated: hot and dry. The second Hamburg raid ignited the war's first great firestorm.

It was a meteorological phenomenon in its own right. Dropped by 731 attacking bombers, incendiaries started thousands of fires while high explosives blasted open paths by which they could rapidly travel. As they merged and intensified, their greed for oxygen sucked in the fresher air from the fringes of the cauldron, the bellowslike draft creating terrific winds that sent bodies, trees, and parts of buildings flying through air heated to 800° centigrade. Naturally centripetal, a fire that " 'drew' like a giant chimney,"[12] the storm nonetheless expanded as "creep-back" widened the area demanding its gaseous fuel.

The firestorm erupted so rapidly that the population caught in it was trapped. Measures that were sensible in a high-explosive attack—rushing to shelters and basements—were disastrous because the fire drained these quarters of oxygen, asphyxiating inhabitants, then baking the bodies through radiant heat or, if the fire burst through collapsing walls, melting them into "a thick, greasy black mass" or leaving behind what the Germans called *Bombenbrandschrumpfleichen* (incendiary-bomb-shrunken bodies). Radiant heat was particularly deadly, working in the same odd ways it would at Hiroshima and Nagasaki: "In many cases, when stockings were worn, they were not even singed, although the skin and underlying structures were severely damaged." The quick-witted could only flee into "a blizzard of red snowflakes" where they often became human torches in the streets, found "marked with a waxen pallor like dummies in a shop window"; or they succumbed from heat or asphyxiation even if they reached waterways. Probably more than forty thousand Germans died.

As the Hamburg police-president commented, "The calamity is as much perceived in the process of destruction as in the accomplished fact." Not merely death but the manner of death, not merely destruction but its otherworldly suddenness and totality triggered among survivors the sense of a world-ending event, one "transcending all human experience and imagination." Theirs was a speechless horror, one usually identified later only with the victims of atomic bombing. For the few who escaped the vortex of the storm, the experience dwarfed all other emotions. Even the police-president's report allocated few words to "the murderous lust of a sadistic enemy." It was the death of the city itself, not antecedents and results, that he struggled to comprehend.[13]

In its murderousness, the Hamburg firestorm was also a fluke, "like a hole in one in a game of golf," devoutly desired and almost irreproducible. The third and fourth raids on the city produced no comparable toll, in part because a vast exodus limited further casualties. Yet nothing distinguished the second raid from countless others during the war except for the unpredicted convergence of forces which the British routinely tried to exploit. The raid's planning and success simply revealed British intentions more nakedly than usual. All the Hamburg raids targeted residential, especially working-class areas of the city, a frequent RAF practice. But because Hamburg's waterways so clearly separated residential from industrial areas, the subterfuge often permissible during the war—that area raids were only an efficient means of destroying economic objectives, dictated by operational necessity—dissolved, though able historians characterize the area attacks misleadingly as "indiscriminate bombing of industrial targets." Harris, who at least had the virtue of an ugly honesty rare in high circles, was closer to the mark in his memoirs, when he referred to "the destruction of factories" as only "a bonus." The rationale for British bombing methods had clearly changed from the early days of area bombing, when the destruction of workers and their housing had been deemed the regrettable by-product of industrial raids. Hamburg marked grim progress toward a goal for bombing once proposed by Harris's superior, Sir Charles Portal—killing 900,000 Germans and rendering 25 million homeless.[14]

Hamburg revealed that Harris sought victory not by disarming Germans of their sword or disabling the forge that produced it, but by destroying the people manning the forge; and at that not through some sudden shock to their morale, which Harris now thought unlikely, but through sustained attrition of their habitats and lives. Americans knew this, Eaker's spring plan making clear that the RAF was to engage in the "mass destruction" of German cities. The directive for the "battle" of Hamburg had made the RAF's objective the "total destruction" of the city as a method to "achieve immeasurable results in reducing the industrial capacity of the enemy's war machine."[15]

"Immeasurable," perhaps just a slip of the pen, also suggested how soft were the calculations justifying this bombing. British strategists scarcely did more than prewar theorists in detailing the connection between planned destruction and the enemy's defeat. But as Max Hastings has written, "If a precise definition of success was not arrived at, nor was a yardstick of failure." Admirals whose ships sank or generals who lost ground could be sacked. Air marshals could not so clearly be judged. Intangible criteria invited unlimited escalation. As Churchill put it after the war, "the debt" the Germans incurred by their blitz of England "was repaid tenfold, twentyfold, in the frightful routine bombardment of German cities. . . . Certainly the enemy got it all back in good measure, pressed down and running over." "Immeasurable results," then, were commensurate with almost infinite vengeance.[16]

Harris's reasoning might have taken on a brutal legitimacy if consistently implemented. Success at Hamburg demonstrated the virtue of returning relentlessly to a target, and it dismayed the Nazi leadership. True, Hitler had his *Götterdämmerung* fantasies—he once stated that the aerial "devastation actually works in our favour, because it is creating a body of people with nothing to lose . . . who will therefore fight on with utter fanaticism." But the Nazi elite remembered too well the home front's supposed collapse in 1918 to regard the destruction of cities callously. For their part, some British commanders hoped, as one put it, that the Hamburg raids would break "the whole of the Gestapo grip on the population."[17]

Yet the very apathy induced by such a tremendous shock strengthened the grip of the Nazi state, which moved swiftly to succor the city and its survivors. Resentment at the Allies—more noticeable outside the stunned city—may have stiffened the resistance of other Germans. And Harris's bombers, by moving on to other cities, overlooked the virtue of more persistence and allowed the city's industries to recover lost ground. British bombing in the months ahead took on almost an aimless quality, piling up vast rubble, yet too dispersed in time and space to apply a decisive shock to either morale or production. By 1943, the RAF had developed the capacity to do area bombing but not to make it effective. Its bombing was stark testimony to the ease with which men equated the destructiveness of air power with its decisiveness. In this way, too, intentions did not produce results.

The assault on Hamburg also demonstrated the fiction of complementarity. While Harris struck residential areas by night, Eaker hit Hamburg's docks and factories by day. Yet the AAF strikes were too light and scattered—it was not easy to find targets in a smouldering city—to complement the British effort. British and American bomber staffs met frequently, and requests for supporting efforts were usually received cordially, but the process was ad hoc, geared to missions of the moment, not toward sustaining mutually reinforcing efforts over the life of the aerial campaign.

In Britain, few doubts surfaced about the wisdom of the Hamburg raids and their place in overall strategy. American reporters, free to find satisfaction in the British raids without worry of American culpability, frankly described their objective as "the wrecking of all housing." But the British press reported the raids in ways typical of what a restrained English historian has called "a three-year period of deceit practised upon the British public and on world opinion." Newspapers described the targets as "important factories" and "dock quarters" and savaged the few religious leaders who protested. Qualms were recorded by Liddell Hart, two decades earlier the author of a sensational prophecy of air war, and by J. F. C. Fuller, who fulminated against England's "Goths, Vandals, Huns." But they had trouble getting into print and failed to have much impact. Politicians on the left had sometimes criticized the strategic bombing effort, not on moral grounds, but because they believed bombing to be a poor substitute for invasion in assisting the Soviet Union. Among RAF airmen, those most familiar with Hamburg's fate, doubts sometimes arose, but as one later asked, "To whom could you express such doubts? . . . What would have been the result? Court martial!"[18]

American leaders did learn something from the Hamburg assaults. The firestorm was carefully studied by American experts, particularly with an eye to the bombing of Japan. Roosevelt saw in Hamburg "an impressive demonstration" of what America might achieve against Japan, a hope Arnold reinforced for him several months later. Moreover, after Hamburg, and until pragmatic concerns imposed some caution, Anglo-American bombers struck Balkan capitals ferociously, attempting to "terrorize Balkan civilians without appearing to use terror tactics." Planning officers had cause for continued concern, however, for the precise effect of the Hamburg raids on German production was difficult to measure, and intercepts of diplomatic messages from Japan's Berlin embassy offered discouraging evidence. More certainly, American experts appreciated that the "numbness and apathy" caused among Germans by Allied bombing might allow only for the further consolidation of Nazi rule.[19]

Confirmation of that apprehension came over the following winter from a "secret source," apparently an agent in Berlin. True, on many accounts the agent's report was encouraging. It described a capital that, after massive RAF raids in November, "has ceased to exist," mired in defeatism and verging on total anarchy. "To sleep, to take a rest, a bath, or change linen, is the first concern,—not going to work or doing one's duty." Germans resented privileges accorded the Nazi elite and resented the destruction the working population endured. "Everybody may abuse everybody. . . . The only man whom you may not abuse, but whom everybody makes responsible for the destruction of Berlin, is Chancellor Hitler." Pillage and theft were rampant, the native population petrified that "barbaric hordes" of foreign workers "will plunder the houses and shops still undestroyed." Returning soldiers were dispirited, officers and businessmen eager for the opportunity to overthrow the vile regime. Many Germans hoped "for the destruction of the industrial districts of Berlin" and were "astonished that . . . bombs should be showered on spots where no important installations of the war machinery are located." Most hated the Nazi system and relieved "their bad conscience" over supporting it "by hiding Jews and providing them with all things necessary." In short, "the total population of Berlin sits caught in a mouse-trap." Only the grip of the party, the paralyzing fear of the Soviets, and the survival of the factories prevented collapse or rebellion. But these were critical exceptions. For all the report's portrait of appalling death, disintegration, and defeatism—and comments perhaps designed to exculpate the German people—it also hinted at RAF failure.[20]

But American leaders did not complain to the British. They could not easily have done so, given their long-standing acquiescence in British methods, plus the AAF's own experiment that winter with a variation of those methods. As for the moral and political issues raised by indecisive destruction, they emerged most clearly through the threat of reprisals by Germans against captured Allied airmen. Such threats commonly force leaders to erect moral positions they may otherwise neglect, and so it was that winter. For the air force's chief lawyer, the moral defense was that American bombs had been aimed only at "military objectives," Americans had waged only "civilized war," and any reprisals would be "barbaric acts." To deter such acts, the United States should promise in return "the destruction of . . . every village and hamlet." (To avoid needlessly provoking the Nazis, the AAF should remove "all names with a terror connotation, such as 'Murder, Inc.,' from planes, clothing and equipment.")

The judge advocate's willingness to promise destruction to all Germans as punishment for their leaders' acts indicated the scanty restraints holding back Americans from a campaign of terror bombing. It also carried little deterrent value, inasmuch as the British had already embarked on such a campaign. Nonetheless, Marshall recommended to FDR a more guardedly worded version of the judge advocate's warning. The president suggested that German POWs would be a more appropriate hostage than German civilians, and therefore Marshall drafted a statement warning "that for each Allied airman sentenced . . . 10,000 German prisoners, or other German males . . . will be selected and detained subsequently to the imposition of peace terms."[21]

If the moral and political basis for resisting British bombing was weak, strategic objections nonetheless remained substantial. American planners continued to worry about the dispersion of the Allied bombing effort and the need for firmer Anglo-American agreement to limit attacks to "a few really essential industries" in a plan "adhered to with relentless determination."[22] But pending such agreement, whatever success the AAF was to achieve had to be largely independent of the British effort.

1943–44: THE RETURN OF BATTLE

Eaker sought to get it by striking Germany's bottleneck industries, in line with the classic precepts of American bombing doctrine. Unable to persuade Harris to undertake such a campaign, some British experts welcomed Eaker's effort. Even Harris, although unsympathetic to American methods, promised that if diversions could be stopped, "we can push Germany over by bombing this year." Now, too, Eaker had a respectable force—three hundred or more bombers could be sent out with some regularity, and only shortages of crews prevented a higher rate of attack. He was also running out of excuses acceptable to Arnold for failing to make effective attacks on Germany. Curtis LeMay, Eaker's most promising combat commander, later wrote with typical sarcasm that the new offensive "was the outgrowth of a search by those intellectual souls in Plans and Intelligence to find an easy way of winning the war in Europe. That's just about like searching for the Fountain of Youth—there *is* no such thing; never was." But the doctrine behind the summer offensive had been the airmen's own creation. Combined with political pressures, it led Eaker, who earlier had expanded his operations cautiously, to campaign recklessly.[23]

From late July through much of October, Eaker's bombers flew in desperate assaults on German factories, particularly those supplying the Luftwaffe fighter force. On August 17 came the first of two peak efforts. Divided into two forces, 376 B-17s were to strike far into Germany, LeMay's group at the Messerschmitt factory at Regensburg, another at the ball-bearing complex at Schweinfurt. The two forces were to be synchronized to divide and confuse enemy fighters, LeMay's to go in first, then fly across the Alps to a base in North Africa. But because of bad weather LeMay's bombers went on alone, bereft of fighter escort and of the diversion which the succeeding force was to supply. Only hours later could the Schweinfurt group make its strike. Enemy fighters took an awful toll of the two American forces. Sixty bombers were downed, and as always during the war, attrition also took other forms—loss of some of the best crews, battle damage to dozens more aircraft, irretrievable time lost when the North African bases could not service LeMay's planes.

To the bomber commander losses on a given day may mean relatively little. What depleted Eaker's force was the high level of attrition endured for two months more, capped by the Black Week in October, when 148 Flying Fortresses succumbed, 60 alone in one day's dual assault on Schweinfurt, along with six hundred crewmen killed or captured. The Eighth had, in the words of the official history, "for the time being lost air superiority over Germany."[24] In fact, it never really had achieved such superiority, and its position was much like what it had been a year earlier. Although the scale of operations was far vaster in 1943 and the penetration far deeper, the considerable damage done to the enemy seemed almost incidental to the issue of the Eighth's sheer survival.

The Eighth's bomb strikes had been heavy and punishing, particularly when incendiaries struck delicate equipment used in ball-bearing manufacture. The strikes triggered panic in the German high command. Yet the Nazis never suffered seriously from shortages of antifriction ball bearings; fighter output dipped slightly for a while, then rose again. This is not to say that production reached the level it would otherwise have sustained or that production alone measured enemy strength. But American success primarily took subtle, indirect forms: the strain on the Luftwaffe, particularly the depletion of its best crews, encountered in prolonged combat with the day bombers; lost production time as factories were dispersed and reorganized, often into less efficient operations; other demands on German sources—not just aircraft and crews, but the two million soldiers and civilians tied down in ground-based air defense. In short, progress came through grim attrition of the enemy, and in the battle of attrition no clear winner had yet emerged. Even indirect gains had paradoxical effects—dispersal interrupted production but also made enemy factories harder to strike in the long run.

The AAF's troubles derived in part from three miscalculations recurrent in the air war. Allied intelligence usually overestimated damage, especially the long-run disruption it would cause. It also underestimated Germany's resilience. In turn, these Allied miscalculations obscured the virtues of relentless return to the same targets. By the end of October, Eaker's bombers were in no position to be relentless anyway. Yet there is little evidence that air commanders saw the need for early follow-up against ball-bearing manufacture.[25] On a tactical level, lessons were learned better. Opinion was unanimous that the American bomber offensive could not continue without long-range fighter escort. The primacy of the unescorted bomber had always been a boast by the youthful air force, politically useful but not strategically essential. Its weakness had long caused concern, too, but in a war of vast operations and demands only the utmost urgency would counteract prevailing policy. That came only in the summer and fall of 1943, yielding an improved P-51 Mustang fighter that was to play a decisive role in the air battles of 1944.

Meanwhile, OVERLORD, the Allied invasion of France, was fast approaching, and the time fast diminishing before RAF and AAF bombers would be transformed by invasion into little more than a glorified support force for a conventional strategy. And invasion itself would be imperiled if the German air force were not defeated. Far from validating aerial doctrine and rescuing the Eighth's tenuous fortunes, the recent campaign, with losses unavoidably publicized, threw the AAF command into a renewed crisis heightened by the imminence of invasion.

Crisis was also aggravated by a lag in preparations to bomb Japan. Hopes to use Siberian bases for that purpose, as predictably recurrent as the seasons, had generated more staff studies, frustrating negotiations, and no results. Roosevelt on occasion derived optimism from "evidence in the recent disputes between Japan and Russia that the Russians have no cause to love Japan." But Roosevelt felt more urgency about getting bombers into China, a priority still governed, as so often in the long record of American air power in Asia, more by politics than strategy. Nineteen forty-three brought no relaxation of popular pressures to lay waste first to Japan, "the enemy whom the American people really hated," as Stimson once pointedly reminded Churchill. Just as important, the bomber could be offered as the token of American support to a client of doubtful loyalty and perseverance. As FDR advised the Joint Chiefs during the Casablanca conference, "periodic bombing raids over Japan . . . would have a tremendous morale effect on the Chinese people." The hope also persisted that air power would help defeat Japan without an invasion. FDR signaled to the American public his intention to begin the bombing quickly instead of moving "forward inch by inch, island by island," a method that "would take about fifty years before we got to Japan."[26]

After all, Chennault had been promising nothing less than "the collapse of Japan" by methods such that "the lives of hundreds of thousands of American soldiers and sailors will be saved." In turn Roosevelt continued to apply the screws to the War Department, giving the matter far more attention than the much weightier air effort being mounted against Germany. Finally, in April 1943, the Flying Tiger himself, along with General Joseph Stilwell, the American commander in China, returned to the states for discussions that sometimes turned ugly. To Stilwell, Chennault's plans were a pipe dream because the Chinese would never defend the air bases. They "stopped fighting about three years ago," he advised. As for military operations, "The Generalissimo has no plan. If he had one it wouldn't be the one he would have tomorrow morning anyway." He was simply "a very slick political manipulator." In contrast, Chennault promised a big boost to Chinese morale, attacks on Japanese cities, and a fatal assault on Japanese shipping. Marshall and Arnold were eager enough to bomb Japan, but the logistical and military obstacles against doing so from China were staggering. "It requires a massive effort here to get a pin point out there," Marshall lamented. Earlier, he had called Chennault's designs "just nonsense; not strategy, just nonsense." Backed by Roosevelt, Chennault got commitments to increases in aircraft and the supplies coming over the Hump route, but not enough for a blow against Japan or even for success against Japanese forces in China.[27]

Until well into 1943, the political importance Roosevelt attached to bombing from Chinese bases had paralleled the strategic priorities of the military command. The paucity of American resources for the Pacific war, the immensity of Chinese armies, the pull of China's plight all coincided to accord China a pivotal place in American plans. By August 1943, planners recognized how their strategy had been made hostage to China's ill fortunes. The Combined Staff was now projecting a bomber offensive for 1947, a dismaying prospect to Arnold's staff. The 1947 timetable was no less satisfying to Admiral Ernest J. King or to Marshall, who feared that a "growing impatience" for quick victory over Japan would develop among Americans once Germany collapsed. Roosevelt was pressing for a shortcut to Japan lest the war go on for "one hundred years." Referring to Hamburg's recent fate, he suggested, "We can use Siberian air fields . . . to attack the heart of Japan in a manner that she will find it hard to endure."[28]

The air staff began scrambling for other ways to strike Japan. The new B-29 bombers, once slated to go to Europe, promised a greater weight and range of effort if the bases could be found. The staff attempted to cut through the thicket of logistical and political barriers against operating out of China by proposing that B-29s stage out of India, using advance bases in China only to refuel and load bombs. In the longer run, the Mariana Islands promised to provide bases free of the problems arising in flying from Siberia or China. Above all, the political imperative of aiding China drove the planning forward. Arnold's staff set June 1, 1944, as a tentative date for activating B-29s in China. Arnold, despite knowing that B-29 production was lagging, pledged to Roosevelt to advance the date to March 1, though there were few illusions that bombing from China would be decisive.[29]

Arnold's promise only raised Roosevelt's mood from impatience to fury. In unusually sharp words, he wrote to Marshall that he was "still pretty thoroughly disgusted with the India-China matters. The last straw was the report from Arnold that he could not get the B-29's operating out of China until March or April next year. Everything seems to go wrong. But the worst thing is that we are falling down on our promises every single time." In other words, political embarrassment bothered Roosevelt more than strategic delay—a renewed round of complaints from Chiang and Chennault did not help his temper—but he had little choice except to approve Arnold's plan.[30]

Roosevelt's explosion came on October 15, right in the midst of the sickening losses of Black Week. It also came after months of promises, in the high command and in the press, about decisive blows from the air force. Arnold tried to deal with the press. He all but begged Eaker "not (repeat) not [to] miss any symptoms of impending German air collapse," and Eaker offered reassurances about "the last final struggles of a monster in his death throes" and "our teeth in the Hun Air Force's neck"—echoes of the unwarranted optimism of a year earlier. Arnold avoided those particular catchphrases before the press, choosing to emphasize the precision of the attack on Schweinfurt and implying paralyzing damage to the German war economy. "Now we have got Schweinfurt," he said with soldierly simplicity and overstatement. Like Eaker's private comments to Arnold, Arnold's public statements fended off anticipated criticism only by increasing expectations still further.[31]

Meanwhile, more substantive responses to the autumn crisis went forward. Strategists of air war had long maintained that losses would decline and damage increase in geometrical rather than arithmetical proportion to increases in bomber strength. They redoubled their efforts to bring the Eighth Air Force bombers and crews up to planned strengths, which had never been met. By December, the Eighth could send out over seven hundred heavies on missions, and it was joined by then by the Fifteenth Air Force based in Italy. Pending arrival of effective long-range fighter escorts, however, these two forces largely marked time.

By this stage in the war, production lines and training camps ground out the interchangeable parts of the war machine with such efficiency that supply no longer posed formidable problems. Differing strategic and political interests were timeless, however, and still mounting as England and the Mediterranean became an impenetrable tangle of bases, competing commands, overlapping jurisdictions, and baroque lines of authority. Plenty only made this tangle more dense and ambitions more intense. In the fall of 1943, the Allies made one last attempt to unscramble it, with only partial success. A renewed effort to streamline target objectives and tighten Anglo-American coordination fell victim to the differing bombing methods of the two air forces and to their wish to continue informal coordination that allowed each largely to go its own way. A truly unified effort threatened to subordinate one part to another. Simplification of priorities made little headway, and interest in a combined command for all Anglo-American strategic air forces was never serious. Finally in February, the two allies revised priorities by providing for "mutually supporting attacks" on the part of the RAF and AAF to be "pursued with relentless determination against the same target areas or systems."[32] These were fine words, and the priority assigned to the German air force was now incontestable, the essential prerequisite for both OVERLORD and further bombing. But no mechanism yet existed to enforce adherence, particularly on the RAF's part, to stated objectives.

In lieu of such a mechanism, a measure of centralized control emerged only at other levels. A unified command was created for the U.S. Strategic Air Forces in Europe, placed in the charge of General Carl Spaatz. At the tactical level, where no fiction of complementarity could disguise the need for intimate coordination during the coming invasion, an Allied Expeditionary Air Forces was created subordinate to Eisenhower, the newly appointed Supreme Commander. The command structure was thus set by the start of 1944, except for temporary alterations dictated by OVERLORD.

Eaker was the victim of this reshuffling. Arnold made him commander of Allied air forces in the Mediterranean—perhaps not a step downward on paper but one which

Eaker bitterly resented and contested. Arnold, often brutally blunt, offered him only bureaucratic phrases about "the dictates of world-wide air operations."[33] The official line was that Eisenhower wanted Spaatz with him in England because the two had already worked together so closely, and the Supreme Commander was not to be denied. But if Arnold took no overt steps to oust Eaker from the Eighth Air Force, he also did nothing to protect him. His long record of badgering Eaker and other commanders suggests that Arnold had found the convenient opportunity to press for better results, which might come with Spaatz in overall command and General James Doolittle in Eaker's place at Eighth Air Force.

Spaatz inherited an experiment in blind bombing by radar that proved to be a short-run dead end but a significant precedent. Tactical conditions provided the rationale: winter's heavy cloud cover and the long wait for P-51s reduced opportunities for precision attacks, while the RAF's "pathfinder" technique, relying on new devices for direction of bombers by radio beams and radar scanning of targets, offered an attractive alternative. But a blunt desire to terrorize Germans also drew some American leaders to the radar technique. In a series of massive daylight assaults, using up to eight hundred bombers, the AAF tried it out against Germany's western port and industrial cities when weather was foul. Accuracy was too erratic and targets too low in priority to achieve significant results very often. But these assaults served the organizational and political imperatives of the air force to justify its massive resources by increasing operations. There was always a tendency, deriving from the lack of criteria for judging the effectiveness of bombing, to measure the latter in terms of effort made rather than results achieved. Autumn's anxiety over the Eighth's stupendous losses aggravated that tendency to the point that "the 'numbers racket' . . . was responsible for some wasted effort." It was preferable to bomb badly rather than not at all, a preference acted on with far more fury in 1945.[34]

The winter's experiment also found the RAF and AAF stumbling toward each other in technique and rationales because of parallel organizational drives and technological developments. Harris had long measured RAF efforts in terms of tonnage dropped and rubble piled up, positing only the loosest connection between those measurements and the enemy's defeat. Conversely, the AAF had never ruled out its own attacks on enemy manpower and morale, objectives whose attractiveness gained as the precision campaign floundered. By 1944, the two air forces were positioned to cross paths. The RAF was developing techniques that gave the night bombers a precision approaching that of the AAF's Fortresses and Liberators, while the Americans were beginning to loosen their definitions of precision bombing.

Before that trend could fully develop, improving weather, the Luftwaffe's threat, and the demands of OVERLORD forced the AAF back on its original track. In one week in February 1944, the Eighth, often assisted by Eaker's bombers based in Italy, launched a furious series of assaults on Germany's aviation industry. Despite long-range fighter escort, appalling losses of bombers occurred on particular missions, at the expense of twenty-six hundred Americans killed, missing, or seriously wounded. Yet

American fighter losses were astonishingly low, and so huge was the American bomber force that the bomber losses were hardly crippling. The AAF now also practiced complex diversions and maneuvers to divide and confuse the German air force, and for the week at least, the RAF struck some of the same targets, marking an unusually high degree of coordination between the two forces.

The result was success but of a kind not always anticipated or immediately understood. Again the bombs rained down on German factories, often with impressive accuracy. And yet, after a pause to complete the dispersal of the aviation industry, German fighter production began its striking upward curve, one carried through September and accompanied by manufacture of thirty thousand V-weapons. When revealed after the war, that curve seemed astonishing, a final and furious expression of Nazi efficiency.

It was hardly that. It reflected in part the Allies' inability to follow up their success with repeated attacks, in this case because OVERLORD drew many of the bombers to other targets. It reflected the skillful improvisation of Albert Speer, jerry-rigging ways to tap the sizable cushion of Germany's war economy. Speer's prodigies also disguised a slow, subtle defeat for the German air force. Increasingly, Germany's aviation became the wartime version of a shop-window air force—formidable in what it could display on a particular day, weak in those categories (reserves, trainers, transports, ground support) that insure long-run success. Furthermore, the quality and numbers of the fighter force were declining relative to Allied strengths. Above all, the lack of aviation fuel became crippling, though not until the summer of 1944. Planes were still mass produced and crews flowed in sufficient numbers, but they were badly trained because they could not get sufficient time in the air and were wasted too quickly in combat to learn the hard way.

Paradoxically, the Allies had a considerable ally in the Nazi high command. Beneath a shell of authoritarian efficiency there operated a feudal system of commands presided over by Hitler's caprice. He indulged revenge, a luxury he could not afford, in launching the "baby blitz" against England in 1944, first with bombers, then with the V-1, a pilotless plane, and the V-2 rocket. Meanwhile, the Luftwaffe attempted an ill-considered strategic bombing operation against Soviet factories. Both efforts consumed precious resources. Moreover, rockets and jet fighters lacked the numbers or the sufficient technological edge to have a decisive effect, and their development was pursued so erratically that they disrupted each other, not to mention the output of more conventional devices. There were Allied mistakes but some at least had the virtue of consistency. By comparison, Hitler's mistakes, unmonitored (though sometimes subverted) by professional bureaucracy, had consistency only in caprice.

The AAF exploited all these weaknesses through the combat forced on the Luftwaffe. The "Big Week" marked the start of this decisive battle, carried over into March when the AAF repeatedly struck Berlin. The wastage in air combat was vast in February and March. German losses increased to over 2,000 planes a month during the spring as American bombers began the oil offensive, provoking furious German air force resistance, and assisted the Normandy invasion. The German decline was, however, uneven. Flak was becoming more effective, and together with German night fighters it proved deadly in March, downing 9 percent of the huge RAF force attacking Berlin on the night of March 23–24, and 94 out of 795 British bombers dispatched to Nuremburg at the end of the month. Harris had boasted to Churchill, "We can wreck Berlin from end to end" if the Americans joined him, which they did. "It will cost us 400–500 aircraft. It will cost Germany the war." Instead, it forced Harris to suspend much of his city-busting campaign; he never resumed it with the single-minded intensity shown over the previous year.[35]

Meanwhile, Harris, Spaatz, and Churchill were strenuously opposing plans to divert their strategic forces to strike the rail network in western Europe in preparation for the invasion. The bomber commanders wanted to get on with the assault on Germany itself, both still convinced that invasion was not necessary, Spaatz now appreciating the vulnerability of Germany's highly concentrated petroleum industry. If the invasion must go on, Spaatz argued, better to leave the rail system to interdiction by tactical air forces, a method more effective and less likely to inflict casualties on French and Belgian civilians. Besides, another "diversion"—against German V-weapon launching sites—was already diluting the strategic assault on Germany.

But with Harris still scoffing at "panacea" targets like oil, he and Spaatz hardly presented a united front, despite support from Churchill, who moaned that the transportation plan "will smear the good name of the Royal Air Forces across the world." Spaatz himself was willing to place all air forces temporarily under the command of Eisenhower, who threatened to Churchill to "go home" if denied that command.[36] Pressed with special vigor by the young British scientist Solly Zuckerman, the transportation plan for attacking marshaling yards was implemented. Its success, though still disputed forty years later, was considerable, and the thousands of casualties among friendly civilians were still far fewer than anticipated in more dire forecasts. Meanwhile Spaatz, on the cheap and a bit on the sly, began the oil campaign anyway. Whatever their other merits, these splintered campaigns inflicted further attrition on the opposing German air force in the west. By D-Day, Goering's air force could not seriously challenge American day bombers and fighter escorts nor the tactical aircraft spearheading the Allied invasion. Harris had been saved by the unwelcome diversion from the further embarrassment his bombers would have suffered at the hands of flak and fighters protecting German cities.

In these complex and shifting aerial campaigns carried on from February through June, means and ends in Allied air strategy had been neatly reversed from those posited in original plans. Where once defeat of the enemy in the skies had been seen as a preliminary to the bombing of his factories—at that, a preliminary American airmen had hoped to reduce through their bombers' formidable defensive capability—now the bombing was a prod to engage the Luftwaffe, the bombers themselves bait to lure it into combat.

The air force's historians acknowledged this shift but concluded that "in terms of final results it matters little whether . . . the German planes were destroyed in the factories, on the ground, or in the skies."[37] In fact it mattered a great deal, for it greatly altered the costs and nature of victory as well as the doctrine on which the air force rested its claim to supremacy and virtue. If precision attacks did not paralyze the enemy's war economy, then victory could not come until his forces were defeated in battle and his territory occupied, precisely the traditional method of war the air prophets had hoped to avoid. And if victory came in the traditional way, the air force served fundamentally to complement traditional strategies, succeeding by a grinding attrition whose toll for both friends and enemies mocked earlier claims about the merciful speed of strategic air power. This was not the virtual end of battle once promised but only battle in new form.

That outcome was not easily foreseen because of two erroneous judgments about Nazi Germany which lay behind British and American bombing. One was the conviction that the German population would never stand up to bombing in the way the English had. That conviction, more commonly held among British leaders (though Churchill and others sometimes demurred), was self-congratulatory and unfounded. The other belief, shared in London and Washington, was that by 1942 the German economy was so fully harnessed to the war effort that any bombing would subtract from Hitler's capacity to wage war. As it turned out, there was enough slack in the German economy, and the resiliency to exploit it, that Allied bombing was slow indeed to take effect. Beyond the misjudgments about Germany, there was an unfortunate if understandable reading of the last war's lessons. Determined to avoid what one British airman had once called "a succession of Passchendaeles," strategists of air war sought victory in World War II without a land invasion, indeed without battle in the sky in that they hoped to destroy the factories and airfields that put enemy fighters into action. Some commanders doubted these propositions or backed away from them in time to avert disaster. But they were held long enough to risk disaster and pointless destruction.[38]

It has been argued that "every salient belief of prewar American air doctrine was either overthrown or drastically modified by the experience of war. Germany proved not at all vulnerable to strategic bombing." The claim is overstated. Vulnerability is a relative, not an absolute, state deriving not merely from a nation's military and economic condition, but from its willingness to endure and its enemy's capacity to mete out. As some airmen have speculated, a more decisive air war against Germany might have resulted had it enjoyed unchallenged priority, more consistency and simplicity in targeting, and more time. Yet one reason it did not achieve that priority was that airmen, through their tendency to over-promise, lost the credibility needed to sustain their claim. They also posited a purity to war-making that it never achieves, tending to regard rivalries, conflicting priorities, dispersed efforts, politically inspired missions, and impatience all as unnecessary and extraneous conditions of war. But these conditions do not intrude on war-making; they are war. Because they are, criticism of the air strategists of World War II for the randomness and rivalry that plagued their bombing effort must be tempered. Their failures were commonplace, although they had abnormal consequences, and they could not easily reduce war to a rational process that confined killing only to that necessary for victory.[39]

At the same time, air strategists, through some mixture of hubris, desperation, and expediency, had themselves set up rational process as their standard. Strategic air power was to transcend war as traditionally fought, with its futility and irrationality, its wasted effort and senseless killing. It did not because no new method of war can do so. The bombers and fighters succeeded through combat and through aiding traditional forms of combat, not, primarily, by strategic devastation (much less the threat of it once so highly regarded), however vast it was.

1943–44: THE TWISTING PATHS TO TOKYO

The airmen themselves recognized some of these paradoxes and disappointments, which acted as another source of urgency behind the effort to bomb Japan. Until well into 1944, the AAF in the Far East remained scattered over that vast theater, lacking centralized command and sometimes clear strategic direction. By January 1944, the Americans had reclaimed the Aleutians, taken Tarawa, prepared to invade the Marshalls, and were moving through New Guinea and the Solomons. The pace was slow, especially in the China–Burma–India theater. But air power, naval and marine as well as the army's, had its successes, among them the spectacular feat of shooting down Admiral Yamamoto's plane, Chennault's exploits with his shoestring air force, the assistance to MacArthur in his end runs around Japanese strongpoints, and, in combination with American submarines, heavy attrition of Japanese shipping. These achievements, it has been noted, "seem hardly to confirm postwar accusations that the Air Force is interested only in strategic bombardment."[40]

It was just as true that much of this activity, involving dispersion of the air force and its subordination to naval and ground commanders, had incurred Arnold's wrath. Nor did it yet fit into an overarching strategic plan for victory in the Pacific. Even more so than in waging the European war, American and Allied strategists struggled to pin down strategic concepts and timetables. Their conflict and confusion became evident when they debated what use to make of the B-29s earmarked for operations from China–India bases. By November 1943, Arnold's operations analysts had identified merchant shipping and steel production as promising targets. But while the navy, MacArthur, and some air commanders hoped to employ the new bombers out of Australian bases General Haywood Hansell, advancing the viewpoint of Arnold's staff, plugged for attacks on steel production in Manchuria and Japan from bases in China. Only when the issue reached the Joint Chiefs and Arnold took it to Roosevelt was it settled, in the air force's favor. As Roosevelt put it to Chennault, "I have had a hope that we could get at least one bombing expedition against Tokio before the second anniversary of Doolittle's flight. I really believe the morale effect would help!" Bombers in Australia could not do that.[41]

In strategic terms, Roosevelt's decision, based as it was on long-standing political considerations, settled little. The debate had taken place in a familiar vacuum of policy because neither side could relate its position to an agreed-upon strategy for victory. Those seeking to strike at Japan's ships and fuel in the southwest Pacific looked toward a quick payoff that would assist an advance on Japan by ground and sea. Conversely, Arnold's staff stuck to their position because they sought victory without resort to traditional methods. Neither side invoked higher authority because higher authority had made no decision on the ultimate method of victory, whether by strategic devastation, invasion, or a combination of the two. Nor could they relate their preferred methods to a strategic timetable, for none existed.

Indecision stemmed in part from the one premise about global strategy that had governed since 1941: concentration on Europe first. Even in January 1944, invasion of Japan seemed too remote to compel close attention to what role it would have in victory over Japan. In addition, military leaders preferred, as they had often during the war, to address logistical and technological problems before deciding on strategy, and those problems loomed far larger for the Pacific than for Europe. Shipping over vast ocean distances and over the land hurdles of Asia imposed the most intractable obstacle. When Marshall had commented on the "massive effort here to get a pin point out there," he described not only a strategic problem but the orientation of staff in Washington. Admirals and generals often worried about getting the forces out there before pondering what to do with them.

Mundane problems tugged hard at Arnold over the winter of 1943–44, especially regarding the B-29. Embodying several technological advances, it was nonetheless rushed into production without testing of prototypes, so that the new aircraft required extensive modification before they became suitable for combat. In the meantime, the bomber's troubles spawned a highly critical inquiry from Senator Harry Truman's committee watching over mobilization for the war. Because Boeing could not handle all the orders for the new bomber, they were parceled out to automotive and other aviation firms, adding to the complexities of production. More than once delays infuriated Arnold and found him roaming about the country inspecting facilities that left him "appalled."[42]

Preparation of bases for the new Twentieth Air Force involved a trail of operations strung from the United States across the Pacific or the Atlantic-Middle Eastern route to India, where the primary bases were established, and then deep into China. At trail's end work proceeded by impressing a third of a million Chinese using the crudest hand methods in service to the most complex modern technology; perhaps the story was only apocryphal that the hapless Chinese who fell before the giant hand-pulled rollers used to pack runways were simply ground underneath. The building of B-29 bases was a feat that led contemporaries to seek "analogies in the building of the great pyramid of Cheops." And the physical demands of the project were not the only ones preoccupying Washington. Chiang's demands for money to finance the project were so imposing that the Twentieth Air Force's own historian, writing in 1945, reached a coy conclusion:

"One does speak of blackmail on the part of an ally, but at best this was very shrewd trading," so shrewd that it helped make the B-29 operations from China "among the most costly of the war."[43]

The Manhattan Project, itself a worry to a select few in the air force, showed how the disjunction between technical means and strategic ends was not confined to the relatively humdrum novelty of the B-29s but perversely increased in proportion to a weapon's promise. By the winter of 1943–44, all theoretical obstacles to construction of atomic bombs had been solved, and the project had become a massive engineering enterprise. Initiated with a German threat in mind, its potential use against Japan began sliding into plans with scarcely any formal review of the shift. The possibility of Germany's surrender before the bomb was ready was one factor, but both Truk and Tokyo were mentioned as targets as early as May 1943, long before dates for the end of the European war or the bomb's readiness could be predicted with precision. By 1944, the technicians' preparations for using the bomb against Japan were going forward. Apparently policymakers were assuming such use, but they rarely discussed it: their energies were still geared to countless remaining technical problems, and the formal rationale for building the bomb remained the "race between Germany and ourselves on a winner-take-all basis." When Roosevelt in September 1944 asked Vannevar Bush, his chief scientific advisor, about use against Japan, Bush replied that the issue could be "postponed for quite a time." Only Roosevelt, by methods lost to the historian, had made up his mind explicitly, agreeing that month with Churchill (but neglecting to tell his advisors) that the bomb "might perhaps, after mature consideration, be used against the Japanese."[44] To be sure, means did not have to crowd out ends—they did not for Roosevelt. Nonetheless, the pattern of concerns roughly mirrored those evident in development of "conventional" weapons like the B-29.

Finally, articulation of long-range strategy fell victim to interservice wrangles whose dimensions dwarfed what went on in Europe. There the compactness of the theater compelled at least a measure of integration among the three services and the two nations. In the Pacific, Americans were relatively free of pressure from allies. This relative freedom, however, only weakened strategy-making further. Britain in particular generated endless debate over matters peripheral to the main American effort, without forcing articulation of the fundamentals of strategy. Among the American services, the inner war over favored methods, routes, and commanders never ceased. Bound by informal rules of unanimity and watched over by a commander-in-chief tolerant of disagreement among subordinates, the Joint Chiefs did the only thing a committee could do: it compromised. If no choice could be made among approaches to Japan through the central Pacific or north from Australia or in the air with strategic bombers, all three would be taken. If one service's representative could not be granted a supreme command, then give MacArthur one force, the navy's Nimitz another, and Arnold himself command of the new Twentieth Air Force.

This approach to war was not as fractious as it sometimes seemed. The distances involved in the Pacific worked against a centralized command of the sort Eisenhower had in Europe. The services often needed each other, with the air force especially dependent on the navy's plan to seize and supply the Marianas. Less parochial commanders welcomed contributions from rival services; Admiral Chester Nimitz, doubtful that sea power alone could defeat Japan, was eager to see Japan "get the kind of thorough city-by-city demolition Germany is getting now."[45] But compromise bred duplication, and with it bloody campaigns whose ultimate contribution to victory was doubtful. Indeed, Marshall opposed invasion of the Philippines, but Roosevelt finally ruled in MacArthur's favor—another reminder that dubious campaigns were not confined to air force commanders. Furthermore, troubled minds within the services did urge the streamlining of Allied strategy, in much the same way that some officers sought to streamline Anglo-American bombing. Their efforts bore little fruit.

In this climate of strategic indecision, assumptions about the methods and purposes of air war again often revealed themselves in peripheral issues: the fate of American POWs in Japanese hands; release of information about Japanese atrocities; and possibilities of gas warfare. By September 1943, evidence of atrocities against American captives had mounted, and journalists were eager to break the story. Roosevelt and the War Department feared that early release would jeopardize efforts to deliver Red Cross supplies for American POWs in Japanese hands. In the longer run, both strategy and public opinion were at issue. Marshall wanted "the storm of bitterness" sure to arise in the United States upon release of the story to "be directed along carefully thought out lines rather than left to dissipate itself in a lurid press and unpredictable reactions." The problem, that is, was to bend popular reactions toward more effective mobilization of the war effort. More pointedly, as the joint staff planners saw the issue, release of the stories should be saved until later in order to "steel public opinion to the damage which, at that time, we are about to inflict upon the Japanese homeland."

At the Office of War Information, Elmer Davis shared similar concerns. Against the incomprehensible Japanese enemy, he worried, "it is more difficult to demand of the nation the exacting sacrifices" necessary for victory. In January 1944, when the government decided to lift the ban on atrocity stories, Davis got more specific. American knowledge of atrocities "would also serve to nullify any voices that might be raised here if we should undertake bombing of Japanese cities." But what worked at home might backfire against Americans in Japanese hands: playing up atrocity stories only increased the likelihood that Japan "will execute all prisoners" taken from American bombers, perhaps indeed all other Americans the Japanese held as well, so Arnold's intelligence officer warned. The legitimacy of that concern was evidenced by the execution earlier of three Doolittle raiders and by death sentences later imposed on B-29 aviators who fell into Japanese hands. But there was no easy way to avert further Japanese brutalities: few officials wanted to pass up the propaganda opportunity available in publicizing Japanese atrocities, much less act to stop widespread American mistreatment and execution of Japanese captives, a practice that only further sanctioned Japanese wrongdoing. As few Japanese were in American hands, Marshall told the president that the only deterrent to Japanese war crimes was to threaten that "the future of Japan as a nation, in fact that of the Japanese race itself," would be jeopardized if Japan took reprisals against American airmen. Here was a threat of extinction from which Roosevelt had backed away when a similar issue had arisen with respect to Germany.[46]

Responses to the POW dilemma displayed reinforcing anxieties and expectations about the coming air campaign. For all that the Nazis were doing in the death camps, about which American officials now had mounting evidence, they still viewed the Japanese as the more savage enemy, hence less open to limited threats. American leaders were planning their own savage campaign against Japanese cities, their flammability the object of frequent comment and temptation. Japanese savagery served as justification for the American campaign and protection against any moral doubts, official or public, about carrying it out. Countervailing forces that occasionally arose in the European campaign—concern over the fate of friendly civilians and religious institutions—rarely appeared in deliberations about air war against Japan.[47]

Restraints against the use of weapons deemed morally abhorrent were also fewer in the Pacific theater, and insofar as they existed, they arose in part out of European politics and strategy. By 1943, both sides in both theaters had made chemical and biological warfare the object of lavish anxiety, extensive preparations, and grisly testing that sometimes got out of hand. In the Pacific, not even the scruple of the Geneva Protocol bound the Americans and the Japanese, neither having officially signed the agreement. Up to 1944, the United States had concentrated on deterring its enemies' introduction of chemical weapons. The Japanese, never having experienced the use of gas in World War I and the revulsion it triggered, employed it on occasion in China without suffering the American retaliation Roosevelt had promised in 1942. By January 1944, American restraint was weakening. The Army Chemical Warfare Service and some air force officers advocated use of gas in battlefield situations and possibly in mass attacks on Japanese cities. The publication of stories on Japanese atrocities seemed to demolish remaining "compunctions of public opinion," as the New York Times's Hanson Baldwin reported; willingness to initiate gas warfare was given occasional expression in crudely sensational articles. Meanwhile, American officials were feeling the pressure of the Chinese government for retaliation.

Strategy in Europe and an unexpected Japanese move held the American government back. The army wanted "nothing . . . done to give the Germans an excuse to use a potent weapon such as gas, which could cause the failure of OVERLORD-ANVIL." The Allies' D-Day strategists had already been upset when German planes unknowingly attacked and sunk an American cargo ship preparing to unload mustard gas at a Sicilian port, killing hundreds of Americans and Italians and sparking fears that the Germans had been given an excuse to initiate gas warfare by blanketing Allied invasion forces with deadly chemicals, perhaps even radioactive gases or particles. Furthermore, while Americans ran no risk of retaliation at home, European and Asian cities would face reprisal strikes by German or Japanese airplanes carrying gas weapons. At the same time the Japanese government made "one of the unique decisions of the war" by announcing a ban on further use of gas by its forces and by embarking on unilateral disarmament of its chemical weapons. Restraint in chemical warfare, then, arose out of a balance of forces, an informal system of mutual deterrence. Lingering moral inhibitions, along with persistent doubts about the utility of gas and germs, also held the Allies in check. At that the lure to Allied leaders of taking the offensive kept surfacing—as when Churchill groped during the summer of 1944 for any scheme, even anthrax bombs, to counter the new German V-weapons. In the end, neither the British nor the Americans resorted to the more fiendish products of their laboratories. In the Asian conflict, frail doubts and inhibitions would have been even a weaker curb on American use had not global interests come into play.[48]

The temptation to use gas and to bomb in reprisal for Japanese atrocities measured the loosening of remaining restraints on all-out air war against Japanese cities. In February 1944, just as these matters reached a climax, Arnold gave Roosevelt his plan for strategic air assault on Japan. He stressed the potential and the relative ease of a systematic campaign of destroying Japanese cities by fire, creating "uncontrollable conflagrations in each of them." Arnold added, almost as afterthought, that the "urban areas are profitable targets, not only because they are greatly congested, but because they contain numerous war industries." That is, he seemed to regard military objectives as only secondary. But Arnold, now more cautious in his rhetoric, made no promises of victory through air power alone. Bombing would mark "the *second strategic phase,* (the softening up of Japan)," apparently a preliminary to some sort of invasion.[49]

On June 15, the Twentieth Air Force started the second phase. Despite the feverish pace pressed by Arnold down the chain of command, the available force was still small. But after renewed demands by Arnold for quick action and a shakedown mission against Bangkok—"the New Haven tryout before the Broadway opening," as the official history put it—some fifty B-29s struck by night against steel plants at Yawata, on the Japanese island of Kyushu. For the Army Air Forces this was a moment to savor, all the more welcome given the enormous attention the army and navy had received over the D-Day invasion. For the American audience, its message was at once celebratory and misleading: "Note that the 20th air force did not aim at a propaganda center such as Tokio, but at a vital industrial target." In fact, the B-29s could not reach Tokyo from the China bases, and "propaganda centers" were indeed in the target plans.

Arnold's staff was jubilant over the "tremendous enthusiasm" Americans seemed to display upon hearing of the raid. It was equally mindful of the "great opportunity for building confidence in the Air Forces . . . and for carrying out the long-range AAF indoctrination of the public for a strong post-war air arm." Even Japanese responses to the first B-29 raids revealed a sense of desperation there. The only discordant note in the aftermath of the Yawata mission came from the primary base for the bombers at Kharagpur, India, where airmen were "greatly disturbed" by publicity disclosing their targets, their names, and their noncombat losses of airplanes. "It serves to corroborate or bear out exaggerated claims made by the enemy and has [a] disquieting effect on families of command combat personnel." They did not wish to be publicly identified nor subjected to the pressures of "crystal gazing" about the future missions of their force. Washington, already growing cautious about claiming too much, had to control further its desire to exploit the Twentieth Air Force's work in the press.[50]

Well it did, too, for that force's 20th Bomber Command was not destined to achieve much of strategic import. Operating under every imaginable condition of adversity, the gas-guzzling B-29s had to haul most of their fuel, bombs, and other supplies from rear bases in India, on flights so long they burned up most of the fuel to be off-loaded and allowed for only a painfully slow accumulation of stocks at forward bases. The Twentieth Air Force, though commanded from Washington in strategic matters, also had to operate through a labyrinth of rivalrous and overlapping commands in the Far East. The 20th's record became a classic example of how, as Marshall knew, a mammoth effort could yield only a "pin point" effect. Tied to a long and fragile tether, the B-29s could reach only the southernmost targets in Japan, and those only with a reduced bomb load and on infrequent missions.

They should not have been sent to China. The military dividends of their operations mainly took the form of training for crews and commanders and shaking down of the untested bombers—necessities of war which could have been met elsewhere to more effect and with less waste. Even those dividends were compromised by the lead time the early missions offered to the Japanese for testing out their antiaircraft and civilian defenses in advance of the heavy assaults to come. Marshall and his staff had apparently considered junking the whole China project in February; it was scaled back in the spring even before it got started and doubts resurfaced in the summer. What kept the project going was Roosevelt's insistence, rooted in political and diplomatic calculations, and the reluctance of his military subordinates to offer challenge on a matter so dear to him.[51]

Of course, the services had never developed the strategic plan with which to contest such operations. Few criteria existed by which to sift out the essential from the merely possible. Top strategists, often referring to the flammability of Japan's cities, had argued in 1943 that "the defeat of Japan may be accomplished by sea and air blockade and intensive air bombardment." But by the end of June 1944, staff planners were explicitly challenging that assumption as "overly optimistic." Over the succeeding months, British and American strategists treated invasion as a certainty rather than a contingency in case blockade and bombardment failed. As they did so, they breathed precision and integration into strategic plans.[52]

Ironic counterpoint to the inauguration of air attacks on Japan, the new caution about success without invasion was not shared by all, and it resulted from no systematic study of the relative merits of invasion and strategic devastation or the relationship between them. Doubt simply crept in during review of countless plans on the particulars of strategy. The slow progress of the Combined Bomber Offensive against Germany may have dampened optimism; more certainly, it taught Arnold and the air force to promise less, whatever their private hopes. Blockade and bombardment, even if successful—as the navy's Admiral King thought they would be, at less cost in lives—might work too slowly in light of the "American public's distaste for long wars of attrition," a main concern for the army. Nor was there any consensus on which method promised fewer casualties. Too, reliance on naval and air power alone would idle the army's vast forces, which might be employed to speed up victory when finished with Germany.[53]

The shift in emphasis toward invasion also reflected the declining influence in Allied councils of the British, with their preference for patient and indirect methods of war. At the same time, the success of the D-Day invasion probably emboldened army planners by demonstrating the continued effectiveness of conventional strategies and carrying the promise of early victory in Europe, thereby freeing huge armies to turn against Japan. As Marshall told the Combined Chiefs of Staff on July 14, it was "now clear to the United States Chiefs of Staff that, in order to finish with the Japanese quickly, it will be necessary to invade the industrial heart of Japan"; earlier "the means for this action were not available," but now they lay "within our power."[54]

Marshall's remarks also reflected mounting evidence of Japanese resistance—the period of timely Japanese retreats was over—and determination to fight to the end. The Japanese seemed more barbaric, fanatical, and formidable than ever. The stage was set for the final fury of air war, which appeared more justified and necessary than ever and yet less likely to succeed on its own. In 1943, when the bombing of Japan was still months into the future, strategists had contemplated its war-winning potential with considerable relish, even though the same men had mostly abandoned hope for victory over Germany without invasion. By the summer of 1944, when the bombing had commenced, expectations for it were scaled down. It was a final irony that their diminution was unjustified, as events in the summer of 1945 would prove.

ESCALATION AND OPERATIONAL NECESSITY

That irony suggests one of the components of air war's escalation. The decisiveness of air power had always been higher in anticipation than in actuality. Similarly, attention to air power, to the moral and strategic issues it raised, had usually been greatest when the bombers themselves were of little use. By the time they began full operation, these issues faded because expectations themselves had shifted and other strategies demanded attention and created new hopes. In short, the least scrutiny was paid to bombing just when it was wreaking the most havoc. Britain's leaders had anguished over the role of the strategic bomber in the late 1930s and in 1940–42, when large efforts were imagined and small ones begun, but except for the renewed scrutiny demanded by OVERLORD early in 1944, British and American air forces were largely free to go their own way in the last year of the war. With regard to the war against Japan, too, discussion of air power peaked in the winter of 1943–44. After that, attention focused on ground and naval campaigns preparatory to invasion. Similarly, popular attention to air power had been intense when little else was going on but declined by June 1944, despite some more realistic journalism and the air force's momentary ecstasy over reaction to the Yawata mission.

Expectations for how the bomber's record would be revealed also proved to be erroneous. Earlier prophecies and plans, from the 1930s and the first years of the war, had foreseen the period of bomber operations as a chronologically discrete phase: the bombers would wage their campaign, and then, if necessary, other forces would follow. Few had imagined that the bomber war would climax simultaneously with the efforts of armies and navies. It was supposed to exist in splendid isolation, exposed to the undistracted glare of moral and strategic observation.

Expectations for air war were thus doubly erroneous—about its effectiveness and its exposure to scrutiny. Facing the disappointment of politicians and public, the men waging the bomber war redoubled their effort to prosecute it in hopes of seizing a recognizably decisive contribution to victory. At the same time as they escalated, their audiences were less likely to pay attention to what they were doing; their strategic devastation accumulated with few questions asked.

Air war had evolved far from what it had been in 1941, much less from what had been imagined earlier. Yet the distance from which people viewed and understood it persisted. To be sure, ignorance and misunderstanding now sprang less from lack of access to experience, more from willful choices to disregard. And the promise of the bomber, as the weapon of humane decisiveness, was attenuated. But change in circumstances and rhetoric should not be overemphasized. Earlier generations had recourse to less experience, but still to a good deal which they largely chose to ignore. The promise of the bomber had not so much disappeared as taken on more subtle expression. Air war still had a singular capacity simultaneously to attract hope and repel examination. As a weapon of apocalypse, now carrying it out, the bomber still elicited those reactions it had before the war and would after it: the twin temptations to employ it and look away from it.

When the war was just over, Liddell Hart postulated that in warfare

> aggressors—unless they are merely barbaric hordes—tend to rely on improved use of conventional weapons, and to avoid widespread destruction, whereas the incensed victims of aggression tend to be far more reckless. That is a natural tendency—because aggressors are calculating. They plan to achieve their gains with the least possible damage, both to themselves and to their acquisitions, whereas the victims of aggression are driven by an uncontrollable impulse to hit back regardless of the consequences.[55]

Liddell Hart wrote before the shattering of myths about the coolly calculating Nazi regime—which in fact operated like "barbaric hordes"—and before scholars established how calculating Allied leaders often were. Nonetheless he captured one reason that bombing was attractive to Americans during the war: for a nation that coveted not territory but influence and revenge, air power was an ideal weapon. It promised punishment, meted out too impersonally to compel close attention to the motive of revenge, and with no danger the enemy would retaliate in kind. In that sense, the remoteness of air power was not simply a permissive factor—not something that merely allowed air war to go on for other reasons—but was itself one of its appealing characteristics.

That appeal did not alone compel the use of the bomber as an instrument of strategic devastation. Certainly it does not capture the language and reasoning employed by most proponents and agents of the bombing effort. Most often, they cited variations of a necessitarian argument. Strategic bombing, they usually said, was dictated by the requirements of defeating tenacious foes, minimizing losses, and making the best use of resources. The necessitarian argument also informed much of the pioneering scholarship on the air war. Thus Noble Frankland, coauthor of a formidable history of the RAF's strategic air compaigns, argued regarding escalation of British bombing from 1940 to 1942:

> All the arguments based on strategic and economic reasons which have gone on since 1940 and, surprisingly, still go on, about the alternatives of this or that kind of attack are wholly groundless for operational reasons alone. The alternative to area bombing was either no strategic bombing or daylight bombing. In the circumstances of the time, the idea of abandoning strategic bombing was scarcely a practicable proposition though there were those who presently claimed that it might have been.

In *The Road to Total War*, F. M. Sallager reached similar conclusions: "Operational considerations, not moral sentiments or strategic objectives, governed what was actually done as the strategic bombing offensive developed. . . . As the war unfolded, the decisionmakers became as much the prisoners as they were directors of the forces they had unleashed." In short, the RAF had been compelled to attack cities if it was to make use of the bomber resources at hand. A similar argument from operational necessity often informed the American rationale for a different tactic, daylight precision bombing in Europe. Both crew training and the capacities of the B-17 and B-24 bombers made them seem suitable for little else.[56]

The historians who locate escalation in the compelling force of operational necessity are not insensitive to the tragic impact of the bombing that resulted nor to motives for revenge and aggrandizement. But they place such motives on the fringes of policy. While there is no fast distinction between motive and rationalization, the argument from operational necessity must be treated with the greatest caution, inasmuch as it often cloaked in a kind of technological determinism what leaders wanted to do for other reasons they did not often admit openly.

Operational necessities did not appear mysteriously. If leaders were prisoners of a technological determinism, it was one they themselves set into motion. They reasoned in a curiously self-fulfilling fashion when, having first created certain forces with certain capabilities, they then complained that they had no choice but to use them in unfortunate ways. In fact, however, well-placed leaders sometimes revealed how politics rather than technology guided them, as when Roosevelt wanted to placate vengeful Americans, encourage the Chinese, and limit the commitment of ground forces abroad. Moreover, operational necessity was an argument selectively employed—discarded when the Eighth Air Force targeted Nazi submarine pens against mounting evidence of how unsuitable the mission was; discarded when B-29 bombers were sent to China almost in defiance of operational constraints. Selective employment of operational arguments invites skepticism about their compelling force. Operational considerations did impose real limits on bomber forces; they were not always facile rationalizations invoked by men who viewed themselves as prisoners of their own machines; sometimes, they were even invoked to forestall foolish or needlessly destructive action. But operational requirements often translated into organizational convenience, that is, the need to keep a bomber force in action in order to justify its existence.

Finally, making decisions on the basis of operational necessity made sense only if it contributed to winning the war, and doing so at less cost. Often neither was the case. A classic example was the British bombing of Lubeck in 1942, a city almost devoid of military or economic importance but so densely built up that it made an ideal target. As Max Hastings has written, it "did not attract the attention of the bombers because it was important, but became important because it could be bombed."[57] Furthermore, such practices continued long past the point where operational necessity still governed. In the British case, Harris's city-destroying campaign was sustained, albeit over considerable opposition, long after the RAF had developed methods of navigation and targeting permitting far more precise attacks on selected economic and military objectives. In the American case, the campaign from China bases continued until January 1945 despite overwhelming evidence of its futility and the availability of Marianas bases far superior in operational terms.

It is no surprise that the escalation of air war derived from so many considerations. But their multiplicity was rarely recognized. The prophets and proponents of air power had asked it to be judged by rational standards of humane efficiency. Yet more than other methods of warfare, it lacked measurable criteria by which to enforce those standards. Its effects were difficult to assess, even to witness; the indices of success most easily assembled—tonnage delivered, sorties flown, acreage wasted—far from inviting restraint, encouraged escalation; decisions about it were by nature more incremental and less discrete than those about other forms of war. To some degree, any modern warfare conducted at great distance and dependent on prodigies of production inhibits oversight and fosters escalation. In the case of air war, the multiplicity of motives involved, the lack of measurable criteria, and the particular remoteness of its consequences combined to give it a peculiarly unchecked momentum.

7

The Sociology of Air War

Weeks after Hiroshima and Nagasaki, the radical critic Dwight MacDonald attempted to characterize the mentality of the nation and people who built and used the atomic bombs. *"Atomic bombs are the natural product of the kind of society we have created.* They are as easy, normal and unforced an expression of the American Standard of Living as electric iceboxes. . . . Perhaps only among men like soldiers and scientists, trained to think 'objectively'—i.e., in terms of means, not ends—could such irresponsibility and moral callousness be found."[1] MacDonald's characterization applied to the air force as well as to the Manhattan Project, for they overlapped in technology, personnel, organization, and purposes. The organizations fashioned to wage conventional air war and nuclear attack both raised questions about whether the pursuit of means obliterated an awareness of ends and the production of destruction became "normal and unforced."

MacDonald's characterization is a point of departure for exploring the men who waged air war, not a conclusion. But it suggests the need to look at the war's bombing as something more than just the unfolding of a series of strategic campaigns. The distance from which Americans (and others) observed and waged air war derived partly from the historical, political, and strategic circumstances already described. But it also developed out of sources that might be called sociological: the backgrounds, mentalities, and interests of the people who made air war possible. Together these forces, plus additional ones noted in the subsequent chapter, produced something similar to, but more complex than, what MacDonald observed.

THE GENERALS

General Henry Harley Arnold remained the dominant figure in the air force over the summer of 1944. As the 20th Bomber Command began operating from bases in China and India, halfway around the world in Washington Arnold wielded personal authority over it. He had apparently written the 20th's commander, General K. B. Wolfe, that "I do not want ever to put myself in the position of having to, or of feeling that I have to, tell you how to do that job. I have every confidence in your ability."[2] But with Arnold, rituals of reassurance usually signaled sagging confidence in his subordinates. On July 1, only days after the 20th launched its first mission against Japan, Arnold recalled Wolfe, whose forte had been aircraft engineering and whose leadership was too cautious for Arnold's taste. He was replaced with a rising star of combat commanders, Curtis LeMay, who took command at the end of August.

A generation separated Arnold, then fifty-eight and an elder among air force generals, from the thirty-seven-year-old LeMay, who had entered the Air Corps after service in Army ROTC at Ohio State University. The two did not know each other personally. But they saw war in similar ways and they were typical figures in the wartime air force. What was most striking about men like LeMay and Arnold was how little fascination they had with combat. There were exceptions—General Claire Chennault, for example, whose relish for battle never seemed to abate—but the Chennaults rarely rose far. Few airmen entered World War II with combat experience—age, accident, attrition, and heresy had denuded the ranks of the first war's combat aviators. Arnold himself had been kept in Washington during World War I.

When he wrote his memoirs, LeMay thought that what he would rather be doing more "than anything else" was to be "commanding actively—in the field, as one might say—even with no declared war in progress." That qualification may seem dishonest to those familiar with LeMay's reputation for bellicosity in the 1960s. Yet it rang true with the record of his own thoughts and accomplishments. He took greatest delight in his success at forging combat-worthy organizations—commanding the first American bombers in Europe in 1942, when he "felt the intimacy of proven human devotion," deploying the fledgling force of B-29s in the fall of 1944, building the new Strategic Air Command out of the chaos of postwar demobilization.[3]

Of course, LeMay knew that these triumphs bore their fruit in combat. But what he prized most was his leadership in getting men ready for war. He excelled at fashioning reliable crews out of green trainees, ill-prepared for the smoke and confusion of battle. Always willing to experiment, he toyed with different bomber formations and bombing patterns and jerry-rigged new methods of maintenance and repair in order to increase the force available. When crew morale sagged in the face of hopeless odds against survival, LeMay turned despair into expedient fatalism. "Everybody would get shot down, and the last B-17 would take off from Britain in early March; and Ira Eaker, by his own testimony, would be on it. So morale went up. If there's no escape, you don't experience combat fatigue." At the same time, as he was no martinet, LeMay offered escape for some—for those whose nerves were shot, he would prescribe different duty, and for the cowardly, he would "pack up the so-and-so and send him home."[4] Operational challenges preoccupied LeMay, and for him joy lay in command itself—less for the power it bestowed or the victory it promised than for the creative skill it demanded.

LeMay had little time or interest to explore the strategy or politics of air power.

Before the war his rank had been too junior to place him in the service schools and the planning offices where these matters arose. The strategic issues raised by the failure of Germany's blitz against England, the RAF's shift to nighttime attacks against Germany, and the relationship between ground invasion and strategic bombing—these were beyond his province as middle-level operational commander, and he was too busy anyway to worry about them. "The only thing I was thinking about was living for the next twenty-four hours and . . . trying to keep my outfit alive and the airplanes flying. . . . We weren't thinking about strategy at the time. . . . We had to have an air force before we could do anything."[5] In war, commanders in the field and planners in Washington both suffocated under the sheer volume of operational detail, until strategic questions often became merely further matters to be slotted to the appropriate compartments of bureaucracy. LeMay's job was to fashion the machinery of war, not to worry about its purposes.

To a surprising degree, Arnold shared that mentality despite his much loftier perch. Though a veteran of battles over air power and a defender of the AAF's interests, he was never an articulate or visionary exponent of air power on a doctrinal level. Almost everyone close to Arnold saw him as "in no sense a thoughtful, precise thinker but a doer."[6] Had he been a visionary, he might never have become the air force's commanding general, and those who were mostly had fallen from the ranks. Arnold had the doctrinal flexibility to adjust to the shifting strategies of the war. He owed his preeminence not to strategic imagination but to the energy with which he prepared his organization for war and lashed it into operation.

In this regard, Arnold and LeMay resembled the outstanding American military figures of the war, General George C. Marshall and General Dwight Eisenhower, whose greatest talents lay in organization and diplomacy. The airmen differed from the army generals in one important way, however. Marshall and Eisenhower knew history, and by virtue of long association with military and political leaders, they understood politics. They preferred, as the deepest traditions of American civil-military relations taught them, to ground their decisions in arguments from military utility; but they comprehended Clausewitz's precepts about war as an extension of politics, and they willingly responded when civil authority altered strategy to fit political needs.

Arnold and LeMay rarely thought to invoke Clausewitz—or Grant and Sherman. They had defined their service and their careers against military tradition, both doctrinal and ritualistic, and were contemptuous of standard operating procedure. LeMay disdained the conventions of military dress, acknowledgment of superiors, and close-order drill and delighted in the air force's "reputation for sloppy uniforms, slatternly salutes, and general shoddiness," practices which indeed had official sanction in air force policy.[7] Disinterest in military tradition and in strategic doctrine went hand in hand. When LeMay and Arnold wrote their memoirs, neither said much about strategy; their memoirs faithfully reflected the focus of their wartime experience.

Similarly, LeMay and Arnold lacked a strong sense of the political and ideological meaning of war, the one being fought in 1944 or the ones that might come in the future.

Fascism, genocide, hegemony, freedom, national interests—these were simply not in their vocabularies. The task, not the purpose, of winning governed. Much the same was true for other Americans also during the war as well as for ranking officers in other services. But the parochial nature of the air officer's experience exacerbated that tendency—their remoteness from high political circles, the complex demands of the technology they operated, their distance from the fields of combat and the furnaces of mass killing.

At times, this parochialism left the airmen refreshingly free of ideological biases. LeMay recounted with evident appreciation the assistance he received from Mao's communists during the war. When he wrote his memoirs, these men had become the nation's enemies, yet LeMay bore no retrospective animosity, only a casual sense of history's irony, which he also felt about the twists of history that found him first leveling Japan's cities, only to receive an award from the Japanese government at the height of the cold war, and then to drive a Honda in retirement. For men like Arnold and LeMay, it was as if other nations were bad because they were enemies, not the other way around. They rarely articulated how ideology or national interest was at stake. Their job was to win a war.

Such an attitude did not prevent a certain involvement in politics. Air force generals fought relentlessly for the resources necessary to do the job as they saw it. But even in the 1960s, when LeMay gained national visibility for defending the manned bomber, resisting civilian authority, and wanting to bomb Vietnam back to the Stone Age (as he was famous for saying), his politics were highly circumscribed, focused on resentment over being denied the tools to do his job and protect his men. His denunciations of "pacifists," "swivel-chair, intellectual types," and the managerial mentality of Defense Secretary Robert McNamara sprang from the same source. At bottom, LeMay wanted the nation to approach war in the same way that he thought an air force should approach a mission: "Once the decision is *made*. . . . Bang. Everybody complies." Politics (except for the scramble for resources) ended when war began. Some air force officers saw no such dichotomy between peace and war; few of them rose to the top or stayed there long.[8]

LeMay was neither uncomplicated nor unlikeable. He had his internal conflicts. For all his later fulminations against intellectuals, educational metaphors abounded in his memoirs, and for all his pride in his ability to improvise, he regretted missing the formal training that would have permitted him to debate politics and strategy as effectively as civilian intellectuals or studious officers. Too, his role in the late 1940s in developing the air force's relationship with civilian expertise suggests he courted what he also distrusted. Like the RAF's Harris, LeMay also had a refreshing transparency that showed through in his memoirs and his politics. He confessed his own fears of going into combat and of leading other men into combat. Knowing he was not a great strategic thinker, he attributed his rise to fortune—promotion came rapidly when so many died quickly—and to his skills at leadership and organization: "The main thing was to have enough energy to get off your ass and do something."[9]

War penalized the ideologues and rewarded the pragmatists, the men who maximized the number of trained crews, bombers in the air, targets hit. Beyond recognizing that getting bombs on target was more likely to win the war than not getting them on target, most American airmen did little to explain how increased effort would secure speedier victory. The absence of concerted strategic thinking on that problem had the advantage of leaving them free to change tactics, in notable contrast to the RAF's Harris, who clung tenaciously to one method of bombing throughout the war. But improvisation without a clear strategy risked redundant or purposeless destruction and the subversion of ends by means.

In order to amass and employ those means, Arnold and LeMay drove their subordinates hard. In contrast to the orderly way in which Marshall and Eisenhower worked through the staff system, both violated customary procedures of command, consultation, and concurrence. Their casualness reflected a disdain for those procedures as well as the peacetime air force's lack of an established cadre of administrators and its style of personal leadership, one possible when the air officer corps had numbered only in the hundreds. Arnold's genial smile, which had long ago earned him the nickname Hap, barely disguised the ruthless streak he exercised with subordinates, his penchant for hectoring those around him. Only one officer responded to Arnold's fury by falling "dead of a massive heart attack on the carpet in front of Arnold's desk," but countless others felt his wrath. In a typical encounter with subordinates, this one in May 1944 on delays in preparing B-29s for combat, Arnold ended his badgering with another explosion of temper: "I have been fighting can't can't can't can't for eight years, and I don't feel like fighting it much longer," and he got up and stormed out of the meeting. Of course he continued to fight, despite his staff's resolve "to keep him off our backs"; except when bad health sidelined him, it was his method to intrude and explode, to pluck men at random for duties regardless of their formal assignments, to roam about his organization with almost imperial abandon. Under his regime, organizational routine coexisted uneasily with personal rule.[10] Arnold harassed his subordinates, particularly his field commanders, in part because he never had a combat command. He neither understood nor tolerated well the manifold impediments to success faced by his bomber commanders, on occasion blithely distorting the hard facts of the forces they wielded. But he yearned to have field command and meddled in the affairs of his lieutenants abroad as if determined to have in practice what he lacked on paper.

On occasion, Arnold faintly recognized the dangers of driving his staff so hard. As early as July 8, 1942, he urged his staff to relax its pace, arguing that "as far as our creative effort is concerned, we are over the peak." As with Arnold's expressions of confidence in commanders, however, such recommendations thinly disguised his push for performance. Certainly they did not portray reality, for the "creative work" of employing air power effectively had only begun. In any event, Arnold's own work habits, as punishing of himself as of others, hardly set a good example. Little seemed to have changed when General Laurence Kuter roamed headquarters on a Saturday night a year later and found one officer already in a "psychopathic" ward at Walter Reed "as a direct result of overwork," another removed from office in "some form of nervous collapse," and a third under medical observation. On the eve of OVERLORD, Arnold found his staff "so wrapped up in our various and current affairs that we do not take any time to think ahead" and again urged his men to cut down on paperwork and take time off; but few did. "We have placed a premium on the operator rather than the theorist," one colonel dared to complain in November. Arnold's drive to increase operations made the complaint substantially correct. Arnold himself was again that month regretting "that we have probably lost a certain degree of initiative and imagination and that all of us are, perhaps, war-weary."[11]

Arnold's injunctions to his staff to ease up and look ahead were oddly similar to the advice given him regarding his own health. During the war, he experienced four heart attacks, and on orders from his doctors and from Marshall, after each he rested briefly. But he could not really acknowlege the precariousness of his own health any more than he could the dangers of an overtaxed organization. He soon slipped back into a pace that he imposed on others and that helped alienate him from his wife and family. He was, like LeMay, a transparent man who never elicited the contrasting impressions that a Roosevelt or an Eisenhower triggered; he lacked guile and subtlety, the capacity to act deviously or operate on multiple levels. Arnold also differed from some other military leaders—Marshall and Stimson, for example, also tired and overburdened men—in his stubborn refusal to delegate authority and in his inability to find outlets for affection and relaxation. Ambition—for himself and his air force, between which he could not distinguish—was his guiding star.

In personality, LeMay was a different case. Arnold's genial smile obscured his ruthlessness. LeMay's gruff appearance—a touch of Bell's palsy froze his face into a half-snarl—hid a certain gentleness of speech and rough affection for others. He worked his subordinates hard but rarely showed the capriciousness and ruthlessness that Arnold displayed. His job with the 20th Bomber Command was a thankless one. But if critical of the poor quality of his staff, crews, and planes, LeMay made few excuses or complaints, pursued the job of expanding operations with zest, and enjoyed an unreserved praise that Arnold bestowed on few others—all the while knowing that the 20th was not to achieve much of strategic import.

The attributes shared by LeMay and Arnold—their close attention to the air force's interests, their dynamic manner with their organizations—also aided them in the other goal Arnold pursued, the independence and stature of the air force which its wartime success was to enhance. If Arnold lacked a strong conception of strategy and national interests, he had foresight into the political and technological requirements of the postwar air force. By the fall of 1944, two closely related objectives guided him in his quest to make the air force the dominant arm of the peacetime military establishment: the presentation of a favorable image of the air force to politicians and public and the harnessing of civilian expertise to the development of future military technologies. Others joined him in these efforts, although Arnold often set their tone.

The air force's efforts at self-promotion, long intense but rarely subtle, gained a sophistication in 1943 and 1944 for which its civilian leadership was partly responsible. Secretary of War Stimson and Robert Lovett, the assistant secretary for air, warned against a hard-sell campaign that might backfire against the air force by revealing its ambitions too baldly and by promising more than the air force could deliver. Lovett wanted "a conservative and constructive educational campaign." He shifted emphasis in public relations from extravagant pronouncements by airmen to the careful shaping of media reporting.

The shift in tactics did not preclude muscular methods, but they were now employed behind the scenes. Angered by *Newsweek*'s treatment of the Eighth Air Force in 1943, Lovett turned to Averell Harriman, whose brother was Lovett's partner at Brown Brothers and a director of *Newsweek*. Harriman's response was encouraging. "I have not supported *Newsweek* for 10 years through its grave difficulties to allow our hired men to use the magazine to express their narrow, uninformed or insidious ideas." If persuasion would not change the magazine's tune, Harriman gave his brother "my full authority to use any strong arm measures," including forcing out *Newsweek*'s other directors. Lovett also exploited other contacts with eastern financial and publishing elites to bend coverage of the war to favor the AAF. By granting privileged access to newsworthy war stories, Lovett could get trusted reporters to cover the air force. Moreover, privilege was a two-way street—it was helpful that a former *Newsweek* editor, Rex Smith, became public relations officer for the Washington headquarters of the Twentieth Air Force.[12]

The air force was not alone in these practices. The rivalry among the services for headlines was fierce, inasmuch as the stakes were high. But the air force's effort was more intense, for while admirals and ground generals sought only to preserve existing institutional relationships, the air force tried to change them by winning independence from the other services. Whereas Marshall devoted little time to the conduct of public relations, they were a major preoccupation for Arnold by 1944, made more critical by the air force's declining chance to win the war on its own and to secure favorable coverage in the face of accelerating ground and naval operations. "The hot pilot is being supplanted in national esteem by G.I. Joe," warned a staff study in August.[13]

By autumn, the air force's anxiety about its political prospects threatened to spill into the conduct of immediate operations. While not specifically invoking those prospects, Lovett explained to the air staff on November 27 that "the Air Forces are being given a 'second chance' in Europe" and he "urged that something drastic be done in order to take advantage of this second chance." Lovett's favored proposal was for a "Jeb Stuart Air Force" of fighter-bombers "scampering all over Germany . . . shooting up targets of opportunity, strafing rail and communication centers and generally causing a breakdown in morale among the German people." Arnold and his staff were skeptical of the specifics of Lovett's scheme, but it conformed in broad purpose with other proposals they supported to hasten the war's end by a climactic campaign of terror bombing. More than ever, achieving victory and enhancing the air force's reputation were inseparable objectives for the AAF, Lovett adding that his plan would also earn the appreciation of the ground army. As Arnold reminded General Hansell, head of the new 21st Bomber Command in the Marianas, "we must in fact destroy our targets and then we must show the results so the public can judge for itself as to the effectiveness of our operations." LeMay had gotten the same message. [14]

To meet Arnold's objective, the AAF arranged coverage of the Pacific war with special care. It wanted coverage to "emphasize accuracy rather than press-agentry," to "prevent the B-29 from being overevaluated in the public mind," and "to let the results speak for themselves." Caution served several purposes. It limited jealousy and attacks from the other services and it conformed to official policy, which sought to deflate popular expectations that Japan would be defeated quickly by blockade and bombardment alone. It also prevented arousal of expectations for the B-29's performance that might later cause an adverse reaction against the air force. It was no time, as the AAF advised corporate advertisers, to "imply that the B-29 is a mighty juggernaut which almost single-handedly is capable of reducing Japan to the point of surrender." [15]

Caution implied no abandonment of the air force's political goals, however. Arnold wrote LeMay on October 5 that he did "not want a high-pressure B-29 publicity program and we are making no effort to maintain constant publicity," but days earlier he had written to another Pacific commander that he was "extremely concerned" over press attention given MacArthur and Halsey. On October 15, General Lauris Norstad, Arnold's chief of staff for the Twentieth Air Force, issued one of the few wrist-slappings LeMay ever received, chiding him on the matter of press coverage: "We have been seriously upset particularly in our public relations because of the delay in receiving your mission results." [16]

Arnold's staff was especially determined to centralize the release of all information about the Twentieth Air Force through its Washington headquarters rather than through field commanders and correspondents. Centralization facilitated control, and with it consistency and the timing of release for maximum effect. More than that, release from Washington reinforced the image of the Twentieth as a "global" air force whose operations cut across the traditional theaters and lines of command. The image desired was of "a global weapon the organizational and operational concept of which is unique among the Armed Forces of the United States." [17] The insistent use of the term "global air force" established an image weighty in both its geopolitical and bureaucratic content: the promise of a future air force capable of patrolling the globe, one so independent of ground and naval operations that only an independent organization could maintain it.

"I believe the best thing we can do is to continue to report facts only without any emphasis on the interpretation of these facts," Norstad wrote Hansell on December 27. [18] Even among sophisticated proponents of air power like Norstad, it was thought that the air force reported only facts, ignoring the distinction between facts and truth and their manipulation to obscure bureaucratic and national ambition. On November 11, the 21st Bomber Command's public relations officer was directed to stress "that specific objectives within the city were bombed so that nobody will get [the] impression general havoc or general conflagration was intended or accomplished."[19] A narrow, literal truth—Hansell's command was not then attempting to raise a "general conflagration"—disguised the air force's intent to do so. To term the Twentieth a global air force was also a gross distortion—tied to bases in one part of a regional command, operating with bombers of increased but still limited range, it was global only in the sense of air force ambitions, not in terms of current realities.

No such quibbles arose at the time, however, and by the end of 1944 the air force was pleased with the results of its cautious press policy. Norstad noted that the "conservatism of our news has in itself been news," something "commented on editorially in several instances."[20] Conservatism helped the transition of the air force's image from that of brash adolescent to one of a mature organization. And as the press fell in line with official claims of selective attacks on economic targets, no consciences were stirred in advance of the assault by fire still in the planning stages.

Few polls were taken to measure the air force's success in public relations, but by June 1945 a *Fortune* survey indicated progress. As *Fortune* put it, "The people are sold on peace through air power." On more subjective grounds, the air force also had reason for optimism as 1945 approached because doubts were arising within the military establishment about public support for a large peacetime ground army. Arnold believed that Americans would support in its place a powerful air force making few demands on manpower and responding to public anxieties, nourished by the air force itself, about defending against future Pearl Harbors. He pursued that argument with Marshall, Stimson, and the media.[21]

The AAF also benefited from the way some Americans linked their interest in a new international organization with the ascendancy of air power. An international air force, either genuinely multinational or drafted from constituent powers, promised the swiftness and global reach to deter or punish aggression at minimal cost. Roosevelt himself seemed to be thinking along these lines, and widespread public speculation of the same sort measured the benign image of air power possible, despite all the horrors, in part because many Americans assumed that air power would be preeminently an American weapon. Persistent, too, was another optimistic habit, seeing peaceful potential in the enormous expansion of aviation resulting from the war. Though less frequent and grandiose than in an earlier age, predictions continued that the spread of air routes and air commerce would create interdependent economic relationships and a global prosperity that would usher in a "Pax Aeronautica."[22]

There was a darker view. William Bishop, a Canadian air marshall whose *Winged Peace* was published in the United States, wanted all aviation internationalized and used to "police the world" without wasting "one moment in talking before raising ordinary hell" with aggressors. Yet Bishop imagined a horrible war of intercontinental missiles and bombers, and his emphasis was more on saving the world from air power than through it. Another pessimist, Emile Gauvreau, warned of how powerful airplane manufacturers would exert irresistible pressures to secure contracts and promote a new international arms trade in deadly aircraft, throwing in his own prediction, made in 1944, of the dangers of atomic bombs. As visions of evils to come, however, both tracts were limited: danger came less from the potential of modern technology than from the stupidity or evil machinations of great nations or powerful individuals. The dominant impulse remained evident in proposals like Allan Michie's: *Keep the Peace Through Air Power.*[23]

For Arnold and the air force, these proposals were of little concern except as hopeful signs of a coming awareness of aviation's dominance in world relations and national policy. The air force was both an instigator and a beneficiary of the perception of a new air age; in a seamless world, both threats and opportunities for the United States would arise most anywhere in the world, threats arriving with the cataclysmic suddenness of Hitler's V-2 rockets. It was a perception shared by liberal one-worlders, self-conscious practitioners of realpolitik, scientists creating the new technology, and conservators of strategic tradition like Marshall. Of course a common perception did not always lead to the same prescriptions about the future role of American air power. It did encompass anxieties and aspirations on which Arnold's air force capitalized with considerable success.

It also buttressed Arnold's effort to fulfill his second objective in postwar policy: developing the technology for future American air superiority by institutionalizing the air force's relationship with the scientific community. That relationship had been evolving along two related lines during the war. Scientists were inventing new weapons, and they were on occasion assisting in the integration of those weapons into tactics and strategy.

The scientists' role in weapons development was uncontroversial. To perpetuate it Arnold turned to Theodore von Karman, a prominent Hungarian aerodynamicist who had come to the California Institute of Technology in 1926. By 1944, the two knew each other well. To von Karman, Arnold was nothing less than "the greatest example of the U.S. military man—a combination of complete logic, mingled with farsightedness and superb dedication." A "fanatic on air power," perhaps, but all the more admirable for it.[24]

In the fall of 1944, Arnold established von Karman as head of a new Scientific Advisory Group for the air force and ordered him to look far into the technological future. According to von Karman's dramatic account, the two rendezvoused at a remote corner of La Guardia airport, Arnold dismissed his chauffeur ("Not another ear was in sight"), and the general disclosed his plans. As fleshed out by his staff, Arnold's rationale for a permanent alliance of officers and scientists was both political and strategic. The strategic danger to the United States lay largely in the unfolding technological revolution: the United States would face enemies and the possibility of "global war" waged by offensive weapons of great sophistication. But the American response would be shaped by considerations of domestic politics. The United States had to reverse "the mistakes of unpreparedness prior to World War II," particularly the failure to harness civilian science to military needs. And technological development would respond to "a fundamental principle of democracy that personnel casualties are distasteful. We will continue to fight mechanical rather than manpower wars."[25]

Arnold had a certain brutal foresight into the shape of wars to come, a vision of intercontinental aerial struggle extrapolated from the lessons of Pearl Harbor and wartime technology. But the politics and strategy of future conflicts interested him less than their technological basis. "I see a manless Air Force," he told von Karman: "I see no excuse for men in fighter planes to shoot down bombers. When you lose a bomber, it is a loss of seven thousand to forty thousand man-hours, but this crazy thing [V-2] they shoot over there takes only a thousand man-hours." The lure of a dehumanized technology of war, which Twain had recorded so ambivalently and other men of science and war had felt so powerfully, attracted Arnold. While other airmen might wax sentimental about the manned bomber, Arnold asked von Karman to look into "manless remote controlled radar or television assisted precision military rockets" and imagined the day when such devices would "fly over enemy territory and look through the leaves of trees and see whether they're moving their equipment." "Atomic propulsion" and "gas and bacteriological warfare" were also to be scrutinized by the scientists.[26]

Fascinated with the gadgetry that scientists might provide, Arnold was less readily attuned to the role civilians might play in operations and strategy. That role usually seemed more suspect to military men, threatening as it did their prerogative to decide how war should be waged. But Arnold was open-minded when civilians took the initiative to extend their policymaking role. The impetus came in part from Edward L. Bowles, the special consultant on scientific matters to Stimson and Arnold. By the end of 1944, Bowles, like many others, was speculating on the institutions suitable for preserving the wartime partnership between military men and civilian experts. Meanwhile, similar ideas were afoot at Douglas Aircraft Company, whose close professional contacts with Bowles and Arnold had been extended by the marriage of Arnold's son to Donald Douglas's daughter. By the summer of 1945, Bowles, Arnold, Douglas, and others were working out plans for Project RAND, a civilian group attached to the Douglas company which would contract with the air force to plan development and employment of new weapons. At the time, few probably saw the role the RAND Corporation would play in strategic matters. RAND was an acronym for "research and development," implying a more narrowly technological role which probably caught Arnold's attention. Soon, however, as one wag put it, RAND would mean Research and No Development, and its strategic role grew naturally out of the inroads into operations and tactics made by Bowles and others during the war.[27]

THE TRIUMPH OF CIVILIAN MILITARISM

Air war, even more than most modern warfare, was never just the enterprise of generals and fliers, as Arnold knew. It required a vast apparatus of technology, production, logistics, and economic and political analysis. Sustaining that apparatus was largely the task of civilians in the American air force. They too waged air war; similarly, their mentalities as well as their relationships to men in uniform helped to define how Americans regarded and prosecuted strategic bombing.

While the other services were also broadening their use of civilian expertise, Arnold's air force was at the forefront of this development. Its flexibility in employing civilian talent was one key both to American superiority in the air and to the air force's emergence as the dominant military service. Contemporaries generally explained the forging of a close alliance among the air force, industry, and science in the same way they explained so many developments of the war: as a product of technological and operational imperatives. In their view, the very nature of air war—its premium on the most sophisticated technology—compelled a more vigorous use of civilian talent.

As did the argument from operational necessities in its other forms, this version had a truth to it. The cutting edge of military technology did lie largely in the weaponry of air war. But that argument confused effect with cause, technological determinism with elites' choices. The technology of air war was at the cutting edge in part because of the political decisions men made. If the pace of technological change alone had been the determining factor, the navy might have matched the air force's success in employing civilian talent, for it had long pioneered new technologies, and its carrier aviation had many of the same technological needs as the air force. And yet its use of civilian science and industrial technology was generally less aggressive than the air force's and marked by more fractious relations between scientists and the officer corps. Another example is more pointed: despite great technological advances, the Luftwaffe was notably deficient in recognition of civilian talent and ability to work harmoniously with it. Much the same was true of the Japanese air forces as well. At most, technological change offered a broad challenge which nations and particular organizations met in very different ways.

The success of the AAF in meeting that challenge was due substantially to its historical development, the background and temperament of its officer corps, and the political and class relationships among American elites. Oddly, much of that success derived from the prewar air force's alienation from the older services. In its quest for autonomy the air force repeatedly had taken its case to the civilian world and come to distrust the technical services the army bureaucracy performed for the airmen. In institutional mechanisms particularly, the air force had excelled at military–civilian cooperation since the establishment in 1915 of the National Advisory Committee for Aeronautics (NACA), its membership comprising both federal officials and private scientists and developers. While maintaining some facilities of its own, NACA also contracted with universities and private corporations, a method scientists usually preferred because it preserved their professional autonomy. NACA was the prototype for the mobilization of industrial and academic science during World War II, adopted by its prewar chairman, Vannevar Bush of MIT, as a model for the National Defense Research Committee in 1940. Thus well before American entry into the war, the airmen had more experience with the conditions under which scientists and industrial laboratories would help the military.

Its contacts with civilian expertise had also been strengthened by the close relationship between military and civilian technology inherent in the field of aviation. Among all military technologies, aviation had the clearest benefits for civilian commerce. Therefore civilian agencies of government, like the Department of Commerce and the Bureau of Standards, as well as private developers readily cooperated with the prewar Air Corps.

The air force's low peacetime status worked to its wartime benefit in other ways. After World War I, disgruntled airmen often left the service, but in doing so some forged close links with civilian technology—Eddie Rickenbacker in the airline industry, Jimmy Doolittle as head of Shell Oil's aviation department after graduate work at MIT. More broadly, because the officer corps of airmen had been so small before the war and then swamped with demands for expansion, it was forced after 1940 to recruit heavily from the ranks of civilian talent and to turn to private industry for help. This was the case, for example, in organizing a worldwide military air transport system, whose development the airline industry assisted, seeing peacetime advantages in doing so.

Even in rarefied areas of strategy much the same thing happened. Lacking its own intelligence staff, the prewar Air Corps had never examined in depth what target systems of any enemy would be the most vulnerable to destruction. For that reason, in December 1942 Arnold authorized a Committee of Operations Analysts, its members mostly civilians, to supplement the air staff's efforts in that regard. A MacArthur or an Eisenhower rarely had to enlist civilian help to decide which island to take or what part of France to invade—for those decisions ample precedent and talent existed within military circles. As in the army and navy, civilians sometimes aroused the resentment of the air officer: even Arnold's references to the "long-haired boys" assisting the air force mixed affection with the layman's bewilderment about the scientists' curious ways.[28] Yet cultural distance and rivalry for influence never seriously impeded the deepening of the military–civilian alliance.

The air officers' relative lack of isolation from civilian society also arose from their professional and class background. At the top ranks, airmen had followed largely the same professional paths as had ground army officers, but they were somewhat younger and less often the product of the service academies, a substantial number having been educated at prestigious technical institutions.[29] Some divergence between air officers and others was also sustained down through the ranks. Air forces demanded a higher proportion of technically trained personnel and had much higher ratios of officers to men. The American air force thus recruited from a higher level of class and educational background, maintained during the war first through requirements for two years of college education for many personnel and later through other screening devices.

Methods of recruitment also strengthened the airmen's bonds with civilian society. The air force aggressively recruited on college campuses and among clubs for flying and model-building. Furthermore, during the war civilian institutions rapidly expanded their indoctrination of American youth in the virtues and techniques of aviation. In training what contemporaries called the Winged Superchildren of Tomorrow, civilian educators and businessmen forged links between the civil and military spheres that were unique among the armed services to the air force.[30] Moreover, once recruited, men were assigned combat flying roles only if they volunteered for them, a practice which sustained the elite status of airmen, as did the long, sophisticated training they received. Despite their higher educational background, airmen were also younger than army soldiers and officers.

In sum, airmen—by class and education, by their relative youth, by their sheer numbers, and by the era's infatuation with aviation—were attuned to the demands of modern technology, organization, and civilian expertise. Cause and effect may be difficult to sort out—the air force's emerging supremacy both reflected its class composition and gave rise to it. But when contemporaries took note of the elite nature of the wartime air force, they intuitively observed that class was at work, perhaps in ominous ways: as air force historians speculated darkly in 1944, the high casualty rate suffered among air officers might deprive the United States of its elite youth in much the way that Ypres and Passchendaele and other world War I battles had done to England. Whatever the price, the elite composition of the air force helped it forge its alliance with civilian professions and authorities.[31]

At bottom, that alliance also strengthened a broader linkage among American elites, one imperfectly established during World War I, partially dismantled after it, and indissolubly fixed during World War II. It was just this success in linking elites that accounted for much of Allied success in the air—British and Russian as well as American. Their enemies failed in that regard because their rulers relied on ideals of military service and party ideology rather than on "military materialism."[32] Trusting their zeal to win the war, they miscalculated the demands of war and thus postponed until too late the task of conscripting or cajoling the services of civilian science and industry. Even had they appreciated those demands more promptly, they would have been disinclined to share real power with civilian experts because their war, especially the Nazis', was waged against the existing system at home as well as enemies abroad.

In both Germany and Japan, the disadvantages of relying on the fervor and judgment of military and party elites extended further, ironically undermining the air forces as fighting units as well. Both countries began the war with the best-trained pilots and ended with the worst. Trusting the fighting man's virtue to win the war quickly, they failed to amass the reserves of quality pilots needed for further training, and pilot skill and training plummeted. Failing also to exploit their civilian labor pool, both countries placed further demands on their military personnel. In contrast, the American air force employed some 500,000 civilians, including large numbers of women, for maintenance and logistical tasks. Just when production in Germany and Japan peaked in 1944, they lacked the well-trained crews to make use of it.

A narrow definition of military strength also sabotaged Axis industrial production. Just as German leaders wanted the best pilots, they wanted the best weapons, ones that satisfied the leadership's thirst for the miraculous instrument of victory and the developers' competitive quest for technological advance and hegemony. But no consultative authority existed to sort out the wheat from the chaff among these novelties, to balance the benefits of their introduction against the costs of disrupting industrial routine. The triumph of a narrow form of technological creativity seriously impeded Axis efforts to develop assembly-line production, and this curtailed output of some types more seriously than did Allied bombing.

In contrast, the Soviet Union, Britain, and the United States developed effective methods of coordinating the efforts of officers, scientists, developers, and manufacturers. Conflicting claims on resources were monitored. Production models were frozen for extended periods. Modifications were selectively introduced. New projects were put on hold unless they promised a payoff in the current war, sacrificing a measure of technological creativity to reliable abundance. Exceptions occurred but primarily when excess of industrial and technical capacity accrued late in the war (some plants were already scaling back from full production after 1942).

To be sure, Nazi rulers wanted to exploit the existing technical and industrial system, not destroy it. But heavy-handed exploitation denied the state the expertise needed to coordinate highly dispersed and complex institutions, despite belated efforts by Germany and Japan to rationalize production and make use of civilian experts. The latter remained servants, not partners, in the war effort. The final irony was that fascist totalitarianism produced far less centralization than the Allies achieved. Generals or party bureaucrats might rule particular fiefdoms with an iron hand, but no informed authority ruled over them. The Allies excelled in rationalizing production and linking laboratory to industry, the high command and the field. Cooperation proved more efficient than coercion.

The faultline did not lie simply between capitalism and totalitarianism, however, as evidenced by Soviet success in the production war. Perhaps the distinction lay in the Allies' capacity to embrace modernism itself—not so much its gadgetry as its technique, rationalization, and integration of elites into a cooperative effort. That was just what Japan's intellectuals, but not its leaders, realized when they "grasped the meaning of the Pacific war as 'the overcoming of modernity.'" "The important social consequence of the war for the Allied powers," Overy concludes, "was not breaking down social barriers between classes—in fact they were in most cases confirmed—but in breaking down barriers between elites."[33] The Nazis conquered Germany's professional elites without integrating them.

Allied and American material superiority was also a function of the superior resources. But the British, from a smaller economic base, outproduced the Germans in aircraft until 1944, and the Soviet Union did so throughout the war despite massive devastation and the vast expansion of Germany's economic base through conquest. Organizational expertise, not sheer abundance, was the key variable. A good example was British and American skill in converting automobile companies to aircraft production, allowing the use of mass production techniques those industries had pioneered. Only Ford's massive Willow Run plant, churning out B-24 Liberators, approached full employment of those methods; aircraft and aeroengine production was notoriously resistant to rationalization and standardization. But the sympathy of Arnold and Lovett for new methods of production, despite resistance from some aviation firms, stood in notable contrast to Germany's experience. There too a substantial automobile industry was available but hardly exploited. Failure to anticipate a long war, resistance from craft workers and manufacturers, the attempt to preserve consumer-goods production, poor use of native labor and the slave work force, and the dispersal of industry dictated by Allied bombing all retarded German efforts to rationalize production and achieve the Allies' economies of scale. Even in 1944, many German aviation factories were still working only one shift—a remarkable index of failure to exploit and coordinate resources.

Even at the time, some observers appreciated how the fascist states were falling behind the Allies in the application of modern technique to war. Arnold's intelligence chief noted that "American policy is to expend machines rather than men," a policy also comforting to the staff historians. Placing "their faith in the tank, the plane and the armored car," Germany and Japan had "sacrificed to the United States their only major advantage," their superiority in mobilizing and motivating mass armies, by waging a technological and economic struggle at which the United States excelled. "American national military policy," the staff historians concluded, "thus may well have altered the dictum to 'get there fustest with the mostest men' to a more sensible— and more economic—'get there last with the most machines.' Machines are cheap in America; men are not."[34]

Waging mechanical war required more than just the willingness of military elites to utilize civilian talent. It required civilians who would pursue a broadening role and be rewarded for doing so. Only the Allies succeeded fully in identifying the purposes of the war with the interests of powerful segments of civilian society. In the broadest sense, that identification arose simply because the Allied powers sought to preserve the status quo at home, whether corporate capitalism in the United States and Britain or Soviet Communism in the USSR. Where, in Japan and even more Germany, war brought the mounting subordination of powerful interests, a sense of common purpose derived only from ideological and patriotic goals insufficient to induce full cooperation.

Of course, in the United States and Britain, reward for cooperation took more concrete forms. "If you are going to try to go to war, or to prepare for war, in a capitalist country, you have got to let business make money out of the process."[35] Stimson's famous dictum was applied with particular force to the production of aircraft. The payoff for industry lay not simply in the immediate profits—ample though they often were—but in squeezing out marginal competitors, forging permanent links with the national government, gaining the inside track on research into new technologies, and absorbing state-financed capital expansion at highly favorable rates after the war. The last was particularly important for industrialists harboring a "mortal terror of a sudden cessation of hostilities" rooted in their knowledge of the industry's cutthroat ways and its dependence on the boom-and-bust cycles of military spending. The business of aviation reminded one manufacturer "of those toy rubber balloons you buy at the circus. Blow them up and they look like a fat pig. Release the pressure and they collapse with a plaintive dying sequel [sic], a wrinkled remnant of overstressed rubber." Few firms believed they could count on a reliable military market after the war; government guarantees were designed as a hedge against its collapse. Not even a considerate government provided full protection against excess capacity, and wartime profits had to be limited, or at least artfully disguised, lest the industry face again the bitter complaints of profiteering endured after World War I. Still, expansion was remarkable, and government generous. Nearly $4 billion—one-sixth of all wartime investment in manufacturing—went into the aviation industry. Washington provided 89 percent of it.[36]

These wide-ranging differences between the Axis and Allied methods of mobilizing for and waging air war have prompted some to attribute the defeat of the Axis states in part to their being dominated by "militarism." The war, it has been said, pitted Allied industrialism "against a militarism inexpertly binding industrialism to its purpose."[37] The terminology may be misleading, however. Economic power was not an alternative to military prowess but another method of expressing it. What happened in the Allied nations was not the decline of militarism or its failure ever to rise in those countries but its transformation. They departed from the path of militarism in the narrow sense that traditional military institutions, elites, and the values associated with them did not dominate. In another, broader sense—the willing enlistment of the broadest array of national energies and elites into the machine of war-making—militarism triumphed in the Allied powers to an exceptional degree, in a variation of it which Alfred Vagts has called "civilian militarism."

Vagts has provided the classic definition of the term:

> Wartime civilian militarism . . . may be defined as the interference and intervention of civilian leaders in fields left to the professionals by habit and tradition. . . . Civilians not only had anticipated war more eagerly than the professionals, but played a principal part in making combat, when it came, more absolute, more terrible than was the current military wont or habit.[38]

Wartime culture gave evidence of civilian militarism in its hero-worship: more often than not, the most admired Americans were not battlefield leaders but experts in preparing for war—the demigods of science who developed radar and constructed atomic bombs, the organizers of victory like Marshall and Eisenhower. The scientists' role and Roosevelt's aggressive effort to expand the Air Corps testified to civilians' "interference" and their success in making combat "more absolute." Not that generals often disliked the outcome. As Arnold's interest in new technologies suggested, what characterized the Anglo-Americans at war was the coalescence, not the divergence, of civilian and military purpose and values. Military elites embraced civilian expertise, civilian elites embraced military purposes.

THE CIVILIAN EXPERTS

Civilian experts prosecuting the air war are more difficult to characterize than officers because civilians entered war work from far more varied backgrounds. Most officers were American by birth, had followed much the same course of training, education, and advancement, and were bound to similar professional norms. Scientists came to the American war effort from all over Europe; nor were all of them foreign-born refugees; some, like von Karman, had come for the intellectual and financial opportunities offered by American science. They varied enormously in the power, professional roles, interests, and talents they possessed, and some traveled far from their original scientific interests.

Many civilians performed the same tasks that they had in earlier wars, though on a much expanded scale. Phalanxes of businessmen and lawyers handled the intricate details of contracting, procurement, and allocation of resources. More novel was the movement of some into war-marking itself, as they helped to make decisions about how weapons should be used and operations conducted. Their assumption of such roles was an erratic process, more noticeable in England early in the war and accelerating rapidly toward the end of the war. Furthermore, civilians' roles were never clearly sorted out along professional lines. For example, many nominally scientific positions were filled by nonscientists. Operations research was once defined by C. P. Snow as the capacity to "think scientifically about . . . operations."[39] But the AAF's Committee of Operations Analysts (COA) was dominated by lawyers and businessmen, many of national prominence—Elihu Root, Jr., Thomas Lamont of J. P. Morgan, John Marshall Harlan (later a Supreme Court justice), Fowler Hamilton—and others such as the Boston lawyer Guido Perera, the COA's de facto chairman for much of the time. Prominent economists like Edward S. Mason figured significantly, as did the Princeton historian and political scientist Edward Mead Earle, a pioneer in academic service to the military establishment. The task of "thinking scientifically" was never alone the scientist's job.

Lawyers and businessmen found themselves in such work in part because the air force lacked the professional staff to do it itself: analysis of an enemy's strategic systems required a knowledge of foreign industrial economies gained through legal or business experience. More important than their technical expertise was the assumption that businessmen and lawyers possessed the talent to think logically about these problems, the connections to draw in specialized expertise, and the freedom from operational demands to give these matters sustained attention. Perera himself, responsible for recruiting COA staff, naturally turned to men of similar background. Indeed, linkages of class, education, and geography, especially at the top rungs of business and law in the Northeast, were vital in recruiting civilians, all the more so with two elite easterners, Stimson and Lovett, at the highest level of the War Department.

These linkages appeared again late in 1944, when the United States Strategic Bombing Survey was constituted to examine the results of the bombing effort. Franklin D'Olier, past national commander of the American Legion and in 1944 chairman of the board of the Prudential Insurance Company, presided, and Henry C. Alexander, a lawyer and partner in J. P. Morgan, assumed active direction. Boston lawyers, including Perera, again played an important role, as did George Ball and Paul Nitze. There were less conventional figures, such as the economist John Kenneth Galbraith; they were especially evident on the lower levels of the survey staff—the poet W. H. Auden, the young Marxist economist Paul Baran. But by 1944 these class and professional connections, in a war which had already thrown these men together in other duties, were largely self-sustaining. "All in all," notes a historian regarding recruitment of the survey staff, "the process was rather more 'clubby' than most Americans might tend to presume."[40] At bottom recruitment reflected also the rapprochement with corporate and professional elites achieved by the Roosevelt administration at the start of the war.

For professional officers, motivation for war work was in one sense a moot point— war was their job anyway, and no additional motive was needed. Scientists, lawyers, and businessmen had to change what they were doing, and therefore motivation tended to be more discrete and focused. But their diversity was notable. The most famous among them, the atomic scientists, included men fleeing from fascism, determined that Germany not get the bomb first, as well as Americans like Robert Oppenheimer whose ideological revulsion against fascism was strong. But such men composed only a portion of the team working on the bomb, much less of the larger community of civilian experts. To some scientists, antifascism was grounded heavily in professional concerns—Nazism had sabotaged the German science they had held in such respect and the internationalism of science they found essential to progress. Much of von Karman's animus against Germany arose from that source: "The technical people of the world know how to talk to one another. If only one could put all problems on a technical basis, what a blessing for the world." The wartime records and memoirs of many civilians reveal scarcely more concern with the ideological and political issues of the war than generals like LeMay and Arnold displayed. As the British scientist Solly Zuckerman recalled, when Hitler came to power "whatever concern I may have felt, even this I suppressed at the time." Indeed, his interest in the geopolitical, moral, and ideological issues of the war never emerged strongly.[41]

Insofar as a broader outlook united most of these men, it lay in a fairly commonplace desire to assist in securing a rapid victory at minimal cost. Typical in outlook was Edward L. Bowles. Neither a rarefied theoretician nor a simple plodder in the trenches of technology, Bowles was a decent, ambitious, and talented man, reflective without being seriously troubled. As professor of electrical communications at MIT, he had presided over pioneering work in radio communications and radiation and in the process established contacts with leading industrial laboratories and interested individuals in the military. Tapped by Bush in 1939 to work on radar, he carved out a role which included not only responsibility for all AAF communications, radar, and electronics, but, as special consultant to Stimson and Arnold, authority to examine operational difficulties in the antisubmarine war, in Allied countermeasures against German V-weapons, and in the bombing campaign against Japan. "If there was anything I wanted," he later recalled, "it was to be mixed up with the overall operations of the military."[42]

He got what he wanted. Lacking the brilliance of an Oppenheimer or the empire-building talents of a Vannevar Bush, Bowles still knew how to work the fringes of power, eschewing messianic claims for the role of science in decision making and in saving mankind. Instead, in perhaps a reflection of how the engineer's mentality differed from that of the physicist, he relied on a self-effacing demonstration of how scientific expertise could solve military problems, particularly in bridging the gap between the invention of new devices and their effective use in warfare—the heart of operations research. His methods earned from Stimson, Arnold, and Marshall a trust they did not bestow on more strong-willed scientists. Bowles returned respect in good measure. If Arnold was an "opportunist" with "the instincts of a lower animal," insensitive to the issues and nuances of strategy, he was what the air force needed to get a "bunch of overgrown chauffeurs into shape." Bowles himself was after all an opportunist, though of deft skill rather than brutal force, determined to get on with winning the war, as impatient with questions of strategic theory as he was with the grander philosophizing of some of his scientific colleagues. No wonder, then, that he "loved the old man," who in turn "had so much faith in me it was dangerous."[43]

Bowles brought to his far-flung activities the scientist's joy in observing and the wonderment of the small-town boy thrown into high-powered circles. He showed few strong feelings about the enemy or the war's purpose. When he visited Saipan late in the war, he found inspiration in the "spirit of this enterprise, its magnitude and beauty" that carried him "into the realm of enchantment so long as one can throw into the distance the dread and the horror of war." Despite that horror, there was "the thrill and the satisfaction that real achievement carried with it" and admiration for the nation's "ability to do on a big scale" and for the "great silence and seriousness of men" taking off in their B-29s to bomb Japan. Untroubled by the technology of war he helped to develop, he did raise for himself one good question about the future: "Will we be able to restrain our avarice and grasping tendencies, or will we press on and be obliged some day because of our ambitions to engender another great conflict?" Neither duty nor temperament inclined him to seek an answer to that question.[44]

The war offered Bowles a comfortable mix of opportunities for status, creativity, and participation in a cause. A lawyer, Robert L. Stearns, an air force operations analyst on leave from his post as president of the University of Colorado, identified similar satisfactions. "The lawyer makes the Air Force his client, contributes broad judgment and investigative skill," Stearns told his alumni. In return, Stearns received "a series of the richest experiences of my life." He echoed wartime mythology about the homogenizing virtues of military life, only he celebrated camaraderie among diverse professional elites rather than the class and ethnic unity of the all-American platoon. Engineers, corporation scientists, government statisticians, and Harvard professors came together in his team of analysts. They were "men who had never met each other before and who had come from widely different homes and backgrounds . . . and who became, as time went on, one of the most closely knit and harmonious faculties I have ever served with." Like Bowles, Stearns also admired many officers with whom he worked and took pleasure in the little sacrifices of military life, as he "learned to sleep on the mail sacks and cartridge causes on a C-47 cargo plane just as well as on the luxurious canvas cot in our own tent quarters." Though less stridently than earlier generations, elite Americans still found war attractive as a force to discipline and unify a diverse nation. "We have gained stature and strengthened fibre," Stearns remarked of his university. He was not so different from Curtis LeMay in locating the satisfactions of war as much in process as in result.[45]

Similarly, Guido Perera admired the air force officers he met early in the war, finding with them a camaraderie and excitement he had missed in civilian life. Like other members of the Strategic Bombing Survey, he also took pleasure in his cordial interviews with high German industrial and military figures at the close of the war, men who "spoke effectively and well—without rancor," as he recalled of one such occasion. "Toasts were drunk to the U.S. Air Forces, as the winner, to the Luftwaffe, as the loser." Perera "couldn't help wondering . . . how they would have behaved if they had won the war," but it seemed enjoyable to play Grant to Germany's Lees, and not simply for Perera. Men with more evident abhorrence for Nazism—George Ball and John Kenneth Galbraith—also put the whisky on the table and found that Albert Speer "evoked in us a sympathy of which we were secretly ashamed," in part because they still "tended to think those rumors [about Nazi extermination policies] exaggerated," as Ball admitted in his memoirs. Charity operated with these Americans less than a fascination with their enemies, or as Ball put it, with the possibility that Speer "seemed, to use Noel Coward's derisive phrases, 'like us.'"[46]

As Freeman Dyson has pointed out in describing his own experiences, even those who grappled with the moral dimensions of the war found participation in it easy to rationalize and a sense of purpose increasingly elusive. Near the end of the war and of his service as operations analyst with the RAF's Bomber Command, he asked himself how "I let myself become involved in this crazy game of murder."

> At the beginning of the war, I believed fiercely in the brotherhood of man, called myself a follower of Gandhi, and was morally opposed to all violence. After a year of war I retreated and said, Unfortunately nonviolent resistance against Hitler is impracticable, but I am still morally opposed to bombing. A couple of years later I said, Unfortunately it seems that bombing is necessary in order to win the war, and so I am willing to go to work for Bomber Command, but I am still morally opposed to bombing cities indiscriminately. After I arrived at Bomber Command I said, Unfortunately it turns out that we are after all bombing cities indiscriminately, but this is morally justified, as it is helping to win the war. A year later I said, Unfortunately it seems that our bombing is not really helping to win the war, but at least I am morally

justified in working to save the lives of the bomber crews. In the last spring of the war I could no longer find any excuses.

Partly in reaction to the loss of "excuses," Dyson charted a unique course of fascination with the German enemy that slopped over into admiration. By war's end, he "began more and more to envy the technicians on the other side who were helping the German night fighter crews to defend their homes and families." They had "a cause clean to fight for." Dyson concluded: "A good cause can become bad if we fight it with means that are indiscriminately murderous. A bad cause can become good if enough people fight for it in a spirit of comradeship and self-sacrifice." Dyson did not seem fully aware of how Britain's "indiscriminately murderous" methods arose from a war begun "in a spirit of comradeship and self-sacrifice," or how unclean the German cause was even at war's end—how many Germans still killed subject peoples rather than defend the homeland, how their leaders could be more blunderingly wasteful of their own men than Bomber Command was with its cannon fodder. In his own peculiar manner, however, Dyson charted the ethical ambiguity which many civilian experts sustained through the war: their difficulty in ascertaining just what made their cause the right one or sometimes even in making the attempt.[47]

To be sure, unlike Bowles, Perera, and Stearns, men like Dyson, Ball, and Galbraith tried to set an ethical compass by pitting themselves against generals and admirals. They found military bureaucracy stifling and the military mind parochial and self-serving, its methods brutal and wasteful. Yet they recount with such pleasure the various struggles they waged that their claimed distaste for wartime service seems disingenuous. They enjoyed violating military protocol just as the airmen did with the older services; both groups came across a bit like small boys enjoying pranks against their elders. Berating airmen for the wastefulness of their bombing methods and their blindness to the civilians' rational findings, these experts presented themselves, as Ball did in commenting on arguments over targeting in 1944, as "interested only in making as objective an assessment as possible."[48] Yet the tone and substance of their arguments suggested they desired something more: recognition of their status and the superiority of their minds in the making of war.

"Command turned simple men into *prima donnas*," Zuckerman complained of his military superiors, but he did not recognize that war might do much the same to men like himself. Zuckerman's own parochialism mirrored what he attacked in others. "Operational problems, I discovered [after the war], savoured more of the characteristics of biological enquiry than of those encountered by chemists or physicists." Apparently not only were most officers unfit for the task of analyzing operations, but many scientists as well. In arguing for his plan of attack against the German railway network, Zuckerman "constantly resorted to biological analogies," as he recalled—without a hint that such analogies might color his argument. The scientists' pretense to objectivity, so abrasive to military men though they did not know how to challenge it, disguised both professional ambitions and intellectual predispositions.[49]

In truth, scientists like Zuckerman and Dyson were naive and confused about what science had to offer to war-makers. Much of Zuckerman's memoirs presumes that there were "right" conclusions to be drawn by objective analysis from intelligence data, if only air officers had not operated on vested interests. His conviction that postwar systems analysis used in selecting strategic objectives had banished "the kind of naive economic analysis" evident in World War II is almost macabre in its faith in the objectivity of scientific systems. Dyson's confusion ran deeper. On the one hand, his memoirs construct a dismaying account of how British airmen needlessly perished because commanders ignored the advice of scientists. On the other, he concluded that "the more technological the war becomes, the more disastrously a bad choice of means will change a good cause into evil"; no one was more eloquent than Dyson in explaining how "science and technology . . . made evil anonymous." Dyson believed that scientists on a day-to-day level could have made the bombing effort less wasteful and inhumane, even as the ultimate tendency of science was to aggravate those evils. He wanted it both ways—to criticize the contributions of science to war and to condemn those who ignored its contributions. Out of that confusion came Dyson's curious reaction at the end of the war to the American bombing of Japan. "Once we had got ourselves into the business of bombing cities, we might as well do the job competently and get it over with," he had believed. Somehow, a "bad choice of means"—how Dyson earlier described the bombing of cities—became good simply because it was successful. [50]

More often than not, these civilian critics did not want to understand the military men they berated but to score points off of them. The officers' narrow minds were their foils for demonstrating the civilians' breadth and intelligence. More than vanity was at stake, of course. At issue was the fate of civilian militarism—whether the broadening influence and heightened status of civilian expertise in war-making would be sustained. The critics pursued that goal as avidly as cooperative civilians like Bowles and Perera, only through conflict rather than compromise.

Their critique of bombing policies suggests their penchant for enhancing their status by scoring easy points. "The strategic air forces were almost sovereign powers" led by "air barons" who "ruled their commands like feudal lords," Zuckerman complained. Yet Allied victory did not rest only on some triumph of abundance over the failures of command but on the relatively ordered manner in which rivalrous commands cooperated. "To the airmen and soldiers, more meant better," Zuckerman wrote in condemning the pointless destructiveness of much bombing. Yet his own account of the bitter debate over bombing railway targets in France indicated that he had not given the issue of civilian casualties "much, if any, thought when the plan was first conceived. By that stage of the war, I had become inured to the idea of casualties, whether our own or the enemy's." His consuming concern had been economy of operations and acknowledgment of the scientist's gift in achieving it—worthy goals perhaps but ones whose moral dimensions did not clearly separate Zuckerman from his opponents. As another British boffin put it regarding a different argument on bombing, "It was on the grounds of probable effectiveness and not of morality"—between which he apparently saw no connection—"that the battle was fought." [51]

When Galbraith wrote his memoirs, he recalled how he had described the bombing of Japan at the end of the war as " 'this appalling business,' which was how anyone of any sensitivity would have felt." Galbraith's dismay would have been more convincing had he introduced evidence that he felt it while the war was still going on. Galbraith's retrospective critique of bombing's role in winning the war was unfair. "But no more than in Germany was it bombing that won the war. Japan's defeat began with the luminous insanity of its own military leadership," he observed, and "the war was won . . . by the greater weight of industrial power and of manpower and immediately by troops and ships and aircraft in direct and dangerous combat." But enemy incompetence and Allied superiority did not alone decide the war—if they had, there would have been no need actually to fight it; they opened opportunities for victory, but only when transformed by strategy into the fact of defeat and surrender. Galbraith's memoirs glided over the role played by strategic bombing in that regard. He seemed more interested in ridiculing the benighted state of the military mind than in exploring why the course of bombing unfolded as it did.[52]

It would be as foolish to make cardboard figures of the civilian critics as it was for the critics to do with the "air barons" they condemned. At their best, they measured their judgments—Zuckerman, for example, finding much to admire in Eisenhower, Tedder, and Spaatz—and their observations into the organizational mentality of bureaucratic warfare had a special incisiveness. But few civilians joined Dyson in seeing themselves as part of that mentality, not just victims and opponents of it, and few admitted that scientists, academicians, and lawyers brought not only a technique but a set of parochial interests to war-making.

Theodore von Karman showed how those interests could be successfully pursued in the narrowest way. Von Karman was a promoter, globe-trotter, and scientific jack-of-all-trades whose interests spanned rocketry, space travel, jet propulsion, military aviation—any activity where aerodynamics came into play. Although he caught Arnold's attention in the 1930s with his warnings of German and Italian progress in aviation and rocketry, he did not quickly choose sides in the emerging world struggle, content in 1937 to advise both the Chinese Air Force and Japanese universities; at the same time Arnold was using Air Corps funds to rescue von Karman's fledgling program in rocketry and jet propulsion at Caltech. Earlier, he had worked for Germany in World War I and for the aviation industries in Germany, Japan, and the United States in the 1920s. At best, he demonstrated the internationalism of modern science. At worst, he sold his talents to the highest bidder.

During the war, his relations with Arnold and the air force flourished. The AAF funded Caltech's pioneering work in jet engines and then in 1943, upon new disclosures about German advances in rocketry, Caltech's Jet Propulsion Laboratory (JPL). Meanwhile, von Karman helped establish a private company, Aerojet, to manufacture for the AAF the jet-assist engines JPL was developing, with substantial profits for von Karman and other stockholders involved, while Arnold promoted von Karman's role as a key scientific advisor to the postwar air force.

The triangular relationship among private university, government agency, and corporation that centered on JPL was the prototype of the postwar military–scientific–industrial complex. Scientists did not always turn the handsome personal bargain von Karman did, but institutionally they prospered from the war. The benefits derived from war outlasted it, and as hot war turned to a cold one, few asked questions about the wisdom of sponsorship by the military. For some, "a particular view of national security answered any questions about propriety or, indeed, imposed an affirmative obligation to do military research." Others "applied the standard of basic research—at best an elusive criterion"—and thereby "absolved themselves of the question of responsibility."[53]

Scientists offered their creative talents on conditions they measured often with an accountant's exactitude. Lavish contracting to universities and industrial laboratories preserved their institutional integrity, expanded facilities, and guarded what intellectual freedom could be maintained during war. The scientists' entry into the policymaking apparatus, achieved variously by guile, persuasion, and demand, insured for them a role in public policy undreamed of before the war. Scientists and university officials set out to put wartime prosperity on a permanent footing, guided by two assumptions: science would prosper from the government funding deemed necessary for capital-intensive research, while the nation would preserve its technological superiority during the coming age of instant warfare, about which scientists sounded the alarms as loudly as military officers. Quarrels over the terms of partnership persisted. But especially in the air force, military men were generally forthcoming.

Civilian militarism brought status, profit, institutional growth, and creative opportunities to many scientists, academicians, lawyers, and businessmen. A minority passionately saw ideological issues at stake in the war. For most, winning the war was surely a goal but one whose worth seemed too obvious to require much elaboration. The war was more fascinating and attractive as a process to which they could apply their talents than as a crusade. Pursuing civilian militarism, they identified it with broader virtues in the Allied cause: the triumph of cooperative organization over the authoritarian and parochial mentality of the militarist elites ruling Germany and Japan. But the struggle for civilian militarism also turned them inward, concentrating their energies on the perfection of technique rather than on the enemy. The lawyer or for that matter the scientist who regarded the air force as his "client" had something to prove but above all was contributing his craft, his ability to "think objectively," as Dwight MacDonald had called it.

Was there a darker attraction? The core of scientific work, especially for the atomic scientists, was the technology of death itself. Attractive because of the intriguing problems it posed and the promise of victory it carried, that technology also conferred power over life and death itself—with the atomic bomb, absolute power. Some felt angst over creating such power; others perhaps welcomed the opportunity to seize the very powers of the gods themselves. In science, freedom and knowledge had always been inseparable from control—to unlock the secrets of nature is also to subdue and seize its power. It hardly could have been otherwise for the men at Los Alamos.

What makes such speculation hard to confirm is the reticence of men who "let Oppenheimer take protective custody of their emotions"[54] and the difficulty of interpreting those revelations they did offer. Too, the relationship between scientist and invention was far different in the 1940s from what it had been even a few decades earlier, when nothing stood between inventor and invention. The scientist of World War II worked on some highly specialized aspect of the final product, distanced from it by a vast organizational apparatus diluting the expression of whatever psychological or pathological drive may have motivated him. In such an atmosphere, Faustian bargains were not so easily, at least not so obviously, struck.

Yet some physicists had to confront the absoluteness of the atomic weapon, its world-ending potential. Early in the war, Oppenheimer and Edward Teller feared that the atomic bomb might be used to trigger a fusion reaction capable of "setting afire the atmosphere of the entire planet." They did not proceed with their work until they reexamined their calculations and "computed a three-in-a-million chance" that the ultimate catastrophe would occur, a chance which their superior, Arthur Holly Compton, "felt was low enough to be worth taking." Yet it remains unclear whether they were merely trying to eliminate that danger before proceeding or were drawn to it. Even on the eve of the Trinity test of the plutonium bomb in July 1945, the possibility of atmospheric ignition from an atomic bomb alone was sufficient to induce Enrico Fermi to "invite bets . . . against first the destruction of all human life and second just that of human life in New Mexico." The scientists were staring at opposites inextricably joined: ultimate control over the universe (at least humankind's small portion of it) and absolute loss of control. Even if few scientists felt the attraction and danger at such an ultimate level, others continued working despite their warning (signed by Fermi among others) that an international arms race in atomic weapons could spell national suicide for the United States, provoking a sudden attack that "might literally wipe out even the largest nation."[55]

The scientists pondered the nature of uranium and plutonium spheres at the instant before fission: "By their calculations, no living creature could ever see such a sphere. It would destroy itself before the eye could deliver an image to the brain." But before brought to a critical mass, the sphere could be handled, and "the thing was warm," seemingly moving and pulsating with life, creating a "thrill of realization and dread," as if the men held in their own hands the secret of nature and of power over it. Working on the bomb instilled a sense of ultimate potency, a triumph of man over nature. "Nuclear explosives have a glitter more seductive than gold to those who play with them," Dyson has commented. "To command nature to release in a pint pot the energy that fuels the stars, to lift by pure thought a million tons of rock into the sky, these are exercises of the human will that produce an illusion of illimitable power."[56]

Dominated by men, Western science has aspired to unlock the secrets of the natural world. Often its practitioners have also sought immortality through escape from that world, a world so often associated with women and femininity. By their colloquial language, the men at Los Alamos hinted at such aspirations. They asked themselves before the Trinity test "the question whether the first complete atom bomb would be a 'dud' or a success, or as they said at Los Alamos, a 'girl' or a 'boy'."[57] Femininity was weakness, masculinity was the power to transcend nature and its mortal reality. If these men entertained a male fantasy of ultimate potency, it was perhaps not coincidence that they gave their bombs masculine names (Fat Man, Little Boy).

Aspirations for ultimate power seem to have been especially intense among three Hungarian scientists. Von Karman's loftiest dreams were for space travel, and he also involved himself deeply in nuclear strategy and weaponry after the war. Teller was the driving promoter of the super-bomb, as the hydrogen bomb was called during the war. John von Neumann, the foremost intellect behind the modern computer and game theory, wartime consultant on everything from weather forecasting to the most forbidding calculations on chain reactions, completed the trinity. All three sought power in several forms. They shared a deep hostility to the Soviet Union during the war and welcomed using the latent or actual power of nuclear weapons against it. All admired and worked eagerly with military officials and actively courted status and position through work on weapons and strategy during and after the war. Yet these mundane forms of power may have been inseparable from aspirations of immortality. His biographer recounts von Neumann's description of "a subconscious feeling of extreme insecurity in individuals, and the necessity of producing the unusual or facing extinction." Von Neumann quipped after Hiroshima that mankind, "having failed to solve the problem of living together, had at least succeeded in *achieving togetherness* by cosmic suicide." Perhaps he was "vulnerable to seduction by 'the gadget,' that is, by the promise of nuclear weapons as a means to salvation." In the power to inflict total death lay also the power to control life itself—those who could take life could also give it and thereby triumph over their own mortality.[58]

Or so we can speculate, while acknowledging the scantiness of the data on which such speculation rests. But even those—perhaps the vast majority—who felt grave doubts about perfecting the technology of death had ways to ward off those doubts. Trivializing language was one means—the bomb could be regarded as a mere device, a "gadget" (not a term merely serving the needs of security, since some wartime code names did connote the grandness of aspirations—OVERLORD for the Normandy invasion). Destructive intentions could be denied. "The bomb will never be dropped on people," Ernest Lawrence reportedly said. "As soon as we get it, we'll use it only to dictate terms of peace."[59] Here was an echo of hopes that had reverberated through decades of effort to perfect the aerial bomber.

By defining their work as a kind of fail-safe effort against the possibility of a Nazi bomb, scientists also maintained the illusion of benign purposes. At the time of the Trinity test, Samuel Allison offered James Conant his belated realization: "They're going to take this thing over and fry *hundreds* of Japanese!" Somehow, he had believed until then that it would be otherwise. Oppenheimer kept doubt at bay in different ways. Trinity "betokened a greater explosion to come—one that would shake mankind free from parochialism and war." Oppenheimer, like many scientists, also preserved an image of his own restraint and humaneness by measuring these virtues against the aggressive designs attributed to the military. He wanted the bomb made and tested, said a colleague, so that it would not "become a secret of the military which they could use to control the government with after the war." The running battle with General Leslie Groves and the military command engaged in by some scientists reinforced the scientists' sense of moral and intellectual superiority. For some, too, not even this war shattered their faith in an international community of science rescuing the world from stubborn nationalism.[60]

But the most powerful protection against experiencing doubt was immersion in fascinating and demanding work, just as doubt arose when scientists were removed from the mainstream of work on the bomb—among the Chicago scientists, whose more theoretical work had been completed earlier. By contrast, few scientists at Los Alamos, working at fever pitch until the very last moment, felt they had time to question. A sheer delight in problem solving consumed them, heightened by the enormous pressure under which they labored, by the sudden leap into enterprise of such importance that the younger scientists experienced, and by the intellectually charged atmosphere Oppenheimer provided. Freeman Dyson later discovered that "they did not just build the bomb. They enjoyed building it," their pleasure, Dyson believed, the source of the guilt some felt more than the destruction their work caused. But doubt rarely emerged among the scientists until their deeds were done. While the war went on, their mentality resembled the one described by Dwight MacDonald, and prevailing as well in the establishment of nonnuclear scientists, officers, and civilian experts. For most of them, destruction was something they produced, not something they did. Their own president had preferred to view the war in those terms. Others ably acted upon it.[61]

THE WARRIORS

Did the men in American warplanes also regard the war as a matter of production and technique rather than destruction and killing? The question may seem silly, for obviously these men killed and were often themselves killed. Far from being able to separate means and ends, they were the human connection between them. The dangers they faced were awesome, their losses sometimes staggering, though also wildly varying. A closer look, however, suggests that even the warriors often saw the perfection of technique as more important than the tasks of killing.

It is true, of course, that army fliers ran enormous risks. The Army Air Forces, its mean wartime strength one-fourth of the total army, took only about one-ninth of the army's battle casualties. But breaking down that large figure better reveals the risks airmen faced, for it includes the great number of men injured in combat, the one risk which was lower for airmen. They ran almost the same risks as others in the army of being killed, however, suffering 52,173 of the 291,557 battle deaths inflicted on all Americans during the war (the RAF lost 70,253 in operations, 47,268 in Bomber

Command). Since combat personnel comprised a smaller proportion of the air force than they did in the rest of the army, the risks once one was assigned to combat were higher in the air force than in ground forces. Airmen also were more likely to be captured by the enemy, and they ran a much greater chance of being missing in action and later declared dead. Furthermore, officers perished in unusual numbers in the AAF because a far higher proportion of the air force were officers (about half of combat flying personnel): twice as many air officers died in battle than in all the rest of the army, despite its larger size. Moreover, 35,946 airmen died in noncombat situations, about 43 percent of all such deaths in the wartime army. In 1943 alone, 850 airmen died in 298 B-24 accidents in the states, leaving the survivors "scared to death of their airplanes." Away from combat, the airmen's scourge was not the soldier's traditional one of disease, but the severe danger of training, ferrying, and other kinds of aerial accidents. In sum, the risks for airmen, though sometimes peculiar, were large.[62]

During the war, medical statisticians examined the fate of a pool of 2,051 personnel who began a series of twenty-five missions for the Eighth Air Force, the principal American air force bombing Germany. Only 559, or 26.8 percent of these men, completed all their missions. Eleven hundred ninety-five were either killed or missing in action but often later certified as fatalities. Another 15.8 percent were lost to the force because of severe wounds or by death or disease incurred outside combat or by removal from flying for administrative reasons. On average, almost 4 percent of the force were killed or missing in action on each mission, and the mean number of missions completed for the entire group was 14.72, barely past the halfway point.[63] Of course the airmen themselves could calculate these loss rates in their rough and sometimes misleading fashion, as generals like LeMay knew well. But no calculation of odds could anticipate their uneven distribution—how one squadron might be decimated in a few weeks and another emerge almost unscathed after many missions.

The airman's anxiety in combat took peculiar forms. Confinement in a highly cramped machine often caused a sense of helplessness experienced also by the submariner. The greater risk of capture by the enemy was a fearsome prospect in the war against the Japanese, who sometimes tried and beheaded airmen for alleged war crimes. Heavy bomber crews also suffered the special strain of responsibility for comrades. When LeMay and his flight surgeons talked to one squadron commander who "flopped on us" after some brutal missions, they learned he "was not worried about *himself*. He had not gone yellow; he was perfectly willing to see himself expended. . . . But he simply couldn't bring himself to the point of taking another crew into combat, and then losing some of them. It had happened too often."[64]

Indeed, as air force psychiatrists found, emotional collapse often stemmed from the impossible decisions a bomber crewman sometimes had to make:

> So close are the men to each other, so bound together by a common purpose and a common fate, that one individual's combat career cannot come to a different conclusion from that of his comrades without pain. This leads to

innumerable situations where a man must choose between a hero's death, without in the least desiring to be a hero, or life in the future with a bad conscience and a constant feeling of depression and guilt. If he chooses the first course of action, he may receive a posthumous decoration and a place of honor in that section of paradise reserved for airmen, but the act will have been due to the impossibility of leaving his friends or letting them down. . . .

Even when there has been no choice, and survival is due to the sheerest whim of fate, . . . the 'survivor's guilt' haunts the individual; he is 'ghosted,' as one man put it, by his dead friends, who will not leave him alone or give him peace of mind.

The burden of comrades' fate was one reason why the morale of heavy bomber crews tended to drop more steeply once combat missions began than it did for fighter pilots. Fighter pilots also benefited from lower casualty rates and less time in the air, without the attendant fatigue and tension bomber crews experienced and had no way to release. And simply because the fighter pilot did not need to maintain formation and had sole control over his aircraft, his sense of controlling his fate was much stronger.[65]

For British bomber crews, a sense of helplessness took on a peculiar dimension in 1944 because loss rates failed to decrease as men flew more missions, destroying the crewmen's hope that they gained mastery of their fate as they accumulated skill and experience. As Freeman Dyson, who made the statistical findings at the time, observed, "Experienced and inexperienced crews were mown down as impartially as the boys who walked into the German machine gun nests in the battle of the Somme in 1916." Dyson attributed this to failures in the gunnery system of the British bombers, failures he waged a futile battle to correct. A colleague also discovered that the escape rate of British bomber crews—their chances of bailing out from damaged or malfunctioning bombers and surviving—was less than half that for American bomber crews, again because of a technical failure difficult to correct due to "the entrenched inertia of the military establishment." No wonder that RAF fliers found that "the line between the living and the dead was very thin," as one wrote: "it is as if those who have gone have merely caught an earlier train to the same destination." American bomber crews at least had the satisfaction of a declining loss rate as they gained experience, plus the probability that 50 percent of their numbers would escape from bombers downed in operations.[66]

Even for them, however, the emotional toll was exacting, and doctors who treated serious emotional problems among crewmen found themselves in "a wasteland in which to wander, filled with shadows of theories, dusty slogans, and dire predictions." Lack of experience in the stresses of combat aviation was one problem. The flight surgeon also served clienteles with conflicting interests: the operational commander trying to increase missions, the combat crew needing protection from a comrade's dangerous behavior, and the individual flier, who might underestimate his capacity to fly or, just as dangerous, overestimate that ability. The doctor's uncertain middle course between these claims "was to help the men carry on to the limit of their capacity, and then perhaps fly a few more missions." A punitive attitude toward emotional problems was widespread in the armed forces, but it was mitigated by the real affection of some commanders for their men and by the enormous investment the air force had in its flying personnel, who were too few and too expensive to be summarily cashiered. Moreover, although combat aviation offered peculiar stresses, cases of gross regression to infantile states were less common among airmen than among ground soldiers; the precarious task of flying, the fine motor and sensory skills it required, and the AAF's superior psychiatric services led to earlier identification of severe problems.[67]

Still, for both flight surgeons and psychiatrists in rear areas treatment was always a struggle because of the unpredictable or intractable problems they confronted. The best doctors perceived keen limits on their predictive and curative abilities. Proud or frightened men masked symptoms adroitly; the triggers to anxiety and dysfunction were too multiple and environmental; and combat aviation, like other branches of service, did not always reward the "normal" or unconflicted personality. Thus the mildly neurotic man might fare better simply because his previous experience with anxiety left him less surprised and frightened by experiencing it in battle or because for the first time he might "be able to feel as well as his neighbor." More dismaying, models of treatment from civilian life had little relevance. There the environmental stimuli to trauma might be controlled or altered to some extent. "In battle," however, "the stress is never concluded, nor can it be controlled. Rather, the intent is to increase the stress continually in the furious pursuit of victory." In the realm of their work, air force psychiatrists acknowledged, "a hair divides the normal from the neurotic, the adaptive from the nonadaptive. The failures of adaption of the soldier . . . mirror Everyman's everyday failures or neurotic compromises with reality."[68]

Flight surgeons and psychiatrists offered several responses to combat stress, performing a triple role as counselor, paternal figure, and therapist. Severe cases required hospitalization, in the zone of operations or back in the states, where the favored treatment became narcosynthesis—drug-induced reenactment of a traumatic episode to assist the ego in mastering or accepting it. But the best treatment was benign rather than invasive: leaves from combat duty and fixed tours, for which doctors lobbied hard. Even rest was minimally effective, for fear and stress built up regardless of the frequency with which missions were spaced. In short, simple physical and emotional exhaustion from frequent flying was a minor factor.[69]

In the end, morale was the responsibility of military, not medical, men, but there were limits to what commanders could do. The objective, physical risk could be trimmed by provision of protective measures in flight and by better methods of rescue and rehabilitation for fallen fliers. Prompt replacement of lost crewmen was absolutely essential for morale—nothing was more depressing than empty bunks. Scarcely less important was a simple measure like keeping the mail flowing. In coping with anxiety, perhaps LeMay's cheery fatalism was helpful to some. Certainly, as better commanders knew, crews responded badly to aborted or scrubbed missions: the heightening of anxiety to no purpose exacted a special strain. And commanders who failed to notify crews in advance of pending stand-downs, leaves, and passes ran the risk of reinforcing "a conception of higher authorities as remote, detached persons who were indifferent to the welfare of the men." That conception could be more powerfully countered by a commander's willingness to share the danger, as LeMay did. As psychiatrists commented, but good commanders have long known, "Nothing is worse for morale than a leader who leads from the rear," particularly for American soldiers, whose lack of ideological and intellectual commitment to the war made their morale highly dependent on perceptions of equitably shared danger and group cohesiveness. So many officers died, some of considerable rank, that the lower ranks could not easily feel sacrificed to the ambitions of their superiors. Too, because combat commanders were not responsible for aircrews' discipline on the ground, the petty frictions that often arose in the army between officers and enlisted men were rare in the combat air force.[70]

But the manifold strains defeated some men. One Eighth Air Force tail gunner first encountered his dread on a training flight in England during which the bomb-bay door of another plane flew off and sliced away the tail section of his bomber. Trapped in the plummeting tail, the sergeant could not smash the Plexiglas but dug a hole in the metal skin, got his body out of the craft up to his shoulders, finally worked free, and got his parachute open shortly before hitting ground, uninjured. He landed near his crashed plane and, after a failed attempt to rescue his comrades, watched them burn. Insomnia and nightmares then set in, but he insisted on starting combat missions—it was the common pattern for crewmen to save up physical and emotional complaints until their tours of duty were nearly done. But when his bomber was damaged in combat, crew members detected that his strain was getting out of control and reported him to the doctors, who granted his wish to be grounded. His case compressed the multiple sources of strain for fliers: the role of blind chance (facing death even before going to battle), the loss of comrades, the cumulative impact of repeated missions, and the sense of helpless confinement. In the Eighth Air Force, only 2 percent of fliers suffered what the historian Thomas Coffey calls "nervous breakdowns," but such a figure disguises a great deal: a host of lesser emotional disturbances, plus those expressed in or diagnosed as physical disabilities or disciplinary problems.[71] In short, the damage could be staggering, both emotionally and physically, both in the air and on the ground where the bombs were dropped, and those who faced and witnessed it could not regard war simply as an application of technique distinct from killing and destruction.

Yet the emotional mechanisms airmen used to cope with danger necessarily diminished their sensitivity to combat and destruction. They might become, commented air force psychiatrists, "effective, careful fighting men, quiet and cool on the ground and in the air" but "drained of most feelings other than those having to do with combat." Likewise in the RAF: "The men who fared best were those who did not allow themselves to think at all. Many crews argued that emotional entanglements were madness." The nature of combat often aggravated this coolness, this "psychic closing-off" as Robert Jay Lifton calls it in a very different context, making it difficult to sustain a sense of engagement in a human, deadly struggle.[72]

Several factors diminished further the sense of struggle. Most obviously, the enemy was rarely met face to face. His death and destruction were either unnoticed or observed at an impersonal distance, and even his efforts to return fire were wholly impersonal. For American fliers, the enemy's retaliation against the homeland or the home base, with its potential to awaken a sense of hatred, was almost nonexistent. Too, in the heat of combat, the energies of crewmen ran as much toward the technical challenge of manipulating the plane and its equipment as toward bombing, which was often done blindly (by radar or by following the lead of pathfinders), with results often unobserved. In the RAF, the men who unleashed destruction "were the last people to know" its results and

> totally dependent on their commanders for information about the success or failure of what they were doing. An infantry platoon commander . . . could achieve some notion of the army's gains or losses by noticing whether he himself was moving forwards or backwards. A convoy escort officer could judge a great deal from the rate of sinkings around him. But a bomber pilot, with rare exceptions such as the great firestorms of Hamburg and Dresden had to wait for the next bulletin from High Wycombe to learn whether his colleagues were dying to good purpose or in vain.[73]

Even then, headquarters' information might be wrong.

Distance from a human enemy was not unique to air war. Even within its boundaries a sense of distance varied widely. Destructiveness and exposure to danger simply did not correlate with each other: the Twentieth Air Force, the most devastating of all the wartime air forces, took only 2.8 percent of all losses by the American air force during the war—some 3,415 casualties, of whom 576 were killed and 2,406 missing—while the AAF in Europe and the Mediterranean endured 94,565 casualties.[74] Fighter pilots came closer to seeing the whites of the enemy's eyes. But even pilots of naval torpedo bombers reported that they often could not see their torpedoes explode because they had to turn away so quickly.

Often enough narrative accounts indicated the remoteness of what warplanes did to others simply by omitting mention of the matter. It often took the interloper on air combat to notice its special sense of unreality. Charles Lindbergh, denied active duty by Roosevelt, nonetheless remained an informal advisor to Arnold and the aviation industry and flew tactical combat missions in the Pacific. His observations were acute:

> You press a button and death flies down. One second the bomb is hanging harmlessly in your racks, completely under your control. The next it is hurtling down through the air, and nothing in your power can revoke what you have done.
>
> . . . How can there be writhing, mangled bodies? How can this air

around you be filled with unseen projectiles? It is like listening to a radio account of a battle on the other side of the earth. It is too far away, too separated to hold reality. (May 29, 1944)

One is separated from the surface of that island as though he were viewing it on a motion-picture screen in a theater on the other side of the world. A plane in the sky, an island in the water; there is no thread of realization, of understanding, of human feeling that connects the two. In modern war one kills at a distance, and in doing so does not realize that he is killing. (September 10, 1944)[75]

To be sure, the implications of the distance Lindbergh described were ambiguous. Detachment from killing can make it easy but can also provide perspective on it; it can both lessen and increase hatred toward an enemy. Wartime historians noted that men opposing the Germans seemed to be "more vindictive toward the Japanese" than the ground soldiers actually committed to Pacific fighting, an observation confirmed in postwar studies. Men in training displayed more vindictiveness toward both enemies than did men in combat. American soldiers held more vengeful attitudes toward the Japanese than toward the Germans, with whom "identification was relatively easy": many American troops in the Pacific and a majority in Europe and the states wanted to "wipe out the whole Japanese nation." But attitudes toward the Japanese were also more superficial and volatile, and combat often triggered a "discovery that much dirty fighting which to the civilian and the inexperienced soldier seemed a special property of the enemy's viciousness was actually a general characteristic of war." Moreover, in both theaters, hatred of the enemy was apparently a minor motivation for men in combat and regarded by air force psychiatrists as counterproductive, a crippling emotion that was a luxury of the home front.[76]

Wartime data permit few firm conclusions about how the airman's peculiar distance from his enemy affected his attitudes. Most likely, distance did not increase or decrease hatred so much as it altered its forms and manner of expression. It made it easier for more men to hate an emeny but also made that hatred more abstract, less personally and intensely felt. Whatever vindictiveness airmen felt, they had fewer opportunities to express it directly, and it was generally submerged in the performance of highly technical functions, especially for bomber crews. "Their excitement at actually witnessing the destruction of a target was great," Vincent Sheean noted when he accompanied a mission against Japan; but that excitement, he suggested, had little to do with what was done to the enemy, much more to do with the successful completion of a task. Furthermore, the routine postmission interrogation of crews, "such a cut-and-dried, mechanical affair," tended to drain away the crews' emotional reactions.[77]

The dominant focus of bomber crewmen was not on the nature or threat of the enemy, especially not in the last several months of the Pacific war, when the threat had dwindled sharply. The enemy was the void at the center of their wartime concerns and postwar recollections. As public relations officer for the 21st Bomber Command in the Marianas, St. Clair McKelway noted that there was a "letdown" after operations started: "It would just be Big Business from now on, with military perfectionist standards applied all up and down the line until we had become an efficient, well-oiled machine of destruction—a good machine, maybe, but a dull one." McKelway appreciated how much success was defined by efficient routine in which feelings about the enemy played a small role.[78]

Erich Fromm found airmen to be teams of technicians "not concerned with killing and . . . hardly aware of an enemy" and preoccupied "with the proper handling of their complicated machine along the lines laid down in meticulously organized plans." Their destructiveness was "known to them cerebrally, but hardly comprehended affectively; it was, paradoxical as this may sound, none of their concern," and the airmen, like the engineers of the bombing effort, were "completely alienated from the product of their work." Fromm did not appreciate how quickly "meticulously organized plans" could collapse when men set out on a mission (or even before they did). His characterization may conflict with the liveliness evident in some firsthand observations of airmen's personalities, which hardly always seemed dehumanized. But conditions acted to drain men of emotions about the enemy whatever their personalities. Guilt did arise for death meted out to victims below, apparently more often among bomber crews than among fighter pilots because the latter usually knew their attacks were confined to enemy soldiers. But by and large hatred and guilt involving the enemy were out of place in a war of technique or dwarfed by more immediate emotions, anxiety and the grief over loss of buddies.[79]

Distance from the enemy occurred because of the nature of air combat but even more because of demands of aviation that arose outside of combat. Flying itself posed many of those demands, particularly for the men of the Twentieth Air Force, who were required to make round trips of up to four thousand miles, often across the treacherous heights of the Himalayas or the trackless expanses of the Pacific. On those missions, takeoff alone posed peril, for the planes were so heavily loaded with bombs and gasoline that the slightest mechanical or human failure could abort a mission or destroy a bomber. Then came the long flight whose success depended on the most careful calculations of altitude, speed, and fuel consumption. Even in October 1944, when the enemy's air defenses were still formidable, LeMay's crews operating out of China found that "take-off . . . is the high point of any flight. All crews, in discussing a mission, invariably talk about their take-off and not about flak, fighters, or other enemy opposition." Likewise crews operating from the Marianas "began to fear their own aircraft and our field orders more than the devices of the enemy." Ditching was frequent on B-29 flights of some fourteen hours, especially when winds of 150 miles sabotaged calculations of fuel consumption, and in the Pacific the downed flier was often never found and rescued. As Ernie Pyle reported, "They were over the empire for only twenty minutes to an hour. . . . What gave the boys the willies was 'sweating out' those six or seven hours of ocean beneath them on the way back," often at night. By the spring of 1945, crewmen in the B-29s faced greater risk from the hazards of flying than they did from the enemy, who accounted for only one-fifth of the B-29s downed. In those circumstances it was no wonder that the airmen Pyle talked with showed little strong feeling about the enemy.[80]

Conditions within the bomber created a curious sense of unreality and alienation. On B-29s, a thirty-foot tunnel, just big enough to crawl through, was the only way to traverse the length of the plane, adding to the claustrophobia sometimes felt on long missions. On the other hand, comforts could make war seem remote—men could smoke, eat, sleep, and wear regular clothing because the B-29 was pressurized and heated. Adding to the sense of unreality was the public relations policy of the Twentieth Air Force. Crews were "picking up news on their radios, when only halfway home, that their bombing mission had been announced in Washington. All the world knew about it, but they still had a thousand miles of ocean to cross before it was finished"—as if announcement of their attack were more important than their fate and missions had an abstracted reality apart from what men did.[81]

Grappling with the environment in and around the plane was as consuming as engaging the enemy. On the older bombers in service in Europe, cold and fatigue posed special problems. More men were disabled by frostbite than by combat wounds, especially when men came on board wet or sweaty or perspired heavily or urinated in their suits during the stress of combat. Anoxia from shortages of oxygen both compounded the perils of frostbite and posed a serious danger in and of itself.[82] The men also had to cope with damage or malfunctions of the plane, often performing herculean feats to get a plane back to base, in the face of unpredictable changes in weather—an unexpected headwind, a target shrouded by bad weather, a home base sunny when they took off and socked in when they returned. Particularly in the Pacific, where the dominant weather patterns came through Japanese or Soviet territory from which American meteorologists could gain little information, the unexpected often occurred.

In these conditions, the bomber often seemed more important than the enemy. It was the focus and repository of crewmen's fears and hopes, the living creature who controlled their fate and whose fate they tried to control. Or it might become a projection of the flier. "He loves them [the planes] for their strength and beauty," Dixon Wecter commented in 1944. "He looks upon them as extensions of his ego, or friends whose temperaments are more vivid than those of most human beings he knows. . . . A man begins to see his own personality in terms of the machines he loves."[83]

Beyond the conditions of combat and flying, the airman's life on the ground sustained his sense of distance from war and the enemy's threat. By no means could all men boast, as one flier did to Pyle, that "we're living as good here [in the Marianas] as we did in America." Facilities were often primitive when operations began. But airmen enjoyed more rest and comfort than did army soldiers or, in the case of airmen in England, the surrounding native population. Although men in the AAF bitterly complained that naval officers enjoyed scandalous luxuries, most airmen lived in comfortable, heated, often permanent buildings; they ate well, watched movies or slept for long periods between missions, or (in the Pacific) took a leisurely swim. Men in transit to or from combat assignments enjoyed the luxury of redistribution centers at Atlantic City and Miami Beach, the resorts taken over by the air force during the war. They also had the advantage of probably the best medical care of all the services. Given the enormous investment required to train aircrews, it made sense to treat them "with a high degree of indulgence," to do everything to reduce deprivations that impeded morale. The high proportion of officers among combat airmen also insulated them from war's deprivations, for they "enjoyed the special privileges, the higher income and prestige that accrued to officers." Even enlisted men in the air force received higher rank, more rapid promotions, and more awards and decorations than did their counterparts in the rest of the army. Operational circumstances also kept some of war's uglier realities at distance: air bases were usually further behind the lines, less exposed to continuous danger than the bases from which ground soldiers operated.[84]

Airmen also spent more time away from combat assignments. They were in training longer before being sent to war; they were returned to the states or to noncombat duty after shorter overseas service than other men in the army; while stationed abroad, they had more free time away from the base and from military supervision. Of course, rhythms of combat varied enormously among different places and types of combat. Thus infantrymen and marines invading Japanese islands engaged in days or weeks of sustained combat while fliers returned to the relative security of bases, but ground soldiers often spent months behind the lines between assaults while aircrews continued flying missions every day or two. In Europe, the AAF bore the brunt of fighting until 1944, but ground operations, waged over large territories and long periods of time, lacked the episodic quality they often had in the Pacific. Even when placed in a battle situation, men might not actually fight; the army's behavioral experts found that among ground soldiers only a small fraction fired their weapons in any given engagement, and by the same token combat airmen sometimes peeled off from engaging the enemy, dumped their bomb loads far from targets, or in other ways aborted their missions.[85]

In any event, operational circumstances were perhaps not the primary ones conditioning airmen to see themselves as an elite for whom performance of professional skills—a mastery of technique—was more important than engaging an enemy. Before they went into combat and again when they came out of it, powerful factors of class, education, and policy strengthened their status and their elite image. The manner and sources of their recruitment were especially critical. Healthier, drawn from a higher educational and class base than other soldiers, given more specialized training, placed in combat duties only if they volunteered for them, airmen were regarded by themselves and others as "a piece of swank" or the "cream of the crop," while the infantry was "a dumping ground." As the war went on, it is true, the air force's craving for manpower led it to draw in less advantaged men. Still, wartime stereotypes reflected both demographic realities and airmen's self-image. They knew they possessed special prestige and deference, evident in the extraordinarily high ratio of officers to enlisted men and in the dominance of higher grades among the enlisted; in rank terms, the air force almost inverted the pyramid of the army. Awareness of prestige was enhanced by the favorable treatment, rapid promotion, and generous awards and decorations airmen received, and by the AAF's success in public relations.[86]

Of course status could inspire resentment. Other servicemen sometimes thought themselves slighted. Editorials like the New York *Daily News*'s "Rickenbacker Didn't Go to College" argued that taxi drivers "could be turned into swell combat pilots" and was unworried "that we may pick up some pilots who don't know . . . the proper way for a gentleman and an officer to navigate a teacup."[87] The AAF itself dropped its college requirements, but the change did little to alter the status, real and perceived, of the airmen.

Elite status was not confined to the American air forces and was not caused solely by the glamor and role of aviation, for the marines also enjoyed prestige as a select group. But the important difference between the two was their divergent criteria for selection; the marines were an elite but not a technical elite, admirable men but hardly pioneers of modern warfare.

The airmen's higher status and more sophisticated training also reflected and strengthened their stronger drive for upward social mobility. They expected promotion to come faster than other army men did—expectations borne out by practice—and they anticipated greater social and economic rewards to come their way after the war. They might find rewards by staying in the air force, which nearly everyone assumed would be far larger after this war than before it. Believers in the "winged gospel," a vast majority of AAF pilots also expected to own their own planes after the war. Most of all, airmen counted on their technical skills to open up good civilian jobs for them, an expectation wartime commentators encouraged. When Dixon Wecter reviewed the fate of wartime veterans in 1944, he saw the airman's salvation in a "huge peacetime aviation program to cover the earth. . . . On a planet where communication and transportation hold the front rank as never before, American technology is on the march." *Fortune* promised a quick payoff for the airman because American business looked to him more than to other servicemen as the best source of postwar talent. Air force personnel constituted "an ivory hunter's game preserve" for the businessman, and the AAF veteran would go into the airline industry and indeed all forms of enterprise, his preferences having "a great deal to do with the character of U.S. business ten and twenty years from now." In part because of this promised payoff, airmen were more content with their assignments, less desirous of transfer to other duties than other servicemen.[88]

The airman's link with civilian business and technology was also tightened by methods and sources of air force recruitment and by the AAF's reliance on civilian institutions for training and logistical support. Shortages of permanent military personnel and facilities had led it, well before Pearl Harbor, to turn to civilian "contract" schools to provide primary training for pilots and other flying personnel as well as for many technical specialties. The AAF gradually took over or phased out most of the contract schools but not before thousands of pilots received their first instruction from civilians; other flying personnel were trained at institutions like the navigation school operated by Pan American Airways. The influence of a technical model for military service could also be measured in the declining place of military drill and other forms of traditional military training.[89]

In part because of the apparent carryover of their skills to civilian work, airmen could more easily look upon wartime service as part of a career or profession rather than as a duty in which fighting itself was the essence. They differed sharply from other servicemen in their higher sense of satisfaction with the particular jobs and tasks they performed. To a considerable degree, their mentality was occupational rather than military. They saw themselves more as technicians and professionals than as warriors, and the technique learned in war promised social and economic mastery in peacetime.[90]

It also provided a sense of mastery over self and nature, especially for pilots. Flying allowed fulfillment of a "child's dreams of omnipotence in the face of his toddling weakness." These dreams "are usually abandoned with fairy tales and toys," commented air force psychiatrists; but "this supertoy, this powerful, snorting, impatient but submissive machine, enables the man to escape the usual limitations of time and space." Flying created "a feeling of aggressive potency bordering on the unchallenged strength of a superman." When the author of *God Is My Co-Pilot* flew over Mount Everest, "he felt that he had humbled this highest mountain and patronizingly saluted his fallen opponent." The airplane offered "the perfect prescription for those that are weak, hesitant or frustrated on earth. Give them wings, 2000 horses compressed into a radial engine, and what can stop them?"[91]

These satisfactions accorded with Fromm's portrayal of fliers as men alienated from themselves and the natural world. Like some scientists, they used technique to master themselves and the mortality inherent in their place in the natural world. Like some scientists, the search for "aggressive potency" also suggested male needs to define the relationship between femininity and that world. The instruments of destruction often had aggressive generic names such as Superfortresses or Marauders. A crew's own bomber, however, was regarded less as an instrument of destruction than as the symbolic repository of feminine forces of unpredictable nature which men could not control. Crews often gave their bombers feminine names—*Memphis Belle, Tokyo Rose, Enola Gay* (after Paul Tibbetts's mother)—and laced their sides with luridly colorful paintings of women until the air force banned "one of the last personal touches in an already impersonal war." As with the scientists, the airmen's rituals reflected more than the insecurities of a male psychology; they served many functions, not the least of which was the homely but powerful need to maintain symbolic contact with stateside sources of love and security. And in a culture that had made so much of aviation, the twin lures of potency and risk sometimes cut across gender lines. It was, after all, a woman flier who had once rhapsodized about "the feel of strength and power beneath your hands" and the quick "transition from life to death" in flying. Furthermore, hundreds of women flew military aircraft during the war, doing the sometimes fatal tasks of ferrying airplanes, towing targets, even testing rocket-propelled prototypes, and doing so without the lash of conscription, status as military personnel, and tangible benefits and payoff in the civilian marketplace accorded men.[92]

But if aviation did not meet only the needs of men, it remained largely a male sphere, and women (like black men) entered it only when the thirst for manpower impelled male leaders to open the door, only to close it again when a surplus of male crews became available late in the war. Likewise, if aviation did not always appeal to masculine ambitions, the testimony to how often it did suggests that airmen, like some scientists, achieved mastery of the natural world by risking return to it—they conquered death by courting it. "The qualities that make the finest combat pilot are qualities that seem to presage his own destruction. Icarus is his prototype and patron."[93] If scientists conquered nature by risking global suicide, pilots did so by risking personal destruction.

These appeals, confined to a limited number of airmen, could not always be sustained in the face of "reluctant intimacy with the mingled smell of burning paint, fabric, rubber, petrol and human flesh from a crashed aircraft," as the English flier's encounter with reality has been described. Even then, however, some "still very much enjoyed the business of flying an aircraft," reveling in "an overwhelming sense of the vastness of the universe." Many men in war experience a sense of grandeur and beauty in the Olympian scale and visual dazzle of war, but the airman's pleasure differed in that it derived as much from flying itself as from war's drama.[94]

The habit of viewing flying as an act of technique apart from war was critically reinforced by the air force's policies of fixing limits to combat duty for airmen. Washington headquarters never officially prescribed a limit to the number of combat missions crews might fly, but by practice commanders usually set a ceiling like the twenty-five or thirty missions that governed the Eighth Air Force; fixed tours of slightly different length also eventually prevailed in the RAF's Bomber Command. While analogous limits were the rule in the navy and the marines, other army servicemen enjoyed no such luxury, serving for the unspecified duration of combat either in a theater or in the war itself.[95]

Fixing limits on combat service played a major role in the morale of aircrews. The completion of a set tour of missions became their consuming goal. It was one reason they often resisted reporting physical and emotional difficulties, for dropping out of rotation risked diminished status, severance of comradely bonds, and increased danger posed when crewmen unknown to each other worked together. Most important, knowledge that their combat duty was finite gave "the hope of surviving . . . some basis in reality" and helped counteract the acute sense of depression and abandonment that accumulated as comrades were lost and isolation from home increased. It also made airmen, despite the peril they faced, less likely than other army servicemen to regard their work loads as unfair or excessive.[96]

The policy of fixed tours profoundly strengthened the task-oriented mentality of bomber crewmen. Many of them "felt that 30 missions was their 'debt to society'—that in order to do their share they must fulfill their 'contract' by completing the quota." They expressed their investment in a "contractual commitment" through their gallows humor: their tendency to regard every man lost on the last five missions as "an unnecessary tragedy" and their practice of forming Lucky Bastard clubs which awarded certificates to crews completing their duty. The contract spelled out their duties but also their rewards—assured status, transfer out of combat duty, the promise of advancement in military or civilian life.[97]

Sanctioned by the air force, the contractual perception of the airman's duty strengthened the disjunction between means and ends characteristic of the air war. Duty involved the performance of technical tasks. The ethic was not a military one bound to the achievement of victory as it was for most other servicemen, but a professional one, related of course to war but both more finite than the war and transcending it because so many of the rewards were to carry over into the peace. Other men in combat performed tasks—bayoneting an enemy soldier, operating a machine gun—which had little or no counterpart in civilian life, whose only utility lay in war itself. They were simply warriors. To a considerable degree, airmen were technicians and professionals who happened to be waging war.

This model of service in air combat, recognizable as still another expression of air war's inseparableness from a civilian context, placed airmen in the vanguard of a historical transformation in definitions of military service. Traditionally defined, such service was different and apart from the broader society, undertaken by men with a higher sense of duty, whose loyalty lay with the organization, whose objective was to win wars, and whose rewards could not be justified by the civilian marketplace. They had not merely a job but a calling if professionals, an obligation if conscripted. The status, rewards, and duties of combat airmen moved them toward an entrepreneurial or occupational model of service. Self-interest was defined as distinct from the war-winning purpose of the organization; rewards were defined by and carried over into the civilian marketplace; the rituals of military life were subordinated to the attainment of skills and status useful in a larger world. And because the distinction from the civilian world was eroding, civilians performed many tasks once assumed only by military men, and the language and methods of the civilian, particularly of the corporate world, entered military institutions. As volunteers for combat duty (even when initially conscripted), airmen were in a strong position to contract for terms of service. The air force's rotation policy, by limiting risks and establishing rewards validated in the civilian marketplace, looked forward to a practice commonplace in the American armed forces by the 1960s.[98]

To be sure, this evolution was only beginning in World War II. If risks were peculiarly finite for the airman they were nonetheless great; if most airmen calculated tangible rewards flowing from their war contract, others still saw themselves as warriors. Furthermore, wartime promises of GI benefits to veterans in some ways extended the entrepreneurial model to other servicemen. If the evolution toward an entrepreneurial model of service is difficult to date, so too have its causes been difficult for critics to locate. But the emergence of an entrepreneurial model in the air force was certainly hastened by the close connections between military and civilian aviation and the reliance on men well acquainted with the norms of civilian business and technology.

The goals defined for airmen accorded well with those held by civilians and generals serving the wartime air force. For all, there was a definition of goals and rewards distinct from a traditional military ethic of winning wars. Victory could not be forgotten; it had attractions of its own, and it was a vehicle for meeting other goals. But mastery of technique—bureaucratic, intellectual, scientific, mechanical—promised rewards apart from and beyond the objective of winning the war. The inventors, organizers, and handlers of the technique of air war found a satisfaction in war that infantrymen or their commanders could not achieve. Concern with mastering technique was often what the leaders of the air force meant when they referred to the operational necessities that supposedly dictated strategy and tactics.

What we might call the sociological basis of air war had great potential to aggravate the disjunction between means and ends and thereby to accelerate the momentum of air war. Because the criteria governing air war did not relate wholly to war itself, bombing had a momentum apart from the conflict. Because men did not have to view bombing solely as an act of war but could also see it as the perfection of technique, they did not always look at its consequences in war or measure its virtues in terms of its impact on war. In some ways, the tendency of war to assume such a momentum was not unique to strategic bombing campaigns: many another campaign in many a war has been waged with other objectives in mind—the testing of a new tactic, the glory of a commander, the pursuit of imperial ambitions. These temptations operated in air war as well, but they were fused with the enormous technological power and the particular temperament of the men who manipulated such power.

Again, contemporaries had a glimmering of these trends in warfare. AAF psychiatrists emphasized the flier's "passive acceptance of our part in the conflict," behind which lay "little real conviction," only a resigned sense of "a struggle between national states for economic empires." The AAF's staff historians detected an absence of zeal in most American servicemen but especially in the new elite of airmen. "It is an interesting paradox," they concluded, "that the most powerful representative of the democratic faith in the present war consciously has endeavored to foster political sterility among the personnel of its armed services."[99] In one way, the historians were wrong: if the men they observed lacked evident convictions about the war, they zealously pursued the perfection of institutions and techniques that carried important political implications. Technological zeal differed from political zeal, but it too had a political content, if one not so easily recognized. Indeed, the "political sterility" they observed, accompanied by technological prowess, could be a frightening combination.

8

The Sources of Technological Fanaticism

THE DISTANT COMMAND

After November 1942, Lieutenant General Henry Harley Arnold ran the Army Air Forces from his office in the new Pentagon building. This labyrinthine structure, with its "narrow stairways that seemed to end in No Exit passageways suitable for disappearances of Alice's white rabbit," quickly came to symbolize the centralization of American military power. Whereas countless bureaus and commands previously had been scattered all about the Washington area, "'The Pentagon thinks' and 'The Pentagon says' soon became familiar in by-lined stories and 'inside' columns."[1]

In time, and with reason, the Pentagon came to stand for something else. Its confusion of corridors and commands also evoked a bureaucratic maze in which power swirled about in ways that baffled even insiders. From the start, even physical concentration of power was compromised, for the navy declined to install its high command into the new structure, any more than it would countenance unification of the armed forces. The Joint Chiefs of Staff, too, met elsewhere, in the Public Health Building, its presence away from the Pentagon a fitting indication of the legal limbo of this wartime improvisation.

Roosevelt was, of course, commander in chief. But by 1944, his declining energies were devoted to the election campaign and a few issues of paramount urgency. His once firm grip on strategy was slipping. In February 1944, he had put command of the Twentieth Air Force directly in Arnold's hands, thereby reaffirming that the aerial weapon was to play an independent, strategic role in defeating Japan. Thereafter, his contribution to the air war was more than ever indirect or secret: by privately approving with Churchill the possible use of atomic bombs against Japan, he gave tentative sanction to the ultimate use of air power. Except for his forceful interest in bombing Japan from Chinese bases, the president had rarely been directly involved in the conduct of strategic air war, preferring to concentrate on prodding the mobilization of resources for it. Inasmuch as that task was now completed, his active role diminished.

His personal relationship with military leaders remained politely distant. His chief of staff, Admiral William Leahy, chaired the Joint Chiefs but showed little interest in strategy. Harry Hopkins, earlier an intimate link between Roosevelt and Arnold, faced declining health. Rare, too, for Roosevelt were the social occasions with Arnold that Churchill sometimes had with Arthur Harris, the RAF's Bomber Commander. Similarly, the fate of particular operations rarely engaged Roosevelt like they might Churchill. The machinery was in place; Roosevelt was largely content to let it turn. He was neither ignorant nor uninformed, Arnold alerting him, for example, to the first American experiments in firebombing Japanese cities.[2] But Roosevelt showed no interest, at least none recorded. Willing as he was to consider using the atomic bomb on Japan, he would have found it hard anyway to discern a political or moral issue in the escalation of "conventional" bombing.

The War Department's civilian leadership exercised scarcely more oversight. Stimson, Marshall, and Arnold worked together harmoniously. But by the war's last year, Stimson was husbanding his energies for a few problems—a crisis he perceived in army manpower, the army's postwar plans for universal military training, and the development of national policy on atomic weapons. Not until well into 1945 did Stimson begin to link those weapons with the conventional bombing campaign and the development of a final strategy for securing Japan's defeat. Like Roosevelt, Stimson was informed of progress in incendiary tactics against Japan but displayed no immediate concern with them.[3] Among his civilian subordinates, Robert Lovett was the most engaged in strategic matters, but his responsibilities for production, public relations, and management usually came first.

Beyond the air force itself, it was left to the Combined and Joint Chiefs and to Marshall to monitor aerial operations and fit them into a broader strategy. For various reasons they did so gingerly. In the European war, they at least had a supreme command through which to formulate strategy. But in September 1944, Eisenhower relinquished his authority over the British and American strategic air forces to bomber commanders whose cooperation remained minimal and autonomy substantial. In the war against Japan, the chiefs' oversight was even less in evidence. Eisenhower owed his command to the heavy responsibility the army bore for operations and the necessity for some coordination of land, sea, and air forces in the congested arenas of European combat. In the Pacific, the army, navy, and air force so equally carried the burden of prosecuting the war that choosing a representative from any one was sure to enrage the others. The various Allied forces largely fought independently of each other, and the main drive against Japan itself was so exclusively an American affair that the Combined Chiefs had almost no voice in shaping American strategy. Efforts to create a unified command in the Pacific made little headway. Arnold wanted a supreme commander over all Allied forces, or barring that, over all AAF air forces in the theater. So he recommended to Marshall. But when a similar proposal came before one of

Marshall's assistants, he rejected it: "Command of great masses of airplanes from Washington," he told Arnold, "is no more justified than would be the command of the Pacific Fleets by Admiral King from Constitution Avenue, or General Marshall's attempts to fight the ground battles of the Pacific from the Pentagon."[4]

Inasmuch as Arnold already had such a command over the Twentieth Air Force, the rebuff only pointed up the anomalous nature of his authority. Nominally, he commanded the Twentieth as an agent of the Joint Chiefs, but they issued few directives on how the campaign against Japan should proceed, except when coordination with other armed forces seemed imperative. Over the summer of 1944, Marshall had moved the Joint Chiefs to a firm statement of expectations to invade Japan, thereby shaping air strategy insofar as it would have to assist invasion. Thereafter, the Joint Chiefs' meetings, and with them their review of strategy, declined sharply, in part because the strategic course of the war now seemed set.

Like his superiors, Marshall was kept abreast of progress in the air war. But especially with regard to the Pacific, Marshall rarely exercised his formal authority over Arnold and the air force. The AAF staff kept him informed more as a matter of courtesy, and with the expectation of "solidifying the position of the 20th Air Force within the War Department" by notifying Marshall of its triumphs.[5] Now that Arnold was surrounded by some talented staff—notably Brigadier (later Major) General Laurence Kuter and Brigadier (later Major) General Lauris Norstad—Marshall was less inclined to scrutinize the AAF's performance. Furthermore, reorganizations of the JCS committee system and the War Department staff had increasingly enabled the air staff to bypass the army staff structure and deal directly with the Joint Chiefs. Functionally, if not yet legally, the AAF was independent of the army and the bureaucratic equal to it in many ways.

If the supervision given Arnold and the air force was loose, it was hardly understood they would go their own way. Marshall had earlier decided to make Arnold "as nearly as I could Chief of Staff of the Air without any restraint," but he added that Arnold "was very subordinate," and indeed their relationship would have been impossible had the two not been in substantial agreement on most strategic issues.[6] Arnold was simply free to direct the air war within a strategic context shared broadly by his president and his military superiors. After September 1944, no one outside the air force carefully examined its methods of bombing. Whether it chose to blast factories, mine sea-lanes, or level cities was largely for Arnold and his subordinates to decide.

At Arnold's level, however, the decentralization of authority ceased. The AAF's Washington headquarters closely supervised field commanders, above all LeMay and Hansell in the Twentieth Air Force. Spaatz's operations in Europe were well grooved by the fall of 1944; major questions of tactics and strategy had been thrashed out or papered over. Operations against Japan were still embryonic and problematical. Not only was it Arnold's nature to examine them closely, but the peculiar command structure of the Twentieth invited careful oversight. While the American strategic forces in Europe had their headquarters in England, the two bomber commands in the Far

East—LeMay's at Kharagpur and Hansell's in the Marianas—were headless entities, their headquarters lodged far away in the Pentagon. By September, authority over them was held by Arnold himself as commanding general of the Twentieth, assisted by Norstad, who doubled as the Twentieth's chief of staff and AAF's deputy chief of staff, and by Kuter, the AAF's assistant chief of staff for plans.

It was a unique relationship. No other major overseas field force of the American war, in any service, had its operational headquarters in Washington. The contrasting relationship Marshall had with his field commanders is instructive. He was in close contact with them, but it was not Marshall's style to hound and badger. He relied more on persuasion, and by 1944 commanders like Eisenhower and MacArthur had such status, confidence, and experience that close supervision from Washington would have appeared unseemly—indeed, if there was ever a feudal baron in this war, MacArthur outdid the air force generals. Lacking the prestige of the great ground generals, Spaatz and LeMay and Hansell were subject to much tighter control from the Pentagon. Norstad reassured Hansell that he had "the utmost latitude in accomplishing [his] mission," but latitude extended only to "the dates that you select, the size of force, and the sequence of targets within the priority list." As Norstad told a different audience, with coy understatement, the bomber commanders were "not told how to do it [their job] although sometimes they have been, I will admit, subject to a little persuasion." The priority list itself—and with it a host of variables: whether to strike by night or day, at cities or individual factories, with high explosives or incendiaries—came from Washington. And despite Norstad's disclaimer, even the freedom to choose targets from the list was sometimes abrogated. As Arnold reminded LeMay, "I follow the work of the XX bomber Commander in far greater detail than you probably think." Arnold's ambitions for the political future of the air force further put the Twentieth "under extreme pressure to perform." Individual commanders felt the pressure another way, too, for Arnold was not above trying to provoke competition among them.[7]

Ever since the telegraph was invented, and doubtless long before, field generals have complained of interference from superiors safe in capitals and insensitive to war's realities. Oversight—watchful, suspicious, domineering—was not new to warfare in 1944. The novelty lay partly in the technology of control. Through radio and teletype and through the rapid courier service and the personal visits made possible by air transport, Washington's contact with its far-flung Asian bomber commands was even more exacting than it was with the strategic air forces in Europe. The sheer volume of communications—ranging from Arnold's chatty but pointed personal letters to reams of target information and the trivial detritus of military bureaucracy—was also novel. Hansell had earlier presided over the creation of this communications net during organization of the Twentieth's headquarters, but he quickly became "sick of it" when he began commanding bomber missions from the Marianas in November: "The machine worked 24 hours a day all right, without stopping. Most of the messages seemed to consist of questions that I couldn't answer. I began to understand the meaning of the remark ascribed to Lord Palmerston to the effect that the disintegration of the British

Empire had begun with the invention of the telegraph." In Hansell's case, it was his own command that was soon to disintegrate.[8]

More important was the organizational novelty involved. It was one thing for a capital to keep close tabs on what its commanders were doing, another to plan in great detail what they would do, as Washington headquarters did in 1944. To be sure, the long line of communications to Saipan, Guam, and Kharagpur sometimes stretched thin, no flood of directives from on high could entirely substitute for judgment on the spot, the field commander with suitable drive could adapt orders to his purposes, and Arnold's volatile temperament undercut any tendencies to settle into bureaucratic routine.

Nonetheless, the supervision from Washington was at times remarkable. "General Arnold's control of the U.S. Air Force is as complete, virtually, as is Hitler's control of Germany," observed an English officer with pardonable exaggeration. "He is a complete dictator. . . . Be discovered doing something Arnold does not like and Arnold sacks you—like that." No more than Marshall and King could Arnold always play such an imperial role: in an air force huge by 1944, he was more than ever dependent on a growing headquarters staff and on a heart whose failings repeatedly removed him from day-to-day control of the air force. Yet if not always wielded personally by Arnold, power usually remained in his headquarters. "It is a current saying that you cannot run a war from Washington," Norstad commented in September. "The fact is, however, that all of this war has been run to a larger degree than most people realized from Washington." If anything, Washington's grip tightened late in the war, for the completion of the tedious business of mobilizing men and planes by 1944 left headquarters free to exercise the "very real prerogatives of command over world-wide operations."[9]

Officers at headquarters regarded such centralized control as another operational imperative. To weave bomber operations into the broader fabric of strategy, informed judgments had to be made from Washington, by men who had a global perspective on strategy, not by the theater commander who saw "the general situation through glasses prescribed by the local optician," as Arnold pointedly put it to Chennault. In particular, coordination of the widely separated bomber commands of the Twentieth Air Force seemed impossible from any other vantage point, all the more so since the Pacific theater had no unified command. As usual, operational necessities were only part of the story, however. Centralized command also satisfied air force ambitions. Only with it could the airmen prevent theater commanders from seizing control of the bombers in pursuit of "tempting local plums"; only with it could they cultivate the image of a global air force with revolutionary consequences for world geopolitics; only with it could Arnold have the operational command he had never before enjoyed. And only centralization permitted maximum use of the techniques of operations research and bureaucratic management enjoying favor in Washington—the full employment of the forces of civilian militarism.[10]

One result of this centralization was the physical distance it interposed between decision makers on the one hand and the conveyers and victims of destruction on the other. Modern communications and transportation, far from facilitating the close witness of war, impeded it by allowing decisionmaking to take place far away. In such circumstances, William Blanchard speculates, "Man no longer feels his aggressive impulses with the same intensity. Aggression is viewed more with the intellect," through the *"symbolic representation* of events rather than his own awareness."[11] To the authorities in the Pentagon, what the bombers did was represented by strike photos, telegraphed reports, and statistical summaries. They enlivened symbols and abstractions with an occasional visit to the field, but even then they were hundreds of miles away from the action.

Operational commanders also experienced war secondhand, for the notion that the practice of war could be separated from its management was also applied to them. When LeMay insisted that he fly missions with the 21st Bomber Command he headed up in the fall of 1944, he found the "people upstairs were yipping shrilly at the idea." They included "those misguided souls in Washington [who] had the notion that a commanding officer didn't need to be qualified as an Aircraft Commander. He had a lot of *those* folks under him. . . . *His* job was to proceed in his own echelon and on his own exalted level." For LeMay, command meant the sharing of danger, the knowledge derived from firsthand experience, not the bureaucrat's management of men. But his victory in this skirmish was token—permission to fly one mission. The more cerebral Hansell was equally determined to fly but found that his slight familiarity with the atomic bomb (about which LeMay then knew nothing) and Allied code-breaking prohibited his participation in combat missions as well.[12]

Whether Arnold did not feel "his aggressive impulses with the same intensity" because of his distance from the war is difficult to prove. But the difference made by his remote position is suggested by comparing his recollections of the war with those of LeMay, so direct a participant in combat and destruction before he reached India, who portrayed much more frankly and fully the destructive fury of American bombers. Even Marshall, another and more preeminent organizer of victory, seemed more sensitive to the nature and magnitude of death in war, in part because it became more personal with the death in battle of his stepson. For the air force commanding general who never served in combat or overseas, war's remoteness took several forms.

More than most military operations, the Twentieth Air Force waged war by assembly-line procedures that divided tasks and fractioned responsibilities. The end product of its efforts—the target folder, and then the destruction—emerged from a long planning process in which the designers rarely saw their creation, and the operators had little to do with the design. Acting on the broad directives coming from the JCS and Arnold, civilian and military experts examined data on the enemy's military and economic systems and drew conclusions about which target systems would be the most vulnerable to destruction. Much of that work took place outside regular military channels altogether, in the work of the Committee of Operations Analysts, men who had almost no firsthand contact with war. The task of translating those conclusions into specific targets and priorities fell to other men, in the plans and operations staffs of the air force and the Joint Target Group. Staff for the Headquarters Twentieth Air Force also helped to choose the timing and order of attacks on targets. At the bomber commands, LeMay and Hansell then conducted photographic surveillance and analysis, compiled the glossy target folders used by airmen, factored in operational considerations—weather patterns, available strengths, estimates of enemy reactions, and so forth—and, usually, chose the specific days and force assignments for attack. Once a mission was carried out, the whole process was reversed, as streams of information flowed back to Washington for evaluation.

Certain practices diluted the compartmentalization inherent in this method. Some officers like Kuter and Norstad effectively held responsibility for both planning and operations. Rotation among various duties might widen perspectives—before going to the Marianas, Hansell had been the Twentieth's chief of staff and a key strategist at the outbreak of the war. Nonetheless, as the war dragged on, many of the best planners, like Kuter, tended to stay in Washington for long periods, and a topflight commander like LeMay never served in a planning agency. Civilians rarely glimpsed the operational dimension of war, and of course the men who designed and built the bombers rarely accompanied them to battle.

Certainly, as Arthur Harris showed, isolation from war's realities could occur even without the physical distance that characterized command of the Twentieth Air Force. Only miles from the bomber stations and the wreckage of English cities, Harris nonetheless followed a more cloistered and imperious routine at High Wycombe than Arnold ever practiced. Bomber Command's "absolute remoteness from the battlefront has led some historians to compare High Wycombe with the French châteaux from which generals of the First World War directed Passchendaele and the Somme." In its imperviousness to new ideas and outside influence, Bomber Command seemed to Freeman Dyson to have been "invented by some mad sociologist," becoming "a huge organization dedicated to the purpose of burning cities and killing people, and doing the job badly."[13]

The Twentieth Air Force was a less visibly demonic system, softened by Arnold's genial public image and by the informality of the American bureaucratic style. Nonetheless, Washington waged the air war by remote control, thereby reducing a sense of responsibility for the destruction that war entailed. Nor did distance from the enemy and bureaucratic methods of waging war against him create a less vindictive approach to war than that favored by men in the field with more direct contact with the enemy. There was no demonstrable correlation between vindictiveness toward the enemy and proximity to him: Washington, far from acting to curb the excesses of a Hansell or LeMay, often prodded them into more destructive action. Besides, vindictiveness was not a prerequisite to pursuing the most destructive course with the enemy: insofar as airmen viewed their war as the task of applying the proper technique, the motives and rewards for intensifying its fury had little to do with satisfying their visceral hostilities toward the enemy. Washington's distance from the consequences of what it planned and ordered allowed the destruction to go forward smoothly, without engaging emotions and moral questions about its consequences. Nor was physical and bureaucratic remoteness from war the only kind of distance the men in Washington maintained.

THE RHETORIC OF TECHNIQUE

Air force planners employed methods of analysis and styles of language that also distanced them from war's realities. In one way, this was hardly their intention. "It is not sufficient merely to bomb Japan," Norstad reminded an audience. "The targets selected, the timing, the weight must be chosen with surgical skill."[14] It was the planners' job to help connect means and ends, to show how the force available could be used to secure victory. Often enough, the connection was hard to maintain, either affectively or conceptually, as designs for incendiary war showed.

Though central to Marshall's scheme for intimidating Japan on the eve of Pearl Harbor, firebombing as a large-scale practicality became possible only after American entry into the war, when the technical work was carried out by the Army Chemical Warfare Service, the National Defense Research Committee, and the petrochemical industry. Much of their experimental work, presided over by the Harvard chemist Louis Fieser, concerned tactical weapons—flamethrowers and the jellied gasoline that Fieser's scientists produced by adding extracts from aluminum napthanate and aluminum palmitate (from which Fieser drew the name *napalm*). Fieser, although he regarded use of poison gas as "inhumane," relished development of incendiary bombs for strategic use, some of his experiments taking bizarre form. In 1943, he launched a project to release captive bats carrying tiny incendiaries from American bombers. These creatures, given to roosting in dark attics and cellars, would ignite thousands of fires in the highly flammable buildings of Japan's cities. Fieser imagined " a surprise attack on Tokyo" with fires "popping all over the city at 4 A.M." Tests continued for many months until "a number of bat bombs, blown out of the target area by high winds, burned down a theater, the officers' club, and a general's sedan at Carlsbad [New Mexico] Army Air Field." Other impractical but prophetic ideas flowed from the Chemical Warfare Service—experiments in showering incendiary "leaves" over forests and grainfields, an early exercise in the arts of defoliation. In the bizarre, Japan sometimes matched the United States, as in its hapless effort to rain balloon-bombs on the United States.[15]

The major preoccupation of the American chemists was the development of reliable incendiaries to be dropped by aircraft against enemy cities. Much effort was necessary to produce bombs which did not disintegrate under field conditions and which penetrated rooftops and zeroed in on targets without being blown off course. The Chemical Warfare Service was up to the task. Model enemy towns were constructed at proving grounds in the United States, the effort at authenticity measured by the employment of German Jewish architects to design the German towns and by the attention to detail down to "the curtains, children's toys, and clothing hanging in the closets." In testing incendiary attacks on mock Japanese workers' districts, teams of firefighters were brought in to quell the blaze with methods the Japanese would use.

The tests against "Little Tokios" inspired confidence that "fires would sweep an entire community" and cause "tremendous casualties."[16]

The technicians' work was one source of a policy for incendiary war. The Chemical Warfare Service had always been an aggressive bureaucracy, and its personnel took their devices to England, made common cause with the RAF, and pressed them on the Eighth Air Force. American use of firebombs—spurred by LeMay's interest, supported by Arnold from Washington, and reinforced by the powerful British demonstration at Hamburg—accelerated rapidly during 1944. Still, until the last months of the European war, they were only a small part of the American aerial arsenal and were employed largely against German industrial targets.[17]

Interest in firebombing Japanese cities crystalized earlier and more intensely. Initial studies by the air force staff had emphasized the classic precepts of high-explosive bombing of precision targets, but by 1943 incendiary war attracted sustained approval. It was supported by British planners and by the prime minister himself, who in May spoke to the American Congress of "the process, so necessary and desirable, of laying the cities and other munitions centres of Japan in ashes, for in ashes they must surely lie before peace comes back to the world." In Arnold's Committee of Operations Analysts (COA), military members compromised long-standing air force doctrine to press for incendiary bombing, while Guido Perera, the lawyer and leading civilian member, "felt it was wrong for the Air Force to turn from precision bombing to area attacks." As "a cynic might add—it is worse than immoral because it is ineffective." So he recalled in his memoirs at least, but little trace of his doubts or of any discernible difference between civilians and professional officers on firebombing survived among contemporary records.[18]

Indeed, in 1943 much of the impetus behind firebombing came from another civilian, Horatio Bond, consultant to the National Defense Research Committee and chief engineer of the National Fire Protection Association, who was later joined by colleagues from that organization and from the Safety Research Institute. Fire fighters—or fire protection engineers, as they preferred to call themselves—proved to be eager fire starters. Like many another civilian profession, their only regret was that they had not "been given an earlier voice in certain major decisions of the war."[19] Late in 1944, more high-powered civilian scientists joined the cause of war by fire.

Meanwhile, by November 1943, the COA had produced for Arnold its report entitled "Economic Objectives in the Far East," as much of a blueprint as the air war against Japan ever had. The committee implicitly placed "urban industrial areas" below merchant shipping and the steel industry and above the aircraft industry in its priorities. More important, it gathered what became commonplace arguments for attacking Japanese cities by fire: the great concentration of Japanese industry in a few cities, the practice of subcontracting to small domestic producers, and the peculiar vulnerability of those cities to fires. If delivered on target, a few thousand tons of incendiaries, a fraction of the total weight of bombs envisaged for the campaign against Japan, would destroy the central areas of twenty cities, so the committee argued.

It was a telling admission that "the greater number of the more important industrial plants lie outside the specific areas suggested for incendiary attack." But those plants would supposedly be taken care of by precision attacks, and more diffuse economic damage would be inflicted by the destruction of subcontractors, "the dislocation of labor by casualty, homelessness and forced migration," the shattering of morale, and the disruption of economic and administrative machinery. "Uncontrollable conflagrations" would "constitute a major disaster" for the enemy. The committee made no estimate of enemy casualties, preferring to measure the damage with other statistics—180 square miles of urban areas devastated, and 12 million people, or 70 percent of the total population in the twenty cities, rendered "homeless."[20]

The section of the committee report dealing with incendiary attacks was quite brief considering the importance it attached to them and which they would come to play. Brevity measured the ease of this kind of bombing from the planners' perspective. Attack on specific economic objectives like shipping or the steel industry required extended scrutiny of complex economic considerations and the most elaborate photographic surveillance and analysis. Incendiary attacks required only some general assumptions about the nature of the Japanese economy, easy photographic surveys to determine broad areas with dense workers' housing, and the assignment of requisite tonnages. Outside the air force, a few voices offered caution in 1943. The flimsiness of Japanese cities making their destruction so easy also would make their rebuilding "correspondingly simple," argued a State Department expert on Japan, while other officials worried that "the untold destruction" unleashed by incendiaries "would unite the mass of people more closely." But the operations analysts were not examining the politics of surrender, and the destruction they envisioned seemed too extensive to worry about potential for recovery.[21]

After November, the technicians' work went forward, as they revised sharply upward the tonnage requirements for incendiary raids.[22] The high command was preoccupied for months with other matters, but in May 1944, as the Twentieth Air Force prepared for its first attacks, the issue of incendiary bombing resurfaced. On the ninth, Perera recommended that the incendiary campaign begin in March 1945, when wind and weather conditions would maximize its effect. At the same time, chemical and biological warfare again came in for high-level attention.[23]

Before June, the firebombing of Japan had been debated in an operational vacuum. It gained new urgency once the B-29s began flying. Operational considerations plunged the air staff into protracted debate. The ineffectiveness of the Twentieth's early precision raids from China bases was quickly evident, and on August 8 one of the wing commanders due to bomb Japan from the Marianas pointedly raised the issue of bombing strategy with Arnold. Brigadier General Rosie O'Donnell argued that no small force of B-29s could achieve decisive effects on industrial targets: "Steam roller tactics are not applicable out there because while we have the steam, we have no rollers." O'Donnell strongly urged downgrading precision attacks for the moment and instead sending the bombers "singly at night using radar to destroy and burn down the several large cosmopolitan centers" and "thereby striking a tremendous blow at civilian morale." Particularly since most Japanese cities were, like Hamburg, in coastal areas, they seemed "ideal radar targets."[24]

O'Donnell's argument ran up against the hold that precision bombing still had on some of the staff of the Twentieth, especially Hansell. The B-29 itself had been designed with daylight operations in mind. O'Donnell's recommendation conflicted also with prevailing conceptions of operational need. Researchers had already pointed out that small-scale incendiary raids would be counterproductive, for if they burned out small portions of cities, they would only make full-scale conflagrations harder to ignite; better to wait for attacks in force. Furthermore, the air war against Germany had deeply discouraged the air staff about the chances of waging a strategic campaign before destroying the enemy's air force. Arnold, to whom none of O'Donnell's arguments was new, replied that Japan's aircraft industry would have to enjoy first priority.[25]

Arnold was always flexible however. He had repeatedly expressed interest in incendiary attacks, and he was eager to go ahead with experiments recommended by his operations analysts. The tests they proposed would have no immediate military utility—targets were chosen "for their compactness and combustibility rather than for their economic or strategic importance." But test raids would refine calculations on the weight, density, and timing of incendiary attacks. Accordingly, twenty-four B-29s struck Nagasaki on the night of August 10–11, although neither LeMay nor much of his staff was yet eager to give incendiary raids a high priority.[26]

Staff officers and operations researchers continued to press the case for incendiary attacks, first experimental, then comprehensive. A September 4 report by a COA subcommittee acknowledged that full-scale attacks on six large urban areas would not likely "affect front line strength." But there was satisfaction in another projected measurement: the attacks "will produce very great economic loss, measured in man months of industrial labor—probably greater loss per ton of bombs despatched than attacks on any other target system." Damage to industry would merely be a welcome side effect of the general dislocation caused by the "dehousing" of some 7,750,000 workers and the evacuation of many more. The report was a rarity in that it explicitly made an estimate of probable enemy casualties, extrapolating its figures from the great Tokyo fire of 1923: some 560,000 Japanese, almost half in Tokyo, would be killed, missing, or seriously wounded. Otherwise, in applying their skills as economists and lawyers, the experts usually measured the effects of bombing by the statistics and language of cost-benefit analysis.[27]

When the full committee issued revised guidelines in October (omitting any mention of casualties), it recommended an incendiary assault on Japan's cities to come after a precision campaign, when a sufficiently large force of bombers had been assembled to permit highly concentrated fire raids. As usual, the analysts made no attempt to project how such raids would help secure final victory, simply implying their relationship to victory. Shortly thereafter the newly formed Joint Target Group, a Joint Chiefs of Staff agency, gave qualified approval to the COA report.[28]

At the same time, in another indication of civilian interest in incendiary war,

Vannevar Bush forwarded to Arnold the recommendations of an operations researcher on his staff at the Office of Scientific Research and Development. Incendiary bombing, it was argued,

> may be the golden opportunity of strategic bombardment in this war—and possibly one of the outstanding opportunities in all history to do the greatest damage . . . for a minimum of effort. Estimates of economic damage expected indicate that incendiary attack of Japanese cities may be at least five times as effective, ton for ton, as precision bombing of selected strategic targets as practiced in the European theater. However, the dry economic statistics, impressive as they may be, still do not take account of the further and unpredictable effect on the Japanese war effort of a national catastrophe of such magnitude—entirely unprecedented in history.

Still, "dry economic statistics" were what the analyst had to offer, again leaving the impression that "the greatest damage to the enemy for a minimum of effort" had become a goal apart from victory, in part because it was more easily measurable. Bush recognized that the issue of incendiary bombing involved "humanitarian aspects" for which a decision "will have to be made at a high level if it has not been done already." Nothing came of his recommendation, no doubt because the air force believed it had already received sufficient sanction from the president.[29]

Indeed by September, even as the analysts' reports were still coming in, the air staff apparently had committed itself to a major incendiary campaign the following spring. As was often the case, no pronouncement to that effect came from Arnold's headquarters. Rather, the commitment was evident in the increased flow of communications on the subject among the Washington staff and the pressure on field commanders to prepare further tests against Japanese cities. The shift in emphasis may have been hastened by the replacement on August 20 of Hansell (off to the Marianas) as the Twentieth's chief of staff with Norstad, an eager advocate of incendiaries and a recipient of a new team of fire engineers pressing the case for firebombing.[30]

No decision would have been made without Arnold's approval, however, and doubtless the arguments of the operations researchers helped end his vacillation about whether to resort to incendiaries. At bottom, these arguments dressed up Arnold's relentless emphasis on maximum effort in the fancier language of cost-benefit studies and statistical measurements. Arnold had always been inclined to measure effort in quantitative terms, focusing on weight applied and damage done without pressing their connection to victory. To a man of that mentality, elaborate statistics projecting rubble accumulated and man-hours lost on a per ton basis were attractive, all the more so since they were endowed with the aura of scientific expertise.[31]

Furthermore, his closest scientific advisor, Edward L. Bowles, was now weighing in with similar arguments, ones developed by the Special Bombardment Group, a new committee of experts set up by Bowles and drawn from the air staff, the scientific and engineering community, and the aviation industry. Their task was to promote the bombing of Japan "by techniques known to us but not yet fully explored or in use," such as unmanned bombers remotely controlled by radar and television to zero them in on targets.[32]

Citing the urgency of increasing the bomb tonnage dropped, the Bowles group argued for stripping the B-29s of most of their defensive armament to permit a vastly increased bomb load. The risk to the bombers was minimal, the experts argued, because the defensive gunnery was not working well in practice and the increased speed made possible in part by streamlining the bombers' surfaces would enable them to outrun "even the best experimental Japanese fighter." The recommendation elicited a vigorous rebuttal from other operations analysts; it must have come as a shock to the airmen and to General Electric engineers who had designed the B-29's novel centralized fire control by which several guns aboard ship were remotely controlled from a single position. Nonetheless, Arnold (and later LeMay) were open to the proposal, and although Bowles disavowed any intention to meddle in strategy, his staff recognized the strategic implications: defenseless bombers would operate more safely at night, relying on radar techniques which would virtually compel the resort to area, incendiary bombing. High explosives could be mixed with "a large percentage of Napalm incendiary clusters" to help in "dislocating workers." As usual, strategic consequences were drawn from operational considerations but were not dictated by them: they merely led the air force where it was already inclined to go.[33]

To be sure, strategy remained in flux, contested by various bureaucratic interests and buffetted by changing assessments of progress in the war. The possibility of assigning top priority to Japanese shipping was raised again in the fall by a COA subcommittee and by Robert Patterson, the War Department's under secretary. The air staff replied with a rhetorical salute to the importance of attacking shipping followed by reaffirmation of its priority on the aircraft industry and urban areas. It was not about to resort to "another hope for a relatively painless method of winning the war," as one official derisively characterized the shipping plan.[34]

In truth, while the AAF would eventually mount an effective effort at aerial mining, it never had its heart in a campaign it saw as largely the navy's responsibility, which might even imply subordination to the navy's control and which lacked the glamor and directness of an assault on Japan proper. Furthermore, injunctions from the Joint Chiefs to prepare Japan for quick invasion diminished interest in an operation which "would be of interest if we were thinking in terms of a two year's reduction of the Japanese homeland." In an unrecognized irony of the moment, heightened expectations of invasion aggravated the impatience to get on with the destruction of Japan's cities, rather than comprising an alternative to strategic devastation. The air force never denied the efficacy of a mining campaign. It simply lacked the patience, and saw it nowhere else, to give it a try.[35]

In November, as pressure to conduct further incendiary tests mounted, air officers increasingly mimicked the language of the civilian analysts: "Dehousing industrial workers causes a greater loss of man hours per ton of bombs dropped than can be accomplished by any other method." "Dehousing" was becoming the favorite euphemism for a variety of virtues perceived in an incendiary assault, some spelled out—workers' absenteeism, lower morale, paralyzed systems—some usually left unspoken: the maimed bodies and bewildering toll of the dead. Target analysts recognized that such assault would inflict scant damage on primary military and industrial establishments. But few questioned the moral or strategic wisdom of the planned campaign. Some worked very hard to make the enemy population the objective of the bombers. Helmut E. Landsberg, a German meteorologist advising the Twentieth Air Force staff, produced a report entitled "Disease Rates after Tokyo Earthquake of 1923" and concluded that "if an influenza epidemic is started as a result of a saturation attack upon the big cities, absenteeism in industrial plants can be expected to soar." Better yet, he suggested, "the casualty rate will be increased if the attacks are made during the cold season," when survivors crowded into public buildings and hospitals would spread "serious epidemics."[36]

Throughout the war's last year, the attempt to quantify the air war went forward. On May 1, 1945, W. B. Shockley, one of the leading operations analysts, concluded that the B-29 programs was profitable because "the cost of dropping a ton of bombs on Japan is 40 man months of United States war effort and the damage done by one ton costs the Japanese about 600 man months of manufacturing labor." By this measurement, too, the campaign against Japan was some six times more profitable than the attacks against Germany waged from March 1943 to March 1944. Shockley was shrewd enough to acknowledge that it was "a long step to see just how industrial man months are related to this objective"—that is, how the bombing would aid invasion and reduce American casualties. It was unclear who was to take the long step.[37]

Of course the rhetoric of technique was not peculiarly American. It hardly could have been, inasmuch as the British had done so much in the first place to inspire operations research and interest in firebombing. In the lingo of the RAF's target planners and civilian analysts, "dehousing" was both a favored objective and a euphemism for much more. They too made the "fatal error" of trying "to establish an absolute mathematical relationship between acres of urban devastation . . . and loss of production to the German war economy. Bomber Command built its great edifice of self-delusion about the plight of the German war machine on an astonishing foundation of graphs and projections." As a typical intelligence evaluation put it:

> 2,400,000,000 man-hours have been lost for an expenditure of 116,500 tons of bombs claimed dropped, and this amounts to an average return for every ton of bombs dropped of 20,500 lost man-hours, or rather more than one quarter of the time spent in building a Lancaster bomber. . . . This being so, a Lancaster has only to go to a German city once to wipe off its own capital cost, and the results of all subsequent sorties will be clear profit.[38]

On occasion, the effort to quantify the air war aroused suspicions, particularly among some professional officers. Reviewing European operations, the Joint Intelligence Committee once stressed that the benefits of bombing "an organic whole" were not measurable by indices of housing burned down and factories destroyed. Hansell warned in the summer of 1944 that in measuring the effectiveness of the AAF, "Mere tonnage of explosives is a fallacious criterion. In the final analysis, the victories are achieved because of the effect produced, not simply because of the effort expended." As he wrote in his memoirs, however, "statistics of tons of bombs dropped and of sorties flown are easily compiled, seem factual and specific, and are impressive. Photographs of burned-out cities also speak for themselves." No one successfully challenged the general approach whereby numbers measured results, informed rhetoric, and displaced subjective analysis.[39]

To be sure, achieving the proper balance between use of hard calculations and entrapment in them was difficult, all the more so because operations research was new and used in such haste. After all, it had flourished in part in response to the carelessness of the subjective claims previously made for air power—hardheaded men would subject them to proper scrutiny. Operations researchers remained properly appalled at the sloppiness of many of the calculations on which bombing proceeded. Concluding his indictment of one set of figures, Landsberg recalled what was easily forgotten: "No matter how efficient the incendiaries are, if the target is not hit, love's labor is lost." Bowles, too, became "concerned over the insidious practice in the Air Forces of measuring air activity in terms of bombs dropped" instead of "targets damaged or obliterated." At the same time, such complaints stopped well short of the larger problem of how targets destroyed were to end the war.[40]

For their part staff officers sometimes dismissed the experts' speculations as "thoroughly characteristic of the academic, nonpractical attitude which has plagued and beclouded the role of the bomber as a modern weapon of war." The experts seemed far too intent on winning the war by "finding pink pill, Holy Grail targets." Such criticism could easily spill over into diatribes suggesting there was little to do except bomb on: if, as the experts suggested, the lack of data on bombing's effectiveness was "a regrettable state of affairs," then airmen reported that "so is the war. . . . So, in short, is the fact that we're fighting a somewhat complicated war instead of engaging in a research project for the next one."[41] The insight here—that war cannot be neatly planned—was more often appreciated by military men than by civilian analysts; it also implied too easy a capitulation to war's unpredictability, a lack of concern about limiting its waste.

In the end, not surprisingly, military commanders often made critical decisions by seat-of-the-pants methods, oblivious to the expert analyses. For all the specialists in photographic analysis had refined their techniques, Harris still made "judgements from his own interpretations of the photographs on his desk."[42] Arnold proceeded less imperiously, but he also rarely encountered expert advice conflicting with his own predispositions. The talent gathering around the American and British air forces (some four hundred operations analysts, mostly civilian, in the AAF)[43] in the end apparently made little difference in the choices made of strategies and means; much of the expert effort simply provided a quasi-scientific rationale for what the bomber commanders would do anyway.

Yet in a subtle way the civilian experts did make a difference. They did much to refine the means of waging air war by settling straightforward problems of the design of bombs, their distribution over targets, the choice of bombing techniques in different circumstances, and so forth. It was indirectly, through their work in refining those means, that they affected strategy, rather than through explicit efforts to fashion it. For there was no clear distinction between means and ends, only a continuum along which men easily moved. Inevitably, the civilians' efforts to perfect technique, the means of waging air war, also defined ends. Ambitious civilians did not define their role modestly, and Arnold did not ask them to. Most of all, the broader role inhered in what they were doing. "By means of technique," William Blanchard has written, "man changes not only the method by which he thinks *but the content of what he thinks about.*"[44] By the language they used, the methods they employed, and the concerns they focused upon, the experts helped change the content of what decision makers in the air force thought about, permitting them to see air war less as a strategic process aiming at victory and more as a technical process in which the assembly and refinement of means became paramount.

They did so in part because the refinement of means and the achievement of destruction were what operations research could most effectively achieve. Assessment of how means related to ends required subjective judgment resistant to quantifiable measurements. Operations analysts focused on the measurable, and in 1944 the most measurable kind of air war was incendiary bombing, whose gross effects were far more quantifiable than campaigns against enemy shipping or steel production. Furthermore, a concentration on things measurable produced a personal and bureaucratic investment in them. The original purpose of examining incendiary war might only have been to clarify it as a choice, to decide if it was effective. But the method most reducible to quantification also received the closest scrutiny, thereby attracting the greatest investment and the most refined justification.

By one standard, this characterization suggests the indifference of scientists and statisticians to strategic purposes and their immersion into the technique of war. Their mentality was not the one so often ascribed to American war-makers, an exclusive focus on victory, but the pursuit of destruction without a clear notion of its relationship to victory. In another sense, however, ends were not so much abandoned as redefined. For these men, perfecting the technique of war became an end in itself, one that encompassed important goals: professional satisfaction and achievement and air force ambitions for a technology and a war-making record that would enhance its place in the postwar military establishment.

The rhetoric and methodology of civilian expertise also defined goals by the distance they interposed between the designers and victims of destruction. The more sophisticated the methods of destruction became, the less language and methods of measurement allowed men to acknowledge the nature of that destruction. A dehumanized rhetoric of technique reduced the enemy to quantifiable abstractions. Statistics of man-hours lost and workers dehoused objectified many of the enemy's experiences and banished almost altogether one category, his death. Certainly Arnold, LeMay, and Harris were brutally frank in their vocabulary on occasion; dehumanized language alone did not compel men to kill and destroy on the scale they did. But, reinforced by other forms of distance characteristic of the air war, it did allow them to do so while insulating their consciences and souls. And by doing so, it helped to push victory from view and to elevate destruction into a goal. "To all sides in a conflict," Zuckerman has commented, "the goal of war must always be victory, but victory has over the course of history almost always been associated with destruction, so much so that destruction has become a kind of vested characteristic of war."[45] The application of operations research to war, at least as practiced in 1944, was one source of that tendency.

That application should not be blamed solely on the scientists who were coming into power. The urge to quantify was also related to the airman's eagerness to intensify operations and to the difficulties inherent in air war of measuring effects by any but numerical methods. Moreover, many of the operations researchers were not scientists. The language and standards of measurement they employed were often borrowed not from science but from the balance sheet mentality of capitalism. The effort to construct a profit-and-loss statement of air war reflected a belief that entrepreneurial models were appropriate to war.

In the end, one is unsure whether to be impressed by the sophistication evident in viewing Japan as a vast laboratory in destruction or appalled by the naivete and narrowness of what these experts did. For all the weight of intelligence brought to bear on the bombing effort, it was still possible for one analyst, as late as June 6, 1945, to complain that "unfortunately, there has been to date no careful study of bombing accuracy from B-29's."[46] The failure to do something so simple and critical to an evaluation of success suggests how the application of expertise served to make the momentum of destruction more thoughtless than refined.

To be sure, much skill entered into the designation of bomb targets in the war's last two years. Yet the Committee of Operations Analysts, an elite of American experts, was perhaps no more shrewd in its recommendations than the air officers who had far more hastily drawn up rudimentary estimates of air force needs and strategy at the start of the war.[47] That the initial hunches turned out to be so good was perhaps less a reflection upon the skill of the civilian experts than upon the difficulty in reducing decisions about war to systematic formulas. It also reflected the fact that the experts did not see their job to be one of connecting the refinement of means to the pursuit of ends—to a concept of how victory was to be achieved.

It was better to bomb well than badly, as Freeman Dyson once thought of the American effort against Japan.[48] In many ways, the talent available to the AAF helped it to do so. Yet, at a minimum, virtue inhered in a better method of bombing only if it related to the ultimate goal of victory. Even if bombing's ability to win the war could be firmly established, other moral considerations come into play: the humanitarian concerns raised by Bush; the possibility of alternative means that might accomplish the same goal with less bloodshed; the consequences after victory of introducing an especially fearsome method of war. It might, indeed, not be better to bomb well, not if to do so only piled on redundant destruction. Because civilian experts usually avoided looking into the abyss of these issues, they became by default the responsibility of strategists and commanders in uniform, insofar as they were recognized at all.

THE FAILURE OF STRATEGY

By September 1944, strategy for the defeat of Japan had been given a broad formulation which was to remain substantially undisturbed till the last months of the war. As expressed by the Combined Chiefs of Staff, the Allies were "to force the unconditional surrender of Japan by . . . invading and seizing objectives in the industrial heart of Japan" after a campaign of blockade by air and sea; "intensive air bombardment" was designed to lower the enemy's ability and will to resist.[49] Strategic bombing was to play a role complementary to other campaigns, independent in its command and target objectives but harnessed to the ultimate task of invasion and occupation.

The origins of that strategy lay in both American military traditions and the circumstances of the moment. A "strategy of annihilation" aimed at engaging the enemy's main forces and seizing his territory and capital had deep roots in the American style of warfare, especially as it had developed since 1860.[50] The Allied policy of unconditional surrender reflected that strategic tradition as well as the requirements of alliance politics and the ideological nature of the war. Dashing hopes for early victory in Europe, the tenacity of German resistance through the fall and winter of 1944 suggested anew the impossibility of securing unconditional surrender without a fight to the finish. The abundance of resources amassed by the Allies made such a fight possible.

The definition of Allied strategy, along with the vagueness about its details, complicated the task of airmen in articulating a rationale for the bombing of Japan. Some airmen still hoped to force Japan's capitulation through blockade and bombardment alone, and there had been evidence in Roosevelt's own statements and in the media to indicate political support for such a strategy. But the airmen could hardly work out a scenario for victory by the means they preferred without appearing to contest official joint and combined policy. Speculation by airmen certainly occurred, but that did not constitute a strategy. And of course few airmen attached priority to the refinement of strategy.

If invasion was assumed to be the method of securing final surrender, there was in fact little room for imaginative calculations on how force was to be useful. Surrender was simply to be imposed as the inevitable result of the invasion, occupation, and dismemberment of the enemy state. Strategic plans were worked out in detail, but the planners usually worked backward, from the point of invasion to the preliminary operations necessary to make it possible. Accordingly, there was little point in debating how bombing might change the enemy's government or its terms for peace, not unless the air force challenged agreed-upon assumptions. With strategic bombing now viewed as a way of softening up the enemy, airmen had little incentive to defend the strategic vision they had never abandoned.

Some leeway remained for strategic imagination. Air force planners needed to determine which industries, military installations, and geographical areas should be bombed to prepare for invasion, what conditions within Honshu the ground soldiers should expect after the bombing campaign was concluded, and how those conditions would affect requirements for the invading force. But invasion was primarily a responsibility for the army and navy, and a year or more in the offing. The pressing problem was to accelerate the bombing campaign and coordinate it, when necessary, with the preliminary campaigns pending against the Philippines in the fall and against Iwo Jima, Okinawa, and eventually Kyushu in 1945. To the extent that the contribution of bombing to the final invasion was measured, it was primarily in terms of general destruction to Japanese industrial production and morale.

On September 27, Norstad, as the Twentieth Air Force's new chief of staff, offered a view of the strategic task ahead in the Far East: "Whether or not air bombardment alone can defeat a power like Japan is of no concern of ours. Whether or not we can destroy their morale is of no great concern. Our primary interest is the destruction of their means of fighting by destroying those economic and industrial establishments upon which her military strength depends."[51] Inasmuch as airmen remained intent on proving the bomber as a war-winning weapon, Norstad's statement was disingenuous. More important, resolution of the issues he dismissed might vitally affect the course of bombing chosen. As long as the bombers' objective remained only the "Japanese ability to wage war," then it enjoyed only a loose connection to a conception of victory.

"To oversimplify our basic operating policy," Arnold wrote Hansell in December, "it is our purpose to destroy our targets." As a statement of long-range strategy, this oversimplification was not far off the mark. Nor was it clarified in Arnold's memoirs, where he characterized the "two main jobs ahead of us" at the close of 1944: "To complete the bombing of Germany, which was more or less routine, and to deploy our B-29 outfits after the completion of their training for the destruction of the Japanese mainland." The strategic payoff of destruction—surrender—seemed simply to be taken for granted.[52]

Later, Hansell denied that air strategists at the time had a "limited vision and were too much influenced by the need to pave the way for invasion." Invasion was simply the "backup" plan the Joint Chiefs had to have in case blockade and bombardment failed.[53] Perhaps Hansell saw it that way at the time, but the staff back in Washington had worked out no plan for victory by air power; it was an idea they liked but were under no compulsion to defend. In fact, the Joint Chiefs had explicitly rejected the view held earlier in the war that invasion should be regarded only as a contingency.

The political possibility existed for a different course of strategy. The Army Air Forces and the navy might have entered an alliance, based on a strategy of victory without invasion that denied glory to the ground army. Their strategic roles were complementary, inasmuch as the navy was strangling the Japanese economy by sea just as the bombers were trying to devastate it on land. And navy and air forces could directly assist each other: by aerial mining, the B-29s could tighten the stranglehold on Japanese shipping; by carrier attacks, the navy could hit objectives on the land, not on the same scale as the B-29s, but with greater precision.

No alliance was ever joined. The very similarity of functions between the two services had long bred a bitter rivalry. Arnold owed to Marshall too much of his authority over the air force to desert his patron and forge a link with Admiral King. More than these political considerations, little in the mood at the time encouraged making choices between strategies for victory. Marshall, it is true, had raised pointed questions on September 1 about the timing and relationship between invasion and aerial assault of the home islands. On September 5, Admiral Leahy, in a rare thrust into grand strategy, had asked the vital question of whether to proceed against Japan by land invasion or by sea and air blockade—he preferred the latter method as likely to "require a longer time to bring the war to an end, but with less cost to us in life and material." The Joint Chiefs even seemed to agree that so fundamental a decision could be made only by the president himself, but it never came before the president until June of the next year, with a very different man in office.[54]

Most of the time, the high command did not ask which strategy would be the most efficient way to secure victory, but rather how all strategies could be assembled and applied against the enemy. The tenacity of enemy resistance did not seem to permit, any more than the weight of Allied resources seemed to require, a selective use of force against Japan. There was no official sanction for seeing bombing as an alternative to invasion. The engines of war would have to roll on; the problem was how to fuel them, not which ones to run. Command relationships also discouraged refined speculation. With no centralized command in the Pacific war, the selection of strategic alternatives was up to the Joint and Combined Chiefs. The former generally made hard choices only under duress or when the commander in chief directed them to do so; the latter was an ineffective mechanism because the British role in Far Eastern strategy was minimal.

As did other failures of command in the air war, the vagueness of strategy, the failure to establish clear connections between military means and the goal of victory, came in for occasional criticism. Arnold himself sometimes lamented the excessive preoccupation with current operations, though he did little to discourage it. From the ranks came a harsher judgment:

> I believe it to be an unhealthy thing that within the Air Force itself there is presently so little difference of opinion. . . . We are committed to the big bomber and the bomber offensive as surely for the future as we have been throughout this war, and with scarcely a dissenting voice. . . . Our most

persuasive and articulate people are almost without exception bomber-minded, steeped in the tradition of Douhet and Mitchel [*sic*].

This dissenting officer proposed an experiment with "a sustained fighter offensive against Japan" that might achieve the goals of the bombers more economically. The proposal was destined to go nowhere; as its author recognized, the momentum to bomb with B-29s was now irresistible. Moreover, his criticism was directed mainly at the needs of the postwar air force, not at the current war. Dissent, when it arose at all, usually did so through the back door of postwar concerns.[55]

One critique that did focus on the ongoing war arose, but from outside the air force, in the army's high-powered Operations Division, where Brigadier General George A. Lincoln consistently complained of the way operations were planned in a strategic vacuum. As late as June 1945, he still observed "the lack of an integrated strategic air plan for the defeat of Japan." Among air force officers, only Haywood Hansell perhaps would have understood fully Lincoln's complaint. He made much the same point by prefacing his memoirs with a quotation from Douhet: "The choice of enemy targets . . . is the most delicate operation of air warfare. . . . It is precisely in this field that the commanders of future Air Forces will be able to give proof of their ability." In the end, proof was not given.[56]

Bombing threatened to develop a momentum apart from the needs of winning the war. Of course the strategists wanted victory, but the carelessness with which they related destruction to victory provided small check on that destruction until victory was secured. Their plans revealed a kind of strategic distance on the consequences of their actions that paralleled and reinforced the distance created by their professional pursuit of technique, by the command and bureaucratic arrangements they made to organize that technique, and by the language and methodology they employed to use it. The disjunction between means and ends—in effect an operational variation of the long-standing chasm between fantasy and reality in conceptions of air war—took many forms.

THE ELUSIVE ENEMY

Any strategy rested finally on a view of the enemy: a conception of the adversary's resolve, of the conditions under which it would cease fighting, and of the institutions that made decisions. On both sides of the Pacific war and in the American air force no less than in other institutions, the attempt to formulate a useful conception was largely a failure in that no way was found to end the war short of cataclysmic and redundant destruction. Measured against the horror most visible to contemporaries—invasion of Japan's home islands—belated success was achieved. By either standard, the final use of American air power against Japan took place against a curious background of misunderstanding and of failure to relate the preferred means of victory to the final goal.

Certain individuals and institutions on both sides made attempts at understanding. In the manner timeless in war, enemies were thrust together in a common experience that compelled understanding even as it inflamed hatreds. "In the history of misunderstanding across the Pacific," Akira Iriye has written, "the war years mark, not an extraordinary period of distortions and misconceptions, but rather a stage in the gradual expansion of interest in and knowledge about each other."[57]

Even in Japan, where talk of compromise peace was discouraged, the nation's evident weakness cut in a different direction. Recognition of Japan's impossible position varied greatly among Japanese leaders but was certainly widespread by July 1944, when the fall of Saipan breached Japan's inner defenses. Particularly among Japan's senior statesmen, but also among some military officers, a desperation to find some way out of continued war mounted, reflected in the fall of Tojo's cabinet. It focused on reverses abroad and on the threat at home to the imperial institution and Japan's elites. "The more critical the war situation becomes, the louder we hear the cry, 'One hundred million die together!'", Prince Konoe complained to the emperor in February 1945. Although "so-called right-wingers" were "the ones who shout the loudest," communists seemed "the instigators of it all." To secure peace short of national suicide, some Japanese leaders began recasting Japanese purposes in the language of international cooperation and national self-determination articulated by Roosevelt and other American leaders. They curried the impression that Japan now supported genuine independence among its subject peoples and might also welcome an important role for the Western powers in postwar Asia. Put another way, these Japanese leaders were preparing a public to accept defeat "by calling it a victory for certain universalistic principles."[58]

Some Americans, at least hazily aware of this reorientation, hoped to exploit it by clarifying and perhaps moderating the formula for unconditional surrender first spelled out by Roosevelt and Churchill in January 1943. Officials in both the State Department and the services wondered how to apply that formula to Japan in a way promoting an early termination of the war and long-term American interests in Asia. To be sure, other military officers, echoing the popular view set forth by de Seversky, argued that vengeance was the nation's purpose: the Japanese were simply "international bandits," and their country "should be bombed so that there was little left of its civilization." Nothing less than "the almost total elimination of the Japanese as a race" seemed likely to insure long-run peace in Asia.[59]

Yet there was no clear-cut division between vengeful officers and generous civilians. Widely regarded as liberals, men like Harry Hopkins and Archibald MacLeish, though they said little about bombing per se, clung to an unbending definition of surrender. Nothing less, it seemed to them, would give the Allies the mandate to create a new Japan sympathetic to the tenets of a liberal international order. On the other hand, the military command, like many Far Eastern experts, grew increasingly restive with a formula that seemed sure to back the Japanese into a corner, extract a ferocious price in American lives and treasure, tax the patience of Americans at home, and then saddle the military with the task of restructuring an entire society.[60]

Those interested in modifying the unconditional surrender formula had been given some leverage in statements made by Roosevelt, who had explained that destruction of enemy states was not the goal of the Allies. Moreover, unlike Allied policy toward German surrender, that toward Japanese capitulation had spelled out territorial terms with some specificity. At the least by identifying what Japan would lose, they implied that Japan itself would remain intact.[61]

But almost no direction came from on high about how to handle the delicate matter of the emperor's fate, over which much wrangling ensued. Many Far Eastern experts disputed the popular view of an all-powerful monarch indissolubly bound to Japan's militarism. Close to the emperor, they explained, were leaders who might help engineer an earlier surrender. And regardless of views about the emperor's culpability for the war, working with him seemed inescapable: without his authority to impose surrender, the task of obtaining capitulation and governing afterward might become hopeless. "To aim at obtaining surrender while ruling out all bargaining on principle is a contradiction in terms," it has since been pointed out.[62] Some contemporaries appreciated that contradiction.

Likewise, they argued that the emperor and liberal politicians would help Japan return to a system of international cooperation like the one emerging before the 1930s. With its militarists punished, its overseas empire dissolved, and its path to economic expansion opened by abolition of protectionist trade practices, Japan would participate as a constructive partner in a world trade system. As one official argued presciently, the loss of empire was "likely to work" to Japan's "advantage" in economic terms. Some Japanese and American officials were also converging on a similar point of view regarding the disposition of the subject Asian peoples. As Japan's pretensions to empire moderated, American calls for a revolutionary upheaval of national liberation became more subdued. Both Americans and Japanese, that is, became less insistent upon refashioning East Asia in their own images.[63]

Indeed, in retrospect at least, by late 1943 there was already "a rather remarkable parallel between American and Japanese war aims." Intractable hostility between Japanese and Americans was the appearance of things. "In actuality much in their strategies and plans reflected similar assumptions about Asia and the Pacific." Indeed, according to Iriye, had Japan approached the United States after Tojo's fall, it would have found the Americans "more than ready with a peace plan."[64]

Convergence, however at work implicitly, was not to come for a fatefully long time, for its workings were hardly the only "actuality" of the times. On neither side was a "peace plan" ready, but only bruited about by men of limited authority cautiously exploring the possible. On both sides, too, powerful passions arrested the movement toward formulation of compromise peace terms. Japan, having fueled the fires of anti-Western hatred, could not now easily bank them. Most of all, the peace faction felt repeatedly intimidated by militarist die-hards and chastened as well by its fears of triggering revolutionary upheaval. Nor was it clear how much Japanese talk of satisfying the national aspirations of conquered peoples was sincere. In any event, the crudest forms of exploitation continued whatever the rhetoric.

Some of the same forces at work in Japan also arrested the American effort at reformulation. Much that Americans learned in 1944 only strengthened the urge to pursue vengeance, despite occasional restraint in the media. Now that timely Japanese retreats had ceased, the most graphic evidence of Japanese tenacity emerged. During the battle for Saipan in July, even Japanese civilians leaped to their deaths rather than surrender, a grim omen of the response the enemy might make to an invasion of the home islands. No less ominous were official estimates—published to prepare Americans for years more of war—that Japan still had millions of men available for a last-ditch stand.[65]

Moreover, Americans learned of Japanese atrocities as the government parted the gates of censorship in order to stiffen American resolve for bombing and the bloody invasion that might follow. The atrocity stories hardly put many Americans in the mood to support a compromise peace. Their mood was illustrated by Senator Bennett Champ Clark's call "to bomb Japan out of existence." Public opinion polls indicated some sentiment for a lenient treatment of postwar Japan, but also a persistent minority for whom "extermination" and "torture" seemed the only appropriate course. The subtle implications of the unconditional surrender formula were probably unclear to most Americans, but they overwhelmingly approved it despite war's mounting costs, just as they insisted on "fighting until the Japanese armed forces are completely defeated" even if Japan "offered to make peace now." As Garry Wills has written, "To conduct war successfully, a commander must often fight his own side's fighting spirit, wrestle it back into constructive channels." At the close of 1944, no one knew just how to do that.[66]

The problem was not simply the proper manipulation of public opinion, for the war could arouse some professionals' passions as well. General George Kenney, commanding MacArthur's air force, worried, like many a general, that "the Jap is still being underrated." But to Kenney he was still "a low order of humanity," prey to "his Mongol liking for looting, arson, massacre and rape," and bound to a "national psychology" of "win or perish." In the summer of 1944, the Twentieth Air Force's task was characterized as bringing maximum pressure on the "little yellow bellies." Nor can one discount the existence of prejudice at the highest levels of government, either the "malignant racism" of a Churchill or the more casual and genteel forms of it shared by men like Roosevelt and Stimson.[67]

The atrocity stories of 1944 only added more weight to racial images and stereotype long accumulating. Japan seemed to many Americans a kind of racial mutant of the monolithic Nazi state, its aggression and regimentation comparable to Germany's, only springing from different, less eradicable sources. More than most wartime stereotypes, this one did violence to reality, for regimentation in wartime Japan was a far more subtle, porous phenomenon than in Hitler's Germany. To be sure, official policies designed to mold seamless unity among Japanese also strengthened the West's image of the Japanese as an anonymous mass in which no sense of individual values existed. The Japanese state relied on an ethic of blind self-sacrifice among its soldiers and sailors and treated ethnic minorities abroad and at home brutally and often murderously. But terror never took the form of systematic and self-conscious genocide that it did in Germany. Criticism of the government by innuendo or indirection remained possible; political parties, though dissolved, functioned anyway in attenuated form; even elections for the Diet were held, albeit highly circumscribed by the government. The numbers jailed for political reasons ran only to the thousands, those executed only to the dozens—a record simply not comparable to that of wartime Germany or to other forms of totalitarian rule. Leaders still had to balance the conflicting claims of competing armed services, suspicious senior statesmen, wary industrialists, and most of all a powerful civilian bureaucracy. Of course, conflicts of interest also plagued the Nazi state, but with the critical difference that one supreme leader had emerged, with a centralized apparatus of repression. Collective leadership still prevailed in Japan.

More brutal repression did not seem necessary. Although never as harmonious and homogeneous as Westerners imagined, the Japanese were well endowed with traditions of obedience to the collective will. More important, unlike the Nazis, the Japanese leadership never sought to reorder an entire society. Conscious of Japan's place in Nazi racial theory, it had little desire to emulate Nazism, nor a coherent ideology of its own. Much of its apparatus of mobilization moved rather listlessly, and more often it was the war itself—the demands for collective organization and sacrifice it imposed—that mobilized the populace effectively. "Wartime Japan," it has been argued, "happily escaped the nightmare of rootless mass society enslaved by huge centralized institutions."[68]

Even the much-touted anti-Westernism of wartime Japan had contradictions that revealed the regime's lack of ideological focus. At the least, Jews were not treated worse than other westerners—to Germany's consternation, Japan refused to classify them by race rather than nationality for purposes of passports and immigration, allowed substantial numbers to pass through or settle in Japan and its occupied territories, and even permitted a refugee Polish Jew to conduct one of its leading orchestras. Despite much venom toward Anglo-Americans, publication in English of prominent journals and newspapers was maintained, in part because of its importance in scientific work. It was also difficult to teach the masses to hate Americans, and wartime films and song lyrics were notably freer from crude stereotyping of the enemy than they were in the United States.

Difficulty in comprehending an enemy's subtleties was not unique to Americans. In both Japan and the United States, an "exterminationist logic," expressed viciously in both rhetoric and action, hardened as the war reached its climax, deriving much of its force from the racism shared by the two combatants. But Americans' sense of racial contempt—displayed in demeaning depictions of the Japanese as rats and apes—had an edge to it missing in Japanese propaganda and passions, if only because Japan's "indebtedness to the West . . . made a Japanese equivalent to white supremacism improbable if not impossible." Japan's images of its Western enemies, though often ugly, had an ambiguity—a hint of admiration and of recognition of humanness—derived from that indebtedness, and "whereas racism in the West was markedly characterized by denigration of others, the Japanese were preoccupied far more exclusively with elevating themselves." Moreover, strategic circumstances made it harder for the Japanese to act out their racial hatred: by recourse to blockade and bombing, Americans could attack the entire Japanese population, but the Japanese could engage only American servicemen; only against fellow Asians could they fully act out the war's uglier passions. To be sure, there was also ambiguity in Americans' racial hatred toward Asians—after all, they were allied with the Chinese. Yet in embracing the Chinese as honorary westerners, Americans did not so much triumph over their racism as reveal how a "migrating stereotype" might be selectively applied to various Asians as circumstances seemed to permit.[69]

Most tellingly indicative of American racial passions was the persisting image of the Japanese as even more fanatical than the Germans. In the end the Germans proved the more fanatical, both in resisting through the actual invasion and dismemberment of their homeland and in treating captive populations with a disciplined ferocity the Japanese could not match. Yet despite those large differences between their two enemies, Americans consistently indicated that they both hated and feared the Japanese more, regarding them as both more brutal and more determined to fight to the death. True, in the end American leaders showed greater flexibility in handling Japan's surrender than Germany's, backing away from the formula for unconditional surrender imposed upon the Nazis. But that flexibility reflected differing circumstances rather than tolerance: the greater freedom American leaders had to set Japan's surrender terms without worrying about alliance politics, the anxiety they felt about sustaining support for the war against Japan once Germany capitulated, and the simple reality of Nazi refusal to consider anything less than a fight to the finish. American policy on Japanese surrender was at best belatedly related to an underlying realization that Japan might surrender short of suicide.

Circumstances aggravated and confirmed the racial hatreds between Japanese and Americans and the American tendency to regard the Japanese as the more fanatical foe. Few Americans worried that Germany could secure the willing cooperation of other peoples in its cause, but many harbored a fear, well grounded in light of Asian resentment of Western domination, that Japan could enlist other Asians into a race war against the West; consequently, anxieties about Japan easily shaded off into a larger, undifferentiated fear of the Yellow Peril. Conditions of fighting strengthened the stereotype of Japanese fanaticism. American soldiers met their Asian enemy in terribly close combat, on postage-stamp islands where retreat, surrender, or strategic maneuver were rarely possible, and where most Japanese expected torture or execution should they indeed lay down arms. Moreover, circumstances contributed to a skewed perception of the relative brutality of German and Japanese behavior toward captives and subjects: Nazi war criminals largely victimized Europeans but spared American POWs, whereas Japanese brutality fell heavily on American captives, larger numbers of whom remained far longer under Japanese control and died as a result. Unsurprisingly, Americans judged brutality more by the fate of their own countrymen than by the liquidation of distant peoples under Nazi control, just as reports of war crimes committed by an Asian enemy seemed more credible than stories of atrocities committed by Germans, whose ethnic and cultural heritage so many Americans shared.

In the final analysis, what measured American racism was the failure, even among high officials, to take account of these circumstances and the ease with which they attributed the Japanese style to a bestial nature and an indifference to life rooted in racial characteristics. The Germans seemed an enemy only by virtue of transient Nazi rule. The Japanese seemed an enemy by virtue of race.

To Americans, the Japanese were a less worthy as well as a more fanatical foe. "I wish we were fighting against Germans," John Hersey quoted one Marine:

> They are human beings, like us. Fighting against them must be like an athletic performance—matching your skill against someone you know is good. Germans are misled, but at least they react like men. But the Japs are like animals. Against them you have to learn a whole new set of physical reactions. You have to get used to their animal stubbornness and tenacity. They take to the jungle as if they had been bred there, and like some beasts you never see them until they are dead.

This was not just a view from the trenches. Arnold thought that "the Germans are smarter, but the Japs are tougher. When a German outfit is cut off, it is usually smart enough to give up—but not the Japanese. We have to bomb and burn and blast them out."[70] There was a sense among some Americans that fighting Japan was unfair to them and unworthy of them, that they were deprived of the chance to do battle with "real" soldiers who would offer an honorable standard by which to measure American virtue. The Japanese were repugnant not simply for their misdeeds, but for the humiliation of having to fight them.

Thus the humiliation of fighting Japan fused with other emotions—racial hatred, anger at American losses and Japanese brutalities, and desire for revenge—to sanction the utmost destruction. The enemy, at once inhuman and dehumanized, deserved a commensurate punishment, a kind that least soiled American hands by actual contact with the enemy.

For the purpose of punishing such a foe in that manner, strategic bombing was the ideal vehicle—savage in consequences but impersonal in method. Through films and other forms of popular culture, and through occasional but frequent statements by their leaders, many Americans had learned and expressed this view of the bomber's attractiveness. This view only intensified during the war's last year. The president's son, Elliott Roosevelt, wanted Japan bombed "until we have destroyed about half the Japanese civilian population." Paul V. McNutt, chairman of the War Manpower Commission, went on record in April 1945 as favoring "the extermination of the Japanese in toto." A month earlier, the U.S. Marine monthly *Leatherneck*, visually depicting the Japanese as vermin under the caption "Louseous Japanicas," described the American need to combat the Japanese "pestilence" by carrying out "the gigantic task of extermination," one to be finished only when "the breeding grounds around the Tokyo area" were "completely annihilated." An elusive, loathsome, and fanatical foe seemed to deserve nothing less.[71]

Over the war's final year, Japan's fanaticism, real and alleged, was increasingly cited as justification for the destruction of her cities, an act necessary to punish and subdue a suicidal nation. To be sure, American bombers leveled Japan's cities far more systematically than Germany's in part for circumstantial reasons—the RAF usually performed that task for the Allies in Europe. Even when American bombers joined the RAF, however, the enemy's fanaticism was rarely cited as justification. The ultimate fury of American aerial devastation came against Japan not because it was more fanatical, but because it was relatively weaker. Germany's strength and tenacity gave the Allies little choice but to resort to invasion because Germany would not surrender without it. It was the relative ease of attacking Japan by air that tempted Americans into the fullest use of air power. As an image, Japan's fanaticism was real enough in the minds of many Americans. But it served mainly to justify a course of bombing rooted in strategic circumstances and the emotional need for vengeance.

The emotions aroused by the war trapped strategists and policymakers in another way as well. There had always been a flaw inherent in applying a formula of unconditional surrender to Japan. Inasmuch as Japan and the United States had been drawn into war finally through the connection of Far Eastern events to the European crisis, Japan's importance as a threat would vastly decline once that connection became severed by Germany's defeat. Unconditional surrender might still be demanded because Japanese actions now seemed in their own right so abhorrent; because the American people wanted it; because Japan, it seemed, would surrender under no other terms. None of these reasons was a major part of the original rationale for demanding such surrender. But they had gained such force that they constrained policymakers in any efforts to revise the formula in light of the imminent demise of the Axis alliance.

To complicate matters further, the question of surrender terms and their relationship to strategy fell into the bureaucratic no-man's-land that lay between the services, the State Department, and other interested agencies and individuals. For their part, military officials, though vexed about how to secure surrender, hesitated to intrude upon prerogatives deemed the possession of civilian policymakers. Of course, the issue was finally the president's to decide. But Roosevelt rarely indicated his views—it is doubtful that his subordinates even clearly framed the issues for him—and he hardly prepared the ground of public opinion by claiming that "we can force the Japanese to unconditional surrender or to national suicide much more rapidly than has been thought possible."[72]

The air force entered this uncharted jungle of bureaucratic and policy conflicts the least equipped of the three services even to see it, much less to mark a course. In its doctrine, the connection between bombing and surrender had rarely moved beyond the level of assumption. By background, air officers were especially insular—the least traveled, the most poorly versed in language skills and direct knowledge of enemy cultures. Organizationally the AAF had never gone through the experience of securing a surrender; nor did it have the intelligence apparatus of the army and navy for studying the enemy. Responsibility for reading the enemy's mind and formulating a surrender strategy largely lay elsewhere—with the JCS staff, the war and navy secretaries, and the splintered intelligence services of War, Navy, State, the Office of Strategic Service, and the Office of War Information. And since air strategy remained officially subordinate to invasion as the final instrument of defeat, the AAF's views on surrender strategy were not easily voiced. In short, the AAF was the arm of government best poised to inflict destruction upon Japan but least able, sanctioned, and inclined to explore how destruction would fulfill its final purpose.

The air force nonetheless received speculation which challenged or qualified racial stereotypes common in America during the war. In 1943, for example, a Justice Department official proposed "total destruction of the Imperial Palace itself as the 'ace card' of the Allied Nations," an act so degrading to the Japanese that it would "prove conclusively the sacred grounds were not being protected from the ravages of war by a 'Divine Being.'" Army Intelligence sought out the opinion of State's Eugene Dooman, a Far Eastern expert who complained of "a general disposition toward clothing the problem of Japanese mass psychology with a lot of mysticism." Many Japanese, he pointed out, "have a fairly rational point of view concerning the origin of the Japanese people and of the imperial family." Dooman welcomed the most vigorous bombing campaign, but his analysis undercut assumptions that the Japanese, because of their racial nature or their previous experience with earthquake and fire, would be peculiarly vulnerable to panic or despair if their cities were torched.[73]

A similar tone emerged in discussions of psychological warfare planning. The navy's Captain Ellis M. Zacharias, later to gain some fame for his role in surrender and widely regarded as an expert on Japan, viewed Japan as "so rigidly disciplined and indoctrinated as to make Germany seem weak and insurgent in comparison." Army Intelligence dissented, pointing out that "Japanese surrendered from time to time in the Russo-Japanese War" and that while their image was that of "a mysterious and adamantine mentality which defies all foreign influences," still "as human beings they follow certain elementary processes of reasoning." Observers in the Far East reached similar conclusions.[74]

The crosscurrents of prejudice and policy were muddy. Crude stereotypes might be invoked to caution against expecting too much from bombing: the "remarkable stoicism" of the Japanese argued against believing they were "more vulnerable than other peoples to this form of punishment [bombing]." The same document that characterized the Japanese as "fundamentally human" found them also "by nature volatile and of short enthusiasms."[75] What emerges from these documents is no lack of earnestness in the attempts to understand the Japanese, but the intellectual, cultural, and bureaucratic void in which these attempts took place. Few intellectual criteria existed by which to distinguish racial from situational sources of Japanese behavior. Firsthand knowledge of Japan was uncommon, drawn from a handful of Japanese in the states and from diplomats and missionaries, whose experience had been highly limited. Since no agency distilled the information into a coherent picture, military officers hardly knew how to integrate what they learned into their strategic plans.

The best that might be said is that air officers, despite or because of their naivete, did no worse than officers more experienced in Far Eastern relations. By the time the bombing began, official policy was rightfully cautious about the psychological intimidation it might inflict. Japanese air raid protection was known to be weak, but the bomber commanders of the Twentieth Air Force were instructed to question the claim that "in the event of bombing, collapse will be rapid." The airmen who fought the Japanese had learned the hard way to discount coarse stereotypes about how "Japanese airplanes were made out of bamboo and paper" and to regard the Japanese as a formidable, if not altogether comprehensible, enemy. Prewar hopes for decisive psychological effects from bombing, already in decline since the war began, were at odds with the commonplace notion of the Japanese as a docile and regimented people. About the most airmen could hope for was a slowly mounting demoralization and fatigue that would foul the machinery of Japanese production and mobilization.[76]

Rash proposals still came forward, such as Norstad's, late in 1944, to "commemorate December 7th . . . by a large scale attack on the Imperial Palace in Tokyo" in order to demolish the Japanese notion of their emperor as an "invulnerable deity." (Apparently just such a commemorative raid was what Tokyo expected and feared.) But outside experts, including Under Secretary of State Joseph Grew, were consulted, and they pointed to the potential of Norstad's plan to trigger the "grossest mistreatment" of American POWs as well as to play into the hands of the die-hard militarists. Arnold's own objection was more ominous, characteristically resting not on a view of the enemy but on strategic timetables. "Not at this time," he instructed Norstad: "Our position— bombing factories, docks, etc.—is sound—Later destroy the whole city."[77]

Arnold's comments reflected the dominant tone in air force speculation about Japan's fate. As technicians, the airmen placed operational considerations first and said little about the enemy, rarely employing the rhetoric of vengeance found elsewhere. Intent on speeding up operations, seldom called upon to explain how doing so would affect the final political outcome, they used a language and methodology in which the enemy, far from being the central preoccupation, was the void at the center of other concerns. Thus the air force could serve as a vehicle of vengeance while confining itself to the problems of technique.

As such, its leaders may seem to have been amoral technicians, instruments of a nation's anger in which they had no particular investment. It is a characterization reinforced by the willingness of AAF leaders to target German morale and cities in the last stages of the war and by their apparent lack of remorse after the war as well. Regarding the bombing of Japan, General Ira Eaker later said, "It made a lot of sense to kill skilled workers by burning whole areas." He "never felt there was any moral sentiment among leaders of the AAF" nor any lack of willingness to use the atomic bomb on Germany had it been ready, except for the lack of "fruitful" targets there by the war's last months. As Ronald Schaffer has argued, most objections to area bombing of cities that arose among AAF leaders were tactical or political rather than moral ones. The relative ease and swift payoff of bombing Japan simply seemed to argue for a more systematic attack on its cities.[78]

Three considerations serve to soften the hard lines of this picture of air force leaders. First, airmen did not decide to bomb in a moral vacuum. As Eaker later commented, "Arnold feared the reaction of the U.S. public to urban area bombing of women and children. He pointed to the large percentage of German people in this country and those who felt we should not have become involved in a war with Germany at all." In contrast, "Ninety percent of Americans would have killed every Japanese." As Spaatz quite correctly recalled, "We didn't hear any complaints from the American people about mass bombing of Japan; as a matter of fact, I think they felt the more we did the better." When rudderless in their own right, the moral sensibilities of airmen were steered by perceptions of popular moral preferences.[79] To that guidance they did not object. No complaints came from them that public opinion kept their bombers in Europe on something of a leash. It was not their job to designate the nation's enemy or the treatment given to it, except by pronouncing upon what was militarily practical. Certainly, in the eyes of professional officers, it was not their task to rise to a higher level of moral concern than that evinced by the nation and its political leaders.

Second, not all air force officers were so quick to dismiss moral issues. Hansell's memoirs offered a critique of the choices made about bombing policy based on their wastefulness and their damaging consequences for the postwar image of the air force, but also explicitly on the failure to choose a strategy which "would have been far less costly in civilian lives."[80] Even those who asserted that moral concerns did not guide them at the time have since felt compelled to offer a defense of the policies they sanctioned.

A third qualification is broader. When Spaatz later acknowledged that "it wasn't for religious or moral reasons that I didn't go along with urban area bombing," he also recalled how he had believed that precision bombing "could win the war more quickly."[81] That argument was as much a moral as a utilitarian claim, one applied by some to incendiary as well as to precision bombing. Of course, few military men were pressed in wartime to justify strategies in moral terms, except that the protection of American lives and interests was itself a moral concern. But in 1945, as earlier in the war when bombing strategy was formulated, speedy victory at minimum cost remained the implicit moral justification for what the airmen wanted to do.

In moral as in strategic matters, however, the methods used to examine problems shaped the content of thinking about them. Preferring expert analysis, the air force sometimes turned over the problem of "evaluating the 'breaking point' of Japanese populations under air bombardment" to its operations analysts. The analysts' tentative conclusions often followed the prevailing wisdom: for all the harm that bombing of cities might do, it would "not necessarily induce sudden neuropsychological collapse of any widespread character." What was more striking was the language of social and psychological analysis employed. While the "psychologically 'tighter' Japanese," notable for their "sadism-masochism duality," might survive bombing as well as Europeans, "when a 'break' comes the effect is more violent and extreme than with Europeans." The problem was one "of discovering a technic for the demoralization of a community." One promising approach was to exploit class antagonisms by bombing "workers' dwelling regions, while (to some extent) sparing upper-class zones."[82]

These observations drew upon the language, techniques, and sometimes the specific analyses of a pathbreaking group of social scientists working the new field of "national character" studies. At first glance, their contributions promised to offset the crude racial stereotyping of wartime culture, for they explicitly repudiated racist language and biological determinism. In practice, however, they probably strengthened the impulses of that culture. By drawing on cultural anthropologists' work on primitive peoples, which focused on "the web of tribal behavior, communal cults, and the like," wartime students of Japan "reinforced the impression that the Japanese were dressed-up primitives," thus subtly confirming popular stereotypes of a backward, barbaric people. The social scientists' characterization of the Japanese as a culturally and psychologically immature and childish people victimized by repressive toilet training—the "Scott Tissue interpretation of history," as one anthropologist snidely described this line of argument—dovetailed with more vicious popular stereotypes of a simian race arrested in its development. Similarly, the language of individual and social pathology gave sophisticated expression to popular notions of a mad people driven by a lust to torture and conquer. More specifically, the impression they conveyed of a psychologically brittle people provided sanction, if unwitting, to the terror bombing of Japanese cities—a kind of scientific gloss on the widely held (if also disputed) notion that the Japanese would crack under the strain of bombing. In short, the use made of the concept of national character permitted pejorative stereotyping under the guise of social science.[83]

To be sure, not all social scientists wanted to justify indiscriminate bombing, or even did so unwittingly. And certainly their influence was limited; as one complained in a different context, "The administrator uses social science the way a drunk uses a lamppost, for support rather than for illumination." Yet this lamppost was brightly lit—widely noticed in both official Washington and the popular press. Its impact extended beyond the occasional justification for terror bombing it provided. More important was the social scientists' effort to objectify the enemy, reducing him to an anonymous category for the application of technique. In war there are many ways to achieve distance from the enemy and from what is done to him. In fighting an elusive enemy, civilian experts cast that elusiveness in new terms rather than clarifying it. Not for them was there the explicit language of racial vengeance. Rather, the language of pathology sanctioned in more subtle and disguised ways the destruction that others justified in bloodier but franker terminology.[84]

By December 1944, as the final air campaign against Japan began, the distance on air war achievable through bureaucracy, methodology, and strategy was also evident culturally and intellectually. A fanatical and cruel enemy deserved punishment, but an unworthy one did not command a commitment in blood to realize that punishment. Bombing might limit the costs. But if, as one high-ranking officer worried, "they will not give up even when faced with certain annihilation," it was by no means clear if even bombing satisfied the conflicting needs.[85] An enemy that continued to fight beyond the point of defeat, as measured by all the conventional standards, was baffling; hence the conclusions of those who tried to understand the enemy pointed in no certain strategic direction and fell into a system where responsibility for acting on conclusions was diffused.

The American government succumbed to a "failure to distinguish between the problem of inflicting strategic defeat on the enemy and that of inducing him to surrender." Masters at solving the first problem, its leaders had long assumed that its solution compelled capitulation. As Hansell recalled, "We failed to weigh the urban decimation in terms of our national policies and purposes and in terms of alternate strategies, and . . . we were hasty in making a long-term decision in order to provide a solution based upon expediency."[86] For this failure responsibility was widespread and rested to a degree with the enemy. It derived from the newness of total war and of air power's role in such a war, about which calculations had long been facile because they had rarely been tested. It derived from the cultural distance between the two enemies as well as the racism flowing from it, although a similar failure in the air war against Germany is caution against attributing too much to racism. It derived from the indifference of strategic planners to the question of relating destruction to surrender and from the failure of political leaders to provide them leadership when they did become concerned.

Destruction would win the war. As in Harris's approach to bombing Germany, it would win by brutalization; terror and economic decline were hard to calculate and gradually became desirable side effects to a strategy that promised victory by total destruction of the enemy state. Without a clear and accurate model of how the enemy thought and how destruction might compel his surrender, little guided the course of bombing beyond its own internal dynamics and the fearsome prospect of invasion. Once again, intangible criteria invited unlimited destruction.

The formula for unconditional surrender has been faulted often enough for making the enemy fight on. At least as plausibly, it led the Allies to fight on. Particularly in the American war against Japan, it provided few criteria for measuring the relationship of destruction to the attainment of political ends. It seemed only to indicate that the path to unconditional surrender lay through unconditional destruction.

THE PROBLEM OF TECHNOLOGICAL FANATICISM

The leaders and technicians of the American air force were driven by technological fanaticism—a pursuit of destructive ends expressed, sanctioned, and disguised by the

organization and application of technological means. Destruction was rarely the acknowledged final purpose for the men who made air war possible. Rather, they declared that it served the purpose of securing victory and that its forms were dictated by
technological, organizational, and strategic imperatives. In practice, they often waged
destruction as a functional end in itself, without a clear comprehension of its relationship to stated purposes.

To label these men fanatics or their mentality and behavior as fanatical may defy
the usual understanding of the terms, which sees in fanaticism the workings of a
single-minded, frenzied emotional devotion to a cause. Intensity of emotion hardly
seemed to characterize men whose virtue was their capacity for rational examination of
problems. "The fanatic cannot tolerate scientific thought," it has been said. Moreover,
"fanaticism is a megalomaniacal condition," one notable for "a jealous, vindictive and
monomaniacal faith," usually in a party, an organization, or a leader in which is
invested a "unique saving function."[87] The air force certainly inspired among its
professional officers an intense loyalty but rarely a monomaniacal allegiance. While
some wartime scientists maintained an unquestioning faith in their methodology and
its beneficence, by no means did all. Nor was faith in the American or the Allied cause
always intense or evenly shared. What characterized the experts in air war was their
flexibility and control, the ease with which they worked among a variety of organizations serving many purposes, and the skill with which they balanced personal, professional, bureaucratic, and ideological goals. Indeed, the practice of air war grew out of a
convergence of diverse appeals, needs, and opportunities, diversity imparting to the
bombing much of its momentum.

Fanaticism in the context of World War II usually refers to America's enemies—
the Nazis, genocidal in ideology and practice, and the Japanese, whose cult of spiritual
strength sent thousands of men to their deaths in kamikaze attacks. In more recent
expressions of fanaticism—the acts of terrorism carried out by shadowy religious
organizations from the Middle East, for example—self-destructiveness seems the
salient characteristic, indeed the hidden desire of the fanatic. In contrast, if anything
seemed to bind Americans together during World War II, it was self-preservation, the
lowest common denominator of support for the war effort.

Why, then, call the practitioners of air war fanatics, and what shared mentality
constituted their fanaticism? For one thing, fanatical acts are not always the product of
frenzied or hateful individuals, as Hannah Arendt has shown in capturing the banality
of Adolf Eichmann.[88] For another, there was a suggestion of the megalomaniacal
among the practitioners of air war in their aspirations for technological omnipotence:
over the natural universe for some of the scientists, over the geographic and political
world for the airmen striving to achieve a "global" air force, with men like John von
Neumann embracing both aspirations. For sure, these aspirations did not often appear
suicidal or self-destructive to the men who held them. Yet the technology they created
or promoted—finally the atomic bomb but to some degree the apparatus of "conventional" air war as well—carried that self-destructive potential for the nation and the

world, and not simply in retrospect inasmuch as the world-ending potential of aerial warfare had been recognized before the war by writers like H. G. Wells and during the war by some atomic scientists and policymakers.

The shared mentality of the fanatics of air war was their dedication to assembling and perfecting their methods of destruction, and the way that doing so overshadowed the original purposes justifying destruction. Their coolness, their faith in rational problem-solving, did not easily appear fanatical because its language was the language of rationality and technique. It apparently expressed the triumph of a new set of values, ones often called modern or bureaucratic, which displaced more traditional ones by which people were defined according to racial, ethnic, religious, and national differences. Yet it is by no means clear that such values had entirely displaced more traditional ones. For one thing, whatever their individual value system, those who waged air war served as the instrument of national passions that were often decidedly racist in character. For another, their rhetoric, as in the use of the term "dehousing," allowed them to express aggressive and destructive impulses in other terms, impulses that did not necessarily disappear from motivation, simply from view.

It was easier to regard the decisions that took lives as the products of technological, strategic, and bureaucratic imperatives. In the face of these imperatives, men felt a helplessness that allowed them to escape responsibility or fulfilled a wish to do so. Actions ceased to be recognized as the product of aggressive wills and became foreordained, irresistible. Certainly, the complexities of modern technology, bureaucracy, and war-making were real enough. The American political system had built-in impediments to accountability because of its diffuse nature, aggravated by the division of responsibilities among the three services. The functional distribution of power along the chain of command and the compartmentalization that accompanied it had much the same effect. Efforts to centralize power, as with Arnold's command of the Twentieth Air Force, did not necessarily enhance accountability at the top because leaders were so remote from war's realities. Rarely were these arrangements designed deliberately to negate accountability—as usual, they were a response to perceived necessities. Yet, for a nation with a benign image of its role in the world, eager to mete out punishment to its enemies but reluctant to proclaim its intent to do so, these arrangements were also attractive, desirable.[89]

The lack of a proclaimed intent to destroy, the sense of being driven by the twin demands of bureaucracy and technology, distinguished America's technological fanaticism from its enemies' ideological fanaticism. That both were fanatical was not easily recognizable at the time because the forms were so different. The enemy, particularly the Japanese, had little choice but to be profligate in the expenditure of manpower and therefore in the fervid exhortation of men to hatred and sacrifice—they were not, and knew they were not, a match in economic and technological terms for the Allies. The United States had different resources with which to be fanatical: resources allowing it to take the lives of others more than its own, ones whose accompanying rhetoric of technique disguised the will to destroy. As lavish with machines as the enemy was with men, Americans appeared to themselves to practice restraint, to be immune from the passion to destroy that characterized their enemies and from the urge to self-destruction as well.

The distinction between technological and ideological fanaticism was not absolute. It could not be, given how war often elicits similar behavior from disparate combatants. On occasion, particularly when their backs were to the wall early in the war, Americans celebrated the suicidal defense of hopeless positions, and if the rhetoric of technique dominated official expression, a rhetoric of racial and martial passion often dominated the larger culture. Allies like the Soviet Union, although zealous in pursuing technological advantage when possible, also could be profligate indeed in the expenditure of manpower. When conditions were favorable, the Japanese relied on technical superiority; it was not suicidal tactics that destroyed the American fleet at Pearl Harbor. Even when frankly suicidal tactics were employed, they had a military rationale, for the intent was to take the enemy along.

Likewise, the fact that both the United States and its enemies were fanatical did not mean that the differences between them in the forms of fanaticism were inconsequential. Destruction disguised as technique carried the gravest implications for the fate of enemy civilians. At the same time, it had inherent limits because it had little sanction apart from the prosecution of war. Since destruction was felt, but rarely proclaimed officially, as a good in itself, its sanction continued only as long as the war and the mobilization of technique that went with it continued. It made all the difference in the world to the Japanese—if we are to contrast their fate to that of the Jews—that however much vengeance may have motivated Americans, it did not become official policy and remained fulfilled by policies undertaken for other stated reasons.

Technological fanaticism had many sources: in the nature of strategic air power, whose benefits promised to be so large yet whose consequences were so hard to observe; in its demands for technique that distanced men from its consequences; in war's powerful emotions, difficult to recognize given America's strategic position and its own self-image. At bottom, technological fanaticism was the product of two distinct but related phenomena: one—the will to destroy—ancient and recurrent; the other—the technical means of destruction—modern. Their convergence resulted in the evil of American bombing. But it was sin of a peculiarly modern kind because it seemed so inadvertent, seemed to involve so little choice. Illusions about modern technology had made aerial holocaust seem unthinkable before it occurred and simply imperative once it began. It was the product of a slow accretion of large fears, thoughtless assumptions, and at best discrete decisions.[90]

In one sense, the disjunction between means and ends that characterized the bombing seems at odds with the tenor of wartime political culture in the United States. The very vagueness of American purposes and the difficulty of achieving consensus about them in a diverse nation immune to immediate destruction led American leaders to define purposes by the lowest common denominators of survival and victory. If victory was a dominant, rationalizing value, was not a premium placed on how destruction would contribute to it? In practice, the focus on victory tended to validate any form of destruction that vaguely promised to secure it. Since political authority defined the path to victory as lying so substantially through production and technological effort, the focus tended to remain on means rather than ends. And progress by the preferred method of victory, war by air, could be measured most easily in terms of the destruction it wrought; the connection of that destruction to the end of victory was as easily presumed as it was hard to prove.

In their long journey from Pearl Harbor to the enemy's surrender on the decks of the *Missouri,* Americans might be likened to a man forced to set out on a cross-country car trip. As he drives along, the trip gathers its own interest, momentum, and challenge. He finds himself diverting to places he had not imagined; he tinkers with his car and enjoys feeling it run faster and smoother and discovers a power and mastery in manipulating it. Perhaps he did not choose this mode of travel conscious of the pleasures it would bring; he thought it necessary because of the baggage he wanted to bring along and because it was cheaper to travel this way, and after all, he already knew how to drive. Nor does he forget what his destination is, but as he travels he does not dwell on its importance; it will take care of itself if he makes the trip properly. Once the trip is done, it rapidly fades from memory, its pleasures and challenges now comfortably tucked away in his mind as necessities imposed on him in order to enable him to reach his destination, not as choices he had the freedom to make.

By December 1944, Americans were close to their destination, closer than most of them realized. Proximity was not evident, not with one more range of mountains to cross, not with the trip itself generating such excitement and anxiety, not with the machine built to make the trip yet to be fully tested. There was perhaps even a hope that the mountains would stand tall, to provide full measure for the test. "To test the [atomic] bomb's real destructiveness," Arnold later wrote about his concerns near the end of the war, "three or four cities must be saved intact from the B-29's regular operations as unspoiled targets for the new weapon. Which cities should be spared was a problem," he added.[91] To Arnold, it seems, the test was as important as the destination. It lay ahead, with not only the atomic bomb but the "regular" forms of fire his bombers could hurl at Japanese cities. Technological fanaticism, long developing, could now be fully expressed.

9

The Triumphs of Technological Fanaticism

WINTER'S CRISES

On December 18, 1944, Curtis LeMay's 20th Bomber Command sent eighty-four B-29s loaded only with incendiaries to attack Hankow, a Chinese city serving as a base for Japanese operations. At the time, the raid seemed to LeMay and Arnold an annoying diversion from strategic operations against Japan. For months they had rejected Chennault's requests to hit the city, acquiescing only when the Japanese threatened to drive deeper into China. But Arnold did not ignore the results of the raid, which fired residential districts as well as designated dock and warehouse areas. After the fact if not in intention, the raid served as a test of firebombing tactics, its "efficacy," as he blandly informed Stimson, important "from a long range as well as an immediate viewpoint." In the Marianas, Arnold's other B-29 commander, Major General Haywood Hansell, would have been well advised to have heeded the lesson of Hankow.[1]

Hansell had arrived on Saipan on October 12 to considerable fanfare from the press and the men already on hand. Hansell's own words were of soldierly simplicity, to the effect that he could do more talking once he had done some fighting. The tone was appropriate, since formidable obstacles to success lay ahead.[2] A month elapsed before enough bombers had arrived and training flights had been run to consider a mission to Japan. Operating on directives from Washington, Hansell picked aircraft engine plants near a crowded suburb of Tokyo, a target satisfying the needs for both a dramatic first mission (Tokyo had not been visited since the Doolittle raid) and the destruction of the Japanese air force before beginning a full-scale strategic campaign. Trouble arose long before the B-29s got off the ground. Hansell repeatedly had to delay the mission because of bad weather. Moreover, his senior wing commander questioned the readiness of the 21st Bomber Command to attack such a distant and well-defended target in daytime. Worse yet, Arnold raised similar doubts, a warning "coming from the very

256

area in which I had expected firmest support." Hansell later explained Arnold's expression of concern as a political act necessary to protect the AAF: with a mighty force of newsmen in the Marianas to look on, Arnold wanted no inaugural disaster. If Hansell, not Washington, made the decision to go ahead to Tokyo by day, "the ill effects" of any disaster "would be less severe on the future of the Air Forces."[3]

The mission finally got off on November 24, with the feared disaster averted—Japan's air defenses would never match Germany's—but scarcely the achievement implied by newsreels proclaiming "B29's Rule Jap Skies," "Tokyo aflame," and the "setting sun of Japanese aggression."[4] Only a fraction of the bombers hit the designated target.

For a first effort, it was not a bad one. Dedicated to precision bombing, Hansell and other officers would do much to improve accuracy by new methods of crew training, especially in use of electronic equipment. But one obstacle would plague B-29 commanders for the next nine months. They could not change the weather. At high altitudes, the newly discovered jet stream, with winds of 150 miles per hour or more, disrupted formations, sabotaged fuel calculations, deflected bombs, and forced bombers either to race past targets downwind or lumber dangerously over them if they flew into its teeth. At times, when attempts were made to bomb upwind, it seemed that "the damn target backed right off the radar; we were going backward over ground."[5] Foul weather also limited opportunities for visual sighting of targets to a precious few days a month—at that, days not anticipated with the accuracy possible in Europe, where prevailing weather patterns first passed over Allied meteorological stations. All these conditions also compounded navigation over oceans offering few visual opportunities for confirming location.

Weather played havoc with Hansell's subsequent missions against the Japanese aircraft industry. In December, crews repeatedly failed to reach their target or to see it when they did or to hit it even if sighted, much less with the radar equipment often used. The record, hardly impressive, looked even worse because of problems in photographic surveillance and intelligence—Japanese aircraft production began a steep decline at the end of 1944, though it was not solely attributable to the B-29 attacks.

Meanwhile, Washington increased the pressure to test incendiary tactics against large urban areas. The line between those tactics and the ones Hansell preferred was blurred even in precision raids because Hansell often used radar or incendiaries or the cover of night—or all three at once. But Arnold and his deputy, Norstad, wanted to do more than just tinker with the tactics of precision bombing. Backed by the findings of the Committee of Operations Analysts and the Joint Target Group, they wanted a full-scale test of the potential for firing Japanese cities. When Hansell failed to take the hint, Norstad got explicit, relaying on December 18 "an urgent requirement" for a fire raid on Nagoya with at least one hundred B-29s. Hansell, although acknowledging "very deep seated" problems in his precision bombing, had a scholarly and somewhat stubborn temperament. Through years as a top strategist he had advocated precision bombing, and he was not about "to waste our bombs on large urban areas as a secondary effort." Replying directly to Arnold, he opposed Norstad's demand in no uncertain terms. He had "with great difficulty implanted the principle that our mission is the destruction of primary targets by . . . precision bombing methods," which he would not abandon just when he was "beginning to get results." Only after Norstad promised that the fire raid would be only a test for "future planning" would Hansell run the mission, which took place on January 3 with dubious results.[6]

Hansell sensed the pressure he was under but not its nature and intensity. Area incendiary raids, he wrote in his memoirs, "were to be undertaken only as last resort," according to the "original plans." But after Hansell had left Washington, the original plans had been revised to upgrade the priority on incendiary attacks. He had missed out on a crucial stage in planning. Even in Washington, the vague circumlocutions employed and the incremental way by which new assumptions crept into planning obscured the shift. The test raids were repeatedly described as "not a departure from our primary mission to destroy Japanese air power" but as "merely necessary preparation for the future."[7]

Moreover, Hansell was given the usual reassurances of Arnold's confidence in him. "'Who said anything about putting the heat on Possum?'", Norstad quoted the commanding general in a letter to Possum Hansell. On January 1, Arnold sent Hansell a cheerful New Year's testament to his "pride" in the 21st's achievements. But the long arm of Washington, whose grip of command and communication Hansell had helped to mold, was reaching out to him. Later he wished he had rejected Norstad's advice that "the normal run of difficulties will only be an annoyance to him [Arnold]" and instead have passed them on to Arnold "in more detail."[8]

Sometime in December, Arnold decided to sack Hansell. Committed to a doctrine in which for him inhered strategic, political, and moral wisdom, Hansell had aroused his boss's notorious impatience. Determined to try whatever worked and to try a man who shared that determination, Arnold turned to Curtis LeMay. As Hansell commented at the time, "The boss considers LeMay as the big time operator and me as the planner." The boss, he later wrote, was also inclined "to measure strategic air attack in terms of tonnage and sorties." The good soldier, Hansell did not fault Arnold for this inclination, knowing the political pressures on Arnold for results. But he disliked the change in policy his dismissal implied and declined to stay on to assist LeMay, in a relationship he knew would be embarrassing to both men.[9]

If Arnold felt under pressure, it came from an army and navy still eager to make a claim on his big bombers, for neither Roosevelt nor Congress and the press were looking critically at air force operations. Most newsmen fell quietly into line with the Twentieth's centralized press control, writing up their stories on the first B-29 raid on Tokyo even before the mission was run, and conveying uncritically the air force's claim of practicing only precision bombing. The B-29s might eventually be able "to wipe out Tokyo altogether," commented the *Los Angeles Times*. "But it may be taken for granted that we have no such objective. As in Germany, our purpose in air-bombing is to cripple the enemy's war potential and soften up his defenses against invasion." "As the Germans long ago discovered," reported the *Kansas City Star,* "final victories are never gained by terrorizing civilians." Press coverage adopted just the tone the AAF wanted.[10]

Nonetheless, Arnold was worried, not only about the slow progress of the Twentieth Air Force, but about the air war against Germany. Spaatz's devastating campaign against the German petroleum industry—assisted by Allied intelligence that was finally on the mark—was gradually paralyzing the enemy's movement in the air and on the ground. In other ways, however, Allied bombing still seemed adrift among conflicting visions of the road to victory. Renewed attention was given Germany's aircraft industry, whose new jets helped provoke a mood just short of panic among Allied strategists (Spaatz even worried about a German death ray). An ill-chosen attempt to knock out German vehicle production further delayed Spaatz's oil campaign. As always, Harris was inclined to plaster cities. By the fall, Allied air forces were also sliding into a campaign against the German railway system, so dense and blessed with reserve capacity that attacks on it were slow to show results. In addition to all these efforts, the heavy bombers repeatedly laid carpets of bombs in front of advancing Allied ground forces—destroying many occupied and enemy towns, to the consternation of some air commanders. In January, in the wake of the Nazis' Ardennes counteroffensive, some three-fourths of the American strategic bomber effort was in fact not strategic at all, but tactical.[11]

The surprise Ardennes attack was a major setback, making it clear, so Stimson told the president, that the United States could not hope "to break down organized German resistance . . . by constant bombardment."[12] What saved the bombing campaign from at least the appearance of failure was first of all the sheer weight of effort the Allied air forces now maintained, the British and Americans each throwing more than one thousand bombers into daily operations. With so much firepower, dispersion of effort was affordable, if wasteful and destructive. Critics argued that a clear priority, either for oil or transportation, could have saved lives and speeded victory, but largesse did not compel clarity. In effect, strategic bombing climaxed in a broad-front campaign that mimicked as well as complemented the strategy Eisenhower pursued on the ground.

Progress by ground forces also salvaged the campaign in the air. It stripped the Nazis of their western fighter and radar defenses necessary for successful interception of Allied bombers. More than that, it further obscured the issue of whether bombers might win wars substantially on their own. Armies drove into a nation that would not submit to terrifying blows from the air. At the same time, armies proceeded at such a slow pace that no ground general discounted the value of air power, tactical and strategic. Still, it must have distressed Arnold to hear Marshall suggest, even before the Battle of the Bulge, that "long-range objectives of strategic bombardment be abandoned for an all-out effort to force an early victory." Nor could he have been pleased to admit to Marshall on January 8 that strategic bombing was "not having the effect upon the German war effort we had expected and hoped." For all that Arnold and other air officers had muted their rhetoric about the war-winning capability of air power, they had not substantially changed their views. But vindicating those views was something else. Perhaps they thought a final, savage blow by air to the enemy would rescue the air force's fortunes by forcing early capitulation.[13]

Impatience to finish off Germany quickly and by a decisive contribution from the air, along with the collapse of German capacity to defend and retaliate, culminated in the bombing that took place over the war's last winter. The climax came at Dresden, struck on the night of February 13–14 in two ferocious assaults brilliantly executed by British bombers, followed the next day by American bombers (except for forty that mistakenly hit Prague). The resulting firestorm, visible to bomber crews two hundred miles away, struck a city clotted with refugees fleeing other crumbling towns and advancing Soviet armies. Residents of Dresden were also unusually ill-prepared, believing their city exempted from Allied bombing perhaps to save it as the capital of a new Germany. The Dresden death toll, even as later revised downward to thirty-five thousand, was catastrophic and became the focal point of postwar debate about the moral distinctions between the Allies and the Axis. Dresden added to a tally of German civilian fatalities from Anglo-American bombing that reached somewhere between three hundred thousand and six hundred thousand; untold thousands more were killed in other Allied operations, the Red Army in particular razing cities by shelling and tactical air strikes.[14]

The Dresden raids were less the product of conscious callousness than of casual destructiveness. Indeed, so many had a hand in the decision and so many reasons were available to run it that no clear rationale had to be furnished. One source was plans advanced from the previous summer for terror attacks to force the final breakdown of German morale. Supported by some AAF leaders, momentarily resisted by others and by Eisenhower, indirectly encouraged by Roosevelt, those plans—"baby killing schemes," as one AAF officer complained—generated intense debate over whether terror attacks would complement the precision campaign or dilute it, enhance the AAF's reputation or tarnish it, teach Germans a lasting lesson or only embitter them, and inflict righteous revenge or cause American shame. Slow to gain explicit approval, such plans were informally implemented anyway over the winter, particularly in Spaatz's February 3 raid on Berlin, claimed to have taken twenty-five thousand lives.[15]

For the RAF's Harris, the obliteration of cities was routine practice, and Dresden was one city on his list as yet relatively unscathed. Yet the impetus within British circles to attack Dresden itself came more from Churchill, who knew well how "increasing the terror" could take place "under other pretexts." Dresden's marginal war industries, though sometimes cited as justification for the attacks, were not even targeted. With Marshall's support, Eisenhower's headquarters probably cut the explicit orders for Dresden, having in mind German morale, plus assisting the Soviet advance westward by disrupting German rail transport and fouling it with refugees. For their part, the Russians encouraged the assistance, though they did not specifically request an attack on Dresden. At least a few British and Americans also sought to impress and perhaps intimidate the Soviets with Anglo-American air power. Certainly Arnold was chagrined that "Stalin hasn't the faintest conception of the damage done to Germany and Japan by strategic bombing," and his representatives came to the Yalta conference in February with Hollywood pictures and combat footage to make an impression on the assembled Big Three leaders.[16]

But to the bomber commanders involved, the Dresden raids did not appear unusual before they were run except for the circuitous channels and prodding by superiors that produced them. Indeed, had the hands of Churchill, Eisenhower, and Marshall not been evident and had not fortuitous factors produced a firestorm, Dresden would probably have escaped critical scrutiny. Harris's Bomber Command had, on its own authority, already demolished other German cities with a ferocity exceeding that displayed in Dresden. Darmstadt, for example, had been incinerated in a September firestorm because it was destroyable, not because it had even the strategic importance Dresden momentarily possessed.[17] But the world had not noticed, any more than it noticed Hankow or the fate of other German, Italian, and Asian cities.

Dresden also stirred controversy because of its status as the cultural capital of Germany and because of an Associated Press story based on a SHAEF officer's briefing and unaccountably cleared by censors. The AP reported that "the Allied air commanders have made the long-awaited decision to adopt deliberate terror bombing of the great German population centers as a ruthless expedient to hasten Hitler's doom."[18] Both the British and American high commands were shocked by the appearance of such a claim and fearful of the controversy it seemed destined to arouse. An assistant to the ailing Arnold warned Spaatz of the "nation-wide serious effect on the Air Forces as we have steadily preached the gospel of precision bombing against military and industrial targets."[19]

Spaatz's headquarters labored to assure Washington that there had been "no change in the American policy of precision bombing directed at military objectives." In a sense the claim was technically correct, and these men really believed that because American planes still flew under directives assigning precise targets, nothing in American targeting practices had changed. But by the end of 1944, American bombers relied on radar or "blind bombing" techniques so often, for roughly three-fourths of their missions, that terror became their inevitable consequence even when defined targets were the avowed objectives. Because that consequence seemed inadvertent and because it came about through a slow erosion of the distinction between precision and area bombing, any confrontation with moral scruples was forestalled for American commanders, just as it had been earlier for the British until civilians were finally acknowledged as the target. "Radar bombing was better than no bombing," air force historians aptly paraphrased the bomber commanders' thinking. On paper there was a policy against "indiscriminate bombing," Schaffer has pointed out: "Sometimes it was adhered to; often it was not, or it was so broadly reinterpreted as to become meaningless." In those circumstances, it was hard to recognize, or at least easy to deny, when the line to a different kind of bombing had been crossed.[20]

Strangely, a drift in the reverse direction had received equally little recognition from the British. "By a curious development of the war's circumstances," it was explained to Arnold, "the AAF now bombs blind by day, while the RAF bombs visually (through the use of visual markers) by night. RAF bombing is now in fact frequently more accurate than our own."[21] However, although unavoidable inaccuracy had originally justified the RAF's switch to area bombing, Harris refused to redirect his bombers. In general, greater accuracy was employed simply to perfect the wholesale destruction of cities.

In assessing responsibility for this destruction, Marshall's biographer has not exempted the chief of staff. Like other responsible commanders, he "did not so much direct the specific bombing as leave the choice of targets in the hands of subordinates who found it difficult to stop the momentum of attacks on a hated enemy." In fact, Marshall, Arnold, and Eisenhower did more than "leave the choice" to subordinates, for they had often talked of terror bombing and tacitly approved it by offering objections rooted only in timing and tactics. In connection with Operation CLARION, a plan to hit smaller German towns, Marshall had already spoken of bombing Munich "because it would show the people that are being evacuated to Munich that there is no hope." Even after Dresden, CLARION was formally ordered by Eisenhower's headquarters.[22]

Earlier, Eaker had objected that CLARION would show the Germans "that we are the barbarians they say we are, for it would be perfectly obvious to them that this is primarily a large scale attack on civilians, as, in fact, it of course will be." But in a climate of degraded sensibilities and informal encouragement, Dresden, like other cities, was razed as the casually accepted by-product of attacks still designated as precise and limited. Spaatz's deputy revealed as much when he parried Washington's queries about what happened at Dresden. "These attacks [on cities he listed] have not been hailed as terror attacks against populations. . . . There has been no change of policy . . . only a change of emphasis in locale." The wording simultaneously implied that "terror attacks" were taking place, and yet that they were not because they had not been "hailed" as such.[23]

Whatever concern Dresden evoked among American leaders was limited. The matter apparently never came to Roosevelt's attention. Stimson was upset over a German account that made "the destruction seem on its face terrible and probably unnecessary," but his stated reasons for concern were political: since Dresden was in the "least Prussianized part of Germany," he explained to Marshall in an eerie echo of the dashed hopes of its residents, it needed to be saved as the "center of a new Germany." There may have been more than this to Stimson's anxiety. Stimson knew the language of realpolitik, but he was also a moralist. But for the moment Dresden was a passing concern for him. For his part, Arnold's response to Stimson's concern was characteristically brutal: "We must not get soft—war must be destructive and to a certain extent inhuman and ruthless."[24]

The "careful investigation" Stimson requested was pursued with little urgency and came too late to affect the subsequent course of bombing. Dresden itself was struck not only on February 14 by the Americans, but again on February 15, March 2, and April 17. Perhaps the additional raids seemed necessary because for all that the city's marshaling yards had justified the initial firestorm, in fact they had escaped major damage, and railway lines had quickly resumed operations. Only the exhaustion of targets and the desire not to complicate further the task of occupying Germany brought the campaign against its cities to a halt in mid-April.[25]

Meanwhile, there was also little sense of restraint in the consideration given another project, the use of remotely controlled worn-out bombers against Germany. The patent inaccuracy of such bombers stirred Admiral Leahy's fear of an "inhumane and barbarous type of warfare with which the United States should not be associated." But Leahy's doubts were overcome by reassurances from the air force that accuracy had been improved and would not be any worse than in the radar bombing already going on. Besides, the use of war-weary bombers against Germany would be a warm-up for employing them against Japan, and as Leahy advised Roosevelt, tests would be of "inestimable value" for postwar development of guided missiles, a field in which German superiority had caused Anglo-American embarrassment. All of these arguments, plus the dividend of "creating further destruction in an already frantic condition in Germany," appear to have been accepted by Roosevelt. They were also pressed by him on Churchill, who had reneged on his earlier approval by citing the danger of German retaliation—a curious pretext in light of German initiation of pilotless air war and Allied firebombing of German cities. But time ran out to make use of the new weapon.[26]

In the United States, popular reactions to Dresden and to the final fury of bombing in Europe were muted. The print media generally gave routine coverage to the raids on Berlin and Dresden and to the AP report describing "deliberate terror bombing" as Allied policy. At the same time, widely publicized pictures and descriptions of how the great cathedral of Cologne was left standing offered ritual reassurance that for all its destructiveness, Allied bombing had somehow been selective and humane in its targeting. Newsreels did acknowledge that "allied strategy called for the levelling of towns if it meant saving the lives of our boys" and pointed the viewer's attention to a city "literally dying before your eyes." But in February and March, the headlines were usually seized by the advances of ground forces in Germany, the Philippines, and Iwo Jima and by the Yalta Conference. Coverage of the air war had a routine, more-of-the-same tone to it.[27]

That tone even crept into the few blunt criticisms offered in the religious press. *Commonweal* expressed bitter but helpless resignation. It effectively captured how governments had used euphemisms to obscure their barbarism: "'Evacuation of the homeless' creates 'a traffic problem.'" But "all the best violent words were used up long ago," and none seemed "left to argue the question of 'deliberate terror bombing'" or to wonder "about how to win the war without making Europe a desert." The socialist Norman Thomas condemned Allied bombing practices against Japan as well as Germany and correctly linked them to a failure to determine America's objective in the war—to the "incredibly stupid slogan of unconditional surrender." Even Thomas, however, had his eye more on the shape of politics to come than on the present: because American airmen "are burning the cities of Japan and the people in them," Russia will be "the one victor in Asia." Only in England, which bore greater responsibility for the fate of Germany's cities, did a clear debate take shape, beginning the process of "dishonoring" Harris for practices his superiors had sanctioned.[28]

In general, then, American military leaders had feared an outcry that never arose.[29] Yet their nervousness had significance, indicating their perceptions of limits to what the nation might accept in the way of destruction against the Germans. Although uncritical, press coverage of Germany's destruction was notably free of the spirit of revenge, implying that bombing was acceptable only as a military necessity. And as the Joint Chiefs were advised by Elmer Davis, long-standing distinctions made by Americans between their two major enemies were still evident in the muted reactions offered to the winter's bombing campaign: "There did not appear to be a great deal of opposition from the humanitarian point of view to the bombing of Japan," the head of the Office of War Information reported on February 27, "but some opposition is being expressed to the continual bombing of Berlin."[30]

Thus, as the air force stepped up its assault on Japan, it faced diverse needs. It sought an opportunity for a more decisive display of air power than had been possible in Europe. At the same time, though cautious about how attacks on Japan should be portrayed, it had cause for believing that the constraints of public opinion, loose enough in any event, would be few indeed in the Asian war. After all, the enemy there was still identified as "rats" in respectable publications, and Americans were cheered on as "Rodent Exterminators."[31] Indignation was recharged by the sight of gaunt and maimed American POWs rescued in February during the Philippines campaign and by the stories of kamikaze attacks over the winter and spring of 1945. To be sure, the same period brought stunning revelations of Nazi atrocities as concentration camps were at last overrun. But Americans were rarely the victims, Germany was clearly a defeated nation, its performance in the field still commanded grudging respect, and the cruder forms of indignation that emerged were largely confined to its Nazi leaders.

GRAND STRATEGY ON HOLD

Delays in defeating the Germans were worrisome in their own right and also for the general urgency they stirred about B-29 operations against Japan. Their negative repercussions for the Pacific war were also quite specific. For one thing, prolongation of the European war threatened to postpone redeployment of American forces in Europe to the Pacific. The previous summer, in the flood tide of optimism that swept in after the Normandy landings, American planners had hoped that Kyushu and maybe even Honshu could be invaded by October 1, 1945, or perhaps even as early as July 1. After the Ardennes offensive, the summer date, at the least, was out of the question. For the AAF, the delay was something of a mixed blessing. "We may thus be forced," noted the Joint Staff Planners, "from our 'invasion' strategy into a 'blockade' strategy, at least temporarily, by our inability to assemble [the] forces required."[32] The air force thereby gained more time to exercise the muscle of the B-29s. But there was no fundamental reorientation of strategy, not even really a reconsideration of it. And what the air force gained in time it lost in potential bases because Kyushu would provide airfields for B-17s and B-24s flown back from Europe.

To be sure, there were other ways to accelerate the air war against Japan. The B-29s operating out of India and China had never been able to reach Japan with justifiable tonnages. By January the air force had formalized its decision to remove the bombers from the continent, coincident with LeMay's move to the 21st Bomber Command. Many of the planes of his old 20th Bomber Command went to the Marianas. The British offered another source of added firepower. For political reasons, British leaders were loathe to be left out of the final drive against the Japanese homeland. For political reasons, their American counterparts were reluctant to allow the British to, as Mac-Arthur put it, "reap the benefits of our successes." Of course, some contribution from across the Atlantic was acceptable to most Americans. Arnold's air force was willing to entertain the basing of British Lancaster bombers in the Philippines or Okinawa. A more promising British contribution to the air war—the transfer of its famous Mosquito aircraft, for which Americans had no equal—was not pursued by the Americans. In the end, the British aerial contribution was still in the pipeline at war's end, the victim of American delays, the prolonged war in Europe, and the unexpectedly early termination of the Asian war. It cannot be said that Americans pursued their contribution zealously.[33]

They eyed much more eagerly the contribution that might be made by a much less willing partner, the Russians. In that regard, too, however, progress was hampered by developments in the European war, in this case a failed experiment there in Soviet–American military cooperation. In the summer of 1944, the American Eighth and Fifteenth Air Forces inaugurated shuttle bombing operations using bases in Russian-held territory. Nominally strategic in design, these operations really had political purposes: to establish a precedent for American use of Siberian bases against Japan, to demonstrate American commitment to the Grand Alliance and to Germany's defeat, and perhaps to impress the Soviets with the power of America's strategic bombers. In the end, none of these purposes was fulfilled. Strategically, operations were insignificant and costly. Politically, the arrangement dissolved into bitterness over Soviet rejection of American requests to fly missions in support of Warsaw's uprising against the Nazis. Planned as cement for the Grand Alliance, shuttle bombing turned into quicksand.

Efforts to secure cooperation against Japan did not cease. For one thing, more was at stake than just air bases. Russian entry might pin down Japanese armies otherwise free to defend the homeland or save Americans the messy task of securing Japanese surrender on the continent. A seemingly minor matter—Soviet weather reports—also became vital in light of the obstacles facing the B-29s; the only information LeMay was getting from the Russians came through breaking their codes, not the most seemly practice among Allies. Encouragingly, in the fall Stalin had promised American access to air bases in the Maritime Territory, promises renewed at Yalta. American military leaders still welcomed Russian help: MacArthur grasped at the opportunity (just as he had in 1941), though finding it convenient to lie about his views once the Cold War heated up. But particularly for those Americans familiar with the shuttle bombing affair in Europe, hope was tempered by uncertainty about stripping the veil of Soviet secrecy and securing practical arrangements.[34]

For Arnold and his new bomber commander in the Marianas, these complications of global strategy composed the backdrop for vexing operational concerns. On January 6, Norstad had flown out to the 21st's sprawling new headquarters on Guam to give Hansell the bad news and confer with LeMay, who arrived the next day. For the men on Guam, wary of the new general coming in to replace a trusted commander, LeMay provided a bit of surprise. Despite his reputation for toughness, he was quiet to the point of being tight-lipped, his voice barely audible to the men around him. Nonetheless, at least to St. Clair McKelway, the former *New Yorker* editor serving as the command's public relations officer, there seemed "a suggestion of something deeply, bottomlessly disturbing in this stocky, plain-looking new commanding general."[35]

Back in Washington, the change of command did not make Arnold confident of early success. He still worried about the backlash of inflated expectations: "We have built up ideas in the Army, the Navy, and among civilians of what we can do with our B-29s." The enormous investment poured into the B-29 had to be justified. "These airplanes are quite expensive and carry with them a crew of 12 men, and yet our results are far from what we expected and from what everyone else expects." Politics once again accounted for Arnold's demand to step up operations, as Hansell had discerned.[36]

Once again, Washington pressed for an incendiary campaign, now questioning the wisdom of postponing the fire raids until precision targets were finished off. When LeMay, his precision attacks meeting the same fate as Hansell's, urged a switch to less "hotly defended" industrial targets, Norstad suggested—after the usual words about not wanting to erode a commander's prerogatives—an incendiary raid on the most densely settled area of Kobe. In Washington, it now was clear that "the purpose of this attack is not experimental," and LeMay's Kobe strike on February 3 was demonstrably more successful than the earlier tests of incendiary attacks. The same day Washington was preparing plans for a similar strike on an area of Tokyo that "does not include many high priority industrial targets" but had "the highest density of population found" in the city and was "rated as highest in fire hazard for insurance purposes." On the twelfth, Norstad instructed LeMay to prepare for creating a "conflagration" in Nagoya, apologizing for going "into tactical detail that properly is your responsibility."[37]

On February 19, Washington further clarified the priority for incendiary runs. LeMay was informed that Japanese aircraft engine plants remained his primary objective, but now "selected urban areas for test incendiary attack" became a clear "secondary" priority. The next day Norstad told LeMay to launch a maximum mission against

Japan. When LeMay responded with the kind of objection that Hansell had earlier served up—a wish not to interrupt his "rigid training schedule"—Norstad overrode him, citing "circumstances beyond our control," quite possibly the bloody effort to capture Iwo Jima; as the primary beneficiary of that effort, the air force could hardly refuse to support it. LeMay ran the biggest mission yet of the war and the biggest "test" of fire raid tactics. Choosing between Nagoya and Tokyo, he sent out some 231 B-29s to hit the capital on the twenty-fifth.[38]

Pressure on LeMay was communicated in other ways besides the push for incendiary bombing. There was the usual concern about public relations, Washington fearful that "the news interest in [B-29] operations is watered pretty thin." Air force headquarters also noted the difficulty LeMay was having in hitting the Japanese aircraft industry: one important plant had been singled out eight times for attack, to no avail, and yet, embarrassingly, the navy did more damage to the plant with only one carrier strike. True, Japanese aircraft production was falling rapidly by February, but due partly to general shortages and a decision to disperse the industry; the Twentieth could claim only indirect credit for the enemy's decline. Moreover dispersion threatened to make targets harder to find, increasing the urgency of inflicting as "much destruction of existing factories" as possible in the next six weeks, as Norstad told LeMay on February 11.[39]

The movement toward area bombing of cities was accelerating in these weeks but still apart from any sustained effort to rethink strategy for bringing about Japan's surrender. Such bombing had long been in the plans, and the rare attempts to justify hastening it simply cited previous decisions for an early invasion—invasion sanctioned a quick campaign of aerial destruction, not slower paralysis by precision bombing and blockade of economic lifelines. This was also the rationale for resisting Chester Nimitz's pleas to supplement the navy's devastating submarine campaign against Japanese shipping by having B-29s sow the enemy's narrow sea-lanes with mines. In reality the air force remained fearful of being drawn into the navy's war, although in February LeMay began training crews in mine-laying operations, lest the navy have an excuse for acquiring its own long-range bombers for such operations. As the air force's historians noted pointedly, "Evidently the air planners did not envisage the extraordinary success that was to follow, but it is questionable whether they could have acted differently if they had." For them, the only task was to carve out the heart of Japan's industrial economy; veins and arteries had little attraction.[40]

The AAF's resistance to blockade and mining also stemmed from poor insight into the perilous nature of Japan's war economy. The air force's winter attacks on Japan, though disappointing, had far more dire consequences for Japan than did the early bombing of Germany because they struck a nation already mobilized almost to the limit. Whereas the Allies for years had to bomb through a sizable cushion of German productive capacity, any destruction against Japan hurt, far more so when magnified by the navy's efforts. In restrospect at least, the long and vexing delay in air operations against Japan turned out to be a boon for the air force, making almost any bombs dropped count for something—and in the process, making the flaws of tactics, strategy, and moral vision less glaring because quick success seemed to justify what had been done. The relative success against Japan resulted primarily from the accidents of strategic timing and Japan's relative defenselessness.

More sensitive to operational considerations than to grand strategy, air planners in February 1945 worried about the weather. Volatile enough over the winter, it seemed likely to "get progressively worse over the homeland of Japan until midsummer." Forecasters thus sanctioned a hurry-up effort against Japan's aircraft industry while some precision attacks remained possible and then a campaign against cities. Further-more, Germany's collapse seemed likely to coincide with the bad weather campaign, and the effect of its defeat "upon the Japanese people might be significantly if not critically increased by a comprehensive attack on Japan's major urban industrial areas."[41] Speculation about a strategy of early surrender was rare, however; the staff's energies focused on expanding operations and the economic dislocation they would cause.

With the air force attending to operations and the Joint Chiefs' deliberations dwindling, it fell to others to peer into the future of Japan's surrender. At Yalta Churchill had opened a new path by suggesting "mitigation" of the unconditional surrender formula and an ultimatum to call on the Japanese to surrender. Marshall and other military leaders were sympathetic to modification of the formula, particularly on the question of the emperor's fate, but met resistance from State's representatives and apparently had no sanction from Roosevelt to pursue Churchill's idea. Progress in thrashing out a formula would not resume until April.[42]

Secretary of War Henry L. Stimson entered the scene in February, and his meetings with State's Grew (acting secretary for Stettinius) and the navy's James Forrestal provided another stage on which the scene could be acted out. Yet through February and March they dwelt on issues at the fringes of surrender policy—Philip-pine independence, the economic rehabilitation of Japan after the war, the fate of Japan's mandated islands—but not surrender itself. On February 20, the newly re-turned Admiral William "Bull" Halsey warned Stimson against any relaxation of peace terms because too many Japanese were "unregenerate and there was no hope of educat-ing them to a decent life." But neither the talk with Halsey nor other deliberations that month prodded Stimson into immediate action.[43]

Stimson was also critically located to connect atomic policy with conventional military strategy and the concern about surrender. No one else of his stature had given the bomb as much thought. But, as earlier, when leaders lifted their eyes from immedi-ate technical and policy concerns, they looked past the intermediate issue of surrender and gazed into the murkier reaches of postwar policy. Indeed, as his biographer has said, "On the question of whether this power should or should not be applied within the particular context of the war the Secretary said no single word." Just as Arnold's vision oscillated between the daily task of operations and the lure of greatness for the air force after the war, Stimson was pulling away from the rapidly disappearing problems of the bomb's technical development to ponder its place in long-run strategy for handling the Soviet Union. Much the same could be said of scientific advisors like Bush and Conant and of working scientists, who, when not still immersed in just trying "to get the job done," ignored the bomb's use and wondered: "What should be done to make sure the possibilities of atomic weapons in the hand of a future Napoleon or Hitler would not bring world disaster?"[44]

In a way, it was odd that Stimson in particular overlooked the surrender issue. Self-appointed expert on Japan, he might have been expected to take the lead. But when he had a "long talk with Marshall on the coming campaign against Japan" on February 27, he acknowledged that "it is a new problem for me." One difficulty for Stimson, as for many tired leaders late in the war, was a calendar cluttered with more immediate issues. But if a fatigued nearsightedness had been the only problem, Stimson would not have looked so closely at issues of postwar policy. More likely, he saw nothing problematical about securing Japan's surrender and using the bomb to get it. A half century in public life had taught that "power when available but renounced as an instrument of policy—out of fear or guilt or presumptions of kindness—had, in his time, produced meaningless confusions and then the perilous circumstance."[45]

To the extent that Stimson and his staff did think about the bomb's use, politics and public relations were the prods: concern about how to announce the bomb's use and about "a growing restlessness and impatience among Members of Congress on account of the size and cost of the project." No one recorded the possibility of using the bomb in order to justify the lavish expenditures blindly allocated, but the War Department's senior administrators did record threats of congressional investigation and the helpfulness of telling concerned congressmen that the Manhattan Project would provide "the possible ultimate success of the war in case of a deadlock."[46]

Roosevelt himself had his eyes on the postwar implications of atomic energy. He continued, of course, to approve efforts to develop the bomb and deliver it against Japan. But in his last months, perhaps the only major operational issue of the Pacific war to which he made a concrete contribution was one of a very different sort. According to one account, Roosevelt received the approval of Nimitz and the Combined Chiefs for use of poison gas against the Japanese on Iwo Jima but scotched the idea. If he made such a decision, it probably rested on no aversion to new weapons, given his simultaneous support of the bomb's development and the use of war-weary bombers against Germany. But initiating use of a weapon with a loathsome reputation posed a different problem than that raised by atomic bombing, about which no prior judgment could be reached in public and against which no enemy could retaliate. With the grimmest fighting still anticipated in Germany and the Pacific, introducing chemical or biological weapons would have established a nasty precedent.[47]

COMMAND DECISION

Regarding the winter's exercises in grand strategy and diplomacy, LeMay contributed and heard little. He was a field commander, and his job was to mobilize and direct his force. Sometime that winter he was informed about the atomic bomb project because training for an atomic mission had to take place in the Marianas, using the planes in which LeMay was expert and coordinated with the operations he conducted. But he was told the bare minimum, and as he later put it, the news "didn't make much of an impression upon me," for a long time had passed "since my college physics days." It would make "a big bang," but how big he could not imagine.[48]

What he did think about and tackle with his uncluttered intelligence and force of character were the manifold problems still outstanding in the B-29 operations. He reaped the benefits of Hansell's earlier efforts in that regard. He exploited Washington's operations researchers, challenging one to "pick out a couple of the stupidest radar operators they have, and Lord knows that's pretty stupid," and perfect crew training in the use of radar for identifying and hitting targets.[49] The numbers of crews and planes he had grew steadily, though stepped-up training kept combat sorties from rising as fast. In February, he gained another important advantage with the capture of Iwo Jima, robbing the enemy of a forward warning station, placing American escort fighters within reach of Japan, and providing new weather stations and an emergency landing field that reduced B-29 losses dramatically.

The "tender and the trivial" matters that saved crewmen and put bombs on target consumed LeMay. He led men with skill, even though privately he condemned "a blundering staff" that was "practically worthless." He had inherited shoddy outfits before; he knew what to do. Only a few key men were replaced, a few others reshuffled. Otherwise he led by example, by a kind of unadorned optimism, by simple command rather than exhortation or intimidation, and by the good humor men under stress must have. Those who knew him better soon learned that his "grimace is a smile," his Bell's palsy simply inverting what pleasure did to other men's faces. He got the best out of weak men, and more out of the best men. It was not just wartime hyperbole for his public relations officer to write a few months later: "He had trained them heartlessly, having a heart that revolted at the idea of what lack of discipline and training would mean to his young crews."[50]

Still, there was little immediate success. Some precision strikes worked, some incendiary raids showed promise, but the direction of LeMay's command was still indeterminate as February drew to a close, when he "woke up . . . to the fact that I hadn't gotten anything much done any better than Possum Hansell had." Beyond him loomed the Washington command structure, so haltingly trying to get a grip on strategy, so firmly in the grip of continued rivalry among the services. LeMay had never been part of the "skullduggery that went on in Washington" regarding conflict among the armed forces, but he was fully aware of how the services warred for glory and resources.[51]

No one questioned the cooperativeness of Nimitz, whose navy provided so much of LeMay's logistical support. But under Nimitz were the admirals and captains who aroused LeMay's amusement and disgust. While the air force pleaded for supplies and facilities, they built splendid homes complete with "the usual retinue of Filipino boys" and "cocktails and highballs and hors-d'oeuvres such as you might find at an embassy in Washington." Mindful of the courtly customs officers followed, LeMay suffered a round of dinner invitations, finally from the submarine commander, whose "house turned out to be the Vanderbilt yacht, now bravely commissioned in the United States Navy." LeMay "had been a poor relation plenty of times before." Official courtesy demanded that he entertain in return, but he used the occasion to tweak the noses of his blue-water rivals and also to make his needs known, taking "especial pains to serve the best flight-rations available," the "canned stuff" the air force was feeding itself. Eventually he got more of what he wanted out of the navy.[52]

Whatever his troubles with the navy, LeMay's relations with his superiors seemed remarkably free from the intrusions he experienced or heard of in Europe. For one thing, because the Twentieth Air Force was under Arnold's direct control, theater commanders had far less call on LeMay to support the army and navy, and when diversions did occur, Arnold and Norstad assumed responsibility for them. For another, Arnold was convalescing in Florida through much of the winter. "He did not tell me how to do my job! No!" LeMay protested years later when queried about his relationship with Arnold. "I never got a direct order from Arnold that I remember," a recollection generally supported by the documentary record. He doubtless felt less harried than his predecessor, and he was not one to worry about the formalities of command relationships.[53]

Yet with Norstad as a like-minded surrogate for Arnold, communications between Washington and the field had not changed much since Hansell's tenure. As usual, rituals of deference to a combat commander's authority mixed with polite nudges and the occasional injunction. Norstad quickly told LeMay that "what General Arnold wants is the greatest possible number of bombs dropped on our priority targets in any given period of time." He was reminded that he would shortly have "the biggest and best air striking force in the world today." LeMay hardly needed the reminder.[54]

Around the first of March, Arnold, or more likely Norstad, apparently ordered a maximum effort from LeMay against Japan.[55] On his own, LeMay was realizing that his "outfit had been getting a lot of publicity without having really accomplished a hell of a lot in bombing results." Furthermore, by March 3 LeMay knew that Norstad himself would pay a call to Guam within a few days. Anticipating that visit, LeMay gave Norstad a hint of what he might find upon arrival. "We have been having a hell of a time with the weather lately," he commented unsurprisingly. One "out" would be "to try night bombing. I don't believe it is an efficient method of operation but this is another case of a few bombs on the target being better than no bombs at all." He promised to be "working on several very radical methods of employment of the force."[56]

If LeMay was vague, it was because he was uncertain, not evasive, about what he could do to redeem the B-29 operations. In the next several days, a solution jelled. Primarily a commander and tactician, not a strategist, he conceived the solution in tactical terms. He mulled his ideas over with key combat commanders and extracted the statistical information he needed from his staff. Could the bombers fly in at five or six thousand instead of twenty-five or thirty thousand feet? To some, the question seemed absurd. Flak was bad enough at high altitudes; obviously, at six thousand feet it would be "slaughter." But LeMay's statisticians determined that few planes actually had been lost to flak, and he had a hunch that Japanese antiaircraft guns were suitable only for high-altitude fire. At worst, perhaps a one-shot surprise could be pulled on the enemy's defenses, before returning to the safety of great height. Furthermore, the cover of night alone offered safety; perhaps he could strip the bombers of their defensive gunnery and its operators, save weight and risk fewer men, and load instead more tons of bombs. Flying at low altitudes also saved fuel—no jet stream, more room for bombs. Attacking in a bomber stream rather than flying in a fixed formation would save more fuel—load more bombs, six tons for each plane. New incendiaries were available, including napalm: use an all-incendiary load, space its distribution right, drench the most flammable area of Tokyo (103,000 inhabitants per square mile), pray for good surface winds, and the conflagration Washington long sought might be fired, especially now that over three hundred B-29s could be sent out on a mission. The big factories were not there, but the cottage industries that apparently fed them were, and the fires might spread into the factory areas.[57]

Here were the "several very radical methods." Many had been for months proposed by operations analysts and tested cautiously by Hansell, and Washington had repeatedly urged further incendiary runs. How much LeMay improvised with his own staff was unclear, perhaps even to him in the haste to make decisions: ideas and precedents could be in the back of his mind without ransacking the files. His command genius lay in his decision to avoid introducing these methods piecemeal, to take the parts and throw them together at once, producing a whole dwarfing the sum of its parts.

The decision did not come easily. Despite his toughness, the doubts kept bubbling up. There was a career at stake. There was Washington to satisfy, with Norstad due to be on the scene. Above all, there were the men in the bombers, flying in low and defenseless. He could hope for their success; he could not rule out for them suicide. As LeMay later dramatized what went through his mind: "Dear General Washington. Dear General Knox. Dear General Gates. Dear General Greene. This is the anniversary of the day you killed my son Eben, my son Jeremiah, my son Watson, my son John. You killed him at Princeton, at Monmouth, at Saratoga, at Germantown."[58] LeMay had faced this responsibility before but never with so many men, never trying such a sudden leap into new tactics, never with so much anxiety.

There was another anxiety, but LeMay was not in touch with it. Harboring no special hatred for the enemy whom he now proposed to slaughter, he confronted no overt anxiety about doing so. But lack of hateful intent did not entirely placate a primitive sense of uneasiness. Everything that he had learned of command responsibility made it acceptable to be anxious about the fate he might deliver to his own men. On their fate his conscious anxiety comfortably focused. But he was troubled and defensive in other ways which he did not articulate to himself or others.[59]

There was hardly time to do so anyway. The tactical elements involved were assembled in a rush, and no subordinate was likely to question a commander about the ethical and strategic issues posed in changing the course of war. Nor was there time or inclination to consult much with Washington. It is doubtful that "Norstad didn't have an idea what I was thinking about," as LeMay later wrote, for LeMay had offered hints in his March 3 letter, and Norstad himself knew perfectly well the options open to the bomber commander—he had urged them himself. But the teletype machines did not hum with LeMay's ideas, and by the time Norstad arrived on the morning of March 9, the orders for a great fire raid had already been cut, on the eighth.[60]

What Norstad's arrival did provide was an opportunity for LeMay to sound out the Washington brass regarding the mission he proposed to run. Norstad was perfectly willing to give LeMay the rope with which either to hang himself or to run up the banners of glory. Norstad seemed to LeMay "a typical staff man," unwilling to commit himself. LeMay "did gain the impression that being a little unorthodox was all right with Hap Arnold." ("So this is what you call being a little unorthodox?" he joked in his memoirs. "Want to be president of the Department of Understatement?") Norstad and Arnold wanted results. They did not want to commit themselves to the method LeMay proposed to try until they knew the results. LeMay put it this way in his memoirs: "All right, by God. If I do it I won't say a thing to General Arnold in advance. Why should I? He's on the hook, in order to get some results out of the B-29's. But if I set up *this* deal, and Arnold O.K.'s it beforehand, then he would have to assume some of the responsibility. And if I don't tell him, and it's all a failure, and I don't produce any results, then he can fire me." Time had played a few tricks on his memory. On the eighth LeMay had notified Arnold of his pending mission. But LeMay had the essence of it right. He was in much the same position that Hansell had been in during November before the first B-29 raid on Tokyo: the ideas and the pressures, in broad outline, came from Washington, but the commander in the field was to take a hint, not to follow orders, for Washington did not want that responsibility.[61]

Similarly, there was no imperative for LeMay to set down a strategic rationale for running a great fire raid. If the new tactics worked, and LeMay was hardly certain they would, then their implications could be assessed, and a strategic rationale for their continuance worked up. Some things could not wait, the press for one. LeMay, according to his public relations officer, was a master of public relations precisely because he "despised" it. He quickly appreciated that the press—some fifty reporters were now on Guam—was more easily handled if it knew what to expect. The newsmen were briefed about the major mission to come, and their stories were written up partly in advance, ready to be released as soon as "the first bombs-away messages" were received. The method not only protected secrets, it insured the best coverage in the states for the mission: Americans could learn of it before Japanese broadcasts deflated and distorted the news. In short, reporters substantially covered the event before it occurred.[62]

"FLAMING DEW"

On March 9, just before midnight, residents of Tokyo began noticing a strange display in the skies over their city. They had been through air raids before, and some, like their counterparts in Europe's threatened cities, had developed superstitions—food rituals, the wearing of Western clothes—to ward off danger.[63] That night's activities seemed different.

In daylight raids, the B-29s had appeared "translucid, unreal, light as fantastic glass dragonflies." Now, at night, flying low and catching spectral colors from flak bursts and searchlights and explosions below, they evoked more menacing images, one moment "their long, glinting wings, sharp as blades" as they caught the light, another appearing as "black silhouettes gliding through the fiery sky," only to reemerge "shining golden against the dark roof of heaven or glittering blue, like meteors, in the searchlight beams spraying the vault from horizon to horizon." With each flash of light, the bombers would be momentarily frozen in the sky, like giant insects caught in amber. Then, as the fires spread and coalesced to produce a steadier glow, "ghastly reflections of the fire" were seen "on the wings of those silvery ghosts." In the sustained, garish light, the insects gained motion. They appeared to the people below to be "attracted like giant silver moths to the towering blaze," or like huge charcoal bugs when soot from the fires blackened their undersides, hellish incarnations of the pesky moths that circled the lightbulbs of Japanese homes.[64]

Even the bombs themselves were visible. They "descended rather slowly like a cascade of silvery water." These were the M-47 napalm-filled bombs designed to start the big fires, or more likely the five-hundred-pound M-69 clusters which burst above ground into smaller magnesium incendiaries. As the display took on unimaginable proportions, victim and attacker had strangely similar images burned in their memories: of "light flashed everywhere in the darkness like Christmas trees lifting their decorations of flame high into the night," and (from above) of a city "illuminated like a forest of brightly lighted Christmas trees." These things took on an unholy beauty even as the city boiled, as people with the luxury to observe tried to relate an alien experience to something familiar. Like every form of war, this one had its strangely compelling attractions: "All the Japanese in the gardens near mine," recorded a French journalist on the fringes of the holocaust, "were out of doors or peering out of their holes, uttering cries of admiration . . . at this grandiose, almost theatrical spectacle." The men in the bombers smelled the soot and the burning flesh and tried to avoid choking or vomiting, or spotted the cauldron while still far out at sea, or bounced suddenly against the top of their aircraft when uprushes of superheated air—the thermals from the blaze— propelled their aircraft upward thousands of feet in a few seconds or flipped them over. There were unknown sensations, attractive and repellent, in what they were doing.[65]

To people on the ground, the bombs seemed to be sown in a random manner. They were not. First attackers carved out an X of flames across one of the world's most densely packed residential districts; followers fed and broadened it for some three hours thereafter. LeMay's tactical design worked. Another design, the government's plan for defense, was being played out below. "Why should we be afraid of air raids?" a patriotic song had run. "The big sky is protected with iron defenses. For young and old it is time to stand up. . . . Come on, enemy planes. Come on many times." Their government had instructed Japanese that they had "only two choices before them: to be victorious, or perish." Victims of faithful obedience to their leaders' edicts, having at first little reason to know their futility, fire fighters and citizens stayed to quench the flames with their thousands of wet mats and waterbuckets. Or they cowered in the promised safety of shallow slit trenches—Tokyo's water table turned anything deeper into a cesspool— that had indeed earlier provided a little protection when high explosives had fallen. Too quickly to allow easy escape, the bombs "scattered a kind of flaming dew that skittered along the roofs, setting fire to everything it splashed and spreading a wash of dancing flames everywhere."[66]

Tokyo was unprepared. Despite Japan's own experience in bombing others in China, despite the warnings served up in test fire raids, despite some vivid reporting on the fate of Germany's cities, little had been done. Before March 9, perhaps 1,700,000 residents had already left the city. But except for the evacuation of schoolchildren— carried out not to protect them but to save them "as a human resource in the abstract"—their exodus owed little to the government, far more to the lash of fear. Some 6,000,000 remained. On the government's part, waterways had been too much trusted to stop flames, firebreaks had been widely but incompletely cleared, concrete shelters had rarely been constructed. Antiaircraft defenses were technically inadequate except for a fairly efficient radar detection and warning system. With defense overwhelmed, the battle, insofar as there was one, took place between civilians on the ground and technicians in the air.[67]

Tokyo did not explode, it descended into "an 'infernum' . . . like that which Dante . . . describes in his Divina commedia."[68] A few months later, the atomic bombs would erupt without warning and with apocalyptic instancy, most of their fury telescoped into seconds of transcendent destruction. There is no way to compare different experiences of terror when each has its own kind of totality, but Tokyo held a different horror and fascination. It was a process of destruction, not a simple act. As the American bombers poured gasoline and chemicals into the inferno, the observer could see the destruction take place and watch the thing come alive, becoming some living, grotesque organism, ever changing in its shape, dimensions, colors, and directions—as if witnessing a preview of the coming August attraction, one shown in slow motion and stop action. In Hiroshima and Nagasaki, most victims did not know what hit them, confronting personal extinction first; the survivors only later suffered the shock of communal annihilation as they crawled out of their wreckage and met the parade of the damned. Because Tokyo's destruction unfolded, its victims first witnessed their neighbor's or their neighborhood's or their city's demise before making a final decision about self-preservation.

In Tokyo, too, time afforded the agony and illusion of choice. There was time, it first seemed, to decide whether to stay and fight the flames or to gather up a loved one or a treasured item. There was time to select the wrong route or the right one, to make the decision that Yamamoto Katsuko did, who "figured that if we all fled right there in the midst of the fire, scattering in every direction, we'd all burn up and die," and who therefore "felt a rope with my foot and used it to tie the whole family together." Or time to put on the government-prescribed padded hood, which, like bundled babies on the backs of fleeing mothers, often caught fire before the victim knew it.[69]

On the ground, the French journalist Robert Gullain watched. "Sometimes, probably when inflammable liquids were set alight, the bomb blasts looked like flaming hair." To the Japanese journalist Masuo Kato, it seemed that "the wind had whipped hundreds of small fires into great walls of flame, which began leaping streets, fire-breaks, and canals at dazzling speed." Even before the air raid warning had sounded, freakish winds, "almost as violent as a spring typhoon," had worried the people of the city. Now they helped create something more furious in intensity and far different in mechanics than even Hamburg and Dresden had suffered. Unlike the firestorm that sucks everything to its center, the conflagration that swept Tokyo was rapaciously expansive, a pillar of fire that was pushed over by the surface winds to touch the ground and gain new fury from the oxygen and combustibles it seized. LeMay had chanced upon just the right use of incendiaries, and the wind served as a giant bellows to superheat the air to eighteen hundred degrees Fahrenheit.[70]

In flight lay the only salvation, just as at Dresden and Hamburg, but few who fled successfully could recall how they did so. Hisaki Imai remembered deciding to gather up his younger brother and race against the prevailing tide of humanity to strike out for a vacant lot. Then, somehow, when he found the vacant lot was built up with houses sure to catch the flames, the two fled with dampened towels over their faces to the Tokyo waterfront and survived the night. Most made the wrong choice or found their flight blocked by the debris whistling through the air or by the thicket of fallen poles and charged electric wires that clogged the streets. Fire alone was not the only danger. The superheated vapors rushing ahead of the wall of flames killed or knocked unconscious its victims even before the flames reached them, just as "entire block fronts burst into flames before the main body of the fire reached them." The mechanisms of death were so multiple and simultaneous—oxygen deficiency and carbon monoxide poisoning, radiant heat and direct flames, debris and the trampling feet of stampeding crowds—that causes of death were later hard to ascertain, though the position in which many were found indicated, in the misleading words of the Strategic Bombing Survey, that they "died peacefully and without evidence of struggle."[71]

Natural instincts betrayed thousands. Waterways running through the city offered apparent relief: the chance to get across to an area as yet untouched by flame or to douse oneself in the waters. But bridges were often burned out and crowds piled up at their approaches, trampling some and pushing others into the water to drown; on surviving bridges, others were forced to jump when the steel structures became unbearably hot. A head above water was no guarantor of safety, as the noxious fumes and superheated air still snuffed out life or fired the water until "the luckless bathers were simply boiled alive." The few large open areas were also tempting havens, but there too life was sucked from the air, and many died "like so many fish left gasping on the bottom of a lake that has been drained." Most of the few concrete buildings survived the conflagration structurally, "small islands in the sea of destruction," ironic monuments to the legacy the West had given Japan. To these buildings police directed panicked crowds, but sometimes incendiaries pierced roofs of corrugated steel or reinforced concrete, or smoke filtered in and asphyxiated the refugees, or fires sucked out their oxygen, or heat penetrated to ignite the building's interior or bake its inhabitants.[72]

That, at least, is the gruesome speculation about the manner of death left behind by witnesses and survivors who entered the blackened area. But it is almost a black hole of speculation. The number killed was possibly double the number injured, probably a higher ratio than at Hiroshima and Nagasaki,[73] suggesting that escape and survival were harder in this conventional raid than in the atomic blasts. Most survivors started their journey to safety already on the fringes of the storm, and accounts of the struggle at its center are few. Furthermore, the Japanese government made few efforts to study the pathology of death and injury, a contrast to German medical resourcefulness that American survey teams later regarded as "almost unbelievable."[74] Later, the political notoriety, scientific interest, and symbolism attached to Hiroshima and Nagasaki so eclipsed the Tokyo fire raid that far less interest developed in collecting its victims' recollections and examining their experience.[75]

Eastern Tokyo—some sixteen square miles, a larger area than LeMay had even targeted—was totally burned out. With it perished at least eighty-four thousand people, and probably far more—by some reckonings the highest toll of any air raid, conventional or atomic, during the war or for that matter of any single man-made catastrophe.[76] Most likely, with many schoolchildren already evacuated and younger males in military service, women and old people suffered grossly disproportionate losses.[77]

Because the fire burned out so quickly, the carnage was soon visible. A Danish diplomat witnessed "a long procession of silent people, men, women and children," passing by at dawn, "quiet and forlorn." "Refugees began to pour in by the hundreds" to a Catholic university campus: "All were silent and calm, but the horror they went through reflected in their faces. . . . All the caravans I met had an atmosphere of deep silence about them." Only a few sounds were to be heard—the coughing and gasping of victims with scarred lungs, the occasional call of the name of a loved one. Gullain saw "hideous sights: wretches with burnt limbs who showed fleshless hands or feet or bloody masks that once were faces peering through filthy bandages." Soon grotesque keloid scars appeared on burn victims—masses of rubbery tissue detached from underlying structure, migrating over healthy tissue, perversely reappearing in larger form if surgically removed, ripe material for skin cancer and other diseases. On others the scars would be, misleadingly, the emblem of shame reserved for atomic victims.[78]

In the smoking moonscape there were bizarre sights: "seeing a man pausing to light a cigar from a blazing telephone pole," at the same time spotting piles of bodies "looking like misshapen lumps of charcoal," often too melted to be identifiable even by sex, and everywhere giving off a "sickeningly sweet odor." "Long lines of ragged, ash-covered people straggle along, dazed and silent, like columns of ants," another reporter discovered. "They had no idea where they were going; all they knew was that they were still alive. I wanted to interview some of them, but I lacked the courage. My only interview was with this vast desolation." Police officials had no more courage. They "were instructed to report on actual conditions. Most of us were unable to do this, because of horrifying conditions beyond imagination." Almost always the survivors were dazed and aimless, "their eyes dull and uncomprehending," drained of life even when life remained, their recollections having "a dreamlike quality." Like their atomic brethren later, many of Tokyo's survivors felt guilty and embarrassed, perhaps "apologetic because my house had survived the raids," as Kato recalled. "'It will be my turn next,' I was in the habit of saying by way of apology for my relative good fortune."[79]

Unlike many survivors of the atomic bomb, Tokyo's injured and fleeing probably knew in a literal way what hit them, but there was no comprehension of what had happened. For them, it did not seem they had been through a man-made experience. Little in their national history, their encounter with humankind, or their religious traditions allowed them to attribute that experience to fellow humans. Europeans— longer experienced with the mechanical world and with war in their homelands, able to comprehend air war because it escalated there so gradually—rarely regarded the bombers even of their firestorms as demons or mystical creatures or incarnations of the natural world. In their imagery they drew on the rich store of religious mythology about the damnation people create for themselves. Perhaps that is why Europeans in Tokyo sometimes referred to the March 10 raids as a "frightful Pentecost" or a realization of Dante's inferno. But a French priest abandoned religious imagery in trying to describe "that fairy scene" of "shooting stars and meteors" and "comets," "these phenomena of nature." Even more so among Tokyo's natives, images of the great raid usually referred to the natural world, as if what man had destroyed by harnessing nature had sprung from nature herself, as if Tokyo had been visited by a plague of monstrous, demonic, fire-breathing insects. These images occurred readily in a society that placed heavy emphasis on the visual sense; that had a well-developed idiom for describing "a pure and sacred homeland imperiled by bestial and demonic outsiders"; that had, by the style of its residential construction and the abruptness of its modernization, less distance than European societies from the natural world. Moreover, because the conflagration did not simply happen, but evolved and mutated, and because the wind did so much to spawn the conflagration, as it might in the fires following an earthquake, nature herself seemed to have revolted—perhaps why, as Kato noted, "a popular debate" soon developed "about which was more dangerous, earthquakes or bombs." The allusions to nature's revolt reflected and sustained the sense of a horror transcending human capacity and culpability, unleashed on people too numbed anyway to attempt much conscious effort at explanation.[80]

The sense of an incomprehensible experience was borne out in reactions to the enemy. To be sure, the trappings of patriotic resistance were maintained in the raid's wake. Even on March 10, as some fires were still burning, a parade marking armed forces day marched down undamaged sections of downtown Tokyo. "In the heart of the ordinary Japanese," Kato later claimed, "there was hatred and bitterness against the American raiders who left an indiscriminate trail of the blackened corpses of babies and grandmothers."[81] Yet signs of hatred toward Americans were surprisingly few. Whatever the hostility, in overt public behavior at the time and in later responses to American occupiers it rarely emerged, muted as it often was by the prevailing shock, apathy, and mere desperation to survive, or cancelled out by other emotions.[82] Under certain circumstances, in a population fresh and effectively mobilized, bombing may trigger defiance and deepen resolve—supposedly the case with the British in 1940, although American authorities later regarded that case "more propaganda than fact." And Tokyo's loss of confidence was perhaps less severe than that in other Japanese cities, if only because massive evacuation soon culled doubters from its ranks and left behind a core population strongly identified with the war effort. But bombing unleashed on a population already deeply fatigued and dispirited spurred no rallying of the spirit against the enemy.[83]

Besides, the government was not skillful enough to exploit indignation to good purpose. Exploitation competed with the desire to keep secrets. The controlled press, unable to ignore altogether the horrific nature of the raid, still downplayed it even while hurling invective at the American murderers, and the government forbade distribution of urban newspapers to smaller towns and rural areas lest the bad news spread too far. The truth spread anyway, a political virus carried by fleeing victims, and authorities were reaping the fruit of years of deception, which now badly undermined their credibility. In that way, as in others, they never caught up with the Anglo-Americans, or even the Nazis, who came to realize the propaganda value of truth, however selective.[84]

Not only did anger fail to revivify the war effort, it often turned against the government or against its handy or culpable representatives, accused of failing to protect or trust the citizenry. "The value of information lies in its accuracy," one complaint ran after the March 10 raid. "Why have the authorities forgotten this simple truth?" At least among those intact enough to be angry, indignation was widespread against the armed services for failing to fend off the invaders or for prattling on about their ability to do so.[85]

Panic, police control, and passivity toward authority prevented such hostilities from becoming a serious problem. And again the destructiveness of the raid overwhelmed interest in finding humans to blame, for "the B-29 raids were beyond the point of criticism," as a Japanese editorialist later commented. People felt that they "were too big for mere criticism of the government."[86]

The pervasive feeling, local at first but spreading through Japan as the raids and victims fanned out, was a sense of hopelessness regarding the war effort, and for some regarding survival itself. Realization of the futility of Japan's position was cumulative and by no means caused only by the experience of bombing. But the fire raids catalyzed and gave brutal immediacy to the doubts long accumulating, abruptly accelerating the decline in all indices of public morale. Even among those Japanese with no direct experience of the bombing, word of its effect eroded confidence, and even among those who attributed their loss of hope to other tribulations, the fire raids had been a contributing cause. Moreover, disenchantment focused on the failure to protect the home front, indicating that falling morale was linked to bombing, not to a more general failure of the war effort (about which, of course, Japanese knew relatively less). For many Japanese, the March 10 raid and the ones to follow it triggered the plunge into a mood of desperation even more than did the apocalyptic events of August. "Propaganda of the deed," the term used later by American experts for the bombing, was taking its toll.[87]

The dominant reactions were apathy, fearfulness, weariness, work absenteeism, and shame and depression over personal conditions of food and cleanliness—reactions also widespread among survivors of the atomic attacks. Absenteeism, for example, often occurred when family members left behind in the city attempted to visit loved ones or when no productive work could any longer be done. Because many factories remained intact but shut down for lack of raw materials, long lines formed at Tokyo's remaining movie houses "when every able Japanese was supposed to be in the armed forces or toiling long hours in war production."[88]

Some Japanese able to experience rage expressed it in class antagonism. Primarily "tough people from one of the worst slum areas," many of Tokyo's survivors fled into better neighborhoods, whose hosts took pity and offered succor. "Instead of being grateful," however, "the slum people resented the fact that in war . . . people should be having such luxuries, ones they couldn't dream of having even in peace. So they looted houses wholesale." Although not always taking a violent form, bitterness about the advantages of the privileged amid the suffering became widespread, in Tokyo and eventually elsewhere.[89]

That bitterness, linked as it was to criticism of official ineptitude and to a more generalized sense of a disintegrating social fabric, fed official anxieties about public reactions to the raid, enough so that "the customary cobwebs of Japanese bureaucracy were torn away" to provide emergency relief to the city. The emperor himself made a personal inspection of the devastated area on March 18, an experience that "no doubt contributed to his growing realization that the war had to be stopped as quickly as possible." The conflagration certainly added to the devastating reversals that soon toppled the ruling cabinet.[90]

And yet the men around the emperor as well as cabinet officials made little mention of the Tokyo raid in their formal deliberations. Prisoners of a traditional definition of military power, unable to imagine defeat without invasion, they instead chattered on about the state (stark enough in its own right) of ground and naval campaigns.[91] Even fighter defense against the Americans continued to have a weak claim on Japan's dwindling resources, though the suicide tactic of ramming American bombers was sometimes tried. In short, the leaders' preoccupation with reverses abroad neatly inverted the masses' desperate focus on events at home. Perhaps the masses' terror was as yet an unmentionable shame or a fate callously tolerated while conducting a stately and circuitous march to surrender. For the privileged who as yet had suffered little, the quivering of public morale was simply a worrisome but distant consideration in calculations about how to proceed.

Rarely rebellious, many of Tokyo's millions nonetheless implicitly made a political statement by voting with their feet. Fearing more raids or terrified that Tokyo would become the battleground when Americans landed or simply bereft of anything left to stay for, over a million people left the city in the raid's aftermath, desperately trying to sell off whatever possessions they could not drag along. They accelerated what became "one of history's greatest migrations." By summer, one-seventh of the nation's population (and a much larger proportion of urban dwellers) had relocated from the cities to small towns and rural areas. By war's end, Tokyo had lost over four million of its residents. It was as if the vital energy of this and other cities "had suddenly been poured into a few transportation funnels." Even in Germany and Britain, air raids did not induce such a huge movement compressed into so little time. Too, the flight in Japan took place with far less assistance by the central government, going forward largely outside its control. It testified, therefore, to the cohesion and discipline of Japanese society that the exodus rarely erupted into overt panic, which was mostly confined to the raid itself.[92]

As evacuation went forward, the gruesome work proceeded of pulling bodies out of buildings and canals, clearing them from the streets, and piling them up for mass burial or incineration. The city staggered back into some of its normal routines. A few of the more deadly results expected from incendiary raids by some Americans did not take place. An outbreak of contagious diseases, for example, was headed off because incinerated areas "were, in effect, sterilized. Rats and mice, lice and fleas, were destroyed along with other animals," and nothing remained to sustain any new insect or vermin population. Mass exodus also minimized the outbreak of diseases. The raid shattered the medical system, but no immediate medical catastrophe ensued, in part because the wounded were so many fewer than the dead. A crushing burden on the city's housing supply arose, however, despite exodus: housing in Japan's cities, densely packed before the raids, never had the cushion of extra space or the time to recover that characterized the bombed-out cities of Europe.[93]

The city, however, did not die the quick death that some Americans hoped it would. Instead, "the limitless acres of ruin seemed to spread everywhere, like a desert, in a drab and monotonous panorama of hopelessness."[94] As shelter burned, heating and electricity went out (even before March 10), food stocks diminished further, and sanitation systems fouled, a gradual but grim decline set in. The city's experience was still another instance where air power's promise of devastating shock, even in what was by many indices the war's most devastating raid, trailed off into agonizingly slow attrition.

Even as death's hand began gripping Tokyo, it reached out elsewhere. Emboldened by his success against Tokyo, LeMay immediately set out to repeat it. Giving his crews little pause lest the Japanese have time to regroup, he sent the bombers against Nagoya on the eleventh, and then in rapid succession against Osaka, Kobe, and Nagoya again. Yet the countless ingredients of the Tokyo holocaust could not be predictably reassembled. Attempting to widen the area of destruction, LeMay pressed his luck too far in spacing the distribution of incendiaries against Nagoya the first time, though eight square miles of Osaka soon disappeared in one raid. Weather affected success, though not always adversely: bad weather over Kobe forced crews to use radar, which enabled them to lay a more perfectly spaced carpet of bombs than visual methods usually achieved. On occasion Japanese defenses met their test a little better, and most of all, as news of Tokyo rapidly spread, abandonment of primitive shelters and attempts to fight fires, along with general flight from the cities, kept casualties down. Thousands more died, however, and millions were rendered homeless.

LeMay and his crews were immensely satisfied. Losses were neglible and results spectacular, and whereas crew morale had seemed "ominous" before March 9, now cases of "personnel disorders" suddenly dropped almost to nothing, to the point that LeMay's experts believed the crews could be "'flown to death'" without developing "'escape behavior'" (the maladies or excuses that took men out of action). But after ten days of blitzing Japan's greatest cities, LeMay had to pause. Both fliers and ground personnel were exhausted, supplies of incendiary bombs had given out, and orders had come down to support the invasion of Okinawa—like Iwo Jima, an operation whose benefits for the air force and even bloodier consequences gave Arnold and Norstad no choice but to lend a hand. The strategic campaign had to go on hold.[95]

ASSESSMENT AND AFTERMATH

It seemed that LeMay had made one of the supremely important command decisions of the war, one that reversed the fortunes of a faltering air force, set the strategic course for the remainder of the war, and even cast the mold of postwar American air power as a weapon of strategic devastation against cities. As LeMay himself said in November 1945, his actions were "an example of the terrible responsibility upon the shoulders of a commander who must risk thousands of lives and perhaps the future of an entire campaign, or even an entire war and must in the final analysis make that decision himself." Earlier, when the New Yorker published the first extended account of the March blitz, LeMay's skillful public relations officer (and former New Yorker editor) portrayed LeMay's role in even more sweeping terms: "LeMay had settled down to make a decision of the kind that this war has known only infrequently, a decision like Grant's when he let Sherman try to march through Georgia, and like several other sudden, quick, unprecedented tactical decisions of the Napoleonic and other wars." The comparison to Sherman's march, a classic initiative in strategic devastation, seemed especially appropriate. Since 1945, most accounts of the war, if they pause at all on the Tokyo raid before sweeping on to Hiroshima, have echoed McKelway's view of a decisive initiative by LeMay.[96] Apparently, he had acted on his own.

Circumstantial evidence invites that view. Only LeMay and his commanders, not the part-time staff back in Washington, were fully sensitive to the operational obstacles catalyzing the switch to new tactics. Furthermore, had Washington anticipated and authorized LeMay's campaign of fire, it might not have failed so miserably to send the incendiaries he needed to wage it, the supply of which he quickly exhausted. Washington issued no formal directive sanctioning the planning and execution of the Tokyo raid, and Arnold remained a convalescent substantially out of the command picture. LeMay was apparently blessed by an extraordinary suspension of control from Washington.[97]

What he really had was the illusion of making his own choices, an unusual freedom only from the formal constraints of command by superiors. Few orders did come his way, but his March 10 mission was a classic example of "inadvertent aggression," whereby leaders communicate destructive intent to subordinates indirectly, prodding without inquiring about details and assuming direct responsibility.[98] Hints, nods, casual remarks, and failure to inquire all characterized LeMay's relationship with Norstad and Arnold. Often, Washington's wishes were so obvious they were left implicit, with little need for anyone to articulate them further. Hansell's fate, the files about his operations that LeMay read over, the pressures upon and within the air force to secure an incontrovertible success, and to do so before invasion closed the opportunity—these things told him what he needed to do, if not precisely how to do it. When LeMay later boasted about the command freedom he possessed in March, he also acknowledged that "I didn't need any direct orders from Arnold, he expected action out of me." As LeMay later paraphrased his injunction from Norstad: "You go ahead and get results with the B-29. If you don't get results, you'll be fired," and "there'll never be any Strategic Air Forces of the Pacific." But because the details were left to him, LeMay could also sincerely believe that he had made the critical command decision.[99]

There were advantages in leaving those details to LeMay. They went beyond simply his superiors' bureaucratic interest in avoiding responsibility, to other benefits less calculated—the evasion of moral and strategic accountability. The slaughter of the enemy, particularly civilians, could be achieved without its being explicitly ordered and consciously confronted and could be seen as the product not of aggressive designs, but of responses to the tactical and technical obstacles confronting LeMay. Operational considerations seemed paramount. Wind and weather, distance and inexperience, altitude and crew morale were the explicit determinants of a new course.

The pattern of oblique signals was not confined to the air force. Even more so than in Le May's contacts with his superiors, Arnold and the air force had gotten the casual nod from their superiors, the Joint Chiefs and the president. Roosevelt had conveyed his interest in bombing Japan (and Tokyo in particular), though couching it largely in political terms, and he had been informed of the test fire raids, and then of the March 10 raid, but made no recorded inquiries.[100] The Joint Chiefs had sanctioned preliminary plans that included the firebombing of cities but did not direct their preparation or monitor their progress. The destruction proceeded with accountability, beyond LeMay's, poorly fixed.

And yet the destruction was hardly unintended or the outcome primarily of the operational considerations usually cited, for plans to firebomb had emerged well before some of the operational obstacles facing the Marianas bombers were even known. Just as telling an indication of the minimal role those obstacles played was the bomber's record elsewhere in Asia.

Incendiary tactics similar to LeMay's were employed against other Asian cities where the obstacles LeMay faced either did not arise or took very different form. The weather was less ferocious over Formosa and China than over Japan, and so too were the strain of long flights and the enemy's fighter opposition. Furthermore, the bulk of American aircraft in use against Chinese and Formosan targets were medium and heavy bombers regularly flying at lower levels and achieving greater precision than B-29s. And of course the enemy's morale and government were hardly targets in Formosa and China, except for those limited institutions and areas specifically supporting Japanese rule and operations: in American eyes, both China and Formosa were non-Japanese except by virtue of occupation, inhabited by friendly peoples promised liberation from the Japanese yoke.

And yet much the same pattern of bombing unfolded there as in Japan. First came precision strikes, then area incendiary raids, against Hankow in December and especially against Formosan cities in the spring. The progression was similar even though the precision strikes against Chinese and Formosan targets had been demonstrably more successful. Furthermore, the incendiary raids clearly targeted large residential areas and achieved a scale against them proportional to that accomplished against Japan itself. Five of Formosa's eleven principal cities were almost completely destroyed, another four half ruined, with predictable casualties: 6,100 killed and thousands more wounded (by Japanese estimates which, if they followed the homeland pattern, were probably low), and over a quarter of a million people made homeless. The weaponry was the same as LeMay's—at least 62,445 gallons of napalm. Against Chinese cities, area bombing apparently continued until forbidden late in July 1945.[101]

The issue is not whether there were legitimate military targets in Formosa and China. There were and these were hit. Much more was hit. To some degree, the rationale was similar to the one used to justify the torching of Japan's cities. As the official historians wrote, "So many of the significant targets of Formosa were situated in the island's cities and towns that area bombing was frequently employed. The resulting destruction, it was assumed, not only would reach supplies of military importance and many small industrial units, but would impose upon the enemy, through destruction of housing and municipal services, a serious loss of labor." But in this case the "municipal services" also supported friendly civilians, and the "serious loss of labor" was inflicted on the same population. The rationale for area bombing, it seemed, hardly need be confined to the enemy.[102]

Except for his mission against Hankow, this torch of destruction was not even wielded by LeMay. Falling to other air force commands, its systematic employment suggests again how much the decision LeMay made for the March 10 fire raid was not uniquely personal; he grasped a weapon others were free and encouraged to use as well. More than that, it suggests that racist assumptions guided bombing in Asia as much as operational considerations. To be sure, the cities of occupied Europe had often been bombed: thousands were killed in French and Belgian cities by Anglo-American bombers prior to and after OVERLORD. In part simply because the air war in Europe went on far longer, the death toll from bombing in Europe's occupied lands quite possibly exceeded the count in Asia.

But at the least, the bombing in occupied Europe took place only after some of the war's most agonized handwringing by Allied leaders and after considerable effort to minimize destruction of friendly lives and landmarks.[103] Never, for example, was it thought appropriate to cripple the Renault plants making vehicles for the German army by causing "a serious loss of labor" among the Parisian masses. Objectives were targeted, though of course often missed, only if their relationship to the enemy war effort was demonstrably intimate. In Asia the criteria were far looser and their formulation did not even warrant review by heads of states or chiefs of services. There, a different set of standards applied not only to the enemy population, but to conquered friendly peoples as well.

Those standards measure the casual nature of the destruction that took place in Asia. They also suggest that bombing against Japan was shaped not simply by operational considerations or even by the enemy's nature and the lust for revenge it aroused, but by the lower value Americans put on Asian lives whatever their nationality or allegiances. At best, the operational factors cited to justify firebombing Formosa were not compelling but only permissive. Nor did the destruction have the sanction of saving American lives that its counterpart in Japan did. By the spring of 1945, Formosa had been stricken from the list of American objectives for landing, and the gain in American lives came only in the modest attrition in Japanese war production (by then almost nullified anyway by destruction of Formosan railways and shipping to Japan) and in the damage (largely by precision strikes on airfields) done to the fearsome kamikaze effort.

As for bombing the cities of Japan itself, the principal rationale was a vast feeder system of home shops and cottage industries that saturated workers' residential areas and kept the main war industries supplied with parts. The existence and importance of this system ran through virtually every argument offered for incendiary raids against urban areas and was offered after the fact in justification. "I'll never forget Yokohama," LeMay wrote after the war about the sights he saw in Japan. "That was what impressed me: drill presses. There they were, like a forest of scorched trees and stumps, growing up throughout that residential area."[104] With the main factories themselves hard to hit, the only method of disabling Japanese war production was to get those drill presses, and that could be done only with firebombing, so the rationale went.

The feeder system was indeed extensive and commented on by Japanese as a target whose destruction did serious damage to Japan's war economy and thereby was implicitly justified.[105] But its importance in 1945 was another matter altogether. Japan's industrial economy, like that of every combatant, had undergone a concentration into larger enterprises to achieve economies of scale and reflect accompanying shifts in the location of economic power. Large numbers of men (by conscription) and women (by economic necessity) had been drawn into the factory system, and "the drift toward oligopoly," Thomas Havens notes, saw "11,000 small shops forced to close in Tokyo alone by mid-1943." Doubtless many of those were in the rapidly collapsing consumer sector, but as the Strategy Bombing Survey later concluded: "By 1944 the Japanese had almost eliminated home industry in their war economy." Factories with fewer than 250 workers still played a vital role, but these were hardly backyard drill presses. Simply the well-known dispersal of war industry out of the cities made the cottage industries a less practical source of supply.[106]

Beyond industrial concentration and relocation, other factors reduced the importance of the feeder system. The war plants it fed were themselves caught in a spiral of declining production, partly because of the direct destruction in some precision attacks and in area raids that spilled over onto them, even more because the lifeline of supplies from outside Japan was being strangled by American attacks on shipping. The attacks on Japanese cities hastened that decline, but LeMay's bombers destroyed a feeder system that would soon have had few working factories to feed, killed or "dehoused" workers from factories whose machines were starting to go silent, and smashed plants whose chimneys were already going smokeless. In short, much of LeMay's bombing simply made the rubble of Japan's war economy bounce. Furthermore, by an economist's standard the destruction achieved was an inefficient way to secure desired ends. Targeting housing, firebombing "hit what was physically the most vulnerable but socially the least effective component of a city," for even in Japan housing was a relatively "elastic" commodity, improvised arrangements would work for a while, and few factories shut down because workers fled cities. Finally, other methods remained to still the factories and the feeder system. They were wholly dependent on electric power systems and (except for accumulated stocks) on rail transport and shipping lines; of those, only the last was the air force beginning to attack in the spring, and then only reluctantly.[107]

So it appears in hindsight, a luxury LeMay of course did not have. The question is whether it was known or could have been known at the time. Through increasingly sophisticated photographic intelligence and other sources, much was understood about the collapse of the Japanese merchant marine, and therefore the sharp decline in raw materials for factories. The decline in home industries was less visible, although American economists and intelligence experts had considerable insight into how war was changing industrial production in the major powers; even in the winter, air force experts had commented on the dispersal of Japanese industry out of the cities, begun in response to precision attacks and reducing the value of urban cottage industries. Attacks on the German petroleum industry and other German economic objectives were already discrediting the value of incendiary attacks on cities there. And Hansell, among others, had already mounted a considerable case for the efficacy of precision attacks.

The answer, then, is that a good deal of knowledge was available and more could have been assembled. To be sure, some of it was only arriving in the spring of 1945, but as events that summer showed, it was often resisted by airmen asked to confront it. Much of it suggested the navy's critical role in shutting down Japanese industry, a role airmen were reluctant to acknowledge. None of it directly addressed the harsh fact that operational limitations made precision bombing difficult, but incendiary attacks persisted after those difficulties moderated. LeMay and the air force had chosen a kind of bombing they could do best, without a compelling rationale for the economic benefits claimed.

What is striking is that so few in the air force asked questions. There had at least been some discussion and action about attacking Japanese shipping but virtually none about the changing structure and dynamics of Japanese industrial production. No one thought to check on whether the feeder system remained economically important or vulnerable to paralysis by less gruesome but still feasible methods. The legitimacy of it (and therefore its people) as a target was simply assumed.

Of course, an alternative bombing strategy, one that extended the blockade of oceanic shipping to all forms of transportation, would have been cruel in its own right, killing thousands when targets were in urban areas. accelerating Japan's devastating decline in food stocks, and perhaps, if its effects had worked more slowly, prolonging the suffering of civilians and of Japanese and American soldiers. Still, there would have been a difference: less destruction. Malnutrition was occurring anyway—at most, it would have been worse. Factories shuttered but not destroyed could have been reopened; malnourished but alive children and workers could be returned to health; isolated but uncharred cities could have revived.

Yet even if LeMay and his superiors had grasped the weakness of their economic argument for area attacks, it is doubtful that they would have acted differently. The momentum behind razing Japan's cities had developed too long and too intensely to be arrested by the collapse of any one argument. Others were available. If not the workers' drill presses, then their contribution to the factory system would have justified attacking their lives and housing; or there would have been arguments for undermining the entire urban infrastructure of Japan or for creating class animosities and mob terror to corrode the enemy's will to fight. Each of these justifications had already been voiced months or years before the March 9 raid. If each successively posited a more distant connection between what the worker did and what Japan needed to sustain war, such looseness would have bothered few, certainly not LeMay. In his opinion, expressed after the war, "There are no innocent civilians. It is their government and you are fighting a people, you are not trying to fight an armed force anymore. So it doesn't bother me so much to be killing the so-called innocent bystanders." Even if the "innocent bystanders," in an atomic conflict, "might be entire nations that aren't even at war," that would be a situation which "bothers me," but "it doesn't change the picture of what you are trying to do any."[108]

However, LeMay's conscience could not rest with his claim for the totality of war and the legitimacy of anything that wins. To establish collective guilt, he pointed also to "the way they were treating their prisoners and their captured people," a justification many Americans cited during the war. But his main justification, if pressed to a moral argument, was a classic one of moral reasoning about war, one that cannot be facilely dismissed—and one that turned 180 degrees away from the enemy civilian's guilt, to claim instead a favor for him: "Actually I think it's more immoral to use *less* force than necessary, than it is to use *more*. If you use less force, you kill off more of humanity in the long run because you are merely protracting the struggle." As he later put it, referring with heavy irony both to firebombing and nuclear attacks: "To expunge a few people to stop a war right at the start is unacceptable. Or a few hundred people, or a few thousand. Or—go all out on it—a few hundred thousand. But over a long period of time, wearily killing them off, killing millions under the most horrible circumstances—That is acceptable." A homely analogy made his point better: "I think now of that elderly wheeze about the stupid man who was not basically cruel—he was just well-meaning. The guy who cut off the dog's tail an inch at a time so that it wouldn't hurt so much."[109]

Not a bad argument—but there is no evidence that LeMay made it in 1945. He never thought through whether the only alternative to firing Japan's cities was to kill off its population an inch at a time, particularly when the enemy was already deeply wounded, not fresh and girded for protracted war. In truth, though he needed a moral argument to still his conscience, he probably rebelled against the demand to have to make it. For a soldier "to worry about the *morality* of what we were doing—Nuts. A soldier has to fight. We fought. If we accomplished the job in any given battle without exterminating too many of our own folks, we considered that we'd had a pretty good day."[110] One moral argument was compelling to LeMay: his overriding duty to limit the losses of the men in his unit. On that score, his firebombing tactics succeeded brilliantly, as American losses declined sharply after March 9. Having met that test, he cut off further argument.

At the same time, officers like LeMay did not want to admit how brutal their method of war had become. Of course there was no confusion among AAF officers about what they had done. "The heart of the city is completely gutted by fire," LeMay commented in his diary immediately after the raid. "It is the most devastating raid in the history of aerial warfare." It was equally clear what lay ahead—as Arnold wrote LeMay, the air force would destroy "whole industrial cities."[111]

Still, even in statements not designed for public consumption, air officers sometimes wrote as if LeMay's fire raids represented no change in policy. Thus the official mission report on the March 10 assault stressed that its purpose "was *not* to bomb indiscriminately civilian populations. The object was to destroy the *industrial and strategic targets* concentrated in the urban areas." In reasoning similar to that employed in defense of bombing Dresden, it seemed that because "these operations were not conceived as terror raids against the civilian population," they were in fact not such. LeMay's raids were undertaken "without abandoning the concept of precision destruction." Because the shift to area incendiary raids had been so long in the making, because precision attacks did continue, because economic effects (however diffuse) remained an objective, and because precision methods remained so central to the defense of American strategic air power, even airmen did not always realize they were crossing a threshold.[112]

But the denial of intent to destroy entire cities and create terror became increasingly hard to maintain. The weeks following the March 10 assault saw self-deception gradually transformed into the conscious deception of others. The air force was alert to any signs that the criticism it feared after the Dresden raids might reappear regarding Tokyo. Already on March 11, as the chief public relations officer in Washington noted, "Some speculation [has] begun here on shift from selected military targets to area bombing." The next day, McKelway on Guam was informed that "commentators [were] having [a] field day searching implications . . . which imply this is area bombing and speculating whether this means departure from policy of precision bombing." McKelway was quickly instructed to counteract "editorial comment . . . about blanket incendiary attacks upon cities. . . . Guard against anyone stating this is area bombing."[113]

On March 23, Norstad stepped in to silence any incipient criticism. Holding a Washington press conference on Arnold's behalf, he faced a familiar dilemma: wanting on the one hand to exploit LeMay's blitz for all the prestige and publicity it was worth, on the other to head off the growth of a barbaric image for the air force. One solution was the resort to a rhetoric of cost-benefit analysis, contrasting the B-29s' strikingly low loss rates with stunning statistics: "1,200,000 factory workers . . . made homeless" and "at least 100,000 man-months" of labor lost to Japan and "369,000,000 sq. ft. of highly industrialized land . . . leveled to ashes" in the Tokyo raid alone. Of course the human carnage was implicit in such statistics, but they kept the emphasis on the economic objectives of precision bombing. Of course there was no denial that incendiaries were the weapon and great conflagration the result, but incendiary attack was simply "the economical method of destroying the small industries in these areas . . . of bringing about their liquidation."

When asked about "the reasoning behind this switch from explosives to incendiaries," Norstad denied any switch because the mission still remained "the reduction of Japanese ability to produce war goods." Even off the record he would not budge. Asked for "any idea how many civilians might have been effected [sic]," Norstad only repeated the figure on homeless. Was there any change in "the basic policy of the Air Forces in pin-point bombing [and] precision?" "None." At the same time, Norstad stressed that the incendiary raids were just beginning; one thousand B-29s would soon fly whereas only three hundred had gone against Tokyo. Every Japanese city was deemed a legitimate target. Who would decide the limits of the forthcoming attacks? "The Japs will decide it"—that is, the raids would continue as long as "they can take it."[114]

A few months later, McKelway's article in the New Yorker nicely brought together the same contradictions maintained by Norstad. True, LeMay was prepared to see all of Japan's cities "wiped right off the map." At the same time, McKelway did not find it contradictory to say that the "incendiaries were dropped with precision." McKelway also tried to distinguish LeMay's methods from those of the RAF against Germany: "It was pin-point, incendiary bombing from a low level, designed not simply to start fires or destroy a single factory but to start one great conflagration whose fury would double and redouble the destructive force of the bombs." It was hardly what most Americans understood by "pin-point, incendiary bombing," but it was useful to keep repeating the phrase.[115]

In one sense, the media's reporting of the March 10 raid seemingly stripped away the veneer of official obfuscation. Certainly the raid received due play, given "eight column banners" in great metropolitan newspapers, as the AAF public relations officers proudly noted.[116] Often, coverage was also graphic. *New York Times* headlines proclaimed that "300 B-29's FIRE 15 SQUARE MILES OF TOKYO," hitting "Thickly Populated Center of Big City." A day later, the *Times*'s headline drove home the same message: "CENTER OF TOKYO DEVASTATED BY FIRE BOMBS," with "CITY'S HEART GONE." The *Times* described precisely the density and size of the area hit and invited readers to imagine the destruction of a comparable area in New York City. Readers were told of the "jellied gasoline" used and were given a vivid report by a correspondent who accompanied the mission: "I not only saw Tokyo burning furiously in many sections, but I smelled it." And though given no figures by the air force, the *Times* at least acknowledged that the civilian toll constituted "a holocaust."[117]

Yet there were limits on what press coverage could communicate. In lieu of good film footage, newsreel companies were first forced to show only stateside tests of napalm bombs. Later newsreels conveyed verbally the message of Tokyo's destruction, but pictures were usually confined to the better-quality footage available for day raids. In that sense, the historical void into which the Tokyo conflagration fell was not created simply by the nature of the atomic attacks: for the media whose message was primarily visual, events that left little visual record tended to disappear. Perhaps the closest the newsreels came to spelling out the truth visually came in the scenes released in May of firebombed German cities. Even that footage showed only the still aftermath of destruction, not the act of destruction itself. Perhaps the lack of good photographs also led *Life* to give the fire raids little play. As always there was a preference for action pictures whose heroic or grisly content was immediate. One consequence was continued attention to men and planes, not to the destruction they did on the ground; even Japanese newsreels featured the brave handfuls of fighter pilots still rising to meet the enemy hordes. Another consequence was enormous attention to the final drama of Germany's defeat, a story photographers could capture graphically.[118]

Yet the dominant limitation in reporting was ideological and imaginative. Reluctant to challenge authority, most papers and editorialists followed the air force line by emphasizing the economic purposes and effects of the fire raids and raising few questions about whether the raids represented a departure from previous policy. They were equally reluctant to speculate whether this new form of bombing might change official strategy for an invasion. Because officials repeatedly described the bombing as still only in an initial phase—a stance that further minimized sensitivity to the damage already done—it seemed premature to speculate on it as an instrument of imposing surrender. In the press as well as in government, a preoccupation with analogies to the manner of Germany's defeat, secured only with bloody invasion, also discouraged such speculation. In addition, there was the familiar tendency to look past the surrender issue to more distant matters, particularly the role of air power in the postwar world. With the battle over postwar unification of the armed forces heating up, that role was ripe material for commentary. The more expansive view was that the Twentieth Air Force showed the way to the "future global air power upon which American security will proportionately rest" and through which the nation would achieve "realistic world influence."[119]

Amid these commercial and political preferences, little inclination was left for pondering what happened on the ground in Japan. If noted at all, loss of enemy life was sometimes mentioned with passing regret, but also the reminder that "Tokyo is a prime military target, so recognized under the rules of war and . . . civilians remain there to man Japan's armament industries at their own peril." More often, the attacks were just described as "the bombing of factories and plants," undertaken against "a fanatical foe prepared to fight to the death." The *New York Herald Tribune* followed a more tortured path around the humanitarian issue. "Any impression that precision bombing is abandoned by the 20th [Air Force] should be corrected." It was simply the case that Japan's "unique industrial set-up . . . makes area bombing necessary." Anyway, "the incendiary raids cause little loss of life but drive inhabitants into the country and destroy their industrial utility."[120]

Only the vengeful (plus a handful in left-wing, religious, and pacifist journals) acknowledged bluntly the scale of human destruction. The *Atlanta Constitution,* finding it "shocking to think of the thousands who must be burned to death," wrongly characterized the fatalities as unavoidable by-products that can occur even in "the most perfect precision bombing." Still, the paper also took satisfaction:

> If it is necessary, however, that the cities of Japan are, one by one, burned to black ashes, that we can, and will, do.
>
> And with each city thus attacked, we remember the treachery of Pearl Harbor and find calm satisfaction in the knowledge that the Japanese of one more city have learned there is a bill, which must be paid, for treachery, that retribution for such a deed is implacable.

Only those willing to proclaim vengeance could admit the carnage—had to admit it to have the full satisfaction of vengeance. Similarly, only those who admitted the carnage acknowledged vengeance as an American motive. Those who did not profess hatred saw the bombing as just a necessary act of technique against an enemy whose fanaticism was singular, carried out by men with "a peculiarly detached and scientific attitude."[121]

There was, then, the familiar pattern: relief at the prospect of quicker victory; celebration of American technical genius, courage, strategic superiority, and war-borne potential for world mastery; and denial or silence about destructive and vengeful instincts. Terror was acceptable as long as it seemed inadvertent. Since the acts that inflicted revenge also seemed militarily necessary, vengeance could be secured without often being spoken.

Impatience and exhaustion with the war that spring strengthened the impulse to destroy the Japanese. Observing that impulse, a British official in the United States noted how long Americans had wanted to finish up in Europe "in order to throw themselves with all their strength upon the hated Japanese savages." But the war's conclusion in Europe also produced a letdown, and the Japanese lacked the "dramatic identities and historical associations of the Nazi or even Fascist leaders." Therefore the Pacific war was relegated to the "category of a bitter and heavy duty" to be completed as rapidly and cheaply as possible. "It is as if all available emotion had been expended upon the great individual monsters like Hitler, Goebbels, Goering, Mussolini, with little feeling left, at any rate at the moment, for the nameless mass of vermin as the Japanese are conceived to be."[122] The American hatred of Japanese was intense but formless. A faceless and despised enemy made revenge welcome for its evil deeds, and now also for the burden placed on Americans to continue a war now won against the more identifiable villain.

What LeMay had done on March 10 was to bring Americans the pleasure of revenge in the guise of military necessity. His own deliberations were of course much narrower in scope, and his genius lay less in recognizing the potential of firebombing than in pulling together the tactical factors that realized it. Without creating the momentum to destroy cities, he skillfully channeled it. Similarly, his decision to carry out the March 10 raid was not particularly influential; it was success itself that guided the course of bombing in the war's remaining months.

THE MOMENTUM OF DESTRUCTION

However destructive, the March fire raids produced no dramatic reorientation in the policies of either of the warring governments. On both sides, officials were aloof to the destruction, glimpsed few dramatic possibilities in the bombing, and worked through cumbersome bureaucracies responding slowly to changing conditions. Circumstances of the moment also delayed quick response. Leadership changed on both sides in April, with the fall of Koiso's government and Roosevelt's death; cautious men searched for their footing in the new political terrain. The fire raids had momentarily halted, and the drama of Okinawa seized attention.

At the time, then, the fire raids only lubricated the wheels of slow change. Though a naval officer, the new premier, the frail and elderly Admiral Suzuki, was not closely associated with the war effort; army influence in his cabinet declined in favor of the navy, long less hopeful about the rewards of a fight to a finish and, unlike the army, virtually without an armed force to carry it on. Fear that American bombing would unleash revolutionary upheaval did motivate some senior statesmen at the time; dark prophecies of prewar years about proletarian uprising, seemingly undercut by the actual experience of war, now were borne out, at least in the fantasy life of some leaders. But the fear that triggered a sense of urgency also bred extreme caution: A radical move toward peace seemed impossible without setting off the very violence that such a move was supposed to forestall. So the Suzuki government tried to straddle two horses. It probed the possibilities for peace, fruitlessly and strangely by negotiation with the Soviet Union—still officially a neutral but Japan's mortal enemy at home and abroad, many of its leaders thought. At the same time, the new government tried to strengthen Japan's resistance to the Allies, hoping to placate die-hards at home and to wrest some victory-in-defeat forcing the Americans to a compromise peace. Militarily, the only recourse was massive kamikaze attacks by sea and air against American forces.

In retrospect, the hope invested in kamikaze tactics seems both ludicrous and fanatical. American forces were too mammoth to be stopped; kamikazes were almost useless against the B-29s, Japan's worst scourge; and fanatical resistance might only harden the enemy's attitude. Yet American losses to kamikazes were indeed appalling (so much so that the American government wrapped them in censorship). Coming when American "war-weariness" was already pronounced, when leaders like Marshall wondered if the nation would even stay the course, the kamikaze attacks may well have had the desired effect.[123] Without the threat of greater losses in invasion they seemed to prophesy, it is doubtful that American leaders would ever have compromised on the critical issue of the imperial throne, on whose preservation Japan's civilian leaders pinned hopes for their continued role in Japanese life.

But if successful in this way, suicide tactics worked at a great price: countless servicemen's deaths on both sides and the continued exposure of Japan's cities to destruction while the tactics were given time to work. Drawing on deeply rooted cultural notions of Japanese purity and outsiders' defilement of it, government propaganda now spoke of "the shattering of the hundred million like a beautiful jewel." As one historian has summed up the mood instilled in Japanese as the bombing climaxed, "The supreme sacrifice and ultimate state of purification, by this terrible logic, had finally come to mean readiness to embrace extermination." "The 'national polity' took precedence over the people," concludes another historian.[124] In any calculus of blame for the destruction of Japan's cities, its leaders figured alongside America's, just as Germany's did in the case of its destruction.

On the American side, too, leaders reacted cautiously to new possibilities. Age was no barrier to Stimson's realization of the atomic bomb's novelty, which he had conveyed to Roosevelt and now made emphatic to Truman: "The world in its present state of moral advancement compared with its technical development would be eventually at the mercy of such a weapon. In other words, modern civilization might be completely destroyed." Yet Stimson still did not connect the issue for mankind raised by the bomb with the immediate conduct of the war against Japan. He and most others who thought about the bomb overlooked the moral issue at hand and its connection to the larger matter of mankind's fate: the possibility that the bomb's use against Japan might establish a precedent for future use and intensify an international arms race. That connection was suggested only by those on the fringes of nuclear policy, among the Chicago scientists, and by that somewhat mysterious gadfly to Roosevelt, Alexander Sachs.[125]

As Stimson later suggested, no one at his level questioned the assumption that the bomb would and could be used against the enemy: "At no time, from 1941 to 1945, did I ever hear it suggested by the President, or by any other responsible member of the government, that atomic energy should not be used in the war. . . . The entire purpose was the production of a military weapon; on no other ground could the wartime expenditure of so much time and money have been justified." And yet Stimson's recollections on this point were confusing, for he also claimed that "the first and greatest problem was the decision on the use of the bomb—should it be used against the Japanese, and if so, in what manner?" Clearly, given unquestioned acceptance of the bomb's use, any "decision" about use was no decision at all. Without some event or realization suddenly intruding upon official deliberations, leaders could only reaffirm an assumption long held.[126]

In military terms, the most relevant event was the firebombing of Tokyo. Its success might have raised questions about the need to use the bomb: was not LeMay achieving roughly the same effect with his incendiaries that the atomic scientists could promise? Conversely, it might have stilled residual moral concern about the bomb's use: had not the very horror of the March 10 conflagration made the bomb's legitimacy a moot point? Contemporary records leave unclear the extent to which these questions were raised in the spring of 1945. Because the orders for Tokyo's firebombing had not come from Stimson's level and because the nuclear bomb's use was largely unquestioned there was little immediate incentive to connect the two. Stimson's records, however, do reveal a tenuous connection, made in a way that diminished concern over use of the atomic bomb—by downplaying the destructiveness of both kinds of bombing rather than comprehending it.

Although Stimson accepted the bomb's use, he could not accept a claim that any use of weapons was legitimate during war. At least momentarily troubled by Dresden, he needed reinforcement against residual doubts about American bombing. Sometime, probably early in the spring of 1945, he had extracted a "promise from [Assistant Secretary for Air Robert] Lovett that there would be only precision bombing in Japan." Despite the March 10 and subsequent fire raids, he remained convinced as late as May 16, as he told Truman, that he was holding the air force, "so far as possible, to the 'precision' bombing [of Japan] which it has done so well in Europe." It seemed important to do so because "the reputation of the United States for fair play and humanitarianism is the world's biggest asset for peace in the coming decades." Similar rules for "sparing the civilian population," he added, to Truman, "should be applied as far as possible to the use of any new weapon," that is, the atomic bomb.[127]

Stimson convinced himself that "precision" bombing remained American practice in part through unwillingness to confront the contrary evidence in the press and to penetrate the transparent distinctions about targeting offered by the air force. After the war he wrote: "In March, 1945, our Air Force had launched the first great incendiary raid on the Tokyo area. In this raid more damage was done and more casualties were inflicted than was the case at Hiroshima." But there is no evidence that Stimson at the time appreciated the magnitude of the March 10 raid, unless it provided him the spur to approach Lovett—if so, he did not note it at the time. To the contrary, only the renewed fire raids on Tokyo at the end of May caught his attention and led him to query Arnold about "my promise from Lovett that there would be only precision bombing in Japan." Stimson was disturbed by press reports indicating a "bombing of Tokyo which was very far from that." Arnold explained that Japan presented a "difficult situation" because industries were scattered about in cities and were "closely connected in site with the houses of their employees," but promised to limit "damage to civilians."[128]

Arnold's explanation was, of course, misleading in implying that civilians were the victims only of unavoidable spillover from attacks on economic objectives. But more important, Stimson declined to question him critically. As in his response to Dresden, Stimson did not want to confront the brutality of American bombing: he merely wanted reassurance that it had been reduced to the minimum. His self-deception played an important role in his acceptance of the atomic bomb's use against cities. "The war," particularly LeMay's firebombing, it is often said, "had so brutalized the American leaders that burning vast numbers of civilians no longer posed a real predicament by the spring of 1945."[129] But Stimson's case showed that something more subtle and self-deceptive sometimes took place. He responded to LeMay's firebombing by bolstering in his mind a fraudulent image about what restraints remained in force. As an incident legitimizing the bomb's use, the horror of March 10 figured largely in the moral defense he constructed after the war, not in his thinking at the time.

Stimson also achieved reassurance by striking Kyoto from the target lists for both conventional and atomic attacks. Having visited Kyoto before the war and discussed its significance in private conversations that spring, Stimson appreciated its similarity to Dresden as a cultural and historical city of unique importance. His motives for exempting Kyoto were complex and shifting. On the one hand, he exhibited the wartime habit of elevating preservation of monuments above preservation of lives. Arthur Holly Compton later recounted a conversation with Stimson on May 31 which proved to Compton that Stimson was

> a man of wide culture and broad sympathy, to whom Japan was a living reality. To him Japan was not just a place on the map, not only a nation that must be defeated. The objective was military damage, he pointed out, not civilian lives. To illustrate his point he noted that Kyoto was a city that must not be bombed. It lies in the form of a cup and thus would be exceptionally vulnerable. But this city, he said, is no military target. It is exclusively a place of homes and art and shrines.

In fact, sparing Kyoto while bombing other cities saved few civilian lives, but as

Stimson told Truman in connection with firebombing, he "did not want to have the United States get the reputation of outdoing Hitler in atrocities." Military men regarded it as unthinkable that a city of Kyoto's size would be spared; General Leslie Groves, whom Stimson had to overrule persistently, saw in Kyoto an experimental opportunity beyond military need, the chance "to gain complete knowledge of the effects of an atomic bomb." Against such utilitarian arguments Stimson offered his own tough-minded case. With respect to firebombing, he worried that Japan might become "so thoroughly bombed out that the new weapon would not have a fair background to show its strength." (Truman "laughed and said he understood.") Later he insisted on protecting Kyoto from atomic attack lest it become "impossible . . . to reconcile the Japanese to us . . . rather than to the Russians."[130]

The nub of the matter was the connection Stimson made in his own mind between power and morality. For him, power was not just a necessary evil, but a potential way to serve moral ends, victory over Japan and a reordering of international relations. Little in Stimson's long record of government service had led him to doubt that connection. But firebombing and the atomic weapon threatened to sever it, for their destructiveness created an evil that might overwhelm any good that could come from them. At the same time, Stimson could not resist the temptation to employ them for desired short-run gains. He wriggled free of this dilemma by his ritual of scrutinizing air force bombing policy and preserving Kyoto. That ritual was not meaningless: if it sanctioned a course of bombing whose nature Stimson refused to acknowledge, it also preserved the residue of moral concerns that might be acted upon later, foreshadowing the final breakdown of the connection between power and morality which Stimson had so long confidently posited. For Japan, however, the ritual offered scant protection.

For the moment it was sufficient to quell any doubts about targeting and move on to the real moral issue he saw, the bomb's dual potential either to destroy "modern civilization" or "to bring the world into a pattern in which the peace of the world and our civilization can be saved."[131] For Stimson and for most others advising the American government that potential translated into an immediate issue with reference to the Soviet Union. For all the controversy among historians regarding "atomic diplomacy," the importance for the bomb's use of the developing antagonism between the two great powers was limited and indirect: there was no particular correlation between attitudes on the Soviet question and stance on the bomb's employment. But that antagonism, and the long-range issues it raised regarding nuclear policy, did diminish attention to the bomb's use in the context of war against Japan. It became hard to ask what would secure Japan's capitulation without drawing in so many other matters that the immediate question became lost. The pursuit of victory, though often seen as the dominating concern of Americans in wartime, was sometimes crowded out by other anxieties.

Such a claim seems to fly in the face of evidence offered by high officials about the gravity with which they viewed the attainment of victory over Japan. Stimson later testified eloquently to the decisive role the pursuit of victory played in motivating his acceptance of the bomb's use. Similarly, Truman later wrote that as of May, "the thought now uppermost in my mind was how soon we could wind up the war in the Pacific." Yet a critical distinction must be made between what was uppermost as a goal and what was paramount as a concern. Neither Stimson nor Truman gave the attainment of victory urgent attention, for victory was assured. Instead, they filled their days with the lengthy and fractious dilemmas arising in Soviet–American relations. Not until May 16, in fact, did Truman even attempt to learn what the military's plans were for securing victory. Only in June did he and Stimson begin thinking seriously about how to speed victory. As for the bomb in the context of the war with Japan, Truman, as he knew, had inherited such a weighty legacy assuming its use that for him to question it would have required exceptional intellectual and political courage.[132]

Military officers, however, were not so complacent about victory, especially in the army, facing as it was a possible invasion. Their job was to win the current war, to which in many ways they devoted themselves with more energy and insight than their civilian superiors, particularly in assessing the possibilities for peace opened by establishment of the "moderate" Suzuki cabinet. Intelligence estimates undertaken at Marshall's urging in April were emphatic: "There are no indications that the Japanese as a whole share the fanatical Nazi psychology of committing national suicide," nor did "any important Japanese leaders," who anyway had "adhered to their established constitutional procedures."[133]

The obstacles to early surrender seemed formidable but not insoluble. They consisted less of the unconditional surrender formula itself than of the Allied failure to interpret it in a way allowing Japan to save face and preserve the imperial institution as well as the effective use made in Japanese propaganda of bloodcurdling statements by some Americans about the wisdom of extermination. It seemed possibile that "clarification of Allied intentions," particularly to the effect that "unconditional surrender does not imply annihilation or national suicide," would hasten Japan's capitulation. So too might news of Germany's defeat and Russia's entry into the war. Furthermore, capitulation might occur before invasion had to take place, perhaps even before the final demolition of Japan's cities, especially if some air effort was shifted to Japan's "limited and vulnerable internal and external lines of communication." Moreover, intelligence experts suggested, a compromise on the emperor's fate might have to be accepted eventually, for otherwise an orderly surrender and occupation would be impossible. The problem, they recognized, was no longer one of inflicting defeat or even a realization of defeat among Japanese—both had been accomplished by April. The problem was one largely unexamined in the annals of military theory and history: how military force could translate defeat into surrender. Guardedly, the military experts indicated there was really no military solution for such a problem except for an invasion that might command alarmingly low support from soldiers, who would see invasion as a "struggle simply to dethrone the emperor or give Admiral William F. 'Bull' Halsey his vaunted ride through Tokyo on the emperor's white horse."[134]

But problems immediately arose in translating these realizations into a working policy. Against unprovable theorems about Japan's future behavior was set the brutal reality of its current fanaticism. Experts themselves were divided about the best military course to accompany political strategy; army representatives still insisted on invasion, about which naval and air officers were dubious while disagreeing about the kinds of bombardment and blockade which would achieve success. These differences might have become a moot point if a change in political strategy had been aggressively pursued, but despite Marshall's backing for it, the State Department balked at change. The new president, in his V-E Day address, had reaffirmed that unconditional surrender "does not mean the extermination or enslavement of the Japanese people." By stating that it also meant "termination of the influence of . . . military leaders," he also implied that civilians like the emperor might escape punishment. Broadcasting to Japan, the navy's psychological warfare experts tried to relay Truman's message, though the American voice was hardly a consistent one. [135]

After that promising start, the new political strategy stalled again. To avoid confrontation with the State Department, Marshall had "put the question of surrender terms on the treacherous ground of psychological warfare." If their objective was to make a psychological impression on the enemy, Stimson and many officers opposed more forthright overtures while the bloody Okinawa campaign hung in the balance, lest they be interpreted as signs of weakness. Political leaders also still feared popular reaction to any promises about an emperor whom Americans had been taught to hate. Inasmuch as the battle for Okinawa dragged on into June, the proper moment for approaching Japan was grievously delayed. [136]

Without refinement of surrender terms, strategists saw little choice but to plan on applying every kind of force against Japan: conventional bombing, use of the atomic bomb, Soviet entry into the war, and of course invasion. Such a broad-front strategy conformed to the dictates of service unity and to the studied caution of military leadership; it was also compelled by the political vacuum in which strategists found themselves. Any attempt to be selective depended on articulation of a political strategy at the highest level, as one staff committee realized: "Unless a definition of unconditional surrender can be given which is acceptable to the Japanese, there is no alternative to annihilation and no prospect that the threat of absolute defeat will bring about capitulation. The accomplishment of the unconditional surrender objectives then must be entirely brought about by force of arms." [137] In short, plans for invasion had to go forward. For the bombing effort the implications were perhaps less clear. But whereas revision of the surrender formula might have sanctioned resort to a more limited attack on lines of communication, the prospect of invasion justified the systematic destruction of all components of Japan's strength, including its cities.

The air force prepared to follow up on LeMay's March successes with little direction from the top and little initiative of its own to refine surrender strategy. To the extent that any such strategy emerged at all, it was more the product than the cause of LeMay's March 10 spectacular. Arnold certainly hoped that bombing alone might end the war, but as usual, his emphasis was on achieving "the maximum weight of effective bombs on Japanese targets" with the intent of destroying "whole industrial cities." It was left to others to translate that effort into a scheme for victory.[138]

It was spelled out by Arnold's staff. Further bombing delivered when Germany collapsed might "bring home the futility of continuing the war" to Japan's masses and leaders. Furthermore, Germany's surrender "might offer Japan's leaders a face-saving basis to end the war" as well as alarm them at the prospect of quick Russian entry into the Asian war. These possibilities, along with some shrewd analysis from army intelligence about the Suzuki cabinet, flowed into Norstad's office. Even before the staff studies were completed, Norstad wrote LeMay anticipating "Japan's hour of decision," and on April 10 he alerted LeMay to the time "very soon when it will be desirable to change the Japanese cabinet by another blitz period," probably when Germany capitulated. Weather experts added their own reasons for a quick resumption of the urban blitz: "Favorable fire weather conditions have almost never occurred from June to October at Tokyo."[139]

In all, LeMay's March triumphs excited expectations for a knockout blow, delivered by bombers before invading troops need storm ashore. LeMay responded accordingly, relaying to Norstad his "conviction that the present state of development of the air war presents the AAF for the first time with the opportunity of proving the power of the strategic air arm." And yet LeMay's wording betrayed the sharp limitations on his vision. For one thing, the AAF's opportunity for "proving" itself seemed more important than a conception for achieving victory. In turn, he really had no such conception beyond trying to apply "maximum pressure on the Japanese Empire by increasing the sortie rate and bomb load," as he put it to Arnold on April 5. After the war, he described his firebombing as having "whipped the populace into a state where they could—and would—accept the idea of surrender." At the time, LeMay and his staff developed no clear rationale even for that strategy. Youth, inexperience, and his place in the chain of command perhaps discouraged LeMay from connecting his operations to the final goal of victory. And yet Eaker and Spaatz, though senior in age and experience, held comparable commands in Europe and on occasion spoke out forcefully on larger strategic and political issues. The difference lay partly in LeMay's mentality, partly in his unique position as subordinate to Arnold: if not to LeMay, then articulation of strategy fell to Arnold, but he had little interest. To both, converting destruction into surrender was a job for superiors in the chain of command. LeMay's job was to destroy targets. The airmen's hope to prove the B-29s' war-winning capacity was not pressed on higher authority. That hope remained, as the official history put it, "not for public consumption."[140]

LeMay was sent off to destroy more cities without a clear rationale for doing so. The air staff was hedging its bets: "If the . . . incendiary attacks do not weaken the morale of the Japanese people" so that they "terminate the war," they would in any event prepare the way for "invasion and the ultimate defeat of Japan." In short, if bombing did not win the war one way, it would another, and there seemed neither sanction nor compulsion from higher authority to choose. Some air staff officers chafed at this vagueness, but to little avail.[141]

So LeMay pressed on. In April he launched only a few major fire raids, though these, against Tokyo, approached his March 10 success in terms of acreage incinerated. In May, restocked with incendiaries and taxing his crews, he dispatched over five hundred bombers on missions, and he completed the firing of Japan's largest cities. Over one hundred square miles of urban landscape were destroyed, and by early June, Tokyo, Nagoya, Kobe, Osaka, Yokohama, and Kawasaki had been stricken from the target lists for fire attacks. Some precision targets remained in these cities, and many others elsewhere. But the trained crews and radar sets necessary for precision attacks remained slow to arrive in the Marianas, while the urgency to strike at particular factories and fortresses was gone. As Hansell later put it, "The new tactic . . . was both easier to perform and to measure."[142] Earlier, fire raids had been viewed as a backup measure to capitalize on and round off precision attacks. Now that relationship was neatly reversed: the cities would be destroyed, then the remains would be picked over.

In June, Arnold arrived at Guam for discussions with LeMay. LeMay recounted their meeting:

> He asked the question . . . when is the war going to end? Well we've been too busy fighting it to figure out a date. But it's about over though. Give me thirty minutes and I'll give you a date. Well I got my plans and operations fellows and said, look, run in right quick and look see how many target areas we got left. . . . If there is no industry left up there, there can't be much war left going on.

LeMay told Arnold that he would run out of targets by about September 1, and that "with the targets gone we couldn't see much of any war going on." Proudly recounted by LeMay as an indication of his command's efficiency and dedication, the incident was a revelation of the air force approach to war, rich with the emptiness of strategic reasoning about how to win the war and of the desire even to formulate it. Destruction would win the war, and the war would have to end when the destruction was complete. LeMay's statement to Arnold was of a piece with the summary statement of his strategy LeMay offered in his memoirs: first establish bases, then "bomb and burn them until they quit. That was our theory, and history has proved that we were right." It was of a piece with how the United States—not always, but at its worst—waged the war.[143]

10

The Persistence of Apocalyptic Fantasy

THE INVERSION OF DREAM AND REALITY

In the last week of May 1945, American bombers almost fulfilled an old fantasy about air power, that a catastrophic attack on an enemy's capital would shock it into surrender. Like much else in the air war, success came about inadvertently. The fire raids against Tokyo on the nights of May 23–24 and 25–26 were designed to finish off the capital as an incendiary target and speed capitulation. But by now fire raids were almost routine, and nothing beyond scorching the remaining areas of Tokyo was expected. Five years of inconclusive bombing had deflated expectations for the terror value of a single aerial blow, and the great March 10 raid must have seemed the best chance to revive them.

Indeed, the most striking result of the new attacks in political terms, the blaze that roared through the emperor's own quarters, apparently was wholly unintended. The imperial grounds, because they stood out so starkly on photographs and radar scopes, did serve "as a convenient checkpoint for navigators." But bomber crews had been instructed to avoid hitting the imperial quarters "since the Emperor of Japan is not at present a liability and may later become an asset."[1] But both raids were directed at areas adjacent to the imperial grounds. Bombs either fell accidentally into the royal quarters, as some eyewitness accounts suggest, or flames that leaped "like bounding tigers" simply spread there, as the terse official American history implies. Either way the air war now came home to the very seat of imperial authority.[2]

Of course much else perished in these two nights: shrines and temples, hospitals and factories, citadels of commerce and government and learning. Or, to use the familiar American indices of triumph, over five square miles on the first raid and nearly seventeen on the second night. From the Japanese point of view, perhaps the scales of justice were righted a bit because another inadvertent casualty of the raids was apparently the death of sixty-two imprisoned Allied airmen.[3] And yet, just as terror was now delivered more routinely, it was also received more matter-of-factly, without the communal shock felt on March 10 or the same casualties now that the civilian populace had shrunken.

But the men close to the throne, so callous to the mass suffering in previous raids, now flinched even as Tokyo's masses became more resigned. The emperor, the court, and high officials remained safe in underground shelters. But the sights and sounds of the royal quarters burning offered a profound shock. The marquis Kido, always in close touch with the emperor, recorded the shame of officials, who felt dishonored by this desecration of the imperial grounds. Never before or after—not with the March 10 raid or the atomic bombings, much less the hundreds of other raids—did Kido note more than the barest details of air raids. But on this occasion he carefully accounted the destruction, listing the many buildings burned down. He also let his imagination run free regarding the fate which the enemy could mete out. Given the "tremendous effect of his mass incendiary bombing," the enemy had "by no means a difficult task to sweep away, one after another all the cities and towns down to villages in the country by fire," along with "stored up clothing and foodstuffs," creating a situation "really past salvation" with the onset of cold weather. Kido was at last glimpsing what most Japanese already knew.[4]

The precise impact of the May raids on the Japanese government remains difficult to measure. Regarding Japan's political strategy, the raids acted only as another catalyst to the more urgent pursuit of Soviet mediation, though by now Foreign Minister Togo bluntly emphasized the futility of that course. Nor did formal military strategy take a new turn. It remained harnessed to the hope, belligerently expressed but deeply doubted, that fanatical resistance on land and at sea would force the enemy to compromise on peace terms. Invasion, not air raids, would decide Japan's fate.[5] But the raids' impact could not be measured only by formal policy. Given the capacity of Japan's "peace" faction to feel intimidated by die-hard militarists, that policy changed only at a glacial pace. Almost an unmentionable shame, the destruction of the imperial quarters produced a reaction played out less in words than in solemn ritual, particularly the many attempts to resign office. As Kido's diary indicated, in court circles the May raids drove home Japan's hopelessness in a visceral way that no other event of these last months could match.

For the short term at least, these raids also played into the hands of the die-hards. Some of its American proponents had hoped that a direct attack on the emperor would destroy his divine mystique in the eyes of the Japanese masses and thereby crush their last remaining reason for persisting in the struggle. That possibility had been on Norstad's mind back in December, and publicly even the *Christian Century,* among many voices, had speculated that the great March 10 raid had "blasted large cracks in the myth by which a weak and inoffensive little man had become a conquering god."[6] But the May raids, coupled with the emperor's show of compassion after the March 10 firestorm, seemed only to strengthen his bond with the populace. Japanese broadcasts, including one by Suzuki, made no pretense that the emperor's divine powers had spared him a personal tragedy. But with the emperor now sharing the nation's suffering, he also became a symbol of its resistance, and grumbling about the government's failure continued to be aimed elsewhere.

Furthermore, the raids provided another opportunity to mobilize the masses by declaiming against the enemy's bestiality, plus the hypocrisy of his claims to be engaged in precision bombing. "When things come to such a pass"—that is, that the imperial palace is burned down— "we the subjects are simply overwhelmed with awe and, at the same time, we cannot help but renew our indignation from our very hearts against this unscrupulous and atrocious enemy America." Arguing that an enemy "who constantly speaks of humanity and peace" must be judged by deeds and not words, the government also implied that no peace terms the United States might announce could be trusted— to accept them would only entrap Japan in the savagery of its conqueror. "The enemy is talking loudly about International Law and humanity, but the reality is that he bombs Palaces, Shrines, Hospitals, National Schools and today he bombed the Imperial Palace," so Suzuki reminded his listeners. Such statements probably did little to energize the resistance of a beleaguered populace, but they set up backfires against any acceptance of early surrender.[7]

None of this constituted a strategy of truth by government leaders. To them, Robert Butow has written, "The people simply did not count. They would do what they were told, and they would obey to the letter."[8] But the May raids drove home the awesome dangers faced by the elites themselves—their own destruction and the disintegration of the nation they ruled.

The assault on the imperial grounds also found an unintended audience back in the United States. The media gave it considerable play, a hint of satisfaction mixed with the claim that the bombs' effects were unintended. It also played into mounting public attention to the thorny issue of the emperor's fate and the surrender process, to which *Time* devoted its cover story on the eve of the raids. *Time* described the Japanese mind as so "utterly alien" to Americans that it seemed "almost as uncontemporary . . . as Neanderthal man." To Americans, "the Emperor Hirohito was Japan," and "the war against Japan was inevitably a war against its Emperor." But soon *Time*'s writers became impatient with the unconditional surrender formula. Truman "had not said enough. . . . A statement of aims beyond 'Kill Japs—unconditional surrender' was awaited by Americans from Berlin to Okinawa." *Time* did not offer a new formula on the emperor or explicitly link its impatience to the May raids. Others did get specific. In *Newsweek*, Raymond Moley proposed "to drive a wedge between the emperor and the people on one side, and the military class on the other," noting that "the profound devotion of the Japanese people to the emperor is the root of the suicidal trend." Moreover, Moley hoped that the political process could be speeded up if "through intensified bombing the panicky streak in the Japanese mentality may be set off."[9]

Here was a stirring of interest in how the bombing might serve American purposes in a way more discrete than simply by piling up further destruction. Bolder speculation seemed out of place: the political effects of bombing were already rather discredited and almost unfathomable anyway in Japan's case; it seemed risky to force the president's hand in public at such a delicate moment and dangerous to nourish false hopes among Americans, all the more so since journalists shared official fears that Japan would exploit such hopes to no good purpose.

More surprising was the indifference in official circles to the possibilities opened up by the May raids, which were perceived by only one man, Joseph Grew. He was well positioned to state his case. Grew often served as the State Department's de facto head, and now worked under a president who was more dependent on the experts' recommendation than the cavalier Roosevelt had been. Grew also possessed a superior knowledge of the workings of bureaucracy, and as America's longtime ambassador to Tokyo, he claimed special prestige and expertise in dealing with Japan. Anticipating retirement when the war finished, he "considered the restoration of peace in the Pacific to be the last task of his public career," a chance for statesmanship.[10]

At the end of May, Grew saw the opportunity to revive the stalled effort to settle the Pacific war early. He was encouraged by the fall of the Koiso cabinet, some phrases in Truman's V-E Day address, and the dismaying impact on Japan of Germany's surrender and of Russia's likely entry into the war. But Grew's initiative was also intimately bound to the political virtues and dangers he saw arising out of the recent raids on Tokyo. On May 26, he instructed Eugene Dooman, his chief Japan specialist, to draw up a new statement of American surrender terms, and when Dooman seemed to balk, Grew invoked the Tokyo air raids and advised Dooman, "We can't waste any more time." This was a rather delphic warning. Perhaps Grew feared that further bombing would destroy the political mechanism, even the very lives of the emperor and the peace faction, needed to effect a surrender and leave the militarists forced or emboldened to fight on. Given the strength of Grew's personal and ideological bonds with some of Japan's leading "liberals," the prospect of their destruction may have triggered personal emotions as well. Furthermore, Grew's knowledge of American work on the atomic bomb must have doubled these fears.[11]

But Grew saw opportunity as well as danger in the Tokyo raids. On May 28 he took his case personally to Truman, proposing a new statement to Japan promising the Japanese permission "to determine their own future political structure." He emphasized that it would carry "maximum effect if issued immediately following the great devastation of Tokyo which occurred two days ago." Urgently desiring action, Grew wanted his statement incorporated into an address Truman was to make on May 31.[12]

For the moment, Grew gained little. The new president, not about to take a bold initiative, made agreeable noises but asked Grew to take up the matter with Stimson, Forrestal, Marshall, and Admiral King. Grew wasted no time, but a meeting the next day produced no satisfaction. The assembled officials agreed on the principle of clarifying American peace terms but not on the timing of an American statement—"the nub of the whole matter."[13] They decided the moment would not come until Japan's final defeat at Okinawa. Such reasoning revealed how policy remained tied to the progress of traditional military strategies, all the more because no one from the services made a case that blockade and bombing might provide sanctions to induce surrender.

Only in one way did bombing strategy enter the calculations made on the twenty-ninth about delaying a statement to Japan. Delay, Grew noted, was deemed necessary "for certain military reasons, not divulged."[14] Without a doubt, those reasons involved the atomic bomb—unmentioned because some conferees (Eugene Dooman, Elmer Davis) knew nothing of it. Those knowledgeable probably reasoned that whatever the psychological impact of bombing upon the Japanese, it would only be vaster and more certain when it took an atomic form.

Both at the time and after the war, Grew thought the aftermath of the May raids was a missed opportunity to bring peace.[15] Perhaps he was right, but more important was the absence of concerted effort by others even to weigh the possibility. It was as if the political and psychological impact of bombing, having been so long exaggerated when so little had been possible, was slighted now that it approached realization. Bombing had always loomed larger as an idea, an abstraction, than as a practical weapon. Perhaps the idea in its new, nuclear form dazzled men and overwhelmed their attention to the ongoing impact of bombing.

But the bomb hardly explains the indifference to firebombing among people ignorant of the Manhattan Project. Despite exceptions, the media generally treated the bombing as a routine matter disconnected from the question of surrender. A veiled implication of an early peace appeared in LeMay's public statement that "in a few months we will be running out of targets," but the press did not follow it up. In commentaries linking bombing to surrender, the most frequent focus was on the possibility of starving Japan into surrender, a scenario recognized as unlikely to yield early results. Coverage of LeMay's operations also rarely went beyond the usual official statements to evoke its full horror. Just as rare was the hint of criticism evident in a *Time* article describing LeMay's blasting of Hitachi just two days after Halsey's fleet had raked it with gunfire: the city "had long been on their [the airmen's] list of targets and they had bombed it regardless of what Halsey's guns might have done." Perfunctory reporting on Japanese charges that American bombers "massacred innocent women and children" raised a moral issue only to dismiss it by asserting either the dishonesty or the hypocrisy of Japanese accusations. The *New York Times*'s Drew Middleton raised the issue in far more broad terms after viewing Berlin's rubble: "The end of Western urban civilization is no longer an empty phrase but a terrible fact already within the grasp of mankind." That danger, much debated during the infancy of air power, engaged few in 1945 until the atomic bomb invited a new perspective.[16]

Some peculiar circumstances that summer aggravated the long-standing difficulties in grasping the reality of bombing. LeMay's first fire raids, in the spring, had been few in number and launched against Japan's largest cities. After the last Tokyo raids, the trail of destruction ran mostly through unknown towns with unpronounceable names, evoking not even the hazy images that "Tokyo" or "Osaka" might trigger. In contrast to LeMay's routine operations, the shelling and bombing by Halsey's fleet, though far less weighty and destructive, were episodic and glamorous: there was drama, daring, and a more visible kind of supremacy in witnessing a navy steam right up to Japan's shores; it seemed more prophetic of Japan's imminent demise, less messy than the carpet bombing of cities, and comfortably in line with grand naval traditions stretching back to Perry's exploits almost a century earlier.[17]

But, as earlier during the war, immediate circumstances shaped coverage of the bomber war less than political preferences and traditions. Caution in portraying and judging the effects of strategic bombing had been evident since the tacit truce of 1943 regarding public debate on those effects. Politicians and press continued their wait-and-see attitude toward strategic air power. It was not discredited; the hope kept creeping back that it would yet obviate further American sacrifices. But the press could assume little for it, instead focusing on familiar methods of warfare, those whose efficacy, if bitterly costly, seemed more certain in the end.

FIREBOMBING: THE FINAL ROUND

In their own way, airmen also missed the chance that Grew had seen. After the May raids on Tokyo, just as before, they divined no special opportunities to hasten Japan's capitulation beyond piling up more rubble than the enemy could tolerate. Likewise, in June they missed two further chances to express their version of how to win the war.

The first opportunity arose when strategists gathered in Washington and met with Truman on June 18 to determine final strategy against Japan. Unfortunately, slipshod preparations and uninstructive discussions meant that the long-awaited review hardly matched the gravity of the task. In a small way, the responsibility for failure was Arnold's, for he failed to appear. Touring Pacific outposts, Arnold ordered LeMay home to give the air force view on strategy. Furthermore, according to LeMay a mix-up about dates made him arrive too late to make his case. That job fell to General Ira Eaker, a veteran of such high-level conferences, but hardly intimate with operations in the Pacific.[18]

In any event, Marshall dominated the June 18 meeting, and with him the broad-front strategy that also had guided American operations against Germany. By no means did he neglect the bomber. He relayed estimates that by the time of the proposed Kyushu invasion on November 1, "our air action will have smashed practically every industrial target worth hitting in Japan as well as destroying huge areas in the Jap cities." But neither Marshall nor anyone else raised the possibility that action of this sort might obviate the need for invasion. In Marshall's eyes, the United States still could not afford the luxury of choosing one way to beat Japan. It had to assemble all methods—blockade and bombardment; invasion; and "the entry or threat of entry of Russia into the war."

Therefore deliberation focused on the hazards and prospects of invasion—with pointed references to the squeamishness of Churchill, the American public, and the men in arms destined to endure it—rather than on other alternatives. Truman was clearly worried. He feared "creating another Okinawa closer to Japan," a peril the Joint Chiefs could not rule out, and an extended though uninformative discussion took place regarding what the casualties might be. Likewise, he raised the danger of "more closely uniting the Japanese" if "white men" landed on their shores. At the same time, Truman would take no bold step away from the invasion dilemma, such as modifying the surrender formula. He "did not feel that he could take any action at this time to change public opinion on the matter." And though the possibility of a speedy end to the war through atomic bombing hung over all the deliberations, it went unmentioned until the War Department's John J. McCloy raised it as the meeting was breaking up. The ensuing talk, not officially recorded, drifted back to the issue of the surrender formula and pointed to no clear alternatives. McCloy's suggestion that Japan be warned in advance of the bomb's use had already been rejected by the Interim Committee on the atomic bomb. That the bomb might preempt invasion was hardly a new idea and hardly one that many were yet ready to count on.[19]

More surprising, no other military advisor suggested alternatives. Marshall came to the meeting presenting the hard-fought consensus of all the Joint Chiefs, none of whom would reopen old wounds by breaking ranks, though Leahy did ask for a change in surrender terms. Speaking for Arnold, Eaker was particularly deferential, embracing the invasion of Kyushu and specifically repudiating "those who advocated use against Japan of air power alone."[20]

What happened to victory through air power? The problem was not LeMay's absence. He would have spoken on Arnold's instructions, just as Eaker explicitly did, and those instructions were to back Marshall to the hilt. The real problem was Arnold's priorities and temperament. He may have deferred to Marshall out of loyalty: the chief of staff had given much support to air power and might do so again in the AAF's final quest for independence. More than that, Arnold, who had repeatedly passed such presentations on to his subordinates, did so again in June partly because he had no clear scheme for winning the war with his bombers. His uncertainty was evident by the way he pegged support for Marshall's Kyushu plan to the acquisition of vast new bases there from which to hit Japan. Clearly those bases would be ready only sometime in 1946, but lacking a plan to end the war earlier, he needed the Kyushu bases.

After the war, Arnold proclaimed his wartime confidence that air power could win the war. At the time, he had no clear idea how or when that would happen. Though given a September 1 victory date by LeMay, he made no concerted case for it. Later, at Potsdam, Arnold hinted at it, maintaining that by then Japan "will have tremendous difficulty in holding her people together for continued resistance to our terms of unconditional surrender." But of course that was arguably the case even in July, and Arnold backed away from a more emphatic prediction. Even in early August, when LeMay's campaign had proceeded further, Arnold suggested to the other Joint Chiefs that bombing might soon win the war, but it "in any event, will assure the success of the land campaign in Japan, and reduce the loss of American lives to a minimum."[21]

Arnold had interest in Washington's June 18 deliberations. The next day, by teletype, he anxiously queried his Pentagon staff about the results: "Do the people in Washington realize that the bombing of Japan—the shortening of war—the saving of American lives all are dependent to some extent on this organization [?]" There was of course a strategic issue tucked away in Arnold's question, but characteristically it was left subordinate to attainment of the recognition Arnold craved and the reorganization of air power he desired. The latter he eventually got in modified form—late in July, the Twentieth Air Force headquarters moved to the Marianas, and Spaatz (with LeMay as chief of staff) headed a new U.S. Army Strategic Air Forces in the Pacific embracing both the Twentieth and Eighth air forces. But in strategic matters, all had not gone well for the air force, either at the meeting with Truman on the eighteenth or the next day, when LeMay made his pitch to the Joint Chiefs and Marshall slept through it (so LeMay recalled).[22]

Another opportunity to reformulate strategy arose when Strategic Bombing Survey (USSBS) experts returned from Europe and made their recommendations for a final course of bombing against Japan. USSBS staff held several conferences with strategists in mid-June, including a meeting on the nineteenth with Stimson, Grew, Lovett, and Marshall. Hedged only by acknowledgment that the German and Japanese cases were not the same, the survey's recommendations constituted a firm plea, based on lessons from Europe, to change LeMay's targeting. The bombers should concentrate on Japanese transportation: the oceangoing fleet had disappeared, but railways and coastal shipping seemed prime targets whose destruction would paralyze the Japanese economy even if remaining factories and cities were left intact. Oil, chemical, and electric power plants were also singled out, the kind of targets with which airmen themselves had once been enamored.[23]

The survey team made slow headway. George Ball's recollections of their reception were acid. "After one long session dominated by General Curtis LeMay, who did most of the talking, I came away dismayed at the shallowness of the views expressed." General Norstad offered his sympathies: "George, never forget that individually many of those men are highly intelligent, but when they meet collectively—did you ever hear such goddam nonsense?" Yet the problem was not simply the obtuseness of generals. Stimson attached great importance to the survey recommendations—one of many signs that no one yet counted on the atomic bomb to end the war early—but he did nothing to follow them up. Nor did Marshall.[24]

Airmen and Joint Staff planners had other reasons for responding tepidly to the survey's ideas. For one thing, they came in from outside normal bureaucratic channels and had to move through a bureaucratic maze of ever-growing intricacy. In the end, the survey's recommendation to attack transportation was acceptable to the airmen but only formalized at the end of July, when Spaatz took command of the Pacific air forces. In the meantime, the survey's ideas were subjected to the pull and haul of timing and tactics, those factors a military bureaucracy is most attuned to calculating. LeMay's staff argued that "bombing must proceed according to its own time table, recognizing weather as the controlling factor, rather than the time table for surface operations." These tactical considerations, which the Twentieth elevated into a "fundamental principle," led it to insist on "rapid destruction of a large number of Japanese cities," with precision attacks saved for the few days of good weather and the main assault on transportation saved for October 1945. Besides, the timetable for invasion provided a good excuse to postpone precision raids—an early blitz against transportation might give the enemy time to recoup before Kyushu's beaches were assaulted. Moreover, by October the weather would be better, the radar techniques nearer perfection, and smaller bombers ready for action from Okinawa. In the interim, the B-29s would go on doing what they did best, making Japan "a nation without cities" but leaving its rail transport largely intact at the time of surrender. There would be no bold departure from proven success, only a gradual assimilation of the survey's recommendations into air force strategy.[25]

After the war, Hansell constructed a powerful case that the survey's recommendations, along with the review at the White House, comprised a final lost opportunity to devise a more efficient and humane strategy for victory over Japan. Hansell pointed to LeMay's surprising success in mining sea-lanes and in carrying out limited attacks against precision targets. Had similar methods been employed on a larger scale against all of Japan's internal transportation system plus its electric power grid, the United States would have achieved the same paralysis of Japan as it did with the wasteful method of firebombing. Even allowing for foul weather, limitations in radar, and other tactical obstacles, the more efficient method, aided by carrier planes, was within LeMay's grasp. The United States would have needed a few fire raids only as a coup de grace to a precision campaign, climactic demonstrations of power to drive home Japan's helplessness. The benign alternative was neglected, he argued, not because the AAF was unwilling or unable to act on it. Rather, the obsession of American grand strategy with quick victory and invasion denied the airmen the opportunity to change their targeting toward a true air strategy for victory. Compelled to soften up Japan for invasion, they had to wage systematic destruction.[26]

Hansell effectively critiqued the course of blockade and bombing that made the rubble bounce in so many redundant ways. But he was wrong in exonerating the air force from responsibility for the holocaust over Japan. Invasion sanctioned but did not compel all-out destruction, which might have been pursued as readily even if invasion had been foresworn. American war-making by the summer of 1945 was characterized by a broad-front strategy permitting each service to pursue its favored course, to avoid choices and do everything within the limits of American resources and of public demands for complete victory at minimal cost. The imperatives of invasion were not the foremost considerations leading the AAF to firebombing; it made that choice in March because incendiary bombing was easy and because doing it rescued the AAF's flagging fortunes. Even in the summer Arnold and his staff had no clear alternative to Marshall's strategy. They pursued the campaign of fire as zealously as the invasion strategists, offering only the vague promise that destruction would make Japan surrender. Furthermore, the only pressure on the AAF to restrain its targeting came from Stimson, a man firmly reconciled to the necessity of invasion unless the atomic bomb forced surrender. Hansell was right on one score: the bombing campaign revealed the bankruptcy of American strategy. But it was the air force as much as the army that had exhausted its storehouse of ideas.[27]

The bombing campaign waged and planned over the summer of 1945 indicated as much. Like Harris's RAF late in the European war, LeMay's air force had trouble reorienting itself despite improving technical proficiency. At the least, having incinerated Japan's major cities, LeMay or Arnold might have concentrated on remaining military or industrial objectives. Instead, the summer campaign of fire turned against nearly five dozen lesser urban areas. With the targets much smaller and the bomber force increasing to seven hundred or more, several cities could be attacked in one mission. The results were immensely gratifying, destruction reaching 99.5 percent of one city's acreage (Toyama), and American losses astonishingly low.

If in the spring the rationale for fire attacks had been casual, in the summer it rested even more on what was operationally easy rather then strategically vital. On the night of July 16–17, for example, B-29s unloaded 790 tons of incendiaries on Oita, a town of some 60,000 people that had, in the words of the later survey report, "no major industry," though "a vital naval air depot" that apparently was not attacked. Railyards did lie in the targeted area, but the survey's listing of buildings destroyed in the raid ran to the distressingly unimportant: banks, a soya sauce factory, two schools, a Presbyterian church. On the night of August 1–2, 1,593 tons—as the survey report noted, incendiary tonnage often far exceeded target requirements—fell on a town of similar size, Hachioji. "Industrially, economically, militarily, and commercially the city was unimportant, except for being a railroad junction and a refugee center for Tokyo."[28]

To be sure, airmen could not always gauge in advance a city's importance. But by now a great deal could be learned, for photographic surveillance went on unimpeded. Some cities attacked did have demonstrable importance to Japan's war effort. Ammori, a city of 100,000 people, lay at the "choke point" in the transportation corridor between Honshu and Hokkaido. LeMay's attack there on the night of July 28–29 produced a conflagration killing 728 people and burning out most of the city, although it was unclear whether the transportation facilities themselves had been disabled. Likewise, against the industrial city of Ube on July 2, "the usual 'fire storm' phenomenon" occurred, but it did not spread to the large industrial buildings in the city. Hamamatsu was, in LeMay's words, "the garbage-can target," the place where B-29 crews that aborted missions to assigned targets regularly dumped their bomb loads. To boot, Halsey's battleships also raked the city, though LeMay "was too busy from then on to pay much attention to the fleet bombardment episode."[29]

On the few days of good weather and on occasional night missions LeMay turned away from the urban areas. The attacks on oil tanks and refineries were successful, if largely meaningless since Japan could no longer import oil anyway. Far more valuable was "the heaviest aerial mining campaign ever waged," one that now exceeded even the damage done by American submarines. Yet the precision attacks were often labeled as "experimental" in the air force's official history, a neat reversal from when that term was applied to fire raids. Most of LeMay's tonnage still hit urban areas, for with a huge force at his command, he could dabble in other operations without seriously diluting the incendiary campaign. Doing so placated critics, satisfied the AAF's residual interest in the doctrine once its mainstay, and prepared for the day when urban areas had become so obliterated that other targets would have to be hit.[30]

Of course, the B-29s' operations were by summer complemented by other air forces which to some extent carried on the precision side of the aerial campaign. Carrier-based planes as well as fighters and smaller bombers with the army's Fifth Air Force roamed over Japan with impunity, attacking airfields, factories, railroad yards, bridges, trains, and what the official history called "other such targets of opportunity." In practice, the tactical fighters and bombers were often doing something more akin to the Jeb Stuart campaign that Lovett had once proposed for Germany in its waning days. The impulse to engage in "general Hell raising" was no longer confined to the big bombers, and in bombing civilians no clear distinction remained between precision bombing and area attacks. Noting the Japanese government's announcement that all men from fifteen to sixty and all women from seventeen to forty would be called up for defense, the Fifth Air Force's intelligence officer declared on July 21 that "the entire population of Japan is a proper Military Target . . . , THERE ARE NO CIVILIANS IN JAPAN." The goal was to do anything "which saves American lives, shortens the agony which War is and seeks to bring about an enduring Peace."[31]

The strafing of passenger trains became a favored action. It may have aroused Japanese indignation even more than the fire raids. There was, after all, some appreciation that B-29s hit general areas because they could not easily target anything else. But there was something gratuitous about the way fighter pilots, flying at low levels and able to discern their targets, singled out civilians for attack. "The Japanese," noted an American visitor in October 1945, "classed such attacks as atrocities, because the passenger trains were not thought to be military targets." Those attacks suggest that even if implemented, Hansell's favored transportation strategy would have been only marginally more discriminate in its treatment of civilians: with the impulse to kill so widely shared, the nature of target selection made only limited difference. So too did the tactical potentialities of the various forces involved. Even though B-29s were clearly best equipped for incendiary raids, other bombers sometimes resorted to the same tactics against Kyushu. "It seemed," commented the official history, that the tactical forces "were prepared to obliterate whatever the B-29's may have left of Japan's urban centers."[32]

Summer plans for future bombing campaigns, those not carried out because of the war's sudden end, measured the widening circles of the destructive impulse. When the last cities were finished off, targets would still have to be found, and it was doubtful that transportation alone could absorb all the capacity. Operations analysts proposed moving on to "all urban areas with a population greater than 30,000 peoples," some 180 towns in all. They could be wiped out by November, when, it was said, "the back of Japan thus will have been completely broken," as if it was not already and as if planners had no idea of effecting earlier surrender. Another possibility lay in new methods of starvation to supplement the interdiction of food transport: the rice paddies might be sprayed with oil, defoliants, or biological agents, and the production of fertilizer further attacked. Because such a campaign would be slow to work its effects, it elicited a doubtful response from some air planners, but given the disappearance of other targets, the air force probably would have implemented it had the war continued into 1946.[33]

The use of gas was also pondered, for old restraints were slipping away: FDR, committed at least in public against American use, was dead; Germany's surrender removed the threat of retaliation against European allies (though not against the Chinese), and the toll of American soldiers and sailors in Pacific combat was mounting. Arnold probably had gas in mind in May 1945 when he asked Eaker to ferret out any "Buck Rogers' ideas" that would effect "Extermination of by-passed Jap Garrisons in [the] South Pacific," though Arnold did not spell out why extermination was needed. Marshall apparently considered using gas, though perhaps only of a nonlethal variety, against those garrisons and in landing operations planned to follow Okinawa. If nothing else, it also seemed advantageous to make the Japanese *think* the Americans might employ gas in urban bombing raids, providing a "tremendous psychological effect on an already jittery populace" that might make it "crack" before invasion had to occur. Nonetheless, the services were not yet at the brink of initiating chemical warfare: popular aversion remained, Truman and American allies had yet to be sounded out, preparation was incomplete, and the payoff had not been convincingly established. Gas might have been used had the war dragged on another year; in 1945, the United States was not ready.[34]

Beyond increasing the intimidation and destruction, strategists had as much difficulty as ever expressing how present and future operations would bring about surrender. The closest they came to a political strategy was the summer's massive effort to blanket Japanese cities with leaflets warning of impending aerial attacks and urging surrender. The operation "irked us a bit," LeMay recalled; "we'd rather drop bombs than leaflets." Nonetheless, it made a formidable impression on the Japanese that Americans could bomb with such impunity that they could announce targets in advance, and perhaps the campaign helped prepare the Japanese to accept surrender when it came. Designed to hasten that surrender, leafleting also saved an immeasurable number of lives by advance notice to targeted cities, meeting the air force's desire to "lessen the stigma attached to area bombing."[35]

In turn, that was part of the broader effort, more than ever guiding Arnold, to capitalize on the war experience to the AAF's benefit. Public relations remained the art of balancing deception and truth, depending on which enhanced that benefit. "In the event of incendiary missions directed at sections of cities," policy was to "continue to maintain that same is precision rather than area bombing." The long-range goal was still to cultivate an image favorable to securing autonomy and maximum resources for the postwar air force. "This policy will never be stated in so many words for public consumption," however.[36]

New weapons were another field of battle in the struggle for independence. "The Army Air Forces is now proceeding on an unauthorized project to manufacture 12,000 JB-2 buzz bombs" (modified German V-1s), Eaker was reminded. He had "no doubt but that neither the V-1 nor V-2 is as effective as bombing." But the AAF wanted the V-1 used for experimental reasons and to lay its claim to these new devices, Arnold worrying that "Ground Forces are about to take over rocket development." Airmen were not naive about the dangers of plunging into the next stage of the century's technological revolution. Arnold was reminded that because of rocketry and nuclear weapons, the United States and other nations "will face destruction on a scale undreamed of in the wildest, most sensational fancies of fiction writers and comic strip artists," ultimately "endangering human survival." But to the air force the only recourse was to beat any potential enemy in the race to possess ultimate terrors.[37]

Many Japanese had by now experienced the science-fiction fantasy. With variations due to the changing nature of targeting and the hard-won lessons of the Japanese, the hardships they endured were essentially extensions of those observed in the spring, and only a few salient features of the summer need be noted. Despite the accelerated pace of bombing, its economic effects were perhaps least important, certainly less dramatic than those of the spring raids. More workers fled factories and cities, but their absence made little difference because industrial capacity had been so reduced that a surplus of usable labor still remained. Industrial capacity probably declined only by a marginal amount as a result of the summer's area bombing; only a systematic attack on coastal shipping and inland transportation could have significantly magnified the economic paralysis caused by blockade and the initial spring fire raids. Of course the Japanese economy was sheared in so many ways that measuring the effect of one kind of destruction is difficult. But in economic terms the summer's fire attacks largely inflicted redundant destruction and missed those components of the economy that were still functioning.[38]

Not so with the impact of the fire raids on the morale and vigor of the Japanese people, whose decline rapidly accelerated. Scarcely less than the deindustrialization and deurbanization of modern Japan was now taking place. In the process, the social structure of Japan was also momentarily upended. Farmers and small-town inhabitants, previously in the social backwater of modern Japan, now had the resources that urbanites coveted. They sometimes lorded it over their hapless city cousins, seeing the bombing as due punishment for the evil ways of the modern city and resenting the demands made by refugees. The very suddenness of Japan's modernization provided a backstop against social disintegration, however. Many urbanites were still familiar with and adaptable to rural ways; most still had relatives in the country; family members went to extraordinary lengths to stay together. As other social institutions—the vaunted neighborhood associations, the modern business corporation, the state bureaucracy—fell into various degrees of chaos, the family became the central social unit.[39]

But few could escape the effects of bombing. If some got used to air raids, far more experienced bombing for the first time. What was most striking in the many indices of morale was how consistent the precipitous decline was among all strata of the Japanese population. Partly this was because so many forces lowered morale besides bombing—news of defeat abroad, food shortages, and the like—but even more because so much of the population had experienced the bombing in one way or another: in raids on smaller cities, by word from the cities' refugees, even in the occasional raids and more frequent alerts that occurred in rural communities. Indeed, the bombing survey found that "57 percent of even the native rural population had experienced air raids and alerts, and about one-sixth said they had actually been bombed." Just as terrifying to rural dwellers was the ominous pattern of American bombing; since it was clearly descending from the big cities to smaller communities, their day might come.[40]

There were backstops in regard to morale too. The police were still powerful. Mere preoccupation with the struggle to live—food became the national obsession—left little energy for politics. For those still peering into the future, deep fears, abetted by state propaganda, curbed any desire to see the war's end; if postwar opinion surveys were correct, 68 percent of Japanese expected that defeat would bring "brutalities, starvation, enslavement, annihilation." A frenzy of actions and exhortations to prepare for invasion also characterized the summer months.[41]

As a consequence, all the bewilderment, anxiety, depression, and anger still did not add up to an immediate threat to the government or constitute the lever Americans could work to effect surrender. The key to capitulation still lay in the machinations of court circles, to whom the danger remained subtle: the venting of pent-up anger against the elites when the inevitable surrender came and a newer prospect, that the masses might lack the strength or will to support any fight to the finish. As official reports noted with uncharacteristic bluntness, "The people are losing confidence in their leaders and the gloomy omen of deterioration in public morale is present." Here was ammunition, used only cautiously, for the peace faction, and later a source of its hope that surrender would not be resisted once it came. The American attack on Japanese morale was having its effect, although as with most of bombing's results, in circuitous ways.[42]

Finally there was the added human carnage of the summer, a tangible matter hopefully more precisely measurable than morale and public opinion. But no reliable figure exists, either for the summer raids or for the entire bombing campaign. The survey's own claims for that campaign differed wildly, ranging from 268,157 to 900,000 killed. If near the latter figure, a minimum of 100,000, and probably far more, died in the war's forgotten raids, especially the dozens of area raids on smaller cities during the summer. Though the death count of March 10 was never repeated in later fire raids, a gruesome toll still mounted because so many raids took place even as each inflicted relatively few fatalities. Whatever the total, it was only a fraction of the war-related civilian deaths (excluding those by extermination) suffered by some warring nations, particularly China and the Soviet Union, where perhaps 900,000 died in Leningrad's siege alone. It was probably comparable to German deaths from air raids. Weighed against Japanese battle deaths, however, it probably means that more Japanese civilians than soldiers died at the hands of American weapons. And measured in terms of the short period in which substantial bomb casualties occurred, it was a uniquely devastating loss.[43]

After the war, the survey commented: "It was not necessary for us to burn every city, to destroy every factory, to shoot down every airplane or sink every ship, and starve the people. It was enough to demonstrate that we were capable of doing all this."[44] Airmen understood the physical destructiveness of the bombing they carried out, but they did little to define a strategy on the basis of it. Vaguely they knew that the Japanese government, not the Japanese people, would make the final decision, but they still could imagine no way of getting at the former except through the latter. They did not try hard to find a way because they still measured organizational success in terms of destruction delivered rather than political results achieved and because other leaders did not work with them to find a way.

Outside the air force, Allied policymakers were, it would seem, ignorant of or indifferent toward the crude facts of destruction. Neither in their official deliberations nor in their diaries and memoirs did they often note even the physical dimensions of the air assault on Japan, much less its consequences for victory over Japan and the world's course after the war. This indifference characterized men holding widely varied political and geographical responsibilities. Adolf A. Berle provides a curious but revealing case study in that regard. Though his tasks were regional (he was the State Department's top Latin Americanist), his copious diaries revealed global preoccupations, and he had occasion to muse on the course of bombing. General Arnold, touring Latin America, inspired Berle's extravagant praise, Berle thinking that "he had probably done as much as any one military man to win this war." But regarding what Arnold's bombers actually did, Berle found nothing to ponder. Neither did most civilian officials in Washington. Across the Pacific, army commanders like General Robert Eichelberger had good reason to pay attention to the air war but did so very late or not at all.[45]

British leaders showed that intimate familiarity with the effects of bombing did nothing to enhance awareness of its course in the war's final months. Among Churchill's colleagues, silence, ignorance, or illusion prevailed. Even Churchill, for years a close observer and shrewd protagonist of air power, followed this distant war only as a series of battles and campaigns on land and sea. His blind spot was not confined to the Pacific war: "In Churchill's voluminous war memoirs . . . Bomber Command's whole campaign [against Germany] received less space than the sinking of a single German warship," one writer has acidly noted. But his only comment on the Pacific aerial campaign suggested he was simply unaware of its scale:

It appeared [he wrote in justifying the atomic bomb's use] that the American Air Force had prepared an immense assault by ordinary air-bombing on

Japanese cities and harbours. These could certainly have been destroyed in a few weeks or a few months, and no one could say with what very heavy loss of life to the civilian population. But now, by using this new agency, we might not merely destroy cities, but save the lives alike of friend and foe.

In fact, by August the assault on most of those cities had been executed, not simply prepared. Churchill seemed to believe that the atomic bomb would short-cut, rather than climax, the American assault on Japanese cities. Truman may have shared the same misconception. "Our air and fleet units," he recalled in his memoirs, "had begun to inflict heavy damage on industrial and urban sites in Japan proper." The notion that American bombing had only "begun" in the summer of 1945 would have been baffling to the Japanese.[46]

LeMay's bombing proceeded largely unmonitored and unnoticed by diplomats and statesmen in London and Washington. Preoccupation with the atomic bomb might explain the indifference, except that it was shared by officials ignorant of the bomb. Like all men, wartime leaders reacted to concrete experiences, and for those who journeyed to Potsdam in July, the sight of Berlin's ruins provided occasion to break silence. For Truman, it inspired a rare flight into moving rhetoric, as he recorded his "fear that machines are ahead of morals by some centuries. . . . We are only termites on a planet and maybe when we bore too deeply into the planet there'll [be] a reckoning—who knows?"[47] But high-level officials rarely had occasion to view Japan's scorched cities, and even if they had it would probably have made little difference. The bombing of Asians simply aroused less interest and concern. At least Berlin's ruins could be viewed with a kind of sorrow and foreboding, as a crumbled monument to Western civilization. Few Americans recognized much of value being lost in Japan.

Compared to other forms of warfare, the bombing of cities retained an unmentionable and inexpressible quality, lying variously beyond or beneath description. With exceptions, that quality had characterized the predictive literature before the war, and it now persisted despite changed circumstances. Whereas in prospect bombing had been an almost unimaginable horror, by 1945 it was also a numbing but distant commonplace. Celebration and aversion, deliverance and doomsday remained the contrasting ways in which bombing was viewed, categories that allowed peoples and nations to avoid confronting the realities of mass destruction.

THE NUCLEAR "APPARITION"

The tenacity of those categories was most tragically demonstrated in the final deliberations upon the atomic bomb, for in them the bomb's use was never seriously debated and its destructive consequences were barely examined. Truman did agree in May to the establishment of the Interim Committee to consider issues raised by the bomb's development. But though its decisions were crucial, it was never charged with weighing whether to use the atomic bomb against Japan, only with how its use would affect the many problems of domestic and international control of atomic energy sure to arise. One member, James Conant, later claimed that the bomb's use against Japan was "the most important matter" on which the committee rendered judgment. But that matter was never formally on its agenda.[48]

The committee's composition and its relationship to the rest of the policymaking community further weakened its attention to the bomb's employment against Japan. Stimson chaired the committee, with his trusted aides Harvey Bundy and George Harrison doing much to shape its agenda and speed its workings. State was represented by its new secretary-designate, Jimmy Byrnes, and by Assistant Secretary Will Clayton, and navy by Under Secretary Ralph Bard. Three barons of science were also represented—Conant, Vannevar Bush, and Karl T. Compton—and attached to the committee was a scientific panel comprised of Oppenheimer, Lawrence, Arthur Compton, and Enrico Fermi, all men involved with the bomb's development. None of these men, except Bard and Stimson in limited ways, was responsible for or familiar with military operations against Japan. By "invitation," Marshall and Groves did attend many committee meetings, but establishment of a military panel was never carried out, and even as conceived it included no air force officer. Likewise, again with Stimson and Marshall as exceptions, committee members had not been involved in the formulation of surrender strategy.

Skewed by composition, the committee was also insulated by operation. Beyond the informal contributions of Stimson and Marshall, it was not directly coordinated with either military strategists in the air force or political strategists in the foreign policy bureaucracy. Except to anticipate arguments that might later arise, the committee had no public to persuade and dealt even with the scientific community at arm's length. For the bomb's use, wartime agreements required British concurrence, but on both sides it was treated as a formality. In general, concerns about secrecy and the hopes and fears aroused by the bomb itself shaped the committee's isolation. But the bomb was first and foremost a weapon of air war, and in that context the committee's focus reflected familiar continuities: the use of strategic air power during the war had rarely been graced by articulate rationales and extended deliberation.

When the committee met, however, questions about employing the atomic bomb inevitably crept into discussion. The residual doubts of some committee members were a consideration. They also faced questions and dissents from outside the committee. In practice it was impossible to attend to the committee's formal agenda without at least obliquely considering rationales for the bomb's use against Japan. How the bomb was first revealed to the world would affect its fate in international politics. There was even speculation that it might be best not to use the bomb against Japan, lest revelation of it speed its development by other nations and thereby erode the American advantage.[49] That was a passing thought; there was still a war to be won, and the bomb's use in that cause was generally taken for granted. Still, the committee considered how the manner of its use would affect the speed with which the war was concluded. In turn, deciding how to employ the bomb sometimes slipped over into pondering whether to use it at all.

To that degree, and in that roundabout way, the atomic bomb's novelty did compel the high-level attention and decisions absent in the recourse to firebombing.

Marshall raised the issue of the atomic bomb's use on May 29 while consulting with Stimson and McCloy to prepare for the Interim Committee's meetings. Marshall suggested the bomb's first use come "against straight military objectives such as a large naval installation." If that achieved "no complete result," Marshall wanted "to designate a number of large manufacturing areas from which people would be warned to leave," without identifying the specific target in advance. "Every effort should be made to keep our record of warning clear. We must offset by such warning methods the opprobrium which might follow from an ill considered employment of such force." Marshall was suggesting more restraints on the bomb's use than any other official at his level ever proposed; some of them were consistent with those offered by dissenting scientists. But choosing to regard the bomb's use as raising moral and political issues beyond his purview as a general, Marshall did not press his argument; McCloy advanced it in modified form at the June 18 meeting with Truman, but Marshall did not support him, deferring instead to contrary recommendations from the Interim Committee.[50]

The question of use arose again during a luncheon break in the committee's long meeting of May 31. Either Ernest Lawrence or Arthur Compton broached the possibility of some sort of demonstration of the weapon short of full use against a city. The question emerged once more during the afternoon's formal deliberations. Perhaps because Marshall missed the luncheon and the afternoon session, exploration of the possibility of a demonstration did not go far. By addressing it, committee members were implicitly recognizing the horror of the bomb. Yet their discussion also revealed the limits of recognition, for attention focused on what Oppenheimer called its "visual effect," which "would be tremendous" in the bomb's use on a city. As Stimson summarized the group's consensus, with the bomb *we should seek to make a profound psychological impression on as many of the inhabitants as possible.*" To insure that impression, surprise seemed essential—one reason among many for rejecting a demonstration, which would limit the numbers observing the blast.[51]

Stimson and his colleagues presumably meant by "psychological impression" that the bomb's terror would drive home the futility of further kamikaze resistance. Some, most likely Stimson, also imagined that the bomb's impact would strengthen the position of the peace faction and allow Japan's leadership to save face in surrendering.

A clue to their intentions is found in the earlier deliberations on the atomic bomb by the Target Committee. First convened on April 27, it consisted of a few military officers associated with the bomb project and a large group of operations researchers and scientists, among whom the most illustrious were Von Neumann and Oppenheimer. Oppenheimer and Groves in turn conveyed its findings to the Interim Committee, and subject to civilian approval, Groves had final authority to choose targets. From the start, the Target Committee dealt mainly with technical and tactical factors involved in the atomic attack, attending to the political and strategic dimensions of targeting in a hurried and ambiguous fashion. At the first meeting, some attempt was made to single out military or industrial targets. The Yawata steelworks were suggested, and target analysts were instructed that "the target and/or aiming point should have a high strategic value." Even that phrasing was equivocal, however, and since the target criteria also included "large urban areas . . . in the larger populated areas," they were expansive from the start.[52]

Soon the committee slipped into the murkier realm of nuclear psychology, developing the phrasing and orientation which Stimson's group inherited. In meetings on May 10 and May 11, participants noted the tactical and industrial importance of several proposed targets. But the first choice was clearly attractive for different reasons. Kyoto possessed from a "psychological point of view" an advantage as "the former capital of Japan" and "an intellectual center for Japan," for "the people there are more apt to appreciate the significance of such a weapon as the gadget." As the committee later put it, the people of Kyoto were "more highly intelligent and hence better able to appreciate the significance of the weapon." This was a leap more into nuclear absurdity than nuclear psychology, for it was not clear how "highly intelligent" people could appreciate if they were dead nor what difference it would make if they could. Nor was the reasoning clear for discussing the "possibility of bombing the Emperor's palace."[53]

The truth was that the committee was casually speculating on this critical matter. Everything else it discussed—weather, height of detonation, radiological effects—was in some measure calculable. But no one could suggest anything precise about how to define or measure "psychological" effect, the committee had few criteria from on high to guide it, and its members included no one versed in Japanese political psychology or the psychological effects observed in earlier bombing raids.

Nonetheless, the Target Committee concluded that "psychological factors in the target selection were of great importance." Or more accurately, that they were overriding. For in discussing *"Use against 'Military' Objectives"* the quotation marks around "Military" indicated that these men were discussing a euphemism, and their concluding words suggested that they regarded the bomb's effect on "any small and strictly military objective" as incidental. Even the audience for the bomb's psychological effect was ambiguous: the Japanese of course, but the initial use also had to be "sufficiently spectacular for the importance of the weapon to be internationally recognized when publicity on it is released."[54]

By the time the Target Committee reconvened on May 28, LeMay had eliminated Tokyo and the emperor's grounds as targets. To be sure, by the standard of psychological effect, Tokyo might still have seemed attractive; after all, Japan's government still resided there. But psychological impression was defined in part by destructiveness, which Tokyo's rubble would not reveal starkly, and anyway Groves wanted that destructiveness demonstrated boldly for reasons unrelated to the war. Perhaps too, the Target Committee had been told that the emperor was off limits, and through Stimson's intervention Kyoto too was later dropped. But the brief discussion of targets that occurred on the twenty-eighth still left psychological effects as paramount, since the committee decided "to neglect location of industrial areas as pin point target."[55]

The names of target cities changed but not the preoccupation with making a psychological statement. It guided others who deliberated on the bomb. To Churchill, too, the bomb was less a device that killed than an "apparition," an "almost supernatural weapon" which would give the Japanese people "an excuse" to surrender without losing face.[56] That persistent way of imagining the bomb's use arose in part because the task of defeating Japan was seen largely in terms of the "Oriental" psychology, whose workings Stimson often mused upon. With the enemy already defeated, the added physical destruction the bomb inflicted was seen as incidental; its decisive impact would be on the minds of men.

Guiding those like Stimson who were attuned to surrender strategy, that reasoning did not shape the preoccupation with psychological impact shown by many others involved in nuclear policy. Another explanation may have been simply an underappreciation of the bomb's killing effect. Until the first nuclear test on July 16, many scientists guessed far too low on the bomb's destructive yield. Compton also claimed later that he and Oppenheimer grossly underestimated fatalities—they would number "some 20,000 people"—because they had "not anticipated that when the attack was made practically no one would have sought shelter." The recollection hardly seems credible, since both Compton and Oppenheimer knew that the bomb would be delivered without warning and by a single plane unlikely to prompt war-weary Japanese to flee to shelter.[57]

A focus on the psychological impact of the bomb also arose out of uncertainty about how to distinguish it from LeMay's firebombing in its purely destructive and lethal impact. Oppenheimer had turned to discussing the bomb's "visual effect" after noting that the result of "one atomic bomb on an arsenal would not be much different from the effect caused by any Air Corps strike of present dimensions." At the same meeting, Groves had offered as one reason against making several simultaneous atomic strikes the assertion that the "effect would not be sufficiently distinct from our regular Air Force bombing program." Earlier, the Target Committee had been firmly told, in words that hinted almost at a rivalry between the nuclear and incendiary bombers, that the Twentieth Air Force had "the prime purpose in mind of not leaving one stone lying on another." It was "laying waste all the main Japanese cities," and its commanders "do not propose to save some important primary target for us if it interferes with the operation of the war from their point of view." If the atomic bomb had little to add in the way of carnage and rubble except its singular efficiency, attention naturally turned to other dimensions of its novelty.[58]

The apparent similarity between atomic bombing and firebombing caused anxiety as well as uncertainty, a fear that the incendiary attacks would eliminate the virgin targets needed to reveal the true force of the atomic bomb. Sometimes, too, the similarity led to surprising misconceptions. LeMay, treating the atomic operation as an extension of his fire raids, recommended that the bomb be dropped from a low altitude, the same technique he used for showering incendiaries. Paul Tibbets, the commander of the first atomic mission, advised him that "the weapon would destroy a plane using it at an altitude of less than 25,000 feet."[59] It was all too easy for some to see Fat Man and Little Boy as little more than bigger bombs.

Firebombing was a crude standard of reference for measuring the atomic bomb. In retrospect at least, the destructiveness of incendiary attacks invited attention to the bomb's psychological effect and obliterated any perceptible moral difference between bombing in its old and new forms. Like Stimson, many made that claim after the fact. Bush recalled later that he had "felt sure that use of the bomb, far less terrible in my mind than the fire raids on Tokyo, if it brought a quick end to the war, would save more Japanese lives than it snuffed out." Conant's recollections were similar. Byrnes argued that the atomic bombs, for all their casualties, did not cause "nearly so many as there would have been had our air force continued to drop incendiary bombs on Japan's cities."[60]

Yet such arguments rarely entered moral reasoning while the war was still going on. A Monsanto employee, urging the bomb's use, argued that "a more fiendish hell than the inferno of blazing Tokyo is beyond the pale of conception. Then why do we attempt to draw the line of morality here, when it is a question of degree, not a question of kind?" It was a good question from a very obscure project worker whose superiors left little record indicating that they raised it. Indeed, given that most high-level officials comprehended the firebombing so inadequately and indifferently, it could not have served as a point of departure for reasoning about the bomb.[61]

Furthermore, the claim that the atomic bomb saved the Japanese from the horror of continued fire raids was loose indeed, leaving unclear whether Japan was saved from a day's fire raids or a month's or a year's. The calculus of alternative carnage was haphazard. It rested on unprovable assumptions that without use of the bomb the war would have continued for some lengthy period and on confidence—which most of the bomb's managers refrained from claiming they had—that the bomb's use would terminate the war quickly. It also rested on the assumption that without employment of the bomb, the Twentieth Air Force would have inflicted an unending succession of holocausts on the Tokyo model. But March 10 was not a repeatable success. It would have required many dozens of incendiary raids to inflict a death toll comparable to Hiroshima and Nagasaki. To be sure, only a handful of fire raids would have piled up a similar record of destroyed urban acreage but without the same loss of life.

Clearly there was something different about nuclear weapons. The comparisons to firebombing later made to justify use of the atomic bomb revealed the difficulty scientists and politicians had in grasping that difference. Nuclear weapons had peculiar consequences, radiation and fallout, whose insidious and persistent potential the bomb's managers understood poorly. But the bomb's uniqueness lay less in its lethality, either immediate or lasting, than in the certainty of its effects. An incendiary firestorm, its creation so dependent on the vagaries of both man's and nature's behavior, was not predictably repeatable. It also could not erupt without some warning to its victims. It was a kind of planned accident, like "a hole in one in a game of golf," as Freeman Dyson said.

The atomic holocaust was a planned certainty. Of course, no one knew the thing would work until it did, and depending on just how and where it was delivered its effect might be marginally raised or lowered. (Hence the bomb's managers pondered whether surrounding hills might focus the blast or low-level detonation might create radioactive dust or explosion in a rainstorm blanket the surrounding area with fallout.) But once perfected, the thing itself would create its own firestorm: certainty inhered within the device itself, while the incendiary technique carried a cataclysmic potential only in relationship to a host of other circumstances. To be sure, when the planned accident did occur, the horror for its victims approached that visited upon cities hit with the atomic device. As a discrete event, March 10 neatly balanced the scales of cruelty. But in the grim game of air war, it was only a chance event.

The distinction is not just a neat abstraction, for it bore decisively upon any moral equation offered between use of the atomic bomb and continued firebombing. Insofar as the bomb's managers believed they were only choosing between similar forms of destruction, they deluded themselves and subsequent observers. It became commonplace for historians to argue that "in fact the atomic bomb used against Hiroshima was less lethal than massive fire bombing," that the bomb's managers expected it "to be less destructive than the average fire raid," and that "it is hard to see how a long-continued aerial bombardment of Japan would have cost fewer lives than the two atomic bombs."[62]

Something else, more emphatically recognized by its managers, made the atomic bomb different from the apparatus of incendiary warfare. Firebombing was a well-established and nearly perfected technique of war. The weight and efficiency of its use might be marginally raised in days and years to come, but its evolution was substantially complete. The hundreds of thousands of lives bombing took in the war were still commensurate with losses inflicted by more conventional forms of warfare, in the siege of Leningrad, for example, or in the battle for Manila in 1945, where perhaps one hundred thousand civilians died mostly from ground fighting and artillery. In August 1945, the further use of firebombing opened no new vistas, taught the world's powers nothing they did not already know, and led to no new arms race. Atomic warfare was secret and its introduction was likely to speed up a competition for arms carrying grave consequences. And its spread would threaten lives and habitats on a scale dwarfing anything achievable through known means of warfare (except possibly chemical and biological weapons). In political terms, nearly all parties to the bomb's development recognized this; hence the concern with secrecy and the desperate attempts to peer into the future. In moral terms, however, in assessing the presumed equation between the evil of continued firebombing and that of using the new weapon, these considerations either disappeared or were seen as further justification for rushing the weapon into battle.

The legacy of firebombing was not technical, for the atomic bomb still involved a quantum leap in that regard. It lay instead in the ways of thinking about bombing that it perpetuated. The persistent focus on the bomb's visual and psychological effect fell squarely in the long tradition of regarding bombing more as an idea, an "apparition," than as a reality of war. The technology was revolutionary, as the bomb's managers appreciated to a degree, but the perspective was traditional. Imagined as conventional bombing had been, the atomic bomb would smite the enemy and reorder the affairs of man because the very appearance of it, over a city and the globe, would be awesome. As such, it would establish at last the validity of powerful fantasies about the shock value of bombing.

Just how far men went to deny the physical reality of the atomic bomb—and in doing so draw on the legacy of earlier bombing—was evident in their language. Even as nuclear policymakers played down the value of the bomb against military or industrial targets, they labored successfully to convince themselves that indeed those targets were their objective. The Interim Committee's initial formulation, stated by Stimson, was ambiguous enough to satisfy a diversity of consciences. The committee agreed *"that we could not concentrate on a civilian area"* while at the same time the bomb should make as *"profound psychological impression on as many of the inhabitants as possible."* The target should *"be a vital war plant employing a large number of workers and closely surrounded by workers' houses."* It was as if the workers could just watch, and any harm done to them would be incidental or inadvertent.[63]

Stimson, having resolved these ambiguities by ruling out Kyoto as a target, helped Truman to do the same. The two took up the matter of target selection on July 25. Truman later wrote that he "had realized, of course, that an atomic bomb explosion would inflict damage and casualties beyond imagination." At the time, however, he had a more comforting way of looking at the bomb's use. He told Stimson "to use it so that military objectives and soldiers and sailors are the target and not women and children. Even if the Japs are savages, ruthless, merciless and fanatic, we as the leader of the world for the common welfare cannot drop this terrible bomb on the old capital or the new." Truman's diary did not record how he reasoned that avoiding Tokyo and Kyoto constituted sparing women and children. Presumably they lived in other cities as well, though after the war Truman wrote that he had asked Stimson "which cities in Japan were devoted exclusively to war production," as if there were such cities. His memoirs noted Stimson's insistence on Kyoto as "a cultural and religious shrine of the Japanese," and apparently he accepted the familiar equation between a "shrine" and human lives. "The target will be a purely military one," he noted at the time. Furthermore, he found reassurance in the Potsdam ultimatum: by "asking the Japs to surrender and save lives . . . we will have given them the chance" to avert the holocaust. Apparently Churchill saw the ultimatum in much the same light.[64]

After years of bombing cities and after the creation of rationalizations and euphemisms to mask the terror, the distinction between "military target" and "city" had totally collapsed. The attention to Kyoto indicated that the shell of a distinction remained, but not its substance, reflecting less a confrontation with the moral issue than a wish it need not even arise. That failure shaped not only the fact but the manner of the bomb's use. It helps to explain why no serious consideration was given to confining use to a military or industrial target that would have limited civilian casualties while still revealing the awesome power of atomic energy. Such targets were of course few by the summer of 1945, and the bomb was far too powerful for its destruction to be limited to them. But they were ruled out for other reasons, because the bomb's managers wanted to do much more than destroy a target, while the collapse of a meaningful distinction between target and city allowed them to do so under the guise of abiding by the rules of the war.[65] Just as almost all of Tokyo could be regarded as a military target, so could Hiroshima and Nagasaki. Just as workers could be "dehoused" without being killed, they and their leaders could be impressed without being incinerated. Just as it had rarely been clear whether conventional bombing aimed to achieve practical effect against the enemy's war-making power or psychological impact on his "will" to fight, so too was the distinction blurred in rationales for the bomb's use.

Nuclear policymakers also ignored the bomb as a reality of war by drawing upon another tradition of looking at air power: viewing it as a transcendent force offering opposed and mutually exclusive possibilities. It was a commonplace to recognize, as Truman did, that the bomb gave Americans "possession of a weapon that would not only revolutionize war but could alter the course of history and civilization." As Stimson put it, and Marshall concurred, "This project should not be considered simply in terms of military weapons, but as a new relationship of man to the universe." The bomb's advent seemed to offer only two possibilities: it "might even mean the doom of civilization or it might mean the perfection of civilization. . . . It might be a Frankenstein which would eat us up or it might be a project 'by which the peace of the world would be helped in becoming secure.' "[66]

Viewed that way, the bomb's use seemed as compelling as it did revolting. Only "the actual use with its horrible results," Stimson later paraphrased the advice he received from scientists like Conant, could "awaken the world to the necessity of abolishing war altogether." If the bomb promised either deliverance or doomsday, if it loomed as either scourge or savior of mankind, then its psychological awesomeness became all-important, and questions regarding its immediate consequences for Japan's cities seemed almost trivial in comparison. Of course the war had to be won, and no responsible official ignored the bomb's potential in that regard, but it was not about that potential that they worried. Instead, they acted in that tradition of prophecy whereby the most farsighted about air power were the most nearsighted about its actual consequences in war. That predilection, so easily associated with the nuclear dilemma, in fact preceded and helped define it, for it allowed destruction to proceed almost unquestioned, while the moral energies of responsible men remained focused on man's historical fate. Men as diverse as Oppenheimer and Stimson saw immediate employment as necessary if the world were to be forced into a contemplation of the new evil. Even the exercise of concern about that evil played a critical role in allaying doubt, for it proved that they were providing the care and consideration which this awesome new force demanded. "I think we made an impression upon the scientists that we were looking at this like statesmen and not like merely soldiers anxious to win the war at any cost," Stimson noted in his diary.[67]

In their attempt at stewardship and statesmanship, as in their contemplation of the bomb as a weapon of war, men simultaneously derived their categories, assumptions, and language from past experience while failing to make conscious and constructive use of it. They wavered between the temptation to save the world through air power, now in its atomic version, and recognition of the imperative to save the world from it. At times, particularly in Stimson's complex and shifting formulations of the problem, some were tempted to do both. Similarly, in dealing with the Soviet Union, the Interim Committee believed that the United States should "push ahead as fast as possible in production and research to make certain that we stay ahead and at the same time make every effort to better our political relations with Russia."[68] Others more clearly staked out one position or the other, Byrnes becoming the most notable exponent of the virtues of atomic intimidation.

While the choices were posed in familiar terms, discussion proceeded with little reference to the world's recent experience in confronting new military technology. The informal system of deterrents against gas warfare was an encouraging example, the record of the submarine and the bomber disillusioning, and the consequences of interwar agreements on naval arms ambiguous. Neither encouraging, alarming, nor uncertain precedents were reviewed for instruction, even by the few policymakers who had had experience with arms control efforts. When a sense of the past entered into deliberations, other matters were at issue, such as the troubled record of Soviet–American relations. Marshall at least cautioned against disparaging Russian fidelity to wartime agreements and suggested that "it might be desirable to invite two prominent Russian scientists to witness the Trinity test." Even that step seemed too bold for most of the Interim Committee, however.[69]

At bottom, the awesomeness of the new weapon made the past seem irrelevant even as men unconsciously drew upon it. The bomb was seen as severing rather than unfolding familiar patterns in modern technology and international relations. Of course, this was just what many people earlier had thought of air power itself, but that continuity also escaped attention. Thus the bomb lacked reality as a weapon of war and as an instrument of international relations. An "apparition," it could not be placed in the context of the familiar, for that seemed to ignore its awesome power. Yet the familiar guided how men felt and thought about the new weapon.

There was another, even more familiar use of the doomsday-or-deliverance dichotomy. Frightening as it was, the bomb would also liberate the warring nations and perhaps all of mankind from the horror of conventional warfare. Churchill gave this hope particularly vivid expression. An invasion of Japan

> might well require the loss of a million American lives and half that number of British. . . . Now all this nightmare had vanished. . . . We seemed suddenly to have become possessed of a merciful abridgment of the slaughter in the East and of a far happier prospect in Europe. . . . To avert a vast, indefinite butchery, to bring the war to an end, to give peace to the world, to lay healing hands upon its tortured peoples by a manifestation of overwhelming power at the cost of a few explosions, seemed, after all our toils and perils, a miracle of deliverance.[70]

He was echoing the old joy about the rise of air power. No other justification for the bomb's use was more persistent and persuasive.

Of course, arguments for the bomb's use did not go unquestioned. But dissenters showed that they and the advocates usually worked from the same assumptions even as they reached different conclusions about the bomb's use. For both, winning the war was an explicit objective eclipsed by other concerns. Dissenters did raise some questions about the bomb's relationship to the war. The Franck Committee report and the Szilard petition, the most famous pronouncements of dissent, noted briefly how the original justification for the bomb project, fear of Germany's acquisition of the weapon, had been invalidated. O. C. Brewster, an engineer on the gas diffusion project, made the point more emphatic in a letter of May 24 to the president that was brought to Stimson's attention: "So long as the threat of Germany existed we had to proceed with all speed. . . . With the threat of Germany removed we must stop this project." In addition, the efficacy of the bomb against Japan was sometimes questioned, the Franck Committee doubting that "the first available bombs, of comparatively low efficiency and small size, will be sufficient to break the will or ability of Japan to resist, especially given the fact that the major cities like Tokyo, Nagoya, Osaka and Kobe already will largely have been reduced to ashes by the slower process of ordinary aerial bombing." In a sense, this claim involved turning one argument for the bomb's use—the marginal difference between it and conventional weapons—against employment of the atomic device. But most dissenters were too sensitive to their ignorance about the military situation in the Far East and to their lack of responsibility for American lives to press any case that the bomb was unnecessary. Although no dissenter, Oppenheimer aptly characterized the scientists' ignorance: "We didn't know beans about the military situation in Japan" except for being told that "the invasion was inevitable," he recalled in 1954.[71]

Ralph Bard, however, was in the inner councils of nuclear decision making, and as navy under secretary was well acquainted with the war's course. He had assented to the Interim Committee's original recommendation for use against a city without warning, but by June 27 he believed that Japan's leaders "may be searching for some opportunity which they could use as a medium of surrender." He proposed that the triple effects of clarifying the surrender formula, alerting Japan to Russia's likely entry into the war, and issuing a "preliminary warning" to Japan about the bomb might avert the necessity of its use. Those initiatives would preserve America's position "as a great humanitarian nation" and respond to "the fair play attitude of our people." But Bard lacked and apparently did not seek out allies to back him up. By this time, Marshall had deferred to the consensus of the Interim Committee. Bard's superior, Forrestal, was eager to change the surrender formula, but he feared Russian ambitions in the Far East more than the bomb's use. Neither the navy's admirals nor the air force's generals particularly thought the bomb was necessary—tried and true methods soon would win anyway—but by the same token they were not especially opposed to the bomb's employment, as long as invasion was avoided. And the navy, as a latecomer to the bomb project (Bard himself learned of it only in May), lacked the bureaucratic vantage point and intimate familiarity with the bomb to mount an effort against its use. Bard got a hearing from Truman, but it was apparently perfunctory, and shortly thereafter he resigned his post. Like others who questioned the bomb's use, he had been "hammering on locked doors."[72]

Thus the case against the bomb's use mostly fell to men removed from ongoing operations against Japan and was advanced with little reference to the war itself. For most dissenters, the issue was the fate of mankind and their troubled consciences. At times, they seemed more concerned with absolving themselves of responsibility for the bloodbath, although of course absolution might compel efforts to avert the bombing.[73] Their overriding concern was that use, especially without warning, would forever jeopardize global agreement on the control or abolition of the new weapon. In this regard, they did their best to show that national interests were at stake: an unthinking or threatening introduction of the new weapon "will mean a flying start toward an unlimited arms race" in which the United States, though it might win technologically, still would lose. In atomic warfare, the advantage would "lie so heavily with the aggressor" that even an inferior power, appreciating the virtues of a first strike, might launch "a sudden unprovoked blow" or "place his 'infernal machines' in advance in all our major cities and explode them simultaneously." The Franck Committee also argued that if American leaders were willing to run such a race, they would be better off not using the bomb, for use would erode the American advantage by hastening progress in competing nations.[74]

But in their preoccupation with the fate of mankind, dissenters paralleled the advocates in regarding the bomb's decisive quality as its capacity to reorder the affairs of man for good or ill. They recognized the bomb's deadliness, but the fate of Japan became an issue for them only insofar as the bomb's use might act perniciously on the realization of future dreams. In two ways, such an approach yielded vital territory to advocates of use. Downplaying the question of need for the bomb against Japan, it omitted altogether any claim that an atomic attack on a city was inherently evil regardless of long-run consequences, and it avoided portraying what that use would be like. In addition, by basing their argument on long-run consequences, they made it highly speculative. No one could envision those consequences with the certainty that they could predict destructive effects on a Japanese city. Moreover, the dissenters ran into the claim, equally speculative but equally defensible, that only the bomb's use could shock the world into controlling the weapon and war itself.

Only Brewster avoided slighting the immediate in favor of the fateful. For him, too, the paramount evil lay in a speculative future, which he vividly sketched: "The possession of this weapon by any one nation, no matter how benign its intentions, could not be tolerated by other great powers." They would "watch our every move" and regard "everything we did . . . with suspicion and distrust." Any time the United States spoke "we would be charged with threatening to use this weapon as a Club. . . . We would be the most hated and feared nation on earth." The resulting state of mind would crush any hopes for international agreement on atomic weapons, and some day "the spark would be struck that would send the whole world up in one flaming inferno of a third world war."

But Brewster went beyond James Franck and Leo Szilard, who rejected immediate use as setting a bad example but skirted the decision about ending the war. He did not "want to propose anything to jeopardize the war with Japan," but he recognized that victory was no longer the issue, and "horrible as it may seem, I know that it would be better to take greater casualties now in conquering Japan than to bring upon the world the tragedy of unrestrained competitive production of this material." This statement squarely confronted the connection between the immediate and the long-run: the needs of the latter could not be met without short-term sacrifice. Brewster's position probably doomed his appeal, for even superiors straining to fathom the bomb's lasting impact wanted its immediate advantage. But his appeal probably did more to touch Stimson and his colleagues than the cautious documents of Franck, Szilard, and others. In a handwritten note penned on the eve of the Interim Committee's May 31 meeting, Stimson forwarded Brewster's "remarkable document" to Marshall, praising the "logic" of this letter by "an honest man." But however provocative, one letter from an obscure engineer could not carry much weight.[75]

Others had doubts. As Admiral Leahy showed, they could arise from military and technological conservatism. To be sure, Leahy's belittlement of the bomb's feasibility and power meant that the bomb's use was hardly a major issue for him. But after Trinity, and even more after Hiroshima, Leahy reacted sharply, and not only because he thought the navy had already won the war. It was because he placed the bomb in an evolution of modern weaponry he found repugnant, drawing on the same indignation that led him to reject chemical and bacteriological warfare as violations of "every Christian ethic I have ever heard of and all of the known laws of war." In Berlin for the Potsdam Conference, he found himself witnessing "a great world tragedy," a violation of "the civilized laws of war" inflicted by both Allied bombing and Russian artillery. Of course the "civilized laws" had long been violated; even honored, they often allowed great bloodshed. But Leahy properly reflected the sense among some professional officers that modern weaponry had ended war as an honorable fight among men at arms. "'Bomb' is the wrong word to use for this new weapon," Leahy wrote at the end of his memoirs. "It is a poisonous thing that kills people by its deadly radioactive reaction, more than by the explosive force it develops."[76]

Perhaps a similar revulsion led Marshall, after the news of Hiroshima had arrived, to tell Groves and Arnold "his feeling that we should guard against too much gratification over our success, because it undoubtedly involved a large number of Japanese casualties." Groves and Arnold, terribly comfortable with the new technology, pushed aside Marshall's doubts, taking note of "the men who had made the Bataan death march."[77] Marshall and Leahy did not share their interest in revenge. Better than most policymakers, they recognized that the bomb was not an "apparition" making a "psychological" impression or important as only a new device imperiling humanity's future;

it was a military instrument for killing vast numbers of people. There was moral realism in that perspective and political foresight as well, Marshall speaking from experience with how brutal victories complicate the victor's task after war. Those whose perspective on the bomb appeared to be narrowly military were as likely as any to explore restraints on its use, for their military experience led them to recognize the bomb's physical destructiveness. But recognition and cautious exploration were as far as Marshall and Leahy went: their doubts had been too fragile, too wedded to a bygone ethic of warfare, too isolated by their narrow view of the officer's role, and too attenuated by years of urgency to win the war and (in Marshall's case) by personal investment in the bomb project.

Marshall aside, doubt about the bomb's use usually arose when personal investment was weakest. Personal and bureaucratic distance from the Manhattan Project was the necessary precondition, as shown by comparing the passivity among men making the bomb at Los Alamos to the concern among Chicago scientists and with Brewster in Tennessee and by the role that latecomers like Bard and Leahy played. But the distance that made doubt possible also made positive action improbable, for these men were not in a position to change the outcome, and they hesitated to try precisely because of their relative ignorance and lack of final responsibility for decision. Even when they did, the prevailing secrecy, the outright suspicion of disloyalty attached to some dissent, or the adroit deflection of their efforts by Oppenheimer and other officials meant that questioning arguments often did not circulate far.

Eisenhower provided a striking example of how doubt arose outside of normal channels. When he heard about the atomic bomb is unclear, but apparently at the time of Potsdam he learned that an atomic bomb was a weapon in hand. He immediately objected to its use. According to the various accounts of his talk with Stimson, he objected on the grounds that Japan "was already defeated," that the United States "should avoid shocking world opinion" by using the bomb, and that it might prevent a nuclear arms race if (as "I mistakenly had some faint hope") other nations remained "ignorant of the fact that the problem of nuclear fission had been solved." If he also objected against the United States using "something as horrible and destructive as this new weapon," he prefigured the reaction Marshall reported to Groves after Hiroshima.[78]

Marshall and Eisenhower, prestigious mentor and immensely popular protégé, would have formed a powerful alliance against the bomb's employment, even more so if their rival and colleague Douglas MacArthur had joined them.[79] But there is no record of any discussion among the three prior to August 6, and Eisenhower proceeded cautiously. He was not, to be sure, stopped by Stimson's apparently angry reaction to his arguments, for after Trinity he offered the same recommendation to "Truman and other advisors." But Eisenhower regarded his views as "merely personal and immediate reactions; they were not based upon any analysis of the subject." At the height of his fame, Eisenhower was too good an army man to claim authority in a theater of war for which he had no responsibility.[80]

The probability is that more forceful objections would not have changed the outcome. Many reasons have been offered (most at the time, but some more in retrospect) for the atomic attack on Japanese cities: the precedents set by firebombing, the psychological impact of the nuclear bomb, the lives to be saved by quicker termination of the war, the desires for revenge, the assertions of Japanese fanaticism, the need to justify an enormous investment, the technicians' desire to test their creation in the most dramatic way, the alarm that might be felt by the Russians, the supremacy the bomb's use might confer on the United States, and the shock to be given to a war-mad world. Other arguments, about the dangers and impracticality of warnings or demonstration, for example, were more intricate.

Yet it was not as if these many justifications came together to form some critical mass whose force compelled the bomb's use. In the physics of the bomb, the malfunction of one component would prevent formation of a critical mass. But in deliberations about the bomb, the discrediting of one component in the rationale for use would not have disturbed its persuasiveness. Only some shock to an entire system of values would have altered history. There was a parallel to the firebombing. In both cases, the action taken did not hinge on the views or influence of one or a few men or on the persuasiveness of one argument. If one argument was weak, others were mobilized. If, for example, a more convincing case had been presented for the feasibility of a noncombat demonstration of the bomb, it would have changed few minds, partly because men had different reasons for using the bomb and each had several.

Above all, no one at the top regarded the bomb's use as an open question. So much effort had gone into building the bomb, so much virtue was attributed to the perfection of technique, so much energy remained bent toward its perfection rather than its purposes that the matter was effectively closed. The bomb was regarded as horrific as a force in the affairs of humankind and not as a weapon in the current war. Even at that, the bomb's horrific nature remained such a virtue that temptation and loathing could coexist, not in fruitful interplay with each other but in a kind of paralyzing oscillation between hope and fear. Like the bomber had been earlier, the atomic weapon was recognized as a transcendent form of power, only to be conceived and used in the familiar ways.

THE CONUNDRUM OF SURRENDER

Grasping the realities of nuclear and conventional bombs was one challenge over the summer of 1945, but not the only impediment to a successful strategy. A knot of more mundane issues still awaited resolution. If many touched only tangentially on the exercise of air power, in the end they cluttered perception of its use.

The working environment itself was a source of confusion. The issues addressed by the great powers at Potsdam covered a staggering range. Truman also had trouble in guiding his subordinates with a steady hand. His cabinet and inner councils were still in flux, and he was uncertain whom to believe as well as how to act. In policy matters, he veered most wildly on what to expect from and demand of the Soviets. Like Roosevelt, he had a keen eye for public opinion but not the same certainty about how to guide it.

An unsteady guiding hand aggravated confusion about the signals received and sent out by the American government with regard to Japan. From Tokyo they came in clamorous volume, through allies and neutrals, through conventional intelligence methods, and through interception of coded Japanese messages. The latter revealed with particular clarity Japan's desperation to have Moscow mediate an end to the war as well as the coldness of Moscow's response, leaving American intelligence experts with "a mental picture of a spaniel in the presence of a mastiff who also knows where the bone is hidden." Most of all, intercepts outlined the minimum Japan needed to accept surrender, made clear in a July 17 cable by Foreign Minister Togo: "If today America and England were to recognize Japan's honor and existence, they would put an end to the war." It was not hard to see through the euphemisms. "Honor" meant retention of the throne, though whether that meant Hirohito himself was less clear. "Existence" meant that Japan would remain a political entity. Stimson, Marshall, and Grew all roughly grasped what Japan would accept, their interpretation buttressed not only by decoded messages but by a good deal of conventional political analysis. Still, the American intelligence apparatus had gaps; it uncovered much less about what Tokyo's military figures were thinking, except their continued preparation of suicidal methods for resisting an invasion.[81]

The messages Washington sent were at least as confusing as those it received. In the councils of government, Leahy was a blunt, if intermittent, advocate of modifying the surrender formula. But his V-E Day address thundered that "Japan must be beaten into defeat, into unconditional surrender" and invoked memories of Pearl Harbor. On July 31, General Arnold prepared a bellicose speech that struck Stimson as "virtually a new ultimatum to Japan," one that Grew thought would "simply mess up matters and obscure the whole situation." On this occasion at least, the misstep was averted—Grew and Stimson stopped the air force chief.[82]

As in the spring, the timing of messages to Japan proved as vexing as their conflicting substance. Having backed down on sending further signals until Okinawa was conquered, the War Department then discovered new reasons for delay. On June 29, it seemed best to wait until August, when a combination of Russian entry, new air forces on Okinawa, and the bomb would offer the proper psychological moment. That moment kept receding, and placing so much emphasis on finding it made agreement on issuing new signals prey to the conflicting views of several bureaucracies and to intangibles of domestic and enemy public opinion.[83]

In turn, there were problems of audience. Words designed for home front consumption, suited well to placate or instill its belligerence, sent confusing messages to the enemy, even more so when the only way to communicate with Tokyo was through the public word. Of course, the United States might have made a direct approach through diplomatic channels, but the virtues of that method were only belatedly appreciated and pursued, in both Tokyo and Washington. The contradiction of trying to obtain surrender without negotiation persisted.

Therefore any official statement had a dual audience (more, if allies are counted), posing problems that sometimes took on baroque complexity. Messages aimed at home could mislead the Japanese, while messages for Tokyo could disturb Americans. Some messages to Japan were designed only to play at home. The renewed demand for unconditional surrender drafted in the midst of the Okinawa battle was intended to head off any Japanese peace feelers tempting to war-weary Americans. McCloy, the assistant war secretary, recognized the problem in speaking to two audiences: Americans "would properly and promptly resent it if the services seemed to be arguing, without sound reasons, against the possibility of surrender discussions." And while threatening "the extinction of the Japanese people" might please some Americans, "we must not deny the Japanese people all hope," if their suicidal resistance was to be averted. This demand was not issued, but policy on surrender terms remained plagued by the problem of dual audiences. Brigadier General Lincoln, the army's keenest mind on these matters, complained at the end of June that a key State Department official "is trying really only to insure that the terms will *cause no criticism* in the U.S." "Shall we state a flat intention to allow the Japanese to retain the structure of a constitutional monarchy," Lincoln asked, "and tempt the Japanese public, or state the opposite intention and please . . . the US public, or leave the matter vague and impress neither side, probably?" It was a good question, the kind War posed better than State, and an accurate prediction of the course to be taken.[84]

A more subtle problem involving signals, one that bore directly on the bombing campaign, involved the potential for conflict between word and deed. From May to August—in official statements, propaganda, broadcasts, and the shower of leaflets—the United States was trying to suggest that Japan might surrender and still be assured a liberal and humane peace. But even a cursory reading of Japanese statements showed how much the firebombing sent a conflicting message or at least one which the enemy government could use to cry hypocrisy.

Put in slightly different terms, the problem of aligning deeds with words drew some attention, particularly with respect to invasion. It was raised at the June 18 White House meeting and conveyed by Stimson to the president on July 2, when he argued that the proposed ultimatum be "tendered before the actual invasion has occurred and while the impending destruction, though clear beyond peradventure, has not yet reduced her to fanatical despair." In general, however, only lower-level officials spelled out the problem insofar as firebombing raised it. "As greater damage is done to Japanese cities," observed the army's intelligence chief in May, "the Japanese will be more inclined to fanatical resistance to the end." The challenge was to calibrate the infliction of further pain against the need to leave something for the enemy to desire to preserve.[85]

Better recognition in 1945 of how signals could be confused would have raised useful questions about how to proceed with the bombing, how to align it with messages to Japan, and how to interpret Japanese peace feelers. Instead, as Stimson later put it, those feelers "merely stimulated the American leaders in their desire to press home on *all* Japanese leaders the hopelessness of their cause; this was the nature of warmaking. In war, as in a boxing match, it is seldom sound for the stronger combatant to moderate his blows whenever his opponent showed signs of weakening." As Paul Kecskemeti has pointed out, Stimson's reasoning rested on a false analogy: where "the stronger boxer has good reason" to fear his opponent's "lucky blow," at "the terminal stage of war . . . the loser cannot change the strategic outcome," and the victor's task is simply to forestall "superfluous losses." Without a coherent and consistent notion of how to align words and deeds, there was no alternative to ending the war except by the most rapid application of all forms of power against the enemy.[86]

There was a lot of "noise," to use Roberta Wohlstetter's term, in the signals sent out by Washington and flowing into it through its hair-trigger intelligence apparatus. Yet the story of surrender and the atomic bomb was not a kind of Pearl Harbor stood on its head, the Americans now with the upper hand but the perils of bureaucratic confusion the same. Distortions emerged from the swirling signals less because of their sheer volume than because of the predilections of bureaucrats to screen out some signals and emphasize others, on their own initiative or on cue from higher authorities. The confusion about signals reflected disorder in Washington (and in Tokyo as well) about what priorities to pursue.

At issue in the American capital was the relative importance of arresting Soviet influence, securing Moscow's trust, finding solutions to the problem of nuclear weapons, and achieving victory over Japan. Victory itself had different meanings, its virtue measured variously by its speed, its cheapness, or its completeness. To be sure, the various objectives were not necessarily mutually exclusive: quick victory over Japan might deny war's spoils to the Soviets, for example. But the interconnections between objectives were hard to calculate, and pursuing them could complicate as well as clarify matters.

Confusion over what kind and how urgent a victory to achieve over Japan remained the most persistent. The Allies did not pose a major problem in that regard; even Moscow proved pleasantly flexible on the central issue of the emperor's fate.[87] But American public opinion offered vexing guidance. In opinion polls, Americans overwhelmingly preferred the method of victory saving the most American lives even if it resulted in a longer war. But policymakers had to look not only at polls, but at abundant other evidence of intense restlessness to have peace and enjoy its material fruits. Moreover, if Americans wanted quick victory, many appeared reluctant to compromise on objectives whose pursuit might delay it. A third of those polled by Gallup in June wanted Hirohito executed, others hoped to see him imprisoned or exiled. In their very confusion, polls left leeway to policymakers on how to prosecute the war and the peace. But another way to interpret the confusion is that Americans wanted a quick and cheap victory but also a complete one.[88]

Those American leaders who recognized that choices had to be made had done little to prepare Americans to make them. The divergence between the public and private utterances of Leahy was not unique. Grew, the most forceful advocate of an open mind on the emperor's fate, earlier had conjured up visions of a Japan whose fanaticism was almost limitless, whose intent was to invade the United States, whose ambitions were so "overweening" that "even the megalomania of Hitler is surpassed." Privately taking a more textured view, Grew began to offer it publicly in 1944 and 1945. But as late as July 1945, Grew publicly insisted on "unconditional surrender" and dismissed Japanese peace feelers in light of "Pearl Harbor, Wake, Manila." Perhaps he considered public stridency as necessary to protect patriotic credentials and private influence. At no time in his memoirs did he recognize how his public statements encouraged the mood he sought to counter in 1945.[89]

Grew, Stimson, Marshall, and others failed in their efforts to include in the Potsdam declaration a clear assurance to Japan that it could retain the emperor. Even before the Potsdam Conference, Byrnes's State Department watered down the language Stimson and Grew had drafted, validation for Stimson's fear of "the feeling of war passion and hysteria which seizes hold of a nation like ours in the prosecution of such a bitter war." Byrnes also consulted the retired Cordell Hull, who found the assurances "too much like appeasement of Japan." Hull's fears were vague, but like other leaders earlier, he worried that "appeasement" would cause "terrible political repercussions" in the United States and undermine the will of Americans to sustain the costs of invasion.[90]

Hull only told Byrnes, with his keen eye for public opinion, what he wanted to hear. After learning of Hull's position, Grew, Stimson, and Marshall ceased to press their case zealously. Hull, after all, was willing to offer the assurances later, during "the climax of allied bombing and Russia's entry into the war." Though Stimson might have liked those assurances to come earlier, his only binding deadline was the moment of invasion, and Hull's timing accorded with the need to coordinate all forms of leverage against Japan. Besides, when it came to public opinion, Byrnes had Truman's attention. As finally issued—by broadcast rather than through private channels—the Potsdam declaration of July 26 did include a vague promise, salvaged by Marshall, of American withdrawal from Japan when "there has been established in accordance with the freely expressed will of the Japanese people a peacefully inclined and responsible government." Experts in diplomatic code might find buried in that phrasing the assurances Tokyo needed, but in their more explicit form they had been excised.[91]

Since precisely this issue of the emperor's fate held up surrender even after Hiroshima and Russia's entry into the war, until Byrnes and Truman offered firmer assurances, their decision at Potsdam has been widely and rightly condemned as the most tragic blunder in American surrender policy, even by insiders who otherwise supported the bomb's use. There can be no certainty that Japan would have accepted in July what it submitted to in August, but the chance was there, and as Ralph Bard had argued earlier, the risks of pursuing it small. Moreover, the moral risks in the opposite direction, in pursuing an atomic solution before attempting to break the diplomatic impasse, were large. Michael Walzer has explained them persuasively:

> if killing millions (or many thousands) of men and women was militarily necessary for their conquest and overthrow, then it was morally necessary— in order not to kill those people—to settle for something less. . . . If people have a right not to be forced to fight, they also have a right not to be forced to continue fighting beyond the point when the war might justly be concluded. Beyond that point, there can be no supreme emergencies, no arguments about military necessity, no cost-accounting in human lives. To press the war further than that is to re-commit the crime of aggression. In the summer of 1945, the victorious Americans owed the Japanese people an experiment in negotiation. To use the atomic bomb, to kill and terrorize civilians, without even attempting such an experiment, was a double crime.[92]

Of course, the double crime extended beyond use of the atomic bomb. A larger failure in surrender policy had sanctioned the razing of Japan's cities for months.

At bottom, the political question was what kind of Japan the United States wanted when the war was over. Experts debated whether to trust existing elites (minus the more blatant militarists) to make Japan over into a peaceful partner in the postwar order or into an attractive bulwark against the Soviets. They wondered whether to pacify and remold Japan through occupation and tutelage, a task which bombing might complicate, or simply to punish and ravage Japan so that it would never rise again—de Seversky's vision. Even more broadly, the question was whether the American objective was victory or vengeance. To a degree these questions had become moot by the summer of 1945—so far had the destruction gone that vengeance and the obliteration of Japan's war industry were already irreversible. More important, the bureaucracies engaged in answering these questions could not reach a consensus powerful enough to change Truman's mind on the surrender formula or to call into question the further course of bombing.

Even military alternatives were not firmly delineated, a failure most evident in discussions about invasion. The army at least moved to check the more dire predictions floating about. When former President Hoover, among others interested in a compromise on surrender terms, circulated predictions that invasion would take "500,000 to 1,000,000 lives," Marshall's staff dismissed the figure as "entirely too high," one that "appears to deserve little consideration." But the armed services never arrived at a firm figure of their own—nor does it appear they were asked to—and the challenge to Hoover's figure apparently never got passed along to Truman, who had requested a review of Hoover's peace proposal. Though their source remains obscure, casualty estimates similar to Hoover's continued to enjoy credibility. Truman later claimed that Marshall gave him the half-million figure, although records provide no support for the claim, and the dismissal of such a figure by Marshall's staff makes it doubtful. Stimson did not disclose who "informed" him that American casualties alone might exceed one million. Churchill's figures were even more extravagant: a million American dead and half that number of British fatalities. With the documentary record so sparse, it is difficult to determine whether the figures offered by memoirists were inflated after the war to buttress the case for atomic bombing or simply an accurate reflection of the loose calculations prevalent in 1945. Most likely, even a lower or more firmly calculated figure, 100,000 or 300,000 Allied lives lost, still would have seemed to justify the bomb's use. But the fact that policymakers never attempted to calculate firmer figures suggests how loosely they framed their alternatives and how easily they convinced themselves of the bomb's legitimacy as a benign alternative to ground warfare.[93]

Perhaps it is wrong to chastise the Anglo-American leaders for failing to define their alternatives and priorities better. Even before the bomb had been tested, a military aide characterized Truman as feeling that "the U.S. is by far the strongest country in the world and he proposes to take the lead at the coming meeting."[94] Added to the preeminence in so many other ways that the United States held in the summer of 1945, perhaps the atomic bomb made Truman and his advisors believe that no firm choices had to be made about priorities. The bomb would end the war quickly, before the Soviets stole prestige and territory, with minimum loss of American lives and with the assurance of complete power to reshape Japan without compromising on the emperor.

Did such an Olympian temptation guide the Truman administration at the Potsdam Conference? An answer hinges in part on whether Americans thought Russian entry was still "necessary" to win the war, a possibility for which the evidence is complex, ambiguous, and easily misunderstood. For one thing, it was not the successful Trinity test of the bomb that alone changed expectations. The importance attached to Soviet entry had been declining since Yalta: some Japanese armies had already been sent home from the Manchurian frontier, the remainder could no longer be transferred because of the success of the American blockade, and in any event they were now pinned down by the Soviet armies massing on the border; in that respect, Stalin had already met one American objective even without entering the war. Meanwhile, the Americans' seizure of new bases closer to Japan made the Siberian airfields less attractive.

But more important, in Marshall's view the talk of the "necessity" of Soviet entry phrased the issue misleadingly. Victory was no longer at issue, only its costs and duration, and Soviet participation in the war still seemed likely to reduce them, both by the sheer force of arms and by the political shock of its entry. Therefore on July 24, a week after the good news from Trinity, Marshall supported the Combined Chiefs' renewed decision to "encourage Russian entry." He did so in part out of pessimism about Japan's early surrender. In the face of Japanese fanaticism, the Allies' job, as he and Stimson had put it on June 19, was "to coordinate all threats possible to Japan," not to pick and choose among them in a way that might only delay victory. More than that, Marshall was reasoning in a cold-blooded way. The United States had little to lose and much to gain by Moscow's entry, since the Soviets would get what they wanted anyway and might as well pay for it by helping the United States out. As he told Stimson on July 23, "Even if we went ahead in the war without the Russians, and compelled the Japanese to surrender, that would not prevent the Russians from marching into Manchuria anyhow and striking, thus permitting them to get virtually what they wanted in the surrender terms."[95]

Marshall did not speak for everyone. Arnold, for example, later recalled that he and his British counterpart agreed at Potsdam that "our next enemy would be Russia." But any suspicions he had about Moscow did not stop Arnold from welcoming its entry into the war. On July 23, when Stalin restated his intention to enter the war, Arnold's reaction was joyful: "To me, that was good news, because it might mean closer air bases, from which we could literally rip Japan to pieces." Arnold's mind was, as ever, fixed on expanding his operational opportunities. He knew the bomb had been successfully tested, but he did not foresee it as ending the war before the Russians swept in.[96]

Other service leaders, however, may have had such a hope. Even before Trinity, King had insisted that the Russians "were not indispensable," though that was not exactly the issue. His civilian boss, Forrestal, shared similar views. Another navy man, Admiral Leahy, "indulged in a hope that Japan might get out of the war before the Soviet Government came in." None of these men had Marshall's stature or access to Truman, but they had influence. More important were the views of Stimson: "The news from Alamogordo . . . made it clear to the Americans that further diplomatic efforts to bring the Russians into the Pacific war were largely pointless. The bomb as a merely probable weapon had seemed a weak reed on which to rely, but the bomb as a colossal reality was very different." Stimson, caught between the perils and temptations of nuclear diplomacy, did not follow the consistent line this passage from his memoirs might suggest. But the hope, which Stimson also attributed to Truman, was likely there.[97]

It burned with much more clarity in the mind of the new secretary of state, Jimmy Byrnes, a man almost desperate to deny the Russians the concessions in the Far East made at Yalta, which he found acutely embarrassing in light of his service to Roosevelt at the time. The possibility of using the bomb to crowd Stalin out of the war sent Churchill into bellicose ecstasy, although his military chiefs were more cautious. The exhausted and erratic prime minister did not always impress or get his way with Truman. He certainly made his views known.[98]

Nonetheless, at the time and afterward, Truman revealed better than anyone else how difficult it was to fix the possibility that loomed so temptingly. On July 17, after the first sparse message on Trinity had already arrived, Truman recorded good news from Stalin. "He'll be in the Jap War on August 15. Fini Japs when that comes about." But the next day he was convinced that the "Japs will fold up before Russia comes in. I am sure they will when Manhattan appears over their homeland." In the interim, Truman had gotten further details on the Trinity success which may have accounted for his change of mood. In the following days, others repeatedly took note of the confidence Truman now expressed as a result of the successful test.[99]

But consistency was not Truman's virtue. A more surefooted leader might have seized the moment and mobilized his government behind a strategy to preempt Soviet entry. Truman was unsure what to believe. On the eighteenth, despite the excitement over "Manhattan" recorded that day in his diary, he wrote his wife strongly implying that he still desired Russia's entry: "I've gotten what I came for—Stalin goes to war August 15 with no strings on it. . . . I'll say that we'll end the war a year sooner now, and think of the kids who won't be killed! That is the important thing." Six months later, Truman recalled that at Potsdam "we were anxious for Russian entry," just as his memoirs stated that as of July 24 "Churchill was as anxious as I was for the Russians to come into the Japanese war." In turn, Churchill, despite his expressed confidence in a quick, atomic victory, still doubted that Japan would surrender if the terms remained unconditional. In any event, Churchill, defeated in elections at home, had to leave Potsdam, and his successor, Clement Attlee, apparently harbored no hope that the bomb would end the war before Russian entry.[100]

Truman's uncertainty came out in other ways. On the twenty-third, Stimson noted, the president was still "very anxious to know whether Marshall felt that we needed the Russians in the war or whether we could get along without them." Via Stimson's oversimplification of Marshall's views, Truman got the assurance he wanted, but his query alone suggested that his newfound confidence was shaky. Certainly any desire to delay Russian entry was compromised when Truman informed Stalin, if only with euphemisms, of America's possession of its new weapon; if Stalin understood Truman's message, it would only have prompted him to order his armies to march sooner.[101]

Most likely, Truman *wanted* to believe that Trinity eliminated his problems and made all objectives obtainable, and some advisors, most often Byrnes, backed him up in that hope. But Truman was still too untutored in war, too dependent on the counsel of military advisors, too erratic in his own outlook to sustain his hope about the bomb. In turn, Marshall, Arnold, Leahy, and other military advisors—for different reasons but with the same results—still could not promise that the thing would even work in battle, much less that it would end the war before the Russians came in, especially since only two bombs would be ready for immediate use. Indeed, when it occurred, "the abrupt surrender of Japan came more or less as a surprise" to Arnold, the advocate of air power, and the technicians were still busy preparing to deliver more nuclear bombs on Japanese cities.[102]

Without a doubt, questions about Russian behavior and the bomb's advent strongly colored American deliberations in July about the Pacific war. They had a decisive influence on all sorts of peripheral issues. They did not appreciably change decisions on matters of central importance: the content and release date of the Potsdam declaration and the course and timing of bombing operations, incendiary and nuclear.

The Americans certainly would have been pleased to end the war without Stalin's help. After so much expenditure of American blood and treasure, they hardly wanted to share the glory. Hence Truman summarily rejected Moscow's request for the Allies publicly to invite Russia into the war; it looked bad to appear needful of Russian help, even if the United States still was. [103] But the desire to monopolize bragging rights hardly reflected only an incipient cold war, for it kept showing up, sometimes in an even less gracious form, in American treatment of the British. Instead it indicated the search for glory that all great powers engaged in, the quest for an elusive kind of influence that solitary triumph might provide as well as the pride of military services determined to finish on their own what they had been doing so long. Like other temptations, it was hard to translate into consistent policy.

The best argument that attitudes toward the Soviet Union and the new weapon affected American surrender strategy has to do with what was not done. Here the issue is not the failure to offer assurance regarding the emperor; that had little to do with Soviet–American relations. But there was another possibility. Given the importance some Americans attached to Russian entry—in Marshall's words of June, it might be "the decisive action levering them into capitulation at that time or shortly thereafter if we land in Japan"—and given as well the evidence that Tokyo regarded Russia as its last hope in securing a negotiated peace, might the Americans have encouraged Stalin to sign on to the Potsdam declaration? Or might they have held off on using the atomic bomb just the few days needed to suggest the effect upon Japan of Russian action? In his diary on July 17, Truman himself had predicted "Fini Japs" when Stalin entered the war: damning evidence against his later claim that he thought use of the bomb necessary to avert a horrible invasion. [104]

The very silence of memoirists on these critical possibilities as well as on the role Russia in the end played in securing surrender suggests that they did not want them explored. The risks of delaying the bomb's use would have been small—not the thousands of casualties expected of invasion but only a few days or weeks of relatively routine operations. Moreover, there were foreseeable rewards in delaying a short time: buttressing the case for using the bomb if use became necessary. And no American strategist had suggested particular advantage—in terms of beating Japan—in having the bombs go off before Stalin's armies marched; the coordinated threats might follow any of several possible sequences.

The strong possibility exists that few American leaders wanted to wait. Perhaps they felt that immediate use of the bomb was justified because no one could be sure of when Stalin would enter until he did so, but the second atomic attack on Nagasaki *after* Russian entry suggests that assurance on this score would have made little difference. They resisted delay less because they thought they could keep Stalin from grabbing what he wanted (he would grab no matter what the timetable) than because they wished to limit the Russian claim to a role in securing Japan's defeat.

Even that explanation of American behavior is incomplete, however. Had preemption of Russian entry been an overriding objective, Truman and his aides would have more willingly pursued the assurances on the throne and hesitated less about them in the final moment. Even men who shared similar suspicions of Soviet ambitions—Grew and Byrnes are the most notable examples—could not agree about the content of American messages to Japan. Timing the bomb's use to come after Soviet entry was not rejected late in July, but rather it was never seriously considered before then. The timing of the bomb's use always had been dictated by operational considerations— when it was ready—irrespective of other threats to Japan that might be applied. Moreover, just as no one could predict that the bomb would end the war quickly, no one could be certain that Russian entry would do so. Even Marshall had hedged his bets: it would be "decisive . . . at that time or shortly thereafter if we land in Japan." In that climate of uncertainty, it seemed to make little sense to delay on either option, atomic bombing or Russian intervention. And there were palpable risks in forestalling the latter. If then the bomb failed quickly to win the war and if word later leaked out that the war had been prolonged because Americans delayed Russian entry—all this allowing the Russians off the hook and American boys to die in their place—American leaders could have been deeply embarrassed. Sen. Alexander Wiley had made quite clear on July 25 the feeling at home that "countless American lives are at stake in Russia's decisions." Out in the Pacific, MacArthur, belatedly informed of the bomb, told reporters Russian entry was "welcome" for just the same reason: "Every Russian killed was one less American who had to be."[105]

To enter the most speculative realm, it seems likely that even had Russian entry been greeted with open arms, rather than accepted as a painful aid and inevitability, the bomb would have been used on the same timetable. Given the momentum to use the bomb and end the war quickly, the appropriate rationale for the quickest employment could have been assembled: would not the Russian allies themselves be pleased by any action reducing their losses? In the event, Stalin, on hearing from Truman of America's "new weapon of unusual destructive force," did express the hope "we would make 'good use of it against the Japanese.'" The point again is that a different course was not so much rejected as never seriously pondered; its implementation would have required a painful reversal of momentum already deeply established, by an administration whose untidy methods (it took months simply to hammer out the wording of the Potsdam declaration) make it foolish to think it could have abruptly reversed years of interest in bringing Moscow into the Pacific war.[106]

The temptation to regard the bomb as eliminating hard choices among priorities could not become an operating policy in a few weeks. Resistance to making hard choices preceded the bomb's arrival, which at most simply made more tolerable the prevailing confusion. Confusion arose out of uncertainty about America's purposes in the war, out of the disorderly processes of policy, and out of Truman's understandable difficulty in mastering the machinery designed to help him set a course. It also grew out of a long-standing view of air power as a weapon capable of fulfilling so many purposes that hard choices and precise rationales for its use did not seem necessary. In turn, the confusion about methods and goals in achieving Japan's surrender helped men to make decisions without full consciousness of their consequences. Therein lay the tragedy of American policy over the summer of 1945, more than in the specific failure to risk assurances to Japan necessary to secure surrender. American leaders bore a heavy responsibility, and none treated it cavalierly. But war's momentum and confusion, combined with air power's inviting ease and multiple attractions, allowed responsibility to be exercised in decisions whose consequences, for the war and for mankind, were not firmly addressed.

After the war, Truman took full responsibility for ordering atomic bombs to be dropped on Japanese cities. His claim has diminished upon inspection, even of some of the statements Truman himself later made. "The final decision of where and when to use the atomic bomb was up to me. Let there be no mistake about it," Truman later wrote in his memoirs: he decided "where" and "when," not whether to bomb. There was no soul-searching moment when his hand trembled above an order he had to sign. The order to Spaatz for the Twentieth Air Force to "deliver its first special bomb" was dated July 24, citing the explicit "approval of the Secretary of War and the Chief of Staff," and was confirmed on July 25 by Marshall and Stimson in communication between Potsdam and War Department headquarters in Washington. It was signed by General Thomas T. Handy, Marshall's acting chief of staff in Washington. Truman probably gave verbal approval for the order, but he signed nothing. Whether he confirmed the order either verbally or in writing after Japan's response to the Potsdam declaration is doubtful. As Groves recalled the handling of final orders, "I didn't have to have the President press the button on this affair."[107]

To quibble over the technicalities of orders and of Truman's later claims about them may miss the essential point: he did decide that the bomb should be used. Yet the technicalities confirm the truth of Groves's characterization of Truman's role. The burden of decision "fell upon President Truman." Nevertheless, "as far as I was concerned, his decision was one of noninterference—basically, a decision not to upset the existing plans."[108] And if the technicalities made no difference in the outcome, they showed how the outcome could be made more acceptable. Decisions had to be made, yet if no final orders had to be signed, they could be made incrementally and felt to flow from the logic of events. Hamburg, Dresden, Tokyo, and countless other cities had been destroyed without the signed orders of prime minister or president. It was fitting that they were also not required for Hiroshima or Nagasaki.

TRANSCENDENCE AND CONTINUITY

The Japanese government rejected the Potsdam ultimatum, in part for reasons mirroring its enemy's concerns. As in Washington, the public image of messages had to be weighed carefully when the medium was the airwaves. Accordingly, the government censored the ultimatum, leaving bellicose passages intact and deleting phrases that might tempt the Japanese into thinking that peace could come on tolerable terms, though broadcasts and leaflets from the American side released the full text.

Tokyo's reaction to the proclamation also revealed how serious was the American problem of coordinating words and deeds. The Allies had threatened "prompt and utter destruction," but, as Tokyo's thinking has been described, "Japan had already been visited with nearly utter destruction. . . . How, the Big Six wondered, could devastation be made more prompt or utter?" American bombing had gone so far that the threat of its continuance was losing its credibility, and Japan had no reason to suspect something more.

There was also the problem of what would happen to Japan after surrender. If Washington had reached no clear consensus on this matter, Tokyo could not divine it on its own. There were teasing phrases: "unconditional surrender" was limited to Japan's armed forces, not explicitly extended to its government or its dynasty; the "freely expressed will of the Japanese people" to choose their own government was granted under certain conditions. Moreover, the Soviet Union had not signed the proclamation. But none of these signs pointed clearly to the value or necessity of Tokyo's immediate acceptance. Without a Russian signature, time to maneuver still seemed to remain. If the Allies did not declare they would abolish the throne, they did not say they would preserve it. And if they regarded Hirohito as one of those "war criminals" to whom they promised "stern justice," would there be an emperor left whom the "freely expressed will" could enthrone?

In face of conflicting pressures and signals, the government's response to Potsdam was one of caution and delay. Suzuki's famous response to the Potsdam declaration contained the word "mokusatsu," a term subject to various translations ("to kill with silence" or "to ignore") none of which was likely to deflect the Americans from their path.[109]

So preparations to deliver the bomb went forward. For the scientists and officers responsible for its development, the decisive moment had already come in New Mexico on July 16 when the plutonium bomb was tested (no test of the uranium bomb was deemed necessary before its use). They knew then they had captured the power of the gods, knew it when they heard the "awesome roar which warned of doomsday and made us feel that we puny things were blasphemous to dare tamper with the forces heretofore reserved to The Almighty." They knew it when they saw a fireball that "closely resembled a rising sun," when they created "a searing light with the intensity many times that of the midday sun," when they transformed the desert "from darkness to brilliant sunshine in an instant." Even the unsentimental Groves felt a "profound awe." Almost rhapsodic recollections of the moment spoke of an ultimate experience: the fireball "lighted every peak, crevasse and ridge of the nearby mountain range with a clarity and beauty that cannot be described but must be seen to be imagined. It was that beauty the great poets dream about but describe most poorly and inadequately."[110]

A sense of "profound responsibility" arose in the men who witnessed "the birth of a new age." Brigadier General Thomas Farrell recorded the "feeling . . . that those concerned with its [the bomb's] nativity should dedicate their lives to the mission that it would always be used for good and never for evil." Ernest Lawrence noticed a similar mood, "a kind of solemnity in everyone's behavior" and "a hushed murmuring bordering on reverence." No less moved, other scientists found the event "a foul and awesome display," prompting Kenneth Bainbridge's comment to Oppenheimer, "Now we are all sons of bitches."[111]

Each man felt sin, shame, ecstasy, and triumph in his own peculiar combination. Few related those feelings to the bomb's imminent use against Japan or recorded much imagination about how the bomb would function as a weapon of war. To be sure, the explosive power of the bomb was carefully checked, and the experts warned that in use against Japan, detonation near ground level would smother the blast with its own radioactivity and suck up material returning to earth as fallout, complicating the safety of occupying personnel and leaving the United States open to charges of practicing chemical warfare.[112]

Groves and his staff also extrapolated from the test new calculations on what would happen to a city (without mentioning the word) when struck by a blast whose "light will be as bright as a thousand suns." But these calculations were a technical exercise, their tone consistent with the perfunctory and obligatory nature of the comments made about the immediate task ahead after Trinity. Farrell set down the "feeling that no matter what else might happen, we now had the means to insure its [the war's] speedy conclusion and save thousands of American lives." Groves too was "fully conscious that our real goal is still before us. The battle test is what counts in the war with Japan." Yet that test elicited little comment. For most men at Trinity, even for Groves, there was a sense that the "real goal" had already been met. The dominant reaction was enormous relief that the thing had worked, that the huge investment of resources and reputations had been validated, and that the promise of mastery had been fulfilled. If men felt like sons of bitches, it was for creating an instrument of "doomsday" and imperiling "the future of humanity." There were awesome responsibilities to be acted upon in the years to come, but not in the days to come. Though no one would have quite put it this way, there seemed to be, in the face of responsibilities stretching almost to eternity, something almost trivial in the use of the first crude gadget against Japan—a kind of horrid little footnote to the much more grand and grim task of managing the fate of humanity. Earlier, some scientists had argued for the bomb's use as necessary to foster the world's appreciation of the new force. Unknowingly, they had described their own need as well. Between Trinity and Hiroshima, the bomb remained to them a kind of awesome abstraction, now tested to be sure, but not yet imaginable as a weapon of war.[113]

For the bomb's managers, the three weeks after Trinity were tense but essentially routine. With Kyoto dropped, Hiroshima, Nagasaki, Kokura, and Niigata remained as designated targets. The only restatement of the rationale for targeting rehashed old reasoning about psychological effect: "All four cities are believed to contain large numbers of key Japanese industrialists and political figures who have sought refuge from major destroyed cities."[114] Given Japan's response to the Potsdam ultimatum, policy was no longer at issue. Spaatz, Groves, and Stimson did worry about new evidence of POW camps near Nagasaki but did not scratch the city from the target list.

Fortunately, the most likely first target, Hiroshima, seemed to have no POW camps, though as it turned out some Allied POWs died in both cities.[115] Otherwise, when not attending to last-minute technical details, the bomb's managers worked on public relations. They honed the statements to be released when the bomb had been used and cleared away last-minute objections to disclosure of certain scientific information on the bomb. The various proposals and petitions about the bomb's use from the scientific community inched their way through the bureaucracy, reaching the White House too late to influence Truman. Then the managers and their president waited.

On the morning of August 6 (still August 5 in Washington), the untested uranium bomb exploded over Hiroshima, and on August 9, after the aircrew diverted from its primary target, the plutonium bomb struck Nagasaki. At last the overstrained bomber crews could experience the relief that scientists and other officers had enjoyed on July 16. What they had seen was a macabre variation on six macabre years of aerial warfare, as if a film of all that had happened had been rewound and suddenly replayed in an instant. The results both confirmed and mocked the facile comparisons made then and later between incendiary and atomic bombing. Blast and fire killed tens of thousands, as they had at Hamburg and Tokyo, but there were also the special victims of radiation poisoning. Rain fell after the atomic firestorms, as it often had after incendiary raids, but it was a black rain carrying a deadly residue of fallout. The aiming point of the Hiroshima bomb—the Aioi bridge—perversely survived the attack, as other nominal targets had survived other bombing raids, but this time inaccuracy made little difference.[116] Like countless others, two cities had been destroyed, but in seconds rather than hours or days. On August 6 and August 9, and in the stream of deaths that has continued since, a minimum of one hundred thousand and more likely over two hundred thousand Japanese died.[117]

The psychic scars that survivors carried were in many ways similar to those which Germans in Dresden or countrymen in Tokyo had suffered. Many reacted like the Nagasaki victim who felt "no bitterness against the Americans. He would rather blame the Japanese government for prolonging the war."[118] A minority did feel bitter, of course, just as in Tokyo, and as always there were subtle variations among individuals and groups and over time. As earlier, there were also many for whom accusation seemed pointless. What decisively distinguished the atomic bomb survivors was their reactions in the months and years to follow. Knowledge of the long-term lethality of radiation, of their special place in the inauguration of nuclear technology, and of the special attention given them fed a lasting sense of experiencing a life-ending trauma with global implications. Before 1945 it had been possible to see in air war the potential for global destruction, but survivors of Hamburg or Tokyo rarely connected the extinction of their cities with the fate of the species. For atomic bomb victims, that connection became indissoluble.[119]

That implication, however, like many others of the atomic attacks, was not immediately apparent, either in Japan or in the United States, where people struggled to grasp or to ignore what distinguished these two cataclysms from the war's other horrors. Even among men knowledgeable about the bomb in advance of its use, news of Hiroshima produced no quick conviction that they might now halt the making of war. On the eighth, Marshall angrily cabled Spaatz about the "incalculable harm" he and LeMay had done to the army by making public statements "that our present Army is not necessary for the further prosecution of the war in the Pacific," that "invasion will be unnecessary, and that the future of Armies has been decidedly curtailed." Stimson also caught the mood of uncertainty persisting even after Stalin's armies rolled. "The bomb and the entrance of the Russians into the war"—notably enough, he put the two on equal footing—"will certainly have an effect on hastening the victory. But just how much effect is on how long and how many men we will have to keep to accomplish that victory, it is impossible to determine." From his vantage point in the Pacific, MacArthur still insisted on going forward with the planned invasion of Japan. "In my opinion, there should not be the slightest thought of changing the OLYMPIC operation." In a long-run perspective, perhaps these three pillars of the army were not so shortsighted as they might appear; the bomb did not sound the death knell of the foot soldier so readily as many Americans rushed to believe. It is only fair to add that army generals, far from feeling cheated out of the glory of invasion, could feel great relief that it did not have to take place. But the acerbic comment Haywood Hansell later made was also appropriate: "The atomic bomb was needed not only to convince the Japanese that further resistance was futile," but to "save the Army from its obsession with invasion."[120]

Yet the air force was scarcely more capable of reversing course in light of the new developments. Both Spaatz and General Farrell wanted a third atomic bomb to be dropped on Tokyo, although on August 10, when news came of the Japanese response to the Potsdam declaration, Spaatz was uneasy about further area bombing; halting it, he sparked erroneous reports of an American cease-fire. But final settlement of the surrender terms was delayed until the fourteenth, and in the meantime, as the official history puts it, "Arnold wanted as big a finale as possible." He got it on the fourteenth, when 1,014 aircraft, including 828 B-29s, sortied against Japan. Combat flights then ceased, although Spaatz ordered a "display of air power" to continue until the surrender was signed, ostensibly to remind the Japanese die-hards that they had lost the war.[121]

Most of these operations after the tenth were public relations, not strategy. The public relations officers instantly recognized that the atomic bomb story was the biggest of the war, "giving Army Air Forces vast prestige," but they also feared that in the public relations "rat race," the navy was "having the edge." They maneuvered and pleaded to make sure "our Air correspondents go in on the first phase of this occupation, comic opera that it is"; to "get our gang onto the Missouri to witness the signing of the surrender"; and to seize some "Japanese bigshots who might give us the right kind of quotations for publication about what bombing did to win the war." The "whole damn thing from now on is politics and publicity," and it was time the generals realized that "effective public relations is never an immaculate conception—it's generally rape and always at least vigorous courtship." Neither Arnold nor LeMay needed persuasion on that score, and it must have been gratifying that as the surrender was signed, 426 B-29s circled overhead, parading the triumph of "Victory Through Air Power" just as "Caesar's legionnaires had paraded theirs in Rome when the short sword was queen of the battlefield."[122]

Other matters of public image were at stake in the waning days of the war. The AAF's public relations experts were also furious about MacArthur's attempts to convince the press "that the Nips were 'sincere and honest and trying to be helpful'" regarding surrender arrangements. The airmen found "great danger in all this for us," fearing that sympathy for the Japanese would "make the announcement of Jap civilian casualties turn against the Air Force. Make us look like barbarians, the Jap govt an injured, innocent body of harmless little brown men." LeMay was told it was urgent for the air force to release its own version of the casualty figures "at the right time. And the right time is after I've collected some atrocity stories about what Japs did to our B-29 crews when they were shot down."[123]

A "wave of sympathy" for the Japanese also troubled General Groves. Twice on August 25 he talked with Lieutenant Colonel Rea at the Oak Ridge Hospital regarding Radio Tokyo's broadcast about Hiroshima's victims. "'Now it is peopled by [a] ghost parade,'" Groves quoted from the broadcast, "'the living doomed to die of radioactivity burns.'" Since these reports were being picked up by the American media, Groves was angry and incredulous. He thought he had solved the problem of radioactivity by avoiding a ground burst of the bombs, so he blamed "a good dose of propaganda" on the "idiotic performance" of American scientists and the media's exploitation of sensational news. Rea offered reassurance: "The thing is these people got good and burned—good thermal burns." As at Tokyo, many indeed had such burns, but many also suffered from radiation burns and sickness. Neither Rea nor Groves could believe it. Rea thought "there's something hookum" about Japanese claims of grossly abnormal blood counts and told Groves "you had better get the anti-propagandists out." Groves also worried about stories on radiation sickness suggesting that the bomb's managers knew or should have known what would happen when the bomb was used. "Is there any difference between Japanese blood and others?" Groves asked in searching for an explanation for altered blood counts. "It seems to be pretty standard," Rea replied unhelpfully. So instrumental in building the atomic bomb, Groves was still trying hard to regard it as just a bigger version of conventional weapons.[124]

The point man on these troublesome matters, Groves could not entirely ignore them. Others responsible for the bomb, however, often sustained the reticence that had characterized their response both to firebombing and to the Trinity test. They appreciated the use of the bomb as a political and psychological event. But as physical phenomena, Hiroshima and Nagasaki elicited little comment from them. In their memoirs, James Conant and even more so Vannevar Bush hurried past this aspect of atomic bombs and indeed the entire story of their development. The official history of the bomb project suggests that their memoirs faithfully reflected their priorities in

August and September: "Because they had lived for more than four years with the quest for the bomb and knew of its effects at Alamogordo, they were not, like most people, stunned by the news from Japan." For Bush and Conant, "the psychological impact lay rather in the shattering of the little world of secrecy in which they had so long been confined." They were swept up in dealing with the political remifications of public knowledge of atomic energy. Like them, many scientists also experienced a "feeling of emancipation" at the end of years of secrecy imposed on them, their families, their entire lives. One physicist, although "shocked by the effect our weapon had produced," later still had to "confess that our relief was really greater than our horror. For at last our families and friends in other cities and countries knew why we had disappeared for years on end. . . . We ourselves also learned that our work had not been in vain." Another man, responsible for fashioning the plutonium bomb, recalled being "desperately anxious to find out . . . whether its intricate mechanism would work. These were dreadful thoughts, I know, and still I could not help having them." In the face of these emotions, there was little time or inclination to ponder what in human terms had happened in Japan.[125]

For the scientists, part of the problem in confronting the bomb lay in their ignorance of the effects of radiation. It took time to absorb the new knowledge gained from Hiroshima and Nagasaki and courage to admit its implications. Zuckerman later recalled a conversation with "the great Theo von Karman" shortly after the war's end:

> "If you had been one of the dead," he asked, "would it have made any difference to you whether you were incinerated in Hamburg or in Hiroshima?" He seemed to think not. It was the means of destruction, of death, on which all discussion focused in those days. Some of the scientists concerned in the development of "the bomb" may have known about the biological effects of radioactivity, but if they did, these were secondary considerations at the time. What mattered was the enormous explosive and thermal power of "the bomb."

Some scientists did respond with special alarm to the peculiar effects von Karman wanted to overlook. Furthermore, even among some of those accepting of the bomb's use, news of its employment against Nagasaki so quickly after its first application triggered special doubt and revulsion. These reactions, though by no means universal, helped mobilize their aggressive entry into many aspects of postwar nuclear policy. Not surprisingly, their inclination was to grapple with future dangers rather than dwell on recent realities or engage in "brooding about the tragedy of using science for destructive purposes," as one of their chroniclers put it.[126]

The new realities of air war, like the old ones, remained inexpressible or unimportant to other leaders as well. British politicians who had had a hand in the bomb had left office prior to Hiroshima after their election defeat. Perhaps that is why their memoirs said so little about the atomic attacks; Churchill's own account ended on July 26. Attlee may have had a more troubled reaction, but he later claimed that he, Churchill, and

Truman did not know that nuclear explosions differed from the conventional weapons, except in their "much greater explosive force." If scientists shielded themselves from understanding the novel lethality of atomic weapons, surely the politicians could have done so with greater ease.[127]

Reticence also characterized American leaders. To nearly all, of course, the bomb's advent raised important problems. In the armed services, the race was on to grasp the implications of atomic energy for the size and missions of the contesting parties. Within a few weeks of Hiroshima, active imaginations in the air force were proposing that the United States operate "a world wide police system . . . to prevent the manufacture of atomic bombs," complete with orbiting satellites for spying, moon-based rockets with nuclear warheads, and computer guidance controls.[128] At State, Byrnes immediately plunged into an experiment in nuclear diplomacy with the Soviets that quickly failed. Few had much to say about Hiroshima and Nagasaki. In the air force, Arnold and LeMay were unrepentant. Though not inclined to think the bomb necessary for winning the war, they were content in its use even if it had shortened the war only by a few days, and they embraced its entry into the American arsenal.

In the Pentagon, the most deeply worried man was Stimson. He never expressed regret about the bomb's use, although he did about the failure to issue assurances on the emperor. Yet he had long pondered the implications of nuclear energy, and in the knowledge of imminent retirement he cleared his agenda of other matters and focused on the nuclear question. Too, the results from Hiroshima and Nagasaki, which Stimson received in great detail, must have at last undercut his illusions about the air force's targeting. On the eighth, he noted how Truman "mentioned the terrible responsibility that such destruction placed upon us here," and his statements to the press on the bomb, in contrast to the prideful style of the president, stressed that "any satisfaction we may feel must be overshadowed by deeper emotions. The result of the bomb is so terrific that the responsibility of its possession and its use must weigh heavily on our minds and on our hearts."[129]

Looking forward instead of backward, Stimson betrayed his change of mood only indirectly, first as he tried to clear away the remaining obstacles to the war's quick termination. On the eighth he told Truman, " 'When you punish your dog you don't keep souring on him all day after the punishment is over; if you want to keep his affection, punishment takes care of itself." The Japanese "are a smiling people and we have to get on those terms with them." The comment was flavored with Stimson's genteel, unselfconscious racism, and ostensibly it related to Japan's treatment after surrender. But it was also a far cry from the boxing metaphor he used to describe his justification in July for the bomb's use, implying a recognition of the helplessness of a nation whose punishment Stimson had so recently accepted. Now he wanted further bombing halted.[130]

Stimson was also moving toward his eloquent plea to Truman and the cabinet in September for an agreement with the Soviet Union about sharing and controlling the secrets of atomic energy. The agreement should be made, he contended, even if it meant speedier Soviet acquisition of the bomb technology, which Stimson regarded as inevitable within five years in any event. Only concessions and mutual trust could produce the agreement, and it had to be a bargain "that has some chance of being kept and saving civilization not for five or for twenty years, but forever." It was Stimson's finest hour, though his eloquence went unheeded. As with most of the protesting scientists before Hiroshima and with Eisenhower in July, the distance from power that provided Stimson perspective also limited his persuasiveness and influence.[131]

Truman's own reactions to the bomb's use are less clear. He lacked Stimson's capacity for productive doubt, and his brittle defensiveness yielded a stream of contradictory reactions. His initial comment, made to the men of the *Augusta,* was an ill-chosen remark: "This is the greatest thing in history." Once in Washington, he may have momentarily flinched at what he had done. As Secretary of Commerce Henry Wallace recorded the August 10 cabinet meeting: "Truman said he had given orders to stop atomic bombing [no third bomb would be ready for several days anyway]. He said the thought of wiping out another 100,000 people was too horrible. He didn't like the idea of killing, as he said, 'all those kids.' " Whatever doubt he felt on the tenth, he kept it mostly at bay thereafter. "Nobody is more disturbed over the use of Atomic bombs than I am," he wrote in a letter on the eleventh, but then argued the case for retribution: "When you have to deal with a beast you have to treat him as a beast." "It was a terrible decision," he acknowledged later, but then he insisted he had experienced not the slightest hesitation in making it or the slightest doubt about the legitimacy of the targets.[132]

To complicate matters further, his initial public statements were scarcely more his than the decision to use the bomb. They had been substantially worked up in advance by others. But taken together, they neatly parroted the war's diverse and conflicting rationales for air power, with added references to how "Providence" had denied the Germans the bomb. There was unvarnished pride in Anglo-American expertise, which had produced "the greatest achievement of organized science in history." At the same time, there was almost a profession of helpless inevitability to the bomb's use, as if no intent had been felt to create something so destructive. "Having found the bomb we have used it," though of course the bomb was hardly just "found." There was the overt rationale of using the bomb to end the war, Truman promising a further "rain of ruin from the air, the like of which has never been on this earth" if Japan did not surrender. At the same time, there was a scarcely veiled agenda of retribution, as if Hiroshima were the moral equivalent of Japanese misdeeds: "The Japanese began the war from the air at Pearl Harbor. They have been repaid many-fold." As if to drive that point home, on the ninth Truman reminded a radio audience that the Japanese "have starved and beaten and executed American prisoners of war" and "abandoned all pretense of obeying international laws of warfare."[133]

Finally, there was one more statement of the tortured distinctions about target selection that had filled the war years. "We are now prepared to obliterate more rapidly and completely every productive enterprise the Japanese have above ground in any city," as if that could be done without destroying the city itself. "We shall destroy their docks, their factories and their communications." The Japanese government promptly picked up on these words and tossed them back to point out the obvious: "It is technically impossible to limit the effect of its use to special objectives such as designated by President Truman, and the American authorities are perfectly aware of this." To that and succeeding Japanese charges of war atrocities, the American government did not reply, though they were implicitly validated in Truman's own talk of a "rain of ruin" and later his warning that "unfortunately, thousands of civilian lives will be lost." Though little even in American newspapers sustained Truman's claims about targeting, they remained a fixture in his own defense of his actions. "The world will note," he stressed on August 9, "that the first atomic bomb was dropped on Hiroshima, a military base," as if city and base were one and the same. True, in addressing his subordinates amid the Berlin crisis in 1948, Truman seemed to imply something else, emphasizing that the atomic bomb "is so terribly destructive. . . . It is used to wipe out women and children and unarmed people, and not for military uses." But Truman made no explicit reference to Hiroshima on that occasion, and out of office he reasserted that he "had ordered the A Bomb dropped on Japan at two places devoted almost exclusively to war production." Almost nine years later, the phrasing he and Stimson had worked out at Potsdam remained intact.[134]

Like American officials, the America media tried with indifferent success to measure the novelty of the atomic cataclysms. A continuity between reactions to the nuclear bomb and responses to conventional bombing provided steady undercurrent to the surface waves of astonishment, delight, and horror about the bomb's revolutionary nature. Even a casual reading of stories on the bomb would have driven home the quantum leap in destructiveness it represented. Yet the terms understandably used to express that leap—the atomic bombs were commonly equated in destructive force to twenty thousand tons of TNT, or the bomb load carried by some two thousand B-29s in a conventional raid—indicated also that the novel could be understood only in terms of the ordinary. Furthermore, the AAF tended to deemphasize the difference between its conventional and atomic weapons. Knowing that the last ready bomb had been delivered against Nagasaki, Spaatz emphasized that the nuclear bomb "as of now is only a comparatively insignificant weapon in [my] arsenal." The Enola Gay's commander, Paul Tibbets, was quoted about what he witnessed, often to vivid effect, but he also pointed out that his bomber "was not shaken as much by the [atomic] blast as it would have been by thermal updrafts fron an incendiary attack on a Japanese city at low level." Headlines provided another gauge to the media's difficulty in separating the new from the familiar. In the New York Times's August 7 edition, the new bomb had sole billing, but the next day it had to share space with other war news headlined "CARRIER PLANES STRIKE NEAR CHINA COAST" and with reports of an especially devastating fire raid on Yawata.[135]

As throughout the air war, the media also had trouble translating bombing into vivid words and images. The atomic clouds over Hiroshima and Nagasaki made an awesome sight in photographs but obscured what happened on the ground. High-altitude before-and-after photographs were impressive documents to the acreage destroyed, but abstract and similar to earlier images of firebombed cities. The best clue to what happened in Japan came from eyewitness accounts quickly published about the Trinity test—vivid descriptions, but not about a city. Meanwhile, Japanese newspapers and broadcasts reported the destruction in no uncertain terms, but so laced their stories with charges of war crimes that it was easy for the American media, as it had done earlier during the war, to characterize the enemy as "trying to establish a propaganda point."[136]

Of course it was not possible to misunderstand for long what atomic bombs did, as John Hersey's account for the New Yorker showed. Still, even in succeeding months, various difficulties in grasping what had happened in Japan maintained a continuity with the earlier air war. Government officials suppressed information, resorted to euphemisms, or selectively released the truth about the atomic attacks, as they had done earlier with firebombing. Even visual testimony, Japanese film confiscated by the American government and the lengthy color footage shot by army filmmakers early in the occupation, remained hidden for decades, the result of a combination of military secrecy and bureaucratic ineptitude. Censorship expressed rather than defied common assumptions about what was decent or useful for portrayal. An old pattern of looking away from bombing continued, perhaps compounded by the need to deny what the United States itself might experience. As often happened during the airplane's infancy, the immediate was slighted in favor of the transcendent. The reality of Hiroshima and Nagasaki seemed less important than the bomb's effect on "mankind's destiny," on "humanity's choice," on "what is happening to men's minds," and on hopes (now often extravagantly revived) to achieve world government. The bomb's "measurable destruction" seemed less telling to the novelist Mary McCarthy than its explosive impact on "the moral world."[137]

Like American governmental leaders, the American media emphasized the profound novelty of nuclear technology. The bomb story "read like some incredible fiction," commented the New York Times, although it was, as the New Yorker wryly pointed out, something that science fiction writers had merrily published during the war years.[138] It seemed that the bomb's advent, far from being a logical culmination of an air war long practiced, had severed the continuity of history itself. This was what the War Department called the "Cosmic Bomb," and it marked the dawn of a "New Age," not the high noon or sunset of an older one.[139]

Even the few critics of bombing had trouble placing atomic weapons in historical context. The Christian Century mounted a harsh attack on the bomb's use, but its mention of the war's earlier bombing was perfunctory, allowing the magazine to speak of "the impetuous adoption of this incredibly inhuman instrument," when in fact the bomb's use, seen in war's context, was hardly impetuous at all. That characterization was in part a result of the religious community's awkward position regarding America's record in the air war. A few of its representatives had expressed opposition to bombing.

More had recorded the pain felt in accepting it. Most had maintained caution or silence before August 1945, which compromised criticism after it. One way out of the awkward position was a frank admission of error, expressed in letters to the *Christian Century*: "We Christians have been too slow, too afraid, perhaps, to speak and act conscientiously as the war has progressed in its downward spiral of scientific ghastliness," pointed out one writer. "Our gasoline holocausts already exceed all barbaric crucifixions of history," claimed another. The magazine itself preferred a more comfortable course, focusing on the bomb's use as an exceptional act. Moreover, it betrayed a parochial impulse for its condemnation: the church's dream of Christianizing the Orient might fail because a Christian nation had unleashed the atomic weapon.[140]

Some observers quickly recognized how the bomb's use expressed an ongoing quality of American war-making. Dwight MacDonald responded to an official defense of the bomb's development which had argued that it "had been created not by the devilish inspiration of some warped genius but by the arduous labor of thousands of normal men and women." To MacDonald, this "effort to 'humanize' The Bomb by showing how it fits into our normal, everyday life also cuts the other way: it reveals how inhuman our normal life has become." Truman himself had supplied the appropriate characterization of the men and women who built the bomb: "Few know what they have been producing. They see great quantities of material going in and they see nothing coming out of these plants." These were among the people MacDonald criticized as "trained to think 'objectively'—i.e., in terms of means, not ends," and he saw the bomb's use as the product of a process deeply imbedded in American culture, not of a simple decision by a few leaders.[141]

MacDonald's rhetoric did not win him a wide audience in a nation satisfied with the war's end and the triumph of American technology. But a few mainstream observers also tried to set the bomb in a broader context. As *Life* declared, "Every step in the bomber's progress since 1937 has been more cruel than the last. From the very concept of strategic bombing, all the developments—night, pattern, saturation, area, indiscriminate—have led straight to Hiroshima." Unlike MacDonald, *Life* did not criticize the bomb's use. Neither did Hanson Baldwin, the prominent commentator for both *Life* and the *New York Times*. Employment would "probably save American lives" and might "even compel Japanese surrender." Yet even in June he had worried that "strategic bombing is a two-edged sword, and in the decades to come the specter of revenge may arise from the ashes of Tokyo to haunt us." The bomb's use further eroded his confidence that war served the state's rational ends, and he explicitly traced the breakdown of rationality to the nature of air war. Both sides had aimed their bombs "against civilians. Because our bombing has been more effective and hence more devastating," however, "Americans have become a synonym for destruction." Now the "new weapon . . . may bring us victory quickly," but it would "sow the seeds of hate more widely than ever. We may yet reap the whirlwind."[142]

Baldwin tried to resist rash, didactic predictions. The nuclear age might spell "the end of urban civilization as we know it," but Baldwin urged his readers to accept the uncertainty they faced: the "new face" of war was only "chaos." Even Baldwin, however, surrendered to the temptation to see a kind of certainty in the bomb's advent: the existence of only two outcomes for mankind. "Atomic energy may well lead to a bright new world in which man shares a common brotherhood, or we shall become— beneath the bombs and rockets—a world of troglodytes." By choosing that perspective, Baldwin, like many others, revived the tradition by which generations had regarded new weapons simultaneously as horrific and beneficent. As the journalist Max Lerner put it, the choice was "world state or world doom." Or as the *Times* editorial staff observed, "We face the prospect either of destruction on a scale which dwarfs anything thus far reported . . . or of a golden era of social change which would satisfy the most romantic utopian." From the University of Chicago, Robert Hutchins hoped that "the atomic bomb is the good news of damnation, that it may frighten us into that Christian character and those righteous actions and those positive political steps necessary to the creation of a world society, not a thousand or five hundred years hence, but now."[143]

Hope was given several expressions. The *Times*'s editorialists thought that the bomb made it both opportune and necessary to prevent future war by American leadership in democratizing the world. Like many other commentators, the *Times* was unclear whether the world was to be saved from the atomic bomb or through it. But the *Times* saw no danger in American possession of the bomb, and it was sure that "no people will want war if they realize what its consequences with the atomic bomb will be." In short, the old view that bombing was its own deterrent remained strong.[144]

Perhaps sharing the *Times*'s hopes and fears, some American leaders looked to the bomb as the instrument that might force the democratization of the Soviet state or at least arrest its further expansion. Others, like Stimson by September, saw only danger in using the bomb "as a direct lever" but still anticipated a better world emerging through agreement with the Soviets on controlling the new technology. That seemed to be the continued outlook as well of Oppenheimer, who regarded the bomb's use as a "spectacular and terrifying technical development" forcing upon "all the war-weary people of the world a recognition, first, of how imperative it has become to avert future wars, and second, how the cooperation and understanding between nations . . . has become a desperate necessity." Oppenheimer found "hope" as well as "peril" in atomic weapons, for their control "cannot be in itself the unique end" but rather "a world that is united, and a world in which war will not occur." Truman himself, although cautious after the war in pursuing international control of atomic weapons, once struck a similar note in commenting to John Hersey on the president's favorite poem, Tennyson's "Locksley Hall": "Notice also that part about universal law. We're going to have that someday, just as sure as we have air war now. That's what I'm working for."[145]

In its short history, aerial technology had promised benefits in peace as well as war. These seemed attractive in their own right and as impediments to war: new wealth and economic interdependence would discourage nations from taking up arms. The same potential seemed to inhere in the new atomic technology. Of course, its first use had to be military, but Stimson declared that "fission holds great promise for sweeping development by which our civilization may be enriched when peace comes," a limitless source of energy for Americans and for the "well-being of the world." The mushroom cloud loomed too large to allow the optimism earlier experienced about airplane technology. Nonetheless, variations on Stimson's vision continued to offer hopeful counterpoint to the new dangers.[146]

Americans tried to draw satisfaction out of the bomb's advent. Finishing a terrible war and facing a horrifying new technology, they naturally grasped for any sign of better things to come. As they did so, they displayed the power of historical tradition, resorting to familiar categories to try to explain and control the novel. It remained for MacDonald to explain that those categories would not work and simply to point out their reappearance. Regarding the great powers, he asked whether they

> will foreswear war itself because an "atomic" war would probably mean the mutual ruin of all contestants? The same reasons were advanced before World War I to demonstrate its "impossibility"; also before World War II. The devastation of these wars was as terrible as had been predicted—yet they took place. Like all the great advances in technology of the past century, Atomic Fission is something in which Good and Evil are so closely intertwined that it is hard to see how the Good can be extracted and the Evil thrown away. . . . *This* atom has never been split, and perhaps never will be.[147]

MacDonald's point was hard to grasp in 1945, for the good of the atomic bomb seemed blindingly apparent and the evil remote, if fearsome. The bomb, it appeared, had ended an awful war and in so doing realized a half-century's fantasy about transcending and erasing the horrors of conventional warfare.

To be sure, such a view of the bomb's decisive power did not immediately crystallize. To take that crude index of perceptions, the headlines, the story of the atomic bomb competed not only with news of triumph by more conventional weaponry, but with word of the Soviet declaration of war. In Japan, too, the bomb story stood alongside "banner headlines that the Soviet Union had declared war on Japan."[148]

The headlines reflected realities soon easily forgotten: contemporaries attached great importance to Soviet entry into the war, and that entry played a major role in Japan's surrender. For all the complex and loaded arguments about the relative importance of the bomb and of Russian entry in compelling Japan's capitulation, it was probably their cumulative and mutual impact that made them decisive. At that, their decisiveness was limited. It was supplemented by lesser forms of air power; thousands of planes over Japan produced "the most impressive and nerve-wracking demonstration of the whole war." Moreover, none of the events of August 6–9 changed the coalitions in Japan's government or the minds of the major individuals involved. Instead, these events left the war party unbending but "at a loss for words which could make any lasting impression upon the end-the-war faction," the war faction grudgingly yielding to the emperor's intervention on behalf of ending the war. At that, Japan's capitulation remained conditional on the emperor's continued sovereignty. Byrnes, worried about the "crucifixion of the President," at first would brook no waffling on terms. Finally, the clever wording was devised that made the emperor "subject to the authority" of the American occupational commander, a formula saving face on several scores by acknowledging the emperor's place without offending Americans at home and by writing the Russians out of a role in occupation.[149]

Diplomacy still ended the war. In its first use, the unconditional power of the atomic bomb did not compel unconditional surrender. By itself, it neither won nor ended the war, though certainly it hastened that end. Yet it quickly became possible for most Americans to think and speak as if the bomb had "won" the war, and as the cold war heated up, their leaders were disinclined to acknowledge a significant Soviet role in hastening Japan's surrender or a significant limitation on a weapon becoming the mainstay of the American arsenal.

It was probably the conviction that the bomb was winning the war that made Americans, in an August 8 poll, so approving of the bomb's use. The polls soon indicated subtle variations on that approval: many Americans wished the bomb had not been used first on a city or used the second time so quickly; on the other hand, in a *Fortune* poll taken in December 1945, almost 23 percent wished that the United States had "quickly used many more of them before Japan had a chance to surrender," still another measure of the persistent appeal of bombing as act of vengeance. Poll data do not allow precision in measuring how Americans judged the relative role of Russia and the atomic bomb in securing Japan's surrender. But probably most were convinced of the bomb's decisiveness. Because of that dubious assumption, atomic bombing seemed to have met the minimum criteria for legitimacy as an act of war—it was useful—and therefore moral inquiry tended to be limited. Among those who pressed that inquiry a bit further, a common view was that the atomic attacks had saved thousands of Japanese (and of course American) lives; or as the *Chicago Tribune* editorialized about American leaders, "Being merciless, they were merciful."[150]

In any event, there was perhaps another reason, besides relief at the war's end, to embrace the bomb's decisiveness. Only if Americans did so with little qualification could they approach the future with some comfort that the bomb would not be used again and that the world would realize the choice it had to make between doomsday and deliverance. To see the bomb as having a more subtle, qualified impact raised troublesome questions. Would future wars be deterred if nations were unconvinced of the bomb's utter finality? If horror at the thought of nuclear war made deterrence necessary, did it not also require making the most of the bomb's awesomeness in its one battle test? To think anything less of the bomb, in regard to past or prospective use, seemed to invite its employment and to demean the responsibility shouldered by those who possessed it.

The fantasy that had ebbed and flowed for decades—that of a new weapon that transcended and thereby ended war—had been realized. Yet Hiroshima and Nagasaki mocked the fantasy that they seemed to fulfill. For the atomic bomb, like bombing in its other forms, had triumphed not as a weapon of shock that obviated a protracted struggle, but only as a climax to it. Only by forestalling invasion did the bomb lay a limited and highly debatable claim to meeting the test of fantasy. Worse, the very power of the bomb that secured momentary fulfillment of fantasy prevented its realization again. The moment of fulfillment was a fluke made possible only by the extraordinary circumstance under which only one nation possessed the new weapon, and its enemy already lay in ashes. The fantasy momentarily unleashed seemed immediately to rebound. Any attempt to realize it again imperiled those who held it as well as those others whom the bomb was to instruct. Some hoped that air power in its new form would realize its old promise by deterring war altogether. There was no easy or safe way to validate that notion. In an earlier age, it had been possible to test fantasy, even if little enlightenment had been drawn from London in 1917, Barcelona in 1938, and Berlin in 1943. In the new age, it seemed likely there would be no rehearsal for Armageddon.

Epilogue

Today, few Americans know much about what happened at Hamburg, Dresden, Tokyo, and scores of other cities during World War II. The atomic bomb's use against Japan—or rather, how people have chosen to remember and regard it—has largely obliterated awareness of the bomber's earlier toll. In a longer view, however, continuity in the history of aerial warfare seems as striking as change. For all that 1945 demarcates the start of a second age in that history, indeed in human history, the burden of the atomic age has been similar to the one shouldered by an earlier generation.

Continuity has been most apparent in how people have thought and argued about bombing. The disputes they pursued for four decades after 1945, though more arcane because the technology became more rarified, were depressingly similar to earlier debates. Much as they did a half-century ago, for example, the American armed services still quarreled vigorously over which should control aerial technology and which can best survive its advances. Disagreement about the accuracy and potency of air power, though burdened with obscure terms like *fratricide* in recent times, echoed in substance the debates that swirled around Billy Mitchell in the 1920s. Argument about the vulnerability of military forces to an enemy's first strike, renewed with particular force several years ago during the MX missile controversy, played upon much the same nightmare that vexed strategists and statesmen, especially in England, during the 1920s and 1930s.

Just as the issues are often similar, the assumptions behind them have changed little. In both eras, most people assumed that the offensive use of air power would triumph over the defensive. Those who dissented from that proposition—most recently, the proponents of President Ronald Reagan's so-called Star Wars program—still shared another widespread assumption, that the problems created by modern military technology could be solved by further advances in it.[1] Still another persistent assumption underlay the tendency of nuclear powers to construct modern versions of the shop-window air forces constructed by European rivals on the eve of World War II—forces, that is, designed to intimidate or to demonstrate resolve but often backed by an apparatus of command, logistics, training, and reserves of dubious quality.[2] In the nuclear age, as in the 1930s, one of the oldest temptations of air power was evident, the temptation to regard it as serving less the needs of battle than the opportunity to avoid it. Given the frightful consequences of actual war, that temptation has only deepened in the nuclear era. More than ever the aerial weapon promises to provide an emblem of great power status, a threat to an enemy's resolve and psychic stability, and a trump card in diplomatic crises. As an unsurprising consequence of that temptation, new aerial weapons have been accompanied by loose and belatedly assembled military rationales, so that the first impulse is to build and deploy weapons and only later to find a military reason for doing so.

Assumptions that have changed little over more than half a century have yielded consequences that are distressingly similar. In World War II, the intangible criteria by which the bomber was measured invited escalation in its use. So they often did as well in the Vietnam War. In cold war politics, intangible criteria have invited escalation in the development and deployment of nuclear weapons. If those weapons only had the purpose of destroying targets in the event of war, their numbers still would be dismaying, but at least finite, for scientists and strategists can measure with some precision the forces required for destruction. Deterrence and prestige, on the other hand, dealing as they do with subjective considerations, have offered discouragingly few guidelines by which to determine what is "enough."[3] At what level of force can any nation be certain that it has dissuaded its enemy from going to war or convinced the enemy of its status?

A continuity ran through the century at a deeper level, regarding the intellectual challenge faced as well as the assumptions made about weapons. That challenge has been dual: to imagine the unimaginable, for only imagination could illuminate dangers and provide the incentive to avert them, and yet also to confront the essentially unpredictable nature of that future (which is the nature of all war as contemplated). To do both—to imagine without predicting, to alert without preaching—required an unusual combination of modesty and tolerance for uncertainty.

In both eras, responses to that challenge often calmed anxious minds but at a great price. Imagination was sometimes searching, arguably more so early in the century, when the danger was fresh rather than monotonously numbing. More often, people rushed to embrace dogma, coping with uncertainty by denying it. Before World War II, many people did so by conjuring up the comforting horror of an aerial blitz so terrifying that no nation would unleash it or long survive if the victim of it. Similar reasoning, responsive to visions of far greater horror, generally guided people in the nuclear era.

Most commentators confronting the aerial weapon have offered only two mutually exclusive alternatives: doomsday or deliverance. Designed to alert—to express a sense of the immense danger in an uncertain future—their attempts to view that future in either-or terms nonetheless carried a hidden agenda of seeking certainty by imposing simplicity upon the unpredictable. Even Jonathan Schell's justly noted *The Fate of the Earth,* at one level a grim celebration of uncertainty, climaxed with the baldest certitude about the "choice" humankind faced between two paths in the nuclear era: "One leads to death, the other to life."[4]

The continuity in habits of thought and practice regarding aerial warfare arose from several circumstances. The sheer magnitude of the danger, unevenly perceived but relentlessly growing, alone invited an apocalyptic outlook. The peculiar impersonality of long-range bombing made it possible both to imagine the worst and to turn away from it. Above all, the power of historical tradition—the persistence of the original terms on which the bomber was contemplated—was at play. Established at the turn of the century, the positing of a choice between doomsday and deliverance defined the alternatives for most observers throughout the century, even though the meaning of the alternatives and the perceived relationships between them underwent repeated modification.

The continuities of thought and practice in turn easily arouse pessimism about the chance of overcoming the threat of aerial warfare. If both the danger and the ways of thinking about it change so little, what way out can there be? Proposals addressing the danger, advanced with considerable eloquence in a number of recent appeals, would themselves require another book at this point. Some suggestions, however, are possible, and in keeping with the focus of this book they concern how we think about the problem of aerial warfare rather than specific political or strategic solutions.

One suggestion is for a different attitude toward the search for certainty. A notable example of that search in recent decades has arisen in contemplation of the possibility of "limited" nuclear war. Many commentators have deemed it imperative to rule out that possibility and to brand those who foresee it as all too willing to let it happen; otherwise, they suggest, nuclear war might seem in some measure "acceptable." Most likely, those commentators are correct, for the technical and political forces compelling escalation of any limited conflict to all-out war are formidable. But the unlikely often happens in war, as the weak record of prophecy about the bomber before World War II indicates. Limited nuclear conflict can be imagined, even if only as a remote possibility, and then the obvious point still be made about it: that even it is a horror which must be prevented. To appreciate the necessity of averting nuclear war does not require imagining only the destruction of the United States, or of Western civilization, or of all civilization, or of all human life, or of the ecosphere itself. We rule none of them out either; we accept them as points on a continuum of uncertainty.

For the most part, we have regarded the uncertainty in aerial warfare as an enemy. It frays nerves, disturbs sleep, vexes policies, and, so it seems, invites miscalculation. If we must face a terrifying future, we prefer the terrors to be known; simply to define them gives some hope of managing them. But we might better regard uncertainty as a friend, trying of course to fathom it but in the end also embracing it. It may be the best hope that the nuclear powers will be deterred from waging war. The very fact that they cannot know what would happen in war may be more daunting than scenarios filled with certitudes. Moreover, out of uncertainty can spring a continued desire to solve the nuclear problem and avoid a passive fatalism. In that regard, we can recall how, in the 1930s, the great powers found comfort in their terrifying vision that the next great war would begin and likely end with an aerial holocaust. They were right to imagine that such a holocaust was possible but wrong to regard it as almost inevitable, and in their error, and in their fumbling preparations to meet what they anticipated, they created a horror different from, but perhaps also worse than, what they had imagined.

A second suggestion is to be skeptical about technological solutions to the problem of aerial warfare. Of course, such solutions have been recurrently offered in the twentieth century: perhaps precision bombing would replace systematic destruction with selective paralysis, it was argued before World War II, just as others later hoped that precisely guided nuclear weapons might replace "countervalue" incineration of cities with "counterforce" targeting. Or, in another hope running through the history of aerial war (most recently in President Reagan's proposals), perhaps a new technology would so revive the defensive powers of a nation that an enemy attack might be doomed to failure.

Little in the record of air war supports these hopes for a technological solution. In World War II, antiaircraft defenses showed surprising capacities, inflicting a fearsome toll on both German and Allied bombers, but never enough to stop the aerial offensives before they had run at least some of their frightful course. Similarly, Allied bomber forces developed considerable sophistication in guiding their bombs with precision, but in both theaters they generally employed that sophistication to perfect their techniques of destroying cities rather than to steer their bombing back into narrower channels.

The problem, then as now, lay partly with the unpredictable consequences of technological change, but even more with the decisions that governments often make, particularly in wartime. Ignoring standards of rationality that observers like to impose upon war, they may choose, for the variety of reasons explored in this book, to employ new technologies for "irrational" purposes: that is, ones with little military utility or a considerable utility nonetheless overwhelmed by the evils accompanying it. Similarly, whatever current intentions the proponents of the Strategic Defense Initiative may have, their successors may employ the new space technology to different ends. Furthermore, the record of war undermines confidence that democratic states are the more rational actors in this regard.

The behavior of nation-states prompts a third suggestion—to be skeptical about the other (and more widely held) solution to the problem of aerial war, the hope that visions of destruction will shock the world into controlling or abolishing the aerial weapon. That solution, too, has afforded little progress. The shock indeed has been there and felt keenly by many people for many years, but translating it into effective political action has met with only a few limited successes and a general run of failure. It may well be that merely the persistent hope for the potency of the shock has in itself been a crippling illusion.

If technology cannot solve its own problems and if it cannot force the awakening leading to its control or abolition, then what hope is there beyond continued reliance upon the terrors of deterrence? Hope begins with an awareness that air power has prospered through the twentieth century because its destructiveness has been as appealing as it has been repellent. The bomber and the rocket have been embraced not only in spite of their horrors but because of them. Therefore, one path away from the nuclear dilemma lies in the recognition, as Dwight MacDonald suggested in 1945, that the good of atomic fission cannot be separated from the bad. Either both are renounced or neither are, barring some unforeseen technological or political development that allows them to be split. This means renouncing all the intangible gains seen as flowing from the mere possession of nuclear weapons, as opposed to their actual use: the status of a great power, the appearance of overwhelming might in great crises, the signals of support to allies that their deployment seems to send, victory in the neurotic game of "missile envy," as Helen Caldicott has called it.[5] Renouncing those gains means a return to seeing nuclear weapons for what they really are, instruments of war.

Renunciation may seem naive; after all, the use of military weapons to do much more than just fight wars is timeless. But surely it is just as naive to think that much is gained by playing this game. The intangible rewards, though by nature difficult to measure, rarely have matched expectations anyway. In war, enemy populations did not panic and collapse under the weight of bombs; in peace, the rewards of nuclear status have proven elusive, and the deployment of nuclear weapons has been as divisive as cohesive to alliances; in crises (as in the one over Cuban missiles in 1962), rivals backed off less at the appearance of their enemy's superiority than at the prospect of nuclear war itself.

Or—to anticipate another objection—it may seem dangerous to think of nuclear explosives merely as weapons of war. To do so seems almost to belittle them or even to accept their employment in war. But it has been one theme of this book that the failure to view aerial weapons as instruments of war that kill and destroy—the habit of looking away from those obvious consequences—has contributed to their growth and encouraged their use. An appreciation of their destructiveness, although seemingly the easiest task in confronting their peril, has in fact proved perhaps the hardest. Even fiction, whose imaginative potential seems the greatest, generally has failed to illuminate in that regard. The many recent novels on the nuclear danger, it has been said, "simply do not connect with human experience"[6] in portraying either the effects of nuclear weapons if used or their impact on consciousness as people wait in fear.

A further suggestion is to invite humility. It is easy to believe that the nuclear age is different, that perhaps in the 1920s and 1930s people and nations raced toward air war because they were still naive about the dangers they faced or just insufficiently scared, but that nuclear energy compels a restraint and an anxiety impossible at an earlier time. The distinction has some validity, especially with regard to the United States, where the bomber's benign properties were most widely assumed. But much evidence suggests that the fear of air war was nearly as powerful to an earlier generation as it is for today's. Indeed, the generation between the world wars had, in the example of World War I, a more potent reminder of war's irrationality than the nuclear generation possesses today. Their reminder had taken the real-life form of blood and death, but today, with World War II more than four decades in the past, people can be scared only by what they think may happen, not by what they vividly remember to have taken place. To regard the missile generation as the first to confront civilization's destruction is immodest, self-indulgent, and self-defeating as well, for it leads to denial of an often instructive example and of the recognition of that heavy inheritance received from an earlier age.

If humility is appropriate, so too is caution in placing blame for the nuclear predicament. There is reason to hesitate before placing it too heavily on the men and women who operate and manage the weapons. They have comprised, episodically at least, a powerful interest group. Particularly during war, the bureaucratic goals they possessed, the technique they commanded, and the pressures under which they operated led them to escalate their use of force in ways often useless, indiscriminate, and unmonitored. Especially since the 1940s, their elaborate links with other interest groups and the economic interests collectively served often have strengthened their voice. And yet military leaders rarely have been the most visionary exponents of air power. Even prophets of air power like Douhet and Mitchell who worked in the armed services usually found their largest audience outside them. Especially in setting forth the more ambitious (and fuzzy) virtues of air power, civilians generally have been more successful, and civilian leaders—Hitler, Churchill, and Roosevelt, albeit in different ways—have been far more subtle and skillful at translating the appeals of air power to a wider audience as well as in developing the practical apparatus for waging air war. In these regards, they have been ably assisted by scientists and other civilian experts.

Responsibility for danger is widespread. Similarly, solutions can arise from many sources beyond the experts. Many technical matters are within the layperson's grasp, the problem is hardly only technical in nature, and the innocent may bring fresh insights to which professionals, long trapped in debates that run in very narrow channels, may be closed off. In different ways, that potential was shown at the dawn of the air age by H. G. Wells and in its twilight by Jonathan Schell. Even if experts devise good solutions, they make little headway in complex political structures accustomed to channeling or eviscerating the novel, unless supported by larger political forces. "I do not think," Robert Oppenheimer said in November 1945, "that one may expect that people will contribute to the solution of the problem until they are aware of their ability to take part in the solution."[7] Much the same holds true today.

Finally, instruction can be gained from the moral agony some Americans have felt about their nation's use of the atomic bomb in 1945. That agony often represented a wish to minimize accountability. Since August 1945, concerned Americans have focused on the "decision" to use the atomic bomb as the moment of supreme moral choice. By doing so, they telescoped years of moral action into one instant of responsibility. There has been comfort in establishing neat boundaries to the choice supposedly made. If sin lay in the discrete choice of a few men at a definable moment, then the nation as a whole was not responsible. Circumscribed, the act of moral failure became retrospectively almost reversible: if only Truman had known such and such, if only Stimson had realized this or that. Reversible, the act need not be repeated in the nuclear age Americans entered: the next time, the moment of decision might go the other way.

It is almost as if we could reverse our mental film of the summer of 1945 and give Hiroshima the happy outcome that Kurt Vonnegut so compellingly proposed for Dresden. Billy Pilgrim saw that city's fate backward:

> American planes, full of holes and wounded men and corpses took off back-
> wards from an airfield in England. Over France, a few German fighter planes
> flew at them backwards, sucked bullets and shell fragments from some of the
> planes and crewmen. They did the same for wrecked American bombers on
> the ground, and those planes flew up backwards to join the formation.

The process continued, as American bombers "flew backwards" over Dresden, "exerted a miraculous magnetism which shrunk the fires, gathered them into cylindrical steel containers," and returned the instruments of destruction back to the United States, "where factories were operating night and day" to dismantle them, "so they would never hurt anybody ever again."[8]

Vonnegut offers an appealing vision but also an evocation of an intricate process, one that reminds us that the temptation to see the discrete act represents a profound and persistent misunderstanding of the dilemma faced in the 1940s and since then. The sin of atomic bombing, like the sin of the whole war's bombing, certainly resulted from choices but not from a moment of choice. Both were products of a slow accretion of large fears, thoughtless assumptions, and incremental decisions. If anything characterized the earlier era, it was the capacity of leaders to avoid the appearance of choice, to act out the salient quality of technology defined so well by Max Frisch: "The knack of so arranging the world that we don't have to experience it."[9]

We might remember this if now we entertain the fantasy that there will be a moment of supreme decision at the brink of some future world war when a leader, his or her fingers dangling above the nuclear button, ponders what to do. In our uncertainty, we cannot be sure that such a moment will not occur. But as Wells knew, we set a course by the ways in which we think about war or decline to do so in the weeks and months and years prior to the supreme moment of crisis and by the little decisions we make in preparation for it. Just as one generation learned to accept bombing as the terror that could not happen, so too has this generation accepted the bomb itself. The parallel, hardly comforting, may be instructive.

Abbreviations and Guide to Archival Sources

The following list includes only those collections cited in the notes. Despite vast amounts of material, archival and manuscript sources form an uneven and incomplete record often difficult to use. United States Army aviation was a new organization constantly changing in its internal bureaucratic structure and its relationship to its superior authorities, the army and the War Department. Therefore the Army Air Forces and its predecessors were less consistent and thorough in retaining and filing records than the older military services. Many air force records were widely scattered through the records systems; many found their way into the private manuscript collections of leading air force officers; some cannot be located at all. Some specific problems in documentation are discussed in notes and in the comments on sources which precede the notes for chapters. For the purposes of this book the most useful collections pertaining directly to the air force were the AAF Records, the HQ USAF Records, the HQ 20th AF Records, the personal collections of Arnold and LeMay, and the varied materials of AFSHRC. Among other collections, the most useful were the WD Staff Records, the Stimson Diary and SecWar Records, the FDR Papers, and JCS Records. The bulk of archival material on the atomic bomb is in two collections, the Harrison-Bundy Files and the MED Records.

AAF Records	Records of the Army Air Forces, Record Group 18, National Archives Building, Washington, D.C.
AFSHRC	Albert F. Simpson Historical Research Center, United States Air Force, Maxwell AFB, Alabama.
Andrews Papers	Papers of Frank Andrews, Library of Congress, Washington, D.C.
Army AG Records	Records of the War Department Adjutant General's Office, Record Group 407, National Archives, Washington, D.C.

Arnold Papers	Papers of Henry Harley Arnold, Library of Congress, Washington, D.C.
Bowles Papers	Papers of Edward L. Bowles, in possession of Bowles at time of author's use.
Chennault Papers	Papers of Claire L. Chennault, Hoover Institution, Stanford University, Palo Alto, California.
FDR Papers	Papers of Franklin D. Roosevelt, Franklin D. Roosevelt Library, Hyde Park, New York.
G-2 Records	Records of the Army Intelligence Division (G-2), Record Group 165, Washington National Records Center, Suitland, Maryland.
G-2 Regional Files	Regional Files 1933–1944, Records of the Army Intelligence Division (G-2), Record Group 165, Washington National Records Center, Suitland, Maryland.
Hansell Papers	Papers of Haywood S. Hansell, microfilm edition at Albert F. Simpson Historical Research Center, Maxwell AFB, Alabama.
Harrison-Bundy Papers	Harrison-Bundy Files Relating to the Development of the Atomic Bomb, in Records of the Office of Chief of Engineers, Record Group 77 (microfilm edition).
Hopkins Papers	Papers of Harry Hopkins, Franklin D. Roosevelt Library, Hyde Park, New York.
Hornbeck Papers	Papers of Stanley Hornbeck, Hoover Institution, Stanford University, Palo Alto, California.
HQ 20th AF Records	Records of the Headquarters, Twentieth Air Force, in Records of the Army Air Forces, Record Group 18, National Archives Building, Washington, D.C.
HQ USAF Records	Records of Headquarters, United States Air Force, Record Group 341, National Archives Building, Washington, D.C.
JB Records	Records of the Joint Army and Navy Boards and Committees, Record Group 225, National Archives Building, Washington, D.C.
JCS Records	Records of the United States Joint Chiefs of Staff, Record Group 218, National Archives Building, Washington, D.C. (some items cited to microfilm edition).
Kuter Papers	Papers of Laurence S. Kuter, Albert F. Simpson Historical Research Center, Maxwell AFB, Alabama.
LeMay Papers	Papers of Curtis LeMay, Library of Congress, Washington, D.C.
MED Records	Records of the Manhattan Engineer District, Office of the Chief of Engineers, Record Group 77 (most items cited to microfilm edition).

Mitchell Papers	Papers of William Mitchell, Library of Congress, Washington, D.C.
Morgenthau Papers	Papers of Henry Morgenthau, Franklin D. Roosevelt Library, Hyde Park, New York.
MPB Collection	Motion Picture Branch, National Archives Building, Washington, D.C. (specific items listed by record group).
Norstad Papers	Papers of Lauris Norstad, in temporary custody of Modern Military Branch, National Archives Building, Washington, D.C., at time of author's use.
SecWar Records	Records of the Office of the Secretary of War, Record Group 107, National Archives Building, Washington, D.C.
Spaatz Papers	Papers of Carl Spaatz, Library of Congress, Washington, D.C.
Stimson Diary	Diary of Henry L. Stimson, original in Stimson Papers, Yale University Library, New Haven, Connecticut, also on microfilm.
USSBS Records	Records of the United States Strategic Bombing Survey, Record Group 243, National Archives Building, Washington, D.C.
WD Staff Records	Records of the War Department General and Special Staffs, Record Group 165, National Archives Building, Washington, D.C.

Sources and Notes

Citations to published sources that are listed in the bibliography indicate only author's last name and page references, except to distinguish among multiple titles under the same name. A list of abbreviations used in citing archival sources can be found preceding the notes.

PREFACE

1. John Hersey, "Hiroshima: The Aftermath," *The New Yorker*, 15 July 1985, 63.

CHAPTER 1

Sources

This chapter draws heavily on secondary sources. The best brief introductions to the early history of air power are in Kennett, *A History of Strategic Bombing*, and Higham, *Air Power*. Among many good sources on European developments, see Quester, *Deterrence before Hiroshima*; Fredette, *The Sky on Fire*; Powers, *Strategy Without Slide Rule*, and Jones, *The Origins of Strategic Bombing*. Early American military aviation has been less well examined, but see Hurley, *Billy Mitchell*; Craven and Cate, *The Army Air Forces in World War II,* vol. 1; and Holley, *Ideas and Weapons*.

On the culture and qualities of imagination that shaped early expectations of air power, see, specifically on American attitudes, Corn, *Winged Gospel*; Leonard, *Above the Battle*; and Kennedy, *Over Here*. On broader currents, see Ellis, *The Social History of the Machine Gun*; Clarke, *Voices Prophesying War*; Kern, *The Culture of Time and Space*. The analysis of Wells's prophecies is largely mine.

Notes

1. Mark Twain, *A Connecticut Yankee in King Arthur's Court* (1889; 1980), 301, 309.
2. Ellis, 9; Churchill, from speech in 1949, reprinted in Eugene Emme, *The Impact of Air Power* (Princeton, 1959), 87.
3. James Martin Hunn, "Popular Science in Paris in the 1780s: The Example of Ballooning," unpublished paper (1981).

4. Crouch, 287.

5. Hurley, 142, 144; Powers, 109. See also Donnelly's *Caesar's Column* (Chicago, 1890).

6. Quotations from Leonard, 88; Kern, 244 (Zweig); Corn, 38 ("Argonauts"), 30, 31, 39 (Gilman paraphrased and quoted).

7. Quotations from Clarke, 3 (Hugo); Ellis, 33 (on the machine gun); Brodie and Brodie, 70 (Donne).

8. Quotations from Leonard, 90 ("evils of war" and Hay), 92 (London and "images of carnage"); Clarke, 77 (Clarke's judgment and "greatest destroyer").

9. The Hague Convention of 1907, reprinted in Richard A. Falk, Gabriel Kolko, and Robert Jay Lifton, eds., *Crimes of War* (New York, 1971), 33–40.

10. Quotation from Leonard, 89; Clarke, 131.

11. Quotations from Elting E. Morison, *Men, Machines, and Modern Times* (Cambridge, 1966), 35 (Mahan); Leonard, 108 (Leonard).

12. Eliot quotation from Leonard, 104. More generally, see Leonard, esp. chap. 5.

13. Quotation from Clarke, 63.

14. *The War in the Air* (1907, 1908; New York, 1917), 253, 352.

15. Ibid., 205, 211, 252.

16. Orville Wright, letter to Wallace Sabine, 7 November 1918, in Marvin W. McFarland, ed., *The Papers of Wilbur and Orville Wright*, 2 vols. (New York, 1953), 1121. See other passing references to military aviation in McFarland, especially 497, 539–40, 680, 744, 774–75, 802, 1017, 1104–05, 1108–09.

17. Brodie and Brodie, 10; Robert V. Bruce, *Bell: Alexander Graham Bell and the Conquest of Solitude* (Boston, 1973), 363.

18. See Crouch, esp. p. 18.

19. Morison, *Men, Machines, and Modern Times,* 37.

20. Quoted in R. Earl McClendon, *The Question of Autonomy for the U.S. Air Arm, 1907–45* (Maxwell AFB, 1950), 33.

21. On strategic views of the first naval aviators, see Brune, 22–28.

22. Higham, 16.

23. Quotations from Fredette, 31.

24. Basil Collier, *A History of Air Power* (New York, 1974), 74.

25. Quotations from Fredette, 72; Powers, 60 (quoting A. J. P. Taylor).

26. Fredette, 66 (quoting the *New York Times* dispatch of 26 June 1917).

27. Powers's comment and *Daily Mail* quotation in Powers, 62.

28. Quotations from Fredette, 39, and Quester, 24.

29. Quotations from Fredette, 116 (Lord Beaverbrook on Trenchard); Powers, 104; Fredette, 225 (instructions to Trenchard).

30. Fredette, 226; Frankland, 25; Churchill quotation from Emme, *Impact*, 38.

31. Quotations from Fredette, 151, 32.

32. Quotations from Fredette, 68, and Powers, 77, 83.

33. Walzer, 19.

34. Quotations from Powers, 54, and Fredette, 160.

35. Brodie and Brodie, 193.

36. Quotations from Craven and Cate, vol. 1, 6; Benjamin D. Foulois, with C. V. Glines, *From the Wright Brothers to the Astronauts* (New York, 1968), 150 (headlines).

37. Quotations from Arthur Sweetser, *The American Air Service* (New York, 1919), 77, 77–78; Craven and Cate, vol. 1, 6 (*New York Times,* 10 June 1917).

38. William Mitchell, *Memoirs of World War I* (New York, 1960), esp. pp. 43, 59, 76; Mitchell, quoted in Hurley, 29.

39. Quotations from Holley, *Ideas and Weapons,* 135, and Greer, 11.

40. Kennedy, 132.

41. Sweetser, *The American Air Service,* xxvii.

42. Hurley, 36.

43. Flugel, 46; Baker, quoted in Hurley, 37.

44. Leonard, 163.

45. Kennedy, 217, 212.

46. Leonard, 152, 165.

47. Leonard, 141.

48. Corn, 11; Fredette, 55–56 (*New York Times,* 14 June 1917).

49. Quotations from Fredette, 198; Powers, 113.

CHAPTER 2

Sources

Many of the sources described for chapter 1 cover the 1920s as well. My critique of the air power prophets draws heavily on my reading of their major writings, cited below in notes. Douhet has never been adequately studied, but see, among many sources that briefly assess him, Brodie, *Strategy in the Missile Age,* and Kennett, *A History of Strategic Bombing.* Bond, *Liddell Hart,* gives his subject the treatment Douhet also deserves. On Mitchell, the sources are many, but I've leaned most on Millis, *Arms and Men,* which takes a provocative long view; Hurley, *Billy Mitchell;* the probing summary of Mitchell's strategic appeal in Weigley, *The American Way of War,* and Brune's erratic but suggestive *The Origins of American National Security.* The William Mitchell Papers (Library of Congress) were also useful. Among many dissertations, the most helpful was Tate, "The Army and Its Air Corps."

On the political struggles that swirled around Mitchell and the army aviators, the sources, beyond those noted, are few. Copp, *A Few Great Captains,* is detailed and colorful but poorly documented and sometimes weak on ideas. Among other biographical studies, see Coffey, *HAP,* on Henry Harley Arnold. An older book, Levine's *Mitchell,* vividly evokes the Mitchell affair and the many foolish things people said at the time.

On arms control issues, in addition to Kennett's excellent brief treatment, older studies were especially helpful: the Sprouts' *Toward a New Order of Sea Power;* Royse, *Aerial Bombardment and the International Regulation of Warfare.* See also Quester, *Deterrence before Hiroshima;* Buckley, *The United States and the Washington Conference;* Bialer, *The Shadow of the Bomber.* On chemical and bacteriological warfare, see Brown, *Chemical Warfare,* and Harris and Paxman, *A Higher Form of Killing.*

For the cultural context of prophecy, I have relied mainly on contemporary speeches, writing, and journalism. An outstanding interpretation remains Ward, "The Meaning of Lindbergh's Flight." See also Corn, *Winged Gospel.*

Notes

1. Giulio Douhet, *The Command of the Air,* trans. Dino Ferrari (New York, 1942), 151; B. H. Liddell Hart, *Paris; or, The Future of War* (London and New York, 1925), 42, 25.

2. Liddell Hart, *Paris,* 43 (emphasis in original); Douhet, *Command,* 195.

3. Quoted in Quester, 56.

4. Douhet, *Command,* 112. See also 59, 194.

5. Douhet, *Command,* 22, 393.

6. Liddell Hart, *Paris,* 51; Trenchard quotation from Quester, 53. See also Harris and Paxman, 34–35, and Brown, esp. 176–83.

7. Liddell Hart, *Paris,* 43, 39–40; "nerve ganglia" from P. R. C. Groves, "For France to Answer," *Atlantic Monthly,* February 1924, 146.

8. Liddell Hart, *Paris,* 36; Douhet, *Command,* 188; Powers, 126 ("Bolshevik upheaval"), 125 (Powers).

9. Liddell Hart, *Paris,* 47–48.

10. Douhet, *Command,* 196, 282; Liddell Hart, *Paris,* 50.

11. Douhet, *Command,* 103.

12. See Millis, 227.

13. Douhet, *Command,* 145, 147, 25; Liddell Hart, *Paris,* 36.

14. Douhet, *Command,* 181, 185.

15. Liddell Hart, *Paris,* 26, 25, 13.

16. Powers, 133, 134 (Churchill); Kennett, 54; Quester, 89, 69.

17. Clarke, 162.

18. See esp. Mitchell, "Aeronautical Era," *Saturday Evening Post,* 20 December 1924, 3–4+, and *Winged Defense: The Development and Possibilities of Modern Air Power* (New York, 1925).

19. Mitchell, *Winged Defense,* 16; William Mitchell, *Skyways: A Book on Modern Aeronautics* (Philadelphia, 1930), 262, 263.

20. "'Viper' Weapons," *Literary Digest,* 24 December 1921, 8, 9; William C. Sherman, *Air Warfare* (New York, 1926), 213.

21. Mitchell, *Winged Defense,* 16; Air Service Tactical School textbook, as quoted in Hurley, 112.

22. Mitchell, *Winged Defense,* xi, 101.

23. Mitchell, "Report of Inspection of the United States Possessions in the Pacific and Java, Singapore, India, Siam, China and Japan," 24 October 1924, file C33-5, Document Collection of the Air Corps Library, 1917–38, Office of the Chief of the Air Corps, AAF Records. On Japanese fears, see Sprouts, 233, and Neumann, 162. On military planning for the Far East, see Brune, 69–70, 74, and Joint Board Basic War Plan—Orange, accompanying Joint Board letter marked J. B. #325 (Serial #228) of 25 August 1924, in file 325, JB Records. For a published discussion of the possibilities for air power in an American-Japanese war, see Hector C. Bywater, *The Great Pacific War: A History of the American-Japanese Campaign of 1931–33* (Boston and New York, 1925).

24. Quotation from Hurley, 92. On politicians' statements, see, for example, House Committee on Military Affairs, *Hearings, Department of Defense and Unification of Air Service* (Washington, 1926), 796, 804–05.

25. Brown, 68.

26. Irwin, *"The Next War": An Appeal to Common Sense* (New York, 1921), 46, 109, 66.

27. *Report of the President's Aircraft Board* (Morrow Board), 30 November 1925 (Washington, 1925), 7.

28. Norris Hall, in Hall, Zechariah Chafee, Jr., and Manley O. Hudson, *The Next War: Three Addresses Delivered at the Symposium at Harvard University, November 18, 1924* (Cambridge, 1925), 37; *New York Times,* 11 January 1922, as quoted in Sprouts, 231.

29. These claims, oft-repeated, are from Mitchell, "Our Army's Air Service," *American Review of Reviews,* September 1920, esp. 283–84, 289.

30. *Washington Herald,* 16 October 1921.

31. See, for example, Mason Patrick to Assistant Chief of Staff, War Plans Division, 10 November 1921, in folder "Reports 1921–25," Box 49, Mitchell Papers.

32. Levine, 215.

33. Quoted in Hurley, 101.

34. "Lineal prototypes" quotation from Samuel Taylor Moore, "A Bargain in Preparedness," *Harpers,* May 1924, 827. Borah quotation from "Disarmament Winning at Washington," *Literary Digest,* 11 June 1921, 8. All other quotations from Levine, 230–31, 304, 311, 359, 330, 318, 345.

35. Quotations from Levine, 265, 313, 317, 369, 331, and Tate, 72 (Pershing).

36. Tate, 256, 45.

37. Trenchard quotation from Hurley, 97. For examples of limited attention to aviation in the late 1920s, see the April 1927 issue of *World's Work* (vol. 53), and Robert Albion, *Introduction to Military History* (New York, 1929).

38. Arnold, 121.

39. C. Vann Woodward, "The Age of Reinterpretation," *American Historical Review* 58 (October 1960): 7.

40. Arnold, 159.

41. "Deeds of Captain Rickenbacker Whose Middle Name Is 'Victor,'" *Literary Digest*, 5 April 1919, 64. See also Philip M. Flammer, *The Vivid Air: The Lafayette Escadrille* (Athens, Ga., 1981), 184–87.

42. On *Hell's Angels*, see Corn, 12. On *Wings*, see "When War-Planes Flame and Audiences Gasp," *Literary Digest*, 12 November 1926, 36–42. Theodore Roosevelt (Jr.), *Rank and File: Stories of the Great War* (New York, 1928), 23. Leighton Brewer, *Riders of the Sky* (Boston and New York, 1934), 7.

43. For attribution of warrior status to Lindbergh, see Charles A. Lindbergh, *"We," by Charles A. Lindbergh* (New York, 1927), 5, 243, 256. Quotations from Lindberg, 9, 141, and from "Sonnet" to Lindbergh by Judge Wendell Phillips Stafford, in W. Jefferson Davis, *Air Conquest* (Los Angeles, 1930).

44. Quotations from Ward, 13; Lindbergh, *We*, 262; Ward, 15 (Ward's conclusion).

45. Frederick Lewis Allen, *Only Yesterday* (1931; New York, 1964), 184.

46. Corn, 52, 88, 86. See also Kathleen Brooks-Pazmany, *United States Women in Aviation, 1919–1929* (Washington, 1983).

47. Stuart Chase, *Men and Machines* (New York, 1929), 144.

48. Chase, 101, 102.

49. Charles A. Beard, ed., *Whither Mankind* (New York, 1928), 19, 407.

50. Beard, *Whither Mankind*, 168, 170, 180, 182–83, 185. See also Beard, *Toward Civilization* (New York, 1930).

51. On the Hoover committee, see esp. W. F. Ogburn, "The Influence of Invention and Discovery," *Recent Social Trends* (1933), vol. 1, 122–66. For an exception to the prevailing reticence, see Igor Sikorsky, "What Can Aircraft Do in the Next War?" *Independent*, 7 November 1925, 521–23.

52. Lindbergh, *We*, 244; Mitchell, *Winged Defense*, 77; for similar expressions, see comment by Roy Wright in Beard, *Toward Civilization*, 98, and by Anthony Fokker in *Annals, the American Academy of Political and Social Science* 131 (May 1927): 183. Davis, *Air Conquest*, 93, 95. For a more literary expression of the theme of broadened consciousness, see Anne Morrow Lindbergh, *North to the Orient* (New York, 1935).

53. Henry Ford, *Today and Tomorrow* (New York, 1926), 205; M. W. Royse, "The Next War in the Air," *Nation*, 9 May 1923, 537.

54. Quotations from Chase, *Men and Machines*, 307–17, and 296, 339. An almost identical version of this essay appeared in the *New Republic*, 8 May 1929, 325–27.

55. P. M. Swanwick, *Frankenstein and His Monster: Aviation for World Service* (London, 1934), as quoted in Bialer, 7.

CHAPTER 3

Sources

Most of the secondary sources listed for chapters 1 and 2 remained useful for the writing of this chapter, although here I have drawn more heavily on primary materials and archival records. Additional sources on Air Corps doctrine and struggles include Futrell, *Ideas, Concepts, Weapons;* Fabyanic, "A Critique of United States Air War Planning 1941–1944."; Cate, "History of the Twentieth Air Force: Genesis"; Shiner, *Foulois and the U.S. Army Air Corps.* For setting attitudes toward possible air war with Japan in perspective as well as for certain details, see Neumann, *America Encounters Japan;* and Iriye, *Across the Pacific.* On the strategic and ethical issues addressed or ignored in the thirties, I have relied especially on Schaffer, "American Military Ethics in World War II," which is provocative even where I take issue with him; Walzer, *Just and Unjust Wars;* Bialer, *The Shadow of the Bomber;* Quester, *Deterrence before Hiroshima;* Hastings, *Bomber Command,* a savage but valuable account of the RAF; and Smith, "The Royal Air Force, Air Power and British Foreign Policy, 1932–37."

Notes

1. Corn, chap. 5 (quotations from 94, 98).
2. "'Strafing' New York from the Clouds," *Literary Digest*, 8 June 1929, 60.

3. Copp, 168, 187.

4. Tate, 181–82.

5. Tate, 169.

6. Millis, 231; Higham, 87.

7. Haywood Hansell, "General Laurence S. Kuter, 1905–1979," *Aerospace Historian,* June 1980, 81 ("somewhat ridiculous"); Benjamin Foulois, with C. V. Glines, *From the Wright Brothers to the Astronauts: The Memoirs of Benjamin D. Foulois* (New York, 1968), 67. Other quotations from Tate, 257, 258. On casualty rates among airmen, see Shiner, 109.

8. William C. Sherman, *Air Warfare* (New York, 1926), 218.

9. I borrow the phrasing used by Robert Wiebe to describe the appeal and place in American political traditions of fiscal policy; see Bernard Bailyn et al., *The Great Republic* (Lexington, 1977), chap. 31, esp. p. 1199.

10. Quotations from Fabyanic, 42; Greer, 81.

11. *New York Times,* 24 July 1934, 6. See also Flugel, 237–38.

12. "The Air Force and Its Characteristics," 25 March 1938, in ser. 6, Hansell Papers.

13. Quoted in Flugel, 197.

14. Quoted in Fabyanic, 45, retaining the original emphasis.

15. Colonel Charles deF. Chandler, "Air Warfare Considerations," *U.S. Air Services,* November 1934, 13.

16. Fabyanic, 46.

17. Fabyanic, 48.

18. Mitchell, *Skyways: A Book on Modern Aeronautics* (Philadelphia, 1930), 256; Greer, 77.

19. Greer, 41; "A Study of Proposed Air Corps Doctrine . . . ," January 31, 1935, in file 321.9 Doctrines of the Army Air Corps, Central Decimal Files 1917–38, AAF Records. For public position, see Henry Harley and Ira Eaker, *This Flying Game* (New York, 1936), esp. 129.

20. Chandler, "Air Warfare Considerations," 13, and Chandler, "A New Deal for Old Strategy," *U.S. Air Services,* June 1934, 16; Tate, 192.

21. Quotations from Mitchell Papers: Mitchell, undated, untitled article with penciled notation, "To Wash. Times Herald—6/28," probably 28 June 1927, Box 28; Mitchell, "Give Us More Planes or We Perish," undated copy of magazine article, probably 1934 or 1935, Box 27; "Address of Gen. Wm. Mitchell before the Massachusetts Camp of the 5th Division, May 25, 1935, Boston, Massachusetts," Box 28. See also Mitchell, "Suppose Japan Surprised Us," undated (1932–35), Box 30. For a brief discussion of some of Mitchell's published warnings on Japan, see Hurley, 123.

22. Mitchell, "The Present Crisis in Asia," undated, sent by letter to *Liberty,* 18 December 1931, Box 16; Mitchell, "America's Action in Case of War with Japan," undated, sent by letter to Hearst Papers, 20 September 1932, Box 16; Mitchell, "The Strategy of the Pacific," undated (1932), Box 27, all in Mitchell Papers.

23. On Air Corps plans for the Philippines, see Westover to Adjutant General, subject: "Air Plan for the Defense of the United States," 13 July 1933, file AG 580 (6–13–33) and "Air Corps Peacetime Requirements to Meet the Defense Needs of the United States," file AG 580 (3–15–33), both in Army AG Records; memorandum, Spaatz for Executive, 5 January 1935, in file 321.1 Doctrines of the Army Air Corps, Central Decimal Files 1917–38, AAF Records. Quotations: "toward squelching" from Col. H. J. Knerr, Chief of Staff, GHQ Air Force, "Lecture for the Army War Class 1935–36 Upon the Occasion of Their Visit to Langley Field, Va., June 12, 1936," in Box 16, Andrews Papers; "ideal objective" from Thomas D. White, "Japan as an Objective for Air Attack," Air Corps Tactical School, 1937–38, in file 168.7004-10, AFSHRC.

24. Captain Bonner F. Fellers, "The Psychology of the Japanese Soldiers," The Command and General Staff School, 1934–35, in file 142.041-1, AFSHRC.

25. Dana G. Mead, "United States Peacetime Strategic Planning, 1920–1941: The Color Plans to the Victory Program" (Ph.D. diss., Massachusetts Institute of Technology, 1968), 3.

26. Iriye, *Across the Pacific,* 180, 181.

27. On the cabinet meeting, see Neumann, 205. For Roosevelt on Mitchell, see Hurley, 122–23,

and on chemical warfare, see Brown, 123–25. For official condemnations of bombing, see Council on Foreign Relations, *The United States in World Affairs, 1938* (New York, 1939), 311, 164–65 for quotations, and also the Council's 1937 volume (New York, 1938), 212–15.

28. For Hull's threat and the bombing scare, see Neumann, 208–09, and Clark Reynolds, *The Fast Carriers: The Forging of an Air Navy* (New York, 1968), 5. For "peaceful blockade" and similar schemes, see Leutze, 10–28; Reynolds, 28–31. For public commentary, see W. Jefferson Davis, *Japan, The Air Menace* (1927; Boston 1928), 53; Sutherland Denlinger and Charles B. Gary, *War in the Pacific: A Study of Navies, Peoples and Battle* (New York, 1936), 230, 311, 222; R. Ernest Dupuy and George Fielding Eliot, *If War Comes* (New York, 1937), 280 passim; and Eliot, *The Ramparts We Watch: A Study of the Problems of American National Defense* (New York, 1938), 166–67.

29. Quoted in Robert Krauskopf, "The Army and the Strategic Bomber, 1930–39," *Military Affairs* 22 (Summer 1958): 85.

30. Westover, "Our National Air Defense," address before the National Aeronautic Association, 30 November 1936, in *Vital Speeches,* 1 January 1937, 181–84. For other typical public statements, see the speeches by Frank Andrews of 15 October 1935 and 28 January 1937, in Box 15, Box 16, Andrews Papers; Arnold and Eaker, *This Flying Game.*

31. Quotations from Copp, 396, 423. I have drawn heavily on Copp's account of these episodes. See also "East Coast 'Raided'," *Newsweek,* 16 May 1938, 13, and " 'Supercolossal Air Epic': 187 Plane Armada Saves U.S. From 'Black' Invasion," *Newsweek,* 23 May 1938, 36–37.

32. W. B. Courtney, "Our Own War Birds Are Best," *Colliers,* 14 October 1939, 64; Fletcher Pratt, "Can They Bomb Us?" *Saturday Evening Post,* 2 December 1939, 34.

33. Francis W. Drake, "The Air Force We Need," *Atlantic,* January 1940, 41; Congressman J. Parnell Thomas, in House Committee on Military Affairs, *Hearings, An Adequate National Defense as Outlined by the Message of the President of the United States,* 76th Congress, 1st Session (1939), 124, 123; Chamberlain, "The Airplane in War," *New Republic,* 10 August 1939, 51.

34. Arlington B. Conway, "Death from the Sky," *American Mercury,* February 1932, 167; W. F. Kernan, "The Airplane in Future War," *Commonweal,* 1 April 1938, 621.

35. Thomas R. Phillips, "Debunking Mars' Newest Toys," *Saturday Evening Post,* 4 March 1933, 61; W. F. Kernan, "Our Reception for Bombers," *American Mercury,* June 1935, 205–11.

36. John Edwin Hogg, "The Bogey of War in the Air," *Forum,* December 1935, 345; "Background of War, part V: Who Dares to Fight?" *Fortune,* July 1937, 71; J. G. Harbord, "War in the Air," *Vital Speeches,* 22 October 1934, 36, 37; James Warner Bellah, "Bombing Cities Won't Win the War," *Harpers,* November 1939, 659; Kernan, "The Airplane in Future War," 622.

37. Conway, "Death from the Sky," 176.

38. Phillips, "Debunking Mars' Newest Toys," 61, 23, 61.

39. Quotations from Winston Churchill, "Bombs Don't Scare Us Now," *Colliers,* 17 June 1939, 11, 56; speech of July 20, 1934, in Eugene Emme, *The Impact of Air Power* (Princeton, 1959), 54, original emphasis deleted. See also Churchill, "Let the Tyrant Criminals Bomb!" *Colliers,* 14 January 1939, 12–13 passim.

40. Paul Gesner, "The Morning After," *Forum,* 6 October 1931, 240; J. Enrique Zanetti, "Warfare By Fire," *Readers Digest,* March 1936, 28.

41. Quotations from L. E. O. Charlton, *War Over England* (London and New York, 1936), 126, 227; L. E. O. Charlton, *The Menace of the Clouds* (London, 1937), 30, 43; *War,* 237; *Menace,* "Escape from Armageddon," title of part 4.

42. Langdon-Davies, *Air Raid* (London, 1938), 82, 109.

43. Quotations from Fuller, "Terror from the Skies," *Living Age,* April 1937, 117–25 (reprinted from an English journal), emphasis by Fuller. See also Robin Higham, *The Military Intellectuals in Britain, 1918–1939* (New Brunswick, 1966), 76–80, and Smith, "The Royal Air Force," 157.

44. Al Williams, *Airpower* (New York, 1940), 305, 161.

45. George Fielding Eliot, *Bombs Bursting in Air: The Influence of Air Power on International Relations* (New York, 1939), 22, 13; Dupuy and Eliot, *If War Comes,* 58, 60–61.

46. *If War Comes,* 88; Eliot, *Ramparts,* 42.

47. *Ramparts,* 166–67.

48. *Ramparts,* 111; George Fielding Eliot, "The Defense of America," *Harpers,* December 1938, 78.

49. *Bombs Bursting,* 160; see also 166–67.

50. *Bombs Bursting,* 80; *If War Comes,* 224.

51. George Fielding Eliot, "The Impossible War With Japan," *American Mercury,* September 1938, 16; *Bombs Bursting,* 69.

52. Denlinger and Gary, *War in the Pacific,* 25.

53. Pierce, *Air War* (New York, 1939), 8, 32, 63, 57, 139–40.

54. Pierce, 156.

55. Herbert L. Matthews, "When Planes Rain Death on a Big City," *New York Times Magazine,* March 27, 1938, 1. See also "Barcelona Horrors," *Time,* 28 March 1938, and Langdon-Davies, *Air Raid,* 21.

56. Louis Fischer, "Madrid Keeps Its Nerve," *Nation,* 7 November 1936, 539. See also Fischer, "Peace on Earth," *Nation,* 24 December 1938, 686–88; Langston Hughes, "Laughter in Madrid," *Nation,* 29 January 1938, 123–24.

57. Thomas R. Phillips, "Preview of Armageddon," *Saturday Evening Post,* 12 March 1938, 12. For similar conclusions, see Charles A. Thomson, "The War in Spain," *Foreign Policy Reports,* 1 May 1939, 38–48. On army reactions to Spain, see also Futrell, 80–81.

58. *New York Times,* 25 September 1937; W. B. Courtney, "Brown and Yellow Bombers," *Colliers,* 4 February 1939, 46; Council on Foreign Relations, *The United States in World Affairs 1937* (1938), 215.

59. "Background to War," *Fortune,* July 1937, 62; Jonathan Mitchell, "Death Rides the Wind," *New Republic,* 26 May 1937, 63–64. On mass media responses, see, for example, "Japan Resorts to Air Terror in Drive for Final Knockout," *Newsweek,* 13 June 1939, 15–16.

60. Martha Gelhorn, "The Lord Will Provide—for England," *Colliers,* 17 September 1938, 15; Christine H. Sturgeon, "Fear Flies over England," *Forum,* November 1939, 247–51; Eliot, *Bombs Bursting,* 73–74.

61. Archibald MacLeish, *Air Raid: A Verse Play for Radio* (New York, 1938); W. B. Courtney, "Rehearsal in Spain," *Colliers,* 23 January 1937, 34, 36.

62. See especially George Fielding Eliot, "If War Breaks Out Tomorrow," *New Republic,* 24 May 1939, 63–66; Emilio Lussu, "Fascist War Technique," translated from Italian and reprinted in *Living Age,* June 1939, 314–17.

63. Higham, 10.

64. Hopkins, 456; Michael Howard, *War and the Liberal Conscience* (New Brunswick, 1978), 99. On "supreme emergency," see Walzer, esp. 251–55.

65. Sir John Fischer Williams, "Modern War and the Civilian," *Living Age,* December 1937, 295, 297, 298; George Fielding Eliot, "Can War Be Civilized?" *New Republic,* 20 July 1938, 294–96.

66. Jacques Maritain, "War and the Bombardment of Cities," *Commonweal,* 2 September 1938, 460–61.

67. Macmillan, *Winds of Change, 1914–1939* (London, 1966), 575.

68. Millis, 239.

CHAPTER 4

Sources

Excellent overviews of the politics, strategy, and logistics of air power during the period are found in Higham, *Air Power;* Kennett, *A History of Strategic Bombing;* and Overy, *The Air War.* For the Munich crisis, see also Bialer, *Shadow of the Bomber;* Powers, *Strategy Without Slide Rule;* Quester, *Deterrence before Hiroshima;* Bond, *British Military Policy;* Cooper, *The German Air Force;* Smith " 'A Matter of Faith': British Strategic Air Doctrine Before 1939." Taylor, *Munich,* provides indiscriminate detail on Lindbergh's role in the European crisis and should be compared to Cole's sympathetic *Charles A. Lindbergh and the Battle Against American Intervention in World War II.* For the air war in Europe in 1939–41, see also Hastings, *Bomber Command,* and Terraine, *A Time for Courage.*

On diplomacy and grand strategy, particularly for the United States, Reynolds, *The Creation of the Anglo-American Alliance,* is provocative and comprehensive and influenced my interpretation at several points. See also, Leutze, *Bargaining for Supremacy;* Herzog, *Closing the Open Door;* and Dallek, *Franklin D. Roosevelt.* No comprehensive study of FDR's views on air power exists, but see in addition to titles already noted, Leighton, "The American Arsenal Policy in World War II." My analysis of public opinion and its relationships to administration policy draws largely on primary sources, but see, in addition to Reynolds and Dallek, Cole, *Roosevelt and the Isolationists;* Culbert, *News for Everyman;* Leigh, *Mobilizing Consent;* Haight, *American Aid to France.*

There is again no definitive recent treatment of American military aviation, but see, in addition to specialized studies cited for previous chapters, Craven and Cate, *The Army Air Forces in World War II;* Pogue, *Marshall,* vols. 1–2; Holley, *Buying Aircraft;* and Hansell, *The Air Plan That Defeated Hitler.*

Because the development of air strategy against Japan has stirred particular controversy among historians, I have cited secondary sources at length in notes, and I have often cited the original location of important primary sources even when they exist in some published form. A few secondary sources can be singled out. Though dated, Wohlstetter, *Pearl Harbor,* provides essential documentation and perspective. Harrington, "A Careless Hope," offered leads to sources and valuable interpretation even though I dispute it. Another valuable account is in Pogue, *Marshall,* vol. 2, with which I also take some exception. I am also indebted to the George C. Marshall Research Foundation, Lexington, Virginia, for providing me with additional original documentation and correspondence among participants and writers gleaned from its files and from the Hanson Baldwin Papers, Yale University. Schaller, *The U.S. Crusade in China,* includes an essential chapter on early, aborted plans to use China for bombing raids against Japan.

Notes

1. Orville H. Bullitt, ed., *For the President, Personal and Secret: Correspondence Between Franklin D. Roosevelt and William C. Bullitt* (Boston, 1972), 288, letter of Bullitt to Roosevelt, 20 September 1938.

2. Bond, *British Military Policy,* 278 ("*We cannot*") (emphasis in Bond); Quester, 97, 98 ("French cities," "another Commune"). On reactions to Barcelona, see Terraine, 54–55.

3. For Britain's "mirror image" of Germany's air capabilities, see Bialer, especially 133. See also Terraine, 53–70.

4. J. M. Spaight, *Air Power in the Next War* (1938), as quoted in Quester, 102.

5. On Roosevelt's sources of information, see Haight, 15; Lowenthal, 92; Dallek, 1972; Cole, *Lindbergh,* passim; Taylor, passim.

6. Cole, *Lindbergh,* 38 ("sense of decency"); Taylor, 849 ("Germany now," "something akin"). See also Robert Hessen, ed., *Berlin Alert: The Memoirs and Reports of Truman Smith* (Stanford, 1984), esp. 118–20.

7. Bullitt, *For the President,* 188, 288; see also 297–300.

8. Harold L. Ickes, *The Secret Diary of Harold L. Ickes* (New York, 1954), vol. 2, 469.

9. Accounts vary on the figures Roosevelt offered in November. I have relied on Arnold, notes on conference at White House, 14 November 1938, in file Conferences 1938–42, Chief of Staff Secretariat (1938–1942), WD Staff Records. For different figures, see Dallek, 173.

10. Arnold, 177 ("bolt"); Arnold, notes on conference cited in n. 9 ("striking force"); John Morton Blum, *From the Morgenthau Diaries: Years of Urgency, 1938–1941* (Boston, 1965), 49 ("'I am not sure'"); Arnold, 177 ("To the surprise"). See also Dallek, 173; Millis, 242. Both Arnold sources present only paraphrases of Roosevelt's words, while Morgenthau claimed to have remembered almost "his exact words." Arnold's claim in his memoirs that he was not surprised by Roosevelt's comments may have been the product of the same faulty memory that led him to date this conference to September, rather than November 14.

11. Haight, 64 ("table-pounding"); Watson, 143 ("impress Germany"); Haight, 89 ("only check"); Cole, *Roosevelt and the Isolationists,* 305 ("there would not").

12. Arnold, notes on November 14 conference cited in n. 9.

13. Franklin D. Roosevelt, *Complete Presidential Press Conferences of Franklin D. Roosevelt* (New York, 1972), vol. 12, 281; Blum, *Morgenthau Diaries*, 118.

14. Quotations from Lowenthal, 100, 101; Blum, *Morgenthau Diaries*, 76. See also Reynolds, chaps. 1-2, and Haight, passim, on Roosevelt's wariness about reliance on the British and the French.

15. Roosevelt, annual message, 4 January 1939, in Samuel I. Rosenman, ed., *The Public Papers and Addresses of Franklin D. Roosevelt* (New York, 1938-50), vol. 8, 2-4.

16. On polls, see Cantril, 939-43, 976-78. On problems and new methods of reading and shaping public opinion, see Leigh, chaps. 1-2.

17. *Life*, 24 October 1938, 18; *New York Times*, 16 October 1938; Bruce Bliven, "Picking Up the Pieces," *New Republic*, 19 October 1938, 295; George Fielding Eliot, *Bombs Bursting in Air: The Influence of Air Power on International Relations* (New York, 1939), 73-74; Lewis Mumford, *Men Must Act* (New York, 1939), 102-03. See also Eliot, "The Military Consequences of Munich," *Foreign Policy Reports*, 15 December 1938, 222-28, for his earlier views, and Vera Micheles Dean, "Diplomatic Background of Munich Accord," *Foreign Policy Reports*, 1 January 1939, 230-48.

18. *New York Times*, 15 November, 16 November 1938; Rosenman, *Public Papers*, vol. 7, 600-01; Johnson's statement is quoted in *Army and Navy Journal*, 16 November 1938, 243, 263; for Morgenthau's opposition to public statement on European air strengths, see Haight, 59. For Roosevelt's continued acceptance of German air superiority, see the account of his talk with Josephus Daniels on January 14, 1939, in Gloria Barron, *Leadership in Crisis* (New York, 1973), 27.

19. Bennett Champ Clark, "The Question of National Defense," radio address, 19 December 1938, in *Vital Speeches*, 15 January 1939, 219. See also "Rearmament vs Balderdash," *Time*, 19 December 1938, 11.

20. See esp. Haight, 94-95.

21. I prefer the terms *unilateralist* and *anti-interventionist* rather than *isolationist* to characterize shades of opposition to FDR's foreign policy. For a good definition of *isolationists* as bound together by little more than their unilateralist outlook, see Manfred Jonas, *Isolationism in America, 1935-1941* (Ithaca, 1966).

22. Quotations from Beard and Bliven in "Should Congress Approve the Proposed National Defense Program?" *Congressional Digest* 17 (March 1938): 90-93. For continued concern with naval policy, see also Beard's numerous other writings in 1939-40, Eliot's writings (many cited in chap. 3), and Hanson Baldwin, "Our New Long Shadow," *Foreign Affairs* 17 (April 1939): 465-76, and Baldwin, "Impregnable America," *American Mercury*, July 1939, 257-67. For additional discussion and sources, see Cole, *Roosevelt and the Isolationists*, 303-09, and Brune, 132-33. Other quotations: Clark, "The Question of National Defense" (see n. 19), 218 ("Hitler or someone"), and Josh Lee, "Roosevelt Policy Promotes Peace," speech of 12 February 39, *Vital Speeches*, 1 March 39, 306 ("restraining"). On Lindbergh's support of the heavy bomber's development in 1939, see Morrison, 9-10.

23. Herbert Hoover, "Our New Foreign Policy," speech before Council on Foreign Relations, 1 February 1939, in *Vital Speeches*, 15 February 1939, 258-61. See also Hanson Baldwin, "Impregnable America," and Baldwin, "Our New Long Shadow," both cited in n. 22; John Chamberlain, "The Airplane in War," *New Republic*, 10 August 1939, 51.

24. Quotations from Haight, 204. On the politics and fate of the French orders, see Haight, chaps. 6-9.

25. Memorandum by the Army Chief of Staff, 17 December 1938, quoted in Haight, 61-62.

26. Watson, 143, paraphrasing Roosevelt. On the possibility that Roosevelt had floated extravagant figures for political purposes, see Holley, *Buying Aircraft*, 170-74. See also Reynolds, 48-49; Haight, chap. 3; Keith McFarland, *Harry H. Woodring* (Lawrence, 1975), chap. 9; Pogue, vol. 1, chap. 19; Watson, chap. 5. On Hitler's efforts, see Cooper, 77-79.

27. Quotations from Larry I. Bland, ed., *The Papers of George Catlett Marshall*, vol. 1 (Baltimore, 1981), 690, 694, 691, 676, 644.

28. Hoover, "Our New Foreign Policy" (cited in n. 23); Reynolds, 49-50.

29. Haight, 55. On Arnold's view of Hitler's use of air power, see his speech of 25 January 1939, in

Speech, Article and Book file, Box 226, Arnold Papers. See also Arnold, testimony before Congress on 18 January 1939, in "Should America's Defense Frontiers Extend Beyond the American Continent?" *Congressional Digest* 18 (March 1939): 93.

30. "The Unwaged War," unsigned typescript article, n.d. (Fall 1938), in folder "Munich—influence of Air Power . . ." file 168.7012–18, Kuter Papers.

31. Wilson, memorandum, "Long Range Airplane Development," November 1938, in folder "Airplanes—Long Range—Need for—Col. Wilson's paper—after Munich," file 168.7012–20, Kuter Papers.

32. Andrews, "Modern Air Power," in *Vital Speeches,* 15 February 1939, 278–81. On tactical school ideas for transoceanic bombers, see Brune, 131.

33. Hansell, 56 ("national existence," etc.). See also Greer, "Development of Air Doctrine," and Fred Greene, "The Military View of American Foreign Policy, 1904–1940," *American Historical Review* 66 (January 1961): 367–75.

34. Copp, 477–79 (and n. 3) implies otherwise in an undocumented account.

35. Sources on heavy bomber orders and deliveries during this period are many and confusing, but see esp. Tate, 226; Futrell, 90; Haight, 184.

36. See Greer, 119; Craven and Cate, vol. 5, 3–11, 243–46.

37. Memorandum, Spaatz to Arnold, "Strategically offensive operations in the Far East," 1 September 1939, in Air AG file 381 Bulky (9–12–39), AAF Records.

38. Quotations from Joseph Alsop and Robert Kintner, *American White Paper* (New York, 1940), 60. For Spaatz recommendation of the B-29, see Greer, 119.

39. Quotations from Alsop and Kintner, *White Paper,* 65, 82.

40. Rosenman, *Public Papers,* vol. 9, 198–202.

41. Al Williams, radio address delivered 29 May 1940, "Real Air Power for the Defense of the United States," in *Vital Speeches,* 1 July 1940, 565–68.

42. Dallek, 225 ("this youngster"); Cole, *Lindbergh,* 189 ("If we say"), 89 ("Air defense"). On Lindbergh, I have drawn especially on Cole, chap. 11, for his views on air power, and chap. 19, for reactions to Lindbergh.

43. See, for example, Francis W. Drake, "Air Power: A Specific Proposal," *Atlantic,* June 1941, 673–80; Alexander de Seversky, "Twilight of Sea Power," *American Mercury,* June 1941, 647–58, and Seversky, "Why We Must Have a Separate Air Force," *Readers Digest,* March 1941, 197–213.

44. Hanson Baldwin, "Military Lessons of the War," *Yale Review,* n.s., 30 (June 1941): 665 ("the plane has"); Baldwin, "Blueprint for Victory," *Life,* 4 August 1941, 40 ("precision bombing"). Other quotations are, in order, from Baldwin, *United We Stand!* (New York, 1941), 188, 190, 5, 222. See also Baldwin, "U.S. Air Power," in *Fortune,* March 1941, 76ff.

45. Arnold and Eaker, *Winged Warfare* (New York, 1941), 132–34, 144–45, 240; Arnold and Eaker, *Army Flyer* (New York, 1942), 263–64; *Winged Warfare,* 260 ("threat").

46. Hastings, 116 ("absolutely devastating"); Higham, 130 ("If the object"); Walzer, 259 ("supreme emergency").

47. Culbert, 206; see also 201–09.

48. Culbert, 194 (MacLeish), 207 ("made Americans"); Edward R. Murrow, *This Is London* (New York, 1941), 152–53 ("There's almost"), 177 ("there are no words"), 149 ("talk about"), 161 ("serious and sensational"), 135 ("fanaticism"), 186–87 ("who had been").

49. Willy Ley, *Bombs and Bombing* (New York, 1941), 121; White et al., *Zero Hour* (New York, 1940), 161; "Beneath the Bombardment," *Commonweal,* 27 December 1940, 247–48.

50. Joseph C. Harsch, *Pattern of Conquest* (New York, 1941), 303 ("a greater proportion"); "Airpower," *Life,* 1 December 1941, 115; "British Bombers Launch the Battle of Germany," *Life,* 4 August 1941, 20–21.

51. Gertsch, 40; Hopkins, 458.

52. Quotations from Holley, *Buying Aircraft,* 244, 235. For an able description of these dilemmas, see Holley, chap. 11.

53. See Holley, *Buying Aircraft,* 221–28.

54. The overriding importance of logistical rather than strategic genius is demonstrated in Overy, *Air War*.

55. Matloff and Snell, 14 ("The United States," quotation from staff memorandum of 26 June 1940 paraphrasing Roosevelt's comments); Wilson, *The First Summit*, 135 ("desperate"); Norman Beasley, *Knudsen: A Biography* (New York, 1946), 309 ("command of the air"; also has full text of Roosevelt's May 4 orders). See also Robert Sherwood, *Roosevelt and Hopkins: An Intimate History* (New York, 1948), 272. On Arnold's return to the White House, see Coffey, *HAP*, 220. On May 14, 1941, orders, see also Holley, *Buying Aircraft*, 237.

56. Francis L. Loewenheim, Harold D. Langley, and Manfred Jonas, eds., *Roosevelt and Churchill: Their Secret Wartime Correspondence* (New York, 1975), 151 (Churchill quotation); Reynolds, 212 ("a believer in"); Henry H. Adams, *Harry Hopkins: A Biography* (New York, 1977), 235 ("airplanes tonight"); Reynolds, 201 ("as a stepping stone"); Henry Morgenthau, Presidential Diaries, vol. 4, 4 August 1941 entry ("lick Hitler," etc.), Morgenthau Papers.

57. Dallek, 285 ("wished to"), 310–11 (Douglas); Leighton, 234–35 (Lippmann). On polls, see above, n. 16. My analysis here draws in part on Dallek, Leighton, and Reynolds.

58. On American reactions to the British experience, see Hansell, *Air Plan*, 53; Pogue, vol. 2, 67; Arnold, 215–28; Coffey, *HAP*, 227–32, 233–34, 239; Greer, 116–18; Fabyanic, 66–74.

59. Leutze, 190–96, 202–03, is among the best of many descriptions of Stark's plan.

60. Craven and Cate, vol. 1, 137 ("a sustained"); Memorandum, Joint Board No. 325, Joint Board to the Special Naval Observer and Special Army Observer, London, n.d. (probably September 1941), in file WPD 4402-64, WD Staff Records.

61. Watson, 338–39.

62. Hansell, *Air Plan*, 74, 79.

63. Hansell, *Air Plan*, 304 ("heavy and sustained").

64. Dallek, 242.

65. Wohlstetter, 85, 82; Chihiro Hosoya, "Miscalculation in Deterrent Policy: Japanese–U.S. Relations, 1938–41," *Journal of Peace Research* 5 (1968): 111 (Stimson).

66. Claire Lee Chennault, *Way of a Fighter: Memoirs of Claire Lee Chennault* (New York, 1949), 97.

67. Blum, *Morgenthau Diaries, 1938–1941*, 366, 367.

68. Notes on conference in the Office of the Chief of Staff, 23 December 1940, in Chief of Staff file Conference Sept. 26, 1940–Dec. 31, 1942, WD Staff Records.

69. See Schaller, 79–82, and notes on conference in the Office of the Secretary of War, 10 June 1941, and 21 July 1941, in file Secretary of War Conferences, Chief of Staff Secretariat Records 1938–42, WD Staff Records. Quotations from Schaller, 79.

70. Memorandum, Chief of Staff to Assistant Chief of Staff, WPD, subject: White House Conference on Thursday, 16 January 1941, in file WPD 4175-18, WD Staff Records ("the possibility of"); letter, Stark to Kimmel, 25 February 1941, in Joint Committee on the Investigation of the Pearl Harbor Attack, *Hearings*, 79th Congress, 1st Session, 1946 (hereafter cited as Pearl Harbor *Hearings*), part 16, 2149–50.

71. Quotations from British–United States Staff Conversations: Minutes of Meetings, 3 February 1941, 26 February 1941, in file WPD 4402-89, WD Staff Records; Leutze, 241, suggests that Churchill supported consideration of carrier raids on "the Japanese homeland towns." Stark quotation from letter, Stark to Kimmel, 19 April 1941, in Pearl Harbor *Hearings*, part 16, 2164.

72. The records in the Philippines of what became called the Far Eastern Air Force, which would have carried out aerial missions from the islands, were largely lost or destroyed in the American defeat there in 1941–42, as were the records of its superior organization, the United States Armed Forces in the Far East, MacArthur's command. War Department and particularly Air Corps/Army Air Forces records for 1940–41 maintained in Washington have in many cases been destroyed or widely scattered to personal collections. On some of the problems with the documentary record for this episode, see Robert F. Futrell, "Air Hostilities in the Philippines, 8 December 1941," *Air University Review* 16 (January–February 1965): 33–45.

73. Quotations from Watson, 416.

74. Notes on conference in the Office of the Chief of Staff, 25 February 1941, in file Notes on

Conferences, Chief of Staff Secretariat 1941–42, WD Staff Records (Marshall quotation); Allison Ind, *Bataan, The Judgement Seat: The Saga of the Philippines Comand of the United States Army Air Force, May 1941 to May 1942* (New York, 1944), 53 ("Hainan, Formosa"); letter, Nelson T. Johnson to Stanley Hornbeck, 13 March 1941, in folder Nelson T. Johnson, 1942, Box 262, Hornbeck Papers ("confident that"); Reynolds, 249 ("Wops"); Matloff and Snell, 66 ("which Japan," "It is probable"). On early Air Corps efforts to identify targets in Japan, see letters from Secretary of Air Staff to several officials in other departments, all dated 12 November 1941 and referring to planning dating back to April 1941, in file SAS 360.02 Japan, Box 101, Arnold Papers; and letter, R. C. Candee, Colonel, Air Corps, Chief, Intelligence Division, to Leland Olds, Chairman, Federal Power Commission, 25 April 1941, in file 142.031-1, AFSHRC. On diminishing fears of Japanese capabilities, see Wohlstetter, 91.

75. The phrase is Daniel Harrington's.

76. Wohlstetter, 268, uses "gradual encroachment" phrase and dates the notion behind it especially to the last weeks before Pearl Harbor. But the evidence she presents on anticipation of Japanese attack northward against Russia over the summer and early fall suggests that expectations of "gradual encroachment" may have been even stronger between June and November; see 101, 114, 129–31, 132–34, 136–38, 141, 142, 144, 150–51, 155–66, 232.

77. For early efforts to deploy B-17s see memorandum for Chief of Army Air Forces, unsigned, n.d. (27 July 1941), in file 452.1 A,-Airplanes, Foreign Files Philippine Islands, Air AG Central Decimal Files, AAF Records; Brief of Information and Decisions at War Council Meeting, 28 July 1941, and notes on conference in the Office of the Secretary of War, 28 July 1941, both in file SecWar Conferences, Chief of Staff Secretariat 1938–42, WD Staff Records; Craven and Cate, vol. 1, 178.

78. On these operational difficulties, see, among much literature, Craven and Cate, vol. 1, 178–93; Walter D. Edmonds, *They Fought With What They Had: The Story of the Army Air Forces in the Southwest Pacific, 1941–1942* (Boston, 1951), 7–13.

79. Arnold's journal of the Argentia conference, in folder "Notes—in long hand 'Argentia' Conference," Conference File, Box 181, Arnold Papers; Arnold, 248–50; Costello, 95; Wilson, *The First Summit*, 147–48.

80. Stimson Diary, 12 September 1941.

81. Quotations from memorandum, Marshall to President, n.d. (20 or 21 September 1941), in folder "Information Used by the Chief of Staff at Conference with the President, Sept. 22, 1941," file Chief of Staff Secretariat Conferences 1938–42, WD Staff Records; letter, Roosevelt to Stimson, 14 October 1941, in file "White House Correspondence, June 26, 1940–Dec. 31, 1941," Stimson "Safe" File, SecWar Records. For Stimson's attention to bomber flights, see, among much evidence, Stimson Diary, 16 September, 8 October, 9 October 1941; file on Philippines in Stimson Top Secret Correspondence File 1940–45, SecWar Records; and notes, AWPD–Officers Meetings, for 14 October and 15 October 1941, in file 145.96–93, AFSHRC.

82. Arnold quotation from memorandum, Arnold to Stimson, 16 October 1941, supplied to help Stimson prepare letter to Roosevelt, in Stimson "Safe" File Big Bomber Program, SecWar Records. All other quotations from letter, Stimson to Roosevelt, 21 October 1941, in Stimson Diary, 21 October 1941.

83. Memorandum, Roosevelt to Hopkins, 25 October 1941, written on Stimson's letter to Roosevelt of 21 October 1941, in folder War Department: Henry L. Stimson, 1940–41, Box 106, President's Secretary File, FDR Papers ("a bit bewildered"); memorandum, Marshall and Stark to President, 5 November 1941, in file WPD 4389-29, WD Staff Records ("potency"); Dallek, 303 ("a good deal"); Loewenheim, *Roosevelt and Churchill,* 163–164 ("opposite"); Stimson Diary, 7 November 1941 ("whether the people"). Hull's memoirs stress his warning about the possibility of attack on American forces but do not mention the "poll" noted in Stimson's diary; see Cordell Hull, *The Memoirs of Cordell Hull* (New York, 1948), vol. 2, 1057–58. On Stimson's talks with Hopkins, see Stimson Diary, 30 October 1941.

84. Stimson Diary, 28 October 1941 ("diplomatic arm" etc.); Joint Board minutes, 3 November 1941, JB Records ("some very clever diplomacy," etc.). See also memorandum of conference, 4 October 1941, with Stimson Diary, 6 October 1941; memorandum of conference, 21 October 1941, with Stimson diary entry of that date; letter, Stimson to Hull, 4 October 1941, item 1873, in Classified File (Secret), SecWar Records.

85. On British buildup, see H. P. Willmott, *Empires in the Balance: Japanese and Allied Pacific*

Strategies to April 1942 (Annapolis, 1982), 126–28, and Reynolds, 239–40, 242–43. On pleas from Dutch and Chinese and responses to them, see Stimson Diary, 25 September and 30 September 1941; letter, Chennault to Madame, 28 October 1941, in folder "Madame Chiang Kai-Shek File," American Volunteer Group Files, Box 1, Chennault Papers; memoranda by Bundy and Gerow of 1 November 1941, in OPD Exec 8, Box A, WD Staff Records; memorandum, Marshall and Stark to President, 5 November 1941, in WPD 4389-29, WD Staff Records.

86. Quotation and discussion of reconnaissance missions in notes on conference in the Office of Chief of Staff, 26 November 1941, in Chief of Staff Project Decimal File 1941–43 (Philippines), WD Staff Records.

87. Marshall quotation from ibid.; letter, Roosevelt to Churchill, 15 October 1941, in Warren Kimball, ed., *Churchill and Roosevelt: The Complete Correspondence* (Princeton, 1984), vol. 1, 250. On military estimates of probable Japanese action, see Wohlstetter, 152–58, 292–312.

88. Quotations from memorandum dated 15 November 1941 by one of the reporters attending the conference, Robert Sherrod. This memorandum was sent to me by the George C. Marshall Foundation, which in turn obtained it from the Hanson Baldwin Papers, Baldwin having obtained it from Sherrod. Unlike Sherrod's published account in Overseas Press Club of America, *I Can Tell It Now* (New York, 1964), 39–45, his original memorandum makes no clear distinction between paraphrase and direct quotation of Marshall's remarks. I have relied on Sherrod's original memorandum on the assumption that his later reconstruction of what was direct quotation apparently relied on memory alone. A brief paraphrase by another correspondent, Ernest K. Lindley, also provided by the Marshall Foundation, generally confirms Sherrod's account but because it contains less detail is not quoted here.

89. Quotation from Pogue, vol. 2, 203; see also 186–89, 194–96, 201–03. Harrington, "A Careless Hope," an otherwise probing account, omits the November 15 conference.

90. Letter, Marshall to Hanson Baldwin, 21 September 1949, responding to an accurate paraphrase of the original documents offered by Baldwin to Marshall in letter of 16 September 1949; both in Baldwin Papers, as supplied by Marshall Foundation. Much of the Marshall letter is reprinted in Baldwin, *Great Battles Lost and Won: Great Campaigns of World War II* (New York, 1966), 420–21. Some other officials involved later denied that offensive uses of air power were under consideration; see letter, Lewis Brereton to Forrest Pogue, 2 July 1964, obtained from Marshall Foundation (Brereton was commander of the Far Eastern Air Force), and Futrell, "Air Hostilities," 40.

91. See "Status of incendiary bombs for the Philippines," 5 September 1941, in Diary, Chief of Air Staff, 5 September 1941, file 336, Central Decimal Files (1939–42), AAF Records; memorandum, Arnold for Marshall, 1 December 1941, initialed by Marshall, in Jacket 254 (Philippines), Official Files, Box 51, Arnold Papers; notes on Air Corps staff meetings, 1 December 1941, in file 145.96-220, AFSHRC; Mountcastle, 98–101, 136; Louis F. Fieser, *The Scientific Method: A Personal Account of Unusual Projects in War and Peace* (New York, 1964), 23.

92. See memorandum, Lt. Col. James G. Taylor, Chief, Intelligence Division, Air Corps, to Assistant Chief of Staff, G-2, 20 August 1941, and memorandum, Lt. Col. Ralph C. Smith, Executive Officer, G-2, for Chief of Air Corps, 8 September 1941, in file 384.3 Japan, Project Decimal File 1941–45, G-2 Records; lists of maps and charts sent to the Far Eastern Air Force in September–October 1941, in file 000-800-Misc-A, Foreign Files Philippine Islands, Central Decimal Files Oct 1942–1944, Air AG Security Classified Records, AAF Records; memoranda, L.S.K. (Laurence S. Kuter) to Secretary, General Staff, 21 November 1941 and 4 December 1941, in Project Decimal File 1941–43 (Philippines), WD Staff Records (quotations from one of two November 21 memoranda by Kuter).

93. Quotation from memorandum, Marshall to Stark, 12 September 1941, in Pearl Harbor *Hearings*, part 16, 2211–12; a copy of that memorandum went to Stimson. On Stimson, see also, in addition to the material cited above, memorandum, Gerow to Secretary of War, 8 October 1941, in file WPD 3251-60, WD Staff Records.

94. Quotations from Gerow memo cited in note 93, and from "Strategic Estimate of Situation from Ground, Air and Naval Viewpoints," n.d. (handwritten notation of November 1941), in file WPD 5510, WD Staff Records. For other planning statements, see folder marked "Theater Studies accomplished in War Plans Division prior to U.S. entry into World War II. . . ," in WPD 5510; memorandum, Assistant

Chief of Staff, War Plans Division, to Chief of Staff, 3 November 1941, Annex III, Tab B, in file WPD 4389-29, both in WD Staff Records. On question of information received by MacArthur command, Kuter memorandum of 21 November 1941, cited n. 92, indicates that maps on industrial objectives in Japan had been sent by that date.

95. Bundy, memorandum for record, 1 November 1941, in OPD Exec 8, Book A, WD Staff Records. War Department and AAF records, which might shed further light on preparations for and intentions of the November 15 conference, are substantial for this period but incomplete for November. According to National Archives staff, files on Marshall's conferences with his staff in November were never accessioned by the National Archives, and numerous attempts by this author and archivists at the National Archives and the Marshall Foundation failed to uncover them.

96. For estimates of bombers' radius of action, see memorandum, Air Staff or Chief of Staff, 1 December 1941, in Diary, January 2–December 21, 1941, Box 7, Spaatz Papers; Craven and Cate, vol. 1, 748–50. On use of the B-24, see Sherrod's notes on November 15 conference of Marshall with press (cited n. 88), and memorandum, Arnold to Stimson, 16 October 1941, in Stimson "Safe" file Big Bomber Program, SecWar Records.

97. Memorandum for Chief of Army Air Forces, unsigned, n.d. (27 July 1941), Tab 4, in file 452.1 A,- Airplanes, Foreign Files Philippine Islands, Central Decimal Files, AAF Records ("would be impressed," etc.). On negotiation, see memorandum, Chaney for Harriman, 11 October 1941, in Stimson "Safe" File Russia, SecWar Records; W. Averell Harriman and Elie Abel, *Special Envoy to Churchill and Stalin, 1941–46* (New York, 1975), 88; Lukas, 96–98.

98. Notes on conference in office of Deputy Chief of Staff, 15 August 1941, in Chief of Staff file Notes on Conferences (June 1941–Nov. 1942) 21: August 1941, WD Staff Records; Stimson to FDR, 21 October 1941, Stimson Diary, 21 October 1941 ("the power," etc.); memorandum by Kuter, 21 November 1941, cited in n. 92 ("both airplanes"). On negotiations, see also Stimson, memorandum of conference with Harriman, 21 October 41, Stimson Diary, 21 October 1941; Stimson Diary, 28 October 1941. On staff studies, see "Theater Studies . . ." and "Strategic Estimate. . . ," both in file WPD 5510, and Gerow to Chief of Staff, 3 November 41, in file WPD 4389-29, all in WD Staff Records. On poison gas, see Stimson Diary, 21 November 1941.

99. Points made in letter, Sherrod to Pogue, 28 August 1969, obtained from the Marshall Foundation.

100. Stimson diary, 28 October 1941 ("very anxious," etc.); Stimson to Marshall, 31 October 1941, in file Philippines, Stimson Top Secret Correspondence File 1940–45, SecWar Records ("when the news"); memorandum for record by Bundy, 1 November 1941, in OPD Exec 8, Book A, WD Staff Records. On evidence of Marshall's meeting with Roosevelt, see "President Roosevelt's Engagements with the Secretaries of State, War and Navy, General Marshall and Admiral Stark October 1st to December 7, 1941," in file marked "Copies of Exhibits Belonging to J. Bayard Clark," Army Pearl Harbor Board—Exhibits, Hearings and Investigations, SecWar Records, which indicates Roosevelt met with Marshall at 12:15 but does not note an agenda.

101. Joseph Alsop and Robert Kintner, column from *Washington Post,* 25 March 1941, in folder "Lauchlin Currie," Box 137, Hornbeck Papers. *U. S. News,* 8 August 1941, 10–12, and 31 October 1941, 18–19. Conclusions on public opinion based on standard secondary literature in the field, but precision is difficult in part because Americans were polled far less often about the Far Eastern crisis than about the European war—itself an indication of relative priorities and anxieties. See polls in Cantril, 975, 1076–77, 1173, the latter indicating that in a November 25, 1941, poll, 48 percent of respondents regarded war with Japan as "comparatively easy," while 35 percent termed it "difficult."

102. On doubts about strategic wisdom, see Kuter memorandum of 21 November 1941, cited in n. 92. On Arnold's last-minute efforts, see his *Global Mission,* 268–69.

103. Quotations from Kinoaki Matsuo, *How Japan Plans to Win* (Boston, 1942), 271. See also Robert J. C. Butow, *Tojo and the Coming of the War* (Princeton, 1961), 362–63; Harrington, 236; Wohlstetter, 163–65; Donald S. Detwiler and Charles B. Burdick, eds., *War in Asia and the Pacific 1937–1949* (New York, 1980), vol. 2, part 4, 54, 63–64, 79–80, 81, 89. On Japanese spy network, see Edmonds, *They Fought,* 23, 37. On intercepts, see Department of Defense, *The 'MAGIC' Background of Pearl Harbor* (Washington, 1979), vol. 4, 114–18, A-162, A-168, A-169.

104. Stimson Diary, 27 November 1941 ("glad to have time," etc.).

105. Notes on conference, 26 November 1941, cited in n. 86 ("Thus far," etc.); memorandum, Marshall and Stark for President, 27 November 1941, in Wohlstetter, 248–50 ("to gain time" and listing of possible Japanese objectives); Sherwood, *Roosevelt and Hopkins*, 428 ("would merely use"). See also Stimson Diary, 27 and 28 November 1941.

106. Wohlstetter, 250 ("prior to the"); James Leutze, *A Different Kind of Victory: A Biography of Admiral Thomas C. Hart* (Annapolis, 1981), 222–23 ("*Panay*-type incident," etc.); notes on conference, 26 November 1941, cited in n. 86 ("might cause"). For FDR's statement that Japan had learned about the B-17s, see Blum, *Morgenthau Diaries*, 389.

107. Quotation from interviews with B-17 crews of the Far Eastern Air Force, in file 168.7022-6, AFSHRC.

108. "Picnic" from ibid. On air crews' overconfidence, see also Edmonds, *They Fought*, 5. For Washington, see Wohlstetter, especially 337–38 on the intelligence establishment.

CHAPTER 5

Sources

In describing the nature of decision making for air war and the early plans and operations after Pearl Harbor, I have supplemented archival sources with standard secondary accounts: Craven and Cate, *The AAF in World War II*; Kennett, *A History of Strategic Bombing*; Costello, *Pacific War*; Higham, *Air Power*; Pogue, *Marshall*, vol. 2; Holley, *Buying Aircraft*; Overy, *Air War*; Dallek, *Roosevelt*; and Hayes, *The History of the Joint Chiefs of Staff*. For debate about the ethics of bombing within the American AAF, see Schaffer, "American Military Ethics." That debate within British circles has received far more scholarly attention; see, among many titles, Hastings, *Bomber Command*, and Terraine, *A Time for Courage*. Walzer, *Just and Unjust Wars*, shaped my perspective in many ways.

For expectations of air power outside official circles I have relied mainly on the contemporary record. Two older articles offered useful preliminary judgments with which I sometimes differ: Gertsch, "The Strategic Air Offensive and the Mutation of American Values, 1937–1945," and Hopkins, "Bombing and the American Conscience." On journalism, Knightley, *The First Casualty*, is valuable if sometimes sensational. For the broader contours of American wartime culture Blum, *V Was for Victory*, is essential. Essential assistance in locating and interpreting sources for the visual record of air power came from George Roeder, historian at the Art Institute of Chicago.

Notes

1. General Leonard Gerow, in notes on conference in General Bryden's Office, 9 December 1941, in Chief of Staff file Notes on Conferences (June 1941–Nov. 1942) 29: December 1941, WD Staff Records; U.S. Department of Defense, *The Entry of the Soviet Union into the War Against Japan* (Washington, 1955) 1 (MacArthur); Report from Prime Minister Churchill to Brigadier Hollis, Chief of Staff Committee, part 4: Notes on the Pacific, 20 December 1941, in Box 1, Churchill–FDR, vol. 3, Map Room Papers, FDR Papers; Cordell Hull, *Memoirs* (New York, 1948), vol. 2, 1111–12; Conference with Air Marshal Portal, 22 December 1941, notes in folder "White House Conferences," Conference File, Box 180, Arnold Papers; memorandum, Arnold for Air War Plans Division, 31 December 41, in Jacket 242 (Japan), Official Files, Box 50, Arnold Papers. See also Julian, 22–25; Pogue, vol. 2, 239.

2. AWPD/4, 15 December 1941, quoted in Julian, 24.

3. H. G. Nicholas, ed., *Washington Despatches, 1941–1945* (Chicago, 1981), 67, 108, 180.

4. Blum, 16; Ralph Ingersoll, *The Battle is the Pay-Off* (New York, 1943), 207; "Life on the News-fronts of the World," *Life*, 15 June 1942, 30.

5. The term is used by Walzer, 171, 173–74.

6. Quotations from memorandum, Arnold to Hopkins, 15 July 1942, in file "Army Air Forces," Box 131, Hopkins Papers; memorandum Arnold to Hopkins, 7 October 1942, in Jacket 91 (Mr. Hopkins),

Official File, Box 43, Arnold Papers; memorandum, Arnold for President, 8 October 1942, in Naval Aides File: A/16—General correspondence, Box 164, Map Room Papers, FDR Papers. See also memorandum, Stimson for President, 12 April 1942, in folder War Department: Henry L. Stimson, 1942–45, Box 106, President's Secretary Files, FDR Papers; letter, Arnold for Hopkins, 3 September 1942, in Jacket 95 (Mr. Hopkins), Official Files, Box 43, Arnold Papers; memorandum, Lovett for Secretary of War, 15 November 1942, in file SAS 381 War Plans, Box 113, Arnold Papers; Fanton, chap. 5 passim; Robert Sherwood, *Roosevelt and Hopkins: An Intimate History* (New York, 1948), 581.

7. Craven and Cate, vol. 1, 610.

8. Quotations from Fanton, 76, 79. See Fanton, 71–85; Craven and Cate, vol. 1, 246–47; Overy, 153–54.

9. Roosevelt, State of the Union Address, 6 January 1942, in Samuel I. Rosenman, ed., *The Public Papers and Addresses of Franklin D. Roosevelt* (New York, 1938–50), vol. 11, 36; Roosevelt, fireside chat, 23 February 1942, in Rosenman, vol. 11, 113; campaign radio address, 2 November 1944, in Rosenman, vol. 13, 384. For other examples of how Roosevelt related combat to the production effort, see Message to Congress on the Progress of the War, 17 September 1943, in Rosenman, vol. 12, 396–99; *Complete Presidential Press Conferences of Franklin D. Roosevelt* (New York, 1972), conference of 12 October 1943, vol. 22, 142–43.

10. Fireside chat, 29 April 1942, in Rosenman, *Public Papers,* vol. 11, 229; Message of 17 September 1943, in Rosenman, vol. 12, 392. For reporters' questions and FDR's responses, see especially *Complete Press Conferences,* conferences of 15 February 1944, vol. 23, 47–51; 22 February 1944, vol. 23, 63–64; 10 March 1944, vol. 23, 85–88; 28 March 1944, vol. 23, 121–22.

11. State of the Union Address, 7 January 1943, in Rosenman, *Public Papers,* vol. 12, 23–25; speech of 12 February 1943, in Rosenman, vol. 12, 79; fireside chat, 12 June 1944, in Rosenman, vol. 13, 175.

12. State of Union Address, 7 January 1943, in Rosenman, *Public Papers;* remarks on board the *Iowa,* 16 December 1943, in Rosenman, vol. 12, 547. Churchill statement is in *Complete Press Conferences,* 25 May 1943, vol. 21, 351.

13. For this and succeeding paragraphs, see, in addition to the standard accounts of the Doolittle raid, Arnold, notes on conference at the White House, 26 January 1942, in folder "White House Conferences," conference file, Box 180, Arnold Papers, for Roosevelt on the value of raids from "a psychological standpoint"; memorandum, Scanlon for Arnold, 2 February 1942, file 384.3 Japan, Box 114, Arnold Papers, for quotations; letter, Stanley Hornbeck to Marshall, 14 March 1942, in folder General George Catlett Marshall, Box 293, Hornbeck Papers. Roosevelt's interest in air raids on Japan during this period recurs in primary documents too numerous to mention here.

14. Memorandum, Arnold for President, 21 April 1942, in Naval Aide's Files A/16—Japan and Japanese Islands—1942–1945, Box 167, Map Room Papers, FDR Papers; Roosevelt, fireside chat, 28 April 1942, in Rosenman, *Public Papers,* vol. 11, 230; Doolittle, quoted in Carroll V. Glines, *Doolittle's Tokyo Raiders* (New York, 1964), 86–87.

15. Dallek, 334–36.

16. Or as it has been argued: "Preemptive bellicosity, instead of putting out the popular fires, fans them." See Wills, 285. For reactions to the news of executions, see the newspaper clippings for April 1943 gathered by the AAF and found in file K-141.2424-1, AFSHRC. For quotation about and characterization of the parade, see Dower, *War Without Mercy,* 92.

17. Roosevelt to Arnold, 22 May 1942, in Jacket 150 (President), Official Files, Box 145, Arnold Papers; Roosevelt, memorandum for Stimson, Marshall, Arnold, Knox, King, and Hopkins, 6 May 1942, in file War Plans, Stimson "Safe" File, SecWar Records; letter, Donovan to Hopkins, 11 May 1942, in folder "Russia: Siberia," Box 218, Hopkins Papers; minutes of the Pacific War Council, 17 June 1942, in Naval Aide's Files: Pacific War Council, Box 168, Map Room Papers, FDR Papers; Thorne, 164 (Churchill). On the Chennault plan, see Spector, 341–42.

18. Arnold, "America Takes the Offensive," address of 8 June 1942, in *Vital Speeches of the Day,* 15 August 1942, 642–45; press release, dated 12 September 1943, on statement by Arnold (in *Flying*), in folder General Arnold, Box 19, Hornbeck Papers; Lovett, quoted in Fanton, 171.

19. Advertisements examined were drawn largely from *Life,* but the same ads often appeared in many

other magazines. In describing other aspects of the airplane's wartime image, I have drawn on Corn, chaps. 5–6. I have explored the flourishing of "geopolitical" studies in unpublished writings.

20. Emile Gauvreau and Lester Cohen, *Billy Mitchell: Founder of Our Air Force and Prophet Without Honor* (New York, 1942) 198, 79, 226–27; Arthur Krock, "Mitchell Air Prophecy Comes to Grim Fruition," *New York Times,* 14 December 1941; William Bradford Huie, *The Fight for Air Power* (New York, 1942), 304, 310. Gauvreau's charges were given even more sweeping and turgid expression in *The Wild Blue Yonder: Sons of the Prophet Carry On* (New York, 1944), in which he found what he called "The Slaughter of Inventive Genius" to be a national trait, particularly among "the American ruling class and its Washington bureaucracy." See also Alexander P. de Seversky, *Victory Through Air Power* (New York, 1942), and the more balanced presentations in Louis A. Sigaud, *Douhet and Aerial Warfare* (New York, 1941), and Levine, *Mitchell.*

21. Coffey, *HAP,* 257–58; Fanton, 174–76.

22. Huie, *Fight for Air Power,* 257, 264; William Ziff, *The Coming Battle of Germany* (New York, 1942), 187, 160, 272.

23. Francis Vivian Drake, "Victory is In the Air," *Atlantic Monthly,* March 1942, 303, 305. See also Drake, "The Air Plan: An Expert Proposes a Method of Beating the Axis from the Air Within Six Months," in *Life,* 26 July 1943, 67–72.

24. Allan A. Michie, *The Air Offensive Against Germany* (New York, 1943), 112–13, 116, 12.

25. De Seversky, *Victory Through Air Power,* 11. For an exception to this pattern, see Gauvreau, *The Wild Blue Yonder,* esp. chap. 19, which championed international agreements for the control of air power.

26. *Victory Through Air Power,* 102, 11, 101.

27. Ibid., 101, 120.

28. Hanson Baldwin, *Strategy for Victory* (New York, 1942), 18; George Fielding Eliot, *Hour of Triumph* (New York, 1944), 78, 77.

29. See, for example, the views of Huie and Michie as of March 1943, as expressed in "What Should Be Our Air Strategy Against Germany?", radio broadcast of "America's Town Meeting of the Air," 4 March 1943, transcript in Jacket 36, Official Files, Box 41, Arnold Papers.

30. Lt. Col. Harold E. Hartney, "The Meaning of Air Power," *Saturday Review of Literature,* 2 May 1942, 5–6; Donald W. Mitchell, "The Dominance of Air Power," *Nation,* 23 May 1942, 603–04. See also Hopkins, 466.

31. For the origins and making of the film, see Richard A. Shale, "Donald Duck Joins Up: The Walt Disney Studio during World War II" (Ph.D. diss., University of Michigan, 1976), chap. 5, and, more speculatively, Richard Schickel, *The Disney Vision* (New York, 1968), 232.

32. Shale, "Donald Duck Joins Up," 142, 144–45, ("was saved" and other characterizations of the film, which I have paraphrased); Manny Farber, "Not So Sound as Furious," *New Republic,* 6 September 1943, 336 ("a carnival"). I viewed a black-and-white print of the film at the Library of Congress, Motion Picture and Television Reading Room.

33. Farber, "Not So Sound as Furious"; James Agee, *Agee on Film* (New York, 1958–60), vol. 1, 43–44. For *New York Times* review, see *NYT Film Reviews 1913–69* (1979), vol. 3, 1947–48. The claim about Roosevelt and Churchill is made in Shale, "Donald Duck," 150–51, and in Bob Thomas, *Walt Disney: An American Original* (New York, 1976), 185–86.

34. The characterization of *Winged Victory,* released in December 1944, is in Joe Morella, Edward Z. Epstein, and John Griggs, *The Films of World War II* (New York, 1973), 215. The interpretation of the bomber's image in *Air Force* is mine, but for a valuable discussion of the making and meaning of the film in other ways, see the introduction to the screenplay by Lawrence Howard Suid, *Air Force* (Madison, 1983). On *The Purple Heart,* see Dower, *War Without Mercy,* 50.

35. Murrow, quoted in Knightley, 313. This and the succeeding paragraph draw heavily on Knightley. On British censorship, see especially Longmate, 367–70.

36. Knightley, 333, 326.

37. Robert Sherrod, *Tarawa: The Story of a Battle* (New York, 1944; Fredericksburg, Texas, 1973), 69–70, 149, 150, 151.

38. Quoted in Herbert Parmet, *Jack: The Struggles of John F. Kennedy* (New York, 1981), 112.

39. See, for example, James Saxon Childers, *War Eagles: The Story of the Eagle Squadron* (New York, 1943); many of the accounts from books and magazines collected in *Combat in the Air*, selected by Maude Owens Walters (New York, 1944); Captain Ted W. Lawson, *Thirty Seconds Over Tokyo* (New York, 1943); Robert L. Scott, Jr., *God Is My Co-Pilot* (New York, 1943) (quotation from p. 254), and typical features in *Life*: its cover story on Joe Foss, 7 June 1943, 88–96, and "Aces of World War II," 15 May 1944, 85–88.

40. A. J. Liebling, *New Yorker* story in Walters, *Combat in the Air*, 33; A. J. Liebling, "The Dixie Demo Jr.," *New Yorker*, 7 November 1942, 31. For a good example of the bomber as hero, see the account by an anonymous AAF captain, "24 Hours of a Bomber Pilot," *Harpers*, August 1944, 283–90.

41. H. S. Canby, "A Hero for America," *Saturday Review of Literature*, 22 May 1942, 10.

42. Steinbeck, *Bombs Away* (New York, 1942), 49, 13.

43. Ibid., 32, 66, 23, 46, 17, 34. As John Blum has commented in *V Was for Victory*, 58: "A culture that had made heroes of its athletes could hardly avoid making athletes of its heroes." On postwar notions of the organization man, see William H. Whyte, Jr., *The Organization Man* (New York, 1956).

44. Steinbeck, *Bombs Away*, 72, 45.

45. The quoted phrase is used by Blum in characterizing John Hersey's writings; see Blum, 62.

46. Steinbeck, *Once There Was a War* (London, 1959, 1961), as quoted in Knightley, 276.

47. Steinbeck, *Bombs Away*, 21, 170.

48. Brendan Gill, "Young Man Behind Plexiglas," *New Yorker*, 12 August 1944, 26–35 passim.

49. Wecter, 520.

50. Sherrod, *Tarawa*, preface to the 1973 edition, ix.

51. *Life*: "Second Front," 27 July 1942, 26 ("relatively cheap"); "Hamburg in Ruins," 23 August 1943, 34–35; "The Chimneys of Leipzig," 15 May 1944, 100ff; Charles J. V. Murphy, "The Unknown Battle," 16 October 1944, 97–110. See also Murphy, "The Airmen and the Invasion," 10 April 1944, 94–106.

52. See *Life*: "Speaking of Pictures," 16 August 1943, 10–12; "Jap Suicides on Attu," 3 April 1944, 36–37; Cecil Brown, "How Japan Wages War," 11 May 1942, 98–108; photo essay, "Japan," 18 September 1944, 60–66.

53. Jerome Bruner, *Mandate From the People* (New York, 1944), 151. See more generally Bruner, chap. 7, and Cantril, 500–01, 1090, 1097. On the unquestioned assumption that the Japanese were more hated, see Dower, *War Without Mercy*, esp. 8, 33, 78.

54. For polls on air war, see Cantril, 922, 923, 1067–68. For a different view, see Gertsch, 41, who argues that the prophets' "influence in guiding public opinion was most significant." In fact, Gertsch introduces no evidence to measure what was essentially unmeasurable, and I prefer more modest conclusions about that influence.

55. Hopkins, 463.

56. "Bombers Over Tokyo," *Christian Century*, 29 April 1942, 550–51; *Commonweal*, quoted in Hopkins, 466.

57. *New York Times*, 6 March 1944, 1; for reactions summarized here, see also 8 March 1944, 19. An interpretation of this affair somewhat different from mine appears in Hopkins, 467–70. Eisenhower statement quoted in Roosevelt press conference of 15 February 1944, *Complete Press Conferences*, vol. 23, 49. *New Republic* quotation from "Massacre by Bombing," 13 March 1944, 332.

58. Polls taken particularly in 1940–41 indicated widespread, though not majority, disapproval of "a policy of bombing the civilian population of Germany" and support for an Anglo-German agreement to stop night bombing. Doubtless much of this attitude arose from fear of reprisal rather than moral scruple, and those polled did not necessarily know that bombing of German cities had already begun. Later polls indicated smaller but sustained disapproval of bombing of German civilians. A large minority of Canadian opinion also disapproved of the bombing of civilian populations. See Cantril, 1067–69.

59. Alexander Kiralfy, *Victory in the Pacific: How We Must Defeat Japan* (New York, 1942), 276, 277, 278.

60. De Seversky, *Victory Through Air Power*, 104; Ziff, *The Coming Battle of Germany*, 272.

61. Pogue, vol. 3, 316 (Pogue's italics deleted here); W. Averell Harriman and Elie Abel, *Special*

Envoy to Churchill and Stalin, 1941–46 (New York, 1975), 74. See also Sherwood, *Roosevelt and Hopkins,* 591.

62. Nicholas, ed., *Washington Despatches,* 298.

63. Eaker to Spaatz, 1 January 1945, quoted in Schaffer, "American Military Ethics," 328.

64. Terraine, 549.

65. Morgenthau, quoted in Laurence Wittner, *Rebels Against War* (New York, 1969), 100; Walzer, 323–25. Messenger, 196–98, attempts to refute the claim that Harris was "dishonored."

66. "Talk of the Town," *New Yorker,* 11 December 1943, 25. The substance and tone of these brief comments precisely foreshadowed the kind of commentary on the nuclear dilemma the *New Yorker* made or published throughout the cold war, especially when it printed an early version of Jonathan Schell's *The Fate of the Earth.*

CHAPTER 6

Sources

In addition to selected archival material, many of the secondary accounts described for previous chapters were useful for the 1942–44 period. Though dated, the several volumes of Craven and Cate, *The AAF in World War II,* still provide the essential narrative. But on strategy, see Hayes, *History of the Joint Chiefs;* Matloff, *Strategic Planning for Coalition Warfare.* Cate, *History of the 20th Air Force: Genesis,* is surprisingly effective and critical given its official status and early publication (1945). Two biographies were invaluable: Pogue, *Marshall,* vols 2–3; Ambrose, *Eisenhower,* vol. 1.

Particular aspects of the air war are treated in Coffey, *Decision over Schweinfurt,* in most ways superior to Coffey's biography of Arnold, *HAP.* On the atomic bomb, see Sherwin, *A World Destroyed.* On chemical and biological warfare and its connections to aerial policy, see Harris and Paxman, *A Higher Form of Killing,* a more recent and sensational but less subtle account than Brown, *Chemical Warfare.* On British operations and their relationship to the American effort, I have drawn on, among other sources, Middlebrook, *The Battle of Hamburg;* Hastings, *Bomber Command;* Terraine, *A Time for Courage;* Longmate, *The Bombers;* Frankland, *The Bombing Offensive Against Germany;* Sallager, *The Road to Total War.* A recent, though not always persuasive, defense of Harris is in Messenger, *"Bomber" Harris.* Valuable perspectives on American operations are found in Schaffer, "American Military Ethics," and Emerson, *Operation Pointblank.*

Notes

1. Memorandum, Stratemeyer for several AAF officials, 2 December 1942, in file 385 (case 74), Official Decimal Files, Box 114, Arnold Papers.

2. LeMay, 251. On revisions in the fighter toll and postwar scrutiny of wartime efforts, see Craven and Cate, vol. 2, xiii, 221–25, but also vol. 3, xxviii, for some backtracking on the part of the authors.

3. Quoted in Coffey, *HAP,* 294.

4. Craven and Cate, vol. 2, 305, 307.

5. Craven and Cate, vol. 2, 316.

6. Memorandum, Marshall for President, 22 March 1943, in Miscellaneous Correspondence, Box 3, Arnold Papers; letter, Arnold to Hopkins, 25 March 1943, in Jacket 36 (Bombing), Official Files, Box 41, Arnold Papers. See also minutes, meeting of the Joint Chiefs of Staff, 6 April 1943, JCS Records.

7. H. H. A. Arnold, Observation Memorandum, 1 May 1943, in Miscellaneous Correspondence,

Box 3, Arnold Papers; DeWitt S. Copp, *Forged in Fire: Strategy and Decisions in the Air War over Europe, 1940–1945* (Garden City, 1982), 375 (Eaker); Coffey, *HAP,* 316 (Eaker); Arnold, memorandum for "All Air Force Commanders in Combat Zones," 10 June 1943, in Jacket 36 (Bombing), Official Files, Box 41, Arnold Papers.

8. Quoted in Schaffer, "American Military Ethics," 321.

9. Matloff, 131; Craven and Cate, vol. 2, 371.

10. Craven and Cate, vol. 2, 375.

11. Ibid., 465.

12. Kennett, 147.

13. Quotations from contemporary observations, medical reports, and recollections found in Bond, *Fire and the Air War,* 119, 116, 118; Middlebrook, 257; and the Hamburg police-president's report, most easily found in Wilson, *WW2,* 297–302. The most powerful exploration of the transcendent nature of the atomic bomb experience, Lifton's *Death in Life* does not compare the reactions of Hiroshima's victims to those of victims of firestorms and other conventional bombing during the war.

14. Dyson, 28 ("hole in one"); Overy, 107 ("indiscriminate bombing"); Hastings, 132 (Harris quotation). On Portal, see Terraine, 505.

15. Minutes of Joint Chiefs of Staff meeting, 28 April 1943, in JCS Records; Middlebrook, 95, reprints the Hamburg directive.

16. Hastings, 133; Winston Churchill, *Their Finest Hour* (Boston, 1949), 349. Hastings here makes reference to a slightly earlier period in RAF operations.

17. Overy, 119; Middlebrook, 334.

18. Middlebrook, 343 ("deceit"), 344–45 (newspaper accounts), 349 (airmen's doubts); Hastings, 176 (Fuller). On complaints from the left, see Overy, 116.

19. Minutes of the Pacific War Council, 11 August 1943, in Folder #2, Naval Aide's Files: Pacific War Council, Box 168, Map Room Papers, FDR Papers; Arnold, memorandum for President, 22 February 1944, enclosing "presentation" on role of the AAF in defeat of Japan, in Naval Aide's Files: A/16—Japan and Japanese Islands—1942–45, Box 167, Map Room Papers, FDR Papers; Schaffer, *Wings,* 56, for characterization of Balkan bombing; Estimate of the Enemy Situation, 1944–Europe, Report by the Joint Staff Planners, 9 November 1943, and succeeding reports, in JCS Records (microfilm edition), part I, 1942–45, European Theater, Reel 1. On doubts about targeting morale, see also Schaffer, "American Military Ethics," 323. On evidence from intercepts, see Ronald Lewin, *The American Magic: Codes, Ciphers and the Defeat of Japan* (New York, 1982), 235.

20. Memorandum, Bissell for Marshall, Arnold, Embick, and Handy, 6 March 1944, enclosing "Report on the Effect of 1943 Air Raids on Berlin," in OPD Exec File 9 (Item 16, No. 357), WD Staff Records.

21. Memorandum, Gen. L. H. Hedrick, Air Judge Advocate, to Commanding General, AAF, 25 December 1943; memorandum, Marshall for President, 29 December 1943; memorandum, President for Marshall, 10 January 1944; memorandum, Marshall for President, 22 January 1944; all in Air AG file 385-D, Warfare, AAF Records.

22. Joint Staff Planners paper, Modification of Directive for the Bomber Offensive, 18 October 1943, in JCS Records (microfilm ed.), part I, 1942–45, European theater, Reel 10.

23. Coffey, *Decision,* 256 (Harris quotation); LeMay, 289.

24. Craven and Cate, vol. 2, 705.

25. See ibid., 704–05; minutes of Wing and Group Commanders Meeting, 16 October 1943, Box B8, LeMay Papers.

26. Quotations from minutes of the Pacific War Council, 11 August 1943 (cited in n. 19); Thorne, 288 (Stimson); minutes, meeting of the Joint Chiefs of Staff, meeting with the President, 16 January 1943, in JCS Records; *Complete Press Conferences,* 19 February 1943, vol. 21, 165.

27. Letter, Chennault to Wendell Willkie, 8 October 1942, in Anna Chennault, *Chennault and the Flying Tigers* (New York, 1963), 203; transcript of conference of Stilwell, Chennault, Marshall, Arnold, and others, 30 April 1943, in OPD file ABC 384 China (15 Dec. 43) Sec. 1-A, WD Staff Records, RG 165;

Michael Baru Kublin, "The Role of China in American Military Strategy from Pearl Harbor to the Fall of 1944" (Ph.D. diss., New York University, 1981), 131.

28. Quotations from Matloff, 231, quoting from minutes of Combined Chiefs of Staff meeting, 14 August 1943; minutes of the Pacific War Council, 11 August 1943, in Naval Aide's Files: Pacific War Council (Folder 2), Box 168, Map Room Papers, FDR Papers. See also memorandum, Kuter for Chief of Air Staff, 10 August 1943, in file 168.7012-1, Kuter Papers.

29. See esp. Cate, 66–67.

30. Memorandum Roosevelt for Marshall, 15 October 1943, in folder War Department: George C. Marshall, Box 106, President's Secretary's Files, FDR Papers; see also accompanying memorandum, apparently by T. V. Soong for Roosevelt, 26 September 1943, and message from Roosevelt to Churchill, 15 October 1943. For Arnold's reply, see his letter to Roosevelt, 18 October 1943, in Jacket 150 (President), Official File, Box 43, Arnold Papers.

31. Quotations from Coffey, *Decision,* 332–33, 336; further information on sources in Craven and Cate, vol. 2, 705, 711, and accompanying notes.

32. Craven and Cate, vol. 3, 28.

33. Coffey, *Decision,* 346.

34. Craven and Cate, vol. 3, xi. See also Schaffer, *Wings,* 60–70.

35. Kennett, 154, quoting Webster and Frankland, vol. 2, 190. On attrition of the German air force, see especially Cooper, chaps. 10–11, and Craven and Cate, vol. 3, esp. chap. 6.

36. Ambrose, 288–89.

37. Craven and Cate, vol. 3, xxviii.

38. Quotation from Terraine, 509, quoting a remark by John Slessor made in November 1939. My critique in this paragraph draws on Terraine and other histories of British bombing, and on Emerson.

39. Emerson, 40–41. For a good example of the airman's quest for purity in war-making, see Hansell, *Air Plan That Defeated Hitler,* especially 270–78; Hansell, it should be noted, does not dispute the right of political authorities to make decisions that disrupt strategic plans.

40. Craven and Cate, vol. 4, xiii.

41. Letter, Roosevelt to Chennault, 15 March 1944, in file "Army Air Forces," Box 1, President's Secretary's Files, FDR Papers. See also minutes of Joint Staff Planners meetings, 9, 16, 24 February 1944, in file CCS 373.11 Japan (8–20–43) pt. 4, JCS Records; Craven and Cate, vol. 3, 27–31.

42. Arnold, 479. Wheeler, *Bombers Over Japan,* contains an excellent description of the B-29s' teething problems.

43. Cate, 166, 170, 171. For the possibly apocryphal story, see Morrison, 37. See also Arnold, 479.

44. Quotations from letter, Groves to Bush, 6 April 1944, in file 14, subseries I, reel 2, MED Records; Sherwin, 123, 111. See also Sherwin, 209–10; Hewlett and Anderson, 253.

45. *New York Times,* 9 February 1944, p. 4, paraphrasing Nimitz.

46. Memorandum, Marshall for Stimson, 8 October 1943, file "Japan (after Dec 7/41)", Stimson Safe File, SecWar Records; see also, in the same file, JCS 504, 17 September 1943, enclosing memorandum, Roosevelt to Secretary of War and Secretary of the Navy, 9 September 1943; JPS 276/2, 3 January 1944, in Plans and Operations Project Decimal File 383.6 Japan (9–17–43) Atrocities, HQ USAF Records. Davis's comments are in letter, Davis to Leahy, 24 December 1943, in JCS Records (microfilm ed.), World War II: Pacific Theater, Reel 1; minutes of the meetings of the Information Board of the Office of War Information, 26 January 1944, Entry 16, RG 208, Records of the Office of War Information, Washington National Records Center, Suitland, Md. For warning of execution, see memorandum, Assistant Chief of Air Staff, Intelligence, for Arnold, 2 February 1944, in file 384.5 Japan, Foreign Files Japan, Air Adjutant General Central Decimal Files Oct. 42–44, AAF Records. Marshall's recommendation to Roosevelt is in memorandum, 22 January 1944, cited above, n. 21.

47. For a few instances in which deliberations did occur, see memorandum, Lt. Gen. P. E. Beynet, Chief, French Military Mission, 29 December 1943, and undated memorandum by Marshall, in Important Memos for the C/S, OPD Exec File #10, WD Staff Records; and file CCS 373.11 Tokyo, Japan (3–3–44), JCS Records.

48. Quotations from Brown, 248–49 (fn. 143), 260, and memorandum, Maj. Gen. Thomas T. Handy, Assistant Chief of Staff, for Deputy Chief of Staff, 27 December 1943, in Chief of Staff file 441.5 (Top Secret), WD Staff Records. See also Brown, 198–207, 246–61; letter, Maj. Gen. William N. Porter, Chief of the Chemical Warfare Service, to Arnold, 7 January 1944, in file "385-D, Warfare," Air Adjutant General Files Oct. 42–44, AAF Records; memorandum, Kuter to Chief of Air Staff, 3 February 44, in file 145.81-151, and "Selected Aerial Objectives for Retaliatory Gas Attack on Japan," April 1944, in file 142.621-8, both at AFSHRC. See also Harris and Paxman, esp. chap. 5.

49. Memorandum, Arnold to Roosevelt, 22 February 1944, cited in n. 19. Two meetings took place between the president and his military staff earlier in February regarding basing, command, and mission of the B-29s; see memorandum, Arnold for Chief of Air Staff, 20 February 1944, in file 334 (case 63), Official Decimal Files, Box 94, Arnold Papers.

50. Craven and Cate, vol. 5, 94. Material for Army Hour broadcast, 18 June 1944, in file 000.77 Broadcasts; extract of teletype conference between Washington and Kharagpur, 17 June 1944, in file Telecons Kharagpur 1944; unsigned memorandum for Chief of Air Staff, Twentieth Air Force, 27 June 1944, in file Telecons Kharagpur 1944, all in HQ 20th AF Records. For "great opportunity," see memorandum, Maj. J. H. Spence to Chief of Staff, Twentieth Air Force, 23 June 1944, in file "1st and 2nd B-29 Raids," Records of the Office, Chief of Air Staff, Scientific Advisory Group (Von Karman Files), 1941–47, AAF Records; for Japanese broadcasts, see also file "1st and 2nd B-29 Raids."

51. See memorandum, Marshall for Secretary of War, 17 February 1944, with memorandum, Somervell for Marshall, 14 February 1944, in OPD Exec File #9 (Book 15, case 241), WD Staff Records, for doubts about China project.

52. CCS 417, "Overall Plan for the Defeat of Japan," 2 December 1943, in OPD file ABC 381 Japan (8–27–42) Sec. 6, WD Staff Records; JCS 924, Report by the Joint Staff Planners, 30 June 1944, JCS Records (microfilm ed.) 1942–45: Pacific Theater, reel 9. See also Hayes, 492–507, 627–28.

53. Matloff, 487–89.

54. Extract from minutes of the CCS meeting, 14 July 1944, in OPD file ABC 381 Japan (8–27–42), WD Staff Records.

55. Basil H. Liddell Hart, *The Revolution in Warfare* (New Haven, 1947), 99–100.

56. Frankland, 61–62; Sallager, 131–32.

57. Hastings, 148.

CHAPTER 7

Sources

I have drawn extensively on primary sources, archival and published, for this chapter. Nearly all the vast literature on air war touches on the sociological qualities of concern in this chapter, but few make those qualities the object of intensive study. Overy, *Air War,* is the best in that regard, though less useful on the men who actually flew; it provided a more valuable source than the mere repetition of footnotes could indicate. See also, Craven and Cate, *The AAF in World War II,* vols. 6–7, and on the aviation industry: Holley, *Buying Aircraft;* Fernandez, *Excess Profits;* Rae, *Climb to Greatness.* Wheeler, *Bombers Over Japan,* is a rich visual and verbal record of the B-29 in construction and operation.

No air force leader has been the subject of the complex and comprehensive biographical study given major army leaders like Marshall and Eisenhower. Many air officers have, however, left useful oral interviews, obtained from the USAF Historical Division, Air University (Maxwell Air Force Base). See also the various publications of the Military Symposia of the United States Air Force, especially Hurley and Erhart, eds., *Air Power and Warfare.* I have concentrated on Arnold and LeMay not only because of their importance, but because they are among the few air officers to write autobiographies; a lengthy interview with LeMay also proved useful. On the air force's postwar ambitions, I have also drawn on my earlier study, *Preparing for the Next War.*

On the role of science in the air war, there is a large literature of institutional studies published after the war and the scientists' autobiographies, of which three were especially valuable: von Karman, *The Wind and Beyond;* Dyson, *Disturbing the Universe;* Zuckerman, *From Apes to Warlords.* Among many sources on atomic scientists, I have relied especially on two problematic studies: Nuel Pharr Davis, *Lawrence and Oppenheimer;* and Heims, *John Von Neumann and Norbert Wiener.* Although not cited in notes, the opening chapters of Smith, *A Peril and a Hope,* were valuable. On institutional relationships of scientists, see especially Koppes, *JPL and the American Space Program.* For Edward L. Bowles, I relied primarily on my lengthy interviews with him and the access to his files he generously granted me. Among other civilians' recollections, I especially drew on Ball, *The Past Has Another Pattern,* and Galbraith, *A Life in Our Times.* On contrasts between the Anglo-American and the enemies' experience, see, in addition to Overy: Wright, *The Ordeal of Total War;* Beyerchen, *Scientists under Hitler.* For the nature and consequences of "civilian militarism," I found that an older study, Vagts's *A History of Militarism,* allowed me to go beyond the understated analysis in Overy.

On airmen there are abundant sources compromised by a bureaucratic quirk: since the AAF was still a part of the United States Army, demographic and medical data on airmen are not easily separable from the many statistics on army officers and enlisted men more generally; most of the data used in this chapter are derived from sources cited in note 62. The most valuable published source was Stouffer et al., *The American Soldier.* Narrower in focus but rich in detail and observation is Grinker and Spiegel, *Men Under Stress,* which emphasizes battle as the defining experience for airmen more than I do. Craven and Cate, *The AAF in World War II,* vols. 6–7, are also essential. Wecter, *When Johnny Comes Marching Home,* a bittersweet wartime study of returning servicemen, has brief but penetrating characterizations of airmen. Fromm, *The Anatomy of Human Destructiveness,* has probing insights resting on little clinical data; I have tried to use it with caution. Among more recent accounts, the most deft portraits of bomber crewmen are in Hastings, *Bomber Command,* on the RAF, and Coffey, *Decision over Schweinfurt,* on the AAF. Gabriel and Savage, *Crisis in Command,* and Moskos, "The All-Volunteer Military: Calling, Profession, or Occupation?" suggest, in ways that others have challenged, how attitudes toward military service have changed in the mid-twentieth century; they helped to sharpen my analysis of how means and ends were separable in the wartime air force.

Notes

1. Dwight MacDonald, editorials from *Politics,* August and September 1945, reprinted in Bernstein, *The Atomic Bomb,* 145, emphasis in Bernstein.

2. Letter, Arnold to Wolfe, draft dated 25 May 1944, in file 201 Wolfe, HQ 20th AF Records.

3. LeMay, 3, 310.

4. Ibid., 357, 365.

5. Author's interview with LeMay, 29 June 1981.

6. Guido Perera, "Memoirs" (1973), frame 0457, Microfilm A1926, file 168.7042, AFSHRC.

7. LeMay, 263. On official policy, see Stouffer et al., vol. 2, 348.

8. LeMay, 311; "swivel-chair," etc. from LeMay's interview with Wilbur Morrison, 31 October 1977, obtained through the courtesy of Morrison and the American Heritage Center of the University of Wyoming.

9. Author's interview with LeMay.

10. Incident about heart attack recounted in Coffey, *HAP,* 265; other quotations from transcript, "Special Meeting on B-29 Project," 27 May 1944, in file 353.01 B-29 Training Program, HQ 20th AF Records.

11. Minutes of Air Staff meeting, 8 July 1942, and 29 May 1944, both in file 337 Boards-Committees-Meetings (Air Staff Meetings), Air AG Central Decimal Files Oct. 42–1944, AAF Records; memorandum, Kuter to General Grant, 15 September 1943, in file 168.7012-1, Kuter Papers; memorandum, Colonel S. F. Griffith for General Wilson, 25 November 1944, in Official Decimal File 385 Japan (77),

Box 115, Arnold Papers; minutes, "Special Meeting of the Air Staff in General Arnold's Conference Room with Mr. Lovett," 27 November 1944, in Official Decimal File 337 (Air Staff Meetings, 1944), Box 96, Arnold Papers.

12. Fanton, 175, 177–78; for the role of Lovett and Stimson in public relations, see more generally in Fanton, 173–83. See also Hansell, *Strategic Air War,* 29.

13. Historical Division, Air Staff/Intelligence, "Comparison of Air and Ground Warfare, 1941– 1944; And of Ground Warfare in Two World Wars and the Civil War," August 1944, in Scientific Advisory Group files, AAF Records.

14. Quotations from minutes of meeting, 27 November 1944, cited in n. 11. For plans, and arguments against them, similar to Lovett's at this time, see Schaffer, "American Military Ethics," 324–30. Arnold reminder to Hansell in letter drafted by Norstad on 27 December 1944, in file 201 Hansell, HQ 20th AF Records; see also letter, Norstad to LeMay, 23 September 1944, in file 201 LeMay, HQ 20th AF Records.

15. Memorandum, Hansell for Commanding General, 21st Bomber Command, 4 August 1944 ("emphasize accuracy"), and memorandum, Smith for assistant to the director [public relations] for Army Air Forces, 8 September 1944, ("to prevent," "imply"), both in file 333 Inspections, 20th AF Units, HQ 20th AF Records; letter, Arnold to Hansell, drafted 27 December 1944 by Norstad, in file 201 Hansell, HQ 20th AF Records ("to let").

16. Letter, Arnold to LeMay, 5 October 1944, in Section III—21st Bomb Command, 20th Air Force Official File, Norstad Papers; letter, Arnold to Lt. General George C. Kenney, 26 September 1944, in file Pacific II (August 18, 1944–October 5, 1944), Records of the Deputy Chief of Staff (Operations), Director of Plans, HQ USAF Records; message, Norstad to LeMay, 15 October 1944, in 20th AF Message File (Telecons Kharagpur 1944), HQ 20th AF Records.

17. Hansell memorandum, 4 August 1944, cited in n. 14.

18. Letter, Norstad to Hansell, 27 December 1944, in 20th Air Force Official File, Norstad Papers.

19. Message to Harmon for Hartwell and McKelway from Smith, 11 November 1944, in 20th AF Message File (Telecons, Guam to Honolulu, 1944), HQ 20th AF Records.

20. Norstad to Hansell, 27 December 1944, cited in n. 18.

21. "The Fortune Survey," *Fortune,* June 1945, 272. See Sherry, 108–19.

22. Alice Rogers Hager, *Wings for the Dragon* (New York, 1945), 307.

23. Air Marshall William A. Bishop, *Winged Peace* (New York, 1944), 173; Emile Gauvreau, *The Wild Blue Yonder: Sons of the Prophet Carry On* (New York, 1944), esp. chap. 19; Allan Michie, *Keep the Peace Through Air Power* (New York, 1944).

24. Von Karman, 225, 268.

25. Von Karman, 267, 268 ("not another," "the mistakes"); other quotations from memorandum, Arnold for von Karman, 7 November 1944, in Numeric File 67, Records of the Deputy Chief of Staff (Operations), Director of Plans, HQ USAF Records.

26. Von Karman, 271 ("I see," "fly over") (von Karman's brackets); other quotations from memorandum, Arnold for von Karman, cited in n. 25.

27. On establishment of RAND, see Bruce L. R. Smith, *The RAND Corporation: Case Study of a Nonprofit Advisory Corporation* (Cambridge, 1966), chap. 2; Fred Kaplan, *The Wizards of Armageddon* (New York, 1983), chap. 4.

28. See Craven and Cate, vol. 6, 41–42; Coffey, *HAP,* 351.

29. The average age of nineteen leading air officers during the war was 47.11, that of twenty-eight leading army generals 52.07. Of the latter 85.7 percent were products of West Point or the Virginia Military Institute, 63.2 percent of the same group of air officers (including one graduate of the Naval Academy). The median date of birth was about the same for both groups, but included among the air officers were several, like LeMay, much younger than the norm. Information drawn largely from *Webster's American Military Biographies* (1978).

30. Corn, *Winged Gospel,* chap. 6.

31. Unfortunately no precise and comprehensive demographic profile exists comparing personnel in the AAF with those in other services. Much of the information here is derived from Stouffer, et al., vol. 1,

250, and vol. 2, chap. 7. Additional demographic data are presented below in the section on airmen. Quotation from "Comparison of Air and Ground Warfare . . . ," cited above, n. 13.

32. See Overy, 148–58 passim.

33. Ibid., 210; Iriye, *Across the Pacific,* 229.

34. Quotations from "Comparison of Air and Ground Warfare . . . ," cited above, n. 13, and from memorandum, Brigadier General Thomas White, Assistant Chief of Air Staff, Intelligence, to Commanding General, Army Air Forces (Arnold), written 26 August 1944, same file location.

35. Quoted in Richard Polenberg, *War and Society: The United States, 1941–1945* (Philadelphia, 1972), 12.

36. Craven and Cate, vol. 6, 317. Quotations from Fernandez, 145, 155.

37. Overy, 210; see also 208.

38. Vagts, 463; see also 452 for discussion of whether the term *civilian militarism* is not a "contradiction in terms."

39. C. P. Snow, *Science and Government* (Cambridge, 1960, 1961), 29.

40. MacIsaac, 56.

41. Von Karman, 279; Zuckerman, 83.

42. Dorothea Wolfgram, "ELB," *Washington University Magazine* (Winter 1980): 37.

43. Quotations from author's interview with Bowles, 3 September 1980. On Bowles's career and role, see also Wolfgram article cited in n. 42; John Burchard, *M.I.T. in World War II: Q.E.D.* (New York, 1948), passim; Smith, *The RAND Corporation,* 34–38; Kevles, 310–13.

44. Bowles, "Diary of Pacific Trip, November–January 1944–45" Bowles Papers.

45. Robert L. Stearns, "Remarks at University of Colorado Alumni Dinner in New York City 21 November, 1944," in file 319.1 Reports-Progress Reports-II (Entry 57), HQ 20th AF Records.

46. Perera quotations from his memoirs, cited in n. 6, frame 0594; Ball, 63, 66.

47. Dyson, 30, 31, 39, 40–41.

48. Ball, 45.

49. Zuckerman, 366, 363, 240.

50. Ibid., 357; Dyson, 41, 30, 44.

51. Zuckerman, 353, 260, 246; R. V. Jones, *Most Secret War* (London, 1978), 303.

52. Galbraith, 233, 231–32.

53. Koppes, 28.

54. Davis, 230.

55. Ibid., 130, 131, 235. Groves, *Now It Can Be Told,* 296–97, interpreted Fermi's invitation as a device to "ease the tension." The warning Fermi signed was in "Prospectus on Nucleonics," with letter of 18 November 1944, in folder 59, reel 4, Harrison-Bundy Files.

56. Davis, 128, 233; Dyson, 91.

57. Jungk, 197. For an evocative discussion of the attitudes toward women and the natural world embedded in Western science, see Susan Griffin, *Woman and Nature: The Roaring Inside Her* (New York, 1978).

58. Heims, 198, 197.

59. Quoted in Davis, 142.

60. Ibid., 241, 224, 228.

61. Quotation from Dyson, 53. See also The Bulletin of the Atomic Scientists, *All In Our Time: The Reminiscences of Twelve Nuclear Pioneers* (Chicago, 1975), especially the recollections of the then youthful Frederic de Hoffmann.

62. Casualties derived from Adjutant General, United States Army, *Army Battle Casualties and Nonbattle Deaths in World War II—Final Report,* RCS CSCAP (OT) 87 (Washington, 1954), 5, 7; Mae Mills Link and Hubert A. Coleman, *Medical Support of the Army Air Forces in World War II* (Washington, Office of the Surgeon General, United States Air Force, 1955), 707; *Annual Report of the Surgeon General, U.S. Navy, for the Calender Year 1945* (Washington, 1948), 18. Mean strengths are in Medical Department, U.S. Army, *Medical Statistics in World War II* (Office of the Surgeon General, Department of the Army, Washington, 1975), 68. Deaths in B-24 accidents and quoted reaction to found in Craven and Cate, vol. 7, 444. British figures are given in Terraine, 682. On percentage of airmen who were officers, see

Stouffer et al., vol. 2, 326. Overall American battle deaths are from Department of Defense, *Selected Manpower Statistics* (Washington, 1974), 282.

63. Link and Coleman, *Medical Support,* 704–05.

64. LeMay, 363.

65. Grinker and Spiegel, 113, 114. For some of these differences between fighter pilots and bomber crews, see Stouffer et al., vol. 2, 407–09.

66. Dyson, 21, 28; on escape rates, see Dyson, 27; on declining loss rates in the American Eighth Air Force, see Link and Coleman, *Medical Support,* 705; quotation from English flier in Hastings, 222.

67. Quotations from Craven and Cate, vol. 7, 403. See also Grinker and Spiegel, 149–53, for the conflicting claims on doctors and 60–61, 136, on comparisons to ground soldiers.

68. Grinker and Spiegel, 16, 28, vii.

69. Grinker and Spiegel review the various methods of treatment; see chap. 7 for detailed discussion of narcosynthesis. On correlations of morale with frequency and number of missions, see Stouffer et al., vol. 2, 389ff.

70. Quotations from Stouffer et al., vol. 2, 396; Grinker and Spiegel, 47. On discipline, see Stouffer et al., vol. 2, 348–50; on aborted and scrubbed missions, Coffey, *Decision,* 245–46.

71. Coffey, *Decision,* 248–49, tells the story summarized here; on saving up complaints, see Stouffer et al., vol. 2, 373–83. On breakdowns, see Coffey, *Decision,* 250; for more detailed figures, see Link and Coleman, *Medical Support,* 679–80.

72. Psychiatrists quoted in Coffey, *Decision,* 245; RAF fliers characterized by Hastings, 221; Lifton, 31–34 and passim.

73. Hastings, 102, 103.

74. Link and Coleman, *Medical Support,* 707; other air forces in the Pacific suffered more severely than the Twentieth, but total losses in that theater made up only about 20 percent of the total wartime figure for the Army Air Forces.

75. Charles A. Lindbergh, *The Wartime Journals of Charles A. Lindbergh* (New York, 1970), 835, 920.

76. "Comparison of Air and Ground Warfare . . . ," cited above n. 13 ("more vindictive"), an observation confirmed in Stouffer et al., vol. 2, 157; other quotations from Stouffer, et al., vol. 2, 157–59, and see more generally in that volume, 108–12, 156–91; Grinker and Spiegel, 43.

77. See Sheean's notes on 20th Bomber Command mission of July 29, 1944, in file 384.5 Aerial Attacks and Raids (Entry 57), HQ 20th AF Records; Sheean's published account of his experiences with the 20th is in *This House Against This House* (New York, 1945, 1946).

78. McKelway, II, 28.

79. Fromm, 346. See also Grinker and Spiegel, 35.

80. Letter, LeMay to Arnold, 19 October 1944, in file 201 LeMay, HQ 20th AF Records; 21st Bomber Command, "Analysis of Incendiary Phase of Operations Against Japanese Urban Areas," n.d. (April 1945), in Box B37, LeMay Papers; Ernie Pyle, *Last Chapter* (New York, 1945, 1946), 31–32. On ratio of accidental to combat losses of B-29s, see Wheeler, *Bombers Over Japan,* 143.

81. Pyle, *Last Chapter,* 37.

82. See Coffey, *Decision,* 242–44.

83. Wecter, 519.

84. Pyle, *Last Chapter,* 43; Stouffer, et al., vol. 2, 353, 344; see also 342–48.

85. See Stouffer et al., vol. 2, 352–61; Grinker and Spiegel, 29; S. L. A. Marshall, *Men Against Fire* (New York, 1947, 1961).

86. Forrest Davis, "The Eighth Came Back," *Saturday Evening Post,* 13 November 1943, 20 ("a piece of swank"); other quotations from Stouffer et al., vol. 1, 309 ("dumping ground"), and vol. 2, 340. On distribution of rank and grades, see Stouffer et al., vol. 2, 326. On limits to the wartime stereotype, see Grinker and Spiegel, 8–9.

87. Quoted in Craven and Cate, vol. 6, 435, no date of editorial given.

88. Wecter, 521; "The Next Business Generation," *Fortune,* August 1945, 151. See also Stouffer et al., vol. 1, 301–03, 308–09, and vol. 2, 352; Grinker and Spiegel, 6; Corn, 108.

89. Various aspects of the AAF's use of civilian institutions in training, recruitment, and logistics are discussed in Craven and Cate, vol. 6, chaps. 13–20 passim.

90. Wartime polling of servicemen measured attitudes on these matters in a bewildering variety of ways suggestive of different conclusions, but see particularly Stouffer, vol. 2, 328–39.

91. Grinker and Spiegel, 4–5.

92. American correspondent's comment on "one of the last personal touches," as quoted in Wheeler, *Bombers Over Japan,* 172; Kathleen Brooks-Pazmany, *United States Women in Aviation, 1919–1929* (Washington, 1983), 46. On women and aviation, see also Corn, chap. 4; Craven and Cate, vol. 7, chap. 16.

93. Wecter, 520.

94. Hastings, 89, 102.

95. Craven and Cate, vol. 7, 421–22; see also the material in Stouffer et al., cited in succeeding notes. On British practice, see Terraine, 523–26.

96. Quotation from Stouffer et al., vol. 2, 385; see also 353–57, 379–87; Grinker and Spiegel, 36.

97. Stouffer et al., vol. 2, 384, 383.

98. For commentary on changes in models of military service, see Moskos, and Gabriel and Savage, chap. 1.

99. Grinker and Spiegel, 38–39; "Comparison of Air and Ground Warfare . . . ," cited above n. 13.

CHAPTER 8

Sources

My analysis here draws on many of the sources also described for chapter 7. On patterns of power, organization, and command relationships, see Craven and Cate, *The AAF in World War II,* especially volumes 5–6. Pogue, *Marshall,* volumes 2–3, and Ambrose, *Eisenhower,* provide more recent perspectives on the same patterns as well as guiding my comparison of command relationships. On these matters as well as on the nature of rhetoric and methodology Hastings, *Bomber Command,* illuminates the British experience, while Blanchard, *Aggression American Style,* while sometimes weak in its use of historical evidence, provided broader generalizations that I have incorporated, with qualifications, into my analysis of technological fanaticism. Schaffer, "American Military Ethics," has been again used with reservations. My material on incendiary war and the rhetoric of technique draws largely on archival sources. Wills, "Critical Inquiry (*Kritik*) in Clausewitz," has informed my understanding of the emotional climate and the nature of momentum in the war. On the politics of surrender, two older studies remain important: Butow, *Japan's Decision to Surrender,* and Kecskemeti, *Strategic Surrender;* Iriye's sharply revisionist study, *Power and Culture,* is provocative but problematical and usefully supplemented, for the Japanese side, with Dower, *Empire and Aftermath.* Villa, "The U.S. Army, Unconditional Surrender, and the Potsdam Proclamation," effectively places American deliberations in their bureaucratic and political context. For the sources, complexities, and consequences of Japanese and American racism, Dower, *War Without Mercy,* is by far the superior study. Thorne, *Allies of a Kind,* also traces the persistence of racist attitudes toward Japan and China among Western leaders. Contrasting views of conditions inside Japan and its empire during the war are offered in Havens, *Valley of Darkness,* Ienaga, *The Pacific War,* and Shillony, *Politics and Culture in Wartime Japan.*

Notes

1. Pogue, vol. 3, 38; see his evocative description, 38–42.

2. Memorandum, Arnold to President, 11 January 1945, in file "Arnold," Box 105, President's Secretary's File, FDR Papers.

3. Letter, Arnold to Stimson, 13 January 1945, Official Decimal File 370.2 China, Box 106, Arnold Papers.

4. Quoted in Craven and Cate, vol. 5, 680; see also 679–80.

5. Memorandum, Kuter to Giles, 8 December 1944 addendum, in Diary of Events and Decisions Made in Absence of Arnold, Box 223, Subject File, Arnold Papers.

6. Marshall interview, 1957, quoted in Pogue, vol. 2, 290.

7. Letter, Norstad to Hansell, 7 December 1944, in file 201 Hansell, HQ 20th AF Records; Norstad, address at the Joint Army-Navy Staff College, 27 September 1944, in file 350.001 Speeches, HQ 20th AF Records; letter, Arnold to LeMay, 17 December 1944, in file Special Official Correspondence (Arnold), Box B31, LeMay Papers; Hansell, *Strategic Air War,* 31.

8. Hansell, *Strategic Air War,* 28. In his interviews, LeMay's recollection of the degree of control of Washington over the bomber commands of the Twentieth Air Force emphasized that it was less than he experienced in Europe; LeMay's perceptions of that control will be treated in detail in the following chapter.

9. English officer quoted in Craven and Cate, vol. 1, 266; Norstad address, 27 September 1944, cited above, n. 7; Craven and Cate, vol. 6, 47.

10. Letter, Arnold to Chennault, 25 February 1944, in Box 8, Chennault Papers.

11. Blanchard, 240, 242 (Blanchard's emphasis).

12. LeMay, 328–29; Hansell, *Strategic Air War,* 36–37.

13. Hastings, 243; Dyson, 29. For a defense of Harris against these charges, see Messenger, esp. 195–205.

14. Norstad address, 27 September 1944, cited above, n. 7.

15. Louis F. Fieser, *The Scientific Method: A Personal Account of Unusual Projects in War and in Peace* (New York, 1964), 14, 133; Mountcastle, 209; Harris and Paxman, 98.

16. Mountcastle, 148; memorandum, Gross for Chief of Air Staff, 5 May 1944, in Official Decimal File 400.112 (74), Box 117, Arnold Papers; memorandum, Kuter and Loutzenheiser to Commanding General, Twentieth Air Force (attention: Colonel Combs), 24 April 1944, in folder "Plans for Incendiary Attacks," Numeric File 11, HQ 20th AF Records. See also report of New York fire chief, "Report on interview with Mr. Daniel Deasy, Battalion Chief New York City Fire Department," in file #9984 (Incendiary Area Study of Tokyo 7–26–43), Project Decimal File (1941–45) 384.5 Japan, G-2 Records.

17. See Mountcastle, 135–46; Schaffer, "American Military Ethics," 321.

18. For initial studies, see "Vulnerability of Japanese Industry to Air Attack," prepared by Target Information Section, Far Eastern Unit, Operational Intelligence Division, AAF, 2 September 1942, in file 142.041-31, AFSHRC; USAF "Japanese Target Data," prepared by Assistant Chief/Air Staff, A-2, March 1943, in file 142.621-1, AFSHRC; Hansell, *Strategic Air War,* 15. On Churchill, see Thorne, 372. On COA deliberations, see Guido Perera, "Memoirs" (1973), frames 0546, 0553, 0635-636, microfilm A1926, file 168.7042, AFSHRC.

19. Bond, *Fire and the Air War,* 188.

20. "Report of Committee of Operations Analysts on Economic Objectives in the Far East," memorandum for Arnold, 11 November 1943, in Air Force Plans Project Decimal File Japan 384.3, HQ USAF Records. See also Bond, *Fire and the Air War,* 41.

21. Quotations from letter, Eugene Dooman to Colonel Martin, 20 July 1943, and Ewing C. Sadler and John A. Eble (Department of Justice) to Fowler Hamilton (Board of Economic Warfare and COA), "Report on Strategic Objectives in Tokyo Area and Postwar Planning Suggestions," 5 May 1943, both in file "Japan", #9900, G-2 Regional Files.

22. See Bond, *Fire and the Air War,* 130–32.

23. See memorandum, Perera and Leach to Hansell, 9 May 1944, in Subject File "Preliminary Studies May '44," HQ 20th AF Records; memorandum, Perera to Lindsay, 8 June 1944, in Air Force Plans Project Decimal File Japan 384.3 (1943) Section 4, HQ USAF Records; letter, Stimson and McNutt to President, 12 May 1944, and letter Roosevelt to Stimson, 8 June 1944, in file "Biological Warfare," SecWar Records; memorandum, Kuter to Chief of Air Staff, 29 June 1944, in file 385 Warfare, Foreign Files Japan, Air AG Central Decimal Files October 1942–1944, AAF Records.

24. Letter, O'Donnell to Arnold, 8 August 1944, in file 381-H War Plans (Misc) National Defense, Air AG 1942–44 Files, AAF Records. For an earlier version of O'Donnell's arguments, see memorandum, O'Donnell to Arnold, 7 February 1944, in file 373.2 VLR Night Operations, HQ 20th AF Records.

25. Letter, Arnold to O'Donnell, 19 August 1944, in Air AG file noted in n. 24.

26. Memorandum, Stearns to Chief of Staff, Twentieth Air Force, 10 August 1944, enclosing other documents, in Numeric File 11 (Plans for Incendiary Attacks), HQ 20th AF Records. On Nagasaki raid, see Craven and Cate, vol. 5, 111–12.

27. "Economic Effects of Successful Area Attacks on Six Japanese Cities," report to Committee of Operations Analysts, 4 September 1944, in Subject File (Report to Committee of Operations Analysts), HQ 20th AF Records.

28. "Revised Report of the Committee of Operations Analysts on Economic Targets in the Far East," memorandum for Arnold, 10 October 1944, in Air Force Plans Project Decimal File Japan 384.3 Section 1/2, HQ USAF Records. See also Craven and Cate, vol. 5, 26–27, 551–53.

29. Memorandum, Ewell to Bush, 12 October 1944; letter, Bush to Arnold, 13 October 1944; memorandum, Arnold to Norstad, 14 October 1944; all in file 373.2 Report of Operations—General, HQ 20th AF Records. For air force response to Ewell's recommendations, see memorandum, Stearns to Combs, 27 October 1944, in Numeric File 11 (Plans for Incendiary Attacks), HQ 20th AF Records.

30. See Hansell, *Strategic Air War*, 50–51; Bond, *Fire and the Air War*, 132–33.

31. Some indication of Arnold's view on incendiary bombing by September is evident in memorandum, Arnold to President, Army Air Forces Board, 26 September 1944, in file 353.41 -K Aerial Gunnery and Bombing, Air AG Central Decimal Files October 1942–1944, AAF Records.

32. Memorandum, Bowles for Arnold, 28 August 1944, with Arnold's approval, dated 2 September 1944, typed on it, in folder "Bowles Edward L.," Numeric File 68, HQ 20th AF Records.

33. Quotations from summation of interim report of Special Bombardment Group, 7 October 1944, in "A Summary of the Activities of Dr. Edward L. Bowles . . . ," 1 November 1945 (pp. 117–18), Bowles Papers; memorandum, Raymond to Bowles, 7 October 1944, in folder "Bowles Edward L.," Numeric File 68, HQ 20th AF Records. Paragraph also based on author's interviews with Bowles, 3 September and 15 December 1980. See also Bruce L. Smith, *The RAND Corporation: Case Study of a Nonprofit Advisory Corporation* (Cambridge, 1966), 35–36.

34. Quotations from office memorandum by Major P. G. Bower, 26 October 1944, in Numeric File 2 (B-29 Mining Plans), HQ 20th AF Records. See also memorandum, Combs for Assistant Chief/Air Staff, Plans, 26 October 1944, and "Report of Sub-committee on Japanese Shipping, Committee of Operations Analysts," 20 October 1944, both in same file location; and memorandum, Combs to Norstad, 4 November 1944, in file 373.11 Bombardment, HQ 20th AF Records.

35. Quotation from Bower memorandum, cited n. 34; see also other documents cited in n. 34.

36. Extract of Teletype Conference between Washington and Kharagpur, 5 November 1944, in folder "Teletype Conference XX Bomber Command," Message File (Telecons Kharagpur 1944), HQ 20th AF Records; memoranda by Landsberg, "Disease Rates after Tokyo Earthquake of 1923," and "Possible Additional Influence of Temperature on Casualty Figures in Attacks on Japanese Cities," both dated 3 November 1944, in file 760.310 1944–45 (vol. 2), AFSHRC. For a more bizarre proposal at this time, see memorandum for Chief of the Air Staff, 14 December 1944, subject: "Employment of Sound in the War Against Japan," file Japan-D, Air AG Files 1942–44, AAF Records.

37. W. B. Shockley, "A Quantitative Appraisal of Some Phases of the B-29 Program," Forwarded to Bowles by Shockley memorandum, 1 May 1945, in Chief of Staff file 384.5, WD Staff Records.

38. Quotations from Hastings, 253.

39. JIC 125/2, 14 August 1943, in Reel 9, JCS Records (microfilm ed., part I, 1942–45, European Theater); memorandum, Hansell to Arnold, 26 July 1944, in file 373 Employment of Aviation, HQ 20th AF Records; Hansell, *Strategic Air War*, 48.

40. Landsberg, "Report on Discussion on and Demonstration of M26 Aimable Incendiary Cluster at Bayway Refinery, Standard Oil Company of New Jersey on 14 November 1944," in Numeric File 11 (Plans for Incendiary Attacks), HQ 20th AF Records; Bowles memorandum for files, 26 February 1945, correspondence files, Bowles Papers.

41. Memorandum, Bower to Posey and Combs, 20 February 1945, in folder "Target Selections," Numeric File 18, HQ 20th AF Records; memorandum, Bower to Posey, 3 February 1945, in Numeric File 21 (Weapons—Bomb Requirements and Effectiveness), HQ 20th AF Records.

42. Hastings, 254.

43. Futrell, 128.

44. Blanchard, 248 (Blanchard's emphasis).

45. Zuckerman, 353–54.

46. Memorandum, Miser to Rowland, 6 June 1945, in file 471.6 Bombs, HQ 20th AF Records.

47. See Craven and Cate, vol. 2, 367–70.

48. See chap, 7. p. 199.

49. CCS 417/9, "Over-all objective in the War Against Japan," as quoted in JCS 924/5. "Operations for the Defeat of Japan," 27 October 1944, in OPD file ABC Japan (8–27–42) Section 7, WD Staff Records.

50. See Weigley, *The American Way of War.*

51. Norstad address, 27 September 1944, as cited above, n. 7.

52. Letter, Arnold to Hansell, written 27 December 1944, in file 201 Hansell, HQ 20th AF Records; Arnold, 532.

53. Hansell, *Strategic Air War,* 35.

54. Memorandum, Marshall for Embick, 1 September 1944, in Chief of Staff file 381, WD Staff Records; minutes of JCS meeting, 5 September 1944, JCS Records.

55. Memorandum, Colonel S. F. Griffin for General Wilson, 25 November 1944, in Official Decimal File 385 Japan (77), Box 115, Arnold Papers.

56. Lincoln paraphrased in memorandum, undated (probably 9 June 1945) and unsigned, titled "Discussion on JWPC 353/1," in OPD file ABC 370.01 (7–25–42), WD Staff Records; for a similar statement on Lincoln's part in March, see notes on the Joint Staff Planners' meeting, 7 March 1945, in file CCS 373.11 Japan (8–20–43), JCS Records; Hansell, *Strategic Air War,* xiii.

57. Iriye, *Across the Pacific,* 227.

58. Quoted in Butow, 49; see also Dower, *Empire and Aftermath,* chaps. 7–8; Iriye, *Power and Culture,* 121.

59. Quoted in Iriye, *Power and Culture,* 123.

60. See especially Villa, 70–71.

61. See Kecskemeti, 157–58.

62. Ibid., 236.

63. Quotation in Iriye, *Power and Culture,* 126–27; see also 47–63, 121–29, 149–53, 190ff.

64. Ibid., 129, 148, 225.

65. See, for example, "U.S. Experts Believe Jap War May Last Years After Nazis Fall," Washington *Evening Star,* 27 September 1944, article clipped and filed with OPD file ABC 381 Japan (8–27–42) Section 7, WD Staff Records.

66. Clark as paraphrased in Spector, 398. Cantril, 1118, 1143. Wills, 285.

67. Kenney letter, 1 January 1943, as quoted in Arnold, 381–83; transcript of teletype conference, 26 July 1944, in Message File (Telecons Kharagpur 1944), HQ 20th AF Records; characterization of Churchill is by Thorne, 725.

68. Havens, 89; a far more brutal picture of wartime Japan emerges in Ienaga, but even he acknowledges holes in the apparatus of state repression.

69. On the differences and similarities between Japan and the United States noted here and in the following two paragraphs, see Dower, *War Without Mercy;* quotations from 245, 204, 204–05. On the concept of the migrating stereotype, see Sheila K. Johnson, *American Attitudes Toward Japan, 1941–1975* (Washington 1975), 7–10; on the role of racist attitudes in American relations with China, see Thorne, passim.

70. John Hersey, *Into the Valley* (New York, 1944), 56, as quoted in Johnson, *American Attitudes Toward Japan,* 37. Arnold, speech of 8 November 1944 in Detroit, in Binder 5, Speech File, Box 226, Arnold Papers.

71. Quotations from Dower, *War Without Mercy,* 55, 184–85.

72. For some of these problems in formulating surrender policy, see Villa, 66–78. Quotations from Roosevelt's fireside chat, 12 June 1944, in Samuel I. Rosenman, ed., *The Public Papers and Addresses of Franklin D. Roosevelt* (New York, 1938–50), vol. 13, 175.

73. For quotations, see documents cited in n. 21; see also "General Notes on Incendiary Bombing of Japanese Cities," unsigned, undated (1943), in Project Decimal File (1941–45) 384.5 Japan, G-2 Records.

74. Memorandum, Zacharias to Horne, 14 June 1943, and memorandum, George H. Kerr to Chief, Japan Branch, War Department Military Intelligence Service, 19 June 1943, both in file CCS 385 Japan (4–27–42) Section 2, JCS Records.

75. Quotations from Joint Planning Staff report, 9 July 1943, in file 381 Japan (8–27–42) Section 2, WD Staff Records; and from CPS 123/1, "Anglo-American Outline Plan for Psychological Warfare Against Japan," 1 April 1944, in file CCS 385 Japan (4–27–42) Section 2, JCS Records.

76. Quotations from "Summary of Japanese Preparedness for Air Raids," unsigned and undated memorandum, with handwritten memorandum by Arnold, 21 July 1944, directing that copies be furnished to the 20th and 21st Bomber Commands, in file 350.09 Combat Intelligence Correspondence, HQ 20th AF Records; interview with air force officer as quoted in report from the Office of the Assistant Chief/Air Staff, A-2, 9 September 1944, in file 401 Supply Japan, Foreign Files Japan, Air AG Central Decimal Files October 1942–1944, AAF Records.

77. Quotations from memorandum, Norstad for Arnold, 29 November 1944, with Arnold's handwritten comments addressed to Norstad, 1 December 1944, in file 373.2 Operations and Reports—Aviation, HQ 20th AF Records; for the responses of Grew and others consulted, see memorandum, Hodges to Assistant Chief/Air Staff, Plans, 6 December 1944, in file "Japan—D", Air AG Records 1942–1944, AAF Records. On Tokyo's expectations see Gullain, 177.

78. Interview with Eaker, May 1962, copy in file K239.0512-627, AFSHRC; see also Schaffer, "American Military Ethics," passim.

79. Eaker interview cited in n. 78; interview with Spaatz, May 1965, copy in file K239.0512-755, AFSHRC. See also Schaffer, "American Military Ethics," 323–24.

80. Hansell, *Strategic Air War,* 90.

81. Interview with Spaatz, 21 February 1962, copy in file K239.0512-754, AFSHRC.

82. Memorandum, W. J. Crozier to Chief of Staff, Twentieth Air Force, 13 December 1944, in file 760.310-7, AFSHRC.

83. The specific implications of the social scientists' work for bombing policy are largely mine, but the more general analysis draws heavily on Dower, *War Without Mercy,* chaps. 5–6; quotations from 123, 138. See also Richard H. Minear, "Cross-Cultural Perception and World War II: American Japanists of the 1940s and Their Images of Japan," *International Studies Quarterly* 24 (December 1980): 555–80.

84. Quotation from Dower, *War Without Mercy,* 138.

85. Statement by General Barney M. Giles, Deputy Commander, AAF, in minutes of special meeting of the Air Staff, 31 August 1944, in Official Decimal File 337 (Air Staff Meetings, 1944), Box 96, Arnold Papers.

86. Kecskemeti, 236; Hansell, *Strategic Air War,* 75.

87. Andre Haynal, Miklos Molnar, Gerard de Puymege, *Fanaticism: A Historical and Psychoanalytical Study* (New York, 1983), 41, 38, 33; the authors of this formidable study of fanaticism would probably disagree with my application of the term but have nonetheless informed my understanding of it.

88. Hannah Arendt, *Eichmann in Jerusalem: A Report on the Banality of Evil* (New York, 1963).

89. For an exploration of these themes in other contexts of American policy, see Blanchard, passim.

90. For an older and somewhat narrower formulation of this view, see Basil H. Liddell Hart, *The Revolution in Warfare* (New Haven, 1947), 95: "It was the combination of an *unlimited aim* with an *unlimited method*—the adoption of a demand for unconditional surrender together with a strategy of total blockade and bombing devastation—which, in the recent war, inevitably produced a deepening danger to the relatively shallow foundations of civilized life."

91. Arnold, 492.

CHAPTER 9

Sources

The principal sources for my account of LeMay and American bombing of Japan are archival. The official record, however, has been incompletely preserved: in particular, no large body of internal records for

LeMay's 21st Bomber Command could be located. Interview material on LeMay fills in some gaps; I have tried to use it with discretion, less to reconcile factual disputes than to confirm impressions of LeMay's personality, methods of command, and attitudes toward his actions.

Several published works also supplement the primary record. Although flawed, Craven and Cate, *The AAF in World War II*, volumes 3 and 5, remain the essential secondary source, supplemented by Hayes, *History of the Joint Chiefs*, and Matloff, *Strategic Planning for Coalition Warfare, 1943–44*. Hansell, *Strategic Air War Against Japan*, is the single best insider's account and an important critique of air force strategy. LeMay, *Mission with LeMay*, is loose on strategy, revelatory on the man. My interpretation of LeMay's decisions and the manner in which they have been remembered draws on Blanchard, *Aggression American Style*, a critique not directly concerned with the policies I examine.

On the bombing of Dresden, I have relied largely on secondary sources. See Irving, *The Destruction of Dresden*, and Smith, "The Bombing of Dresden Reconsidered," less imaginative but better documented and a valuable corrective on some points. The account in Pogue, *Marshall*, volume 3, is brief but judicious; equally valuable is Schaffer, "American Military Ethics." Among accounts of the British role, see Hastings, *Bomber Command*, and Webster and Frankland, *The Strategic Bomber Offensive Against Germany*, volume 3. Once again, Walzer, *Just and Unjust Wars*, is essential.

Documentation on and accounts of the March 10 fire raid on Tokyo are incomplete, but several valuable English-language sources are available. The best secondary account is Daniels, "The Great Tokyo Air Raid, 9–10 March 1945." Caidin, *A Torch to the Enemy*, an older, vivid popular account, was notable as the first large-scale attempt to remember the March 10 raid in the face of postwar preoccupation with the atomic attacks; long out of print, some of it is excerpted in Wilson, *WW2*. Among firsthand accounts, see especially Gullain, *I Saw Tokyo Burning*, and Kato, *The Lost War*. Voluminous if sometimes flawed data and observations are available in many reports of the United States Strategic Bombing Survey, and in the survey's unpublished interrogations, in RG 243, National Archives. Early postwar studies, some written by the survey's experts, include Bond, *Fire and the Air War*; Janis, *Air War and Emotional Stress*; Ikle, *The Social Impact of Bomb Destruction*. Havens, *Valley of Darkness*, and Shillony, *Politics and Culture in Wartime Japan*, supersede the earlier studies by setting the bomb destruction in the broader context of wartime Japanese culture and politics.

Among many examinations of the politics and strategy of unconditional surrender, I have relied especially on Sherwin, *A World Destroyed*; the older but perceptive study, Batchelder, *The Irreversible Decision*; and Villa, "The U.S. Army, Unconditional Surrender, and the Potsdam Proclamation." For Stimson, I have relied mainly on primary sources, but Morison, *Turmoil and Tradition*, is perceptive, if sympathetic.

Notes

1. Quotations from letter, Arnold to Stimson, 13 January 1945, in Official Decimal File 370.2 China, Box 106, Arnold Papers. See also Craven and Cate, vol. 5, 142–44 and n. 46; Claire Chennault, *Way of a Fighter* (New York, 1949), 328–30. Even before the Hankow raid, the navy's carrier-based bombers allegedly had inflicted "indiscriminate carpet bombing" on Naha, the capital of Okinawa, and provoked a protest from Japan through diplomatic channels which the American government ignored. But it does not appear that the navy's action served as an instructive example to the air force. See Usui Katsumi, "On the Duration of the Pacific War—A New Look at the Accepted View," in *Japan Quarterly* 28 (October–December 1981): 484, and U.S. Department of State, *Foreign Relations of the United States: 1945; Diplomatic Papers*, vol. 6, 470–72.

2. On Hansell's arrival at Saipan, see Craven and Cate, vol. 5, 546, and the film coverage in the AAF Combat Weekly Digest, Number 58, 4 December 1944, in RG 18, MPB Collection.

3. Hansell, *Strategic Air War*, 37–38; see also Craven and Cate, vol. 5, 548–58.

4. See the lead story in Universal Newsreel, vol. 17, release 356, 18 December 1944, in RG 200, MPB Collection.

5. Quoted in Spector, 493.

6. Quotations from Craven and Cate, vol. 5, 564 ("urgent requirement"); letter, Hansell to Norstad, 2 December 1944, in file 201 Hansell, HQ 20th AF Records ("very deep seated"); letter, Hansell to

Arnold, 16 December 1944, in file 201 Hansell, HQ 20th AF Records ("to waste any bombs"); telecon, Hansell to Arnold (through Norstad), 19 December 1944, in file Mission Reports (Mission 17, Nagoya, 3 January 1945), HQ 20th AF Records ("with great difficulty"); Craven and Cate, vol. 5, 564 ("future planning"). See also Hansell, *Strategic Air War,* 51.

7. Quotations from Hansell, *Strategic Air War,* 48 (see also p. 50); memorandum, Norstad to Arnold, 19 December 1944, in file 373.2 Operations and Reports (21st Bomber Command), HQ 20th AF Records; memorandum, Norstad for Arnold, 2 January 1945, in Jacket 203 (War Council), Official Files, Box 47, Arnold Papers.

8. Letter, Norstad to Hansell, 7 December 1944, in file 201 Hansell, HQ 20th AF Records; letter, Arnold to Hansell, 1 January 1945, in Series 2, Box 2, Hansell Papers; letter, Hansell to Arnold, 14 January 1945 in file 201 Hansell, HQ 20th AF Records.

9. McKelway, II, 32; Hansell, *Strategic Air War,* 48. See also letter, Hansell to Arnold, 14 January cited above, n. 8, and letter, Arnold to Hansell, 1 February 1945, in Series 2, Box 2, Hansell Papers.

10. "How Long to Smash Tokyo?" *Los Angeles Times,* 1 December 1944; "Tokyo Targets," *Kansas City Star,* 29 November 1944. See also Hansell, *Strategic Air War,* 29.

11. Much of this story is covered in detail in Craven and Cate, vol. 3; see 666 for Spaatz's worries about death ray; 722 for figures on weight of effort devoted to tactical missions; on consternation of some air commanders, see Terraine, 665–67.

12. Stimson Diary, 11 January 1945.

13. Marshall, paraphrased in Craven and Cate, vol. 3, 649; memorandum, Arnold for Bissell, 8 January 1945, with copy to Marshall and initialed by Marshall, in Chief of Staff file 384.5, WD Staff Records.

14. On the controversy over Dresden's death toll, see esp. Smith, "The Bombing of Dresden," 265–69. Many histories of the bombing campaigns are largely silent on the matter of total civilian casualties during the war, but see esp. Hastings, 352, for some summary and analysis.

15. On the Berlin figure, see Craven and Cate, vol. 3, 726; Irving, 104; "Berlin Can't Take it," *Newsweek,* 5 March 1945, 30–31. Plans for climactic morale attacks are discussed in many accounts, but see esp. Irving, 110; Schaffer, "American Military Ethics," 324–32, and Schaffer, *Wings,* chaps. 4–5 (quotation from p. 83).

16. For Harris's independence from his superiors, see Hastings, 330–36. On Churchill, see Smith, "The Bombing of Dresden," 82–83, 225–28, 246; the quotations are phrases Churchill first chose and then deleted in March while addressing the controversy over Dresden. On the role of SHAEF and the Russians, see among many sources, Smith, 237–47, and Pogue, vol. 3, 540–47. Other quotations from Arnold in memorandum, Arnold to Lindsay, 13 January 1945, in Jacket 59 (Conference), Official File, Box 42, Arnold Papers. On suspicions that some British and Americans sought to impress or intimidate the Soviets, see, for example, Irving, 93, 117; Smith, 19–20; Schaffer, "American Military Ethics," 330; Laurence S. Kuter, *Airman at Yalta* (New York, 1955), 32–33.

17. See Hastings, chap. 13.

18. Quoted in Smith, "The Bombing of Dresden," 72; see Smith, 70–73, for origins of the AP story, and 280–81 for its complete text.

19. Message, Rex Smith to Spaatz, signed Arnold, 18 February 1945, quoted in Smith, "The Bombing of Dresden," 73. See also memorandum, Giles to Arnold, 19 February 1945, in Diary of Events and Decisions Made in Absence of Arnold, Box 223, Subject File, Arnold Papers. Arnold was in Florida convalescing from his fourth heart attack.

20. Message, Anderson (signed Spaatz) to Arnold, 19 February 1945, UA 64470, in CM-IN Top Secret file Jan–Feb 1945, WD Staff Records. On the use of radar techniques and the quoted comment by air force historians, see Craven and Cate, vol. 3, 666–69. For Schaffer's comment, see "American Military Ethics," 332, where his conclusions about the consciousness of commanders differ somewhat from mine.

21. Memorandum, Wilson to Arnold, 30 March 1945, in Numeric File # 8 ("Plans and Sortie Rates—20th AF"), HQ 20th AF Records.

22. Pogue, vol. 3, 547, 544 (quotation from Marshall).

23. Eaker to Spaatz, 1 January 1945, as quoted in Schaffer, "American Military Ethics," 328; it was on this occasion that Eaker issued his oft-cited warning against allowing "the history of this war to convict us of throwing the strategic bomber at the man in the street." Message, Anderson to Washington, 17 February 1945, quoted in Smith, "The Bombing of Dresden," 78.

24. Quotations from Stimson Diary, 5 March 1945; see also memorandum, McCarthy to Arnold, 6 March 1945, and accompanying documents, in Chief of Staff file 384.5, WD Staff Records. Arnold quotation from his comments penned on copy of memorandum, Giles to Arnold, 7 March 1945, in Diary of Events and Decisions Made in Absence of Arnold, Box 223, Subject File, Arnold Papers.

25. On subsequent raids, see memorandum, Marshall for Stimson, 6 March 1945, in Chief of Staff file 384.5, WD Staff Records; Webster and Frankland, vol. 3, 108–09 (n. 5); Irving, 191–94; Craven and Cate omit mention of April 17 raid.

26. Minutes of Joint Chiefs of Staff meeting, 8 February 1945, in JCS Records; memorandum, K.W.T. to Hull, 11 March 1945, in Item 71 (Information from the White House), OPD Exec # 10, WD Staff Records; Leahy to President, 26 March 1945, in Leahy file # 125 (Memoranda to and from President, 1945), JCS Records. See also Francis L. Loewenheim, Harold D. Langley, and Manfred Jonas, eds., *Roosevelt and Churchill: Their Secret Wartime Correspondence* (New York, 1975), 688–89, for FDR's final request, 29 March 1945, to Churchill on this matter, and Schaffer, "American Military Ethics," 326–27.

27. *Newsweek:* "Now Terror, Truly," 25 February 1945, 34–35; "Berlin Can't Take It," 5 March 1945, 30–31; "Here was Dresden," 12 March 1945, 33. *Time:* "Mission Accomplished," 19 March 1945, 31 (on Cologne); Universal Newsreel, vol. 18, release 381, 15 March 1945, in RG 200, MPB.

28. C. G. Paulding, "Terror Bombing," *Commonweal,* 2 March 1945, 485; Norman Thomas, "War, Peace and the Churches," *Chritian Century,* 11 April 1945, 458–60. On Harris, see Walzer, 323–25.

29. Curiously, historians have neglected the popular response to the final days of the bombing of Germany, simply assuming that the leaders' fears were well founded.

30. Minutes of Joint Chiefs of Staff meeting, 27 February 1945, in JCS Records.

31. See "Halsey on Rats," *Newsweek,* 5 March 1945, 32–33; "Rodent Exterminators," *Time,* 19 March 1945, 32–33.

32. Notes for Joint Staff Planners meeting, 21 February 1945, in Air Plans Project Decimal File 381 (1943) Section 1, HQ USAF Records. For earlier assumptions about invasion, see Hayes, 627–28, 629–30.

33. MacArthur quoted in Hayes, 632. On responses to British participation in the war, see Thorne, passim; Hayes, passim; Robert M. Hathaway, *Ambiguous Partnership; Britain and America, 1944–1947* (New York, 1981), 57–62; and the documents in file CCS 373.11 Japan (9–18–44) British Participation in VLR Bombing of Japan, JCS Records.

34. On Soviet–American military cooperation during the war's last year, see Craven and Cate, vol. 3, 308–19; Julian, especially 342–49; Hayes, 668–76, 683–85; Lukas, passim; James, 763–65; Walter Millis, ed., *The Forrestal Diaries* (New York, 1951), 27–29, 31; John R. Deane, *The Strange Alliance* (New York, 1947), 107–25; memorandum, Marshall to President, 23 January 1945, in file Memoranda to and from President (1945), JCS Records.

35. McKelway, II, 37.

36. Memorandum, Arnold to Norstad, 14 January 1945, in Jacket 286 (B-29 Project), Official File, Box 54, Arnold Papers.

37. Quotations from Craven and Cate, vol. 5, 568 ("hotly defended"); memorandum, Samford to Combs, 1 February 1945 ("purpose of this attack"), and memorandum, Samford to Combs, 3 February 1945 ("does not include," etc), and telecon, Norstad to LeMay, 12 February 1945 ("conflagration," etc.), all in Numeric File #11 ("Plans for Incendiary Attacks"), HQ 20th AF Records. For staff arguments against postponing the fire campaign, see memorandum, Bower to Posey, 16 January 1945, in Numeric File #11, cited above. See also Craven and Cate, vol. 5, 568–70, 611.

38. Telecon, COMAF 20 to BOMCOM 20 and BOMCOM 21 (Norstad to LeMay and others), 19 February 1945, in Numeric File #4 ("Directives"), HQ 20th AF Records; teletype conference, Norstad and LeMay, 20–21 February 1945, in Numeric File #47 ("Special Conference—20 Feb. with LeMay"),

HQ 20th AF Records. On the February 25 raid on Tokyo, see Craven and Cate, 572–73, who cite it as the "conclusive 'test' of the fire bomb that the Twentieth Air Force had been asking for," but since the priority for fire raids had already been upgraded, the February 25 mission was probably more a confirmation than a source of policy.

39. Telecon, Rees to McKelway, 15 February 1945, and telecon, Norstad to LeMay, 11 February 1945, both in file Telecons Out G-H-K 1945, Message File, 20th AF Records. On embarrassment over the navy's success, see Craven and Cate, vol. 5, 573.

40. See memorandum, 16 January 1945, cited above, n. 37, and Craven and Cate, vol. 5, 661–66 (quotation from 664).

41. "Air Estimate and Plans for Twentieth Air Force Operations, February–March–April 1945," n.d. (1–10 February 1945), in Subject File, HQ 20th AF Records.

42. Villa, 74–80; Matloff, 341–42. For a more optimistic view of progress in these discussions, see Iriye, *Power and Culture,* 233–34.

43. See Stimson Diary, 8, 20 February 1945; minutes of Committee of Three meetings, 8, 20 February 1945, with memorandum on Halsey conversation attached, in Stimson Top Secret Safe File (Committee of Three), SecWar Records.

44. Morison, 513; Batchelder, 43–44.

45. Stimson Diary, 27 February 1945; Morison, 514.

46. Memorandum, Patterson to Stimson, 25 February 1945 ("growing restlessness") in folder 2, reel 1, Harrison-Bundy Files; Stimson Diary, 10 June 1944 ("the possible ultimate success"). See also Stimson Diary, 26 February 1945; Sherwin. 199–200.

47. The analysis of FDR's possible motives is mine. The story appears to have been first told in S. Lovell, *Of Spies and Stratagems* (New York, 1963); was rejected by Brown, 283 (n. 48); presented with caution in Stockholm International Peace Research Institute, *The Problems of Chemical and Biological Warfare,* vol. 1 (Stockholm, 1971), 298; and repeated with less caution in Harris and Paxman, 135. Consideration of use of chemical and biological weapons was certainly widespread in Anglo-American military circles in 1945, though by no means uniformly favorable and opposed especially by Admiral Leahy. On buildup and consideration, see Harris and Paxman, chaps. 4–5, and Brown, chap. 6.

48. LeMay's interview with Wilbur H. Morrison, 31 October 1977, copy obtained from American Heritage Center, University of Wyoming. Norstad took his January trip to the Pacific apparently intending to tell Hansell of the atomic bomb project and may have told LeMay at that time. See memorandum, Derry to Groves, 1 January 1945, on meeting with Norstad and others, in File 5, Subseries I, reel 1, MED Records. By spring, LeMay was closely involved in operational planning for the atomic bomb mission. See memoranda, Derry to Groves (10 March 1945), Norstad to LeMay (29 May 1945), Kirkpatrick to Groves (10 June 1945), same file location.

49. LeMay, 345.

50. LeMay, 14; letter, LeMay to Norstad, 31 January 1945, in Box B31, LeMay Papers; McKelway, III, 27, 32.

51. LeMay's interview with Sherry, 29 June 1981; LeMay's interview with Morrison.

52. LeMay, 340–42.

53. LeMay's interviews with Morrison and Sherry.

54. Letter, Norstad to LeMay, 19 January 1945, in Box B31, LeMay Papers.

55. Claimed in McKelway, III, 26, but the surviving documentary record seems to contain no such order, and it is unmentioned in Craven and Cate.

56. Ibid., 27; letter, LeMay to Norstad, 3 March 1945, in Box B31, LeMay Papers. LeMay noted that his letter might not reach Norstad before his visit to Guam.

57. Quotation from LeMay, 346. This portrayal of LeMay's process of reaching a decision is based on the account in LeMay's memoirs; the McKelway series, III; LeMay's interviews; and Major Gene Gurney, "The Giant Pays Its Way," in Colonel James F. Sunderman, ed., *World War II in the Air: The Pacific* (New York, 1963, 1981), 247–65.

58. LeMay, 351.

59. These observations rest primarily on interpretations of two kinds of evidence. In his memoirs,

the narrative of his wartime career became unglued and broke down into a kind of staccato, stream-of-consciousness style just at the point where he began discussing the command decision to launch low-level incendiary raids. The formal content of these interruptions concerned his anxiety about the fate of the men he sent to battle. We need not discount it (or the skillful hand of his collaborator, MacKinlay Kantor) to wonder if the anxiety articulated did not also express concerns less visible to LeMay. Furthermore, when in interview I probed him regarding the moral and strategic issues raised by firebombing and the atomic bomb, LeMay's pattern of rather pat and well-formulated answers to questions broke down, he became restless and nervous, and finally he angrily broke off the interview. Of course that anxiety partly expressed exasperation with questions he thought inappropriate; but the content of the questions and the contradictions into which they sometimes led him were also upsetting. Furthermore, LeMay struck me as a largely transparent man in the best sense—not uncomplicated, but also not inclined to hide his emotional state. Therefore, I took the evident signs of distress as related to the manifest content of the questions thrown at him. Whatever the confidence he asserted regarding his solutions to the moral dilemmas posed, he could not escape a sense of the terribleness of the deeds he ordered done. Occasional passages in his memoirs suggest how that sense arose and then was quickly suppressed; see, for example, LeMay, 425.

60. LeMay, 347. On the timing of Norstad's arrival, see the March 9 entry in LeMay's daily diary, in Box B9, LeMay Papers, and Craven and Cate, vol. 5, 614.

61. LeMay's interview with Morrison ("a typical staff man"); LeMay, 348. On LeMay's notification to Arnold, see Craven and Cate, vol. 5, 614 and n. 25.

62. McKelway, III, 27, 36.

63. U.S. Strategic Bombing Survey, The Effects of Strategic Bombing on Japanese Morale (Washington, 1947), 36.

64. Gullain, 178, 182 ("translucid," etc.); recollection of Rev. Bruno Bitter, a Catholic priest in Tokyo, in Assistant Chief of Air Staff—Intelligence, Headquarters Army Air Forces, Mission Accomplished: Interrogations of Japanese Industrial, Military and Civil Leaders of World War II (Washington, 1946), p. 100 ("ghastly reflections," etc.); Kato, 210 ("attracted").

65. Lars Tillitse, "When Bombs Rained on Us in Tokyo," Saturday Evening Post, 12 January 1946, 82 ("descended"); Gullain, 182 ("light flashed); Caidin, in Wilson, WW2, 312 ("illuminated"); Gullain, 182 ("All the Japanese," etc.). For other sensations of American crews described here, see Caidin, in WW2, 312–19, and Martin Sheridan, "Giant Tokyo Fires Blackened B-29's," New York Times, 11 March 1945.

66. Kato, 205 (patriotic song); Dower, War Without Mercy, 247 (paraphrasing government instructions); Gullain, 184.

67. Havens, 162. On evacuation and other preparations prior to the March 10 raid, see also in addition to Havens, Daniels, 121–23, and U.S. Strategic Bombing Survey, Field Report Covering Air Raid Protection and Allied Subjects, Tokyo, Japan (Washington, 1947).

68. Bitter, in Mission Accomplished, 100.

69. Havens, 179. See also Gullain, 185.

70. Gullain, 182; Kato, 210; Gullain, 181 ("almost as"). For intensity and dynamics of the conflagration, see esp. Caidin, in Wilson, WW2, 317–18, and Bond, Fire and the Air War, 181. Accounts of the surface winds prevailing before the attack vary widely. Most American sources reported little wind prior to the conflagration: Bond, Fire and the Air War, 165; Field Report Covering Air Raid Protection and Allied Subjects, Tokyo, 63; "300 B29's Fire 15 Square Miles of Tokyo," New York Times, 10 March 1945. Witnesses on the ground reported strong winds before the raid: Gullain, 181; Kato, 209; translation of article in French by Father Flaujac on the bombardment of Tokyo, in Donald S. Detwiler and Charles B. Burdick, eds., War in Asia and the Pacific, 1937–1949 (New York, 1980), vol. 12. On wind, see also USSBS, Effects of Incendiary Bomb Attacks on Japan: A Report on Eight Cities (Washington, 1947), 90, 94.

71. Hisaki Imai's story is recounted in Kato, 211–13; USSBS, Effects . . . Report on Eight Cities, 94; U.S. Strategic Bombing Survey, The Effects of Bombing on Health and Medical Services in Japan (Washington, 1947), 150.

72. Gullain, 186 ("luckless bathers"); Kato, 211 ("so many fish"), 5 ("small islands"). For effects of the firebombing on sturdier buildings, see section on Tokyo in USSBS, Effects . . . Report on Eight Cities.

73. For this comparison, see esp. Daniels, 129. Further evidence is in U.S. Strategic Bombing

Survey, *Final Report Covering Air-Raid Protection and Allied Subjects in Japan* (Washington, 1947), 197, and USSBS, *Field Report Covering Air Raid Protection and Allied Subjects, Tokyo,* 3, 79. The Manhattan Engineer District estimated the ratio of dead to injured was about one to one in Hiroshima, somewhat higher in Nagasaki; see "The Atomic Bombings of Hiroshima and Nagasaki," p. 18, in *Manhattan Project: Official History and Documents* (microfilm ed., University Publications of America), Reel 1. In contrast, The Committee for the Compilation of Materials on Damage Caused by the Atomic Bombs in Hiroshima and Nagasaki, *Hiroshima and Nagasaki,* 420–21, suggests a much higher ratio of dead to wounded in Hiroshima and Nagasaki than in Tokyo. As discussed below in notes at greater length, casualty estimates vary widely and are hard to validate.

74. USSBS, *Health* report, 146.

75. No work of the scope and power of John Hersey's *Hiroshima* emerged after the war regarding Tokyo, and in the preoccupation with preparing for a possible atomic war, most postwar studies of the wartime bombing concentrated on the atomic blasts. Janis's *Air War and Emotional Stress* (1951) ably demonstrated this emphasis. Opening with a complaint about the "dearth of relevant material on atomic warfare" as opposed to " 'conventional' " bombing (p. 1), Janis focused on Hiroshima and Nagasaki and implied their uniqueness in ways both valid and misleading. One problem that many scholars faced was that much of the information available in American sources, particularly the Strategic Bombing Survey reports, distinguished poorly or not at all between the March 10 raid and other "conventional" attacks on Japan.

76. Casualty figures on Tokyo and in comparison to the atomic attacks are variable and much debated. The Strategic Bombing Survey itself offered conflicting figures on the March 10 raid, though they generally fell in the range of 79,000–84,000 dead, the discrepancies due in part to conflicting Japanese sources and the different methodologies used by different survey teams. The problems of ascertaining reliable figures are discussed at some length in the survey's *Health* and *Morale* reports. One survey tally offered in the *Final Report Covering Air Raid Protection,* 197, suggested that the Tokyo death toll was much higher than that in Nagasaki, slightly higher than in Hiroshima. Manhattan Engineer District estimates (see n. 73) indicated death tolls of 66,000 in Hiroshima and 39,000 in Nagasaki. Another report, *Field Report Covering Air Raid Protection and Allied Subjects, Tokyo,* 63, simply called the March 10 raid "the greatest disaster ever visited upon any city." In this grim search for first ranking, more recent sources drawing on Japanese investigations give Hiroshima the nod: Tokyo, 100,000; Hiroshima, 130,000; Nagasaki, 60–70,000; see Committee For Compilation, *Hiroshima and Nagasaki,* 420–21, and my chapter 10, n. 117. But it also seems probable that more effort has gone into determining a precise figure for the atomic attacks than for Tokyo and that the cessation of the war immediately after those attacks probably facilitated more accurate scrutiny of the death toll. In most cities the task of recovering bodies went on for weeks; few tallies can claim to be authoritative. The best brief account of conflicting estimates of Japan's casualty figures is in Daniels, 129, and his notes. See Gullain, 187, for speculation, echoed in many firsthand accounts, on figures much higher than that of 84,000 used here; similarly, Dyson, 43, who gives the Tokyo toll as 130,000. The claim that the March 10 raid "killed more Japanese than both atomic bombings combined" (Gregg Herken, *The Winning Weapon* [New York, 1980], 212) persists but now seems inaccurate.

77. Available figures do not break down losses by sex or age, but see Ikle, 205–06, for suggestive comment on the British experience. In subsequent incendiary raids, far less costly anyway, evacuation of Japanese cities, leaving behind primarily a work force to run remaining industries and government offices, probably lowered sharply the proportional losses of women and the elderly.

78. Tillitse, "When Bombs Rained," 82, 85; Bitter, in *Mission Accomplished,* 100, 101, attributing the silence to the fact that "orientals are fatalists"; Gullain, 193–94. On keloids, see Stockholm International Peace Research Institute, *Incendiary Weapons* (Cambridge, 1975), 146–48.

79. Kato, 214, 215 ("seeing a man," etc.); Pacific War Research Society, 102 ("Long lines," etc., quoting Japanese reporter); Strategic Bombing Survey interview with Nobushige Nishizawa on police reaction, 17 November 1945, in USSBS Records; Kato, 215, 211, 198 ("their eyes," etc.).

80. Gullain, 183 ("frightful Pentecost"); Flaujac article, cited n. 70 ("fairy scene," etc.); Dower, *War Without Mercy,* 249; Kato, 217.

81. Kato, 9, a recollection not specific to the March 10 raid.

82. For a good discussion of the many problems in gauging the hostilities of bomb victims, see Janis, esp. 129–33. See also USSBS, *Morale* report, 38–39.

83. Quotation from USSBS, *Morale* report, 56. On Tokyo's divergence from patterns of morale in other Japanese cities, see the *Morale* report, 48, 49, 50–51.

84. On prohibition of distribution of newspapers, see Shillony, 106. Some leaders had already begun to see the value of more truthful propaganda; see Havens, 161.

85. Quotation from Shillony, 106. For further evidence of hostility toward leaders, see Janis, 138, 144; Ienaga, 221–22; USSBS, *Morale* report, 28–30, 38–39, 45–46, a discussion of patterns throughout Japan, not just in Tokyo.

86. Comments of a Stanford-trained Japanese editorial writer for the English-language *Nippon Times*, as quoted in *Mission Accomplished*, 27.

87. USSBS, *Morale* report, 33. See also the entire report, but esp. 28–29, and *Mission Accomplished*, for much anecdotal testimony to the impact of the March 10 raid.

88. Quotation from Kato, 12. On the range and content of personal reactions to incendiary bombing, see USSBS, *Morale* report, passim; Janis, parts 1, 2, passim; Kato, chap. 1; Haven, chaps. 9–10.

89. *Mission Accomplished*, 28. See also *Morale* report, 27, 30–31, 44–45, 85.

90. Daniels, 127; Shillony, 76. See also USSBS, *Morale* report, 30; Toshikazu Kase, *Journey to the Missouri* (New Haven, 1950), 103; Premier Suzuki's interrogation by the strategic survey, 26 December 1945, in USSBS Records.

91. For a sense of the content and tone of official deliberations at this time, see Koichi Kido, *Translation of the Diary of Marquis Kido* (Washington, 1955).

92. Quotations and much of the information about evacuation are from Havens, 167–68. See also Daniels, 127; USSBS, *Final Report Covering Air Raid Protection*, 171.

93. Quotation from USSBS, *Health* report, 4. More generally, see that report, and USSBS, *Field Report Covering Air Raid Protection and Allied Subjects, Tokyo*, 74, 79. Few victims could be identified; see *Field Report*, 83, 187. On housing, see especially Ikle, 61–62. Havens, 158–59, notes that one-fifth of Japan's wartime housing loss occurred to create firebreaks.

94. Kato, 6.

95. Quotations from 21st Bomber Command, "Analysis of Incendiary Phase of Operations Against Japanese Urban Areas," n.d., in Box B37, LeMay Papers. I have drawn on this document for this and the preceding paragraphs as a valuable supplement to standard secondary sources.

96. LeMay, speech before Ohio Society of New York, "Air Power," 19 November 1945, in Box B42, LeMay Papers. McKelway, III, 30. Much of the initial press coverage of the March 10 raid gave considerable attention to LeMay. Some examples of later historical treatment might be noted. A pioneer study, Bernard Brodie, *Strategy in the Missile Age*, commented with some circumspection on "some radically new tactics worked out in General Curtis LeMay's headquarters" (p. 127). More recently, Russell Weigley, in *The American Way of War*, 364, commented more sweepingly on the "wide discretion in the determination of bombing strategy for Japan given to Major General Curtis E. LeMay's XXI Bomber Command." A recent history of the war against Japan was even less cautious in finding that "LeMay took only forty-eight hours to decide to 'throw away the book' and abandon precision bombing in favor of incendiary bombing" (Costello, 347). Two recent, authoritative histories of strategic bombing make similar claims: Kennett, 170; Overy, 98. Similarly, the Pacific War Research Society found LeMay deciding on "a bold, indeed a revolutionary plan," and doing so "on his own initiative " (*The Day Man Lost*, 99). Some of these accounts mention the pressures on LeMay for a different course but emphasize the solitary initiative he took. Other accounts treat the issue with more complexity or ambiguity; some of their evidence and arguments are introduced below.

97. On incendiaries, see Craven and Cate, vol. 5, 540–41. Arnold's hospital stay ended on March 15; see his *Global Mission*, 542.

98. See Blanchard, 192.

99. LeMay, interview with Sherry; LeMay, 347. LeMay backtracked somewhat from his claim of having had a free hand under questioning during his interview with me.

100. For the information conveyed to Roosevelt, see War Department Operational Summaries (entry for Pacific Ocean Area 10 March 1945), in Box 63, Map Room Papers, FDR Papers.

101. Account and figures in the above two paragraphs based on Craven and Cate, vol. 5, 479–89, 695. The deaths were not limited to China and Formosa, for "U.S. air raids and naval blockade from late 1944 . . . contributed greatly to the starvation of 1945, in which over a million Vietnamese died in Tonkin and Annam." See Dower, *War Without Mercy,* 297.

102. Ibid., 485. Craven and Cate add: "The missions were [also] used to experiment with different types of bombs and fuzings and with the tactics best suited to a variety of objectives." Besides Hankow and the Formosan cities and certain others in China, many other Japanese-held Asian cities were hit, in China and on down through Indochina and on to Singapore, but despite some use of radar techniques, wholesale destruction of these cities was apparently neither the intention nor the result. See the references in Craven and Cate, vol. 5, as indexed under the names of the relevant cities.

103. For the magnitude, details, and limits of high-level Allied efforts to limit damage to civilians and artifacts in occupied Europe, see Schaffer, *Wings,* 38–59.

104. LeMay, 384. LeMay offered much the same image in many interviews and speeches. Nor was it just the airman's impression—see Arthur Holly Compton, *Atomic Quest,* 228–29, on his brother Karl Compton's observations of Tokyo's ruins, and Compton's use of them to justify both atomic and conventional bombing.

105. See, for example, Kato, 8–9.

106. Havens, 92; USSBS, *Summary Report (Pacific War)* (Washington, 1946), 18.

107. Ikle, 75. Much of this analysis is suggested, explicitly or implicitly, in many of the Strategic Bombing Survey reports, and in Hansell, *Strategic Air War,* chap. 10, which also draws heavily on the survey reports.

108. LeMay's interview with Sherry.

109. LeMay's interview with Sherry; LeMay, 382, 384.

110. LeMay, 383.

111. LeMay's "Daily Diary," March 10 entry, in Box B9, LeMay Papers; letter, Arnold to LeMay, 21 March 1945, in Box B31, LeMay Papers.

112. Tactical Mission Report, Mission No. 40, 10 March 1945, in file Mission Reports 1944–45, HQ 20th AF Records (emphasis in original); "Analysis of the Incendiary Phase . . . ," cited above n. 95; letter, Combs to Hansell, 28 March 1945, in file 201 Hansell, HQ 20th AF Records.

113. Telecon, COMAF 20 (Col. Rex Smith) to COMGENBOMCOM 21, 11 March 1945, in file Telecons G-H-K out 1945, Message File; telecon, Spence to McKelway, 12 March 1945, in folder for Mission No. 41 (11 March 1945, Nagoya), file Mission Reports, 1944–45; telecon, Spence to McKelway, 14 March 1945, in folder for Mission No. 42 (13 March 1945, Osaka), file Mission Reports 1944–45; all in HQ 20th AF Records.

114. "Verbatim transcript" of Norstad press conference, 23 March 1945, in file 201 Norstad, HQ 20th AF Records.

115. McKelway, III, 36, 35.

116. Telecon, Spence to McKelway, 12 March 1945, cited above, n. 113.

117. *Times* quotations all taken from the several stories and headlines in its editions for 10–11 March 1945. See also *Time* and *Newsweek* issues for 19, 26 March 1945, and Hopkins, 470–72.

118. See Universal Newsreels for 29 March 1945 (release 385), 10 May 1945 (release 397), 17 May 1945 (release 399), all in vol. 18, RG 200, MPB Collection. Observation on Japanese coverage based on the collections of Japanese newsreels in the Library of Congress and the National Archives.

119. Gill Robb Wilson, "The Air World," *New York Herald Tribune,* 30 April 1945.

120. "Incendiaries Over Tokyo," *Kansas City Star,* 12 March 1945; David Lawrence, "Air Power Now Seen in Proper Perspective," *Washington Star,* 14 March 1945; "Japanese Battleground," *New York Times,* 26 March 1945; Gill Robb Wilson, "The Air World," *New York Herald Tribune,* 23 April 1945.

121. "Tokyo—Osaka—Nagoya—Kobe—?" *Atlanta Constitution,* 20 March 1945; Gill Robb Wilson, "The Air World," *New York Herald Tribune,* 30 April 1945.

122. H. G. Nicholas, ed., *Washington Despatches 1941–1945* (Chicago, 1981), 558 (May 13).

123. For examples of the American leadership's anxiety about "war-weariness," see Villa, 84; Arnold, 560. Public opinion polls, however, found that respondents in May preferred to "take time and save lives" rather than to "end war quickly despite casualties" (see Cantril, 1073). For public speculation about Washington's fear of war-weariness and relaxation after V-E day, see "Washington Trends," *Newsweek,* 14 May 1945, 26.

124. Dower, *War Without Mercy,* 233. Ienaga, 231. Daniels, 131, makes the same criticism just as harshly.

125. Stimson, memorandum discussed with Truman, 25 April 1945, in Stimson Diary, and published in many sources; see Bernstein, *The Atomic Bomb,* 5–7. On Sachs, see Sherwin, 131–32. On the Chicago scientists, see my chap. 7.

126. Stimson, "The Decision to Use the Atomic Bomb," *Harper's,* February 1947, as reprinted in Bernstein, *The Atomic Bomb,* 4; Henry L. Stimson and McGeorge Bundy, *On Active Service in Peace and War* (New York, 1947), 617. As ably summarized by Bernstein (p. 1), Stimson's recollections on the decision to use the bomb simultaneously maintained that "policymakers had long regarded the bomb as a 'legitimate' weapon; [and] that they carefully considered the decision."

127. Stimson Diary, 1 June 1945 (clearly referring to an earlier conversation with Lovett), 16 May 1945. In regard to Stimson's May 16 statement, Sherwin's interpretation (p. 197) seems inadequate: "The possibility that its [the bomb's] extraordinary and indiscriminate destructiveness represented a profound qualitative difference, and so cried out for its governance by a higher morality than guided the use of conventional weapons, simply did not occur to him." On its own right, Sherwin's point is correct, but it must also be stated that Stimson arrived at his indifference in part because he also failed to recognize the moral issue involved in "conventional" bombing.

128. Stimson, *Harper's* article, in Bernstein, *The Atomic Bomb,* 15–16; Stimson Diary, 1 June 1945. Suggesting a different view from mine is Robert Oppenheimer's recollection, vague and offered many years later, that Stimson found it "appalling" that the bombing of Japan elicited so little protest; see Giovannitti and Freed, 36.

129. Gabriel Kolko, *The Politics of War: The World and United States Foreign Policy, 1943–1945* (New York, 1968), 539. Stimson's biographer makes the point more obliquely; see Morison, 515.

130. Compton, 237; Stimson, memorandum of talk with the president, 6 June 1945, in Stimson Diary; Groves, 273–75; Stimson Diary, 24 July 1945. See also Arnold, 492, 589, and Otis Cary, "The Sparing of Kyoto—Mr. Stimson's 'Pet City,'" *Japan Quarterly,* October–December 1975, 337–47.

131. See n. 125 for Stimson's April 25 statements.

132. Truman, 235 (quotations and Truman's review of military plans).

133. Memorandum, McGuire to Chief of Staff, Twentieth Air Force, 6 April 1945, in file 091.1 Governments, HQ 20th AF Records; J.I.S. 141/2, 11 April 1945, in Air Force Plans Project Decimal File PD 341 Japan (4–3–43) Sec. 9, HQ USAF Records. J.C.S. Memorandum for Information No. 390, 29 April 1945, in file CCS 387 Japan (4–6–43), JCS Records. Villa, 80–83, reviews much of this material in more detail.

134. J.I.S. 141/2, cited above, n. 133; Villa, 81, 84 (Villa's words).

135. Truman, 207. On broadcasts, see Allan M. Winkler, *The Politics of Propaganda: The Office of War Information, 1942–1945* (New Haven, 1978), 144–45.

136. Quotations from Villa, 85 (his words). See also Villa, 84–86, and documents in Chief of Staff file 091 Japan (Top Secret), WD Staff Records, and in file CCS 387 Japan (5–9–45), JCS Records.

137. J.C.S. 924/15, 25 April 1945, in Air Force Plans Project Decimal File 341 Japan (4–3–43) Sec. 9, HQ USAF Records; also quoted in Villa, 83.

138. Letter, Arnold to LeMay, 21 March 1945, in Box B31, LeMay Papers.

139. "Twentieth Air Force Staff Study," 24 March 1945, Numeric File # 20 ("Future Operations"), HQ 20th AF Records; letters, Norstad to LeMay, 3 April 1945, 10 April 1945, in 20th Air Force

Official File, Norstad Papers; staff study, "Weather Conditions in Relation to Incendiary Bombing of Tokyo area," n.d., with cover memorandum, 24 April 1945, in Numeric File # 10 ("Weather and Weather Reconnaissance"), HQ 20th AF Records.

140. Telecon, LeMay to Norstad, 25 April 1945, in Message File (21st February to April 1945, Ins), HQ 20th AF Records; letter, LeMay to Arnold, 5 April 1945, in Box B31, LeMay Papers; LeMay, 368; Craven and Cate, vol. 5, 627.

141. Staff study, 24 March 1945, cited above, n. 139. For a hint at internal staff discontent, see memorandum, Combs to Assistant Chief of Air Staff, Plans, 12 May 1945, in Numeric File #15 ("Reports to Higher Headquarters"), HQ 20th AF Records. Hansell's dissatisfactions, though not a clear dating of them, are expressed in his *Strategic Air War;* Hansell, now in a minor position, could do little to influence planning.

142. Hansell, *Strategic Air War,* 61.

143. Quotations from LeMay's interview with Sherry; LeMay's interview in film *The Bomb* from "The World At War" series; LeMay, 381. Though he did not do so in his memoirs, LeMay frequently recounted the story of his meeting with Arnold in the many interviews he has given, some of which indicate October 1 as the date he gave Arnold. Arnold's more brief account in *Global Mission,* 564, 576, largely confirms LeMay's recollection. The meeting probably occurred on June 15; see Arnold's account, and LeMay's "Daily Diary," entries for 12, 15 June 1945, in Box B9, LeMay Papers.

CHAPTER 10

Sources

Most of the sources listed for chap. 9 remain pertinent to my account of the war's last months. In light of the large amount of material published on use and consequences of the atomic bomb, I have relied less in this chapter on archival materials. Among the many accounts, Sherwin, *A World Destroyed,* is important but less detailed for the summer of 1945 than for the earlier period. Four older studies remain surprisingly useful: Batchelder, *The Irreversible Decision;* Hewlett and Anderson, *The New World;* Butow, *Japan's Decision to Surrender;* and Kecskemeti, *Strategic Surrender.* Brief but again essential is Villa, "The U.S. Army, Unconditional Surrender, and the Potsdam Proclamation." On Jimmy Byrnes, see the excellent study by Messer, *The End of an Alliance.* Problematical but useful is Rose, *Dubious Victory.* Much of the literature on atomic policy is directed toward explaining its relationship to the onset of the cold war, while I have placed that policy more in the context of the wartime struggle. Judicious observations about interpreting use of the atomic bomb are offered by Bernstein in his introductory and editorial comments and his own essays in Bernstein, *The Atomic Bomb.* Boyer, *By the Bomb's Early Light,* exhaustively documents the persistence into the atomic age of many themes I examine here, though with less emphasis on their continuity with the preatomic era.

In the large literature on the atomic bomb oriented toward a lay audience, a few accounts stand out not only for their vividness but their contributions to scholarly debate: The Pacific War Research Society, *The Day Man Lost;* Giovannitti and Freed, *The Decision to Drop the Bomb,* incorporating a wealth of interview material; and Wheeler, *The Fall of Japan,* which includes a striking visual record. Committee for Compilation, *Hiroshima and Nagasaki,* is in most ways definitive regarding the bomb's destruction in Japan. The most recent popular account is Wyden, *Day One.*

In interpreting Marshall's views on the atomic bomb, I have benefited from advice offered by his biographer, Forrest Pogue.

Notes

1. Craven and Cate, vol. 5, 638, the second quotation from instructions given bomber crews in March.

2. Quotation from Gullain, 210. Kato, 216, offers a different view of how the flames reached the imperial grounds. The official explanation is in Craven and Cate, vol. 5, 638–39.

3. The claim is made in John Toland, *The Rising Sun: The Decline and Fall of the Japanese Empire, 1936–1945* (New York, 1970), 837.

4. Koichi Kido, *Translation of the Diary of Marquis Kido* (Washington, 1955), entries for 25 May 1945, 8 June 1945.

5. See, among many documents, "Translation of 'Estimate of Situation for Spring of 1946' compiled by Imperial Headquarters Army Department and dated 1 Jul 45," in Donald S. Detwiler and Charles B. Burdick, eds., *War in Asia and the Pacific 1937–1949* (New York, 1980), vol. 12.

6. "Can Divinity be Bombed?" *Christian Century,* 21 March 1945, 358. On Norstad, see chap. 8, p. 248.

7. Quotations from broadcasts of 26 May by Suzuki and President Shimomura of the Information Board, as excerpted in "Reports from Japanese Radio, 14 May 1945–31 May 1945," in Narrative History, Headquarters, 21st Bomber Command, 1 May 1945–31 May 1945, in file 762.01 May 1945, vol. 1, AFSHRC.

8. Butow, 80.

9. "The God-Emperor," *Time,* 21 May 1945, 33. "Power vs. Statesmanship," *Time,* 16 July 1945, 13, and for similar thoughts in *Time*'s sister publications, see the editorial in *Life,* 16 July 1945, 22–23. Raymond Moley, "Attacking the Jap Mentality," *Newsweek,* 2 July 1945, 92.

10. Makoto Iokibe, "American Policy Towards Japan's 'Unconditional Surrender,'" *The Japanese Journal of American Studies,* no. 1 (1981): 47.

11. Ibid., 45–47.

12. Joseph Grew, *Turbulent Era: A Diplomatic Record of Forty Years* (Boston, 1952), vol. 2, 1429. Even the statement Grew proposed was still not explicit on the emperor's fate; see Waldo Heinrichs, Jr., *American Ambassador: Joseph C. Grew and the Development of the United States Diplomatic Tradition* (Boston, 1966), 379–80.

13. Grew, *Turbulent Era,* vol. 2, 1434. See also Truman, 416–17; Walter Millis, ed., *The Forrestal Diaries* (New York, 1951), 66; Stimson Diary, 29 May 1945.

14. Grew, *Turbulent Era,* vol. 2, 1434.

15. See Grew's letter to Stimson, 12 February 1947, in Bernstein, *The Atomic Bomb,* 30–32.

16. "Battle of Japan," *Time,* 2 July 1945, 26; "How to Starve Out Japan: Bomb the Rice Paddy Dikes," *Newsweek,* 28 May 1945, 41; Fletcher Pratt, "The War in the Pacific," *New Republic,* 28 May 1945, 737–39, also on attacking Japan's food supplies; "Pacific Compromise," *Time,* 30 July 1945, 28, on attacks against Hitachi; "Propaganda Voice," *Time,* 6 August 1945, 13; Middleton, quoted in "Terrible Fact," *Time,* 18 June 1945, 26.

17. See, for example, "Military Review," *New Republic,* 23 July 1945, 93–94.

18. LeMay recounted the story of the mix-up in his interview with Morrison, and it is noted in Morrison, 221.

19. The formal record of the June 18 meeting is in file CCS 383 Japan (6–14–45) Sec. 1, JCS Records, reprinted with one deletion in U.S. Department of State, *Foreign Relations of the United States: The Conference of Berlin (The Potsdam Conference) 1945,* vol. 1, 903–10. For a sampling of the divergent interpretations of the discussion triggered by McCloy and the conflicting documents they rest on, see Hewlett and Anderson, 363–64; Morison, 523–24; Rose, 227–29.

20. Notes on June 18 meeting, cited above, n. 19.

21. Arnold, 566, for his claim about wartime confidence in air power, and 596 for August quotation. For his statement at Potsdam, see JCS 1421, "Report on Air Operations in the War Against Japan," 15 July 1945, in OPD file ABC 384.5 Japan (9 Nov 43) Sec. 3, WD Staff Records, and the indication in *FRUS, Potsdam,* vol. 2, 38, of its presentation by Arnold to the Combined Chiefs on July 16. The AAF's operations researchers and social scientists were starting their own effort to estimate a date when the war would conclude, relying on "historical and statistical materials concerning casualties of past battles and wars." Their pessimistic first hunch, that "we shall probably have to kill at least 5 to 10 million Japanese" in an invasion, suggested the wisdom of an air strategy. Their effort appears to have been inspired partly by Quincy Wright, then in the midst of his monumental studies on war. Needless to say, their work was not completed before the war's end. Its backers also revealed again the faith of operations researchers that

war's intangibles could be quantified. See memorandum, Shockley to Bowles, 21 July 1945, and memorandum by Quincy Wright, "Historical Study of Casualties," 21 July 1945, and other materials in folder "Misc. materials relating to study on war casualties," Bowles Papers.

22. Transcript of Arnold-Ankenbrandt—Norstad-Proctor Conference, apparently by teletype, 19 June 1945, in Message File (20th AF POA Aug. 45 to Special Conf. Only), HQ 20th AF Records. On LeMay's meeting with Joint Chiefs, see the materials cited in n. 18.

23. MacIsaac, 100–01.

24. Ball, 60. On the June 19 meeting, see the perfunctory notes in Stimson Diary, 19 June 1945, and minutes of meeting of the Committee of Three, 19 June 1945, in file Minutes of Meetings, SecWar Records.

25. On acceptance of recommendations for transportation, see MacIsaac, 101–02, and memorandum, Lovett to Secretary of War, 31 July 1945, in file "Aircraft, Air Corps, General," SecWar Records. Quotations from LeMay's staff are taken from memorandum, Kissner to Kuter, 22 June 1945, in file 142.66021-12 (20 May 45), AFSHRC. "A nation without cities" is the phrase in JCS 1421, cited above, n. 21. See also letter, Eaker to Arnold, 18 July 1945, in folder "Conference—Germany—July 1945," Box 181, Arnold Papers, and memorandum, Posey to Lindsay, 24 July 1945, in Numeric File # 49 (Reader's File—Private Kimball), HQ 20th AF Records.

26. See Hansell, *Strategic Air War,* 60–93. For a summary of the survey's reasoning insofar as it supported Hansell, see USSBS, *Summary Report (Pacific War)* (Washington, 1946), 19–20.

27. The arguments about bombing strategy over the summer of 1945 did not follow the neat lines Hansell later thought he saw. He singled out the Joint Target Group, a JCS agency, as advocates of an invasion strategy and the "major influence on the change to urban incendiary attacks" (Hansell, *Strategic Air War,* 62). While the Joint Target Group and the air force staff sometimes differed over the timing of various kinds of attack, their differences were not clearly argued out over the distinction between an air strategy and an invasion strategy.

28. USSBS, *Effects of Incendiary Bomb Attacks on Japan: A Report on Eight Cities* (Washington, 1947), sections on Oita and Hachioji.

29. Ibid., sections on Ammori, Ube. LeMay, 378.

30. Quotation from Craven and Cate, vol. 5, 674; for descriptions of experimental nature of precision attacks, see 645–53. In all, 88 percent of Japan's merchant marine was sunk in the war, and submarines accounted for 55 percent of that total; see USSBS, *Japan's Struggle to End the War* (Washington, 1946), 11.

31. Quotations from Craven and Cate, vol. 5, 696–97. Of the 160,800 tons of aerial bombs aimed at the home islands, B-29s dropped 147,000, naval and other air force planes the rest.

32. Otis Cary, ed., *War-Wasted Asia: Letters, 1945–46* (Tokyo and New York, 1975), 116; Craven and Cate, vol. 5, 699.

33. Quotations from letter, Griggs to Bowles, 18 July 1945, in file B-29 Radar Bombing, Scientific Advisory Group Files, AAF Records. On proposals for a starvation campaign, see message, COMAF 20 to COMGENBOMCOM 21, 6 MAY 1945, in Numeric File #18 (Target Selections), HQ 20th AF Records; letter, Samford to Bertrandias, 4 June 1945, in Official Decimal File 385 Japan (92), Box 115, Arnold Papers; letter, Chennault to LeMay, 9 July 1945, and letter, LeMay to Chennault, 20 July 1945, in file Special Official Correspondence (General Officers), Box B31, LeMay Papers; Harris and Paxman, 38–39.

34. Arnold's request was made in memorandum, Arnold to Eaker, 25 May 1945; responses suggested gas and bacteriological warfare as well as starvation, bombing by rockets, and other methods; for Arnold memorandum and responses, see Project Decimal File 383.6 Japan (10 April 1944) By-passed Garrisons, HQ USAF Records. On threat to use gas against cities, see memorandum to Joint Staff Planners, 27 July 1945, and enclosed report, "Gas Deception Against Japan," in Project Decimal File 471.6 (8–28–42) Sec. 5, HQ USAF Records. On Marshall, see memorandum, Marshall to Leahy, 21 June 1945, in OPD Exec File # 10 (Item 64) Admiral Leahy, WD Staff Records; McCloy, "Memorandum of Conversation with General Marshall, 29 May 1945," copy provided by Marshall Foundation National Archives Project (Verifax 2798, Item 2678), original in folder S-1, Secretary of War Safe File, SecWar Records; and David Lilienthal, *The Journals of David E. Lilienthal: The Atomic Energy Years, 1945–1950* (New York, 1964),

199–200. See also Brown, 267–89, which minimizes more than I the military's interest in strategic employment and its general willingness to resort to the new weapons, and James, 730.

35. LeMay's interview with Sherry. Craven and Cate, vol. 5, 656, paraphrasing contemporary documents ("lessen the stigma").

36. Quotations from memorandum, Spence to Norstad, 22 May 1945, in file 322.01 (Commander and Staff—20th AF), HQ 20th AF Records. See also telecon, Spaatz to Giles, 17 July 1945, in Message File (20th AF July to Aug 1945 Outs), HQ 20th AF Records.

37. Memorandum, Timberlake to Eaker, 17 May 1945, in Numeric File # 70, and memorandum, Eaker for G-2, 9 June 1945, in Numeric File #57, both in Records of Deputy Chief of Staff (Operations), Director of Plans, HQ USAF Records; see also memorandum, Norstad to Arnold, 8 June 1945, for Norstad's recommendation against using V-2s against Japan, in Numeric File #57. Quotation from Arnold is taken from memorandum, Arnold to Eaker, 4 July 1945, in Jacket 39, Official Files, Box 41, Arnold Papers. Warning to Arnold about "human survival" is in "Potentialities of New Developments in Warfare," n.d., with memorandum, Arnold to Chief of Air Staff, 28 May 1945, in file 400.112 Research and Development, Official Decimal Files, Box 117, Arnold Papers.

38. USSBS, *The Effects of Air Attack on Japanese Urban Economy* (Washington, 1947), v–vi, but see also p. 11 and other parts of this report that suggest that the economic impact of bombing may have been higher, and *Summary Report,* esp. 17–20.

39. USSBS, *The Effects of Strategic Bombing on Japanese Morale* (Washington, 1947), 78–79, 85–88; Havens, 161–66, 171–73; Frederick S. Hulse, "Some Effects of the War Upon Japanese Society," *Far Eastern Quarterly* 7 (November 1947): 31–32.

40. USSBS, *Morale* report, 55, see also 19–23, 47–56.

41. Ibid., 23. On the critical decline in food stocks, see in addition to many primary sources, Alan S. Milward, *War, Economy and Society, 1939–1945* (London, 1977), 256–59.

42. Quotation from "A Survey of National Resources as of 1–10 June 1945," as quoted in USSBS, *Morale* report, 137; see also 137–46, and Pacific War Research Society, 191.

43. Not only for Japan but for most countries, casualty figures are extremely varied and unreliable, and sources for those figures are often vague. Comparison among countries is even more difficult than comparison among the various raids suffered within one. USSBS figures based on Japanese sources ranged from 268,157 killed and slightly more injured, given in *Final Report Covering Air-raid Protection and Allied Subjects in Japan* (Washington 1947), 197, to 330,000 killed in air raids, the figure more often cited, as in *The Effects of Bombing on Health and Medical Services in Japan* (Washington, 1947), 5–6, 143, and in *Summary Report,* 20. The Japanese government in 1949 estimated total home front fatalities at 323,495 (see Committee for Compilation, *Hiroshima and Nagasaki,* 367, whose authors clearly regard the official figure as low). But using polling techniques, survey researchers estimated 900,000 killed and another 1,300,000 wounded, figures they acknowledged are probably high, though certain characteristics of the polling techniques also kept them down (*Morale* report, 194–95); since the figure of 1,300,000 injured was apparently subject to less sampling error, and since most other estimates have placed the number of injured at only slightly more than the number of dead, 900,000 fatalities appears more plausible. If one subtracts from the higher figure the highest estimates for fatalities in the March 10, August 6, and August 9 attacks—130,000, 130,000, and 70,000 (the latter two figures, from *Hiroshima and Nagasaki,* 363–69, 420–21, exclude deaths from atomic bomb related injuries after 1945)—one arrives at a death toll of 550,000 in other raids, doubtless a very high estimate.

More detailed than the usual calculations, Robert Goralski, *World War II Almanac: 1931–1945* (New York, 1981), lists civilians killed in air raids at 668,000, and those in the three great raids as 174,000 (see 427, 385). Havens, 176–77, implies a lower figure, while Dower, in *War Without Mercy* (298, 362–63), suggests 86,336 killed in the "63 other cities." Partly because the counting of the dead was even less reliable in the smaller cities raided over the summer, I believe the death toll in them was higher than the figures indicated by Havens and Dower would suggest.

As for Japanese military deaths, there is scarcely more agreement. The survey put them at 491,000 (*Health* report, 143). Goralski, 427, totals them for the years 1937–1945 at 1,140,429 for all theaters, and

485,717 in action against American forces. Many other sources do not specify their time frame, an especially troublesome habit since for Japan the onset of World War II can be variously dated to 1931, 1937, or 1941.

44. *USSBS, Japan's Struggle,* 10.

45. Beatrice Bishop Berle and Travis Beal Jacobs, eds., *Navigating the Rapids, 1918–1971: From the Papers of Adolf A. Berle* (New York, 1973), 533–35, entries for 4 May and 6 May 1945; see also Jay Luvaas, ed., *Dear Miss Em: General Eichelberger's War in the Pacific, 1942–1945* (Westport, 1972).

46. Longmate, 366, commenting on Churchill's memoirs; Winston Churchill, *Triumph and Tragedy* (Boston, 1953), 639–40; Truman, 416. Comments on other British and American leaders based on examination of standard autobiographical and biographical sources.

47. Ferrell, 52–53 (bracketed material in Ferrell).

48. James Conant, *My Several Lives* (New York, 1970), 302. On the agenda for the committee, see Sherwin, 169; letter, Karl Compton to George L. Harrison, 10 May 1945, in folder 76, reel 6, Harrison-Bundy Files, and committee logs and letters to appointees in Harrison-Bundy and Manhattan Engineer District files.

49. Compton, 237, 276–77.

50. McCloy, "Memorandum of Conversation with General Marshall," as cited in n. 34. A postwar comment by Marshall suggested that he had entertained a slightly different possibility for the bomb's use, viewing it as "a wonderful weapon as a protection and preparation for landings." See Lilienthal, *Atomic Energy Years,* 198. For evidence that Marshall did not support McCloy at the June 18 meeting, see John J. McCloy, *The Challenge to American Foreign Policy* (Cambridge, 1953), 43: "Not one of the Chiefs nor the Secretary thought well of a bomb warning."

51. Notes of the Interim Committee meeting, 31 May 1945, in folder 100, Harrison-Bundy Files, underlined in the original. A good brief review of issues regarding the luncheon discussion is in Sherwin, 207–08.

52. Notes on initial meeting of Target Committee, 27 April 1945, in file 5 (subseries I), reel 1, MED Records.

53. Memorandum, Derry and Ramsey to Groves, 12 May 1945, "Summary of Target Committee Meetings on 10 and 11 May 1945," same file citation as n. 52.

54. See n. 53.

55. Minutes of third Target Committee meeting, 28 May 1945, same file citation as n. 52. Groves, 267, also makes clear that the enemy's "will" was the overriding target, and military and industrial objectives secondary.

56. Churchill, *Triumph and Tragedy,* 639.

57. Compton, 236–37.

58. Notes of the Interim Committee meeting, 31 May 1945, cited above, n. 51; notes on initial meeting of Target Committee, 27 April 1945, cited above, n. 52.

59. Memorandum, Kirkpatrick to Groves, 10 June 1945, reporting on Guam meeting among LeMay, Giles, Tibbetts, and others, in file 5 (subseries I), reel 1, MED Records (microfilm ed.).

60. Vannevar Bush, *Pieces of the Action* (New York, 1970), 62–63; Conant, *My Several Lives,* 302; James Byrnes, *Speaking Frankly* (New York, 1947), 264.

61. Letter, Even J. Young to M. D. Whitaker, 14 July 1945, in folder 76, reel 6, Harrison-Bundy Files. There is some evidence that in a passing way the firebombing of Tokyo entered discussion about the atomic bomb's use, for it was on Grew's mind during his May 29 meeting with Stimson, Marshall, and King, and Stimson mentioned "the burning of Tokyo" later that day in meeting with Marshall and McCloy. In both instances, however, it was apparently the late May raids, not the more devastating attack on March 9–10, that drew mention. After Hiroshima, Ernest Lawrence recalled that at the May 31 luncheon of the Interim Committee, someone argued that the "number of people that would be killed by the bomb would not be greater in general magnitude than the number already killed in fire raids," but there is no record of whether that comment provoked extended discussion. For sources on the May 29 meetings, see n. 13 and the McCloy memorandum cited in n. 34; on Lawrence's recollection, see Sherwin, 209–10.

62. Gabriel Kolko, *The Politics of War: The World and United States Foreign Policy, 1943–1945* (New

York, 1968), 539, 542; Spector, 558. The pervasiveness of the acceptance of this claim since the war is measured by its repetition by scholars of quite different political and intellectual orientations. Thus Samuel Eliot Morison, in his unqualified defense of the bomb's use, wrote, "The stepped-up bombings and naval bombardments, had they been continued after 15 August, would have cost the Japanese loss and suffering far, far greater than those inflicted by the two atomic bombs." (See Morison's October 1960 piece for *Atlantic Monthly,* as contained in Bernstein, *The Atomic Bomb,* 50.) Herbert Feis, the former State Department official and prolific commentator on strategy and diplomacy at the war's end, put the matter more colorfully: "A glance at the chart kept in the Headquarters of the U.S. Strategic Force at Guam, with its steeply ascending record of bombing flights during the summer of 1945 and scheduled for the next month or two, leaves visions of horror of which Hiroshima is only a local illustration. Observation of the plight of the country and its people made soon after the war ended left me appalled at what those would have had to endure had the war gone on" (see Feis, *The Atomic Bomb and the End of World War II* (Princeton 1966), 193). All such arguments assume, without making the assumption time-specific, that the war would have gone on for a substantial period of time without the bomb's use.

63. 31 May 1945 Interim Committee meeting, cited above, n. 51 (emphasis in original).

64. Truman 419, 420; Ferrell, 55–56; Truman's reference to asking Stimson about cities devoted to war production was in his letter to James L. Cate, 12 January 1953, reprinted in full in Craven and Cate, vol. 5, opposite p. 712. On Churchill, see *Triumph and Tragedy,* 644–45. For Stimson's earlier discussion of Kyoto with Compton, see chap. 9, p. 295–96.

65. For an illuminating discussion of how language operated and distinctions broke down, see Batchelder, especially 155–60.

66. Truman, 415; 31 May 1945 Interim Committee meeting, cited above, n. 51; Stimson Diary, 31 May 1945.

67. Stimson to Raymond Swing, letter of February 1947, as quoted in Sherwin, 200; Stimson Diary, 31 May 1945.

68. 31 May 1945 Interim Committee meeting, cited above, n. 51.

69. Ibid.

70. Churchill, *Triumph and Tragedy,* 638, 639.

71. Franck Committee Report, 11 June 1945, and letter, Brewster to President, 24 May 1945, in folders 76 and 77, respectively, reel 6, Harrison-Bundy Files. Oppenheimer quoted in Batchelder, 70, from testimony at Oppenheimer's 1954 security hearing.

72. Bard memorandum, 27 June 1945, in folder 77, reel 6, Harrison-Bundy Files. See also Robert Greenhalgh Albion and Robert Howe Connery, *Forrestal and the Navy* (New York, 1962), 174–75; Smith, *A Peril and a Hope,* 37; Sherwin, 217. For "hammering on locked doors," see Wyden, 166.

73. Many scientists, Szilard reported in the letter accompanying a famous petition of protest, wanted "clearly and unmistakably on record . . . their opposition on moral grounds to the use of these bombs in the present phase of the war." See letter dated 4 July 1945 in folder 76, reel 6, Harrison-Bundy Files.

74. Franck Committee Report, cited above, n. 71.

75. Brewster letter, cited above, n. 71. Letter, Stimson to Marshall, 30 May 1945, same file as Brewster letter.

76. William D. Leahy, *I Was There: The Personal Story of the Chief of Staff to Presidents Roosevelt and Truman, Based on His Notes and Diaries Made at the Time* (New York, 1950), 440, 396, 395, 441.

77. Groves, 324. Marshall's statement to Groves did not mean that he regreted use of the atomic bomb. After the war, he offered David Lilienthal the standard rationale: the bomb's use "had actually been humane because it shortened the war and made it unnecessary to exterminate the Japanese." But other statements to Lilienthal, considered also in light of Marshall's comments to McCloy and Stimson on 29 May 1945, suggest that he was troubled by the *way* in which the new device was employed—without warning and against cities. See Lilienthal, *The Atomic Energy Years,* 198–99.

78. Quotations from Ambrose, 426, and Eisenhower, *Crusade in Europe* (Garden City, 1948, 1961), 470–71. Because Eisenhower's objections are documented largely in postwar accounts, my phrasing regarding them is tentative. On Eisenhower's earlier knowledge of atomic energy, see *Crusade,* 275, and

the correspondence prior to D-Day on defense against possible German employment of radioactive poisons against Allied forces or cities, in subseries II, reel 5, MED Records.

79. MacArthur was informed of the imminent use of the bomb very late to offer an opinion, and though at the time he may have regreted both its use and the content of the Potsdam ultimatum, it is hard to separate his views at the time from opinions he later expressed as well as from his ire about being informed so late and at learning that Eisenhower had been told first. See James, 775–76.

80. Ambrose, 426; Eisenhower, *Crusade*, 471.

81. American intelligence experts and intercepts of Togo's message are quoted in Ronald Lewin, *The American Magic: Codes, Ciphers and the Defeat of Japan* (New York, 1982), 274, 282. The War Department's view was stated in memorandum, Craig to Handy, 13 July 1945, in OPD file ABC 387 Japan (15 Feb 45) Sec. 1-B, WD Staff Records.

82. Leahy, *I Was There*, 365; Stimson Diary, 31 July 1945.

83. See memorandum, "Subject: Timing of Proposed Demand for Japanese Surrender," 29 June 1945, with memorandum, McCloy to Stimson, 29 June 1945, in file "Japan (After Dec 7/41)," Stimson Safe File, SecWar Records.

84. Memorandum, McCloy to Chief of Staff, 20 May 1945; memorandum, Lincoln to Hull, 29 June 1945, both in OPD file ABC 387 Japan (15 Feb 45) Sec. 1-B, WD Staff Records (emphasis in original).

85. Stimson, memorandum for the president, 2 July 1945, in Stimson Diary, 2 July 1945; memorandum, Bissell to Assistant Chief of Staff, OPD, 15 May 1945, in file cited in n. 84.

86. Kecskemeti, 196, 197.

87. *FRUS, Potsdam*, vol. 1, 43–45.

88. Cantril, 1073, 1119; Gallup poll described in Bernstein, "The Perils and Politics of Surrender," 5.

89. Grew, *Turbulent Era*, vol. 2, 1391, 1394; Grew, as quoted in Butow, 111. For a more sympathetic review than mine of Grew's public statements, see Heinrichs, *American Ambassador*, 362–69.

90. Stimson Diary, 2 July 1945; Cordell Hull, *Memoirs* (New York, 1948), vol. 2, 1594 ("too much"); *FRUS, Potsdam*, vol. 2, 1267.

91. *FRUS, Potsdam*, vol. 2, 1267 ("the climax"). The Potsdam declaration is reprinted in many primary and secondary accounts; see Truman, 390–92. See also Villa, 88–92. Stimson's thoughts on when a declaration or "warning" should be issued to Japan kept shifting; see his postwar account as reprinted in Bernstein, *The Atomic Bomb*.

92. Walzer, 268.

93. Hoover's proposal was attached to memorandum, Truman to Secretary of War, 9 June 1945, although the War Department had already begun reviewing it by that date (see Stimson Diary, 1 June 1945); staff comments on such casualty figures can be found in memorandum, no author and no addressee (initialed: "HLS"), 4 June 1945, and memorandum, GAL (Lincoln), 14 June 1945; all in file "Japan (After Dec 7/41)," Stimson Safe File, SecWar Records. Truman's recollection is in Truman, 417; Stimson's in his postwar article, reprinted in Bernstein, *The Atomic Bomb*, 10; Churchill's in *Triumph and Tragedy*, 638.

94. Quoted in Robert M. Hathaway, *Ambiguous Partnership: Britain and America, 1944–1947* (New York, 1981), 168.

95. *FRUS, Potsdam*, vol. 2, 1463; Stimson Diary, 19 June 1945, 23 July 1945. My views on this issue are developed in more detail in Sherry, *Preparing for the Next War*, 186–89.

96. Arnold, 586, 590.

97. King's comments were made at the June 18 White House meeting (see n. 19); Leahy, *I Was There*, 419, see also 422; Henry L. Stimson and McGeorge Bundy, *On Active Service in Peace and War* (New York, 1947), 637.

98. On Byrnes, see Messer's account; on Churchill, see his *Triumph and Tragedy*, 639, 640, and Arthur Bryant, *Triumph in the West* (Garden City, 1959), 363–64.

99. Ferrell, 53, 54.

100. Robert H. Ferrell, ed., *Dear Bess: The Letters from Harry to Bess Truman, 1910–1959* (New

York, 1983), 519; Ferrell, *Off the Record,* 80; Truman, 387; Churchill, *Triumph and Tragedy,* 641–42; Francis Williams, *A Prime Minister Remembers* (London, 1961), 75.

101. Stimson Diary, 23 July 1945. On information to the Russians, see Feis, *The Atomic Bomb,* 82. Although Churchill and Truman believed that Stalin misunderstood, most likely he did not; see David Holloway, *The Soviet Union and the Arms Race* (New Haven, 1983), 15–23.

102. Arnold, 598.

103. See Truman, 402–03.

104. Quotation by Marshall from June 18 White House meeting; see n. 19. On the implications of Truman's diary entry of July 16, see Robert Messer, "New Evidence on Truman's Decision," *Bulletin of the Atomic Scientists,* August 1985, 55.

105. Wiley as quoted in Rose, 334; notes on MacArthur's press conference of August 6, 1945, as quoted in James, 774.

106. The arguments in the preceding paragraphs exist piecemeal in many secondary accounts, but see especially Bernstein's comments in Bernstein, *The Atomic Bomb,* 94–96. Quotation from Truman, 416.

107. See Pacific War Research Society, 182, quoting Truman, 419. The order to Spaatz is printed in Truman, 420–21. Groves's quotation from interview quoted in Giovannitti and Freed, 251 (Giovannitti and Freed's italics deleted here). On orders, see also Ferrell, 55–56; Feis, *The Atomic Bomb,* 125; Hewlett and Anderson, 394. Giovannitti and Freed, 243–56, review much of the conflicting evidence in detail.

108. Groves, 265.

109. Except for those from the Potsdam declaration, quotations as well as much of the interpretation come from Pacific War Research Society, 213–17.

110. Quotations from "impressions" of Brigadier General Thomas Farrell ("awesome roar," "searing light," "lighted every peak"), and from unnamed liaison officer, both contained in Groves's report on the Trinity test, memorandum to Stimson, 18 July 1945, in *FRUS, Potsdam,* vol. 2, 1361–68, which also has Groves's statement on "profound awe." Lawrence, "Thoughts by E. O. Lawrence," 16 July 1945 ("from darkness"), in *FRUS, Potsdam,* vol. 2, 1369–70.

111. Sources for Farrell and Lawrence comments cited in n. 110; Bainbridge's recollections are in Bulletin of the Atomic Scientists, *All In Our Time: The Reminiscences of Twelve Nuclear Pioneers* (Chicago, 1975), 230.

112. On hazards to occupying personnel, see memorandum, Nichols to Groves, 5 July 1945, in file 6 (subseries I), reel 1, MED Records. On fears of being charged with practicing chemical warfare, see Jungk, 228, and John Ehrman, *Grand Strategy,* vol. 6 (London, 1956), 296. Groves, 269, maintained that "I had always insisted that casualties resulting from direct radiation and fallout be held to a minimum," though his method of minimizing them—blast at a higher altitude—maximized casualties from blast and fire; see also 286. Contemporary documents confirm Groves's later account of his expectations regarding fallout and radiation. On July 30, he wrote Marshall, "No damaging effects are anticipated on the ground from radioactive materials. These effects at New Mexico resulted from the low altitude from which the bomb was set off." See Groves, memorandum to Chief of Staff (titled "Memo to Secretary of War" on pp. 2–3), 30 July 1945, in Folder 4 (Trinity), Gen. Groves Top Secret Correspondence Files, MED Records (does not appear in microfilm ed.).

113. On new calculations, see Groves to Chief of Staff, 30 July 1945 (cited in n. 112), which estimated radius within which certain types of personnel injuries from light, blast, and gamma rays would occur, though without an estimate of number of casualties. Quotations from Farrell and Groves from sources cited in n. 110; "future of humanity" from I. I. Rabi, as quoted in Wyden, 213. See also Groves, 298; Smith, *A Peril and a Hope,* 60–61, 76–77; and the recollections in Bulletin of the Atomic Scientists, *All In Our Time.* For one attempt after Trinity to reopen the question of the bomb's use, see Wyden, 216–17.

114. Memorandum, Stone to Arnold, 24 July 1945, in file 5 (subseries I), reel 1, MED Records.

115. See Groves, 312–13; Sherwin, 234 and notes; and Committee for Compilation, *Hiroshima and Nagasaki,* 479–81, a detailed review of the conflicting evidence on deaths among POWs.

116. On black rain, see Committee for Compilation, *Hiroshima and Nagasaki*, 92–94, 101.

117. Initial estimates largely relying on Japanese sources and incorporated into the USSBS reports were at the low end of the range. The most thorough review, and the most recent of consequence, is in Committee for Compilation, *Hiroshima and Nagasaki*, especially 363–69, 420–21. Though it cannot resolve all the contradictions in evidence, it appears to settle on figures of 130,000 dead by November 1945 from Hiroshima's attack, and 60–70,000 dead from Nagasaki's, with additional deaths in the several tens of thousands in the years since 1945. The problem of determining a toll is complicated by the continuing deaths of atomic bomb victims due to the effects of radiation and other forms of trauma, though to be sure victims of incendiary raids continued, in lesser numbers, to die as a result of bomb-related injury and disease.

118. Tatsuichiro Akizuki, *Nagasaki 1945*, trans. Keiichi Nagata (New York, 1981), 154.

119. See Lifton.

120. Eyes Only message, Marshall to Spaatz, 8 August 1945, in Project Decimal File 384.5 Japan (8 Aug 45), HQ USAF Records; Stimson Diary, 9 August 1945; Eyes Only message, MacArthur to Marshall, 9 August 1945, in Leahy File 55 Pacific Area, JCS Records; Hansell, *Strategic Air War*, 92. See also Luvaas, *Dear Miss Em*, 299–300, for relief at war's quick end.

121. On targeting a third atomic bomb against Tokyo, see memorandum, Groves to Arnold, 10 August 1945, in file 5 (subseries I), reel 1, MED Records, and Craven and Cate, vol. 5, 732. Quotations from Craven and Cate, 732–33. See also Bernstein, "The Perils and Politics of Surrender," 14–17.

122. Message, Higgins to Finney, 7 August 1945, in Message File (20th AF August Outs), HQ 20th AF Records ("giving Army Air"); message, McCrary to LeMay, n.d. (mid-August 1945), in Box B31, LeMay Papers (other quotations on public relations). On need to have an AAF representative at surrender signing, see message Giles to Norstad and Eaker, date unclear (mid-August 1945), in Message File ("Special Conference Only"), HQ 20th AF Records. On B-29s overflying surrender ceremonies, see Craven and Cate vol. 5, 734, and Theodore White, *In Search of History: A Personal Narrative* (New York, 1978), 230.

123. Message, McCrary to LeMay, cited n. 122.

124. Memoranda of telephone conversations, 25 August 1945, in file 5 (subseries I), reel 1, MED Records. For further efforts to muffle public debate on fallout and radiation, see Boyer, 187–88.

125. For their explanations of autobiographical brevity, see Bush, *Pieces of the Action*, 8; Conant, *My Several Lives*, 302. Quotations: Hewlett and Anderson, 415; Smith, *A Peril and a Hope*, 81 ("feeling of emancipation"); recollections of attitudes toward use of the bomb from Jungk, 222, 223.

126. Zuckerman, 359; Smith, *A Peril and a Hope*, 80; see also 78–79.

127. Williams, *A Prime Minister Remembers*, 73–74; see also 95–101.

128. USAAF Scientific Advisory Group, "Defense Against the Atomic Bomb," 28 August 1945, in file "Defense Against the Atomic Bomb," Scientific Advisory Group Files, AAF Records. See also Sherry, *Preparing for the Next War*, chap. 7; Gregg Herken, *The Winning Weapon* (New York, 1980); David Alan Rosenberg, "American Atomic Strategy and the Hydrogen Bomb Decision," *Journal of American History* 66 (June 1979): 62–87.

129. Stimson, memorandum of conference with the president, 8 August 1945, filed with 9 August diary entry; Stimson, memorandum for press, 9 August 1945, with diary.

130. Stimson, memorandum of conference cited in n. 129; for Stimson's suggestion to the cabinet on August 10 of a bombing halt, see Millis, *Forrestal Diaries*, 83.

131. Stimson, memorandum for the president, 11 September 1945, with Stimson Diary that date, also reprinted in many published sources. Although not always accurate, Henry Wallace's account of the response to Stimson's proposal is among the most detailed and illuminating of several firsthand sources; see John Morton Blum, ed., *The Price of Vision: The Diary of Henry A. Wallace, 1942–46* (Boston, 1973), 481–87. I am indebted to my former student William McCulla for further insights and documentation regarding Stimson's course in August and September.

132. Truman, 421; Blum, *Price of Vision*, 474; Bernstein, "The Atomic Bomb and American Foreign Policy: The Route to Hiroshima," in Bernstein, *The Atomic Bomb*, 113 (letter of August 11); Margaret Truman, *Harry S. Truman* (New York, 1972), 5–6. See also Millis, *Forrestal Diaries*, 84.

133. Truman statement dated August 6, in *New York Times*, 7 August 1945; Truman radio report, 9 August 1945, in *New York Times*, 10 August 1945.

134. Ibid. Truman's 1948 comment recorded in Lilienthal, *The Atomic Energy Years*, 391. Truman's later comment made in memorandum, 24 April 1954, in Ferrell, 304. Japanese government's protest in cable to Swiss legation forwarded to the American Department of State, in U.S. Department of State, *Foreign Relations of the United States: 1945; Diplomatic Papers*, vol. 6, 472–73.

135. On Spaatz, see "Nagasaki Flames Rage for Hours," *New York Times*, 10 August 1945; on Tibbetts, see "5 Plants Vanished," in *New York Times*, 8 August 1945.

136. See *Life*, 20 August 1945, 26–31, which also includes an artist's depiction of Hiroshima showing the huge cloud as the only distinctive feature and photographs of firebombed Japanese cities. Characterization of Japanese reports in "2D Big Aerial Blow," *New York Times*, 9 August 1945. On August 10, the *New York Times* ran a "photo-diagram" showing a circle around the area of Hiroshima's destruction and listing objectives damaged or destroyed; all were military facilities, industrial structures, utilities, or bridges, conveying by silence the impression that these were the targets of the American bomb and the kinds of objectives destroyed.

137. On American-made footage, see "38 Years after Nagasaki, a chronicler of the horror returns to an unfaded past," *Chicago Tribune*, 5 January 1984; on Japanese footage, finally released in 1968 and first shown on American television in an edited version in 1969, see Erick Barnouw, "The Hiroshima-Nagasaki Footage: A Report," *Historical Journal of Film, Radio and TV* 2 (March 1982): 91–100. For quotations, and numerous other indications of "the focus shifting abruptly from the immediate reality to some more generalized context," see Boyer, esp. 193–94.

138. Editorial, "Heard Round the World," *New York Times*, 7 August 1945. The *New Yorker* waited until its August 25 edition to take notice of the bomb, and then did so in its characteristically arch manner, publishing an account of how the editor of *Astounding Science Fiction* continued to publish stories of the atomic bomb all through the war's censorship on such matters. He simply told the army "that atomic bombs had been our stock in trade for years and that it would look terribly suspicious if we suddenly dropped them. . . . The Army said they guessed so, too. They probably figured nobody would believe us anyhow." Imbedded in the *New Yorker* story was a justified distrust of official information about the bomb. Addressing readers desirous of knowing more about the bomb, the magazine told them "you had better bypass Dr. Vannevar Bush and Dr. James B. Conant and Secretary Stimson and go to the pulps, preferably *Astounding*." See "1945 Cassandra," *New Yorker*, 25 August 1945, 15. By later publishing John Hersey's account of Hiroshima, the magazine operated in that spirit.

139. "New Age" and "Cosmic Bomb" in "NEW AGE USHERED," *New York Times*, 7 August 1945.

140. See "America's Atomic Atrocity" and letters to the editor in *Christian Century*, 29 August 1945, 974–76, 982–84.

141. MacDonald in *Politics*, August 1945, September 1945, as found in Bernstein, *The Atomic Bomb*, 147, 145. Truman quotations from his August 6 statement, in *New York Times*, 7 August 1945.

142. Editorial, "The Atomic Age," *Life*, 20 August 1945, 32. Baldwin, "The Atomic Weapon," *New York Times*, 7 August 1945; Baldwin, "1000 Plane Blows Daily in Prospect for Japan," *New York Times*, 4 June 1945.

143. Baldwin, "The New Face of War," *New York Times*, 8 August 1945; Baldwin, "The Atomic Weapon," *New York Times*, 7 August 1945; editorial, "Science and the Bomb," *New York Times*, 7 August 1945; Lerner, quoted in Boyer, 34; Hutchins in *University of Chicago Round Table*, No. 386 (12 August 1945), as quoted in Lawrence S. Wittner, *Rebels Against War* (New York, 1969), 125. For these themes in popular culture, see Spencer R. Weart, "The Atomic Age: The Heyday of Myth and Cliché," in *Bulletin of the Atomic Scientists*, August 1985, 38–43. Boyer persuasively documents the persistence of what he calls the "'either/or' formulation" in American culture after Hiroshima; see esp. 65–81, 94, 125–26.

144. Editorials, "Heard Round the World" and "Our Answer to Japan," in *New York Times*, 7 August 1945.

145. Stimson, letter to president, 11 September 1945, with Stimson Diary, 12 September 1945; article by Oppenheimer for North American Newspaper Alliance, in *New York Times* as "Atom Held Peace Agent," 9 August 1945; Oppenheimer, Speech to the Association of Los Alamos Scientists, 2

November 1945, in Alice Kimball Smith and Charles Weiner, eds., *Robert Oppenheimer: Letters and Recollections* (Cambridge, 1980), 315–25. Oppenheimer quickly objected to an effort to build the "super-bomb" (hydrogen bomb), arguing that the nation's safety "cannot lie wholly or even primarily in its scientific or technical prowess. It can be based only on making future war impossible." Byrnes and others feared that Oppenheimer and other scientists would "prefer" not to work on the hydrogen bomb "unless ordered or directed to do so by the Government on the grounds of national policy." See letter, Oppenheimer to Stimson, 17 August 1945, in file 3 (subseries II), reel 4, MED Records; George L. Harrison, memorandum for the record, 18 August 1945, reprinted in Sherwin, 314–15. Truman's comments to Hersey are quoted in Alonzo L. Hamby, *Liberalism and Its Challengers: FDR to Reagan* (New York, 1985), 72.

146. Stimson's statement on the atomic bomb, in *New York Times*, 7 August 1945. See the wealth of speculation, sometimes ludicrous and sometimes cautious, that immediately appeared in the American press regarding peaceful uses of atomic energy, much of it documented in Boyer.

147. MacDonald in *Politics*, as found in Bernstein, *The Atomic Bomb*, 145–46.

148. Shillony, 108. The *New York Times*'s headline for August 9 ran: "SOVIET DECLARES WAR ON JAPAN; ATTACKS MANCHURIA, TOKYO SAYS; ATOM BOMB LOOSED ON NAGASAKI." I am indebted to Ellen Bible, a former undergraduate student of mine at Yale University, for her survey of newspaper reaction to Russia's entry into the war.

149. Butow, 181 (quotation on reaction to conventional planes), 180; Messer, 118.

150. See polls in Cantril, 20–24. *Chicago Tribune* quoted in Boyer, 186, which documents many similar expressions.

EPILOGUE

Notes

1. For a more sophisticated version of this hope, suggesting that new advances can make nuclear armaments technology obsolescent, see Freeman Dyson, *Weapons and Hope* (New York, 1984).

2. See, for example, Daniel F. Ford, *The Button: The Pentagon's Strategic Command and Control System* (New York, 1985).

3. See, among many recent critiques, Richard J. Barnet, *Real Security: Restoring American Power in a Dangerous Decade* (New York, 1981), esp. 39–40.

4. Jonathan Schell, *The Fate of the Earth* (New York, 1982), 231.

5. Helen Caldicott, *Missile Envy: The Arms Race and Nuclear War* (New York, 1984).

6. Jack Fuller, "The Day Before: Human Survival in Contemporary Literature," *Chicago Tribune Magazine*, 18 November 1984, 30.

7. Alice Kimball Smith and Charles Weiner, eds., *Robert Oppenheimer: Letters and Recollections* (Cambridge, 1980), 319.

8. Kurt Vonnegut, Jr., *Slaughter-House Five* (New York, 1968, 1969), 74–75.

9. Frisch, the Swiss novelist, is quoted on the title page of Daniel J. Boorstin, *The Image: A Guide to Pseudo-Events in America* (New York, 1961, 1980).

Select Bibliography

This bibliography consists mostly of secondary sources frequently cited in the notes. A few additional secondary sources, not cited but broadly pertinent to the history of air power or influential on this account, are also listed. Less important or less frequently cited secondary sources are indicated only in notes. Except for a few that are recurrently cited in this account, published primary sources do not appear in this bibliography.

Ambrose, Stephen. *Eisenhower: Soldier, General of the Army, President-Elect, 1890–1952.* New York, 1983.

Arnold, H. H. *Global Mission.* New York, 1949.

Aron, Raymond. *The Century of Total War.* Garden City, N.Y., 1954.

Ball, George. *The Past Has Another Pattern: Memoirs.* New York, 1982.

Batchelder, Robert C. *The Irreversible Decision, 1939–1950.* Boston, 1962.

Bernstein, Barton, ed. *The Atomic Bomb: The Critical Issues.* Boston, 1976.

_____. "The Perils and Politics of Surrender: Ending the War and Avoiding the Third Atomic Bomb." *Pacific Historical Review* 46 (February 1977): 1–27.

Best, Geoffrey. *Humanity in Warfare.* New York, 1980.

Beyerchen, Alan D. *Scientists under Hitler: Politics and the Physics Community in the Third Reich.* New Haven, 1977.

Bialer, Uri. *The Shadow of the Bomber: The Fear of Air Attack and British Politics, 1932–1939.* London, 1980.

Blanchard, William H. *Aggression American Style.* Santa Monica, 1978.

Blum, John M. *V Was For Victory: Politics and American Culture During World War II.* New York, 1976.

Bond, Brian. *British Military Policy between the Two World Wars.* New York, 1980.

_____. *Liddell Hart: A Study of His Military Thought.* London, 1977.

Bond, Horatio, ed. *Fire and the Air War.* Boston, 1946.

Boyer, Paul. *By the Bomb's Early Light: American Thought and Culture at the Dawn of the Atomic Age*. New York, 1985.

Brodie, Bernard. *Strategy in the Missile Age*. Princeton, 1959.

———. *War and Politics*. New York, 1973.

———, and Fawn Brodie. *From Crossbow to H-Bomb*. 1962. Bloomington, Ind., 1973.

Brown, Frederic J. *Chemical Warfare: A Study in Restraints*. Princeton, 1980.

Brune, Lester H. *The Origins of American National Security Policy: Sea Power, Air Power and Foreign Policy, 1900–1941*. Manhattan, Kan., 1981.

Buckley, Thomas H. *The United States and the Washington Conference, 1921–1922*. Knoxville, 1970.

Butow, Robert J. C. *Japan's Decision to Surrender*. Stanford, 1954.

Caidin, Martin. *A Torch to the Enemy: The Fire Raid on Tokyo*. New York, 1960.

Cantril, Hadley. *Public Opinion, 1935–1946*. Princeton, 1951.

Cate, James Lea. *History of the 20th Air Force: Genesis*. Washington, 1945.

Clarke, I. F. *Voices Prophesying War, 1763–1984*. New York, 1966.

Coffey, Thomas M. *Decision over Schweinfurt: The U.S. 8th Air Force Battle for Daylight Bombing*. New York, 1977.

———. *HAP: The Story of the U.S. Air Force and the Man Who Built It, Gen. Henry H. "Hap" Arnold*. New York, 1982.

Cole, Wayne S. *Roosevelt and the Isolationists, 1932–45*. Lincoln, Neb., 1983.

———. *Charles A. Lindbergh and the Battle Against American Intervention in World War II*. New York, 1974.

The Committee for the Compilation of Materials on Damage Caused by the Atomic Bombs in Hiroshima and Nagasaki, *Hiroshima and Nagasaki: The Physical, Medical, and Social Effects of the Atomic Bombings*. New York, 1981.

Compton, Arthur Holly. *Atomic Quest: A Personal Narrative*. New York, 1956.

Cooper, Matthew. *The German Air Force, 1933–1945: An Anatomy of Failure*. New York, 1981.

Copp, DeWitt S. *A Few Great Captains: The Men and Events that Shaped the Development of U.S. Air Power*. Garden City, N.Y., 1980.

Corn, Joseph J. *The Winged Gospel: America's Romance with Aviation, 1900–1950*. New York, 1983.

Costello, John. *The Pacific War, 1941–1945*. New York, 1982.

Craven, Wesley Frank, and James Lea Cate, eds. *The Army Air Forces in World War II*. 7 vols. Chicago, 1948–58.

Crouch, Tom D. *A Dream of Wings: Americans and the Airplane, 1875–1905*. New York, 1981.

Culbert, David Holbrook. *News for Everyman: Radio and Foreign Affairs in Thirties America*. Westport, Conn., 1976.

Dallek, Robert. *Franklin D. Roosevelt and American Foreign Policy, 1932–1945*. New York, 1979.

Daniels, Gordon. "The Great Tokyo Air Raid, 9–10 March 1945." In W. G. Beasley, ed., *Modern Japan: Aspects of History, Literature and Society*. London, 1975.

Davis, Nuel Pharr. *Lawrence and Oppenheimer.* New York, 1968.

Dower, J. W. *Empire and Aftermath: Yoshida Shigeru and the Japanese Experience, 1878–1954.* Cambridge, Mass., 1979.

_____. *War Without Mercy: Race and Power in the Pacific War.* New York, 1986.

Dyson, Freeman. *Disturbing the Universe.* New York, 1979.

Ellis, John. *The Social History of the Machine Gun.* New York, 1975.

Emerson, William R. *Operation Pointblank: A Tale of Bombers and Fighters.* USAF Academy, Col., 1962.

Fabyanic, Thomas A. "A Critique of United States Air War Planning, 1941–1944." Ph.D. diss., Saint Louis University, 1973.

Fanton, Jonathan Foster. "Robert A. Lovett: The War Years." Ph.D. diss., Yale University, 1978.

Fernandez, Roland. *Excess Profits: The Rise of United Technologies.* Reading, Mass., 1983.

Ferrell, Robert H., ed. *Off the Record: The Private Papers of Harry S. Truman.* New York, 1980.

Finney, Robert T. *History of the Air Corps Tactical School, 1920–1940.* Maxwell AFB, 1955.

Flugel, Raymond Richard. "United States Air Power Doctrine: A Study of the Influence of William Mitchell and Giulio Douhet at the Air Corps Tactical School, 1921–1935." Ph.D. diss., University of Oklahoma, 1965.

Frankland, Noble. *The Bombing Offensive Against Germany.* London, 1965.

Fredette, Raymond H. *The Sky on Fire: The First Battle of Britain, 1917–1918.* New York, 1966, 1976.

Fromm, Erich. *The Anatomy of Human Destructiveness.* New York, 1973.

Futrell, Robert Frank. *Ideas, Concepts, Doctrine: A History of Basic Thinking in the United States Air Force, 1907–1964.* Maxwell AFB, 1971.

Gabriel, Richard, and Paul L. Savage. *Crisis in Command: Mismanagement in the Army.* New York, 1978.

Galbraith, John Kenneth. *A Life in Our Times: Memoirs.* Boston, 1981.

Gertsch, W. Darrell. "The Strategic Air Offensive and the Mutation of American Values." *Rocky Mountain Social Science Journal* 11 (October 1974): 37–50.

Giovannitti, Len, and Fred Freed. *The Decision to Drop the Bomb.* New York, 1965.

Greer, Thomas. *The Development of Air Doctrine in the Army Air Arm, 1917–1941.* Maxwell AFB, 1955.

Grinker, Roy R., and John P. Spiegel. *Men Under Stress.* Philadelphia, 1945.

Groves, Leslie. *Now It Can Be Told: The Story of the Manhattan Project.* New York, 1962.

Gullain, Robert. *I Saw Tokyo Burning: An Eyewitness Narrative from Pearl Harbor to Hiroshima.* Garden City, N.Y., 1981.

Haight, John McVickar, Jr. *American Aid to France, 1938–1940.* New York, 1970.

Hansell, Haywood S., Jr. *The Air Plan That Defeated Hitler.* Atlanta, 1972.

_____. *Strategic Air War Against Japan.* Maxwell AFB, 1980.

Harrington, Daniel F. "A Careless Hope: American Air Power and Japan, 1941." *Pacific Historical Review* 48 (May 1979): 217–38.

Harris, Robert, and Jeremy Paxman. *A Higher Form of Killing: The Secret Story of Chemical and Biological Warfare.* New York, 1982.

Hastings, Max. *Bomber Command: The Myths and Reality of the Strategic Bombing Offensive 1939–1945.* New York, 1979.

Havens, Thomas. *Valley of Darkness: The Japanese People and World War Two.* New York, 1978.

Hayes, Grace Person. *The History of the Joint Chiefs of Staff in World War II: The War Against Japan.* Annapolis, 1982.

Heims, Steve J. *John Von Neumann and Norbert Wiener: From Mathematics to the Technologies of Life and Death.* Cambridge, 1980.

Herzog, James H. *Closing the Open Door: American Japanese Diplomatic Negotiations, 1936–1941.* Annapolis, 1973.

Hewlett, Richard G., and Oscar E. Anderson, Jr. *The New World, 1939–1946.* University Park, Pa., 1962.

Higham, Robin. *Air Power: A Concise History.* New York, 1972.

Holley, I. B. *Buying Aircraft: Material Procurement for the Army Air Forces.* Washington, 1962.

Holley, I. B., Jr. *Ideas and Weapons: Exploitation of the Aerial Weapon by the United States during World War I: A Study in the Relationship of Technological Advance, Military Doctrine, and the Development of Weapons.* New Haven, 1953.

Hopkins, George. "Bombing and the American Conscience During World War II." *The Historian* 28 (May 1966): 451–73.

Howard, Michael. *War in European History.* New York, 1976.

Hurley, Alfred F. *Billy Mitchell: Crusader for Air Power.* 1964. Bloomington, Ind., 1975.

———, and Robert C. Ehrhart, eds. *Air Power and Warfare: The Proceedings of the 8th Military Symposium, United States Air Force Academy, 18–20 October 1978.* USAF Academy, 1979.

Ienaga, Saburo. *The Pacific War, 1931–1945: A Critical Perspective on Japan's Role in World War II.* 1968. New York, 1978.

Ikle, Fred Charles. *The Social Impact of Bomb-Destruction.* Norman, Ok., 1958.

Iriye, Akira. *Across the Pacific: An Inner History of American-East Asian Relations.* New York, 1967.

———. *Power and Culture: The Japanese-American War, 1941–1945.* Cambridge, 1981.

Irving, David. *The Destruction of Dresden.* 1963. New York, 1965.

James, D. Clayton. *The Years of MacArthur, 1941–1945.* Boston, 1975.

Janis, Irving L. *Air War and Emotional Stress: Psychological Studies of Bombing and Civilian Defense.* New York, 1951.

Jones, Neville. *The Origins of Strategic Bombing: A Study of the Development of British Air Strategic Thought and Practice up to 1918.* London, 1973.

Julian, Thomas A. "Operation 'Frantic' and the Search for American-Soviet Military Collaboration, 1941–1944." Ph.D. diss., Syracuse University, 1968.

Jungk, Robert. *Brighter Than a Thousand Suns: A Personal History of the Atomic Scientists.* New York, 1958.

Karman, Theodore Von, with Lee Edson. *The Wind and Beyond: Theodore Von Karman, Pioneer in Aviation and Pathfinder in Space.* Boston, 1967.

Kato, Masuo. *The Lost War: A Japanese Reporter's Inside Story.* New York, 1946.

Kecskemeti, Paul. *Strategic Surrender: The Politics of Victory and Defeat.* Stanford, 1958.

Kennedy, David M. *Over Here: The First World War and American Society.* New York, 1980.

Kennett, Lee. *A History of Strategic Bombing.* New York, 1982.

Kern, Stephen. *The Culture of Time and Space, 1880–1918.* Cambridge, Mass., 1983.

Kevles, Daniel J. *The Physicists: The History of a Scientific Community in Modern America.* 1978. New York, 1979.

Knightley, Phillip. *The First Casualty, From the Crimea to Vietnam: The War Correspondent as Hero, Propagandist, and Myth Maker.* New York, 1975.

Koppes, Clayton R. *JPL and the American Space Program.* New Haven, 1982.

Leigh, Michael. *Mobilizing Consent: Public Opinion and American Foreign Policy, 1937–1947.* Westport, Conn., 1976.

Leighton, Richard M. "The American Arsenal Policy in World War II: A Retrospective View." In Daniel R. Beaver, ed., *Some Pathways in Twentieth-Century History.* Cincinnati, 1969.

LeMay, Curtis E., with MacKinlay Kantor. *Mission with LeMay.* Garden City, N.J., 1965.

Leonard, Thomas C. *Above the Battle: War-Making in America from Appomattox to Versailles.* New York, 1978.

Leutze, James R. *Bargaining for Supremacy: Anglo-American Naval Collaboration, 1937–41.* Chapel Hill, 1977.

Levine, Isaac Don. *Mitchell: Pioneer of Air Power.* New York, 1943.

Lifton, Robert Jay. *Death in Life: Survivors of Hiroshima.* New York, 1967.

Longmate, Norman. *The Bombers: The RAF Offensive against Germany, 1939–1945.* London, 1983.

Lowenthal, Mark Martin. "Leadership and Indecision: American War Planning and Policy Process, 1937–42." Ph.D. diss., Harvard University, 1975.

Lukas, Richard C. *Eagles East: The Army Air Forces and the Soviet Union, 1941–1945.* Tallahassee, 1970.

MacIsaac, David. *Strategic Bombing in World War Two: The Story of the United States Strategic Bombing Survey.* New York, 1976.

Matloff, Maurice. *Strategic Planning for Coalition Warfare, 1943–1944.* Washington, 1959.

———, and Edwin M. Snell. *Strategic Planning for Coalition Warfare, 1941–42.* Washington, 1953.

McKelway, St. Clair. "A Reporter with the B-29s." In *The New Yorker,* I: June 1945. II: 16 June 1945. III: 23 June 1945. IV: 30 June 1945.

Messenger, Charles. *'Bomber' Harris and the Strategic Bombing Offensive, 1939–1945.* New York, 1984.

Messer, Robert L. *The End of an Alliance: James F. Byrnes, Roosevelt, Truman, and the Origins of the Cold War.* Chapel Hill, 1982.

Middlebrook, Martin. *The Battle of Hamburg: Allied Air Forces Against a German City in 1943.* New York, 1981.

Millis, Walter. *Arms and Men: A Study in American Military History.* New York, 1956.

Morison, Elting E. *Turmoil and Tradition: A Study in the Life and Times of Henry L. Stimson.* 1960. New York, 1964.

Morrison, Wilbur H. *Point of No Return: The Story of the 20th Air Force.* New York, 1979.

Moskos, Charles. "The All-Volunteer Military: Calling, Profession, or Occupation?" *Parameters, Journal of the U.S. Army War College* 7 (1977): 2–9.

Mountcastle, John W. "Trial by Fire: U.S. Incendiary Weapons, 1918–1945." Ph.D. diss., Duke University, 1979.

Neumann, William. *America Encounters Japan: From Perry to MacArthur.* Baltimore, 1963.

Overy, R. J. *The Air War, 1939–1945.* New York, 1981.

The Pacific War Research Society. *The Day Man Lost: Hiroshima, 6 August 1945.* Tokyo and New York, 1972.

Pogue, Forrest C. *George C. Marshall.* 3 volumes. New York, 1963–73.

Powers, Barry D. *Strategy Without Slide Rule; British Air Strategy, 1914–1939.* London, 1976.

Quester, George H. *Deterrence before Hiroshima.* New York, 1966.

Rae, John Bell. *Climb to Greatness: The American Aircraft Industry, 1920–1960.* Cambridge, 1968.

Reynolds, David. *The Creation of the Anglo-American Alliance 1937–1941: A Study in Competitive Co-operation.* London, 1981.

Rose, Lisle A. *Dubious Victory: The United States and the End of World War II.* Kent, Ohio, 1973.

Royse, M. W. *Aerial Bombardment and the International Regulation of Warfare.* New York, 1928.

Sallager, F. M. *The Road to Total War: Escalation in World War II.* Santa Monica, 1969.

Schaffer, Ronald. "American Military Ethics in World War II: The Bombing of German Civilians." *Journal of American History* 67 (September 1980): 318–34.

———. *Wings of Judgment: American Bombing in World War II.* New York, 1985.

Schaller, Michael. *The U.S. Crusade in China, 1938–1945.* New York, 1979.

Sherry, Michael S. *Preparing for the Next War: American Plans for Postwar Defense, 1941–45.* New Haven, 1977.

Sherwin, Martin J. *A World Destroyed: The Atomic Bomb and the Grand Alliance.* New York, 1975, 1977.

Shillony, Ben-Ami. *Politics and Culture in Wartime Japan.* London, 1981.

Shiner, John F. *Foulois and the U.S. Army Air Corps, 1931–1935.* Washington, 1983.

Smith, Alice Kimball. *A Peril and a Hope: The Scientists' Movement in America, 1945–1947.* Chicago, 1965.

Smith, Malcolm. "'A Matter of Faith': British Strategic Air Doctrine Before 1939." *Journal of Contemporary History* 15 (July 1980): 423–42.

———. "The Royal Air Force, Air Power and British Foreign Policy, 1932–37." *Journal of Contemporary History* 12 (January 1977): 153–74.

Smith, Melden E., Jr. "The Bombing of Dresden Reconsidered: A Study in Wartime Decision Making." Ph.D. diss., Boston University, 1971.

Spector, Ronald H. *Eagle Against the Sun.* New York, 1985.

Sprout, Harold and Margaret. *Toward a New Order of Sea Power.* Princeton, 1943.

Stouffer, Samuel, et al. *The American Soldier.* 2 volumes. Princeton, 1949.

Tate, James Phillip. "The Army and Its Air Corps: A Study of the Evolution of Army Policy Towards Aviation, 1919–1941." Ph.D. diss., Indiana University, 1976.

Telford, Taylor. *Munich: The Price of Peace.* Garden City, N.Y., 1979.

Terraine, John. *A Time for Courage: The Royal Air Force in the European War, 1939–1945.* New York, 1985.

Thorne, Christopher. *Allies of a Kind: The United States, Britain and the War against Japan, 1941–1945.* New York, 1978.

Truman, Harry S. *Memoirs.* Volume 1: *Year of Decisions.* Garden City, N.Y., 1955.

Vagts, Alfred. *A History of Militarism, Civilian and Military.* 1937. New York, 1959.

Villa, Brian L. "The U.S. Army, Unconditional Surrender, and the Potsdam Declaration." *Journal of American History* 63 (June 1976): 66–92.

Walzer, Michael. *Just and Unjust Wars: A Moral Argument with Historical Illustrations.* New York, 1977.

Ward, John William. "The Meaning of Lindbergh's Flight." *American Quarterly* 10 (Spring 1958): 3–16.

Watson, Mark Seton. *Chief of Staff: Prewar Plans and Preparations.* Washington, 1950.

Webster, Sir Charles, and Noble Frankland. *The Strategic Air Offensive Against Germany, 1939–1945.* 4 vols. London, 1961.

Wecter, Dixon. *When Johnny Comes Marching Home.* Cambridge, 1944.

Weigley, Russell F. *The American Way of War: A History of United States Military Strategy and Policy.* New York, 1973.

Wheeler, Keith. *Bombers Over Japan.* Alexandria, Va., 1982.

———. *The Fall of Japan.* Alexandria, Va., 1983.

Wills, Garry. "Critical Inquiry (*Kritik*) in Clausewitz." *Critical Inquiry* 9 (December 1982): 281–302.

Wilson, Theodore A. *The First Summit: Roosevelt and Churchill at Placentia Bay, 1941.* Boston, 1969.

_____, ed. *WW2: Readings on Critical Issues.* New York, 1974.

Wohlstetter, Roberta. *Pearl Harbor: Warning and Decision.* Stanford, 1962.

Wright, Gordon. *The Ordeal of Total War, 1939–1945.* New York, 1968.

Wyden, Peter. *Day One: Before Hiroshima and After.* New York, 1984.

Zuckerman, Solly. *From Apes to Warlords: The Autobiography (1904–1946) of Solly Zuckerman.* London, 1978.

Index

238, 306–08; on bombing of Germany, 150, 152, 157, 259, 260–62; on bombing Japan from China, 159–60, 167, 172; on reprisals for mistreatment of POWs, 157, 169–70; in Dresden controversy, 260–62; on Japanese surrender terms, 268, 297, 298, 304–05, 306–07, 331, 334; fears war-weariness, 293; on atomic bomb, 304–05, 317–18, 325, 326, 328–29, 336–37, 338, 340, 341, 345, 415n; on Soviet-American relations in 1945, 325, 336–37, 338, 340; on costs of invasion, 335–36
Marx, Karl, 20
Mason, Edward S., 194
Matthews, Herbert L., 69
McCormick, Anne O'Hare, 140
McKelway, St. Clair, 211, 266, 282, 289, 290
McLoy, John J., 307, 318, 332
McNutt, Paul V., 245
Michie, Allan, 128, 186
Middleton, Drew, 305
Midway, Battle of, 123, 136
Mitchell, William (Billy): before World War I, 11; in World War I, 18, 19; struggle with army and navy, 22, 34–37, 39, 357; views and predictions, 29–31, 34, 38, 43, 49, 52–59 passim, 89, 128; on ease of bombing Japan, 31, 58–59; court-martial, 35, 36, 37; influence on American doctrine, 52, 128, 239, 362; death, 61; celebrated after Pearl Harbor, 127
Moley, Raymond, 303
Morgenthau, Hans, 145
Morgenthau, Henry, 79, 81, 83, 85, 97, 101, 102
Mumford, Lewis, 83
Munich crisis: 21, 67–68, 70, 75; role of air war in, 76–78; influence on American air power, 76, 77–82, 83, 87–89, 101, 114
Murrow, Edward R., 94–95, 132
Mussolini, 23, 152
MX Missile, 357

Nagasaki: 177; as incendiary target, 229; atomic attack on compared to firebombing, 275, 277, 344; planning for atomic attack on, 339, 341, 343; reactions to attack on, 346, 347, 348, 350–51, 355–56; casualties in atomic attack, 406n, 413n, 418n
Nagoya, 257, 282, 300, 326

National Advisory Committee for Aeronautics (NACA), 188
National Defense Research, 188, 226, 227
National Fire Protection Association, 227
Navy, United States: early aviation, 10, 11; conflict with army aviators, 34–38, 52; in pre–World War II planning, 59, 98, 101, 103, 114; operations in Pacific war, 122, 166, 169, 231, 267, 287, 293, 311; conflict with AAF, 147, 168–69, 219, 220, 231, 238, 258, 267, 270–71, 287; in intelligence-gathering, 247; in shelling and bombing Japan, 267, 305–06, 311, 401n; in deliberations on atomic bomb, 326–27
Nelson, Donald, 121
von Neumann, John, 203, 252, 318
Nicaragua, 22
Nimitz, Chester, 169, 195, 269, 270–71
Norstad, Lauris: as chief of staff for Twentieth Air Force, 184, 221, 222, 223, 225; in air force public relations, 184–85, 289; on strategists' task, 226, 237; supports firebombing, 230, 248, 257–58, 266–67, 271–72, 273, 283, 289, 302; relationship with LeMay, 273, 283, 308; criticizes AAF generals, 308
North Africa, 94, 118, 119, 120, 147–48
Nuremburg, 164

O'Donnell, Emmett, 228
Office of Scientific Research and Development, 230
Office of Strategic Services, 247
Office of War Information, 247
Okinawa, 237, 292, 298, 304–05, 331, 332, 401n
Oppenheimer, Robert, 195, 202–04, 317, 318, 324, 326, 353, 362, 420n
Osaka, 109, 116, 282, 300, 326
OVERLORD, 159, 161, 162, 163, 164, 170, 173, 264

P-51 Mustang, 159, 162
Pan American Airways, 215
Paris, 12
Patterson, Robert, 231
Pearl Harbor, Japanese attack on: 114, 120, 254, 333; in American justification for bombing Japan, 115, 116, 117, 123–24, 291, 331, 349; in political debates, 126–27;

influence on postwar air policy, 187
Pentagon, 219, 222–24
Perera, Guido, 194, 195, 197, 198, 199, 227, 228
Pershing, John J., 18, 37, 86
Philippines: foreseen as air base, 11, 31, 53, 59; in 1941 plans for bombing Japan, 103–15; destruction of American bomber force, 114, 116; as object of dubious campaign, 169
Pierce, Watson O'dell, 68–69, 154
Potsdam Conference, 307, 316, 330, 334–41 passim, 343, 345
Precision bombing: doctrine developed by Americans, 49–58, 72, 93; in prewar media, 62, 64, 74, 93; abandoned by British, 94, 162, 262; Anglo-American disagreement on, 120–21, 148–49, 156, 157–59; and Doolittle raid, 123; in wartime media, 126, 127–29, 131, 160–61, 171, 184–85, 263, 289–91, 312–13; by Eighth Air Force against Germany, 148–49, 155, 160–61, 162–63, 175; diminishing role in Eighth Air Force, 162, 164–65, 260–62; by Twentieth Air Force, 171, 256–58, 266–67, 270; in plans against Japan, 227–34; diminishing role in Twentieth Air Force, 269–73, 282–83, 286–89, 300, 308–12; against China and Formosa, 284; Stimson's concern over, 294–95
Predictive literature: before World War I, 4–9; in 1920s, 23–33, 44–46; in 1930s, 61–69; in World War II, 126–31; recent fiction on nuclear war, 361
Public opinion polls, 82–83, 98, 138, 185, 242, 333, 355, 387n, 409n
Pyle, Ernie, 133, 211–12

Rand Corporation, 187
Rea, Lieutenant Colonel, 346
Reagan, Ronald, 357, 360
Reid, Frank, 37
Republic Aviation, 127
Rickenbacker, Eddie, 39, 66, 189
Rome, 144, 152
Roosevelt, Elliott, 245
Roosevelt, Franklin D.: 140, 182, 258, 293; in air mail controversy, 48; early views on military aviation, 49, 59–61; publicly criticized on air policy, 62, 83, 85, 87; air policy in response to Munich, 76, 77–89; on rearma-